Essays on Saving, Bequests, Altruism, and Life-Cycle Planning

Laurence J. Kotlikoff

The MIT Press
Cambridge, Massachusetts
London, England

This book was set in Palatino in '3B2' by Asco Typesetters, Hong Kong, and was printed and bound in the United States of America.

Library of Congress Cataloging-in-Publication Data

Essays on saving, bequests, altruism, and life-cycle planning / Laurence J. Kotlikoff.
p. cm.
Includes bibliographical references and index.
ISBN 0-262-11262-0 (hc.: alk. paper)
1. Saving and investment—United States. 2. Retirement—United States—Planning. 3. Income distribution—United States. 4. Altruism—United States.
I. Kotlikoff, Laurence J.
HC110.S3 E85 2000
339.4—dc21

00-068383

For Alex and David and in memory of Henry—my beloved sons.

Contents

Sources

Chapter 1

"Understanding the Postwar Decline in US Saving: A Cohort Analysis" *Brookings Paper on Economic Activity 1*, (Washington, D.C.: The Brookings Institution, 1996), pp. 315–390. Reprinted by permission. Copyright © 1996, The Brookings Institution.

Chapter 3

"Simulating the Transmission of Wealth Inequality via Bequests," *Journal of Public Economics* 79 (1), 98–128. Reprinted by permission. The North Holland Publishing Co., Copyright © 2001, Elsevier Science.

Chapter 4

"Intergenerational Altruism and the Effectiveness of Fiscal Policy," from Toshiaki Tachibanaki, ed., *Savings and Bequest* (Ann Arbor Michigan: University of Michigan Press, 1994), pp. 167–196. Reprinted by permission. Copyright © University of Michigan Press.

Chapter 5

"Is the Extended Family Altruistically Linked? Direct Tests Using Micro Data," *The American Economic Review* 82 (5), 1177–1198. Reprinted by permission. Copyright © 1992, The American Economic Association.

Chapter 6

"Parental Altruism and Inter Vivos Transfers: Theory and Evidence." *The Journal of Political Economy* 105 (6). Reprinted by permission. Copyright © 1997, The University of Chicago.

Chapter 7

"A Strategic Altruism Model in Which Ricardian Equivalence Does Not Hold," *The Economic Journal* 100 (December 1990), 1261–68. Reprinted by permission. Copyright © 1992, Blackwell Publishers Co.

Chapter 9

"Looking for the News in the Noise: Additional Stochastic Implications of Optimal Consumption Choice," *Annales D'Economie et de Statistique* 9 (1988), 29–46. Reprinted by permission. Copyright © Annales D'Economie et de Statistique.

Chapter 11

"Life Insurance of the Elderly: Adequacy and Determinants," from Gary Burtless, ed., *Work, Health and Income Among the Elderly* (Washington, D.C.: The Brookings Institution, 1987), pp. 229–268. Reprinted by permission. Copyright © 1987, The Brookings Institution.

Chapter 13

"How Much Should Americans Be Saving for Retirement," *The American Economic Review* 90 (2), 288–292. Reprinted by permission. Copyright © 2000, The American Economic Association.

Introduction

This book brings together fourteen articles I've coauthored in recent years. Four of these articles have never been published. Many of the rest were published in specialized books and journals. Consequently, part of my motivation in creating this book was to give this work more visibility. But the main reason stems from my belief that the value of the collection exceeds the sum of its parts.

The articles consider four interrelated topics: saving, bequests, altruism, and life-cycle financial planning. These issues were among those examined in my 1989 MIT Press volume *What Determines Savings?* But the current volume considers each of the subjects from different perspectives and applies different theoretical and empirical approaches.

The book is divided into three parts. The first part contains three chapters focused on saving, bequests, and inequality. The second part has five chapters that study altruism. And the third part offers six chapters about life-cycle financial planning. In this brief introduction I summarize the questions raised by each of the chapters, the methods used to address the questions, and the answers provided.

Saving and Bequests

Postwar America has witnessed a remarkable decline in the rate of national saving. Between 1950 and 1979 our country saved each year over 10 percent of its national income. Since then, we've been saving at about half that rate. What explains this dramatic change? Is it our fiscal policy, our demographic transition, our attitudes toward saving, or some other factors?

The first chapter of part I, coauthored with Jagadeesh Gokhale and John Sabelhaus, addresses these questions. It develops an elaborate cohort database and uses these data to study the different factors involved in postwar changes in U.S. saving. The data construction and analysis are guided by the life-cycle theory of saving. Central to that theory is the proposition that the elderly are society's big spenders when measured in terms of their propensities to consume. Why should the elderly spend more out of each dollar of remaining lifetime resources than the young? The answer, according to the life-cycle model, is simply that they are closer to the end of their lives and have, in effect, less time to shop. The life-cycle theory thus predicts that if the government redistributes from young savers (including those not yet born, whose propensity to consume before they are born is zero) to old spenders, the private sector will, on balance, consume more and the nation will save less. Demographics also matter. Other things equal, having more old spenders relative to young savers around translates into a higher rate of aggregate consumption and a lower rate of aggregate saving. The same outcome will result from changes in behavior that lead to an increase in the propensities of either the young or the old to consume.

Chapter 1 decomposes postwar changes in national saving into those arising from government intergenerational redistribution, changes in demographics, changes in cohort-specific spending behavior, and changes in the rate of government spending. This breakdown shows that two factors explain why our nation is saving at half its former rate. Of the two, the most important is the government's massive postwar intergenerational redistribution, which it has effected primarily through the expansion of the social security, medicare, and medicaid programs.

The second factor is a significant increase in the rate at which the elderly are consuming their resources. The key reason for this appears to be the form in which they are receiving those resources. As chapter 2, written with Alan Auerbach, Jagadeesh Gokhale, John Sabelhaus, and David Weil, demonstrates, the government has not only spent the postwar period taking ever larger sums of money from young and future generations and handing them to contemporaneous older ones. It has also given the elderly these resources in the form of annuities—streams of income or in-kind benefits that continue until death. In so doing, the government has taken away much of the fear of outliving one's money and permitted the elderly to consume their resources at a much faster clip. However one judges the morality of U.S. postwar intergenerational redistribution, the government's effective provision of insurance against lifespan uncertainty via the provision of annuities seems a major achievement. But that achievement may have come at the unintended costs of more consumption by the elderly and less national saving.

Another presumably unintended consequence of the government's implicit annuitization of the elderly is that it has increased inequality in the distributions of net wealth. Feldstein (1976) was the first to point out that social security replaces a much larger fraction of the net worth of lower than of upper income classes. It does this in two ways—by taxing away a larger share of the labor income of those with low earnings and by replacing a larger share of the preretirement earnings of such households with old-age benefits. This leaves the lower income classes with (a) less wherewithal from which to save and (b) less reason to postpone consumption. Chapter 2, which uses Survey of Consumer Finances data as well as aggregate cohort data, considers the entire gambit of government policies in generalizing Feldstein's finding.

The fact that the government has (a) facilitated the decision of the elderly to consume at a faster rate and (b) annuitized a disproportionately large share of the resources of the poor has potentially important consequences not just for the distribution of wealth, but also for the distribution of bequests and inheritances. Chapter 3, written with Jagadeesh Gokhale, James Sefton, and Martin Weale, constructs a simulation model to study the bequest transmission process as well as the government's role in altering that process. The model incorporates lifetime earnings inequality, unintended bequests, assortative mating, the inheritance of skills, social security, and a variety of other factors. Although highly stylized, the model does an excellent job of explaining the wealth distribution among American couples at retirement, including the top tail of the wealth distribution. The study delivers five messages. First, the extent of wealth inequality is highly dependent on the extent of lifetime earnings inequality. Second, intentional bequests are not needed to generate an empirically reasonable distribution of wealth. Third, intentional bequests are not needed to generate a large ratio of inherited to life-cycle wealth. Fourth, absent social security, the random nature of the receipt of unintended inheritances can actually serve to mitigate inequality in accumulated wealth. And fifth, social security and other government annuities play an important role in raising wealth inequality as well as inequality in the receipt of inheritances.

Altruism

The articles in part I proceed from the assumption that bequests are undesired and arise because of imperfections in annuity markets. As Barro (1974) pointed out, the alternative assumption, that bequests reflect intergenerational altruism, has profound implications for the macroeconomic and microeconomic effects of fiscal policy. Strong evidence in support of intergenerational altruism would undercut not just the studies in part I, but major portions of the economics literature and virtually all conventional macroeconomic fiscal policy analysis.

Testing the Barro model carefully is, thus, a task of the first order. The first four articles of part II attempt to do just that. They take the intergenerational altruism hypothesis seriously. Indeed, they take it as the null hypothesis and directly test its predictions using cohort and micro data. The key proposition here is that the distribution of consumption within the altruistically linked extended family is independent of the distribution of resources. Two corollaries of this proposition are (a) the distribution of changes in the consumption of extended family members is independent of the distribution of changes in extended family member resources, and (b) exogenous redistribution of resources within the extended family will be offset by endogenous intrafamily transfers.

I first set about testing the Barro proposition in a paper with Michael Boskin (Kotlikoff and Boskin 1986). We assumed that one big Barro inter- and intragenerationally altruistically linked dynasty determined economy-wide consumption decisions and used dynamic programming to determine how the dynasty would consume given aggregate earnings and rate of return uncertainty. The assumption of one big dynasty is less extreme than it may seem. First, the aggregate consumption decisions of a single big dynasty would be the same as those resulting from altruistically unlinked dynasties, provided they had common homothetic intertemporal preferences. Second, as I showed in Kotlikoff (1983), and Bernheim and Bagwell independently derived in 1988, intermarriage among altruistically linked dynasties effectively links the dynasties themselves into one mega-dynasty.

After estimating our model, Boskin and I tested whether the cross-cohort distribution of economic resources mattered to aggregate consumption given the level of consumption predicted by the Barro model. The answer we found was a strong and statistically significant dependence of aggregate consumption on the intergenerational distribution of resources.

While telling, the aggregative nature of this rejection of Barro's model seemed less than fully convincing. So I next teamed up with Andy Abel to test the Barro model using cohort data derived from the Consumer Expenditure Survey. The result is chapter 4. This article was first distributed as an NBER working paper (no. 2490) in 1988 under the title "Does the Consumption of Different Age Groups Move Together?—A New Nonparametric Test of Intergenerational Altruism," and finally found a publisher in 1994.

The paper showed that altruism imbues consumption with a factor structure, one implication of which is that the Euler errors of altruistically linked individuals and, by extension, households are identical. Assuming time-separable, homothetic preferences, this implies that all altruistically linked households should experience the same percentage change in consumption from one period to the next, independent of their own resource shocks. With some weak additional assumptions, this implies that the average percentage change in household consumption within an age cohort should be the same for all age cohorts and not correlated with their income changes. As we also pointed out in the paper, the nonaltruistic life-cycle model, coupled with the assumption of risk sharing, also delivers these predictions.

Our empirical analysis is nonparametric in that it places no restrictions on preferences besides the assumption of homotheticity and time-separability. The findings indicate that the distribution of average within-cohort consumption changes depends significantly, in both economic and statistical terms, on the distribution of within-cohort average resource changes.

Our derivation of the factor structure of consumption implied by altruism and, in first difference form, by selfish risk sharing suggested yet another source of data to test both altruism and selfish risk sharing, namely the Panel Study of Income Dynamics' (PSID) data on the consumption of parents and adult children living in separate households.[1] Chapters 5 and 6 are two of three papers I wrote with Joseph Altonji and Fumio Hayashi using these data.[2]

Chapter 5 provides more strong evidence against interfamily altruism. It shows that extended family member resources have at most a minor effect on a household's consumption decisions; that is, the distribution of consumption among extended family members is heavily dependent on the distribution of resources across those members.

Chapter 6 plays devil's advocate to chapter 5. It grants that intergenerational altruism is not ubiquitous, but asks whether this behavior is characteristic of a subset of extended families, specifically those who are observed to be making interfamily transfers. To examine this question, we again turned to the PSID data, but this time, the data on transfers. Our objective was to test the Barro restriction on transfer-income derivatives that follows from the fact that exogenously redistributing a dollar of income from the transfer recipient to the transferor should lead the transferor to increase her transfer by a dollar. However, before we could estimate the transfer-income derivatives of parent transferors and child transferees, we needed to resolve two issues. First, we needed to clarify that the timing of transfer payments is not arbitrary, because if it were, we'd need to have data on lifetime, not annual transfers. Such data aren't available. Second, we needed to deal econometrically with the potential sample selection bias arising from focusing on the sub sample of extended families in which parents were making transfers.

We responded to the first issue by positing a model in which the future income of children is uncertain. This simple and realistic assumption has the following implication: unless children are liquidity constrained, their assumed altruistic parents will delay making transfers to them until their income uncertainty is resolved. Intuitively, if altruistic parents think their children may strike it rich and if their children aren't cash-constrained, the parents will take a wait-and-see attitude with respect to making transfers. The observation that parents are making transfers is thus an observation that the children are indeed borrowing constrained and that the amount being transferred has been chosen deliberately. This deliberate choice of the level of transfers is critical for generating the testable restriction on the parent and child transfer-income derivatives. To deal with the second issue—the sample selection problem—we used an ingenious sample selection-corrected derivative estimator developed by Altonji and Ichimura (1996).

Like the other studies in section II, this one also strongly rejects intergenerational altruism. We found that taking a dollar from a transferee child and giving it to a transferor parent would lead the parent to hand back to the child somewhere between 4 and 13 cents depending on the income measure we choose. These responses are not only small economically; they are also not statistically different from zero.

Intergenerational altruism can also be tested along other dimensions and with other kinds of evidence. For example, chapter 2 shows that the government's forced annuitization of the elderly was not undone or, indeed, even offset, by the elderly purchasing more life insurance as would be predicted in an altruistic setting. And chapter 1 shows that the dramatic postwar increase in the consumption of the elderly relative to the young coincided with a dramatic increase in their relative resources.

As a group, chapters 1, 2, 4, 5, and 6 represent a fairly definitive rejection of the specific model of intergenerational altruism posited by Barro. But does this mean that altruism is decisively ruled out as an important component of preferences? The answer, as chapters 7 and 8 indicate, is not necessarily. Chapter 7, written with Assaf Razin and Robert Rosenthal, shows that Barro's proposition (also known as Ricardian Equivalence after a seemingly off-the-cuff paragraph by David Ricardo)—that altruistically linked individuals will base their economic decisions on collective rather than individual resources—is predicated on special assumptions about the strategic interaction between donors and donees. In particular, Barro assumes that donees take their transfers from donors as given and that donors believe any transfer they make, no matter how large or small, will be accepted.

This Nash assumption seems plausible until one contemplates the behavior of two mutually altruistic individuals who each wish to transfer income to the other. If their mutual altruism is sufficiently strong, no Nash equilibrium will emerge. Instead they will pass money back and forth to each other forever. In light of this problem, chapter 7 considers an alternative game that both selfish and altruistic children can play with their altruistic parents. This game permits children to refuse the receipt of transfers if they think these transfers are too small, or, if they care about their parents, too big. If one assumes that the conflict between parents and children is resolved via the extended Nash bargaining solution, the threat points of the parents and children will influence the game's outcome. Consequently, with this formulation of economic behavior, which seems as plausible as that entertained by Barro, Ricardian Equivalence will almost never hold. Why? Because exogenous redistribution between parent and child alters their threat points and, thus, their strategic interaction.

While chapter 7 questions the assumption that Barro makes about the strategic behavior of altruists and their loved ones, chapter 8, written with Assaf Razin, questions Barro's implicit assumption that the altruist has full information about her loved one's economic circumstances. If one introduces, as does chapter 8, asymmetric information between donors and donees, Ricardian Equivalence again loses purchase. In this case, the donor's problem becomes isomorphic to Mirrlees's (1971) optimal tax problem. In the optimal tax problem, the government tries to redistribute among agents of different, but unobserved ability. Here, parents play the role of government and children play the role of agents. Parents not only determine the absolute amount of funds to transfer to their children, but also how those transfer payments will vary with the earnings of the child. Thus inter vivos transfers will be structured just like tax and transfers programs and generate the same kind of work disincentives.

Life-Cycle Planning

Following the use of neoclassical frameworks to study saving, bequests, wealth inequality, and altruism, the final section asks whether households are actually making life-cycle economic decisions in the manner suggested by neoclassical theory. The first chapter in this part, chapter 9, was written with Ariél Pakes. The chapter points out in general terms that if households are, over time, rationally processing new information about their earnings, the changes in their consumption will imbed extractable information about the extent and time resolution of that earnings uncertainty. Stated differently, in a context of earnings uncertainty, new information about lifetime earnings and only new information about lifetime earnings should explain revisions in consumption plans. If consumption is measured accurately and is fluctuating through time to a much greater extent than can be rationalized by changes in information about future earnings (i.e., if the noise in consumption is much greater than the news about lifetime earnings), then households are failing to intertemporally optimize. Chapter 9 uses time series data on consumption to compare the noise in consumption with the news in earnings. Its findings are not particularly supportive of optimal intertemporal consumption choice; virtually all the noise in consumption is unrelated to the news about earnings.

Chapter 9's findings are illustrative and suggestive, but hardly convincing evidence against rational consumption choice. First, the particular time series application relies on the kind of infinite horizon dynastic preferences rejected in the studies of the previous section. Second, the chapter's framework entertains one and only one form of uncertainty, namely uncertainty in labor income. Third, the high ratio of noise to news in consumption innovations may simply reflect substantial errors in measuring national per capita consumption.

Chapter 10, written with Stephen Johnson and William Samuelson, takes a more direct approach to testing the rationality of intertemporal consumption choice. It presents results from an experiment conducted at Boston University in which subjects were asked to make preferred consumption choices under hypothetical life-cycle economic conditions. The subjects' responses suggest a widespread inability to make coherent and consistent spending and saving decisions. Their errors in decision-making were not only substantial, they were, in many cases, systematic. To be more precise, subjects made substantially different choices in identical economic situations because they systematically over-discounted future earnings. They also systematically oversaved, apparently out of a failure to appreciate the power of compound interest.

Like the findings in chapter 9, those in chapter 10 are not entirely convincing. In this case, the participants in the experiment—primarily students at Boston University—while being paid to participate, had no personal stake in providing correct answers. In addition, the students were being asked to imagine themselves in a very simple economic world with no uncertainty—a situation different quite from their reality. Many of the subjects may simply have failed to set their own circumstances aside when asked to think how they would behave in a quite different environment.

In contrast to chapters 9 and 10, chapter 11, written with Alan Auerbach, looks at actual individual choice, in this case the purchase of life insurance, to assess the rationality of life-cycle decision-making. The chapter starts with the premise that life insurance, while not perfectly actuarially fair, is sufficiently cheap to permit households to attain close to full insurance when it comes to preserving the living standards of survivors. The chapter also shows that rational choice of life insurance can be tested not simply by looking at the degree to which it is purchased, but also by considering how the amount purchased responds to the government's provision of survivor insurance through social security. The data used in the study come from the Retirement History Survey.

The chapter finds the following: first, life insurance holdings are inadequate for almost half of the sample households. Second, life insurance holdings are grossly inadequate for a significant minority of sample households. Third, empirical estimation of the demand for life insurance produces results that are, in most cases, greatly at odds with theoretical predictions. And fourth, households do not reduce their own purchase of life insurance in light of the implicit life insurance they are provided by social security.

The chapter's finding of severe under-insurance among an important minority of American households has been confirmed in my subsequent work with Auerbach (Auerbach and Kotlikoff 1991a,b), in a recent coauthored study that used the Health and Retirement Survey (Bernheim, Forni, Gokhale, and Kotlikoff 1999), and in studies by Holden, Burkhauser, and Myers (1986), and Hurd and Wise (1989).

Chapter 12, written with B. Douglas Bernheim, takes yet another approach to understanding whether households are able to plan rationally and appropriately for their economic futures. The approach is to look at their financial literacy and to examine the kind of advice households are securing from financial planners and, presumably, following when it comes to making their consumption and saving decisions. The chapter reaches the following three conclusions. First, most Americans are not making prudent financial decisions. Second, many Americans are unaware of their financial vulnerabilities and lack the knowledge and sophistication to make proper financial decisions. Third, the financial planning industry's approach to financial planning, which is based on targeted saving, produces prescriptions that are, in many cases, inappropriate and unreasonable.

Chapter 12 introduces a new financial planning tool, Economic Security Planner (ESPlanner), which I codeveloped with Jagadeesh

Gokhale, Lowell Williams, and Douglas Bernheim. Since writing chapter 12, we have developed ESPlanner into a much more sophisticated life-cycle consumption-smoothing tool.

Chapter 13, written with Bernheim, Lorenzo Forni, and Gokhale, uses the current version of ESPlanner to address the normative question of how much should the respondents in the Health and Retirement Survey, a group that is approaching retirement, be saving. The answer is a lot except for low-income Americans for whom social security replaces a very high fraction of preretirement income. A lot here means between 10 and 20 percent of income, with the recommended saving rate rising with age and income. Such high saving rates are to be expected given that these households have spent their younger years raising families, paying off mortgages, and paying for college tuition. High preretirement saving also accords with the typical cross-section profile of financial wealth by age of household head. This profile features hump savings for retirement, but the hump in savings occurs in the last 40s and 50s.

In addition to pointing out how much typical preretirees should be saving, the chapter notes the critical role of future social security benefits in making that decision. Specifically, it asks how much higher prescribed saving rates should be, under the assumption that social security benefits will be substantially cut in the medium term. The answer is that all households, particularly low-income ones, need to save at substantially higher rates than would otherwise be the case. The chapter argues that the social security system's long-run finances are in such precarious condition that major benefit cuts are almost inevitable. The fact that most Americans approaching retirement appear to be saving at lower rates than ESPlanner recommends, especially given prospects for major social security benefit cuts, represents further reason to question the quality of Americans' intertemporal economic decision-making.

In chapter 14, Gokhale, Mark Warshawsky, and I used ESPlanner to compare the recommendations of conventional financial planning software with those flowing from the economic approach imbedded in ESPlanner. The differences in recommended saving and insurance holdings are, in many instances, dramatic. The paper suggests that large segments of the American public are being persuaded to make saving decisions that leave them consuming either far too much or far too little in the present compared to what they'll be able to consume in the future.

Conclusion

This book tries to explain why our nation is saving so little, why its bequest behavior is changing, why wealth is so unequally distributed, whether altruism influences household responses to fiscal policies, how altruism might be modeled, how to formally test the rationality of intertemporal economic choice, whether people are capable of making consistent and appropriate intertemporal decisions, whether they do make such decisions, whether they have the knowledge and tools to help them in that process, and, finally, what they should be doing to prepare for the future. While the articles are not perfectly interlinked, they do, I think, feed on and nourish each other.

In trying to briefly summarize and connect the chapters of this book, I've had to restrain myself from pointing out many of the things I like about each chapter and some of the surprises they contain. For example, chapter 1 shows that the U.S. government has rearranged our net nonasset income (nonasset income after taxes and after in-kind and in-cash transfers) such that postwar cohorts can now expect to receive higher net nonasset income after retirement than prior to retirement. This depends, of course, on the government's ability to deliver on its promised transfer payments, but it provides a graphic explanation for the disappearance of personal saving in the United States. Another example is chapter 11's derivation of how Heckman's correction for sample selection bias neatly generalizes to the case in which sample selection is occurring based on two correlated processes. A third example is the subtle way one can extract new information about future earnings distributions by considering the covariance of consumption changes and ex-post realizations of lifetime earnings.

These and other discoveries as well as the opportunity to work with such a distinguished group of coauthors made these chapters great joys to write. I hope that their reading provides a small fraction of the pleasure I derived in their construction.

Notes

1. Townsend (1989) independently derived this factor structure.

2. Hayashi, Altonji, and Kotlikoff (1996) is the third. This paper provides a broader framework for analyzing the factor structure of consumption, but reaches the same negative conclusion about the existence of either widespread altruism or selfish risk sharing.

References

Altonji, Joseph G., and Hidhiko Ichimura. 1996. "Estimating Derivatives in Non-Separable Models of with Limited Dependent Variables." Manuscript, Evanston, Ill.: Northwestern University.

Auerbach, Alan J., and Laurence J. Kotlikoff. 1991a. "Life Insurance Inadequacy—Evidence from a Sample of Older Widows," National Bureau of Economic Research working paper no. 3765.

Auerbach, Alan J., and Laurence J. Kotlikoff. 1991b. "The Adequacy of Life Insurance Purchases," *Journal of Financial Intermediation*. 1(3): 215–41.

Barro, Robert J. 1974. "Are Government Bonds Net Wealth." *Journal of Political Economy*. 48(6): 1095–118.

Bernheim, B. Douglas, Lorenzo Forni, Jagadeesh Gokhale, and Laurence J. Kotlikoff. 1999. "The Adequacy of Life Insurance: Evidence from the Health and Retirement Survey," NBER working paper no. 7372.

Bernheim, B. Douglas and Kyle Bagwell. 1988. "Is Everything Neutral?" *Journal of Political Economy*. 96(2): 308–38.

Boskin, Michael J., and Laurence J. Kotlikoff. 1986. "Public Debt and US Saving: A New Test of the Neutrality Hypothesis." *Carnegie-Rochester Conference Volume Series*. 23:55–86. Reprinted in Laurence J. Kotlikoff. 1989. *What Determines Savings?* Cambridge, MA: MIT Press, 455–78.

Feldstein, Martin. 1976. "Social Security and the Distribution of Wealth." *Journal of the American Statistical Association*. 71:800–807.

Gokhale, Jagadeesh, Laurence J. Kotlikoff, and Mark J. Warshawsky. 1999. "Comparing the Economic and Conventional Approaches to Financial Planning." NBER working paper no. 7321.

Hayashi, Fumio, Joseph G. Altonji, and Laurence J. Kotlikoff. 1996. "Risk-Sharing Between and Within Families," *Econometrica*. 64(21): 261–294.

Holden, K. C., R. V. Burkhauser, and D. A. Myers. 1986. "Pensioners' Annuity Choice: Is the Well-Being of Their Widows Considered?" University of Wisconsin, Institute for Research on Poverty discussion paper 802–86.

Hurd, Michael D., and David A. Wise. 1989. "The Wealth and Poverty of Widows: Assets Before and After the Husband's Death." In D. Wise, ed. *The Economics of Aging*. Chicago and London: University of Chicago Press, 177–99.

Kotlikoff, Laurence J. 1983. "Altruistic Extended Family Linkages—A Note." Mimeo, Yale University, and included as part of a 1983 grant proposal to the Sloan Foundation. Published in Laurence J. Kotlikoff. 1989. *What Determines Savings?* Cambridge, MA: MIT Press, 86–7.

Kotlikoff, Laurence J. 1989. *What Determines Savings?* Cambridge, MA: MIT Press.

Mirrlees, James A. 1971. "An Exploration in the Theory of Optimal Income Taxation." *Review of Economic Studies*. 38(114): 175–208.

Townsend, Robert M. 1989. "Risk and Insurance in Village India." Mimeo, University of Chicago.

I Saving and Bequests

1 Understanding the Postwar Decline in U.S. Saving: A Cohort Analysis

with Jagadeesh Gokhale and John Sabelhaus

In 1950 the rate of net national saving in the United States was 12.3 percent. In 1994 it was only 3.5 percent.[1] The difference in these saving rates is illustrative of a dramatic long-term decline in U.S. saving. The U.S. saving rate averaged 9.1 percent per year in the 1950s and 1960s, 8.5 percent in the 1970s, 4.7 percent in the 1980s, and just 2.7 percent in the first five years of the 1990s.[2]

The decline in saving in the United States has been associated with an equally dramatic decline in domestic investment. Since 1990, net domestic investment has averaged 3.6 percent per year, compared with 8.2 percent in the 1950s, 7.9 percent in the 1960s and 1970s, and 6.1 percent in the 1980s. The low rate of domestic investment appears to have limited growth in labor productivity and, consequently, real wages. Since 1979, labor productivity has grown at less than half the rate observed between 1950 and 1979, and total real compensation (wages plus fringe benefits) per hour has grown at only one-seventh its previously observed rate.

This paper develops a unique cohort data set to study the decline in U.S. saving. It focuses on four periods for which Consumer Expenditure Surveys (CEX) are available: 1960–61, 1972–73, 1984–86, and 1987–90. These and a host of other microeconomic surveys are combined with National Income and Product Account (NIPA) data and other aggregates to form measures of cohort-specific consumption and resources. The benchmarking of our cohort data set to NIPA aggregates ensures that our findings relate directly to the decline in net national saving measured by these aggregates.

We use our cohort data within a simple life-cycle framework to decompose the postwar change in U.S. saving in terms of changes in the following factors: the intergenerational distribution of resources, cohort-specific consumption propensities, the rate of government spending on goods and services, and demographics. Our findings are striking. Most of the decline in U.S. saving can be traced to two factors. First, the government's redistribution of resources toward older generations with high consumption propensities from younger ones, including those not yet born, with low or zero consumption propensities. Second, a dramatic rise in the consumption propensities of older Americans. The form of government transfers to the elderly—the fact that they are annuitized and, in the case of health care, made in kind—may help to explain the rise in the elderly's spending rate. For the young and middle-aged, the findings are different. The consumption propensities of most young generations have declined slightly or remained constant over time, and this has bolstered U.S. saving.

The next two sections of this chapter provide a brief discussion of related research and present some stylized facts about recent trends in U.S. saving and consumption. We then describe our method for decomposing changes in national saving. We discuss data construction and data sources in general terms (details are provided in appendix A) and present our findings. We next relate the increase in the propensity of the elderly to consume to the increase in the annuitization of their resources recently documented by Alan Auerbach, Laurence Kotlikoff, and David Weil and Auerbach and others.[3] We address a number of questions about the reliability of our findings and examine the paper's implications for future rates of U.S. saving. We conclude with a summary.

Related Studies

Several recent studies of U.S. saving focus on personal saving, defined as saving out of disposable income. Lawrence Summers and Chris Carroll suggest that younger cohorts may be hoping to rely on social security in their retirement and are, in consequence, saving too little on their own. In contrast, Barry Bosworth, Gary Burtless, and John Sabelhaus compare personal saving rates in the 1960s, 1970s, and 1980s and conclude that all age groups are now saving at lower rates than used to be the case. Orazio Attanasio reaches a third conclusion. He places the blame for current low levels of personal saving on the failure of a particular subset of cohorts to save, namely, those born between 1925 and 1939.[4]

The studies by Bosworth, Burtless, and Sabelhaus and by Attanasio use consumer expenditure data that directly cover only 80 percent of aggregate consumption. Although Bosworth and his coauthors impute some missing consumption components, they ignore health care, as does Attanasio. This is a significant omission. Health care is a large and growing component of national consumption. Moreover, as medical consumption has grown as a share of output, so too has overall consumption, suggesting that medical consumption, or at least its method of finance, has played a key role in the decline in the U.S. rate of saving.

Even were all the studies of personal saving in agreement, it would be hard to assess their implications for national saving. From a theoretical perspective, personal saving bears no necessary relationship to national saving. This point can be understood by considering the standard life-cycle model under certainty. According to this model, the appropriate measure of household saving is the propensity of households to consume out of the present value of their remaining lifetime resources. This propensity will be invariant to present-value neutral changes in the timing of after-tax income flows, each of which will produce a different value of personal saving.

For example, an increase in households' current social security taxes that is offset, in present value, by higher projected social security benefits will leave their consumption and, thus, national saving unchanged, but lower their personal saving. The postwar period has witnessed an enormous growth in social security and other government transfer programs. Hence changes over time in U.S. personal saving rates may simply reflect the life-cycle pattern of these tax and transfer programs, rather than some underlying change in household consumption and saving behavior.

The problem with studying national saving through personal saving is actually deeper than this discussion suggests because the tax and transfer labels of government receipts and expenditure programs are not unique.[5] Assuming that agents are rational, the same fiscal policy can be classified in countless ways without making a difference to economic outcomes, including national saving. But each classification will result in a different measure of personal saving. For example, suppose that the U.S. government had historically classified social security contributions as loans to the government rather than as taxes, and current and past social security benefit payments as the repayment of past loans plus an old age tax rather than as transfer payments.[6] That would have produced an entirely different reported path of personal saving during the postwar period, but it would not have altered national saving, assuming rational consumption and saving behavior. In 1993, as an example, the personal saving rate would have been almost twice as large as the rate reported.

Studies that focus directly on household consumption and, by implication, on national saving are few and far between. The work of David Cutler and others is one example.[7] This study employs an infinite-horizon model to study the response of household consumption to demographic change. Its findings suggest that high rates of household consumption and low rates of national saving reflect households' projections of higher future per capita income levels as a result of the aging of the U.S. population. There are two major problems with this analysis, however. First, the assumed intergenerational altruism underlying the infinite-horizon model is strongly rejected by household and cohort panel data.[8] Second, the study's results are highly sensitive to the authors' assumption about the initial position of the economy.

Michael Boskin and Lawrence Lau estimate an aggregate consumption function, taking into account aggregation over different cohorts.[9] Their results suggest that a decline in saving by generations born after the Great Depression has been largely responsible for the postwar decline in U.S. saving—a finding at odds with those reported here. However, they find that the age distribution of resources is an important determinant of aggregate consumption—a finding consistent with those reported here.

The Postwar Decline in U.S. Saving: Some Stylized Facts

Table 1.1 reports average values of the net national saving rate for the 1950s, 1960s, 1970s, 1980s, and the first four years of the 1990s. The net national saving rate is defined as $(Y - C - G)/Y$, where Y refers to net national product (NNP), C to household consumption, and G to government spending (purchases of goods and services). The table also reports rates of government and household consumption out of output, G/Y and C/Y, respectively. In addition, the table reports our preferred measure of private sector saving, which we call

Table 1.1
Saving and spending rates, percent

Period	Net national saving rate	Government spending rate	Household consumption rate	Household saving rate
1950–59	9.1	21.0	69.9	11.5
1960–69	9.1	22.1	68.8	11.7
1970–79	8.5	21.4	70.1	10.8
1980–89	4.7	21.3	74.0	5.9
1990–94	2.7	20.7	76.6	3.4

Source: Authors' calculations from the National Income and Product Accounts (NIPA).

the household saving rate. This is defined as $(Y - G - C)/(Y - G)$; that is, the share saved of the output left to the household sector after the government has consumed. Unlike the personal saving rate, the household saving rate is not affected by present-value neutral changes in the timing of income flows. Nor is it altered by changes in the classification of government receipts and expenditures, assuming that agents are rational and are not deceived by the government's choice of language.

As table 1.1 indicates, government spending has not been responsible for reducing the rate of national saving. Indeed, the rate of government spending, G/Y, has declined since the 1960s. Furthermore, in the 1990s government spending has averaged just 20.7 percent of output—as low a rate as any observed in the five periods considered. The rate of household consumption, on the other hand, rose from 69.9 percent of output in the 1950s to 76.6 percent in the early 1990s.[10] This increased rate of household consumption is associated with a decline in the household saving rate from 11.5 percent in the 1950s to 3.4 percent in the 1990s.

Table 1.2 considers the role of health care spending in the growth of household spending. It shows that medical expenditures (M/Y) have increased from 3.9 percent of NNP in the 1950s to 12.8 percent in the 1990s. In the 1950s health care spending represented less than 6 percent of household consumption. In the 1990s to date it has represented almost 17 percent. The increase in the rate of medical spending is associated with only a modest reduction in the rate of nonmedical spending. In the 1950s nonmedical consumption averaged 66.0 percent of NNP. In the 1990s it has averaged 63.8 percent.

Table 1.2
Household and medical consumption rates, percent

Period	Household consumption rate	Medical consumption rate
1950–59	69.9	3.9
1960–69	68.8	5.2
1970–79	70.1	7.3
1980–89	74.0	10.1
1990–93	76.6	12.8

Source: Authors' calculations from the NIPA.

Thus, although the rate of medical consumption has risen by 8.9 percentage points between the 1950s and 1990s, the rate of non-medical consumption has fallen by only 2.2 percentage points.

Decomposing the Changes in National Saving

We adopt the no-bequest life-cycle model under certainty as an initial framework for decomposing the postwar changes in national saving. In so doing, we do not belittle other determinants of saving, such as uncertainty and the desire to bequeath. Rather, we believe that this model is a useful starting point. Our analysis relates cohorts' consumption to their resources. In the base case, resources refers to net wealth plus the actuarial present value of future nonasset pretax income, minus the actuarial present value of net taxes (taxes paid less transfer payments received).[11]

The base case assumes that individuals correctly foresee their future resource streams (pretax nonasset income, taxes, and transfer payments) through 1993 and form projections of these variables for the years after 1993. We also present results based on the assumption of myopic expectations. Under myopic expectations, individuals are assumed to extrapolate current age- and sex-specific levels of non-asset incomes, taxes, and transfers into the future on the basis of recently observed rates of productivity growth.

Our results can also be considered from the perspective of a life-cycle model with uncertainty, in which expected, rather than actual realized resources, determine consumption. Realized future income, taxes, and transfers represent an unbiased estimate of the ex ante expected values of these resource streams, since they differ from their expected values by a mean-zero expectation error. If the expectation error in total resources is small, then the use of realized future resources rather than expected future resources, the theoretically more appropriate resource measure, will make little difference to our results. Note that the expectation error in total resources could be small even if expectation errors with respect to particular components of resources were large. The reason is that these expectation errors may be offsetting. For example, the introduction and growth of medicare after 1965 may not have been expected by the young cohorts that were making consumption decisions in the early 1960s. But, presumably, the future slowdown in the growth of their real wages was also unanticipated. This unexpected decline in the human capital component of their resources may have offset much of the unexpected increase in the present value of their medicare benefits.

Our interest is in the net national saving rate, which at time t is given by

$$\frac{S_t}{Y_t} = 1 - \frac{C_t}{Y_t} - \frac{G_t}{Y_t}, \tag{1}$$

where S_t stands for net national saving.

In the standard life-cycle model with certainty and homothetic preferences, each cohort's consumption is proportional to the present value of its remaining lifetime resources ("resources," for short). We denote the per capita resources of the cohort aged i at time t as r_{it}. This is the sum of the cohort's per capita net wealth, nw_{it}, its per capita present value of future labor earnings (human wealth), hw_{it}, its per capita present value of private and government employee pension benefits (pension wealth), pw_{it}, less its per capita present value of future tax payments net of the per capita present value of future transfer payments received (the generational account), ga_{it}.

Since our empirical analysis attributes all consumption to adult cohorts aged eighteen through one hundred, we write aggregate consumption at time t as the sum of consumption of individual cohorts aged eighteen through one hundred;[12] that is, as

$$C_t = \sum_{i=18}^{100} \alpha_{it} r_{it} P_{it}, \tag{2}$$

where i indexes age, α_{it} stands for the average propensity to consume of i-year-olds at time t, and P_{it} stands for the number of i-year-olds at time t. We note for future reference that $\alpha_{it} = c_{it}/r_{it}$, where c_{it} is the average level of consumption of those aged i at time t.

Our goal is to decompose changes over time in the net national saving rate into changes in the rate of government spending, G_t/Y_t, and changes in the determinants of the rate of household spending, C_t/Y_t. These determinants are clarified by expressing the rate of household spending as

$$\frac{C_t}{Y_t} = \left(\sum_{i=18}^{100} \alpha_{it} \frac{r_{it}P_{it}}{r_t P_t} \right) \frac{R_t}{Y_t}, \tag{3}$$

where R_t stands for the total value of resources of living generations at time t (that is, $R_t = \sum_i r_{it}p_{it}$), P_t stands for the total population at time t, and r_t stands for the resources per capita of living generations at time t.

According to equation 3, changes over time in the rate of household consumption can be traced to changes over time in four factors: cohort-specific propensities to consume (α_{it}), the shape of the age-resource profile (r_{it}/r_t), the age-composition of the population (P_{it}/P_t), and the resources-to-output ratio, that is, the ratio of the total resources of current generations to current output (R_t/Y_t).

In our empirical analysis we compute the values of five factors—the four above and government spending—for each of the periods 1960–61, 1972–73, 1984–86, and 1987–90. We then consider how the national saving rate in each of these periods would have differed had one of the five factors not taken its actual value but, instead, a value observed in another period.

This decomposition of changes in life-cycle saving into those due to changes in demographics, saving behavior, and age-resource profiles has a long tradition, dating back to the work of Albert Ando and Franco Modigliani.[13] Their lessons bear repeating. First, increases in any cohort's propensity to consume will, all else equal, raise the rate of aggregate household spending and lower national saving. Second, given the value of R_t/Y_t, higher rates of population growth and real wage growth mean higher rates of national saving for the following reason. In the life cycle model, the propensity to consume is predicted to rise with age. Since growth in both population and real wages raises the values of P_{it}/P_t and r_{it}/r_t for younger cohorts and lowers them for older cohorts, such growth produces a reweighting of α_{it} that reduces the rate of household spending and raises the rate of national saving.

The ultimate effect of growth in population and real wages on national saving is ambiguous, however, because such growth is also likely to raise R_t/Y_t. Faster population growth means that the remaining lifetime resources and incomes of the young play a bigger role in determining the overall value of R_t/Y_t. But since the ratio of future resources to current income is larger for the young than it is for the old, population growth raises R_t/Y_t. Faster real wage growth also raises R_t/Y_t because it raises the resources-to-income ratio of the young, while leaving that of the old unchanged.

The final lesson is that redistribution across generations can alter national saving. It does so by altering the age-resource profile, or the resources-to-output ratio, or both. Government tax and transfer policy can, of course, produce such redistribution. Consider government redistribution among living generations—specifically, from the young to the old at time t—that leaves the resources-to-output ratio unchanged. Such redistribution is accomplished by raising the present value of taxes net of the transfers of young generations (the generational account) and reducing the present value of taxes net of the transfers of older generations, while leaving unchanged the net tax burden faced by current generations collectively. This policy lowers the values of r_{it}/r_t for the young and raises them for the old. Thus it raises the weights applied to relatively high values of α_{it} and reduces those applied to relatively low values, producing a higher rate of aggregate household spending.

Next, consider redistribution from future to current generations that raises the resources-to-output ratio, but leaves the age-resource profile unchanged. This can be accomplished by reducing the generational account of each current generation by just the amount needed to produce the same percentage increase in its remaining lifetime resources. This policy raises the rate of household spending by an amount that depends on the resource- and population-weighted economywide propensity to consume (the bracketed term in equation 3).

Data Construction and Sources

To decompose changes in national saving across the four periods chosen, one needs to know the value of the five factors listed above for each period. Of these factors, the rate of government spending and the age-composition of the population are readily available. This is not the case for the value of c_{it} or r_{it}, both of which are needed to form α_{it}. The value of r_{it} is also needed to form the age-resource profile and the resources-to-output ratio.

Our procedures for calculating c_{it} and r_{it} are described in detail in appendix A. Briefly, we form these variables, or their constituent components, by using cross-sectional profiles and population data to distribute aggregate variables by age and sex. For example, to determine the average value of consumption of fifty-three-year-old males and females in the period 1960–61, we use CEX and other data to determine relative per capita consumption by age and sex during that period, and use this age-sex relative consumption profile and data on the age-sex composition of the population during this period to distribute aggregate personal consumption expenditures from the NIPA for this period by age and sex. As a second example, consider how we calculate the human wealth component of the resources of thirty-eight-year-old females in 1972. For 1972 and subsequent years we distribute actual or projected NIPA labor income by age and sex, using profiles of relative average annual earnings by age and sex derived from the U.S. Census Bureau's annual Current Population Survey (CPS), as well as actual and projected population counts by age and sex. The resulting values for the average earnings of thirty-eight-year-old females in 1972, of thirty-nine-year-old females in 1973, of forty-year-old females in 1974, and so forth are then actuarially discounted back to 1973.

As just suggested, our study treats individuals, rather than households, as the life-cycle decisionmakers. In practice, it is impossible to conduct this type of cohort analysis on the basis of the household as the decisionmaking unit for the simple reason that households are transient entities that appear and disappear through time, as the result of marriage, divorce, separation, and death. The empirical issue arising from treating individual adults within a multiadult household as separate decisionmakers is how to allocate household income and consumption among them. We allocate the total income earned by married couples evenly between the husband and wife, and allocate income earned by other adults to those adults. In allocating married couples' income evenly among spouses, we are, in effect, implicitly viewing marriage as the choice of an occupation that generates income (which may be negative) for each spouse. To examine the sensitivity of our results to this view of marriage, we also present results in which the income earned by spouses is allocated to the nominal recipient of that income.

As described in more detail in appendix A, household consumption taken from the CEX is allocated among adults in the following manner. Wherever it is possible to determine the particular consumer of a good or service within the household, such as the consumer of pipe tobacco, this individual is allocated this consumption. Consumption that is not so easily allocable—such as expenditure on food—is allocated among all adults and children, using a child-adult equivalency scale and assuming equal consumption by all adults. The children's consumption is then reallocated equally to each coresident parent.

Illustrating the Data Construction

Our general method of distributing an aggregate variable in time t, say Z_t, by age and sex can be understood more precisely by considering the following equation:

$$Z_t = z_{40t}^m \sum_{i=18}^{100} (v_{it}^m P_{it}^m + v_{it}^f P_{it}^f). \tag{4}$$

In equation 4, z_{40t}^m stands for the average value of Z for forty-year-old males at time t; v_{it}^m and v_{it}^f stand for the ratios of the average values of Z for males and females, respectively, aged i at time t to z_{40t}^m; and P_{it}^m and P_{it}^f stand for the populations of males and females, respectively, aged i in year t. Given the value of Z_t from the NIPA or another source, the relative age-sex profile of Z (v_{it}^m and v_{it}^f) calculated from a cross-sectional survey, and P_{it}^m and P_{it}^f calculated from population data, one can use equation 4 to solve for z_{40t}^m. One can then multiply this value by $v_{it}^m(v_{it}^f)$ to determine $z_{it}^m(z_{it}^f)$, that is, the average value of Z for males (females) aged i in year t. Finally, one can form a population-weighted average of z_{it}^m and z_{it}^f to produce an average value of Z for age group i at time t.

In the case of c_{it}, we use the 1961–62, 1972–73, 1984–86, and 1987–90 CEX and the 1977 and 1987 National Medical Expenditure Surveys (NMES) to form relative profiles of total consumption by age and sex. By total consumption we mean all of the components of household consumption that are included in the NIPA aggregate, including health care and imputed rent on owner-occupied housing. The age-sex relative consumption profiles for the four periods derived in these calculations are used with period-specific counts of population by age and sex to distribute NIPA values of aggregate household consumption in each of the four periods.

Turning to r_{it}, recall that this variable is the sum of annuitized and nonannuitized resources. We form each of the components of r_{it} separately and then add them together. By annuitized resources we refer to the present value of future labor earnings (human wealth), social security benefits, private and government employee pension benefits, government health care benefits, welfare benefits, and other government transfers; and, as negative annuities, the present value of future taxes. Taxes include labor and capital income taxes, indirect taxes, payroll taxes, and property and other taxes. Nonannuitized resources refer simply to holdings of net wealth.

The computation of cohorts' nonannuitized resources for the four periods involves distributing by age and sex and aggregate value of household net wealth for each year, and then averaging over the years defining the four periods. The computation of each component of annuitized resources is more involved. First, for each year between 1960 and 1993 the national aggregate for a particular type of payment (or receipt) is distributed by age and sex, according to the cross-sectional age-sex relative profile that is applicable to that payment (or receipt). For example, aggregate 1965 social security benefits are distributed according to the age-sex relative profile for these benefits in 1965. This yields per capita estimates of the payment (or receipt) by age and sex for that year. The per capita annuity values for years after 1993 are estimated by either distributing projected aggregate payments (or receipts) according to the latest available cross-sectional relative profile, or assuming that age- and sex-specific per capita values, respectively, equal those in 1993 or some later year, except for an adjustment for productivity growth.

Second, for each generation in a given year t, the present value of all future per capita payments of a particular type (for example, indirect tax payments) is computed by multiplying these future per capita payments by the generation's projected population in the relevant years, discounting these values back to year t, and dividing the sum of the discounted values by the number of members of the generation alive in the base year. This method produces actuarially discounted per capita present values of the particular payment (or receipt) for each generation alive in year t. We consider three pretax real discount rates: 3 percent, 6 percent (our base case), and 9 percent.[14]

As an example of this method for calculating the different components of annuitized resources, consider our estimate of human wealth (HW). The formula for human wealth in year t for individuals of sex x born in year k (HW^x_{tk}) is

$$HW^x_{tk} = \frac{1}{P^x_{tk}} \sum_{s=t}^{k+D} e^x_{sk} P^x_{sk} R^{s-t}, \tag{5}$$

where e^x_{sk} stands for the average earnings in year s of a member of the generation born in year k and of sex x; P^x_{sk} is the population in year s of the same sex-specific generation; $R = 1/(1+r)$, where r is the rate of interest; and D is the maximum age of life. The calculation of e^x_{sk} is given by

$$e^x_{sk} = \frac{d^x_{sk} E_s}{\sum_{s=t}^{k+D} (d^m_{sk} P^m_{sk} + d^f_{sm} P^f_{sk})}. \tag{6}$$

In equations 5 and 6, E_s is aggregate labor earnings in year s, and d^x_{sk} is the ratio in year s of the average earnings of the generation born in year k and of sex x to the average earnings of our reference group—those who were aged forty in year s (that is, those for whom $k = s - 40$).

The construction of relative profiles by age and sex (d^x_{tk}) is described by the following equations:

$$j^x_{sk} = \frac{\sum_{i=1}^{N^x_{sk}} w^x_{ski} j^x_{ski}}{\sum_{i=1}^{N^x_{sk}} w^x_{ski}}, \tag{7}$$

and

$$d^x_{sk} = \frac{j^x_{sk}}{j^m_{s,s-40}}. \tag{8}$$

In equation 7, j^x_{sk} is the weighted average (across cohort members indexed by i) of labor income; N^x_{sk} is the number of observations in year s of individuals of sex x born in year k; j^x_{ski} is the wage and salary income in year s of the i-th individual of sex x who was born in year k; and w^x_{ski} is the person-weight of this observation. Equation 8 shows the calculation for year s of the average labor income of members of the generation of sex x born in year k, relative to that of contemporaneous forty-year-old males.

The national aggregates used in these calculations come from the National Income and Product Accounts, the Federal Reserve System's Flow of Funds (FOF), the American Council of Life Insurance (ACLI), the Current Population Survey, and the Survey of Current Business (SCB). The sources for cross-sectional relative profiles are the CPS, the Survey of Income and Program Participation (SIPP), the Consumer Expenditure Survey, the Survey of Consumer Finances (SCF), the Social Security Administration's Annual Statistical Supplement (SSAASS), and the Health Care Financing Administration (HCFA). The computations also use the historic and projected population counts of the Social Security Administration (SSA).

Looking at the Data

Before decomposing the changes in the U.S. saving rate during the postwar period, it is worth looking at some of the data that we have constructed. Tables 1.3 and 1.4 present the average values of consumption, resources, and the components of resources for males and females within ten-year age groups in each of the four periods under consideration (1960–61, 1972–73, 1984–86, and 1987–90).

To start with consumption, figure 1.1 presents cross-sectional relative age-consumption profiles for total consumption in each of the four periods. Figure 1.2 does the same for nonmedical consumption alone. The periods are based on the availability of CEX data. For each period, the average consumption of forty-year-olds is normalized to one.

The figures document a remarkable increase in the relative consumption of the elderly. This increase is more pronounced if medical care is included in the measure of consumption, but the increase in the relative consumption of nonmedical goods and services is also striking. Figure 1.3 depicts the size of housing, medical, and other consumption for selected cohorts during the periods 1960–61 and 1987–90. The first two panels of figure 1.3 show these components in constant 1993 dollars. Consumption of all three was greater in the late 1980s than in the early 1960s. The third and fourth panels show

Table 1.3
Consumption, total resources, and components of resources, males

	Age group								
Measure and period	20–29	30–39	40–49	50–59	60–69	70–79	80–89	20–89	65–89
Consumption									
1960–61	12.0	15.2	15.6	14.0	11.5	9.4	8.8	13.5	9.9
1972–73	14.8	19.7	20.3	18.8	16.9	14.9	14.0	17.6	15.3
1984–86	15.3	20.6	23.6	22.2	21.7	20.0	21.5	20.0	20.9
1987–90	16.6	21.4	25.4	23.7	23.9	23.4	23.1	21.6	23.7
Percent change[a]	37.7	41.4	62.7	69.6	108.2	148.3	163.8	60.2	138.8
Total resources									
1960–61	269.6	273.4	259.9	224.1	178.6	142.0	103.4	239.6	146.8
1972–73	316.4	338.9	335.2	307.9	255.8	201.1	130.0	304.8	205.3
1984–86	349.5	379.2	394.9	379.3	339.9	259.7	141.3	356.4	265.6
1987–90	364.5	393.6	410.0	399.3	362.3	281.3	154.6	373.6	286.0
Percent change[a]	35.2	44.0	57.8	78.2	102.8	98.1	49.5	55.9	94.8
Human wealth									
1960–61	358.7	315.7	238.5	140.5	48.7	11.3	4.5	224.8	17.5
1972–73	425.6	395.4	292.9	168.9	53.5	10.2	3.8	275.9	16.8
1984–86	479.2	454.0	354.0	189.7	57.5	11.5	3.8	326.5	18.2
1987–90	499.7	471.8	369.9	200.0	59.8	12.9	4.1	339.8	19.8
Percent change[a]	39.3	49.4	55.1	42.4	22.8	14.8	−7.3	51.1	12.6

Table 1.3 (continued)

Measure and period	Age group 20–29	30–39	40–49	50–59	60–69	70–79	80–89	20–89	65–89
Nonhuman wealth									
1960–61	11.8	44.1	81.1	111.3	125.4	118.2	91.8	70.8	118.0
1972–73	13.1	48.9	99.7	141.1	159.7	142.2	88.7	83.4	140.8
1984–86	14.5	50.5	109.1	163.6	185.1	157.0	73.6	87.8	154.5
1987–90	15.5	52.9	113.3	170.8	193.6	164.0	77.0	92.6	161.3
Percent change[a]	31.2	20.2	39.7	53.5	54.4	38.8	−16.1	30.8	36.7
Pension wealth									
1960–61	15.8	20.5	21.7	17.6	14.0	9.5	4.8	17.6	10.3
1972–73	18.2	26.4	36.9	39.5	29.3	18.6	12.1	27.9	20.5
1984–86	19.3	29.0	44.5	62.1	60.1	35.2	18.6	36.9	40.0
1987–90	20.0	29.6	45.3	65.3	65.4	41.0	21.6	39.1	45.4
Percent change[a]	26.8	44.4	108.9	270.5	367.0	331.4	352.5	122.1	339.7
Generational account									
1960–61	116.7	106.9	81.4	45.3	9.5	−3.0	−2.3	73.6	−0.9
1972–73	140.5	131.8	94.3	41.6	−13.3	−30.1	−25.3	82.4	−27.2
1984–86	163.4	154.2	112.6	36.1	−37.2	−55.9	−45.3	94.8	−52.8
1987–90	170.6	160.7	118.5	36.8	−43.5	−63.3	−51.8	97.8	−59.6

Source: Authors' calculations. Cohort per capita consumption numbers are based on the Consumer Expenditure Survey (CEX), the National Medical Expenditure Survey (NMES), and the NIPA. Total resources and the components of resources are based on the Current Population Survey (CPS, March files), the Survey of Consumer Finances (SCF), and the NIPA. The generational account is calculated on the basis of the CPS, the NIPA, unpublished budget projections provided by the U.S. Office of Management and Budget (OMB), and unpublished population projections provided by the Social Security Administration (SSA). See text and appendix A for details.
Note: Population weighted averages in thousands of 1993 dollars.
a. Percent changes is calculated from the first period (1960–61) to the last (1987–90).

Table 1.4
Consumption, total resources, and components of resources, females

Measure and period	Age group 20–29	30–39	40–49	50–59	60–69	70–79	80–89	20–89	65–89
Consumption									
1960–61	12.7	15.4	14.9	12.9	11.0	9.7	8.7	13.2	9.8
1972–73	15.5	20.6	19.7	17.6	16.2	14.6	13.7	17.4	14.8
1984–86	16.0	21.7	22.3	20.3	20.2	19.5	19.6	19.7	19.8
1987–90	17.2	22.6	24.2	22.3	22.2	22.2	21.8	21.5	22.2
Percent change[a]	35.7	46.8	62.5	72.8	101.8	129.7	149.6	62.6	126.8
Total resources									
1960–61	247.7	255.1	255.4	222.3	166.4	119.3	92.4	223.1	127.0
1972–73	296.3	319.0	323.2	297.3	246.2	181.8	106.3	282.8	183.7
1984–86	346.1	380.7	378.1	357.8	325.4	234.0	105.2	337.8	229.7
1987–90	365.8	399.6	397.5	378.3	346.7	253.2	116.8	357.3	247.3
Percent change[a]	47.7	56.6	55.7	70.2	108.3	112.3	26.4	60.2	94.8
Human wealth									
1960–61	328.1	280.0	204.3	109.9	32.1	5.5	1.2	188.1	9.7
1972–73	394.8	346.9	245.6	130.5	33.7	4.8	1.4	225.2	8.4
1984–86	451.1	418.2	303.5	143.1	37.2	6.1	1.7	272.4	9.5
1987–90	472.2	438.1	322.9	154.1	38.4	6.9	2.1	285.7	10.4
Percent change[a]	43.9	56.5	58.1	40.2	19.7	26.0	79.6	51.9	7.7

Table 1.4 (continued)

	Age group								
Measure and period	20–29	30–39	40–49	50–59	60–69	70–79	80–89	20–89	65–89
Nonhuman wealth									
1960–61	7.1	42.6	91.1	117.1	112.8	99.1	87.7	71.6	101.0
1972–73	12.3	54.7	105.6	138.9	144.4	114.7	65.7	83.9	114.0
1984–86	19.7	65.6	109.1	151.2	167.8	121.7	29.6	88.2	115.3
1987–90	21.4	68.7	113.6	157.9	175.5	126.8	31.0	93.0	119.8
Percent change[a]	202.3	61.4	24.7	34.8	55.5	28.0	−64.7	29.9	18.6
Pension wealth									
1960–61	16.9	22.0	21.8	19.0	14.5	7.3	2.9	18.0	8.6
1972–73	19.1	28.6	38.8	38.1	28.3	16.3	7.5	27.9	17.6
1984–86	20.7	31.2	47.0	61.4	52.4	28.5	16.0	36.7	31.1
1987–90	21.4	31.9	47.9	64.3	57.3	32.2	17.9	38.7	35.0
Percent change[a]	26.4	45.0	119.9	238.9	296.4	341.5	526.8	115.7	305.7
Generational account									
1960–61	104.4	89.4	61.8	23.7	−7.1	−7.4	−0.7	54.5	−7.7
1972–73	129.9	111.3	66.8	10.1	−39.8	−46.0	−31.6	54.2	−43.6
1984–86	145.4	134.2	81.5	−2.1	−68.1	−77.6	−57.9	59.5	−73.8
1987–90	149.1	139.1	86.9	−2.0	−75.5	−87.2	−65.9	60.1	−82.2

Source: Authors' calculations, using the data sources for table 1.3.
Note: Population Weighted Averages in Thousands of 1993 Dollars.
a. Percent change is calculated from the first period (1960–61) to the last (1987–90).

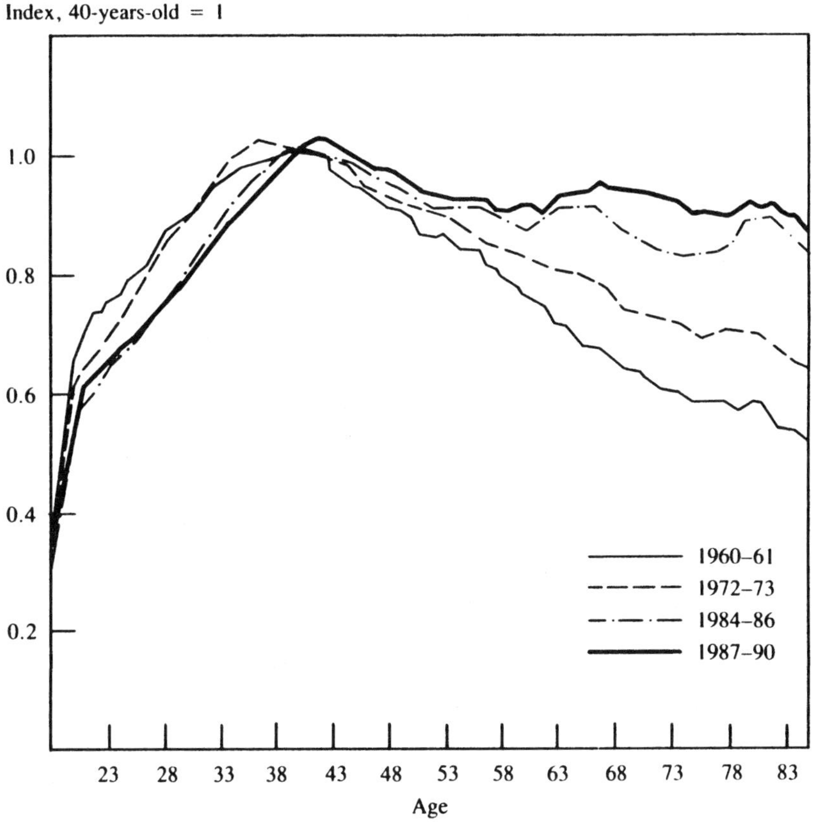

Figure 1.1
Relative total consumption profiles. *Source:* Authors' calculations, based on the CEX.

the shares of the three components. They demonstrate that the share of medical consumption was significantly larger for all cohorts in the later period. For elderly cohorts, the increase in the share of medical consumption was accompanied by a decline in the shares of both housing and other consumption between the early 1960s and the late 1980s.

Table 1.5 examines some of the numbers underlying figures 1.1 and 1.2. It reports the ratio of the average level of total, as well as nonmedical, consumption of sixty-, seventy-, and eighty-year-olds to the respective levels of twenty-, thirty-, and forty-year-olds for each of the four periods. Table 1.5 shows that in 1960–61 seventy-year-olds consumed only 71 percent of the amount consumed by thirty-

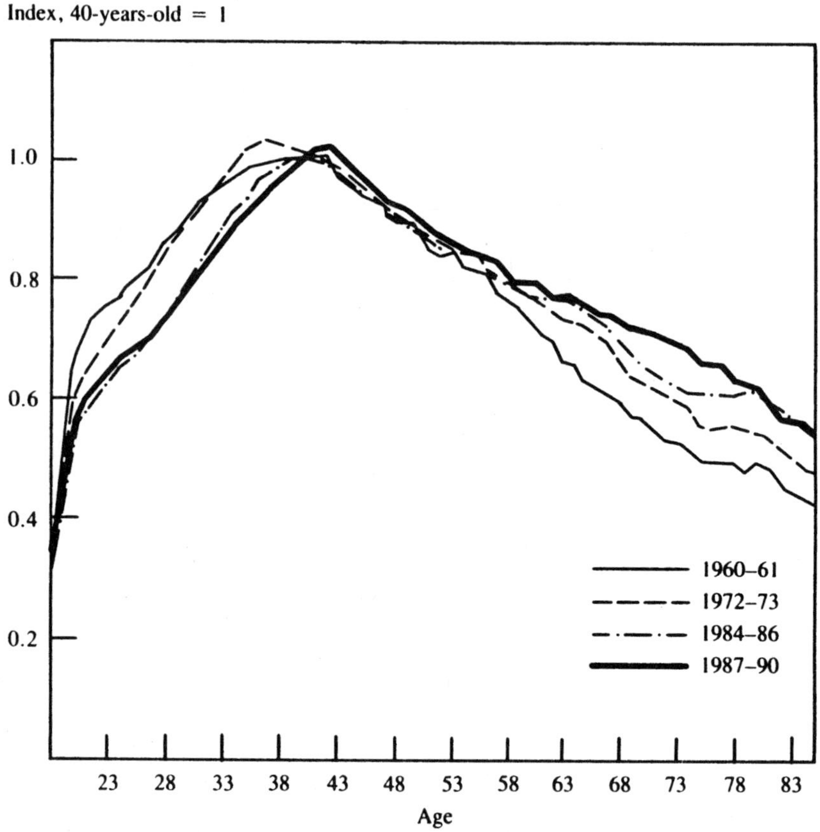

Figure 1.2
Relative nonmedical consumption profiles. *Source:* Authors' calculations, based on the CEX.

year-olds, whereas over the period 1987–90 their consumption exceeded that of thirty-year-olds by 18 percent. In the case of nonmedical consumption, seventy-year-olds consumed only 63 percent of the amount consumed by thirty-year-olds in 1960–61, compared with 91 percent over the period 1987–90. The increase in consumption of the elderly relative to other age groups has been equally dramatic.

Another way to summarize the increase in the relative consumption of the elderly is in terms of their share of total household consumption. In the early 1960s the elderly (those aged sixty-five and over) accounted for 10.6 percent of U.S. household consumption and

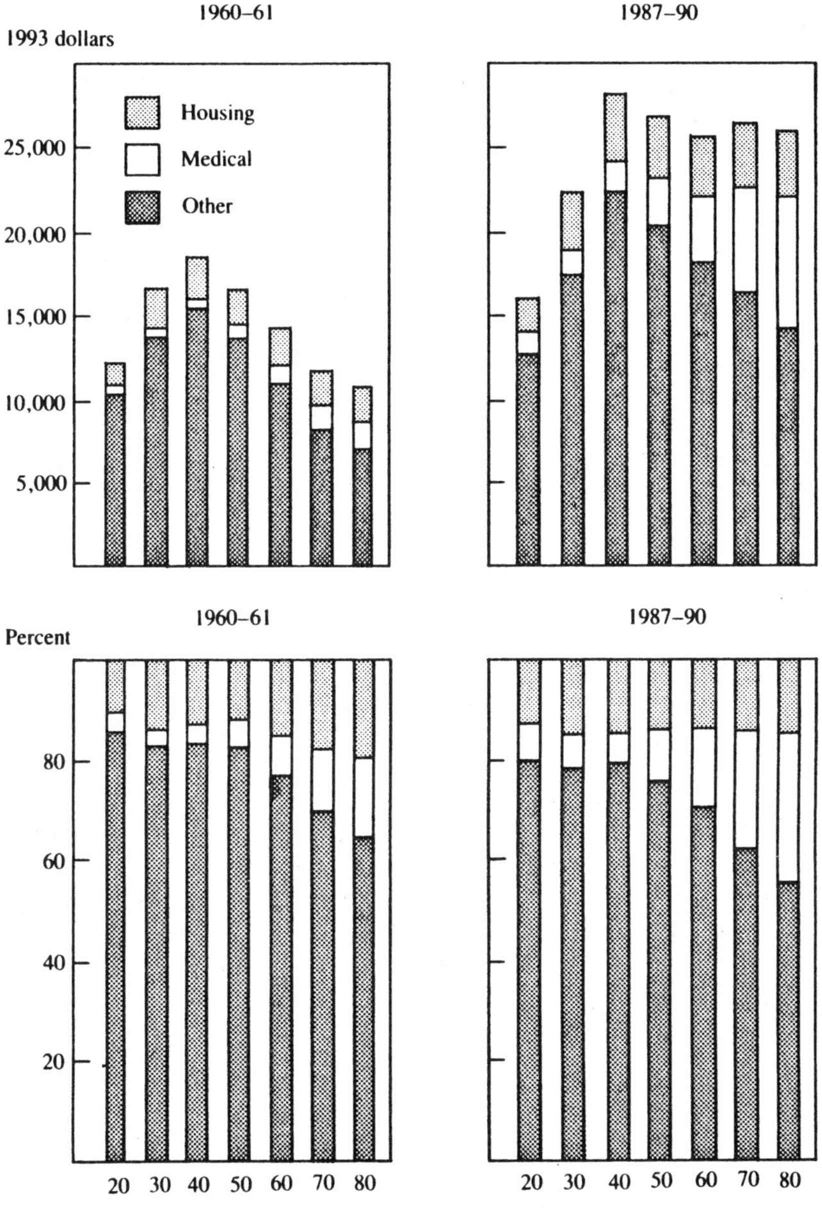

Figure 1.3
Composition of total consumption, by age. *Source:* Authors' calculations, based on the CEX.

Table 1.5
Consumption of the elderly relative to the young, ratio

Age comparison and type of consumption	1960–61	1972–73	1984–86	1987–90
Total				
Age 60/age 20	1.17	1.37	1.58	1.59
Age 70/age 20	0.97	1.21	1.56	1.64
Age 80/age 20	0.89	1.16	1.61	1.60
Age 60/age 30	0.86	0.93	1.09	1.15
Age 70/age 30	0.71	0.82	1.07	1.18
Age 80/age 30	0.65	0.79	1.11	1.16
Age 60/age 40	0.77	0.83	0.87	0.91
Age 70/age 40	0.64	0.73	0.86	0.94
Age 80/age 40	0.58	0.70	0.89	0.92
Nonmedical				
Age 60/age 20	1.11	1.28	1.43	1.42
Age 70/age 20	0.86	1.04	1.22	1.28
Age 80/age 20	0.75	0.91	1.16	1.11
Age 60/age 30	0.81	0.86	0.97	1.02
Age 70/age 30	0.63	0.70	0.83	0.91
Age 80/age 30	0.55	0.61	0.78	0.80
Age 60/age 40	0.73	0.78	0.77	0.80
Age 70/age 40	0.57	0.63	0.66	0.72
Age 80/age 40	0.49	0.55	0.62	0.63

Source: Authors' calculations, based on the CEX and the NMES. See text and appendix A for details.

14.1 percent of the U.S. population. By the late 1980s, they accounted for 17.8 percent of total household consumption and 16.4 percent of the total population. Based on demographics alone, the elderly's share of consumption should have risen by 16.3 percent; instead, it rose by 67.9 percent.

This striking increase in the relative consumption of the elderly has coincided with an equally remarkable increase in their relative resources. Figure 1.4 depicts changes in the age distribution of resources (r_{it}/r_t) across the four periods.[15] Table 1.6 presents ratios of the average resources of sixty-, seventy-, and eighty-year-olds to those of twenty-, thirty-, and forty-year-olds. In 1960–61 the average resources of seventy-year-olds were only 55 percent as large as those of thirty-year-olds. In 1987–90 they were 81 percent as large. The resources of other older cohorts have also grown significantly, relative to those of younger cohorts, over the past three decades.

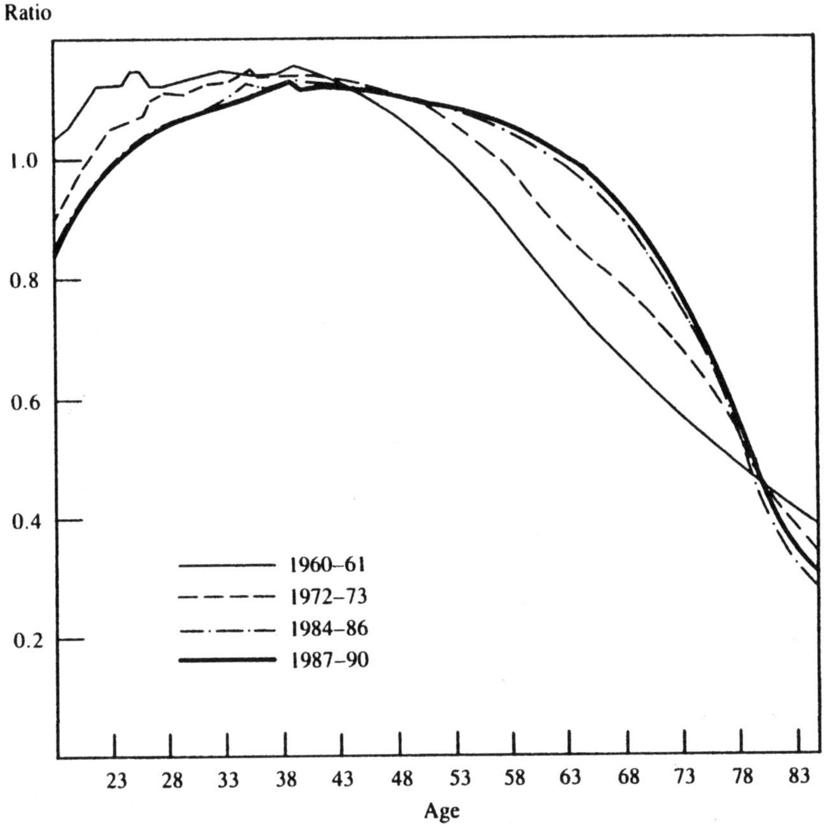

Figure 1.4
Ratio of cohort resources per capita to total resources per capita. *Source:* Authors' calculations, using the data sources for table 1.5.

Figures 1.5 through 1.8 show the components of r_{it}/r_t: the human wealth ratio (hw_{it}/r_t), nonhuman wealth ratio (nhw_{it}/r_t), pension wealth ratio (pw_{it}/r_t), and generational account ratio (ga_{it}/r_t).[16] Figure 1.5 indicates a sizable decline in the human wealth ratio for young cohorts across the four periods. Indeed, this decline accounts for most of the overall decline in r_{it}/r_t for young cohorts. The reduction in the ratio of human wealth to resources at these ages is the result of a low projected rate of labor income growth compared to that of the 1960s and early 1970s. Figure 1.6 shows profiles of the ratio of nonhuman wealth to resources for the four periods. Although this ratio falls for all cohorts over age thirty-three, it falls relatively

Table 1.6
Resources of the elderly relative to the young[a], ratio

Age comparison	1960–61	1972–73	1984–86	1987–90
Age 60/age 20	0.79	0.97	1.10	1.13
Age 70/age 20	0.58	0.78	0.92	0.95
Age 80/age 20	0.43	0.49	0.48	0.50
Age 60/age 30	0.74	0.85	0.95	0.97
Age 70/age 30	0.55	0.67	0.79	0.81
Age 80/age 30	0.40	0.42	0.41	0.43
Age 60/age 40	0.73	0.82	0.90	0.93
Age 70/age 40	0.54	0.66	0.74	0.78
Age 80/age 40	0.40	0.41	0.39	0.41

Source: Authors' calculations, based on the CPS (March files), the SCF, the NIPA, unpublished budget projections provided by the OMB, and unpublished population projections provided by the SSA. See text and appendix A for details.
a. Rate of discount is 6 percent.

more for the oldest age groups. Figure 1.7 presents the ratio of pension wealth to resources for each of the four periods. As indicated, cohorts at preretirement ages experienced especially rapid growth in pension wealth over the last three decades. The increase in pw_{it}/r_t accounts for a sizable part of the overall increase in r_{it}/r_t for these cohorts.

Figure 1.8 shows changes over time in the ratio of the generational account to resources. Note that all cohorts experienced declines in ga_{it}/r_t between the early 1960s and late 1980s. However, the decline was much greater for cohorts aged fifty-five and older. In 1960–61, for example, the present value of net transfers to seventy-year-olds amounted to 3 percent of per capita resources. In the late 1980s the corresponding figure was about 22 percent. Changes in the generational account are clearly responsible for most of the rise in the relative resources of the elderly during the postwar period.

Figure 1.9 graphs age-specific consumption propensities (α_{it}) in the four periods. In each period the propensity to consume is roughly constant for ages up to about sixty, and then rises steadily. There is a local peak between ages thirty-five and forty-five that appears to reflect household expenditures on child rearing. Note that this peak occurs at later ages through time, which is consistent with the trend of parents having their first child at later ages.

The most striking feature of figure 1.9, however, is the very substantial increase in the consumption propensities of older Americans

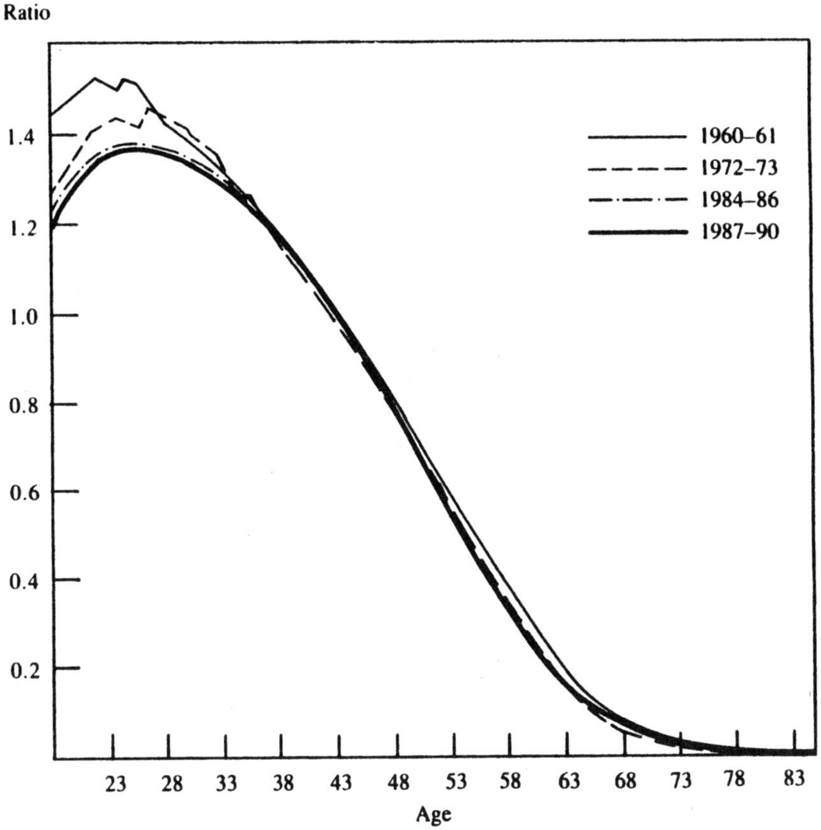

Figure 1.5
Ratio of cohort human wealth per capita to total resources per capita. *Source:* Authors' calculations, based on the CPS and the NIPA.

over time. For example, eighty-year-olds' propensity to consume rose from 8.7 percent in 1960–61 to 13.6 in the period 1987–90. However, there is no corresponding increase in the consumption propensities of the young or the middle-aged.[17]

Returning briefly to the point made above that, unlike propensities to consume out of total remaining lifetime resources that do not change when government receipts and payments are reclassified, propensities to consume or save out of disposable income are creatures of vocabulary, figure 1.10 presents propensities to save out of disposable income by age, in the late 1980s, for two different definitions of disposable income. *Conventional* disposable income is the

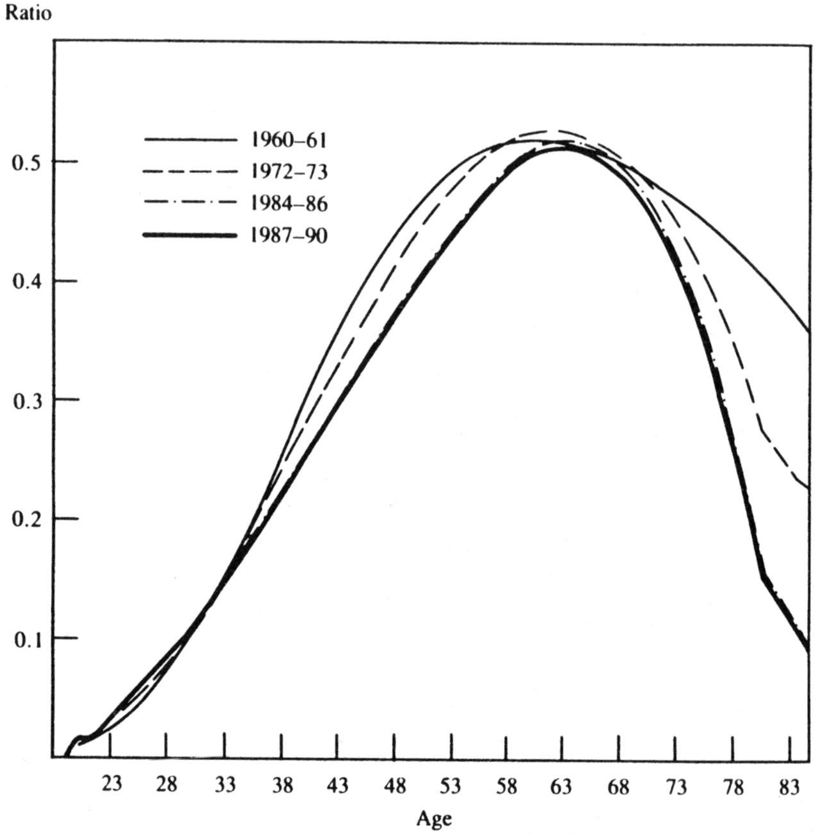

Figure 1.6
Ratio of cohort nonhuman wealth per capita to total resources per capita. *Source:* Authors' calculators, based on the SCF and the NIPA.

sum of labor income, capital income, and pension income less net taxes. *Alternative* disposable income is almost identical, except that all social security contributions are classified as loans to the government, and all social security benefits are classified as the repayment of principal plus interest on past social security loans, less an old age tax.[18] The figure is remarkable in two respects. First, based on the conventional definition, average propensities to save are substantially negative for the young and the old.[19] Second, propensities to save are very different for the two definitions of disposable income. Under the conventional definition, for example, both forty- and

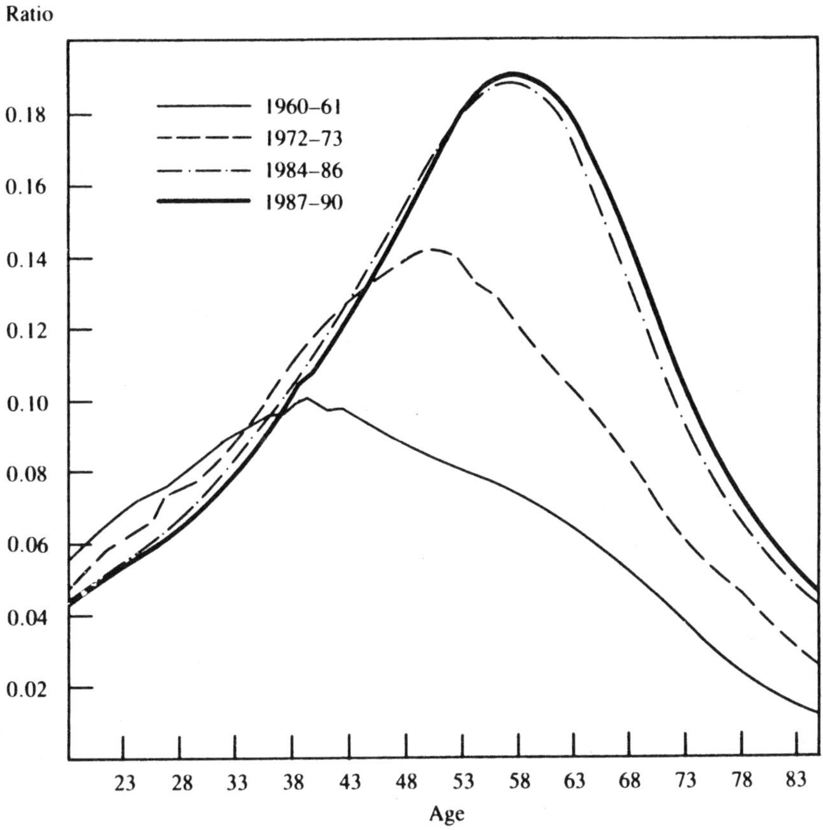

Figure 1.7
Ratio of cohort pension wealth per capita to total resources per capita. *Source:* Authors' calculations, based on the data sources for figure 1.5.

sixty-five-year-olds have zero propensity to save, whereas under the alternative definition their propensities to save are 13 percent and −75 percent, respectively.

Figure 1.11 continues the main thread of the paper by showing changes in the age composition of the U.S. population over the four periods. It indicates a small rise in the share of the population over age sixty-five since the early 1960s. It also indicates that compared with the early 1960s, in the late 1980s there were relatively more adults in their twenties and thirties, and relatively fewer adults in their forties and fifties.

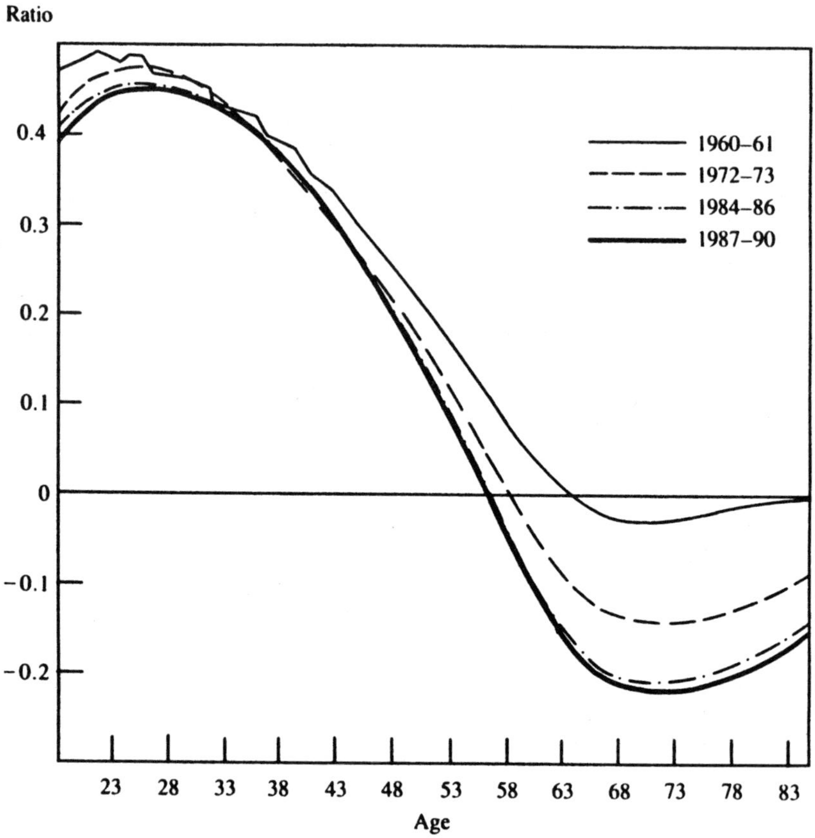

Figure 1.8
Ratio of cohort generational account per capita to total resources per capita. *Source:* Authors' calculations, based on the CPS, the NIPA, the SCF, and unpublished budget projections from the OMB.

Figures 1.12 through 1.14 plot longitudinal profiles of labor and pension incomes and net tax flows. Figure 1.15 plots total nonasset income, computed as labor plus pension income minus the net tax flow. The profiles are shown for cohorts at ten-year intervals, beginning with the cohort aged eighteen in 1920. The labor and pension income profiles exhibit the expected hump shapes. Labor incomes peak at middle age and decline sharply at retirement ages. Pension incomes increase steeply at retirement ages.[20] The longitudinal net tax profiles, however, show an interesting pattern. Generations that reach middle ages later in time pay substantially more in net taxes

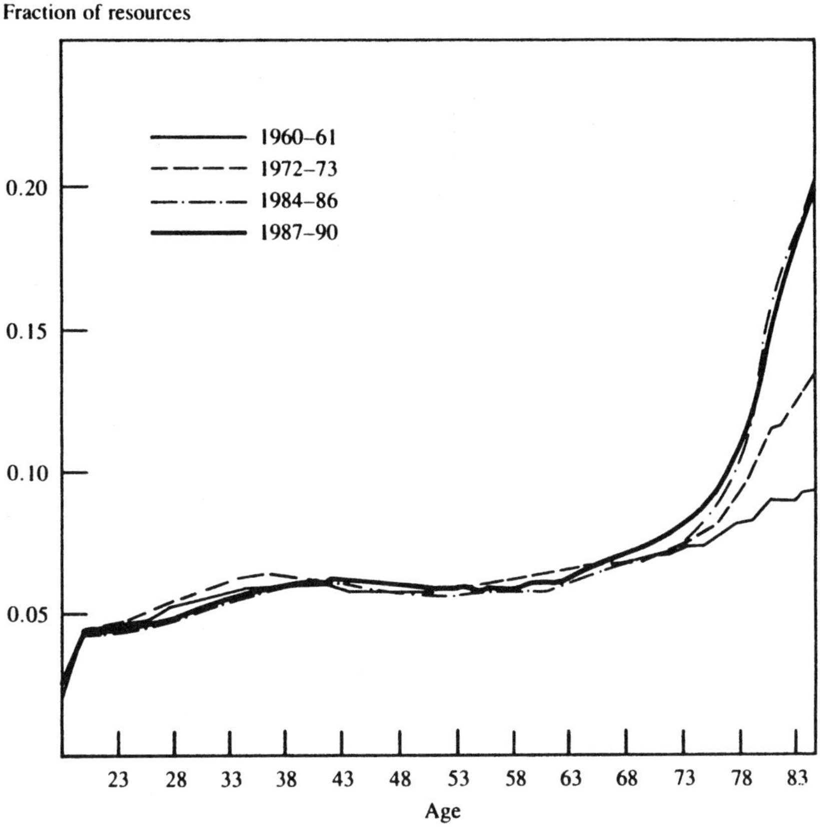

Figure 1.9
Average propensity of consume out of total resources. *Source:* Authors' calculations, using the data sources for table 1.5.

than those that reached these ages earlier. However, cohorts that retire later in time receive substantially greater net benefits from the government than do those that retired earlier.

The total nonasset income profiles are dominated by labor income during youth and middle age. After retirement, however, they are dominated by higher pension incomes and negative net taxes. As a result, nonasset incomes rise sharply at retirement and continue on an upward course thereafter. As was true for those who retired in the 1940s, 1950s, and 1960s, future retirees will receive nonasset incomes that are higher than their peak nonasset incomes when they were

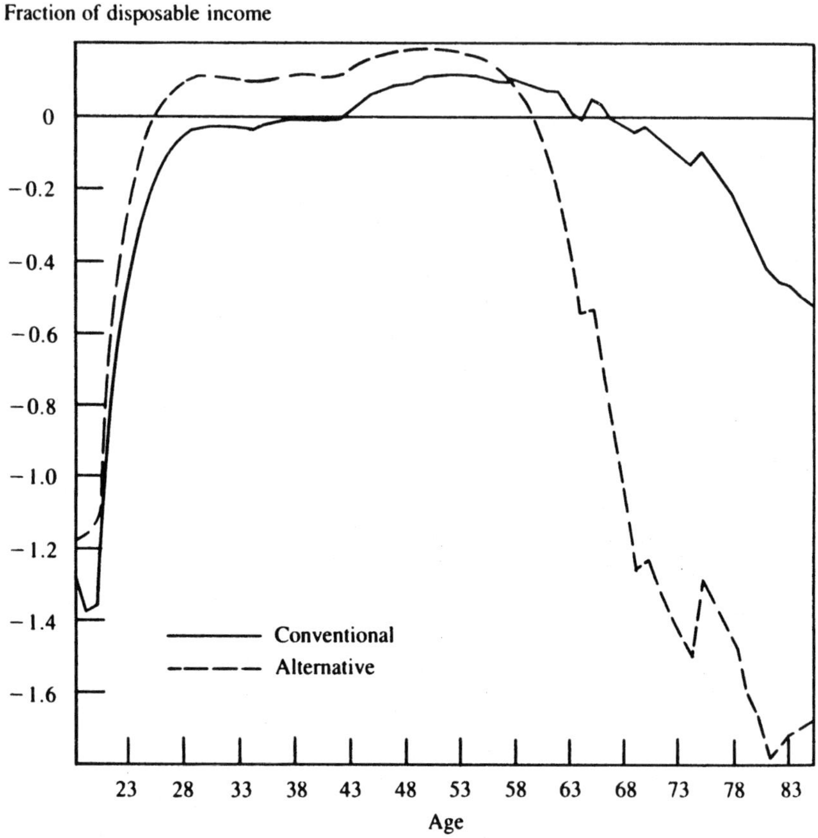

Figure 1.10
Average propensity to save out of conventional and alternative disposable income, 1987–1990. *Source:* Authors' calculations, using the data sources for tables 1.5 and 1.6.

working. This picture differs dramatically from the textbook illustration of life-cycle age-nonasset income profiles.

Explaining the Postwar Decline in U.S. Saving

Table 1.7 examines the effect on U.S. saving of changes in the five factors mentioned above: the age distribution of resources, propensities to consume, the ratio of resources to output, the age distribution of the population, and the rate of government spending. The factors involving resources and consumption propensities are calculated using a real discount rate of 6 percent.

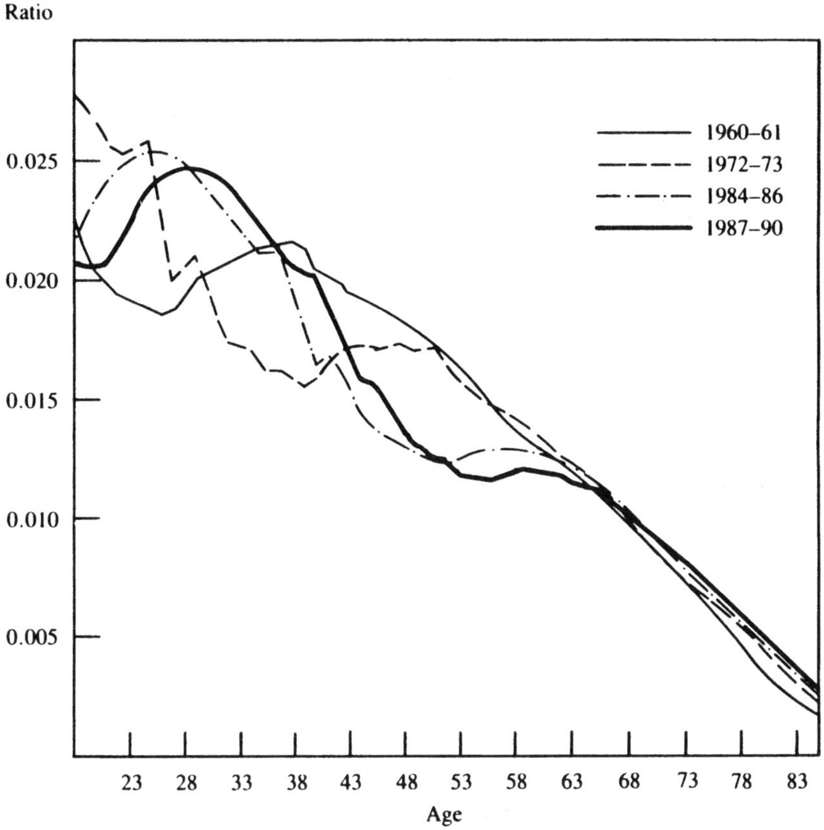

Figure 1.11
Ratio of cohort population to total population. *Source:* Unpublished data provided by the SSA.

In each panel of table 1.7, the numbers along the diagonal are the observed rates of U.S. net national saving in the row period. The other numbers indicate the saving rate that would have been observed in the row period, had the specified saving factor taken its value from the column period.

The counterfactual analysis undertaken here is partial-equilibrium in nature. For example, in asking how much higher U.S. saving would have been in the late 1980s, had cohort-specific consumption propensities been the same as those of the early 1960s, we are ignoring other factors that might have changed as a consequence of a change in consumption propensities. The following exercises are

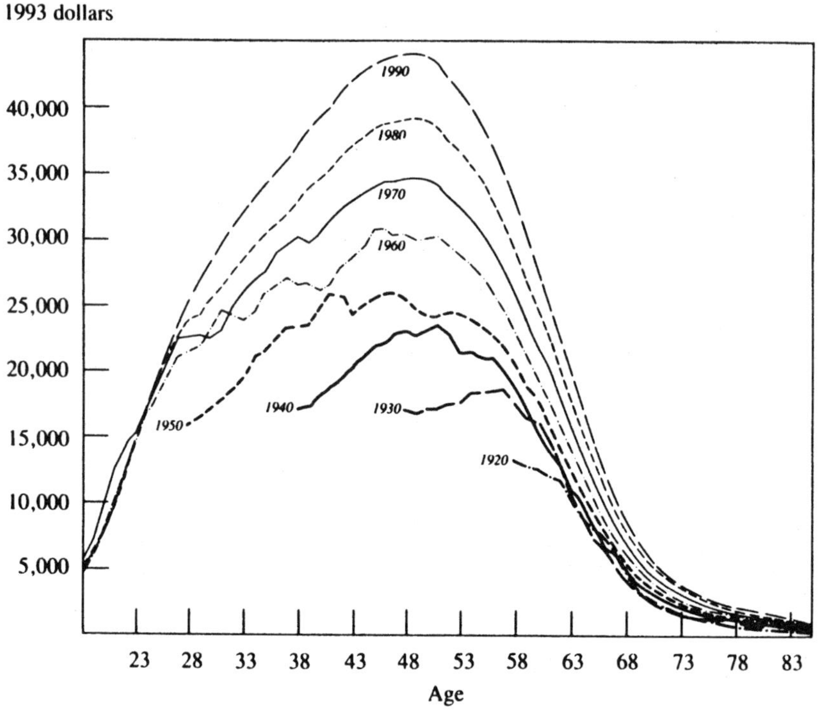

Figure 1.12
Longitudinal profiles of labor income, selected cohorts. *Source:* Authors' calculations based on the data sources for figure 1.5.
a. Cohorts are determined by the year in which they were aged eighteen.

meant to convey the potential importance of various determinants of saving, rather than to indicate precisely what the U.S. saving rate would have been if the world had evolved differently.

Changes in the Age-Resource Distribution

The first panel of table 1.7 shows the effect on the U.S. saving rate of changes over time in the age distribution of resources. The first number in the last row (4.97) is the saving rate that, ceteris paribus, would have been observed in 1987–90, had the age-resource distribution of 1960–61 prevailed during this period. Since the actual saving rate observed in 1987–90 is 3.38 percent, the saving rate would have been 47 percent higher had the age-resource distribution of the late 1980s been that of the early 1960s. Comparison of the last number in the first row of the first panel of table 1.7 (5.53) with the

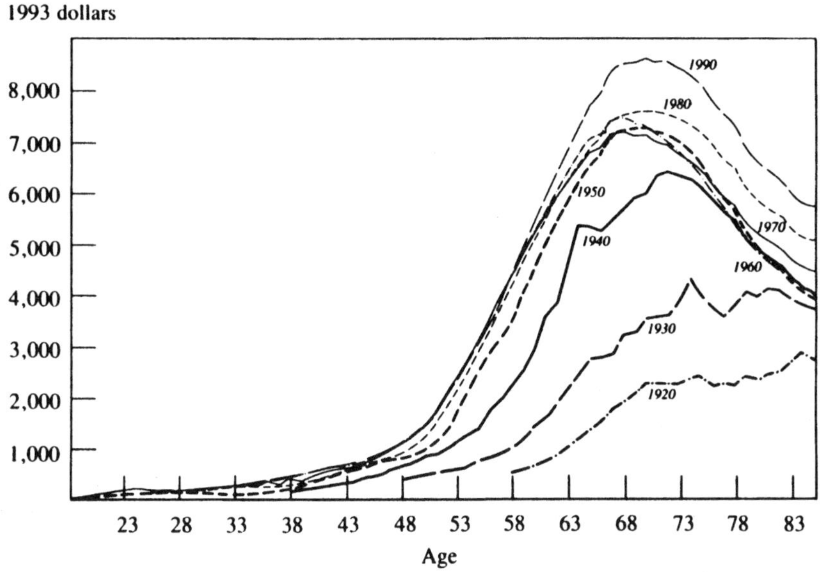

Figure 1.13
Longitudinal profiles of pension income, selected cohorts. *Source:* Authors' calculations based on the data sources for figure 1.5.
a. Cohorts are determined by the year in which they were aged eighteen.

actual saving rate in 1960–61 (7.85), provides another way to assess the importance of the change in the age-resource distribution. It shows that the saving rate would have been 30 percent lower if the age-resource distribution had changed as it did over the three decades, but everything else had remained as it was in 1960–61. The finding that the shift in the age-resource distribution contributed to a decline in the national saving rate is robust to alternative discount rate assumptions.[21]

The changes in the age-resource profile observed between the late 1980s and the early 1960s did not occur overnight. Figure 1.4 points this out, and table 1.7 shows that the shifting age-resource distribution has been responsible for a steady decline in the U.S. national saving rate.

Changes in Average Propensities to Consume

The second panel of table 1.7 shows the effect on the net national saving rate of changes over time in the average propensities to con-

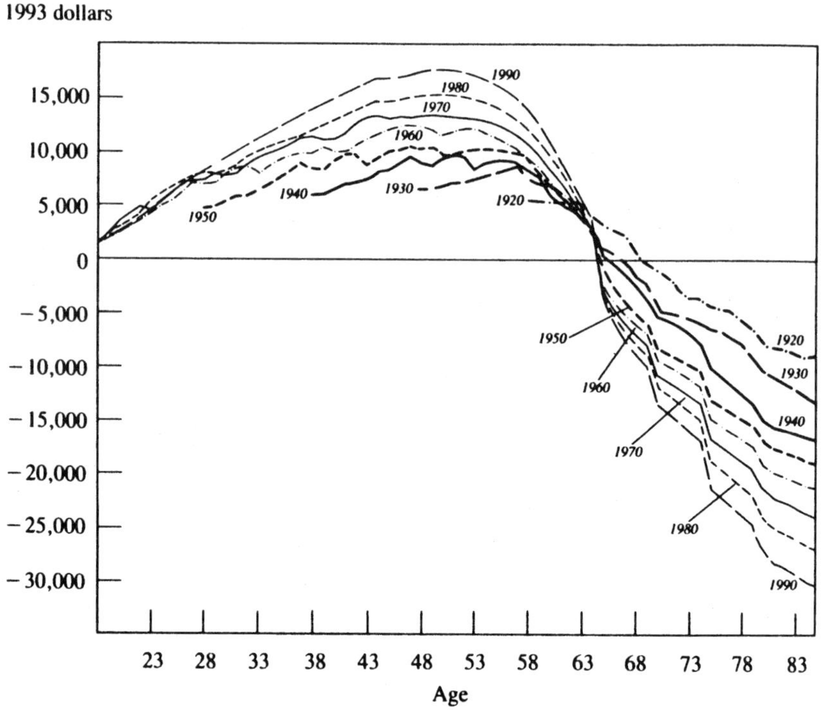

Figure 1.14
Longitudinal profiles of the generational account, selected cohorts. *Source:* Authors' calculations based on the data sources for figure 1.5.
a. Cohorts are determined by the year in which they were aged eighteen.

sume of both young (aged under sixty-five) and old (aged sixty-five and over) cohorts. The last number in the first column (4.85) indicates that, other things equal, the net national saving rate in 1987–90 would have been 43 percent higher had consumption propensities equaled those of 1960–61. This increase in the saving rate is not surprising, given the much larger consumption propensities of elderly cohorts in 1987–90 that are displayed in figure 1.9. However, the result that changing consumption propensities contributed to the decline in the national saving rate is not robust to the choice of the discount rate: at 3 percent, substituting the consumption propensities of 1960–61 for those of 1987–90 produces a lower saving rate (2.55).

Table 1.8 decomposes these changes in saving into those due to changes over time in the consumption propensities of the young and

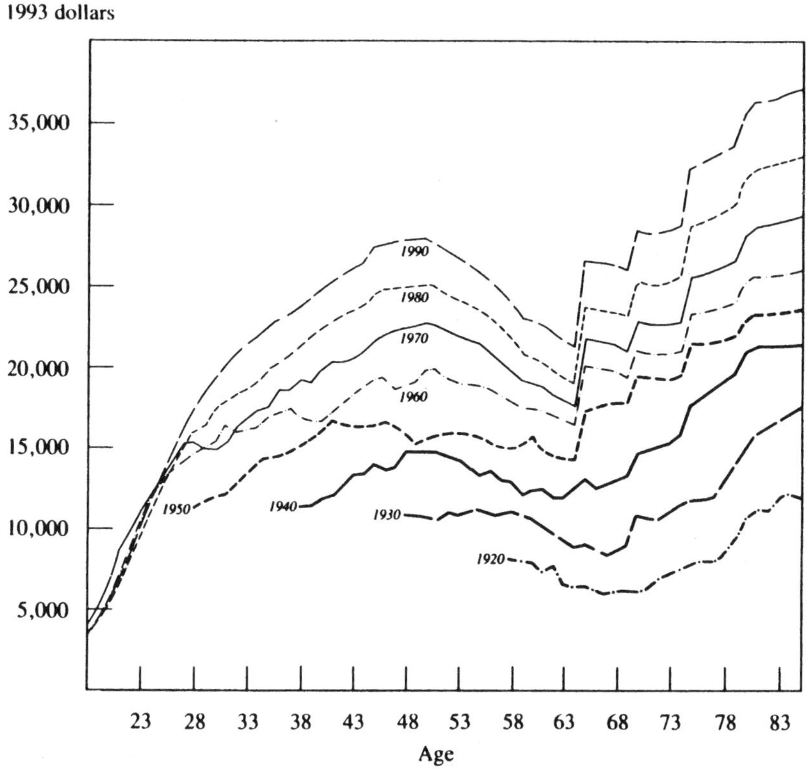

Figure 1.15
Longitudinal profiles of nonasset income, selected cohorts. *Source:* Authors' calculations based on the data sources for table 1.6.
Nonasset income is labor income plus pension income less net tax flow. Cohorts are determined by the year in which they were aged eighteen.

of the old. The first panel of table 1.8 shows the effect on saving rates of changing the consumption propensities of older generations. Had only the consumption propensities of older generations remained at their level in 1960–61, the saving rate would have been 5.74 percent in 1987–90, instead of 3.38 percent. The conclusion that sharp increases in older generations' propensities to consume are partly responsible for the decline in national saving is sustained under alternative rates of discount.

The second panel of table 1.8 shows that replacing the consumption propensities of younger generations in 1987–90 with their values in 1960–61 would actually slightly lower the saving rate—from 3.38

Table 1.7
The effect on the net national saving rate of counterfactual factor values[a], percent

Factor and period of counterfactual saving rate	Period of counterfactual factor value			
	1960–61	1972–73	1984–86	1987–90
Age-resource distribution (r_i/r)				
1960–61	7.85	6.21	5.54	5.53
1972–73	11.10	9.87	9.42	9.37
1984–86	5.87	4.72	4.51	4.38
1987–90	4.97	3.74	3.51	3.38
Consumption propensity (α_i)				
1960–61	7.85	5.01	8.45	6.85
1972–73	12.49	9.87	12.86	11.22
1984–86	4.04	0.98	4.51	2.80
1987–90	4.85	1.73	5.06	3.38
Age distribution (P_i/P)				
1960–61	7.85	9.60	9.01	8.57
1972–73	7.97	9.87	9.23	8.69
1984–86	2.93	4.89	4.51	3.85
1987–90	2.44	4.24	4.01	3.38
Resources-to-output ratio (R/Y)				
1960–61	7.85	11.84	4.33	5.42
1972–73	5.75	9.87	2.11	3.24
1984–86	8.03	12.01	4.51	5.60
1987–90	5.90	10.01	2.26	3.38
Government spending rate (G/Y)				
1960–61	7.85	8.16	8.03	8.27
1972–73	9.57	9.87	9.74	9.98
1984–86	4.33	4.64	4.51	4.75
1987–90	2.96	3.27	3.14	3.38
Addendum	1960–61	1972–73	1984–86	1987–90
Actual ratios[b]				
R/Y	12.53	11.82	13.15	12.96
HW/Y	11.45	10.38	11.59	11.31
NHW/Y	3.69	3.20	3.21	3.18
PW/Y	0.95	1.10	1.37	1.36
GA/Y	3.56	2.86	3.02	2.88
G/Y	21.59	21.28	21.41	21.17

Source: Authors' calculations, using the data sources for tables 1.5 and 1.6.
a. In each panel except the last, the numbers along the diagonal are the observed rates of net national saving in the row period. The other numbers indicate the saving rate that would have been observed in the row period if the specifed saving factor had taken its value from the column period.
b. $R/Y = (HW + NHW + PW - GA)/Y$, where R is total resources, HW is human wealth, NHW is nonhuman wealth, PW is pension wealth, GA is the generational account, and Y is the net national product. G denotes government purchases of goods and services.

Table 1.8
The effect on the net national saving rate of counterfactual propensities to consume of the old and the young[a], percent

Cohort and period[b]	Period of counterfactual factor value 1960–61	1972–73	1984–86	1987–90
Old				
1960–61	7.85	7.30	6.61	6.28
1972–73	10.52	9.87	9.06	8.70
1984–86	6.22	5.45	4.51	4.03
1987–90	5.74	4.91	3.88	3.38
Young				
1960–61	7.85	5.57	9.69	8.42
1972–73	11.84	9.87	13.67	12.40
1984–86	2.33	0.03	4.51	3.28
1987–90	2.50	0.21	4.57	3.38

Source: Authors' calculations, using the data sources for tables 1.5 and 1.6.
a. See table 1.7, note a for organization of this table.
b. Old cohorts are defined as those aged sixty-five or older and young cohorts as those younger than age sixty-five.

percent to 2.50 percent. The somewhat higher consumption propensities of those in their twenties and early thirties in the early 1960s, compared with the late 1980s, is responsible for this result. This finding is strengthened if one discounts at 3 percent, but reversed if one discounts at 9 percent.

Changes in the Age Distribution of the Population

The third panel of table 1.7 shows the effect on U.S. saving rates of changes over time in the age composition of the population. As indicated, had the age distribution of the population in 1960–61 prevailed in 1987–90, the U.S. saving rate would have been 2.44 percent, rather than 3.38 percent. This result can be understood by recalling that the propensity to consume rises with age and, as shown in figure 1.11, that the age distribution of the early 1960s featured relatively more middle-aged individuals and relatively fewer younger individuals than did the age distribution of the late 1980s.

These results are independent of the choice of discount rate. To see why, note that the product $\alpha_{it}(r_{it})$ in equation 3 equals the per capita consumption of cohort i in year t, which is the same regardless of how one decomposes this quantity between α_{it} and r_{it}. Further, R_t/r_t equals P_t, which is also independent of the discount rate. Hence the effect of changes in the ratio P_{it}/P_t on the national saving rate will be the same for all discount rates.

Changes in the Ratio of Resources to Output

Values of R_t/Y_t and its components for the four periods are reported in the bottom of panel of table 1.7. This ratio rises over time, from 12.53 in the early 1960s to 12.96 in the late 1980s. As the table shows, the principal reason for the rise is the decline in the ratio of aggregate generational accounts to income (GA_t/Y_t). In other words, the government's redistribution of resources from future to living generations is the main reason for the increase in the resources-to-income ratio.

Recall that, ceteris paribus, a higher ratio of resources to output means a higher rate of consumption out of net national income and a lower net national saving rate. The fourth panel of table 1.7 shows the effect of changes over time in the resources-to-output ratio (R_t/Y_t). The number in the last row of the first column number (5.90) indicates that saving rates would have been 75 percent higher if the 1960–61 ratio had prevailed in 1987–90. The number in the first row of the last column (5.42) shows that if the 1987–90 ratio had prevailed in 1960–61, the saving rate would have been one-third smaller. The magnitude (but not the sign) of the effect on saving of the increase in the resources-to-output ratio is sensitive to the choice of discount rate.[22]

Changes in the Government Spending Rate

The fifth panel of table 1.7 considers how changes in the government spending rate (G_t/Y_t) have affected national saving. As reported in the bottom panel of table 1.7, this rate fell slightly, from 21.6 percent in 1960–61 to 21.2 percent in 1987–90. Had G_t/Y_t taken its 1960–61 value in 1987–90, the U.S. saving rate would have been 12 percent smaller; that is, the change in the rate of government spending during the last three decades was not responsible for the low rate of national saving in the late 1980s.

The Annuitization of the Elderly's Resources and Their Increased Propensity to Consume

One likely explanation for the postwar increase in the propensity of the elderly to consume is the remarkable increase in the extent to which the elderly's resources are annuitized. Moreover, a significant share of these annuities are medicare and medicaid benefits that are provided in kind, in the form of the consumption of medical goods and services.

The data in tables 1.9–1.12 are similar to those reported by Auerbach and others.[23] Tables 1.9 and 1.10 decompose total resources into bequeathable resources and their components, nonhuman wealth and the term value of life insurance, and annuitized resources, which equal the difference between total resources and bequeathable resources. Tables 1.11 and 1.12 report these components as a fraction of total resources. The extent of resource annuitization (R^a) is computed as the ratio of annuitized to total resources, that is

$$R^a = 1 - \frac{TERM + NHW}{HW + NHW + PW - GA}, \tag{9}$$

where *TERM* stands for the average term value of life insurance, *HW* stands for average human wealth, *NHW* stands for average nonhuman wealth, *PW* stands for average private pension wealth, and *GA* stands for the generational account.

Table 1.11 shows that for males aged sixty-five and over, R^a was two-and-a-half times larger in 1990 than it was in 1960, reflecting an increase from 0.16 to 0.41. For elderly females, the increase was even bigger—from 0.18 in 1960 to 0.50 in 1990 (table 1.12). This larger share of elderly persons' annuitized resources implies an equal and opposite decline in their share of bequeathable resources.

Increased annuitization of resources means that the elderly have less reason to fear that they will run out of resources if they live longer than expected. Consequently, they are likely to choose to consume at a higher rate. As demonstrated by Kotlikoff and Avia Spivak, the availability of annuities can make a great difference to the consumption levels of the elderly, even when the elderly are not very risk averse.[24] For example, according to their simulations, moderately risk-averse elderly persons with no bequest motive, nor any explicit or implicit means of acquiring annuity insurance will, on average, fail to consume a third of their resources before they die.

Table 1.9
Decomposition of total resources into annuitized and bequeathable resources, males

	Age group								
Measure and period	20–29	30–39	40–49	50–59	60–69	70–79	80–89	20–89	65–89
Total resources									
1960–61	269.6	273.4	259.9	224.1	178.6	142.0	103.4	239.6	146.8
1972–73	316.4	338.9	335.2	307.9	255.8	201.1	130.0	304.8	205.3
1984–86	349.5	379.2	394.9	379.3	339.9	259.7	141.3	356.4	265.6
1987–90	364.5	393.6	410.0	399.3	362.3	281.3	154.6	373.6	286.0
Percent change[a]	35.2	44.0	57.8	78.2	102.8	98.1	49.5	55.9	94.8
Annuitized resources[b]									
1960–61	239.8	203.0	153.8	94.2	42.5	19.2	9.9	149.4	23.0
1972–73	281.5	250.3	196.5	138.2	80.7	53.2	39.3	194.1	57.0
1984–86	313.7	282.0	237.7	181.8	138.0	97.6	66.1	237.4	103.7
1987–90	323.6	286.4	240.6	188.9	149.3	111.4	75.7	243.9	116.2
Percent change[a]	35.0	41.1	56.4	100.4	251.0	479.9	660.7	63.2	406.1
Bequeathable resources[c]									
1960–61	29.8	70.5	106.1	129.8	136.1	122.8	93.5	90.2	123.8
1972–73	35.0	88.6	138.8	169.7	175.1	147.8	90.6	110.7	148.3
1984–86	35.8	97.2	157.1	197.5	201.9	162.1	75.2	119.0	161.9
1987–90	40.9	107.3	169.4	210.4	213.0	169.9	78.9	129.8	169.8
Percent change[a]	37.4	52.2	59.7	62.1	56.5	38.4	–15.5	43.9	37.1

Table 1.9 (continued)

Measure and period	Age group 20–29	30–39	40–49	50–59	60–69	70–79	80–89	20–89	65–89
Nonhuman wealth									
1960–61	11.8	44.1	81.1	111.3	125.4	118.2	91.8	70.8	118.0
1972–73	13.1	48.9	99.7	141.1	159.7	142.2	88.7	83.4	140.8
1984–86	14.5	50.5	109.1	163.6	185.1	157.0	73.6	87.8	154.5
1987–90	15.5	52.9	113.3	170.8	193.6	164.0	77.0	92.6	161.3
Percent change[a]	31.2	20.2	39.7	53.5	54.4	38.8	–16.1	30.8	36.7
Term value of life insurance									
1960–61	18.0	26.4	24.9	18.6	10.7	4.6	1.6	19.4	5.8
1972–73	21.9	39.7	39.0	28.6	15.4	5.7	1.9	27.3	7.5
1984–86	21.3	46.7	48.1	33.9	16.8	5.1	1.6	31.2	7.3
1987–90	25.4	54.3	56.1	39.6	19.4	5.9	1.9	37.2	8.5
Percent change[a]	41.4	105.7	124.7	113.1	81.7	29.0	16.4	91.3	45.8

Source: Authors' calculations, using the data sources for tables 1.5 and 1.6. Life insurance relative profiles by age and sex are based on the SCF, using aggregate life insurance estimates from American Council of Life Insurance. *1993 Life Insurance Fact Book Update* (Washington, 1993).
Note: Population weighted averages in thousands of 1993 dollars.
a. Percent change is calculated from the first period (1960–61) to the last (1987–90).
b. Total resources less bequeathable resources.
c. Nonhuman wealth plus term value of life insurance.

Table 1.10
Decomposition of total resources into annuitized and bequeathable resources, females

Measure and period	Age group								
	20–29	30–39	40–49	50–59	60–69	70–79	80–89	20–89	65–89
Total resources									
1960–61	247.7	255.1	255.4	222.3	166.4	119.3	92.4	223.1	127.0
1972–73	296.3	319.0	323.2	297.3	246.2	181.8	106.3	282.8	183.7
1984–86	346.1	380.7	378.1	357.8	325.4	234.0	105.2	337.8	229.7
1987–90	365.8	399.6	397.5	378.3	346.7	253.2	116.8	357.3	247.3
Percent change[a]	47.7	56.6	55.7	70.2	108.3	112.3	26.4	60.2	94.8
Annuitized resources[b]									
1960–61	221.8	187.7	142.6	90.4	46.1	17.4	3.3	134.5	22.3
1972–73	261.1	227.5	184.5	136.4	91.8	64.2	39.5	175.9	65.7
1984–86	304.5	272.9	228.9	181.5	147.6	110.5	75.2	224.2	111.5
1987–90	318.4	281.8	237.1	191.0	159.7	124.3	85.4	234.2	124.2
Percent change[a]	43.6	50.2	66.3	111.2	246.4	613.0	2449.0	74.1	456.9
Bequeathable resources[c]									
1960–61	25.9	67.4	112.8	131.9	120.3	101.9	89.1	88.6	104.7
1972–73	35.2	91.5	138.7	160.9	154.4	117.6	66.8	106.8	118.0
1984–86	41.6	107.8	149.2	176.4	177.8	123.5	30.0	113.6	118.3
1987–90	47.4	117.8	160.4	187.4	187.0	128.9	31.4	123.1	123.2
Percent change[a]	82.9	74.7	42.2	42.1	55.4	26.6	−64.8	39.0	17.7

Table 1.10 (continued)

	Age group								
Measure and period	20–29	30–39	40–49	50–59	60–69	70–79	80–89	20–89	65–89
Nonhuman wealth									
1960–61	7.1	42.6	91.1	117.1	112.8	99.1	87.7	71.6	101.0
1972–73	12.3	54.7	105.6	138.9	144.4	114.7	65.7	83.9	114.0
1984–86	19.7	65.6	109.1	151.2	167.8	121.7	29.6	88.2	115.3
1987–90	21.4	68.7	113.6	157.9	175.5	126.8	31.0	93.0	119.8
Percent change[a]	202.3	61.4	24.7	34.8	55.5	28.0	−64.7	29.9	18.6
Term value of life insurance									
1960–61	18.9	24.9	21.6	14.8	7.5	2.8	1.3	17.0	3.7
1972–73	22.9	36.7	33.1	22.0	10.0	2.9	1.1	22.9	4.0
1984–86	21.9	42.2	40.1	25.2	10.0	1.8	0.4	25.4	3.0
1987–90	26.1	49.1	46.8	29.5	11.5	2.1	0.4	30.1	3.4
Percent change[a]	38.2	97.4	116.2	99.8	53.0	−25.5	−68.5	77.5	−7.3

Source: Authors' calculations, using the data sources for table 1.9.
Note: Population weighted averages in thousands of 1993 dollars.
a. Percent change is calculated from the first period (1960–61) to the last (1987–90).
b. Total resources less bequeathable resources.
c. Nonhuman wealth plus term value of life insurance.

Table 1.11
Share of annuitized and bequeathable resources in total resources, males

Measure and period	Age group 20–29	30–39	40–49	50–59	60–69	70–79	80–89	20–89	65–89
Annuitized resources[a]									
1960–61	0.89	0.74	0.59	0.42	0.24	0.14	0.10	0.62	0.16
1972–73	0.89	0.74	0.59	0.45	0.32	0.26	0.30	0.64	0.28
1984–86	0.90	0.74	0.60	0.48	0.41	0.38	0.47	0.67	0.39
1987–90	0.89	0.73	0.59	0.47	0.41	0.40	0.49	0.65	0.41
Bequeathable resources[b]									
1960–61	0.11	0.26	0.41	0.58	0.76	0.86	0.90	0.38	0.84
1972–73	0.11	0.26	0.41	0.55	0.68	0.74	0.70	0.36	0.72
1984–86	0.10	0.26	0.40	0.52	0.59	0.62	0.53	0.33	0.61
1987–90	0.11	0.27	0.41	0.53	0.59	0.60	0.51	0.35	0.59
Nonhuman wealth									
1960–61	0.04	0.16	0.31	0.50	0.70	0.83	0.89	0.30	0.80
1972–73	0.04	0.14	0.30	0.46	0.62	0.71	0.68	0.27	0.69
1984–86	0.04	0.13	0.28	0.43	0.54	0.60	0.52	0.25	0.58
1987–90	0.04	0.13	0.28	0.43	0.53	0.58	0.50	0.25	0.56
Term value of life insurance									
1960–61	0.07	0.10	0.10	0.08	0.06	0.03	0.02	0.08	0.04
1972–73	0.07	0.12	0.12	0.09	0.06	0.03	0.01	0.09	0.04
1984–86	0.06	0.12	0.12	0.09	0.05	0.02	0.01	0.09	0.03
1987–90	0.07	0.14	0.14	0.10	0.05	0.02	0.01	0.10	0.03

Source: Authors' calculations, using the data sources for table 1.9.
a. Total resources less bequeathable resources.
b. Nonhuman wealth plus term value of life insurance.

Assuming that individuals do not have access to annuity insurance, either explicit or implicit, at the margin, they will likely plan to spend down their net wealth to zero and then consume their annuity income. At this point, their average propensity to consume is mechanically determined and is guaranteed to rise with age. This is because consumption equals annuity income, and resources equal the present expected value of annuity income. So the average propensity to consume (APC) is equal to one divided by the actuarial value of $1.00. Assuming that survival probabilities decline with age, this ratio will rise with age. For example, if the discount rate is zero, the APC will simply equal the individual's life expectancy. This line of argument suggests that the government's annuitization of the

Table 1.12
Share of annuitized and bequeathable resources in total resources, females

Measure and period	Age group 20–29	30–39	40–49	50–59	60–69	70–79	80–89	20–89	65–89
Annuitized resources[a]									
1960–61	0.90	0.74	0.56	0.41	0.28	0.15	0.04	0.60	0.18
1972–73	0.88	0.71	0.57	0.46	0.37	0.35	0.37	0.62	0.36
1984–86	0.88	0.72	0.61	0.51	0.45	0.47	0.71	0.66	0.49
1987–90	0.87	0.71	0.60	0.50	0.46	0.49	0.73	0.66	0.50
Bequeathable resources[b]									
1960–61	0.10	0.26	0.44	0.59	0.72	0.85	0.96	0.40	0.82
1972–73	0.12	0.29	0.43	0.54	0.63	0.65	0.63	0.38	0.64
1984–86	0.12	0.28	0.39	0.49	0.55	0.53	0.29	0.34	0.51
1987–90	0.13	0.29	0.40	0.50	0.54	0.51	0.27	0.34	0.50
Nonhuman wealth									
1960–61	0.03	0.17	0.36	0.53	0.68	0.83	0.95	0.32	0.80
1972–73	0.04	0.17	0.33	0.47	0.59	0.63	0.62	0.30	0.62
1984–86	0.06	0.17	0.29	0.42	0.52	0.52	0.28	0.26	0.50
1987–90	0.06	0.17	0.29	0.42	0.51	0.50	0.27	0.26	0.48
Term value of life insurance									
1960–61	0.08	0.10	0.08	0.07	0.05	0.02	0.01	0.08	0.03
1972–73	0.08	0.12	0.10	0.07	0.04	0.02	0.01	0.08	0.02
1984–86	0.06	0.11	0.11	0.07	0.03	0.01	0.00	0.08	0.01
1987–90	0.07	0.12	0.12	0.08	0.03	0.01	0.00	0.08	0.01

Source: Authors' calculations, using the data sources for table 1.9.
a. Total resources less bequeathable resources.
b. Nonhuman wealth plus term value of life insurance.

resources of the elderly has, in effect, forced the elderly to consume a larger share of their resources in each successive year.

Questioning the Findings

This section addresses various questions about the reliability of our findings.

Allocating Couples' Incomes to Nominal Recipients

The results presented above are based on income, tax, and transfer profiles that were constructed from microeconomic data sets. In the

Table 1.13
The effect on the net national saving rate of counterfactual factor values—Allocating income to nominal recipients[a], percent

Factor and period of counterfactual saving rate	Period of counterfactual factor value 1960–61	1972–73	1984–86	1987–90
Age-resource distribution (r_i/r)				
1960–61	7.85	6.19	5.52	5.55
1972–73	11.16	9.87	9.39	9.36
1984–86	6.00	4.75	4.51	4.40
1987–90	5.07	3.75	3.49	3.38
Consumption prospensity (α_i)				
1960–61	7.85	4.88	8.39	6.78
1972–73	12.59	9.87	12.94	11.32
1984–86	4.10	0.92	4.51	2.81
1987–90	4.93	1.68	5.05	3.38
Resources-to-output ratio (R/Y)				
1960–61	7.85	11.98	4.46	5.51
1972–73	5.59	9.87	2.07	3.16
1984–86	7.91	12.05	4.51	5.57
1987–90	5.81	10.08	2.29	3.38
Addendum	1960–61	1972–73	1984–86	1987–90
Actual ratios[b]				
R/Y	12.68	11.94	13.29	13.10
HW/Y	11.56	10.45	11.66	11.39
NHW/Y	3.69	3.20	3.21	3.18
PW/Y	0.96	1.11	1.37	1.36
GA/Y	3.53	2.82	2.95	2.82

Source: Authors' calculations, using the data sources for tables 1.5 and 1.6.
a. See table 1.7, note a, for organization of this table.
b. See table 1.7, note b, for definitions of variables shown.

case of married households, we allocate equal amounts of these flows to each spouse. An alternative procedure would be to allocate income to the person who nominally received it. Table 1.13 shows that the results produced by implementing the latter method are almost identical to those in the earlier tables. For example, the saving rate for 1987–90 with the resource distribution of 1960–61, all else remaining the same, is 5.07 under the alternative method, instead of 4.97 (see the first panel of table 1.7). Using the consumption propensities of 1960–61 yields a saving rate of 4.93 in 1987–90 under the alternative method, compared to 4.85 under the former procedure (see the second panel of table 1.7). Finally, using the ratio of resources to output of 1960–61 produces a saving rate of 5.81 in 1987–90 under the alternative method, instead of 5.90 under the former procedure (see the fourth panel of table 1.7).

If There Were No Annuity Markets

The base case assumes that individuals can convert future income flows into current consumption at actuarially fair rates of discount—that is, using the pretax rate of interest and the probability of death conditional on age. This is equivalent to assuming the existence of actuarially fair annuity insurance, whether explicit or implicit. To investigate the robustness of our results to this assumption, we now consider the opposite assumption—that no annuity insurance is available at the margin. In this case, the appropriate rate for discounting future flows is simply the pretax rate of interest.

Table 1.14 shows average resources for ten-year age groups in the four periods under the assumption of no annuity markets. Compared to the results of tables 1.3 and 1.4, total resources are higher under the no annuity markets assumption, as would be expected from the lower rate of discount. Also, because of the greater annuitization of the resources of older cohorts in the late 1980s, compared to the early 1960s, for older cohorts the difference between resources under the two cases is greater in the late 1980s, compared to the early 1960s.

Table 1.15 indicates that the assumption of no annuity insurance does affect the magnitude, but not the sign, of the saving factors considered in table 1.7.[25] Under this assumption, applying the propensities to consume of 1960–61 to the cohort-specific resource levels of the late 1980s increases the saving rate from 3.38 percent to 6.23 percent, rather than to 4.85 percent under the base case (see the second panel in table 1.7) Substituting the age-resource distribution and resources-to-income ratio of 1960–61 in place of their respective 1987–90 values also leads to an increase in national saving. In the case of the age-resource distribution, the saving rate increases from 3.38 percent to 5.23 percent, instead to 4.97 percent under the base case. Finally, using the ratio of resources to output of 1960–61 in place of that of 1987–90 increases the saving rate from 3.38 percent to 4.60 percent, instead of to 5.90 percent under the base case. Sub-

Table 1.14
Total resources—No annuity markets

Sex and period	Age group								
	20–29	30–39	40–49	50–59	60–69	70–79	80–89	20–89	65–89
Males									
1960–61	290.6	314.0	317.6	291.4	245.0	199.8	143.0	288.0	205.2
1972–73	336.7	379.3	400.6	395.5	355.3	294.7	205.2	363.0	298.5
1984–86	365.0	422.0	461.6	476.3	464.0	393.4	254.5	419.4	394.8
1987–90	378.4	435.6	478.4	496.9	490.5	423.0	279.5	438.2	422.6
Percent change[a]	30.2	38.7	50.6	70.5	100.2	111.7	95.4	52.1	105.9
Females									
1960–61	256.7	278.7	289.8	264.9	212.2	159.1	117.1	253.1	166.6
1972–73	304.4	342.3	362.7	351.7	312.8	249.8	162.9	320.6	249.6
1984–86	348.3	405.1	419.3	419.0	407.7	328.9	190.6	379.9	320.2
1987–90	364.9	422.0	440.1	439.8	431.6	353.2	211.0	400.2	343.1
Percent change[a]	42.2	51.4	51.9	66.1	103.4	122.0	80.2	58.1	106.0

Source: Authors' calculations, using the data sources for table 1.6.
Note: Population weighted averages in thousands of 1993 dollars.
a. Percent change is calculated from the first period (1960–61) to the last (1987–90).

Table 1.15
The effect on the net national saving rate of counterfactual factor values—No annuity insurance[a], percent

Factor and period of counterfactual saving rate	Period of counterfactual factor value			
	1960–61	1972–73	1984–86	1987–90
Age-resource distribution (r_i/r)				
1960–61	7.85	6.41	5.78	5.97
1972–73	11.06	9.87	9.43	9.57
1984–86	6.29	5.01	4.51	4.61
1987–90	5.23	3.86	3.29	3.38
Consumption propensity (α_i)				
1960–61	7.85	4.40	7.36	5.30
1972–73	12.88	9.87	12.36	10.29
1984–86	5.07	1.57	4.51	2.33
1987–90	6.23	2.71	5.50	3.38
Resources-to-output ratio (R/Y)				
1960–61	7.85	12.19	5.41	6.70
1972–73	5.36	9.87	2.82	4.16
1984–86	6.99	11.39	4.51	5.82
1987–90	4.60	9.16	2.03	3.38
Age distribution (P_i/P)				
1960–61	7.85	9.60	9.01	8.57
1972–73	7.97	9.87	9.23	8.69
1984–86	2.93	4.89	4.51	3.85
1987–90	2.44	4.24	4.01	3.38
Addendum	1960–61	1972–73	1984–86	1987–90
Actual ratios[b]				
R/Y	14.56	13.66	15.06	14.80
HW/Y	11.91	10.64	11.70	11.38
NHW/Y	3.69	3.20	3.21	3.18
PW/Y	1.45	1.54	1.82	1.78
GA/Y	2.49	1.73	1.67	1.54

Source: Authors' calculations, using the data sources for tables 1.5 and 1.6.
a. See table 1.7, note a, for organization of this table.
b. See table 1.7, note b, for definitions of variables shown.

stituting the population shares of 1960–61 in place of those of 1987–90 results in the same saving rate as in the base case (2.44 percent). The reason, as mentioned earlier, is that the rate of discount does not affect the calculated effect on national saving rate changes in the age composition of the population.[26]

Future Growth in Medicare and Medicaid

The future course of fiscal policy is uncertain. However, by incorporating federal revenue and outlay projections that differ from the baseline used in our analysis, we can consider the implications of alternative future policies. For example, the resolution considered by the Congress in December 1995 to balance the federal budget by the year 2002 proposed cuts in the growth of medicare and medicaid and in projected government purchases. It also included reductions in taxes, mainly in the form of additional deductions against taxable income. As table 1.16 shows, projecting future transfer payments on the basis of these budget proposals does not materially alter the level or the distribution of resources across cohorts.

Table 1.17 shows that under this case, the results of our counterfactual saving rate exercises are quite similar to those reported in table 1.7. The second panel of table 1.17 shows that the saving rate would be 5.52 percent if the consumption propensities of 1987–90 were replaced by those of 1960–61. This is a bigger effect than under the base case. The reason is that lower spending on medicare and medicaid under the balanced budget scenario reduces the resources of the middle-aged and elderly in 1987–90 and raises their consumption propensities. Also, relative to the base case, post-1990 reductions in federal health outlays have a smaller effect on the resources of most middle-aged and elderly generations in 1960–61. Consequently, the increases in the consumption propensities of these age groups associated with the alternative fiscal policy are larger for the late 1980s than they are for the early 1960s. This, in turn, means that substituting consumption propensities from the early 1960s for those of the late 1980s has a larger effect on saving rates.

Replacing the age-resource distribution of 1987–90 with that of 1960–61 results in a saving rate of 4.98 percent, which is very close to the base case rate of 4.97 percent (table 1.7). Applying the ratio of resources to output of 1960–61 in the period 1987–90 results in a saving rate of 5.25 percent. This increase is less than that in the base

Table 1.16
Total resources—Balanced federal budget by 2002

	Age group								
Sex and period	20–29	30–39	40–49	50–59	60–69	70–79	80–89	20–89	65–89
Males									
1960–61	268.6	272.7	259.6	224.0	178.6	142.0	103.4	239.2	146.8
1972–73	314.9	337.0	333.4	307.1	255.7	201.1	130.0	303.5	205.2
1984–86	347.0	376.2	390.9	374.9	337.2	258.8	141.2	353.5	264.4
1987–90	361.6	390.2	405.6	393.6	357.8	279.3	154.0	369.9	283.5
Percent change[a]	34.6	43.1	56.2	75.7	100.3	96.7	49.0	54.7	93.1
Females									
1960–61	246.6	254.2	254.9	222.2	166.4	119.3	92.4	222.5	127.0
1972–73	294.6	316.8	321.1	296.1	245.9	181.8	106.3	281.3	183.6
1984–86	342.8	377.4	373.9	352.9	322.0	232.6	104.9	334.4	228.2
1987–90	361.8	395.7	392.8	372.2	341.5	250.5	115.9	353.0	244.4
Percent change[a]	46.7	55.7	54.1	67.5	105.1	110.0	25.4	58.6	92.5

Source: Authors' calculations, using the data sources for table 1.6 with budget plan figures from Congressional Budget Office, *Economic and Budget Outlook: December 1995 Update.*
Note: Population weighted averages in thousands of 1993 dollars.
a. Percent change is calculated from the first period (1960–61) to the last (1987–90).

Table 1.17
The effect on the net national saving rate of counterfactual factor values—Balanced federal budget by 2002[a], percent

Factor and period of counterfactual saving rate	Period of counterfactual factor value			
	1960–61	1972–73	1984–86	1987–90
Age-resource distribution (r_i/r)				
1960–61	7.85	6.23	5.59	5.59
1972–73	11.10	9.87	9.45	9.41
1984–86	5.89	4.72	4.51	4.40
1987–90	4.98	3.73	3.50	3.38
Consumption propensity (α_i)				
1960–61	7.85	4.82	7.94	6.19
1972–73	12.65	9.87	12.54	10.75
1984–86	4.56	1.33	4.51	2.64
1987–90	5.52	2.24	5.21	3.38
Resources-to-output ratio (R/Y)				
1960–61	7.85	12.00	4.85	6.06
1972–73	5.58	9.87	2.46	3.72
1984–86	7.54	11.71	4.51	5.73
1987–90	5.25	9.57	2.12	3.38
Addendum	1960–61	1972–73	1984–86	1987–90
Actual ratios[b]				
R/Y	12.50	11.77	13.03	12.82
HW/Y	11.45	10.38	11.59	11.31
NHW/Y	3.69	3.20	3.21	3.18
PW/Y	0.95	1.10	1.37	1.36
GA/Y	3.59	2.92	3.14	3.02

Source: Authors' calculations, using data sources for tables 1.5 and 1.16.
a. See table 1.7, note a, for organization of this table.
b. See table 1.7, note b, for definitions of variables shown.

case because, in this case, the aggregate generational account component of the resources-to-output ratio only falls from 3.59 to 3.02 over the period, instead of from 3.56 to 2.88.

Bias from Error in Measuring Resources

Given income uncertainty, our preferred resource measure would be expected, rather than actual realized, resources. But, as indicated above, our measure of a cohort's resources is not exactly actual realized resources. In fact, it is based partly on the cohort's actual realized future income streams and partly on projections of its income streams from the mid-1990s onward. Assuming that our method of projecting cohorts' future incomes properly captures cohorts' own expectations about future incomes, we would except the error in measuring expected resources to be smaller in the later periods than in the earlier periods. Since the measurement error we introduce by using actual incomes is an expectation error, it has a mean of zero. Thus its presence will impart an upward bias to our measurement of average propensities to consume, because of Jensen's inequality and the fact that this error shows up in the denominator of the APC formula. And since this bias is likely to be greater in the earlier period than in the later period, our analysis likely understates the relative importance of rising APCs over time to reducing U.S. saving rates.

Myopic Expectations

Our measure of a cohort's resources in a given period assumes that members of the cohort, on average, accurately foresaw the nonasset income that they would receive and the net taxes that they would pay through 1993. In addition, the measure assumes that their expectations of nonasset income and net taxes after 1993 correspond, on average, to the values that we project. These assumptions may, of course, be invalid.

An alternative is to assume myopic expectations concerning future nonasset income and net taxes. Under this case, we assume that cohorts expect, on average, to receive the same nonasset income and pay the same net taxes at future ages as do cohorts of the same sex at those ages currently, except for an adjustment for growth; that is, we assume that cohorts expect the current cross-sectional age-nonasset income and age-net tax profiles to shift proportionally through time due to economic growth, but not to twist.

The rate of economic growth projected for each period is assumed to equal the average growth rate of output per hour over the ten years before the period. Thus the growth rate is 2.79 percent for 1960–61, 2.71 percent for 1972–73, 1.09 percent for 1984–86, and 1.03 percent for 1987–90. Table 1.18 shows total resources for different age groups under myopic expectations. For all except the youngest generations, total resources are somewhat lower under myopic expectations than under the base case (tables 1.3 and 1.4).[27]

Table 1.18
Total resources—myopic expectations

	Age group								
Sex and period	20–29	30–39	40–49	50–59	60–69	70–79	80–89	20–89	65–89
Males									
1960–61	280.1	267.6	245.2	208.5	165.4	135.0	101.1	232.9	138.4
1972–73	398.3	384.0	348.7	301.8	247.1	196.4	125.8	335.1	199.5
1984–86	354.7	375.9	381.6	361.6	324.6	251.9	138.9	350.3	256.4
1987–90	367.7	391.0	397.8	379.7	341.3	268.1	148.6	365.9	271.7
Percent change[a]	31.3	46.1	62.2	82.1	106.4	98.6	46.9	57.1	96.3
Females									
1960–61	250.6	239.2	230.1	194.7	142.5	106.9	89.1	206.6	112.5
1972–73	360.4	352.0	325.6	281.3	227.7	166.6	96.8	297.9	168.7
1984–86	326.0	358.7	354.5	336.7	306.8	224.1	99.6	318.3	218.8
1987–90	353.9	384.1	375.8	354.6	324.9	239.7	109.1	340.3	233.1
Percent change[a]	41.2	60.5	63.3	82.2	128.0	124.3	22.5	64.7	107.2

Source: Authors' calculations, using the data sources for table 1.6. See text for computational details.
Note: Population weighted averages in thousands of 1993 dollars.
a. Percent change is calculated from the first period (1960–61) to the last (1987–90).

Table 1.19
The effect on the net national saving rate of counterfactual factor values—myopic expectations[a], percent

Factor and period of counterfactual saving rate	Period of counterfactual factor value			
	1960–61	1972–73	1984–86	1987–90
Age-resource distribution (r_i/r)				
1960–61	7.85	7.45	4.68	4.75
1972–73	10.01	9.87	7.22	7.25
1984–86	5.89	6.07	4.51	4.48
1987–90	5.05	5.26	3.41	3.38
Consumption propensity (α_i)				
1960–61	7.85	13.03	9.44	8.10
1972–73	4.30	9.87	5.78	4.19
1984–86	2.90	8.19	4.51	2.97
1987–90	3.44	8.58	4.89	3.38
Resources-to-output ratio (R/Y)				
1960–61	7.85	2.40	3.71	4.54
1972–73	14.81	9.87	11.06	11.81
1984–86	8.62	3.21	4.51	5.33
1987–90	6.77	1.20	2.54	3.38
Addendum	1960–61	1972–73	1984–86	1987–90
Actual ratios[b]				
R/Y	11.97	12.89	12.67	12.53
HW/Y	12.27	13.04	11.28	11.24
NHW/Y	3.69	3.20	3.21	3.18
PW/Y	0.55	0.91	1.23	1.29
GA/Y	4.54	4.26	3.05	3.17

Source: Authors' calculations, using data sources for tables 1.5 and 1.18.
a. See table 1.7, note a, for organization of this table.
b. See table 1.7, note b, for definitions of variables shown.

Table 1.19 shows that when resources are computed under the assumption of myopic expectations, the base case conclusions from our counterfactual saving rate experiments are sustained for changes in the age-resource distribution and the resources-to-output ratio. Substituting the age-resource distribution of 1960–61 in place of that of 1987–90 produces a saving rate of 5.05 percent under myopic expectations, compared to 4.97 percent in the base case. Using the resources-to-output ratio of 1960–61 instead of that of 1987–90 produces a saving rate of 6.77 percent, which is even higher than the

5.90 percent rate under the base case. The same experiment with consumption propensities produces a saving rate of 3.44 percent under myopic expectations, which is only slightly larger than the actual saving rate of 3.38 percent.

Bequests and Inter Vivos Transfers

Our life-cycle framework ignores inherited resources and resources received through inter vivos gifts. If we had data on cohorts' expected future receipts of inheritances and gifts, we would include their present expected value in our measure of resources. This would lower cohorts' measured propensities to consume, particularly for young and middle-aged cohorts whose parents and grandparents are still alive, but would raise the aggregate ratio of resources to income.

If, as we suspect, bequests and inter vivos transfers have been declining over time in the United States, relative to the size of the economy, our failure to include the present expected value of future inheritances and gifts in measured resources would mean that propensities to consume are biased upward by more in the earlier periods than they are in later periods. Consequently, we may overstate the degree to which the consumption propensities of the young and the middle-aged have declined and understate the degree to which the consumption propensities of older Americans have increased. We may also understate the degree to which the age-resource profile has tilted toward the elderly. Finally, we may overstate the degree to which the resources-to-output ratio has risen.

Accounting for Uncertainty

An obvious criticism of our analysis is that it ignores the fact that consumption decisions are made under uncertainty. As Angus Deaton and Carroll point out, propensities to consume out of certain resources will, in general, exceed those out of uncertain resources.[28] This is only true in general, because there are utility functions, specifically quadratic and constant absolute risk aversion functions, for which current consumption is a linear function of the present expected value of future resources.

But even if utility is of a different form than quadratic or constant absolute risk aversion (for example, isoelastic), one can still define the propensity to consume out of total expected resources. The difference is that this propensity to consume will depend on the degree of uncertainty that consumers face. It follows that the changes in propensities to consume out of expected resources that we have reported may reflect changes in the degree of resource uncertainty. This, indeed, is the point we argue above, when relating the rise in the propensity of the elderly to consume to the increased annuitization of their resources.

Furthermore, uncertainty (for example, in the context of isoelastic preferences) requires one to think somewhat differently about our counterfactual saving rate experiments. In addition to all the other factors that these experiments implicitly hold constant, they should also be understood to hold constant the degree of resource uncertainty.

Considerations of uncertainty, however, do not alter our conclusion that the government's intergenerational redistribution has been the major cause of the postwar decline in U.S. saving. Although this redistribution has undoubtedly altered the nature and degree of resource uncertainty, government policy has produced a major systematic change in the distribution of expected resources among current and future generations. This intergenerational redistribution of resources would produce a predicted decline in national saving in any life-cycle model, with or without uncertainty. Indeed, since the social insurance policies that have effected the redistribution are likely, on balance, to have raised, rather than lowered, consumption propensities, the effect of these policies on U.S. saving rates is probably understated by our findings that focus on changes over time in the age-resource distribution and the ratio of resources to output.

Do Future Resources Affect Consumption?

A final concern is whether, in our analysis, cohorts are consuming in accordance with the life-cycle model. There is a voluminous literature testing the life-cycle model, most of which seems to be highly supportive. Can our data also be used to test this model? The answer appears to be no.

The tests that immediately come to mind involve regressing cohort consumption against variables that capture the level, composition, and timing of cohort resources. The life-cycle model under certainty predicts that the level, but neither the composition nor the timing, of resources matters to current consumption. This point can be seen in the following linear model of cohort consumption:

$$c_{it} = h(i) + g(i)r_{it}, \tag{10}$$

where $h(i)$ and $g(i)$ are functions of age, and $g(i)$ represents the marginal propensity to consume out of resources. This model is appropriate if, first, there is no uncertainty; second, preferences are identical across cohort members; and third, preferences are either homothetic, or quadratic, or exhibit constant absolute risk aversion.[29] In this case, since consumption depends on resources only through r_{it}, regressing consumption on a polynomial in age and the components of resources (human wealth, net wealth, pension wealth, and the generational account) interacted with a polynomial in age will yield the same propensity to consume out of each component of resources. Furthermore, if one decomposes those components of resources that involve present values into a current flow and the present value of future flows, the propensities to consume out of the current flows and the present value of future flows will be identical. For example, if human wealth is divided into current labor earnings and the present value of future labor earnings, the propensity to consume out of current labor earnings will equal the propensity to consume out of the present value of future labor earnings.

Although testing the equality of marginal propensities to consume out of the various components of resources seems simple enough, one practical difficulty of a cohort data set is that the components of resources are, themselves, nonlinear functions of age and other data, and therefore are highly colinear. Current labor earnings, for example, is large and positive at young and middle ages and essentially zero at older ages; so this variable has a definite pattern with age. Furthermore, if the cross-sectional age-earnings profile is fairly smooth between ages eighteen and sixty-five, the current earnings for all cohorts under age sixty-five at a point in time will be proportional to a polynomial in age. As a second example, the present value of future social security benefits (excluding current benefits) also has a definite pattern with age; it is small for young cohorts that are years away from collecting benefits, large for middle-aged cohorts that are approaching retirement, and small for old cohorts that are approaching their maximum lifespan. Moreover, although variables such as current earnings and the present value of future social security benefits exhibit variation over time, our data set contains only four periods.

Without the assumption of certainty, the difficulty in using our data to test the life-cycle model is compounded. First, if preferences are neither quadratic nor exhibit constant absolute risk aversion, the propensity to consume out of resources will depend not only on age, but also on the composition of resources, in terms of those that are safe, like current net worth, and those that are risky, like future labor earnings.[30] Since we do not know the form of this dependence, we have no way to control for it when testing for equality of marginal propensities to consume.

If preferences are quadratic or exhibit constant absolute risk aversion, consumption is linear in the expected value of resources, and therefore the propensity to consume depends only on age. But in our model, the present value of the variable for future flows of resources incorporates the actual realized values of these flows, rather than the expected values. Consequently, our present-value realized resource components will differ from their expected-value counterparts by component-specific expectation errors. Hence our use of realized rather than expected resources in a consumption regression introduces classical measurement error in the variables. This problem will contaminate not only the coefficients on the present values of future resource flows, but also the coefficients on current flows. Indeed, one can show that the coefficients on current flows will be biased upward. Thus coefficients on current flows may be much larger than those on the present values of future flows not because cohorts ignore the future or fail to optimize intertemporally, but simply because current flows are, in part, proxying for expected future flows.

In principle, one can instrument the variables measured with error to avoid these biases. Lagged income variables, such as a cohort's lagged labor earnings, represent natural instruments since they are, presumably, correlated with individuals' expected future incomes but not with their expectation errors. However, the orthogonality of lagged incomes and expectation errors is a time-series property, and we have only four time-series observations.

Notwithstanding this litany of admonitions, table 1.20 presents marginal propensities to consume out of alternative resource variables at ages twenty, forty, sixty, and eighty, as predicted by four ordinary least squares (OLS) regressions, estimated separately for males and females. Each regression includes an intercept, age, age

Table 1.20
Marginal propensities to consume out of specified resource components at selected ages[a]

Equation	Sex and age	Total resources	Net worth	Human wealth	Pension wealth	Generational account	Current human wealth	Current pension wealth	Current net taxes	Future human wealth
	Males									
1	20	0.06	...	...	...	...	...	...	...	...
	40	0.06	...	...	...	...	...	...	...	...
	60	0.06	...	...	...	...	...	...	...	...
	80	0.10	...	...	...	...	...	...	...	...
2	20	...	0.23	0.09	0.14	−0.18	...	...	...	...
	40	...	0.22	0.07	0.02	−0.15	...	...	...	...
	60	...	0.12	0.00	−0.01	−0.07	...	...	...	...
	80	...	0.05	−0.02	0.40	−0.10	...	...	...	...
3	20	...	0.07	...	...	...	−0.50	−2.19	1.12	0.18
	40	...	0.05	...	...	...	0.10	−0.59	0.70	0.09
	60	...	−0.02	...	...	...	0.38	1.87	0.25	−0.05
	80	...	−0.11	...	...	...	−1.12	2.29	1.29	−0.05
4	20	...	−0.03	...	...	...	−0.60	−0.25	...	0.05
	40	...	−0.21	...	...	...	−0.02	1.21	...	0.02
	60	...	−0.44	...	...	...	0.17	2.37	...	0.24
	80	...	−0.62	...	...	...	−1.65	1.25	...	1.02
	Females									
1	20	0.06	...	...	...	...	...	...	...	...
	40	0.06	...	...	...	...	...	...	...	...
	60	0.05	...	...	...	...	...	...	...	...
	80	0.08	...	...	...	...	...	...	...	...
2	20	...	0.04	−0.01	0.49	0.07	...	...	...	...
	40	...	0.05	0.02	0.27	−0.02	...	...	...	...
	60	...	0.02	0.07	0.00	−0.12	...	...	...	...
	80	...	−0.04	0.10	0.35	−0.07	...	...	...	...
3	20	...	0.00	...	...	...	−0.04	4.20	−0.09	−0.01
	40	...	0.00	...	...	...	0.51	4.42	−0.32	0.00
	60	...	0.00	...	...	...	1.00	3.03	−0.36	−0.01
	80	...	−0.02	...	...	...	0.74	2.40	0.14	−0.10
4	20	...	−0.09	...	...	...	−1.55	−1.58	...	0.08
	40	...	−0.13	...	...	...	−0.97	−1.39	...	−0.06
	60	...	−0.13	...	...	...	−0.86	0.42	...	−0.37
	80	...	−0.11	...	...	...	−3.84	3.69	...	−0.78

Source: Authors' calculations, using the data sources for tables 1.5 and 1.6.
a. The dependent variable is consumption (c_{it}). Each regression includes an intercept, age, age squared, and a third-order polynomial in age interacted with each of the resource variables that appear in the table.

Future pension wealth	Future net taxes	Current social security benefits	Current medicare & medicaid benefits	Current welfare benefits	Current tax payments	Future social security benefits	Future medicare & medicaid benefits	Future welfare benefits	Future tax payments
...	...	...	...	...	...	...	...	...	...
...	...	...	...	...	...	...	...	...	...
...	...	...	...	...	...	...	...	...	...
...	...	...	...	...	...	...	...	...	...
...	...	...	...	...	...	...	...	...	...
...	...	...	...	...	...	...	...	...	...
...	...	...	...	...	...	...	...	...	...
...	...	...	...	...	...	...	...	...	...
0.14	−0.43	...	...	...	...	...	...	...	...
0.10	−0.31	...	...	...	...	...	...	...	...
−0.08	−0.17	...	...	...	...	...	...	...	...
−0.39	−0.53	...	...	...	...	...	...	...	...
0.25	...	−10.48	−1.12	−2.43	0.73	−0.80	0.29	0.79	−0.03
0.14	...	−3.00	2.26	4.77	2.01	−0.60	0.16	−0.52	−0.10
0.11	...	8.80	8.72	9.42	4.22	−1.02	−1.28	−4.15	−0.71
0.57	...	11.29	16.83	−0.66	7.72	−3.69	−4.94	−10.31	−2.37
...	...	...	...	...	...	...	...	...	...
...	...	...	...	...	...	...	...	...	...
...	...	...	...	...	...	...	...	...	...
...	...	...	...	...	...	...	...	...	...
...	...	...	...	...	...	...	...	...	...
...	...	...	...	...	...	...	...	...	...
...	...	...	...	...	...	...	...	...	...
...	...	...	...	...	...	...	...	...	...
0.45	0.06	...	...	...	...	...	...	...	...
0.15	0.01	...	...	...	...	...	...	...	...
−0.20	−0.07	...	...	...	...	...	...	...	...
0.10	−0.10	...	...	...	...	...	...	...	...
−0.33	...	19.17	0.06	13.72	5.08	−0.37	0.01	−0.58	−0.27
−0.22	...	14.49	3.01	7.57	4.27	0.10	0.47	−0.49	0.01
−0.03	...	6.11	7.01	2.30	2.82	0.80	1.01	2.14	0.45
−0.11	...	14.17	10.23	18.71	5.99	1.10	1.30	9.18	0.63

squared, and a third-order polynomial in age interacted with each of the resource variables.

Regression 1 considers only total resources; as indicated, marginal consumption propensities are flat at around 6 percent for males and females through age sixty, and rise to 10 percent for males and 8 percent for females at age eighty. Regression 2 breaks total resources into net worth, human wealth, pension wealth, and the generational account. Although an *F*-test strongly rejects equality of marginal propensities to consume out of these components of resources, certain results (such as the generally negative predicted marginal propensities to consume out of the generational account) provide support for the life-cycle model.

This support evaporates when we further disaggregate the four main components of resources and the components of the generational account into current flows and the present value of future flows (regressions 3 and 4, respectively). As the table shows, both the signs and the magnitudes of calculated marginal propensities to consume are highly sensitive to the precise combination of variables that are included in the regressions. These basic findings also pertain to regressions using data constructed under the assumptions of 3 and 9 percent discount rates; data constructed using simple, rather than actuarial, discounting; and data constructed under the assumption of myopic expectations. Finally, the findings also pertain to instrumented regressions, using as instruments age and age squared interacted with six lagged values each of per capita labor earnings, pension benefits, social security benefits, and other per capita taxes and transfers.[31]

From these results we must conclude that our data are not up to the task of testing the life-cycle model. This does not, however, invalidate their use for the main purpose of this study, namely, decomposing changes over time in U.S. saving rates.

Implications of Projected Demographic Change for Future U.S. Saving Rates

One final issue is the prognosis for U.S. saving rates in light of projected demographic change. To consider this issue, we use the consumption propensities, relative resource profiles, and resources-to-output ratios of the late 1980s to calculate the national saving rate for alternative projections of the future age structure of the population.

Table 1.21
The effect of demographic change, percent

Year	Saving rate	Year	Saving rate
1995	2.1	2025	1.4
2000	1.7	2030	1.3
2005	1.7	2035	1.3
2010	1.9	2040	1.3
2015	1.9	2045	1.3
2020	1.7	2050	1.3

Source: Authors' calculations, using the data sources for tables 1.5 and 1.6.

Table 1.21 shows that, all else equal, projected changes in the population structure will produce a further decline in the U.S. saving rate. The projected rate for 2000 is only 1.7 percent. Over the period 2000–20, the saving rate will oscillate around this value. But after 2020, when the baby boom generation has completely retired, the saving rate is predicted to decline to 1.3 percent.

Conclusion

This chapter traces the dramatic postwar decline in U.S. saving to two factors: government redistribution from current young and future generations to current older ones, and a sharp increase in the propensity of older Americans to consume out of their remaining lifetime resources. Absent these factors, the current U.S. rate of national saving would be roughly three and a half times as large. The increase in the resources of the elderly relative to those of younger generations, as well as the increase in their propensity to consume out of their resources has produced a remarkable increase in their relative consumption. Today, seventy-year-olds are consuming, on average, roughly one-fifth more than thirty-year-olds; in the early 1960s, they were consuming slightly more than two-thirds as much. The increase in the relative consumption of the elderly is dramatic even if one considers only nonmedical consumption.

The fact that propensities to consume were not systematically larger, and indeed, were smaller for most young and middle-aged cohorts, in the late 1980s than in the early 1960s indicates that "spendthrift" young and middle-aged Americans are not to blame for the decline in U.S. saving. This is not to say that young and middle-aged Americans are saving enough. Given the severe imbalance in long-run U.S. fiscal policy, these groups need to save significant amounts simply to safeguard themselves against future tax increases or reductions in transfer payments.[32]

Since there is every reason to believe that intergenerational redistribution will continue apace in the United States, there is every reason to believe that U.S. saving rates will remain extremely low, if they do not decline even further. Anemic rates of saving will spell anemic rates of domestic investment, labor productivity growth, and real wage growth. This is the legacy of the uncontrolled intergenerational redistribution from young savers to old spenders that has been fueling ever-higher rates of consumption in the United States.

Appendix A: Data Construction

In allocating income, taxes, and benefits to household members, we distribute various income, tax, and transfer aggregates according to age-sex relative profiles obtained from various microeconomic surveys described below. Two methods are followed in constructing the relative profiles for the various types of payments and receipts. In both methods, children's amounts are attributed equally to the head and the spouse (if present). In the primary method, nominal receipts and payments by married individuals are divided equally between the head and the spouse before averaging within each age-sex category. This is done for labor income, all tax payments, and all benefit receipts except for medicare and medicaid—which are in-kind benefits and cannot be shared with the spouse. The other method involves allocating the amounts to the nominal recipient before averaging within each age-sex category. The detailed description of data sources and construction that follows should be read with these alternative methods of allocating payments and receipts within the household in mind.

Labor Income

Aggregate labor income between 1960 and 1993 is calculated as labor's share of national income as reported in the NIPA. For each of these years, labor's share of national income is calculated under the assumption that it is the same as its share of proprietorship income.[33] Relative profiles of labor income by age and sex are calculated for each year between 1963 and 1993, using CPS data. The 1963 profile is used to distribute aggregate labor income for earlier years. Per capita labor income for years beyond 1993 is projected under the assumption that, except for an adjustment for growth, cohorts of a given age and sex earn the same average labor income in future years as cohorts of that age and sex earned in 1993. For example, males who are aged 50 in years after 1993 are assumed to earn the same amount, on average, apart from an adjustment for growth, as males who were aged 50 in 1993. The growth adjustment is 1.2 percent per year. Thus the projected average earnings of males aged 50 in 1996 equals the average earnings of males aged 50 in 1993 multiplied by $(1.012)^{33}$.

Pension Benefits

Pension benefits include private pension benefits, workers' compensation, veterans' benefits, and government employee pension benefits. Aggregate private pension benefits for the years 1960–88 are taken from Park (1992). In this case, we use the NIPA estimates primarily because estimates based on administrative reports are generally deemed more reliable than those based on household surveys. The estimates for the years through 2030 are derived by assuming that the ratio of pension benefits to GDP remains as its 1988 level. Actual GDP through 1993 and unpublished GDP projections made by the Office of Management and Budget (OMB) through the year 2030 are used to extrapolate aggregate private pension benefits into the future. The aggregates for the other three types of benefits through 1993 are taken from SCB, and the same procedure is used to extrapolate these aggregates through the year 2030.

The relative profiles for all four types of pensions are computed from the March CPS for the years 1972–93. This survey contains information on various types of pension income, including company or union pensions, workers' compensation, veterans' benefits, and government employee pensions, and receipts from annuities and other regular contributions. For all categories, retirement, disability and survivor benefits are included. The 1972 profile is used to distribute the aggregates in earlier years, and the 1993 profile is used to distribute the projected aggregates through 2030. For years after 2030, it is assumed that real average pension benefits for a given age and sex equal their 2030 values adjusted for growth at an annual rate of 1.2 percent, as assumed in the base case.

Social Security Benefits

Aggregate social security benefits between 1960 and 1993 are those reported in the NIPA. For the years between 1993 and 2030, we use unpublished projections (on a NIPA basis) provided by the Office of Management and Budget. Relative profiles of social security benefits by age and sex, obtained from the CPS for the years 1968–93, are used to distribute aggregate benefits in those years. Aggregate benefits in earlier years are distributed according to the relative profiles for 1968, and the OMB's projected benefits for the years 1994 through 2030 are distributed according to the relative profiles for 1993. Per capita benefits by age and sex beyond the year 2030 equal those in that year, adjusted for productivity growth at an annual rate of 1.2 percent.

Medicare and Medicaid Benefits

Aggregate medicare and medicaid payments are reported in the NIPA from the inception of these programs through 1993. The OMB has provided us with unpublished projections (on a NIPA basis) of aggregate medicare payments for the years 1994 through 2030. In the case of medicaid, we apply the OMB's projected annual growth rates for grants in aid to state and local governments between 1994 and 2030 to the aggregate value of medicaid for 1993 from the NIPA. For each year beyond 2030, total medicare and medicaid payments to individuals of a given age and sex are calculated by multiplying the projected number of individuals of that age and sex for the year by the per capita level of benefits to individuals of that age and sex in 2030, adjusted for post-2030 growth in the level of per capita benefits (using the 1.2 percent productivity growth rate of the base case). Relative profiles of medicaid benefits are based on HCFA data on average benefits by age and sex. Relative profiles of medicare benefits are based on data from McClellan and Skinner (1996).

Unemployment Insurance, Aid to Families with Dependent Children, Food Stamps, and General Welfare Benefits

Aggregate values of these federal, state, and local transfers are reported in the NIPA. General welfare benefits include federal black lung benefits, state general assistance, state energy assistance, education benefits, and other federal, state, and local transfers. The age-sex relative profiles used to distribute these benefits are obtained from March CPS data on public assistance for the years 1972 and 1993. These relative profiles are used to distribute their respective aggregate expenditures for each year between 1960 and 1993, and the 1972 profiles are used to distribute benefits in the years before 1972. For future years, we assume that the age- and sex-specific values of each type of transfer payment keep pace with productivity growth of 1.2 percent.

Labor Income Taxes

Aggregate federal, state, and local income taxes for 1960 through 1993 are reported in the NIPA. For 1993 through 2030, we use unpublished projections of federal income tax revenues provided by the OMB. State and local income taxes for 1993 through 2030 are projected by using the OMB's unpublished forecast of GDP and assuming that the ratio of state and local income taxes to GDP in 1993 prevails between 1993 and 2030.

Aggregate labor income taxes in each year are calculated as the product of total federal, state, and local income taxes and labor's share of national income. We distribute aggregate labor income taxes on the basis of the CPS profiles of labor income described above. For the years after 2030, we assume that age- and sex-specific values of labor income taxes keep pace with productivity growth of 1.2 percent.

Payroll Taxes

The NIPA reports aggregate values of payroll taxes from 1960 through 1993. The OMB has provided us with projections of aggregate federal payroll taxes from 1994 through 2030. Aggregate state and local payroll taxes for 1994 through 2030 are calculated on the basis of the OMB's projection of GDP between 1994 and 2030 and the assumption that the ratio of state and local payroll taxes to GDP in 1993 prevails through 2030. Aggregate payroll taxes in the years 1960–2030 are distributed by age and sex, according to CPS profiles of covered earnings (that is, labor earnings subject to social security payroll taxes) from 1963 through 1993.[34] Age- and sex-specific values of payroll taxes beyond 2030 are assumed to equal their values in 2030, adjusted for growth at 1.2 percent.

Excise and Sales Taxes

The NIPA is our source for aggregate excise tax (including property tax) and sales tax revenue from 1960 through 1993. For the period 1994–2030, we use unpublished projections of federal excise and sales tax revenues provided by the OMB. State and local excise and sales tax revenues between 1994 and 2030 are calculated by using the ratio of these revenues to GDP in 1993 and applying the OMB's unpublished forecasts of GDP through 2030.

Age-sex relative profiles of excise and sales taxes are calculated from the 1960–61, 1972–73, 1984–86, and 1987–90 CEXs. Separate profiles are constructed for tobacco, alcohol, property taxes, and all other sales and excise taxes. The 1960–61 profiles are used for the years before 1966; the 1972–73 profiles are used for the years 1967 through 1978; the 1984–86 profiles are used for the years 1979 through 1986; and the 1987–90 profiles are used for 1987 and beyond. Age- and sex-specific values of sales and excise taxes beyond 2030 are assumed to equal their values in 2030, adjusted for growth at 1.2 percent.

Capital Income Taxes

Aggregate capital income taxes between 1960 and 2030 are calculated as capital's share of national income multiplied by actual or projected values of aggregate federal, state, and local income tax revenues. Relative profiles for capital income taxes come from the 1962 and 1983 SCFs. These profiles are based upon weighted (SCF person weights) average net worth holdings, by age and sex. This procedure could not be applied to individuals over age eighty because of the paucity of data. The profile of average net worth holdings by age and sex are smoothed and extrapolated through age one hundred using a fourth-order polynomial. Age- and sex-specific values of capital income taxes after 2030 are assumed to equal their values in 2030, adjusted for growth at 1.2 percent.

Nonhuman Wealth

Age- and sex-specific values of nonhuman wealth for each year between 1960 and 1993 are constructed by distributing by age and sex the total private net wealth in that year. Aggregate private net wealth for these years is reported in the Flow of Funds.[35] The relative profiles of wealth holding by age and sex are calculated with data from the 1963 and 1983 SCFs. The 1963 profiles are used for the years before 1963, and the 1983 profiles for years after 1983. The profiles for intermediate years are constructed by interpolating linearly between the profiles for 1963 and 1983.

Determining Average Consumption by Age and Sex

The data used to determine average consumption by age and sex for the years 1960–61, 1972–73, 1984–86, and 1987–90 are from the NIPA; the 1960–61, 1972–73, and 1984–90 CEXs; and the 1977 and 1987 NMESs. Aggregate NIPA household consumption expenditure is allocated to adults on the basis of four relative profiles of consumption by age and sex—for the years 1960–61, 1972–73, 1984–86, and 1987–90.

To use the 1960–61 CEX, we have to impute particular demographic information to its households. The reason is that this CEX provides only general indicators of the ages and sexes of household members other than the head and spouse. We impute this information by means of a statistical match with the 1960 decennial census. Specifically, we sort the census data by a set of variables that are also available in the CEX. These include demographic variables such as the number of children under age eighteen, the ages and sexes of the household head and spouse, household income, the sex and marital status of the household head, an urban versus rural indicator, region, and housing tenure. For each 1960–61 CEX household with members other than the head and spouse, we randomly select a census household from the set of census households with the same matching data. The ages and sexes of census household members other than the head and spouse are then attributed to the CEX household.

Each of the four age-sex relative consumption profiles is formed in a similar manner. First, we divide the NIPA consumption aggregates into thirty-five separate components. For most of these components, such as clothing, there are corresponding data in the CEX that can be used to distribute the aggregate values of these components. For three components, imputed rent, financial services, and expenditures by charitable institutions, there is no corresponding direct measure in the CEX, but there are other variables that can be used for purposes of distribution (for example, house value in the place of imputed rent). However, there is no CEX variable that is comparable to the NIPA's health care component, so we use the NMES to distribute health care.

The second step in forming the age-sex relative consumption profiles involves benchmarking the distribution data to the relevant component of the NIPA consumption aggregate. For example, we divide the NIPA clothing component by the total CEX clothing expenditure, computed using the CEX household weights. The resulting ratio is used to rescale the clothing expenditure of each household in the CEX. Clothing expenditure is rescaled separately for each of CEX surveys used in the study, based on the contemporaneous value of clothing from the NIPA. This procedure is used to rescale the CEX data for each of the NIPA components for which there are also direct CEX measures. The rescaling factors for easily verified or remembered spending categories, like automobiles and rent, are generally very close to one. CEX aggregates for spending on other goods and services, such as food and alcohol, are generally underreported by roughly 20 percent.[36]

In the case of imputed rent, we calculate the ratio of the NIPA aggregate imputed rent to total CEX reported house values (again, computed using the CEX household weights). We then multiply each household's reported house value by this ratio to produce a NIPA-benchmarked estimate of the household's imputed rent. This procedure is also used in the case of financial services, expenditures by charitable institutions, clothing provided by the military, net foreign remittances, and food produced and consumed on farms, using, respectively, CEX reported totals for checking plus saving accounts, charitable contributions, number of members in the military, and other consumption, and a dummy variable equal to one if the household owned a farm and equal to zero otherwise.

In the case of health care expenditure, we benchmark the NMES data using the five broad components in the NIPA: physician's services, hospital services, private health insurance, prescriptions, and other medical. Specifically, we form the ratio of each of these components to the corresponding NMES totals (based on the NMES population weights) and then rescale the NMES data on the basis of these ratios. We use the 1977 NMES for the years 1960–61 and 1972–73, and the 1987 NMES for the years 1984–86 and 1987–90.

As the third step in forming the age-sex relative consumption profiles, we allocate the rescaled (NIPA-benchmarked) actual or imputed CEX data to individuals within the CEX household. (This was not necessary for the NMES data because this survey takes the individual as the unit of observation.) For certain types of expenditure, the method of allocation is fairly clear. For example, expenditure on boy's clothing is divided evenly among the household's male children, and pipe tobacco is divided evenly among the household's adult males. For other types of expenditure, we have developed particular rules. Housing expenditure, including imputed rent, is allocated evenly to the head and spouse. Food, vacations, and other items of expenditure that are not readily allocable are divided evenly among the household's adult equivalents, where adults (those aged eighteen and over) have an equivalency factor of 1.0, and children have an equivalency factor that increases linearly from 0.3 for newborns to 1.0 for eighteen-year-olds.

The fourth step entails using the NIPA-benchmarked NMES data to calculate age- and sex-specific weighted average values of each of the five types of health care expenditure. These values are then attributed to individual members of the CEX households, on the basis of their age and sex. We also allocate to individual members of the CEX households, on the basis of their age and sex, average values of privately paid educational expenditure. These average values are determined by calculating average elementary and secondary school expenditures per child aged five through eighteen and average college expenditures per person aged eighteen through twenty-four.

In the fifth step, we reallocate all of the children's expenditure from the CEX, including the imputed health care expenditure, evenly to the head of household and spouse. We then combine these NIPA-benchmarked, actual or imputed CEX data for particular years (1960–61, 1972–73, 1984–86, and 1987–90) to form the ratio of the average value over these years of the total expenditure of adults of a particular age and sex to that of forty-year-old males. This provides our four age-sex relative consumption profiles.

We use our four age-sex relative consumption profiles and our age- and sex-specific population data to allocate total NIPA consumption over the four periods by age and sex. This may seem an unnecessary second round of benchmarking of aggregate NIPA consumption, but in so doing, we ensure that our final calculated values of average consumption by age and sex are consistent with the census population data that we use to calculate age- and sex-specific values of average remaining lifetime resources. In particular, we avoid the under- or overestimates of average age- and sex-specific consumption that would arise if the CEX household weights were systematically too high or too low.

Notes

We thank the Office of Management and Budget and the Social Security Administration for providing long-term fiscal and population projections, and Jonathan Skinner for providing health expenditure data. We also thank Orazio Attanasio, Barry Bosworth, Robert Haveman, Andrew Samwick, Jonathan Skinner, and numerous seminar participants for helpful comments. The opinions expressed in this paper are those of the authors and are not necessarily shared by the Federal Reserve Bank of Cleveland or the Congressional Budget Office.

1. The net national saving rate is defined as net national product less national consumption (household consumption plus government purchases), divided by net national product. The National Income and Product Account (NIPA) data used in the body of this paper do not incorporate recently revised NIPA data for the years starting in 1959.

2. The recently released revised NIPA data also show a dramatic decline in the U.S. net national saving rate. For example, during the 1960s the saving rate based on the revised data averaged 12.1 percent compared with 4.6 percent during the period 1990–95. Saving rates in the revised data are higher than in the unrevised data because government consumption has been redefined to exclude government purchases of durables, but to include the imputed rent on the stock of government durables. The Commerce Department appears, however, to be understating this imputed rent because its measure includes only the depreciation on the stock of government durables.

3. Auerbach, Kotlikoff, and Weil (1992); Auerbach and others (1995).

4. Summers and Carroll (1987); Bosworth, Burtless, and Sabelhaus (1991); Attanasio (1993).

5. See, for example, Kotlikoff (1993).

6. Such reclassification is not merely a hypothetical possibility. The so-called privatization of the Chilean social security system amounts, in large part, to classifying workers' social security contributions as loans, rather than taxes. Under the Chilean "reform," workers contribute to pension funds. But the pension funds then lend most of these funds to the government, which uses them to make benefit payments to current social security recipients.

7. Cutler and others (1990).

8. See Altonji, Hayashi, and Kotlikoff (1992, 1995), Abel and Kotlikoff (1994), and Hayashi, Altonji, and Kotlikoff (1996).

9. Boskin and Lau (1988a, 1988b).

10. The rise in the rate of household consumption began in the 1970s. The household consumption rate rose by 1.6 percentage points between the early 1970s and the late 1970s (that is, from 1970–74 to 1975–79), by 2.1 percentage points between the late 1970s and the early 1980s, by 2.0 percentage points between the early 1980s and late 1980s, and by 1.6 percentage points between the late 1980s and the early 1990s.

11. Discounting is at a constant real interest rate. The "actuarial" value of income, taxes, and transfers received or paid in future years is that discounted by the probability of surviving to these years.

12. Cohorts over the age of one hundred are grouped together with those aged one hundred.

13. Ando and Modigliani (1963).

14. These rates bracket the pretax real rate of return observed, on average, between 1961 and 1992, where the rate of return in year t is calculated as $[(NW_t - E_t - P_t + C_t + T_t)/NW_t - 1] - 1$, such that NW_t is household net worth in period t; E_t is aggregate labor income, excluding contributions to private pension funds; P_t is pension income, including private pensions, government employee pensions, workers' compensation, and veterans' benefits; C_t is personal consumption expenditure; and T_t is aggregate net tax payments.

15. The kinks at age eighty in figure 1.4 reflect our method of imputing relative nonhuman wealth for individuals of this age and above. The small number of observations at these ages in the Survey of Consumer Finances precludes forming separate estimates of average nonhuman wealth at these ages. Here, we assume that the relative nonhuman wealth of those aged eighty or above equals that of eighty-year-olds of the same sex.

16. Note that our base case calculations assume a 1.2 percent annual growth of labor productivity after 1993, and a discount rate of 6 percent.

17. The findings that the consumption propensities of the very old have risen and that those of the young and middle-aged have remained relatively constant are robust to different assumed values of the discount rate. At a discount rate of 3 percent, for example, eighty-year-olds' propensity to consume rises from 8.6 percent in 1960–61 to 12.4 percent in 1987–90. At a discount rate of 9 percent, it rises from 8.9 to 14.9 percent. Detailed consumption propensities by age under alternative discount rate assumptions are available from the authors upon request.

18. The old age social security tax is negative (positive) if the social security benefits received by a cohort exceed (are less than) the return of principal plus interest on the cohort's past social security contributions. The calculation assumes that the timing of the payment of this old age tax coincides with the time at which the cohort actually receives social security benefits. For example, if the present value (to age zero) of the old age social security net tax of a generation is 30 percent as large as the present value (to age zero) of its lifetime social security benefits, we assume that each year the generation faces a tax equal to 30 percent of its social security benefits, and otherwise treat payments to and benefits received from social security as equivalent to investing in a financial asset.

19. The fact that other studies (for example, Bosworth, Burtless, and Sabelhaus, 1991) report positive propensities to save out of disposable income at all ages, notwithstanding their use of conventional classifications, appears to reflect their failure to include all the components of consumption, in particular, medical goods and services.

20. Pension incomes include survivor, disability, and retirement benefits from private and government employee pension plans, workers' compensation, and veterans' benefits.

21. This result is sustained under the alternative discount rate assumptions of 3 and 9 percent. The results from all the counterfactual experiments under these alternative discount rates are available from the authors upon request.

22. Assuming a discount rate of 3 percent yields a saving rate of 7.49 percent when the 1960–61 value of R/Y is substituted for the 1987–90 value; using a 9 percent discount rate produces a saving rate of 4.46 percent.

23. Auerbach and others (1995).

24. Kotlikoff and Spivak (1981).

25. All the results in table 1.15 use the base case discount rate of 6 percent.

26. In equation 2, $\alpha_{it}r_{it}$ is simply equal to c_{it}, which is independent of the definition of resources.

27. Levels of human wealth for both male and female working generations are higher for the 1960–61 period under myopic expectations than under the base case. This results from the high growth rate used to compute 1960–61 human wealth under myopic expectations, relative to the actual growth of labor income in subsequent years. The actual growth of pension income in later years, however, was more rapid than that used to form pension wealth under myopic expectations. In addition, the generational accounts of all cohorts are much higher in 1960–61 under myopic expectations, primarily because the creation and growth of the medicare and medicaid programs were excluded when forming myopic generational accounts for that period. For the 1960–61 period, the lower cohort pension wealth and higher generational accounts more than offset the higher cohort human wealth for all except the youngest generations. For 1987–90, cohort pension and human wealth are not much different under myopic expectations, compared to the base case. Detailed data on the components of resources under myopic expectations are available from the authors upon request.

28. Deaton (1992); Carroll (1992).

29. The function $h(i)$ is equal to zero if preferences are homothetic.

30. More precisely, the propensity to consume will depend on the amount of safe resources and the distribution of risky resources.

31. We do not have lagged values of resource flows on a generation-specific basis for the years before 1960 that we could use as instruments.

32. See, for example, Auerbach and Kotlikoff (1994) and Bernheim (1993).

33. The share of labor income in national income is ϕ, where ϕ satisfies $C + \phi PI = \phi NI$. In this equation, C is compensation paid to employees less employer contributions to employee pension plans, PI is proprietorship income, and NI is national income. The calculated values of ϕ are quite stable over the period 1960–92, ranging between 0.76 and 0.82.

34. The data do not permit the calculation of separate profiles for state and local payroll taxes, which are not necessarily subject to earnings ceilings. However, payroll taxes other than social security are a small fraction of the total (less than 30 percent), so the bias associated with using profiles of covered earnings is likely to be quite small.

35. Our aggregates are net of the Flow of Funds's estimate of the value of residential structures, plant, and equipment owned by nonprofit institutions.

36. See Bosworth, Burtless, and Sabelhaus (1991) for a general comparison of CEX and NIPA aggregates.

References

Abel, Andrew B., and Laurence J. Kotlikoff. 1994. "Intergenerational Altruism and the Effectiveness of Fiscal Policy—New Tests Based on Cohort Data." In *Savings and Bequests*, edited by Toshiaki Tachibanaki. Ann Arbor, Mich.: University of Michigan Press.

Altonji, Joseph G., Fumio Hayashi, and Laurence J. Kotlikoff. 1992. "Is the Extended Family Altruistically Linked? Direct Tests Using Micro Data." *American Economic Review* 82(5): 1177–98.

Altonji, Joseph G., Fumio Hayashi, and Laurence J. Kotlikoff. 1995. "Parental Altruism and Inter Vivos Transfers: Theory and Evidence." Working Paper 5378. Cambridge, Mass.: National Bureau of Economic Research (December).

Ando, Albert, and Franco Modigliani. 1963. "The 'Life Cycle' Hypothesis of Saving: Aggregate Implications and Tests." *American Economic Review* 53(1): 55–84.

Attanasio, Orazio P. 1993. "A Cohort Analysis of Saving Behavior by U.S. Households." Working Paper 4454. Cambridge, Mass.: National Bureau of Economic Research (September).

Auerbach, Alan J., and Laurence J. Kotlikoff. 1994. "The U.S. Fiscal and Savings Crises and Their Impact for Baby Boomers." In *Retirement in the 21st Century ... Ready or Not ...*, edited by Dallas L. Salisbury and Nora Super Jones. Washington: Employee Benefit Research Institute.

Auerbach, Alan J., Laurence J. Kotlikoff, and David N. Weil. 1992. "The Increasing Annuitization of the Elderly—Estimates and Implications for Intergenerational Transfers, Inequality, and National Saving." Working Paper 4182. Cambridge, Mass.: National Bureau of Economic Research (October).

Auerbach, Alan J., and others. 1995. "The Annuitization of Americans' Resources: A Cohort Analysis." Working paper 5089. Cambridge, Mass.: National Bureau of Economic Research (April).

Bernhein, B. Douglas. 1993. "Is the Baby Boom Generation Preparing Adequately for Retirement?" Summary report prepared for Merrill Lynch and Co., Inc. (January).

Boskin, Michael J., and Lawrence J. Lau. 1988a. "An Analysis of Postwar U.S. Consumption and Saving: Part I The Model and Aggregation." Working Paper 2605. Cambridge, Mass.: National Bureau of Economic Research (June).

Boskin, Michael J., and Lawrence J. Lau. 1988b. "An Analysis of U.S. Postwar Consumption and Saving: Part II Empirical Results." Working Paper 2606. Cambridge, Mass.: National Bureau of Economic Research (June).

Bosworth, Barry, Gary Burtless, and John Sabelhaus. 1991. "The Decline in Saving: Evidence from Household Surveys." *BPEA, 1:1991*, 183–241.

Carroll, Christopher D. 1992. "The Buffer-Stock Theory of Saving: Some Macroeconomic Evidence." *BPEA, 2:1992*, 61–135.

Cutler, David M., and others. 1990. "An Aging Society: Opportunity or Challenge?" *BPEA, 1:1990*, 1–56.

Deaton, Angus. 1992. *Understanding Consumption*. Oxford: Clarendon Press.

Hayashi, Fumio, Joseph Altonji, and Laurence J. Kotlikoff. 1996. "Risk-Sharing Between and Within Families." *Econometrica* 64(2): 261–94.

Kotlikoff, Laurence J. 1993. "From Deficit Delusion to the Fiscal Balance Rule: Looking for an Economically Meaningful Way to Assess Fiscal Policy." *Journal of Economics*, supplement 7: 17–41.

Kotlikoff, Laurence J., and Avia Spivak. 1981. "The Family as an Incomplete Annuities Market." *Journal of Political Economy* 89(2): 372–91.

McClellan, Mark, and Jonathan Skinner. 1996. "The Distribution of Medicare Benefits: A Lifetime Perspective." Unpublished paper. Stanford University (April).

Park, Thae S. 1992. "Total Private Pension Benefit Payments, 1950–88." In *Trends in Pensions 1992*, edited by John A. Turner and Daniel J. Beller. Washington: U.S. Department of Labor.

Summers, Lawrence H., and Chris Carroll. 1987. "Why Is U.S. National Saving So Low?" *BPEA, 2:1987*, 607–35.

2

The Annuitization of Americans' Resources: A Cohort Analysis

Alan J. Auerbach, Jagadeesh Gokhale, Laurence J. Kotlikoff, John Sabelhaus, and David N. Weil

I. Introduction

Chapter 2 examines changes since the early 1960s in how elderly Americans hold their wealth. We distinguish between two forms of wealth-holding. Nonannuitized wealth refers to assets which can be sold, transferred, or, in the event of an individual's death, bequeathed.[1] Annuitized wealth, by contrast, is the claim to a stream of future payments that will cease upon the person's death. Social security or pension payments are examples of annuitized wealth.

Examining the changes in resource annuitization is important. Generations whose resources are more annuitized will consume more and bequeath less to their children and others.[2] This has implications for national saving as well as for the intergenerational transmission of inequality. In the extreme case in which bequests arise solely because annuities are unavailable, the provision of annuities can lead the elderly to consume all the resources that they otherwise would have bequeathed to younger generations. Although the young would respond to the elimination of their expected bequests by reducing their consumption, the net change in the economy's consumption would be positive because of differences in propensities to consume between the young and old. Hence, the availability of annuities will decrease national saving absent an intrinsic desire to bequeath. Simulation exercises (e.g., Kotlikoff and Spivak 1981; Davies 1981; Abel 1985; and Kotlikoff, Shoven, and Spivak 1986) suggest that the availability of annuities could increase the elderly's consumption by over a third and produce an even larger percentage reduction in the long run stock of wealth.

The distribution of resources could also be greatly affected by a reduction in bequests due to greater resource annuitization of the elderly. In the United States the one percent of households with the most net wealth own 34.3 percent of total net wealth. The distribution of bequests is similarly skewed. If all bequests were eliminated, one would expect the distribution of net wealth to resemble more closely the distribution of human wealth, which is much more equally distributed than is nonhuman wealth: only 9.5 percent of wage income is received by the one percent of households with the highest wages.[3]

Despite the importance of the issue, there appears to be no previous systematic study of changes over time in the annuitized and bequeathable shares of resources of America's elderly. Several recent studies (Radner and Vaughn 1987; Greenwood 1987; Avery and Kennickell 1990) have examined the distribution at a point in time of U.S. net wealth. Other studies by Feldstein (1976), Avery, Elliehausen, and Gustafson (1986), Wolff (1987a), and McDermed, Clark, and Allen (1989) have examined the distribution of broader concepts of wealth, including some annuitized components of wealth. These studies indicate the importance of annuitized wealth in the total resources of the elderly.

In this paper, we construct two data sets to study the change in resource annuitization in the United States and its implications for the aggregate flow of bequests and inequality. First we construct a unique *cohort* data set to study the trend in annuitization in the United States: annuitized and bequeathable resource components of total resources are constructed for individual cohorts alive in four periods—1960–61, 1972–73, 1984–86, and 1987–90. Specifically, we use cross-section surveys to distribute to cohorts the annual aggregate flows of income reported in the National Income and Product Account (NIPA) and other sources. The cohort data set is used to evaluate how the shares of bequeathable and annuitized resources in total resources have changed between the early 1960s and the late 1980s. In order to examine the implications for inequality, we construct measures of *household* net worth, total resources, and life insurance coverage based on the 1962 and 1983 Surveys of Consumer Finances (SCF). With this data we address two questions: first, have U.S. households counterbalanced the changes in resource annuitization by adjusting their purchases of life insurance?, and second, what are the implications of the change in resource annuitization for the distribution of bequests and, hence, for the transmission of inequality via bequests?

Our findings are striking. Across all Americans, the annuitized share of resources remained roughly constant between the early 1960s and the late 1980s. However, among *elderly* Americans (age 65 and over), the annuitized share rose from 16 percent to 41 percent for men and from 13 percent to 54 percent for women. Without this increase in the degree of annuitization, we estimate that U.S. aggregate bequests would have been 44 percent larger in the late 1980s. Although the precise impact of the elderly's increased annuitization on their consumption is unclear, it appears to be substantial. Indeed, it appears to explain a significant fraction of the decline in national saving.

Based on household-specific measures of total resources, net worth, and life insurance from the SCF, we find no evidence that life insurance has been used to offset the increased annuitization of America's elderly. Indeed, between 1962 and 1983, the amount of insurance protection, as represented by the ratio of the term value (face value less cash value) of insurance to total resources, declined by more than half for those aged 65 or more. Because the increase in annuitization is least pronounced among the richest older Americans, the increased annuitization is likely to have increased inequality in the distribution of bequests.

The rest of the chapter is organized as follows: section II presents a very simple model showing how annuitization can affect aggregate wealth accumulation. Section III presents an overview of the factors that have affected the degree of resource annuitization in the United States. Based on the cohort data set on resource components, section IV describes the changes in resource annuitization between the early 1960s and the late 1980s and examines the sensitivity of the results to alternative assumptions. Section V explores the implications of greater resource annuitization for the size of aggregate bequests and national saving.[4] Section VI turns to the SCF's household data set to address the issue of whether U.S. households have offset their greater resource annuitization by purchasing additional life insurance coverage.[5] Section VII discusses the issue of inequality and points out that the inequality in total resources is considerably smaller than the inequality in net wealth. This section also suggests how the increased annuitization of the elderly's resources may affect the distribution of net worth over time. Section VIII summarizes findings and draws conclusions.

II. A Simple Model of the Effects of Annuitization

Analysis of the following simple two-period life-cycle model clarifies the theoretical argument connecting increased annuitization to the decline in bequests and national saving.[6] Agents live for two periods. They work full time when young (earning W_y), do not work when old, and consume C_y when young and C_o when old. Population is stationary, and the size of each cohort is normalized to unity. Each agent survives with probability $(1-p)$ to old age. There is no private annuities market. However, the government provides annuities by taxing each cohort an amount T when young and returning this amount with interest to surviving members of the cohort when they are old. Since there are $(1-p)$ survivors in each cohort, each survivor receives an annuity of $T(1+r)/(1-p)$, where r is the real interest rate. If T does not exhaust private saving, those who die prior to their last period of life will leave a bequest. Assuming bequests are divided equally among the young, the bequest received per young person is pB, where p is the fraction of each cohort that dies prior to old age, and B is the bequest made per decedent.

At the beginning of any period (before anyone has died), total wealth in the economy, K, equals the sum of private wealth of the elderly plus the wealth held by the government. The wealth held by the government is just T—the aggregate tax payments of each generation. Private wealth of the elderly can be traced to their saving when young, $W_y + pB - T - C_y$. Total wealth is just this sum plus T, so

$$K = W_y + pB - C_y. \tag{1}$$

Bequests equal the accumulated value of saving when young, that is

$$B = (W_y + pB - T - C_y)(1+r). \tag{2}$$

For those agents who survive to old age, their consumption, C_o, is given by

$$C_o = (W_y + pB - T - C_y)(1+r) + T(1+r)/(1-p), \tag{3}$$

where the first term on the right hand side of equation (3) represents principal plus interest on private savings, and the second term is the government's annuity payment to survivors. We close the model by assuming that agents maximize an expected time-separable, homothetic utility function over consumption when young and old, given by

$$U = u(C_y) + (1 - p)\alpha u(C_o), \tag{4}$$

where α is the time preference parameter. Maximization of utility subject to the budget constraint given in (3) implies that consumption when old is proportional to consumption when young, that is

$$C_o = \theta C_y, \tag{5}$$

where the factor of proportionality, θ, depends on α, r, and p.[7] These equations imply

$$K = \frac{W_y - pT(1 + r)[1 + (1/\theta)]}{1 - [(1 + r)/\theta] - p(1 + r)}. \tag{6}$$

According to equation (6), aggregate wealth is a decreasing function of T, the amount of saving which is annuitized by the government. The intuition for this result is clear from equations (1)–(3) and (5). According to (1) and (2), raising T lowers the steady-state level of bequests as well as the steady-state capital stock ignoring induced changes in consumption when young. If consumption when young were to fall as much as inheritances received when young (pB), aggregate wealth would remain unchanged. But, according to equations (3) and (5), consumption when young falls by less than pB for two reasons. First, the propensity to consume when young is less than unity. Second, the annuity provided by the government increases the amount each generation can afford to consume over its lifetime because it reduces undesired bequests.[8]

In our model, agents have no interest in leaving bequests and, therefore, no interest in purchasing life insurance. As Yaari (1965) first demonstrated, the purchase of term life insurance is equivalent to the sale of an annuity. If we modified our model to include a bequest motive and the voluntary purchase of life insurance, we would find that government annuitization of the saving of the young would simply lead them to purchase more life insurance; that is, the annuities purchased by the government would be immediately resold.

III. Factors Affecting Resource Annuitization in the United States

Certain stylized facts suggest that resources of U.S. households are now more annuitized, while others suggest that they are less so. Social security benefits currently represent almost 10 percent of U.S. personal income compared with only 4 percent in 1960. The increase in private pensions in the last three decades has also been dramatic. In 1962 9 percent of elderly Americans received income from private pensions. By 1988 the figure had risen to 29 percent.[9] In 1960 pension funds represented only 5.2 percent of U.S. household net wealth; by 1990 they represented 16.5 percent.[10] The combined effect of increases in social security and pensions raised the fraction of the income of the elderly represented by annuitized sources from 40 percent in 1967 to 55 percent in 1988.[11]

While the share of household resources tied up in annuitized social security and pension benefits has increased over time, for older Americans the annuitized share of resources represented by future streams of survival-contingent earnings has declined. This is due to the continuing trend toward earlier retirement. Between 1963 and 1983, for example, the labor force participation rate for men aged 60–64 fell from 80% to 57%, while the rate for men aged 65–69 fell from 41% to 26%. The fraction of elderly Americans' income represented by earnings fell from 30 percent in 1967 to 17 percent in 1988.[12] Earlier retirement may have partially or fully offset the increased annuitization of the resources of older Americans.

A second way in which older Americans could have maintained their net degree of annuitization in the face of increases in social security and private pensions is by purchasing additional life insurance. As Yaari (1965) showed, purchasing life insurance is equivalent to selling off one's annuities. While such a possibility exists, Auerbach and Kotlikoff (1987) find no evidence that households use life insurance to offset government-induced changes in their degree of annuitization. Specifically, they report that survivor insurance provided by social security does not lead to offsetting reductions in the private purchase of life insurance. The Auerbach-Kotlikoff study considers the demand for life insurance to protect surviving spouses. In contrast, Bernheim (1991) treats married couples as single agents who purchase life insurance solely as a means of providing bequests for children. He reports that households do increase their life insurance purchase in response to the government's provision of social security annuities, but the life insurance offset appears to be quite modest. Taken together, the Auerbach-Kotlikoff and Bernheim findings suggest very considerable scope for increased annuitization to raise the consumption of the elderly and to lower their bequests.[13]

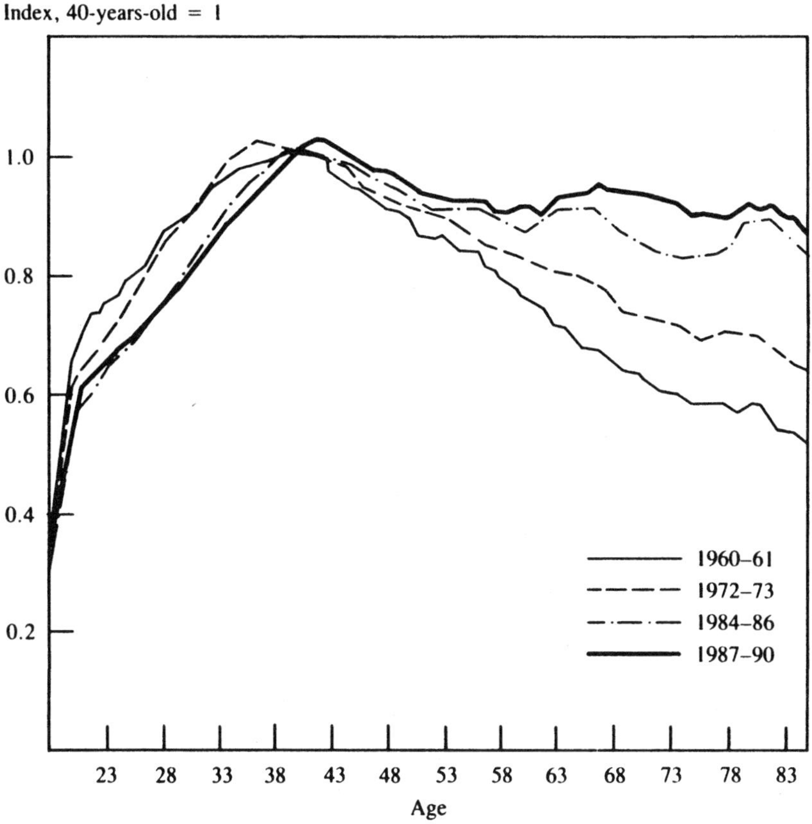

Figure 2.1
Relative total consumption profiles. *Source:* Authors' calculations, based on the CEX.

In the United States the increase in annuitization, which is documented below, has coincided with both a dramatic decline in national saving and a dramatic increase in the relative consumption of the elderly. In the 1980s, the net national saving rate averaged 5.4 percent. In contrast, it averaged 9.0 percent in the 1960s, and 8.7 percent in the 1970s. In the 1990s it has averaged only 3.8 percent. A comparison of the 1960–61, 1972–73, 1984–86, and 1987–90 Bureau of Labor Statistics (BLS) Consumer Expenditure Surveys (CEX) shows an equally remarkable rise in elderly persons' relative consumption. Figure 2.1 presents indices of average consumption by age for each of the four periods.[14] For each period, the average consumption of 40-year-olds is normalized to 1.

Table 2.1
Consumption of the elderly relative to the young

Comparison	1960–61	1972–73	1984–86	1987–90
Age 60 / Age 20	1.17	1.37	1.58	1.59
Age 70 / Age 20	0.97	1.21	1.56	1.64
Age 80 / Age 20	0.89	1.16	1.61	1.60
Age 60 / Age 30	0.86	0.93	1.09	1.15
Age 70 / Age 30	0.71	0.82	1.07	1.18
Age 80 / Age 30	0.65	0.79	1.11	1.16
Age 60 / Age 40	0.77	0.83	0.87	0.91
Age 70 / Age 40	0.64	0.73	0.86	0.94
Age 80 / Age 40	0.58	0.70	0.89	0.92

Source: Authors' calculations.

As the figure indicates, the age-consumption profiles for later years are tilted upward compared to those for earlier years, indicating a rise over time in the relative consumption of the elderly. Table 2.1 reports the ratios of average levels of consumption of 70-year-old males and females to those of 30-year-old males and females for each of the four periods. It shows that 70-year-olds in 1960 consumed about two-thirds the amount consumed by 30-year-olds in 1960, whereas their consumption now exceeds that of 30-year-olds.

The increase in the annuitization of the elderly is certainly not the only, nor necessarily the most important, explanation for the increase in their relative consumption and the concomitant decline in national saving. Indeed, much of the explanation for these outcomes appears to lie in the government's massive transfers to the elderly, which have raised their incomes relative to those of young people (see Boskin, Knetter, and Kotlikoff 1985; and Gokhale, Kotlikoff, and Sabelhaus 1996).

IV. Findings

Changes in the Cohort Distribution of Resources

The total resources of a cohort is the sum of its human, nonhuman, and pension wealth, less its generational account. Generational account refers to the present value of a sex-specific generation's future tax payments net of the present value of its future receipts of transfer payments. Our calculations include all tax payments made to, and transfer payments received from, federal, state, and local governments.[15]

Tables 2.2a and 2.2b contain per capita values of total real resources and resource components for male and female cohorts in 10-year age groups for the years 1960–61, 1972–73, 1984–86, and 1987–90. The tables also show the per capita resources of all cohorts aged 20–89 and of older cohorts aged 65–89. For the entire populations of males and females, total resources grew substantially over the three decades since 1960, but they grew more rapidly for the elderly and for women. For males as a group, per capita resources rose by 55.9 percent. For older males, they grew by 94.8 percent. For females as a group, per capita resources rose by 60.2 percent. For older females, they grew by 94.8 percent.

Some of the reported differences across ages and sex in resource growth are particularly striking. For example, males aged 20–29 experienced only a 35.2 percent increase in their average resources over the 30 years, whereas males aged 60–69 experienced a 102.8 percent increase; and females aged 20–29 experienced a 47.7 percent increase whereas those between 70–79 experienced a 112.3 percent increase.

The relative growth in elderly Americans' resources appears primarily to reflect government intergenerational redistribution coupled with increased longevity. Between 1961–62 and 1987–90 the generational account of older males fell from –\$900 to –\$59,600. The decline was even larger for older females. Their average generational account was –\$7,300 in 1960–61, but in 1987–90 period it was as low as –\$82,200. Over the same period the generational accounts of younger cohorts rose dramatically. For example, the accounts of males aged 20–29 rose from \$116,700 to \$170,600 and those of females aged 20–29 rose from \$104,400 to \$149,100. The components of generational accounts shown in tables 2.3a and 2.3b clearly indicate that the changes in the relative values of generational accounts of the old and the young primarily reflect increases in social security and government-provided health-care benefits (medicare and medicaid), on the one hand, and increases in labor income and payroll taxation, on the other.

The Decomposition of Total Resources into Annuitized and Bequeathable Resources

The degree of resource annuitization, R^a, is computed as one minus the ratio of bequeathable to total resources, that is,

Table 2.2a
Total resources and resource components—male cohorts

Age Group:	20–29	30–39	40–49	50–59	60–69	70–79	80–89	20–89	65–89
Total Resources									
1960–61	269.6	273.4	259.9	224.1	178.6	142.0	103.4	239.6	146.8
1972–73	316.4	338.9	335.2	307.9	255.8	201.1	130.0	304.8	205.3
1984–86	349.5	379.2	394.9	379.3	339.9	259.7	141.3	356.4	265.6
1987–90	364.5	393.6	410.0	399.3	362.3	281.3	154.6	373.6	286.0
% Increase									
87–90/60–61	35.2	44.0	57.8	78.2	102.8	98.1	49.5	55.9	94.8
Human Wealth									
1960–61	358.7	315.7	238.5	140.5	48.7	11.3	4.5	224.8	17.5
1972–73	425.6	395.4	292.9	168.9	53.5	10.2	3.8	275.9	16.8
1984–86	479.2	454.0	354.0	189.7	57.5	11.5	3.8	326.5	18.2
1987–90	499.7	471.8	369.9	200.0	59.8	12.9	4.1	339.8	19.8
% Increase									
87–90/60–61	39.3	49.4	55.1	42.4	22.8	14.8	−7.3	51.1	12.6
Nonhuman Wealth									
1960–61	11.8	44.1	81.1	111.3	125.4	118.2	91.8	70.8	118.0
1972–73	13.1	48.9	99.7	141.1	159.7	142.2	88.7	83.4	140.8
1984–86	14.5	50.5	109.1	163.6	185.1	157.0	73.6	87.8	154.5
1987–90	15.5	52.9	113.3	170.8	193.6	164.0	77.0	92.6	161.3
% Increase									
87–90/60–61	31.2	20.2	39.7	53.5	54.4	38.8	−16.1	30.8	36.7
Pension Wealth									
1960–61	15.8	20.5	21.7	17.6	14.0	9.5	4.8	17.6	10.3
1972–73	18.2	26.4	36.9	39.5	29.3	18.6	12.1	27.9	20.5
1984–86	19.3	29.0	44.5	62.1	60.1	35.2	18.6	36.9	40.0
1987–90	20.0	29.6	45.3	65.3	65.4	41.0	21.6	39.1	45.4
% Increase									
87–90/60–61	26.8	44.4	108.9	270.5	367.0	331.4	352.5	122.1	339.7
Generational Account									
1960–61	116.7	106.9	81.4	45.3	9.5	−3.0	−2.3	73.6	−0.9
1972–73	140.5	131.8	94.3	41.6	−13.3	−30.1	−25.3	82.4	−27.2
1984–86	163.4	154.2	112.6	36.1	−37.2	−55.9	−45.3	94.8	−52.8
1987–90	170.6	160.7	118.5	36.8	−43.5	−63.3	−51.8	97.8	−59.6

Source: Authors' calculations.
Note: Population weighted averages in thousands of 1993 dollars.

Table 2.2b
Total resources and resource components—female cohorts

Age Group:	20–29	30–39	40–49	50–59	60–69	70–79	80–89	20–89	65–89
Total Resources									
1960–61	247.7	255.1	255.4	222.3	166.4	119.3	92.4	223.1	127.0
1972–73	296.3	319.0	323.2	297.3	246.2	181.8	106.3	282.8	183.7
1984–86	346.1	380.7	378.1	357.8	325.4	234.0	105.2	337.8	229.7
1987–90	365.8	399.6	397.5	378.3	346.7	253.2	116.8	357.3	247.3
% Increase									
87–90/60–61	47.7	56.6	55.7	70.2	108.3	112.3	26.4	60.2	94.8
Human Wealth									
1960–61	328.1	280.0	204.3	109.9	32.1	5.5	1.2	188.1	9.7
1972–73	394.8	346.9	245.6	130.5	33.7	4.8	1.4	225.2	8.4
1984–86	451.1	418.2	303.5	143.1	37.2	6.1	1.7	272.4	9.5
1987–90	472.2	438.1	322.9	154.1	38.4	6.9	2.1	285.7	10.4
% Increase									
87–90/60–61	43.9	56.5	58.1	40.2	19.7	26.0	79.6	51.9	7.7
Nonhuman Wealth									
1960–61	7.1	42.6	91.1	117.1	112.8	99.1	87.7	71.6	101.0
1972–73	12.3	54.7	105.6	138.9	144.4	114.7	65.7	83.9	114.0
1984–86	19.7	65.6	109.1	151.2	167.8	121.7	29.6	88.2	115.3
1987–90	21.4	68.7	113.6	157.9	175.5	126.8	31.0	93.0	119.8
% Increase									
87–90/60–61	202.3	61.4	24.7	34.8	55.5	28.0	−64.7	29.9	18.6
Pension Wealth									
1960–61	16.9	22.0	21.8	19.0	14.5	7.3	2.9	18.0	8.6
1972–73	19.1	28.6	38.8	38.1	28.3	16.3	7.5	27.9	17.6
1984–86	20.7	31.2	47.0	61.4	52.4	28.5	16.0	36.7	31.1
1987–90	21.4	31.9	47.9	64.3	57.3	32.2	17.9	38.7	35.0
% Increase									
87–90/60–61	26.4	45.0	119.9	238.9	296.4	341.5	526.8	115.7	305.7
Generational Account									
1960–61	104.4	89.4	61.8	23.7	−7.1	−7.4	−0.7	54.5	−7.7
1972–73	129.9	111.3	66.8	10.1	−39.8	−46.0	−31.6	54.2	−43.6
1984–86	145.4	134.2	81.5	−2.1	−68.1	−77.6	−57.9	59.5	−73.8
1987–90	149.1	139.1	86.9	−2.0	−75.5	−87.2	−65.9	60.1	−82.2

Source: Authors' calculations.
Note: Population weighted averages in thousands of 1993 dollars.

Table 2.3a
The components of generational accounts—males

Age Group:	20–29	30–39	40–49	50–59	60–69	70–79	80–89	20–89	65–89
Labor Income Taxes									
1960–61	42.51	36.49	26.73	15.18	5.13	1.18	0.46	25.80	1.85
1972–73	55.05	50.52	37.13	21.13	6.58	1.25	0.47	35.27	2.06
1984–86	64.47	59.89	46.01	24.44	7.38	1.48	0.49	43.20	2.34
1987–90	68.32	63.16	48.66	25.98	7.73	1.67	0.53	45.57	2.56
Payroll Taxes									
1960–61	37.43	29.21	20.34	11.15	3.71	0.87	0.31	20.94	1.35
1972–73	57.06	49.28	34.64	19.43	6.16	1.19	0.36	34.78	1.94
1984–86	69.31	64.03	49.02	26.09	7.84	1.58	0.52	46.25	2.49
1987–90	72.61	67.11	51.93	28.04	8.35	1.78	0.56	48.53	2.74
Indirect Taxes									
1960–61	46.81	44.80	37.25	25.88	15.41	8.29	4.53	34.19	9.68
1972–73	51.45	51.16	43.27	32.66	20.51	11.82	6.90	39.86	13.23
1984–86	57.64	56.86	49.75	37.93	26.16	15.76	8.79	46.26	17.39
1987–90	60.44	59.45	52.09	39.88	27.59	17.07	9.09	48.46	18.60
Capital Income Taxes									
1960–61	19.37	27.40	31.80	30.46	23.83	15.60	8.90	25.64	17.13
1972–73	20.22	28.24	33.29	32.65	26.54	16.75	7.78	26.45	18.21
1984–86	25.04	33.79	40.37	39.42	30.81	18.04	6.92	31.28	19.87
1987–90	26.57	36.25	43.66	43.85	34.74	20.62	7.59	34.22	22.57
Social Security Benefits (OASDI)									
1960–61	9.90	13.39	18.67	23.77	29.49	24.81	15.15	18.05	25.79
1972–73	12.60	17.60	24.97	36.86	48.31	42.20	28.83	26.11	42.97
1984–86	16.02	21.90	31.37	46.62	62.08	54.06	36.80	32.07	55.20
1987–90	17.12	23.34	33.10	49.96	65.79	57.37	39.10	34.20	58.15
Health Benefits (medicare and medicaid)									
1960–61	11.46	11.59	10.98	9.90	7.49	3.91	1.37	10.03	4.62
1972–73	18.78	20.67	22.23	22.72	22.67	18.53	11.91	20.72	19.00
1984–86	28.85	31.21	35.82	42.06	46.25	38.48	25.00	34.80	39.34
1987–90	32.52	35.09	39.98	48.28	55.18	46.83	30.33	39.89	47.55
Welfare Benefits									
1960–61	8.10	6.05	5.05	3.72	1.62	0.25	0.02	4.91	0.52
1972–73	11.85	9.10	6.86	4.64	2.07	0.42	0.10	7.15	0.69
1984–86	8.15	7.22	5.33	3.13	1.10	0.26	0.13	5.33	0.37
1987–90	7.66	6.80	4.76	2.69	0.91	0.27	0.16	4.90	0.37

Note: Population weighted averages in thousands of 1993 dollars.

Table 2.3b
The components of generational accounts—females

Age Group:	20–29	30–39	40–49	50–59	60–69	70–79	80–89	20–89	65–89
Labor Income Taxes									
1960–61	38.75	32.24	22.81	11.84	3.38	0.58	0.12	21.53	1.02
1972–73	50.98	44.28	31.09	16.29	4.14	0.59	0.18	28.75	1.03
1984–86	60.57	55.04	39.39	18.42	4.78	0.79	0.21	35.99	1.23
1987–90	64.43	58.49	42.38	19.99	4.97	0.90	0.27	38.25	1.35
Payroll Taxes									
1960–61	34.10	26.21	17.92	9.10	2.53	0.44	0.10	17.77	0.76
1972–73	52.96	43.74	29.67	15.49	4.04	0.59	0.15	28.75	1.02
1984–86	65.43	59.48	42.77	20.14	5.22	0.86	0.24	38.95	1.34
1987–90	68.81	62.85	46.01	22.03	5.49	0.98	0.30	41.17	1.48
Indirect Taxes									
1960–61	46.05	42.96	35.48	25.35	15.19	8.56	4.48	32.20	9.55
1972–73	50.50	49.53	41.42	31.72	20.98	12.15	7.04	37.23	13.21
1984–86	56.43	55.60	48.01	36.71	26.09	16.05	9.38	43.16	16.82
1987–90	59.20	58.27	50.16	38.72	27.28	17.07	9.80	45.19	17.71
Capital Income Taxes									
1960–61	19.46	28.42	33.85	31.52	22.56	14.58	9.55	26.01	15.83
1972–73	21.44	28.98	33.39	31.91	24.66	13.20	6.45	25.77	14.85
1984–86	27.25	34.78	39.02	37.18	27.72	13.20	3.52	29.84	14.49
1987–90	29.15	37.50	42.15	41.18	31.18	14.95	3.93	32.61	16.35
Social Security Benefits (OASDI)									
1960–61	15.50	21.89	30.41	38.65	40.20	26.41	13.07	27.50	28.78
1972–73	18.26	26.60	38.44	54.83	65.83	51.56	32.16	38.55	52.37
1984–86	22.63	31.08	44.94	66.05	80.17	65.43	43.03	45.29	65.18
1987–90	24.24	33.11	46.94	69.86	84.24	69.15	45.50	47.92	68.37
Health Benefits (medicare and medicaid)									
1960–61	11.20	12.69	13.36	12.68	9.64	5.11	1.85	11.32	5.85
1972–73	16.66	20.33	24.38	26.57	26.46	20.73	13.25	21.75	20.98
1984–86	23.77	29.10	36.72	45.29	50.56	42.67	28.02	34.88	42.00
1987–90	26.24	32.12	40.37	50.97	59.03	51.42	34.34	39.58	50.14
Welfare Benefits									
1960–61	7.27	5.80	4.49	2.80	0.88	0.07	0.01	4.15	0.21
1972–73	11.07	8.34	5.98	3.89	1.31	0.26	0.05	6.01	0.37
1984–86	17.89	10.47	6.01	3.18	1.13	0.42	0.18	8.21	0.47
1987–90	21.98	12.75	6.45	3.11	1.10	0.55	0.32	9.59	0.57

Note: Population weighted averages in thousands of 1993 dollars.

$$R^a = 1 - \frac{TERM + NHW}{HW + NHW + PW - GA}, \tag{7}$$

where *TERM* stands for the average term value of life insurance, *HW* stands for average human wealth, *NHW* stands for average non-human wealth, *PW* stands for average private pension wealth, and *GA* stands for the generational account. Tables 2.4a and 2.4b decompose total resources into annuitized and bequeathable components. Tables 2.5a and 2.5b show these components as a share of total resources. Table 2.5a shows that R^a has more than doubled for older males—for cohorts aged 65 and older, it increased from 0.16 in 1960–61 to 0.41 in 1987–90. For older female cohorts the increase reported in table 2.5b is from 0.18 in 1960–61 to 0.50 in 1987–90. This larger annuitized share of elderly persons' resources implies, of course, an equal and opposite decline in their share of bequeathable resources.

The increased annuitization of older generations is not offset by decreased annuitization of younger ones: table 2.5a shows that the value of R^a is roughly constant for males below the age of 60. Although the increase in annuitization is substantial for older males, the increase in overall male resource annuitization is small—from 62 percent in 1960–61 to only 65 percent in 1987–90. This occurs because younger males far outnumber older ones in the population. A similar story is true in the case of females. For the female population as a whole, R^a rises from 0.60 to 0.66 between the two periods.

Sensitivity Analysis

Discount Rate

The calculations reported earlier assume a 1.2 percent rate of productivity growth (g) and a discount rate of 6 percent. We denote these as the base case values for r and g. Table 2.6 examines the sensitivity of R^a to alternative discount rate assumptions.[16] As the table shows, the conclusion that the resource annuitization of the elderly has increased dramatically since 1960 holds for a wide range of values of r. Higher interest rates produce smaller values of annuitized resources, but they do so for each of the years considered. Hence, the result that R^a rises significantly over time is not affected by much.

Table 2.4a
Total resources decomposed into annuitized and bequeathable resources—males

Age Group:	20–29	30–39	40–49	50–59	60–69	70–79	80–89	20–89	65–89
Total Resources									
1960–61	269.6	273.4	259.9	224.1	178.6	142.0	103.4	239.6	146.8
1972–73	316.4	338.9	335.2	307.9	255.8	201.1	130.0	304.8	205.3
1984–86	349.5	379.2	394.9	379.3	339.9	259.7	141.3	356.4	265.6
1987–90	364.5	393.6	410.0	399.3	362.3	281.3	154.6	373.6	286.0
% Increase									
87–90/60–61	35.2	44.0	57.8	78.2	102.8	98.1	49.5	55.9	94.8
Nonhuman Wealth									
1960–61	11.8	44.1	81.1	111.3	125.4	118.2	91.8	70.8	118.0
1972–73	13.1	48.9	99.7	141.1	159.7	142.2	88.7	83.4	140.8
1984–86	14.5	50.5	109.1	163.6	185.1	157.0	73.6	87.8	154.5
1987–90	15.5	52.9	113.3	170.8	193.6	164.0	77.0	92.6	161.3
% Increase									
87–90/60–61	31.2	20.2	39.7	53.5	54.4	38.8	−16.1	30.8	36.7
Term Value of Life Insurance									
1960–61	18.0	26.4	24.9	18.6	10.7	4.6	1.6	19.4	5.8
1972–73	21.9	39.7	39.0	28.6	15.4	5.7	1.9	27.3	7.5
1984–86	21.3	46.7	48.1	33.9	16.8	5.1	1.6	31.2	7.3
1987–90	25.4	54.3	56.1	39.6	19.4	5.9	1.9	37.2	8.5
% Increase									
87–90/60–61	41.4	105.7	124.7	113.1	81.7	29.0	16.4	91.3	45.8
Annuitized Resources (total resources minus bequeathable wealth)									
1960–61	239.8	203.0	153.8	94.2	42.5	19.2	9.9	149.4	23.0
1972–73	281.5	250.3	196.5	138.2	80.7	53.2	39.3	194.1	57.0
1984–86	313.7	282.0	237.7	181.8	138.0	97.6	66.1	237.4	103.7
1987–90	323.6	286.4	240.6	188.9	149.3	111.4	75.7	243.9	116.2
% Increase									
87–90/60–61	35.0	41.1	56.4	100.4	251.0	479.9	660.7	63.2	406.1
Bequeathable Wealth (nonhuman wealth plus term value of life insurance)									
1960–61	29.8	70.5	106.1	129.8	136.1	122.8	93.5	90.2	123.8
1972–73	35.0	88.6	138.8	169.7	175.1	147.8	90.6	110.7	148.3
1984–86	35.8	97.2	157.1	197.5	201.9	162.1	75.2	119.0	161.9
1987–90	40.9	107.3	169.4	210.4	213.0	169.9	78.9	129.8	169.8
% Increase									
87–90/60–61	37.4	52.2	59.7	62.1	56.5	38.4	−15.5	43.9	37.1

Source: Authors' calculations.
Note: Population weighted averages in thousands of 1993 dollars.

Table 2.4b
Total resources decomposed into annuitized and bequeathable resources—females

Age Group:	20–29	30–39	40–49	50–59	60–69	70–79	80–89	20–89	65–89
Total Resources									
1960–61	247.7	255.1	255.4	222.3	166.4	119.3	92.4	223.1	127.0
1972–73	296.3	319.0	323.2	297.3	246.2	181.8	106.3	282.8	183.7
1984–86	346.1	380.7	378.1	357.8	325.4	234.0	105.2	337.8	229.7
1987–90	365.8	399.6	397.5	378.3	346.7	253.2	116.8	357.3	247.3
% Increase									
87–90/60–61	47.7	56.6	55.7	70.2	108.3	112.3	26.4	60.2	94.8
Nonhuman Wealth									
1960–61	7.1	42.6	91.1	117.1	112.8	99.1	87.7	71.6	101.0
1972–73	12.3	54.7	105.6	138.9	144.4	114.7	65.7	83.9	114.0
1984–86	19.7	65.6	109.1	151.2	167.8	121.7	29.6	88.2	115.3
1987–90	21.4	68.7	113.6	157.9	175.5	126.8	31.0	93.0	119.8
% Increase									
87–90/60–61	202.3	61.4	24.7	34.8	55.5	28.0	−64.7	29.9	18.6
Term Value of Life Insurance									
1960–61	18.9	24.9	21.6	14.8	7.5	2.8	1.3	17.0	3.7
1972–73	22.9	36.7	33.1	22.0	10.0	2.9	1.1	22.9	4.0
1984–86	21.9	42.2	40.1	25.2	10.0	1.8	0.4	25.4	3.0
1987–90	26.1	49.1	46.8	29.5	11.5	2.1	0.4	30.1	3.4
% Increase									
87–90/60–61	38.2	97.4	116.2	99.8	53.0	−25.5	−68.5	77.5	−7.3
Annuitized Resources (total resources minus bequeathable wealth)									
1960–61	221.8	187.7	142.6	90.4	46.1	17.4	3.3	134.5	22.3
1972–73	261.1	227.5	184.5	136.4	91.8	64.2	39.5	175.9	65.7
1984–86	304.5	272.9	228.9	181.5	147.6	110.5	75.2	224.2	111.5
1987–90	318.4	281.8	237.1	191.0	159.7	124.3	85.4	234.2	124.2
% Increase									
87–90/60–61	43.6	50.2	66.3	111.2	246.4	613.0	2449.0	74.1	456.9
Bequeathable Wealth (nonhuman wealth plus term value of life insurance)									
1960–61	25.9	67.4	112.8	131.9	120.3	101.9	89.1	88.6	104.7
1972–73	35.2	91.5	138.7	160.9	154.4	117.6	66.8	106.8	118.0
1984–86	41.6	107.8	149.2	176.4	177.8	123.5	30.0	113.6	118.3
1987–90	47.4	117.8	160.4	187.4	187.0	128.9	31.4	123.1	123.2
% Increase									
87–90/60–61	82.9	74.7	42.2	42.1	55.4	26.6	−64.8	39.0	17.7

Source: Authors' calculations.
Note: Population weighted averages in thousands of 1993 dollars.

Table 2.5a
The share of bequeathable and annuitized resources in total resources—males

Age Group:	20–29	30–39	40–49	50–59	60–69	70–79	80–89	20–89	65–89
Total Resources									
1960–61	1.00	1.00	1.00	1.00	1.00	1.00	1.00	1.00	1.00
1972–73	1.00	1.00	1.00	1.00	1.00	1.00	1.00	1.00	1.00
1984–86	1.00	1.00	1.00	1.00	1.00	1.00	1.00	1.00	1.00
1987–90	1.00	1.00	1.00	1.00	1.00	1.00	1.00	1.00	1.00
Nonhuman Wealth									
1960–61	0.04	0.16	0.31	0.50	0.70	0.83	0.89	0.30	0.80
1972–73	0.04	0.14	0.30	0.46	0.62	0.71	0.68	0.27	0.69
1984–86	0.04	0.13	0.28	0.43	0.54	0.60	0.52	0.25	0.58
1987–90	0.04	0.13	0.28	0.43	0.53	0.58	0.50	0.25	0.56
Term Value of Life Insurance									
1960–61	0.07	0.10	0.10	0.08	0.06	0.03	0.02	0.08	0.04
1972–73	0.07	0.12	0.12	0.09	0.06	0.03	0.01	0.09	0.04
1984–86	0.06	0.12	0.12	0.09	0.05	0.02	0.01	0.09	0.03
1987–90	0.07	0.14	0.14	0.10	0.05	0.02	0.01	0.10	0.03
Bequeathable Wealth (nonhuman wealth plus term value of life insurance)									
1960–61	0.11	0.26	0.41	0.58	0.76	0.86	0.90	0.38	0.84
1972–73	0.11	0.26	0.41	0.55	0.68	0.74	0.70	0.36	0.72
1984–86	0.10	0.26	0.40	0.52	0.59	0.62	0.53	0.33	0.61
1987–90	0.11	0.27	0.41	0.53	0.59	0.60	0.51	0.35	0.59
Annuitized Wealth (total wealth minus bequeathable wealth)									
1960–61	0.89	0.74	0.59	0.42	0.24	0.14	0.10	0.62	0.16
1972–73	0.89	0.74	0.59	0.45	0.32	0.26	0.30	0.64	0.28
1984–86	0.90	0.74	0.60	0.48	0.41	0.38	0.47	0.67	0.39
1987–90	0.89	0.73	0.59	0.47	0.41	0.40	0.49	0.65	0.41

Source: Authors' calculations.

No Annuity Markets

The base case assumes that individuals can convert future income flows into current consumption at actuarially fair rates of discount—that is, the sum of the pretax rate of interest and the probability of death conditional on age. This is equivalent to assuming the availability of actuarially fair annuity insurance, whether explicit or implicit. We examine the robustness of our results to this assumption by considering the opposite assumption—that annuity insurance is unavailable at the margin. Under this assumption the appropriate rate for discounting future flows is simply the pretax rate of interest.

Table 2.5b
The share of bequeathable and annuitized resources in total resources—females

Age Group:	20–29	30–39	40–49	50–59	60–69	70–79	80–89	20–89	65–89
Total Resources									
1960–61	1.00	1.00	1.00	1.00	1.00	1.00	1.00	1.00	1.00
1972–73	1.00	1.00	1.00	1.00	1.00	1.00	1.00	1.00	1.00
1984–86	1.00	1.00	1.00	1.00	1.00	1.00	1.00	1.00	1.00
1987–90	1.00	1.00	1.00	1.00	1.00	1.00	1.00	1.00	1.00
Nonhuman Wealth									
1960–61	0.03	0.17	0.36	0.53	0.68	0.83	0.95	0.32	0.80
1972–73	0.04	0.17	0.33	0.47	0.59	0.63	0.62	0.30	0.62
1984–86	0.06	0.17	0.29	0.42	0.52	0.52	0.28	0.26	0.50
1987–90	0.06	0.17	0.29	0.42	0.51	0.50	0.27	0.26	0.48
Term Value of Life Insurance									
1960–61	0.08	0.10	0.08	0.07	0.05	0.02	0.01	0.08	0.03
1972–73	0.08	0.12	0.10	0.07	0.04	0.02	0.01	0.08	0.02
1984–86	0.06	0.11	0.11	0.07	0.03	0.01	0.00	0.08	0.01
1987–90	0.07	0.12	0.12	0.08	0.03	0.01	0.00	0.08	0.01
Bequeathable Wealth (nonhuman wealth plus term value of life insurance)									
1960–61	0.10	0.26	0.44	0.59	0.72	0.85	0.96	0.40	0.82
1972–73	0.12	0.29	0.43	0.54	0.63	0.65	0.63	0.38	0.64
1984–86	0.12	0.28	0.39	0.49	0.55	0.53	0.29	0.34	0.51
1987–90	0.13	0.29	0.40	0.50	0.54	0.51	0.27	0.34	0.50
Annuitized Wealth (total wealth minus bequeathable wealth)									
1960–61	0.90	0.74	0.56	0.41	0.28	0.15	0.04	0.60	0.18
1972–73	0.88	0.71	0.57	0.46	0.37	0.35	0.37	0.62	0.36
1984–86	0.88	0.72	0.61	0.51	0.45	0.47	0.71	0.66	0.49
1987–90	0.87	0.71	0.60	0.50	0.46	0.49	0.73	0.66	0.50

Source: Authors' calculations.

Table 2.7 compares the increase in resource annuitization under the base case to that under the alternative assumption of nonavailability of annuity insurance. Under the latter case, males experience an increase in the share of resources annuitized from 40 percent in 1960–61 to 60 percent in 1987–90. Resource annuitization for females is again more pronounced, rising from 37 percent in the early 1960s to 64 percent in the late 1980s. Thus, the conclusion that resource annuitization has increased significantly for the elderly is robust to assuming the unavailability of annuity insurance at the margin.

Table 2.6
Resource annuitization under alternative interest rate assumptions

	$r = 3.0\%$		$r = 6.0\%$		$r = 9.0\%$	
	20–89	65–89	20–89	65–89	20–89	65–89
Males						
1960–61	0.73	0.20	0.62	0.16	0.53	0.13
1972–73	0.74	0.33	0.64	0.28	0.55	0.24
1984–86	0.77	0.44	0.67	0.39	0.58	0.35
1987–90	0.76	0.46	0.65	0.41	0.56	0.36
Females						
1960–61	0.72	0.23	0.60	0.18	0.51	0.14
1972–73	0.74	0.42	0.62	0.36	0.53	0.31
1984–86	0.79	0.55	0.66	0.49	0.57	0.43
1987–90	0.76	0.56	0.66	0.50	0.56	0.45

Source: Authors' calculations.

V. Implications for Aggregate Bequests and National Saving

As discussed earlier, cohorts with higher degrees of annuitization will, ceteris paribus, bequeath less and consume more. To assess the impact on aggregate bequests of changes since the early 1960s in Americans' degree of annuitization, we first estimate the annual flow of bequests in the late 1980s under base case values of r and g. We do so by multiplying the aggregate 1988 value of bequeathable wealth (net worth plus term life insurance) for individual male and female cohorts by their respective 1988 mortality probabilities.[17] Summing the products over all cohorts yields an aggregate 1988 bequest flow of $218.8 billion (see table 2.8). Next, we calculate 1988 aggregate bequests under the assumption that a cohort's bequeathable resources in 1988 equal its total resources in 1988 multiplied by its 1960–61 ratio of bequeathable resources to total resources. This produces a 1988 bequest flow of $314.6 billion. Thus, without the increase in resource annuitization, aggregate 1988 bequests would have been an estimated 43.7 percent larger, holding, as we are in this counterfactual experiment, the total resources of all cohorts at the 1988 values.

The $95.8 billion difference between these two bequest amounts constitutes the additional amount that generations alive in 1988 appear likely to have consumed as a consequence of this increased annuitization. This $95.8 billion figure is substantial. It represents

Table 2.7
Resource annuitization: Base case vs. no annuity markets

	Base case		No annuity markets	
	(1)	(2)	(3)	(4)
Year	20–89	65–89	20–89	65–89
Males				
1960–61	0.62	0.16	0.69	0.40
1972–73	0.64	0.28	0.70	0.50
1984–86	0.67	0.39	0.72	0.59
1987–90	0.65	0.41	0.70	0.60
Females				
1960–61	0.60	0.18	0.65	0.37
1972–73	0.62	0.36	0.67	0.53
1984–86	0.66	0.49	0.70	0.63
1987–90	0.66	0.50	0.69	0.64

Source: Authors' calculations.

Table 2.8
Annual bequest flows: Alternative interest rate assumptions (billions of 1993 dollars)

	$r = 0.03\%$	$r = 0.06\%$	$r = 0.75\%$
Bequest flows			
1960–61 ratio	331.3	314.6	301.4
1987–90 ratio	218.8	218.8	218.8
Percent difference	51.4	43.7	37.7

Source: Authors' calculations.

47.2 percent of total net national saving in 1988! Table 2.8 also indicates that this conclusion would not be altered under alternative rates of discount. Table 2.9 shows that percentage reduction in estimated 1988 bequests due to the increased resource annuitization would not be much affected even under the alternative assumption of no annuity markets. Under this case, the reduction in bequests would still be a sizable 55 percent.

A different question about the reliability of these findings involves our use of the random bequest method to estimate the flow of bequests. This method assumes that the net worth and life insurance holdings of those people who actually die at age x at time t do not differ systematically with respect to their wealth holdings and life insurance from those who don't actually die at age x at time t.

Table 2.9
Annual bequest flows under the base case and under no annuity markets (billions of 1993 Dollars)

	Base case	No annuity markets
1960–61 ratio	314.6	338.7
1987–90 ratio	218.8	218.8
Percent difference	43.7	54.8

Source: Authors' calculations.

Admittedly, many of those who actually die at age x at time t may know ahead of time that they are about to die and decrease some of their assets through extravagant spending. In addition, those that actually do die may incur particularly large uninsured medical expenses. But this bias in the random death method's calculation of bequests, whatever its size, is a bias that holds for each our calculations of actual bequests in 1988 as well as the hypothetical bequests that would have prevailed in 1988 had the degree of annuitization been that of the early 1960s. Indeed, if one assumes that end-of-life uninsured medical expenses and as well as end-of-life excess consumption in 1988 would have been the same had Americans' annuitization been that of 1960–61, our procedure underestimates the percentage decline in bequests.[18]

VI. Was Greater Resource Annuitization Offset by Life Insurance Purchases?

The increased annuitization of the elderly means that a smaller fraction of resources will be bequeathed. As mentioned earlier, those elderly who want to maintain the fraction of their bequeathable resources in the face of an exogenous increase in annuitized resources could offset their annuities by purchasing life insurance. Table 2.10 examines changes in holdings of life insurance between 1962 and 1983 derived from the SCF for these years. For these calculations, total resources were computed for each household by adding up human wealth, social security wealth, pension wealth, and household net worth.

The SCF data are advantageous because they contain a detailed accounting of households' net worth. However, they also have some shortcomings. First, because the 1962 and 1983 SCFs are cross-sectional surveys, past and future income streams had to be imputed

Table 2.10
Ratios of face and term values of life insurance to total resources

	50–54	55–59	60–64	65–69	70–74	75–79	80+	50+	65+
Married Couples, by age of husband									
1962 F/R	0.077	0.096	0.091	0.074	0.062	0.045	0.031	0.081	0.063
1983 F/R	0.067	0.071	0.061	0.027	0.038	0.018	0.019	0.053	0.028
1962 T/R	0.067	0.085	0.076	0.057	0.043	0.030	0.014	0.068	0.046
1983 T/R	0.063	0.064	0.051	0.020	0.029	0.012	0.014	0.046	0.021
Single men and women									
1962 F/R	0.070	0.094	0.046	0.065	0.021	0.034	0.061	0.060	0.048
1983 F/R	0.054	0.077	0.030	0.013	0.012	0.009	0.011	0.035	0.011
1962 T/R	0.059	0.084	0.041	0.059	0.013	0.030	0.049	0.052	0.041
1983 T/R	0.052	0.073	0.025	0.009	0.007	0.007	0.007	0.031	0.008

Source: Authors' calculations.
F/R—Ratio of face value of life insurance to resources.
T/R—Ratio of term value of life insurance to resources.

to each household to compute human wealth, pension wealth, and social security wealth. Second, the SCF does not contain data on government health care transfers. The omission of this wealth component biases downward the calculation of total resources, especially for middle-aged and older households. Moreover, these data do not include information on taxes and welfare transfers—which, on net, biases the total resources of younger individuals upward. Despite these biases—which may largely cancel out for some households—the data are potentially capable of shedding light on the questions that we use them to address.

Table 2.10 shows the ratios of the face value (the amount paid in the event of death) and the term value (the face value less the cash value of whole life policies) of life insurance to total resources in 1962 and 1983. We separately examine married couples and single individuals. The table shows that for both groups there has been a significant decline in the extent of insurance coverage: for married couples with husbands over 65, the value of insurance as a fraction of resources fell by one half, while for singles over 65, the extent of insurance fell by more than three quarters. It should be noted that because of health care transfers—an important component of the elderly's total resources in 1983 relative to 1962—these results understate the extent of the decline in life insurance coverage as a percent of total resources.

In the case of married couples, this change is potentially explained by the increased generosity in the survivorship provisions of social security and private pensions. In the case of single individuals (who among the older age groups are mostly widows and widowers), the decrease in the degree of insurance coverage seems clear evidence of a decline in the desire to bequeath resources to the next generation. Hence, our calculations show that changes in life insurance holdings not only have failed to offset the increased annuitization of the elderly, but actually have reinforced the reduction in the bequests/resources ratio associated with increased annuitization.

VII. The Impact of Increased Annuitization on Inequality in the Distribution of Bequests

This section examines the effect that changes in the degree of annuitization have on the distribution of bequests—again based on the SCF data. If changes in the degree of annuitization are different for groups that hold different amounts of wealth, then changes in annuitization will change the distribution of bequests. To the extent that bequests received from past generations are a major determinant of the wealth-holding of those currently alive, changes in the distribution of bequests will induce changes in the distribution of wealth.

Table 2.11 shows the shares of total resources and net worth held by different ranges of the total resources and net worth distributions, for both 1962 and 1983. We confine our analysis to individuals aged 65 and over. As one would expect, the distribution of net worth is more skewed than the distribution of total resources. Among men, for example, the top decile of the resource distribution held 49 percent of total resources in both 1962 and 1983, while the top decile of the net worth distribution had 65 percent of net worth in 1962 and 66 percent in 1983. Since net worth and resources are correlated, this implies (and the next table shows) that people with low resources also have high fractions of their resources held in annuitized form.

Table 2.12 shows the degree of annuitization for men and women over 64 in different ranges of the total resource distribution for the two years—1962 and 1983. It shows that the fraction of resources held in annuitized form declines markedly as one moves up the resource distribution. Thus differences in annuitization act to make the distribution of bequests more skewed than the distribution of

Table 2.11
The distributions of total resources and net worth of the elderly, 1962 and 1983 (share of resources or net worth)

	Resources		Net Worth	
	1962	1983	1962	1983
Men				
First Quartile	0.046	0.054	0.008	0.010
Second Quartile	0.099	0.108	0.050	0.046
Third Quartile	0.167	0.170	0.125	0.114
75th–89th Percentile	0.197	0.180	0.164	0.169
90th–94th Percentile	0.105	0.105	0.154	0.115
95th–99th Percentile	0.386	0.382	0.499	0.547
Women				
First Quartile	0.059	0.066	0.011	0.009
Second Quartile	0.102	0.125	0.057	0.056
Third Quartile	0.178	0.194	0.141	0.129
75th–89th Percentile	0.183	0.202	0.175	0.173
90th–94th Percentile	0.105	0.097	0.133	0.126
95th–99th Percentile	0.373	0.317	0.484	0.507

Table 2.12
The elderly's annuitized shares of resources by their position in the resource distribution

Position in the resource distribution	Men		Women	
	1962	1983	1962	1983
First quartile	0.723	0.812	0.742	0.763
Second quartile	0.592	0.724	0.547	0.741
Third quartile	0.533	0.627	0.443	0.621
75th–89th percentile	0.483	0.522	0.332	0.519
90th–94th percentile	0.365	0.458	0.208	0.514
95th–99th percentile	0.196	0.265	0.054	0.132

resources: the richer a person is, the higher the fraction of his or her wealth that is bequeathed.

For all of the groups examined, the degree of annuitization rose between 1962 and 1983. This rise is especially pronounced among women. The annuitization rate among women is particularly significant for intergenerational wealth transmission because women are most commonly the last surviving member of a household. Women in the 50th through 89th percentiles of the resource distribution increased their rate of annuitization by approximately 50 percent of its initial value, while for women in the top decile, the rate of annuitization more than doubled. On the other hand, the rate for women in the top 5 percent of the resource distribution rose very little as a fraction of total resources (from 5.4 percent of resources to 13.2 percent of resources) when compared with other parts of the resource distribution. For example, women in the rest of the top half of the resource distribution saw their rate of annuitization rise by at least 18 percent of total resources. Thus it seems that changes in annuitization acted to increase the inequality of the distribution of bequests.

To further examine how changes in the form in which resources are held have affected the size and distribution of the bequest flow, we projected expected bequests by the elderly in 1983 (in the manner of section VI above) by different parts of the distribution of total resources. We then inflated bequeathable wealth of individuals so that the bequest/resource ratio in each resource class would match the bequest/resource ratio for that class in 1962, and re-estimated the flow of bequests in 1983. The results of this exercise are presented in table 2.13. The table shows how changes in the fraction of resources that are bequeathable have made the distribution of potential bequests more unequal. Among men, the fraction of bequeathable resources within the top five percent of the resource distribution rises from 39.5 percent (10.4 divided by 26.3), using the 1962 pattern of asset-holding, to 42.8 percent (9.3 divided by 21.7), using the 1983 pattern. Among women the change is more dramatic: From 30.4 percent using the 1962 pattern to 38.4 percent using the 1983 pattern. Our calculations show that if the elderly had held bequeathable resources to total resources in the same proportion in 1983 as they had in 1962, the flow of bequests from the elderly would have been 29 percent higher in 1983.[19]

Table 2.13
Projected bequests by the elderly in 1983 using 1962 and 1983 ratios of bequests/resources (billions of dollars)

	Men		Women	
Bequest/resource ratio:	1962	1983	1962	1983
Position in the resource distribution				
First quartile	0.7	0.4	1.2	0.9
Second quartile	1.9	1.2	2.9	1.6
Third quartile	5.5	4.0	6.7	4.4
75th–89th percentile	3.1	2.7	4.8	3.4
90th–94th percentile	4.7	4.0	3.8	2.1
95th–99th percentile	10.4	9.3	8.5	7.8
Total	26.3	21.7	28.0	20.3

Note: The second and fourth columns of this table present projections of the flow of bequests in 1983 using the methodology described in section VI of this paper. The first and third columns inflate bequeathable wealth for individuals in each resource class in 1983 such that the mean ratio of bequeathable wealth to total wealth is the same as that for the corresponding resource class in 1962. All of the calculations are performed only for men and women aged 65 and over.

VIII. Conclusion

This chapter combines a large array of micro and macro data to study changes since the early 1960s in the degree of annuitization of Americans' resources. Although we find no increase in the annuitization of younger Americans, we find a dramatic increase in the degree of annuitization of older Americans. This finding is robust to alternative assumptions about interest and growth rates as well as various possible courses of future U.S. health-care policy.

The increase in the annuitization of the elderly reflects increases in their receipt of social security and health transfers coupled with their failure to increase their purchase of life insurance. Since the elderly have much higher mortality probabilities, their degree of annuitization is critical to the flow of bequests. According to our base case estimates, holding fixed the total resources of each cohort, current aggregate U.S. bequests would be 44 percent larger if these resources, particularly those of older Americans were annuitized to the same degree as they were in 1960. The reduction of bequests and, by implication, the reduction in national saving is not a one-time event. Rather the increased annuitization means an ongoing reduction in national saving and the national investment that saving finances.

While increased annuitization cannot explain all of the remarkable recent decline in U.S. saving, it appears to be an important piece of the puzzle.

An increase in the annuitized share of resources can be undone by an increase in the purchase of life insurance. Such an increase in life insurance purchase did not, however, occur over the period. On the contrary, both the face and term values of life insurance were substantially smaller relative to the elderly's resources in 1983 than they were in 1962.

Changes in resources annuitization hold implications for the transmission of inequality via bequests. Because those with larger resources also have a smaller share of their resources in annuitized form, greater annuitization has increased inequality in the distribution of bequests. The bequests of the rich now account for a larger share of total bequests than before.

Appendix 1: Estimating Cohort-Specific Total Resources and Resource Components

Estimating Annuitized and Nonannuitized Resources

In this study we calculate the amounts of nonannuitized and annuitized resources for all male and female adult cohorts for the periods 1960–61, 1972–73, 1984–86, 1987–90.[20] The components of annuitized resources are the present values of future labor earnings (human wealth), social security benefits, private and government employee pension benefits, government health care benefits, welfare benefits, and other government transfers, and, entering as negative annuities, the present values of future taxes. Taxes include labor and capital income taxes, indirect taxes, payroll taxes, and property and other taxes. Nonannuitized resources refer to holdings of net wealth.

The computation of cohorts' nonannuitized resources for the four separate time periods involves distributing by age and sex each year's aggregate value of household net wealth. The computation of each annuitized resource component employs a common strategy. First, for each year, the national aggregate for a particular type of payment (or receipt) is distributed by age and sex according to the cross-sectional age-sex relative profile that is applicable to that payment (or receipt). For example, aggregate 1962 social security benefits are distributed according to the age-sex relative profile for these benefits that prevailed in 1962. This yields estimates of the per capita amounts of the payment (or receipt) by age and sex for that year. The per capita annuity values for years after 1993 are estimated by either: (a) distributing projected aggregate payments or receipts according to the latest available cross-section relative profile, or (b) assuming that age- and sex-specific per capita values equal their respective values in 1993 or some later year except for an adjustment for productivity growth.

Second, for each generation in a given year t (say, males born in 1966), the present value of all future per capita payments of a particular type (say, indirect tax payments) is computed by multiplying these future per capita payments by the generation's projected population in those years, discounting these values back to year t, and dividing the sum of the discounted values by the number of members of the generation alive in the base year. This method produces actuarially discounted present values of the particular receipt or payment for each generation alive in period t.

As an example of this method for calculating the different components of annuitized resources, consider the estimate of human wealth (HW). Our formula for human wealth in year t of a person of sex x born in year k, $HW^x{}_{t,k}$, is

$$HW^x{}_{t,k} = \frac{1}{Px_{t,k}} \sum_{s=t}^{k+D} \hat{e}^x{}_{s,k} P^x{}_{s,k} R^{s-t}, \tag{A1.1}$$

where $\hat{e}^x{}_{s,k}$ stands for the average earnings in year s of a member of the generation born in year k and of sex x; $P^x{}_{s,k}$ is the population in year s of the same generation; $R = 1/(1+r)$, where r is the rate of interest; and D is the maximum age of life. The calculation of $\hat{e}^x{}_{s,k}$ is given by

$$\hat{e}^x{}_{s,k} = \frac{d^x{}_{s,k} E_s}{\sum_{s=t}^{k+D} [d^m{}_{s,k} P^m{}_{s,k} + d^f{}_{s,k}{}^{Pf}{}_{s,k}]}. \tag{A1.2}$$

In this equation, E_s is aggregate labor earnings in year s, $d^x{}_{s,k}$ is the ratio in year s of the average earnings of the generation born in year k of sex x divided by the average earnings in year s of our reference group—those males who were age 40 in year s (i.e., those for whom $k = s - 40$). The construction of relative profiles by age and sex, $d^x{}_{t,k}$, is described in equations (A1.3) and (A1.4):

$$j^x{}_{s,k} = \frac{\sum_{i=1}^{N^x{}_{s,k}} w^x{}_{s,k,i}\omega^x{}_{s,k,i}}{\sum_{i=1}^{N^x{}_{s,k}} w^x{}_{s,k,i}}, \tag{A1.3}$$

and

$$d^x{}_{s,k} = \frac{j^x{}_{s,k}}{j^m{}_{s,s-40}}. \tag{A1.4}$$

In equation (A1.3), $j^x{}_{s,k}$ is the weighted average (across cohort members indexed by i) of labor income. $N^x{}_{s,k}$ is the number of observations in year s of individuals of sex x born in year k, $\omega^x{}_{s,k,i}$ is the wage and salary income of the ith individual of sex x in year s who was born in year k, and $w^x{}_{s,k,i}$ is the person weight of this observation. Equation (A1.4) shows the calculation in year s of the average labor income of members of the generation with sex x who were born in year k, relative to that of contemporaneous 40-year-old males.

Data Sources

The national aggregates used in our calculations come from the National Income and Product Accounts (NIPA), the Federal Reserve System's Flow of Funds (FOF), The American Council of Life Insurance (ACLI), the U.S. Census Bureau's Current Population Survey (CPS), and the Survey of Current Business (SCB). The sources for cross-section relative profiles are the CPS, the Survey of Income and Program Participation (SIPP), the Consumer Expenditure Survey (CEX), the Survey of Consumer Finances (SCF), the Social Security Administration's Annual Statistical Supplement (SSASS), and the Health Care Financing Administration (HCFA). The computations also use the historic and projected population counts of the Social Security Administration (SSA).[21] For a more detailed description of the computation method and data sources, we refer the reader to Gokhale, Kotlikoff, and Sabelhaus (1996). Here we only describe the computation of the distribution of term life insurance by age and sex.

Aggregate face values of life insurance for the years 1960 through 1993 are reported by the ACLI. Relative profiles of the distribution of term life insurance are obtained from the 1962 and 1983 SCF. Fortunately, the SCF reports term as well as face values of life insurance.

Consequently, we were able to calculate the ratio of term value to face value of life insurance on an age- and sex-specific basis for the years 1962 and 1983. Multiplying these ratios by the aggregate face values of life insurance produced age- and sex-specific term values of insurance for 1962 and 1983, and, after interpolating, for other years as well.[22]

Appendix 2: Computing Total Resources and Resource Components: Survey of Current Business

The Data

The data used in this chapter come from two sources: the Survey of Financial Characteristics of Consumers (SFCC), conducted in 1962 and 1963, and the 1983 Survey of Consumer Finances (SCF), conducted in 1983. The 1962 SFCC sampled 2,557 households. A total of 429 of these households have heads age 65 and over. The 1983 SCF contains data on 4,103 households, of which 774 have heads age 65 and over. The interviews for both surveys were conducted in person.

Income totals in the 1962 and 1983 surveys refer to income in calendar 1962 and 1982, respectively. Asset totals in the 1962 survey refer to assets as of December 31, 1962. Asset totals in the 1983 survey refer to assets at the time of the survey. The strength of these surveys lies in their coverage of asset-holding, but neither provides the kind of detailed breakdown of certain types of income that one would like. For example, in 1963 households were asked only about their combined 1962 social security and pension income, not about each component separately. In addition to not distinguishing the source of pension income, the 1962 survey provides only the household total for this income, rather than the separate amounts received by the husband and wife. Hence, for 1983, as for 1962, we rely on the variable indicating the total receipt of social security plus private pension income. This is but one example of our use of parallel methodologies to construct resource components for 1962 and 1983.

Benchmarking

In order to deal with the problem of possible under- or over-reporting of assets and income in the Surveys of Consumer Finance, we compare the totals in the survey to aggregate totals, and adjust (benchmark) the survey data so that the two match. Our survey totals are computed using the surveys' household weights.

In the case of assets, our benchmarks come from the Federal Reserve's (1992) *Balance Sheets for the U.S. Economy.*[23] We divide assets into three groups: housing wealth, non-housing wealth excluding life insurance, and life insurance. For nonhousing, nonlife-insurance wealth our benchmark is total household net worth less assets of nonprofit organizations, pension reserves,[24] life insurance reserves,[25] and net housing wealth. We compare this benchmark to net worth excluding both net housing wealth and the cash value of whole life insurance policies in our surveys. For 1962, the benchmark total is \$1,360 billion and the survey total is \$1,097 billion, implying that an upward adjustment of 24.1 percent to the data. For 1983, the benchmark total is \$6,870 billion and the survey total is \$7,387 billion, implying a downward adjustment of 7.0 percent. We also apply these same benchmarking factors to life insurance. For net housing wealth, the 1962 benchmark total is \$377.0 billion, and the survey total is \$316.4 billion, implying an upward adjustment of 19.2 percent, while for 1983, the benchmark total is \$2,875 billion and the survey total is \$2,883 billion, implying a reduction of 0.3 percent.

Labor earnings form the basis for our calculation of both the human wealth and social security wealth of those in our sample who are working at the times of the surveys. Hence, benchmarking labor earnings is our means of benchmarking these two components of total resources. To benchmark labor earnings we compare aggregate wage and salary income of the nonself-employed in the two surveys to the total compensation of employees in 1962 and 1982 reported by the U.S. Department of Commerce. The benchmark totals are \$299.3 billion in 1962 and \$1,586.1 billion in 1982. The respective 1962 SFCC and 1983 SCF totals are \$277.6 billion and \$1,468.5 trillion. Based on these figures we adjust upward reported wages and salaries by 7.8 percent for 1962 and by 8.0 percent for 1983.

For respondents who report receiving social security plus private pension income we use their reported receipts of this income to form estimates of their social security plus private pension wealth. For both 1962 and 1982 we compared total pension and social security income for all households in the survey to the sum of aggregate social security payments plus aggregate public and private pension payments. Aggregate social security payments is determined as the sum of 1962 or 1982 OASI and DI aggregate payments reported in *The 1983 Social Security Bulletin Annual Statistical Supplement.* Aggregate pension payments are those calculated by the Bureau of Economic Analysis and reported in the National Income and Product Accounts (Park, 1992). For 1962 the benchmark value is $21.1 billion, while the SFCC value is $17.3, implying an upward adjustment of 22.0 percent. For 1982 the benchmark value is $264.8 billion, while the SCF value is $191.2 billion, implying an upward adjustment of 38.5 percent.[26]

Calculation of Social Security and Private Pension Wealth

For current social security and private pension income recipients we calculate social security and pension wealth for the two periods in exactly the same manner. First, in the case of married couples, we allocate two-thirds of our benchmarked value of social security plus pension income to the husband and one-third to the wife. This is the split that would be in effect if all of this income represented social security retirement benefits and if the wife collected social security dependent benefits.

The resulting individual values of social security plus pension income are then used to determine the net present value of benefits for each respondent in our sample. Specifically, we calculate the actuarial discounted value of future social security plus private pension income taking into account social security survivorship benefits. Our actuarial discounting assumes a 3 percent real interest rate and uses sex-specific life tables from 1960 and 1980. In 1982 social security survivorship rules provided surviving spouses with the maximum of their own benefit or that of their deceased spouse. In 1962 the survivor benefit equaled the maximum of one's own benefit or 82.5 percent of one's deceased spouse's benefit.

One bias in this variable arises from our assumption that the private pension income component of total social security plus private pension income is subject to the same survivorship provision as is the social security component. This assumption leads to an upward bias in the calculated value of 1962 social security plus pension wealth because survivor benefits in private pension plans have become more generous over time. In addition, in 1983 a greater fraction of private pension recipients chose joint survivor pensions than was the case in 1962.[27]

A second upward bias in our calculated value for 1962 of social security plus private pension wealth arises from our treating social security and pension income in 1962 as if it were fully indexed for inflation. Unlike the situation in 1982, in 1962 there was no such formal indexation of social security benefits. In addition, very few, if any, firms had legal commitments to index their pension benefits in 1962. While this income was not formally indexed, post-1962 adjustments to the benefit levels of social security and private pensions amounted to partial indexation. In assuming full indexation we overstate the 1962 value of social security plus private pension wealth relative to the 1982 value. Correcting for these two biases would strengthen the finding reported below that the elderly's resource annuitization increased between 1962 and 1982.[28]

Calculation of Social Security Wealth for Households Still Working

For nonretired men and women we calculated separate values for social security and private pension wealth. Our social security wealth calculation requires a wage history which we base on the respondents' reported current wage. We project the current wage forward until retirement and backward until the beginning of working life. In the 1962 data, we assumed an annual growth rate in the real wage of 2 percent. In the 1983 data, we assumed an annual growth rate of average real wages of 1 percent. In addition, in 1983 we applied to each worker the cross-sectional growth in wages for their three digit industries and age group. These cross-sectional growth rates are those calculated by Avery et al. (1988) based on data from the Bureau of the Census Current Population Survey.

The first step in the calculation of social security benefits is the calculation of the average value of wages entering the Social Security Primary Insurance Amount (PIA) benefit formula. Before 1977 the calculation of the PIA was based on Average Monthly Wages (AMW). After 1977 the PIA was based on Averaged Indexed Monthly Earnings (AIME): past wages were inflated by the ratio of average wages in the economy in the year the individual reaches age 60 to average wages in the year in which income was earned. Thus in 1983, past wages were adjusted for both inflation and real wage growth.

We replicated these rules in our calculations. In 1962, we assumed a 3.5 percent annual growth rate of nominal wages (2 percent real growth plus 1.5 percent inflation). For 1983 the rate of growth of prices and, thus nominal wages, does not affect the calculation of expected real benefits. Given the calculated values of AMW and AIME, we determined each working respondent's prospective PIA at his or her age of retirement using the rules in force in 1962, in the case of the 1962 survey, and 1983 in the case of the 1983 survey.

Calculation of Private Pension Wealth for Those Still Working

The 1983 SCF contains a calculated value for private pension wealth which we adopt as our measure of private pension wealth for working respondents in 1983. Since the 1962 SFCC contains no comparable calculation of private pension wealth, we imputed 1962 private pension wealth for current workers, based on a regression of 1983 pension wealth, on the incomes and characteristics of 1983 SCF respondents. The 1983 data is converted into 1962 dollars before the regression is run. These regression coefficients are then applied to the 1962 data. We adjust for the increase in the prevalence of pension coverage by multiplying imputed pension wealth in 1962 by the ratio of the fraction of the labor force covered by pensions in 1962 to the fraction covered in 1979 (the last year for which we have data). Kotlikoff and Smith (1983) report that the fraction of workers covered by private, federal, or state and local pension plans (not including social security) rose from 39.7 percent in 1962 to 48.2 percent in 1979.

Calculation of Human Wealth for Those Still Working

We used the future real wage profiles calculated above to determine what our working respondents would earn in future years were they to continue working. To predict retirement ages for working respondents we used the cross-sectional sex- and age-specific labor force participation rates for 1962 and 1983[29]: if the participation rate for men aged 65 was x and the rate for men aged 70 was y, then we assign a man who was working at age 65 a probability of y/x of working when he was 70. We also use the period-specific mortality probabilities (by age and sex) to discount human wealth.

Tricky Cases and Sample Selection

There are a number of respondents in both surveys for whom it is difficult to calculate some or all resource components. Self-employed respondents are one example. Since we are not sure how much of their income reflects labor as opposed to capital income, we have little basis for assessing their human wealth and their social security wealth. Rather than make heroic assumptions to deal with the self-employed, we simply exclude them from our analysis.

A second group consists of respondents over 62 who both receive social security and/or private pension benefits, but who also report positive labor earnings. For such respondents we assume they will cases working immediately and apply the 1962 or 1982 social security earnings test to calculate the size of the full social security benefit they would receive if they earned zero labor income. We use this calculated benefit to form the social security wealth for these respondents. In those cases that the calculated benefit exceeds the maximum social security benefit for the year in question, we simply attribute the maximum social security benefit to these respondents.

A third group are respondents age 62 and under who report receiving both social security and private pension income as well as labor income. We use the following ad-hoc rule, which we derived from looking at the data: for people with earnings in excess of four times their reported social security and private pension income, we use only the wage information and ignore the social security and private pension benefit. For respondents with wages less than four times the benefit, we use the benefit and ignore the wage. Our reason for using this rule is that there are many people with very small benefits and moderate-sized wages, so using their benefits make little sense. Similarly, there are people with very small wages and moderate-sized benefits. The factor of four was chosen because it neatly divides the two groups and because someone with a ratio of 4 at age 60 would have approximately equal social security wealth calculating using either wages or benefits.

A fourth group of potentially problematic respondents are those over 65 who indicate that they neither receive wages nor any social security and private pension income. For such respondents we ascribe zero human wealth and zero social security plus private pension wealth.

Finally, there are respondents age 65 and under who report neither the receipt of current social security and private pension benefits nor current income. Unfortunately, the 1962 SCF does not allow for people under 65 and not working to be counted as retired. Thus everyone in the category is either self-employed (52.5 percent), a farm operator (18.0 percent), or simply described as not working (27.5 percent) (we presume that these people are unemployed). Since we cannot trust reported wages in any of these cases, we exclude all of these respondents.

In addition to the sample selections described above, for most of our analysis we limit our sample to all males and females over age 50. For some parts of our analysis we also consider all households whose heads are age 50 or more.

Notes

We thank Jinyong Cai, Douglas Gale, and Mark Schweitzer for helpful comments, Felicitie Bell for providing us with critical data on United States' population projections, the Brookings Institution for permission to reprint some of the tables and one of the charts contained in Gokhale, Kotlikoff, and Sabelhaus 1996, and Jean MacIntire for excellent research assistance. Auerbach and Kotlikoff also thank the National Institute of Aging for research support.

1. In the rest of the chapter we use the term *bequeathable wealth* to describe non-annuitized resources.

2. In this chapter a *generation* refers to persons of a given sex born in the same year.

3. Authors' calculations from the 1983 *Survey of Consumer Finances*. Note that the relative skewness of inheritances compared to bequests depends on how the number of heirs varies with the size of bequests, a point on which we have no information.

4. The methods and data sources for estimating cohort-specific annuitized and non-annuitized components of resources is described in Appendix 1.

5. The methods for computing household-specific measures of net worth, resources, and life insurance coverage based on SCF data are described in appendix 2.

6. This model is also presented in Auerbach, Kotlikoff, and Weil 1992.

7. In this model we are assuming that one cannot purchase annuities at the margin from private insurance companies. Allowing for such purchases would change the value of θ.

8. Note that the reduction in aggregate wealth arising here is not, as in Feldstein (1974), the result of the government directly transferring resources from the young to the old, but rather the result of the government indirectly assisting the old in reducing their transfers to the young.

9. Chen (1992), table 15.3.

10. Federal Reserve, Flow of Funds Accounts.

11. Chen (1990), table 15.11.

12. Ibid.

13. A final reason why the elderly's annuitization may not have increased involves the possible role of children in providing their older parents with annuity insurance. Kotlikoff and Spivak (1981) showed that the family can substitute quite well for a complete annuities market. If families do indeed provide this form of insurance, their response to the increased provision of annuities by social security and private pensions would be to reduce their own provision. While family risk sharing may characterize some families, a recent study by Altonji, Hayashi, and Kotlikoff (1992) tests for and strongly rejects family risk sharing behavior as a ubiquitous phenomenon.

14. The source for this figure as well as table 2.1 is Gokhale, Kotlikoff, and Sabelhaus (1996). Their study describes their method of allocating household consumption to the adults residing in the households interviewed in the various CES. It also describes their methods of allocating by age and sex those components of household consumption expenditure included in the NIPA but excluded in the CES. Examples of such components include imputed rent and medical care. The calculated average values of consumption by age and sex used in this figure and table 2.1 are benchmarked on a component by component basis against the NIPA totals of household expenditures for the various years in question.

15. Many (but not all) of the results reported here are from Gokhale, Kotlikoff, and Sabelhaus (1996).

16. The effects of varying the rate of productivity growth were insignificant and are not reported.

17. Mortality probabilities are calculated as one minus the ratio of the number of people of a given age alive in 1989 and the number of the same cohort alive in 1988. These two years were chosen because they lie in the middle of the last period for which we computed the share of bequeathable and annuitized resources—1987–90.

18. The reason is that the difference in bequests is the same, but the level of actual 1990 bequests is smaller, producing a larger percentage change in bequests in the hypothetical exercise.

19. The percent change in the bequest flow in this table is smaller than that presented in section VI because of the different data source.

20. This section draws heavily upon Gokhale, Kotlikoff, and Sabelhaus (1996).

21. SSA's projections are available through the year 2066. These projections were extended to the year 2200 by using SSA's mortality, fertility, and immigration assumptions for the year 2066.

22. Note that the cash value of life insurance is counted as part of nonhuman wealth.

23. The 1992 edition of the Federal Reserve's *Balance Sheets* contains upwardly revised estimates of the market value of land.

24. Pension reserves, though part of household wealth in the *Balance Sheets*, do not correspond to any of the wealth items that we benchmark in the surveys. We include

the present value of future pensions receipts as part of household annuitized wealth later in this appendix.

25. Life insurance reserves include reserves against both term and whole life policies, while only the value of whole life policies is counted as part of net worth in our survey measure. Thus we exclude life insurance from both the benchmark and from the survey total.

26. As a check on the effects of our benchmarking procedure, we report below some of our key results using nonbenchmarked data.

27. Beller and McCarthy (1992) report that for married men retiring and receiving a defined benefit pension before 1974, 24.8 percent of pension plans provided protection for a surviving spouse. By the period 1979–82, the comparable figure was 59.5 percent.

28. In fact, because of double indexation during the 1970s, ex-post the social security wealth of some cohorts was higher than the values we calculate. Since this phenomenon was clearly not anticipated in 1962, however, we do not include its value in calculations of 1962 social security wealth. Rather, we would argue, double indexation constituted a transfer to the relevant cohorts at the time that it occurred.

29. The data we started with were participation rates for five-year age groups up through age 74, and the rate for people 75+. We smoothed these with a polynomial and assumed that the participation rate for people 80 and above was zero.

References

Abel, Andrew B., "Precautionary Savings and Accidental Bequests," *American Economic Review*, vol. 75, no. 4, 1985, 777–91.

Auerbach, Alan J., Jagadeesh Gokhale, and Laurence J. Kotlikoff, "Generational Accounting: A Meaningful Alternative to Deficit Accounting," *Tax Policy and the Economy*, ed. David Bradford, National Bureau of Economic Research, vol. 5, 1991, 55–110.

Auerbach, Alan J., Laurence J. Kotlikoff, and David N. Weil, "The Increasing Annuitization of the Elderly—Estimates and Implications for Intergenerational Transfers, Inequality, and National Saving," National Bureau of Economic Research working paper no. 4182, October 1992.

Avery, Robert B., and Arthur B. Kennickell, "Household Saving in the U.S.," *Review-of-Income-and-Wealth*, 37(4), December 1991, 409–32.

Avery, Robert B., Gregory E. Elliehausen, and Thomas A. Gustafson, "Pensions and Social Security in Household Portfolios: Evidence from the 1983 Survey of Consumer Finances," in Gerard F. Adams and Susan M. Wachter, eds. *Savings and Capital Formation: The Policy Options*. Lexington, Mass.: Heath, Lexington Books, 1986, 127–60.

Beller, Daniel J., and Helen H. Lawrence, "Trends in Private Pension Plan Coverage," in John A. Turner and Daniel J. Beller, eds. *Trends in Pensions 1992*. Washington, D.C.: U.S. Department of Labor, Pension and Welfare Benefits Administration; distributed by the U.S.G.P.O. 1992, 59–96.

Boskin, Michael, Michael Knetter, and Laurence J. Kotlikoff, "Changes in the Age Distribution of Income in the United States, 1968–1984," mimeo, Center for Economic Policy Research, Stanford University, October 1985.

Davies, James, "Uncertain Lifetimes, Consumption and Dis-saving in Retirement," *Journal of Political Economy*, vol. 89, 1981, 561–77.

Feldstein, Martin S., "Social Security, Induced Retirement, and Aggregate Capital Accumulation," *Journal of Political Economy*, vol. 82, 1974, 905–26.

Feldstein, Martin S., "Social Security and the Distribution of Wealth," *Journal of the American Statistical Association*, vol. 71(356), Dec. 1976, 800–807.

Gokhale, Jagadeesh, Laurence J. Kotlikoff, and John Sabelhaus, "Understanding the Postwar Decline in U.S. Saving: A Cohort Analysis," *Brookings Papers On Economic Activity*, vol. 1, 1996, 315–390.

Greenwood, Daphne T., "Age, Income, and Household Size: Their Relation to Wealth Distribution in the United States," in Edward N. Wolff, ed. *International Comparisons of the Distribution of Household Wealth*. Oxford: Oxford University Press, Clarendon Press, 1987, 121–140.

Kotlikoff, Laurence J., John Shoven, and Avia Spivak, "The Impact of Annuity Insurance on Savings and Inequality," *Journal of Labor Economics*, vol. 4, no. 3, pt. 2, 1986, 5183–207.

Kotlikoff, Laurence J., and Daniel E. Smith, *Pensions in the American Economy*, NBER volume, Chicago, IL: University of Chicago Press, 1983.

Kotlikoff, Laurence J., and Avia Spivak, "The Family as An Incomplete Annuities Market," *Journal of Political Economy*, vol. 89, no. 2, April 1981.

McDermed, Ann A., Robert L. Clark, and Steven G. Allen, "Pension Wealth, Age-Wealth Profiles, and the Distribution of Net Worth," in Lipsey, Robert E.; Tice, Helen Stone, eds. *The Measurement of Saving, Investment, and Wealth*. National Bureau of Economic Research Studies in Income and Wealth, vol. 52, Chicago: University of Chicago Press, 1989, 689–731.

Park, Thae S., "Total Private Pension Benefit Payments, 1950–88," *Trends in Pensions, 1992*, eds. John A. Turner and Daniel J. Beller, U.S. Department of Labor, Pension and Welfare Benefits Administration, 1992, 271–83.

Radner, Daniel B., and Denton R. Vaughan, "Income, and the Economic Status of Age Households," in Edward N. Wolff, ed. *International Comparisons of the Distribution of Household Wealth*. Oxford: Oxford University Press, Clarendon Press, 1987, 93–120.

Shyrock, Henry, S., and Jacob S. Seigel and Associates, *The Methods and Materials of Demography*, U.S. Department of Commerce, Bureau of the Census, vol. 1, 1971, 365–6.

Wolff, Edward N., "Estimates of Household Wealth Inequality in the U.S., 1962–1983" *Review of Income and Wealth*, vol. 33(3), September 1987, 231–256.

Yaari, Menahem E., "Uncertain Lifetime, Life Insurance, and the Theory of the Consumer," *Review of Economic Studies*, vol. 32, April 1965, 137–50.

3 Simulating the Transmission of Wealth Inequality via Bequests

Jagadeesh Gokhale,
Laurence J. Kotlikoff,
James Sefton, and
Martin Weale

I. Introduction

Does inequality in inherited wealth exacerbate wealth inequality? If so, by how much? These fundamental questions remain unresolved. Although it may seem counterintuitive, inherited wealth may be more evenly distributed than noninherited wealth and may reduce overall wealth inequality. The reason is that the distribution of inheritances is largely governed by the random nature of longevity, whereas the distribution of noninherited wealth is largely governed by the distribution of labor earnings.

Theoretical research has identified many of the channels through which inheritances influence wealth inequality, but their relative importance is unresolved. Empirical analysis of inheritances has been limited by the availability of reliable data. An alternative approach initiated by Blinder (1974, 1976) and Davies (1982), and the one taken here, is to simulate the transmission of inequality via bequests. Unlike previous simulation studies, this study focuses on unintended inheritances arising from random dates of death and the dynamic impact of these inheritances on the distribution of wealth.

To study this process, we construct an overlapping generations model with uncertain lifespan. Each agent lives for at most 88 years—the first 22 years as a child, the second 22 years as a young adult who marries and has children, the third 22 years as a married, middle-aged adult who has no additional children, and the last 22 years as a married or widowed older adult facing lifespan uncertainty. Agents who die prior to reaching age 88 bequeath their wealth to their spouses. If their spouses are no longer living, they bequeath in equal amounts to their children, all of whom are alive given the model's timing. Agents have life-cycle preferences, meaning they have no bequest motive per se and leave bequests only because their resources are not fully annuitized. Our model follows the economy and its existing and new agents through time. This is a prerequisite to determining the impact of random inheritances on the long-run distribution of wealth.

The bequest/inheritance process is complicated. Other things equal, children whose parents die relatively early receive larger inheritances than children whose parents die relatively late. But how much one inherits depends both on the number of one's siblings sharing the bequest and on the amount of nonannuitized wealth one's parents accumulate prior to their deaths. Parents' wealth accumulation depends, in turn, on how much they themselves inherited (which depends on when their ancestors died), the level of their earnings and the percentage of those earnings saved, the rate of return received on their savings, the number of children they had to support, and their own time preference rates (which influences their desire to save). Hence, earnings inequality, the transmission of earnings inequality across generations, the number and spacing of children, assortative mating, heterogeneous rates of return, time preference, the annuitization of retirement savings through social security, and the progressivity of the income tax system can all play important roles in influencing inequality in inheritances. We consider each of these factors and their interactions in trying to account for wealth inequality and immobility.

To parse our life-cycle effects and to ensure that we capture the receipts of all inheritances, we measure intra-cohort wealth inequality at retirement. In studying wealth mobility, we consider the wealth holdings of the children of rich and poor retirees when these children reach retirement. Our results suggest that whether inheritances dampen or exacerbate wealth inequality depends very strongly on social security's annuitization of retirement savings. Absent social security, inheritances somewhat reduce wealth inequality among members of the same birth cohort. In social security's presence, however, inheritances play an important role in increasing wealth inequality. Social security aside, the main determinants of our model's wealth inequality are inequality in lifetime earnings (skill differences), assortative mating based on skills, and the rate of time preference. Interestingly, holding constant inequality in skills, the fact that agents inherit their skills from their parents does not materially alter wealth inequality.

When all of the factors that influence wealth inequality are included and calibrated to what appear to be the most realistic set of parameter values, our model generates a distribution of wealth that closely approximates the degree of inequality and skewness in the actual U.S. data. In particular, the richest 1 percent of our model's retiring households holds 32.8 percent of total wealth, which is quite close to the corresponding 30.4 percent figure in the Survey of Consumer Finances (SCF). Our model also generates a reasonable degree of wealth immobility. Under our most realistic set of assumptions, 15.9 percent of the children of the super rich end up super-rich themselves.

Our findings are striking, but their relevance to the U.S. economy is a matter of opinion. True, we've considered a large set of important determinants of wealth inequality. But we haven't considered all determinants; and although we've tried to calibrate the model carefully, our calibration is limited by the availability of data. These points should be kept in mind in judging whether this paper's findings are telling us about the real world or just about the life-cycle model.

The chapter proceeds in Section II with a literature review.[1] Section III presents our simulation model and its calibration. Section IV presents simulation results. Our strategy here is to start with extreme assumptions to illustrate the roles played by different factors and then turn to a more realistic set of assumptions. Section V discusses the impact of inheritances on the transmission of wealth inequality across generations, and Section VI summarizes and concludes the chapter.

II. Literature Review

Early studies of the like between inheritance and inequality focused on the relationship between the values of the estates of fathers and their sons (Wedgwood 1929, Harbury and Hitchens 1979). Wedgwood considered a sample of 99 people who left estates of at least £200,000 (just under $1,000,000) between 1924 and 1925. He found that 60 percent had a predecessor who died leaving at least £50,000, and that about one-third of the wealthy owed their position entirely to inheritance. Harbury and Hitchens reported that in 1973, 58 percent of those men who died leaving at least £100,000 had fathers who had left at least £25,000 at 1973 prices and that 67 percent of the variance in a son's estate was explained by the variation in the father's estate.

Interesting as they are, these data do not prove that inherited wealth is a source of inequality. The data relate to the total value of the father's estate and not to the amount inherited by the son, which may have been much less if the estate was divided equally among a number of children. And they are perfectly consistent with the view that wealthy fathers endowed their children with other advantages in life that helped them become wealthy. Nevertheless they reinforce the widely held view summarized by Meade (1976) that inheritance is a source of inequality in the distribution of wealth, a conclusion supported by the theoretical model of Wilhelm (1997) and the empirical work of Menchik (1979). This view underlies support for estate taxation as a potential mechanism for redistributing wealth.

The alternative idea—that intergenerational transfers can be equalizing—can be traced to Stiglitz (1969). In common with most of the growth literature of the day, Stiglitz assumed that each individual's consumption was a linear function of her total income. He demonstrated that a stable, egalitarian distribution of wealth would emerge if inheritances were distributed evenly among all of one's children.

Subsequent work focussed on the impact of inheritance on income inequality rather than wealth inequality. Atkinson and Stiglitz (1980) used the same model, but added earnings heterogeneity, to show that an increase in the size of inheritances, caused by an increase in the rate of savings, would decrease income inequality. In essence, inheritances act as insurance against the random receipt of lower-than-average labor income. If an agent's earnings end up below (above) the average for his cohort, chances are his parents' earnings were higher (lower) than the average for their cohorts, and their bequest will permit his parents to share with him their better (worse) luck. Atkinson and Stiglitz also pointed out that for inheritances to increase inequality in these linear models, an additional mechanism needed to operate to offset this insurance effect. Stiglitz (1969) suggested primogeniture (the oldest son receives the entire estate). Blinder (1973) suggested class mating.

The models of Becker and Tomes (1979) and Tomes (1981) highlight the joint role that inheritances and earning power (human capital) play in determining whether intergenerational transfers are equalizing. Their condition for this outcome is that the propensity of parents to transfer financial and tangible resources to their children exceeds the *inheritability* of human capital—the correlation coefficient between the parents' and the child's human capital. Solon (1992) and Solon and Zimmerman (1992) have recently tried to estimate the inheritability of human capital in the United Kingdom and the United States, respectively. Their results suggest a coefficient of 0.5 for the correlation between a father's and a son's earnings. Although this is a large correlation, it's not clear whether it arises because of genetics or parents' human capital investment in their children.

Laitner (1979a, 1979b) constructs a utility-maximizing framework in which parents care about both their own and their children's consumption, bequests must be non-negative, and there is no inheritability of human capital. He shows that an equilibrium wealth distribution exists and that inheritances are equalizing if there is no assortative mating. The studies of Meade (1964), Stiglitz (1969), Pryor (1973), Atkinson and Harrison (1978), and Atkinson (1980) also point to the role of imperfect correlation of spouses' inheritances in equalizing the distribution of inheritances.

Theoretical work on taxation provides additional grounds for believing that inheritances are equalizing. Becker and Tomes (1979) and Atkinson and Stiglitz (1980) show that inheritance taxation can increase income inequality. However if there are incomplete markets, such as the market for educational loans considered by Loury (1981), redistributive taxation of bequests can reduce intragenerational inequality.

The question of whether inheritances increase or decrease income inequality has also been studied empirically. Tomes (1981) examined this question directly and found evidence in support of an equalizing effect. Davies and Kuhn (1991) suggest that even though inheritances are equalizing in the long run, a rise in inheritance taxation will reduce inequality in the short run, but raise it in the long run.

Previous Simulation Studies

The simulation literature descends from Atkinson's (1971), Flemming's (1976), Oulton's (1976), and Wolfson's (1977) analyses of whether a pure (no-bequest) life-cycle model can explain wealth inequality. The general conclusion of this work is that, sans bequests, the life-cycle model is unable to explain the extreme upper tail of the wealth distribution. For example, Atkinson found wealth shares of the richest 1 and 5 percent of just 2 percent and 10 percent. As pointed out by Davies and Shorrocks (1978), Oulton's (1976) addition to the Atkinson model of a more realistic earnings distribution raised these shares to 6 and 17 percent. These figures are far below the actual U.S. shares.

Blinder (1974, 1976) conducts simulation studies with both intragenerational heterogeneity and life-cycle accumulation. He finds that inheritances are unimportant in determining inequality of annual income and that there is high intergenerational mobility in the distribution of inherited wealth. Unfortunately, he doesn't consider the impact of inheritances on the distribution of total wealth.

Wolfson (1979) and Davies (1982) simulate a behavioral model of life cycle saving and desired bequests. For example, in Davies' Canadian study parents maximize a lifetime utility function defined over their own and their adult childrens' consumption subject to their own and their childrens' lifetime budget constraints.[2] Davies' cross-sectional wealth and income distributions closely match the corresponding 1970 Canadian distributions.[3] Davies explored only the role of intentional bequests on inequality and in a static context, that is, he did not consider how the receipt of inheritances by one generation would influence the receipt of inheritances by the next generation and so on. In contrast, the bequests in our model are purely unintentional. They are also random, and this randomness requires tracing their influence over successive generation, that is, it necessitates a dynamic approach.

Huggett (1996) develops a large-scale life-cycle simulation model with uncertain lifetimes as well as uncertain labor income that follows an autoregressive process. He compares the model's age-wealth distribution to the actual U.S. distribution and finds a fairly close match except at the very upper tail. But unlike our analysis, which considers how the distribution of inheritances alters the distribution of wealth, Huggett assumes that all bequests are collected by the government and divided evenly across the population.

The closest antecedent to our study is that of Flemming (1979). Like us, Flemming considers earnings heterogeneity and unintended bequests arising from uncertain lifetimes and imperfect annuitization. But he also examines intentional bequests and the inheritability of skills. In contrast to our approach, Flemming's model has parthenogenesis, that is, there is no marriage. There is also no heterogeneity in the number and spacing of children. Flemming finds that wealth is much more unequally divided than are earnings, that random mortality in the absence of annuities and desired bequests can increase wealth inequality by roughly a third, and that intentional bequests can play an additional important role in raising wealth inequality.

Empirical Evidence on Altruism

Since our model ignores intended bequests, it's important to consider past research that has examined the motives underlying bequests. Laitner and Juster (1996) find some limited support for altruism in the decision at retirement of most TIAA-CREF participants not to annuitize fully their TIAA-CREF balances. In contrast, Boskin and Kotlikoff (1985), Altonji, Hayashi, and Kotlikoff (1992, 1997); Abel and Kotlikoff (1994); Hayashi, Altonji, and Kotlikoff (1996); Gokhale, Kotlikoff, and Sabelhaus (1996); and Wilhelm (1996) show that (a) the distribution of consumption across cohorts is very strongly dependent on the cross-cohort distribution of resources, (b) the distribution of consumption within extended families is very strongly dependent on the distribution of resources within extended families, (c) taking a dollar from a child and handing it to parents who are actively transferring income to that child leads the parent to hand back only 13 cents to the child, (d) the very major postwar increase in the annuitization of the resources of the elderly has not been even partially offset by an increase in their holdings of life insurance, and (e) the vast majority of bequests are distributed equally among children independent of their economic needs. Individually and as a group, these studies constitute very strong evidence against intergenerational altruism, suggesting that most bequests may be unintended or motivated by nonaltruistic considerations.

Hurd (1992) examines the influence of children on saving by elderly people in the United States. He finds that the elderly with children do save more than those without, but that the effect is statistically insignificant. Thus his findings are consistent with a view that bequests are largely accidental. According to his simulations, the bequest motive is not only statistically insignificant; it's also small in absolute terms.

It is frequently observed that retired consumers save rather than dissave. Prima facie this might indicate a bequest motive in some form (Hurd 1990). However Gokhale, Kotlikoff, and Sabelhaus (1996) and Miles (1997) point out that when wealth is calculated to include the capitalized value of social security receipts, it decreases throughout retirement. Hurd also concludes from a careful analysis of panel and cross-section data that the evidence on wealth change is consistent with the life-cycle hypothesis and the view that bequests are accidental.

A final point concerning the likelihood of altruistic bequests was made by Meade (1966) and Flemming (1976). They pointed out that anything less than very strong altruism would not suffice to generate ubiquitous and significant bequests given that, on average, the lifetime incomes of children significantly exceed those of their parents.

Evidence on Intergenerational Mobility

Paul Menchik's (1979) laborious study of wealth immobility appears to be the most detailed analysis of wealth mobility in the United States. Menchik examined probate records of 1,050 Connecticut residents who passed away in the 1930s and 1940s. Each of these decedents left an estate of $40,000 or more. Armed with these records, Menchik tried to track down probate records of the spouses and well over 1,000 children of the 1,050 decedents. His search ended up locating only 199 children for whom probate records were available for both parents. Menchik then considered the correlation between different measures of parental wealth (such as the average of the father's and mother's estates) with the estates of their decedent children. Menchik reports a child-parent wealth correlation of close to 0.5 and concludes there is fairly high wealth immobility.[4]

III. The Model and Its Calibration

This section describes the model's demographic structure, its marital arrangements, its fertility patterns, its method of constructing an initial distribution of the population, its method of populating the model through time, its allocation of skills to the model's agents, its determination of bequests and inheritance, its time-zero wealth distribution, the length of its simulations, and its consumption and saving behavior.

Demographic Structure

Agents in the model can live for 88 periods. All economic and demographic events (like earnings, consumption, marriages, births, deaths, wealth transfers, and so on) occur at the end of each period. Agents are children during their first 22 periods of life and consume as part of their parents' households from ages 1 through 22. Agents marry on their 22nd birthdays. They give birth to children at ages 22 through 43, depending on their draw from a "birth matrix" described below. They also enter the work force on their 22nd birthday (receiving their first paycheck at age 23), and work through age 66. They face positive probabilities of dying between ages 67 and 88. The probability of an agent's dying on her 88th birthday given that she has lived to that date is one. The probabilities of dying at ages 67 through 87 are taken from U.S. mortality statistics. The number, sexes, and timing of children born to each couple are determined randomly as discussed below. This distribution is aligned to ensure that an equal number of males and females—2,000—are born each year. Hence, each cohort is of equal size, and there is no population growth.

Marriage

Agents marry at age 22, either on a random basis or on the basis of their skill (the present value of their lifetime earnings). In the latter case of assortative mating, agents are married based on their skill rank, with the top skilled female marrying the top skilled male, the next most skilled female marrying the next most skilled male, and so on.

Fertility

An initial population (at time $t = 0$) of 4,000 thousand individuals (2,000 males and 2,000 females) was created for each age between 0 and 87. First, a matrix of "birth ages" was derived from a fertility simulation of CORSIM—a dynamic microsimulation model of the United States economy described in Caldwell, et al. (1998). The simulation considered 40,434 females born between 1945 and 2000 and recorded their ages of giving birth if those ages fell between ages 22 and 43. For each female in our CORSIM sample, we stored this information in our CORSIM birth matrix that accommodates a maximum of 10 birth ages, 5 for male and 5 for female births. Thus, the matrix has 40,434 rows and 10 columns. Table 3.1 shows the distribution of females in the matrix by number and sex of births.

Table 3.1a
Distribution of females by number and sex of births at ages 22 through 43*

Female Births →	0	1	2	3	4	5
Male Births ↓						
0	20.68	**12.94**	**6.96**	**1.49**	**.33**	**.10**
1	**13.64**	**14.77**	**5.32**	**1.38**	**.35**	.13
2	**7.83**	**5.06**	**2.16**	**.70**	.24	.12
3	**1.87**	**1.38**	**.64**	.23	.12	.05
4	**.41**	**.33**	.17	.12	.08	.00
5	**.12**	.13	.11	.05	.00	.00

Source: Authors' calculations based on CORSIM Birth Matrix.
*Females with at least one but less than 5 births numbered 40,434.

Table 3.1b
Distribution of females by number and sex of births at ages 22 through 43

Female Births →	0	1	2	3	4	5
Male Births ↓						
0	.00	**13.00**	**9.00**	**2.20**	**.55**	**.15**
1	**16.05**	**22.40**	**6.45**	**1.60**	**.50**	.00
2	**12.20**	**7.15**	**2.50**	**.80**	.00	.00
3	**2.85**	**.95**	**.75**	.00	.00	.00
4	**.40**	**.40**	.00	.00	.00	.00
5	**.10**	.00	.00	.00	.00	.00

Source: Authors' calculations.
Note: Birth matrix used in simulation.

Since computer memory limitations allowed us to process only 4,000 individuals in each year of birth, we needed to pare down our birth matrix to end up with one that contains exactly 2,000 male births and 2,000 female births. We started by selecting 2,000 rows from the birth matrix. The selection was done at random without replacement, except that rows containing more than 5 births were excluded. The total number of births in the selected 2,000-row matrix exceeded 4,000. Hence, we randomly eliminated male and female births in the rows of this matrix for rows containing more than one birth until we were left with precisely 2,000 male and 2,000 female births. This guaranteed that the 2,000 rows of the final birth matrix would generate exactly 2,000 female and 2,000 male births. Table 3.2 shows the distribution of females by the number and sex of their births in the birth matrix used in the simulation.

Table 3.2
SCF wealth distribution of married households with household heads aged 60–69

	Percent of wealth held by top*									
	99%	95%	90%	75%	50%	25%	10%	5%	1%	Gini coefficient
SCF	100.0	100.0	99.9	98.7	92.9	79.8	62.5	51.0	30.4	0.73

Source: Authors' calculations from the Survey of Consumer Finances, 1995. The 1995 SCF data is available at website: http://www.bog.frb.fed.us/pubs/oss/oss2/scfindex. The net worth calculation employed here is based upon the SAS program provided in the 1995 SCF's documentation.
*Weighted by the SCF's nonresponse adjusted "final weight".

Populating the Model at Time Zero

We populated our model by first creating 2,000 male and 2,000 female older-adults for each age between 67 and 88. These males and females were then married to each other sequentially. Some of these oldsters were treated as dead when we initiated the simulation. But we needed to include their ghosts at this stage of our process of populating the model in order to establish complete family trees. Marriage was allowed only between people of the same age to be consistent with our assumption that marriage occurs at age 22 (i.e., that oldster males married oldster females when they were 22 and their wives were 22). Family relationships were established by exchanging ID numbers. For example, marriage involves entering the spouse's ID numbers in the spouse-ID location of each person's record. Oldsters have no living parents or grandparents.

Drawing from the 2,000 thousand rows of the birth matrix at random and without replacement, the middle-aged and young-adult children of the initial oldsters are created, ranging in age from 24 through 66. Take, for example, the initial 70-year-olds. For each 70-year-old female (including the ghosts), we assigned a row of the birth matrix drawn at random without replacement. This row indicates how many children the female had and the ages at which she had them. We repeated this process of drawing from the birth matrix at random without replacement for each cohort of oldster females; that is, we did it for 66-year-old oldster females, 67-year-old oldster females, and so on through 87-year-old oldster females. In this process, we do not permit oldsters to bear children in their twilight years, rather we are retrospectively considering the births of the initial oldsters' children when oldsters were in their child-bearing years. When each child is created, the parents' ID numbers and years of birth are entered in the child's record, and the child's ID number and year of birth is entered in each of the parents' records.

Given that females give birth between the ages of 22 and 43, oldsters aged 88 at the initiation of our simulation ($t = 0$) have children who are aged 45 through 66; oldsters aged 87 at $t = 0$ have children aged 44 through age 65; and so on, until we reach oldsters aged 67 at $t = 0$ who would have children aged between 24 and 45. Thus, at this stage of our populating procedure, exactly 4,000 (the full compliment of) 45-year-olds and less than 4,000 thousand individuals at other ages between 24 and 66 have been created. The reason is that everyone (including oldster ghosts) who could have given birth to 45-year-olds has been considered, but not everyone who gave birth to those between ages 24 and 44 and those between ages 46 and 66 has been considered. For example, some 25-year-olds are children of the current middle-aged rather than of the current oldsters (including the ghosts), and some 50-year-olds are children of ghosts who are older than the current oldsters.

Since at this stage there are fewer than 4,000 middle-aged males and females at ages 45–66, additional middle-aged males and females are created such that they total 4,000 for each of these age groups. Next, all middle-aged males and females (those 45–66) were married at random, making sure that siblings were not married to each other. Next, the children of middle-aged adults were created, again taking draws without replacement from the birth matrix, for females of a given age and then doing the same for females of another age until all females aged 45 through 66 had been considered. The children produced by this process range in age from 2 through 44.[5] Given that we've already created the children of the $t = 0$ oldsters, the addition of these children leave us with exactly 2,000 males and 2,000 females aged 23 through 44—the young adults. The procedure just described was also used to marry the young adults.

The next step in the creation of the initial population was creating the children of the $t = 0$ young adults that were born at $t = -1$ or earlier. Each young-adult female was assigned a row of the birth matrix at random without replacement, and children were created for all birth ages less than the age at $t = 0$ of the female in question. For example, a 44-year-old female's children were created for birth ages between 22 and 43, but a 23 year-old's children are created only if her birth row assignment contains a birth-age of 22. That is, children that will be born at $t = 0$ or later were not created as yet. At the end of this process, exactly 2,000 males and 2,000 females had been created for each age between 1 and 88. The final step in creating the initial population was to kill off oldsters (make the ghosts disappear) according to their cumulative mortality probabilities.[6]

Each person-record contains ID numbers and years of birth of the spouse, parents, grandparents, and children. Also recorded is the position of the birth-matrix row selected for each adult household, whether the person is alive or dead and, if dead, the year of death.

Populating the Model through Time

In populating the model through time, we engaged in the following steps in each year from $t = 0$ onward. First, for $t = 0$, we allocated, at random and without replacement, a row from the birth matrix to all 22-year-old females. Second, 22-year-old males and females were married to each other (at random, or according to their skill ranks, depending on the case being considered). Third, females aged 22–43 gave birth as determined by their assigned birth matrix row, thereby creating 2,000 newborn (0-year-old) males and 2,000 newborn (0-year-old) females. Fourth, oldsters were killed off at random according to the conditional probability of dying at their respective ages and the existing wealth of those who just died was transferred to the surviving spouse or children. Finally, we aged everyone, excluding those who died, by one year.

Skill Endowments

In our simulations with no skill differences, all working agents are assigned a skill level of 1 and receive an annual wage of $1 because we normalize at unity the wage per unit of skill. In the case of skill differences, but no assortative mating, we assign wage profiles to agents when they reach age 23 and begin earning a living. These profiles are derived from CORSIM simulations.

CORSIM simulates wage trajectories for a representative sample of U.S. individuals either alive in 1960 or born thereafter. We use a subsample of 2,000 male and 2,000 female wage trajectories selected randomly from the CORSIM cohort of individuals born between 1970 and 1974. The wage trajectories are growth adjusted to conform to the earnings of the cohort born in 1970 (aged 23 in 1993). For example, the wages at each age (ranging from 23 to 66) of those born in 1974 are adjusted downward by the compound growth factor applicable between 1970 and 1994. The growth factors are derived from on the U.S. Social Security Administration's average wage index.

These trajectories are placed in two earnings arrays (named M for males and F for females) with 2,000 rows and 44 columns in each. In the simulations with no skill differences, each year's aggregate wages equal $176,000 (2,000 males and 2,000 females earning $1 per year in each of their 44 earning years). To generate the same annual wage flow for the simulations with skill differences, we normalize the two earnings arrays by a factor α such that the $\alpha^*(u'Mv + u'Fv) = 176{,}000$, where u and v are unit vectors of lengths 2,000 and 44 respectively. This yields normalized earnings arrays M' and F'. The 2000 rows of M' and F' are then ranked and sorted according to the present value of earnings for each trajectory. The present values of earnings are calculated using a discount factor of 4 percent. These present values represent the skill level embodied in each of the 2,000 male and 2,000 female wage trajectories.

Each of the 2,000 males (females) in a birth cohort is then assigned one of the 2,000 male (female) rows at random. This assignment is done without replacement to ensure that each cohort that comes along has precisely the same distribution of earnings trajectories. In the case of assortative mating, we repeat the above assignment of skills, but then marry the highest skilled female with the highest skilled male, the second highest skilled female to the second highest skilled male, and so on, where skill is measured by the present value of lifetime earnings. In the case of inherited skills, we assign to each male agent the skill level of his father and to each female agent the skill level of her mother. In the case of inherited skills and assortative mating, males and females inherit their father's and mother's skills, respectively, and assortative mating proceeds based on this skill distribution.

Bequests and Inheritances

When a married oldster dies, his or her spouse retains all the marital wealth. When a widowed oldster dies or if both spouses in a married couple die at the same time, the decedent's (s') wealth is evenly divided among the children.

Initial Wealth Endowments and Length of the Simulations

To initiate a simulation, we give all adults at $t = 0$ an endowment of wealth of 1 unit. We then run the model for enough years into the future until the distribution of wealth of 67-year-olds, as well as the total amount of wealth in the economy, stabilizes. Since the asymptotic wealth distribution and the total level of wealth are independent of the initial level and distribution of wealth, the fact that we start with this particular initial endowment of wealth doesn't alter our results. In practice, both the wealth distribution of 67-year-olds and the total level of wealth converge well before 150 years in each of our simulations. But to guarantee consistency across simulations, we ran each simulation for 150 years.

Consumption and Saving Behavior

Agents' expected utility are time-separable isoelastic functions of their own current and future consumption as well as that of their children through age 22. Consider, as an example, the expected utility of a couple that is age 23 and will have two children, one when the couple is age 25 and the other when they are 28:

$$EU = \sum_{a=22}^{a=87} \beta^{a-22}(p_{ha}c_{ha}^{1-1/\sigma} + p_{wa}c_{wa}^{1-1/\sigma})$$

$$+\delta \sum_{a=25}^{a=46} \beta^{a-22} c_{k1a}^{1-1/\sigma} + \delta \sum_{a=28}^{a=49} \beta^{a-22} c_{k2a}^{1-1/\sigma}. \tag{3.1}$$

In (3.1), the first summation considers the utility of each spouse from his or her own consumption at each possible age to which they could live. The second two summations consider the utility that the couple derives from the consumption of their two children. The terms c_{ha}, c_{wa}, c_{k1a}, and c_{k2a} refer, respectively, to the consumption of the husband, wife, first child, and second child when the couple is age a. The term β is the time-preference factor, σ is the intertemporal elasticity of substitution, and δ is a child-consumption weighting factor. In our first set of simulations, we set the time preference rate (which equals $[(1/\beta) - 1]$) equal to the interest rate. We also set δ equal to 0.4.

As σ approaches zero, households become more and more reluctant to consume (they become more and more concerned about consuming) smaller amounts in the future than they consume in the present. Since the inverse of σ is the household's coefficient of relative risk aversion, a value of σ close to zero translates into a coefficient of risk aversion close to infinity. In our simulations, we assume that σ is very close to zero.[7]

Assuming that σ is very close to zero simplifies enormously household consumption decisions. First this assumption in conjunction with the assumption of a time preference rate equal to the interest rate means that households seek to maintain the same level of consumption over time for each spouse. Households also seek to maintain a constant level of consumption for their children, when they are children. Given the value of δ, this child-consumption level equals 40 percent of the parental consumption level.

But most important, our assumption that σ is very close to zero means that households only consider their safe resources in deciding how much to consume at each point in time. Thus households who expect to receive an inheritance, but don't know for sure that they'll get one (because all of their parents may live to age 88), will ignore this potential source of future income in making their current consumption and saving decisions.

At each point in time, married households will calculate the number of years of remaining life, multiply this amount by 2 (to take into account the presence of both spouses) and then add to the resulting value 0.4 times the number of years of consumption of their children. This total number of effective adult consumption-years is then divided into the household's safe resources to determine consumption per effective adult. The household's safe resources consist of its wealth (which may reflect the receipt of past inheritances) plus the present value of its remaining lifetime labor earnings. Given the level of consumption per effective adult, it's straightforward to calculate total household consumption and subtract it from total household income to determine household saving.

We want to emphasize that inheritances affect consumption behavior, but only once they are received. There is no consumption out of potential future inheritances. Instead households, at each point in time, consider the worst-case scenario and formulate their consumption and saving plans accordingly. Were we to assume a positive value of σ, households would take a gamble and consume more in the present in anticipation of possibly inheriting in the future. But their decision as to how much to consume would be extraordinarily complex. The reason is that they would, at certain ages, have to take into account not simply their own resources, including their own wealth, but also that of their parents and their grandparents, assuming their grandparents are still alive. Take, for example, a 25-year-old couple with two sets of living parents and four sets of living grandparents. In deciding how much to consume, the household has to consider its own current wealth level as well as the wealth levels of all six parental and grandparental households. Formally, the dynamic program that the household must solve to determine how much to consume involves up to seven state variables, namely all seven of these wealth levels.[8] Unfortunately, solving dynamic programs with seven state variables appears to be beyond the capacity of current computers.[9]

Data and Calibration

The mortality probabilities used in the analysis are those released by the U.S. Social Security Administration for 1995. The interest rate (equal to the time preference rate) used in the simulations is 4 percent. As mentioned, the earnings and fertility matrices are derived from the CORSIM module. The CORSIM simulation modules for both are highly detailed. The earnings module was estimated from the Panel Study of Income Dynamics (PSID) data and includes separate logistic and regression equations for determining whether an agent works, whether a working agent works full or part year, how many weeks per year and how many hours per week full-year and part-year workers work, and how much each earns per hour. The intercept of each of these functions is adjusted to align the population-weighted labor supply behavior of CORSIM to national labor supply and earnings aggregates.

The fertility module includes separate logistic functions for 30 different subgroups of women, estimated using data from the National Longitudinal Survey. The subgroups are distinguished by age, the presence of children, marital status, race, and work status. The regressors in the logits are age, duration of current marriage, earnings, family income, homeowner status, marital status, schooling status, work status, and duration since the birth of women's two youngest children. In producing the larger birth matrix from which we selected 2,000 rows, we ran the CORSIM model from its start year of 1960 through 2000. In so doing, we used the entire panoply of CORSIM modules to assign CORSIM agents the various socioeconomic characteristics, such as work status, entering as regressors in the fertility logits.

IV. Findings

Wealth Inequality in the SCF

For reference, we first report findings from the 1995 SCF on the distribution of net worth among married households with household heads aged 60 to 69.[10] The richest 1, 5, and 10 percent of households hold 30.4, 51.0, and 62.5 percent of aggregate U.S. net worth, respectively. The Gini coefficient for this wealth distribution is 0.727. These calculations indicate two things: first, the U.S. wealth distribution is highly unequal among married households whose household heads are of retirement age, and second, the very rich account for a very sizeable fraction of total wealth.

Wealth Inequality Generated by Our Model

Table 3.3 begins to consider wealth inequality generated by our model. In this table, as well as tables 3.4 through 3.6, all households are assumed to earn a 4 percent real rate of return and the distribution of earnings is determined simply by the CORSIM data, that is, there is no adjustment for the upper tail of the earnings distribution.

Table 3.3 reports Gini coefficients of wealth and consumption distributions for households aged 66. It also shows the flow of bequests as a share of labor income, and the flow of bequests left to children (as opposed to spouses) as a share of the economy's labor income. The odd-numbered rows report results without inheritances and the even numbered rows those with inheritances; that is, the odd-numbered simulations assume no mortality prior to age 88.

The first point to make about table 3.3 is that the flow of bequests is a significant fraction—roughly 9 percent—of labor income for each of the simulations involving uncertain lifetimes. The flow of bequests to children, as opposed to spouses, is also significant—roughly 3 percent of labor income. Roughly speaking, the sizes of these flows correspond to estimates of bequest flows in the United States. For example, Auerbach, et al. estimate the 1990 total U.S. bequest flow at $218 billion, which amounts to about 6 percent of the

Table 3.3
Inequality and bequest flows, no social security and no progressive income taxation

Row	Simulation	Gini W	Gini C	Total B/L (%)	X-Gen B/L (%)	C/L (%)
1	No inheritances	0.045	0.045	0.0	0.0	74.6
2	Inheritances	0.075	0.075	9.0	2.9	76.6
3	No inheritances and skill differences	0.460	0.460	0.0	0.0	74.3
4	Inheritances and skill differences	0.441	0.441	9.3	3.0	76.2
5	No inheritances, skill differences, and perfect marital sorting	0.565	0.565	0.0	0.0	74.2
6	Inheritances, skill differences, and perfect marital sorting	0.534	0.534	8.5	2.4	76.2
7	No inheritances, skill differences, and perfect inheritance of skills	0.454	0.454	0.0	0.0	74.3
8	Inheritances, skill differences, and perfect inheritance of skills	0.451	0.451	9.0	3.1	75.8
9	No inheritances, skill differences, perfect marital sorting and perfect inheritance of skills	0.572	0.572	0.0	0.0	74.3
10	Inheritances, skill differences, perfect marital sorting, and perfect inheritance of skills	0.570	0.570	8.8	2.8	76.4

Note: All wealth and consumption distributions are across 66-year-old households in the simulation. W—wealth, C—consumption, B—aggregate bequests, L—aggregate labor earnings, X-Gen—cross generational, I—inherited wealth.

Table 3.4
Wealth distribution—no social security and no progressive income taxation

Row	Simulation	Percent of wealth held by top								
		99%	95%	90%	75%	50%	25%	10%	5%	1%
1	No inheritances	99.2	95.9	91.5	77.7	53.2	27.3	11.1	5.6	1.1
2	Inheritances	99.3	96.1	91.9	78.7	55.1	29.7	13.1	7.0	1.6
3	No inheritances and skill differences	99.9	99.4	98.3	93.6	80.5	57.8	34.4	22.3	7.3
4	Inheritances and skill differences	99.9	99.3	98.1	93.0	79.3	56.4	33.2	21.5	7.0
5	No inheritances, skill differences, and perfect marital sorting	100.0	99.7	99.2	96.4	86.4	66.5	43.0	29.6	11.1
6	Inheritances, skill differences, and perfect marital sorting	100.0	99.7	99.1	95.6	84.6	63.8	40.5	27.7	10.4
7	No inheritances, skill differences, and perfect inheritance of skills	99.9	99.4	98.4	93.6	80.3	57.3	33.7	21.5	6.8
8	Inheritances, skill differences, and perfect inheritance of skills	99.9	99.3	98.3	93.3	79.8	57.1	34.3	22.4	7.5
9	No inheritances, skill differences, perfect marital sorting and perfect inheritance of skills	100.0	99.7	99.2	96.3	86.8	67.2	44.0	30.8	11.8
10	Inheritances, skill differences, perfect marital sorting, and perfect inheritance of skills	100.0	99.7	99.2	96.4	86.5	67.0	43.9	30.4	11.8

Note: All wealth distributions are across 66-year-old households in the simulation.

Table 3.5
Inequality and bequest flows with social security and with progressive income taxation

Row	Simulation	Gini W	Gini C	Total B/L (%)	X-Gen B/L (%)	C/L (%)
1	No inheritances	0.108	0.038	0.0	0.0	56.2
2	Inheritances	0.188	0.040	1.4	0.5	57.6
3	No inheritances and skill differences	0.556	0.424	0.0	0.0	54.2
4	Inheritances and skill differences	0.617	0.418	2.8	0.9	55.6
5	No inheritances, skill differences, and perfect marital sorting	0.639	0.523	0.0	0.0	52.8
6	Inheritances, skill differences, and perfect marital sorting	0.687	0.508	2.4	0.6	54.1
7	No inheritances, skill differences, and perfect inheritance of skills	0.549	0.419	0.0	0.0	54.3
8	Inheritances, skill differences, and perfect inheritance of skills	0.627	0.423	2.8	1.0	55.3
9	No inheritances, skill differences, perfect marital sorting and perfect inheritance of skills	0.649	0.529	0.0	0.0	52.9
10	Inheritances, skill differences, perfect marital sorting, and perfect inheritance of skills	0.711	0.527	2.5	0.8	54.2

Note: All wealth and consumption distributions are across 66-year-old households in the simulation. W—wealth, C—consumption, B—aggregate bequests, L—aggregate labor earnings, X-Gen—cross generational, I—inherited wealth.

Table 3.6
Wealth distribution—with social security and with progressive income taxation

		Percent of wealth held by top								
Row	Simulation	99%	95%	90%	75%	50%	25%	10%	5%	1%
1	No inheritances	99.5	97.2	93.7	81.7	57.8	30.6	12.5	6.3	1.3
2	Inheritances	99.9	98.7	96.3	86.1	63.6	34.9	15.1	8.1	1.9
3	No inheritances and skill differences	99.9	99.4	98.5	94.5	84.3	67.8	46.1	31.8	11.5
4	Inheritances and skill differences	100.0	99.6	98.8	95.6	87.5	73.3	51.9	36.8	13.6
5	No inheritances, skill differences, and perfect marital sorting	100.0	99.7	99.2	96.5	88.1	73.6	55.3	42.0	17.7
6	Inheritances, skill differences, and perfect marital sorting	100.0	99.7	99.3	97.0	90.1	78.1	61.1	47.3	20.8
7	No inheritances, skill differences, and perfect inheritance of skills	99.9	99.4	98.5	94.4	84.1	67.0	45.2	30.8	10.5
8	Inheritances, skill differences, and perfect inheritance of skills	100.0	99.6	98.9	95.8	87.7	73.8	53.5	38.6	14.6
9	No inheritances, skill differences, perfect marital sorting and perfect inheritance of skills	100.0	99.7	99.2	96.5	88.6	74.5	56.6	43.6	18.7
10	Inheritances, skill differences, perfect marital sorting, and perfect inheritance of skills	100.0	99.8	99.4	97.3	91.0	79.9	64.3	51.0	22.7

Note: All wealth distributions are across 66-year-old households in the simulation.

wage flow in that year. Second, the flow of consumption is higher with inheritances than without. This is as expected since inheritances constitute an intergenerational redistribution from the old to the young. This raises the lifetime resources of each successive new generation, permitting it to consume at higher levels.

The first column of table 3.3 indicates that the inclusion of uncertain lifetimes in the simulation has only a modest effect on wealth inequality. Leaving out skill differences and mortality, the Gini is just 0.05. This Gini is nonzero because of differences across households in the number and timing of their children. These differences influence the amounts that households consume when young and, thus, the amounts of wealth they bring into old age. Although the addition of uncertain lifetimes raises the Gini coefficient by almost two-thirds, to 0.08, this is still a very small value and suggests that, by themselves, inheritances arising from random death are not a major source of wealth inequality across members of the same cohort.

In contrast, table 3.3 shows that skill differences are a major force behind wealth inequality in our model. With inheritances, the introduction of skill differences increases the wealth Gini from 0.08 to 0.44 (compare rows 2 and 4). Under our assumptions and parameterization, fertility differences, inheritances, and skill differences jointly explain more than 60 percent of the intragenerational inequality observed in the SCF data, with skill differences being the predominant factor.

The inclusion of marital sorting by skill further increases the Gini coefficient for wealth to 0.53 (table 3.3, row 6). This effect is significant, but not huge. The reason is that the rate of increase in skill levels for each skill-rank increment is small for the first 1,900. Hence, marital sorting by skill class does not imply pairing individuals with very different skill levels relative to marrying them at random. This effect accounts for a further 13 percent of the Gini observed in the SCF data. Adding inheritance of skills only marginally increases the Gini coefficient on wealth to 0.57 (table 3.3, row 10). Thus, inheritance of skills contributes only marginally to intragenerational wealth inequality.

Although uncertainty in dates of death raises wealth inequality slightly in the absence of skill differences, it does the opposite in the more realistic case that skill differences exist. As rows 3 through 10 in table 3.3 indicate, this is true whether or not couples sort themselves in the marriage market based on skills or whether skills are inherited. Under each of these assumptions, the Gini coefficient is somewhat smaller with uncertain lifetimes than without; that is, inheritances reduce, rather than raise, wealth inequality. This result is not surprising. Because only a few households in each birth cohort have very high skills, very large bequests are likely to go to children with skill levels lower than their parents' skill levels. This has a slight equalizing effect on the distribution of wealth at retirement.

Note that the Gini values for consumption at retirement are the same as those for wealth. This is because for a given number of children, lifetime resources, consumption, and wealth at retirement are all strictly proportional in all of the simulations reported in table 3.3. Table 3.4 shows wealth held by households in the top x percentiles for selected values of x. Consistent with the results of table 3.3, wealth held by richer households is much larger when skill differences are present. In the presence of inheritances, for example, the share of wealth held by the richest 5 percent of households increases by more than a factor of three (compare rows 2 and 4 in table 3.4). With inheritances and skill differences, the fractions of wealth held by the richest 1, 5, and 10 percent of households are all higher when marital sorting by skill is introduced (compare rows 6 and 4). They are not very different when children inherit skills from their parents compared to the case that skills are assigned at random to members of each cohort (compare rows 8 and 4). The wealth distributions reported thus far exhibit much less inequality than found in the SCF. In each of the rows in table 3.4, the shares of wealth held by the richest 1, 5, and 10 percent of households are much smaller compared to those reported in table 3.2.

Introducing Progressive Income Taxation and Social Security[11]

We introduce the annuitization of retirement savings via social security by assuming that 15.3 percent (the OASDHI social security and medicare payroll tax rate) of each year's labor income, up to a maximum taxable limit (calibrated to correspond to the U.S. Social Security System's taxable limit), is accumulated at a 4 percent interest rate and converted, at retirement, into an actuarially unfair annuity. Caldwell et al. (1999) estimate that on average, 67 cents of every dollar paid in OASI payroll taxes represents a pure tax. That is, the present value of Social Security OASI benefits at retirement equals the accumulated value of only 33 percent of OASI payroll taxes paid during the working lifetime. Unfortunately, similar "money's worth" calculations are not available for medicare of the disability insurance program. We assume only 30 percent of each person's payroll taxes are converted into an annuity, with the rest representing a pure tax.

Adding social security to the model raises the possibility that households for whom consumption per adult is small relative to annuity income per adult will wish to borrow against their benefits. To prevent households from leaving negative bequests, we subject such households to a borrowing constraint *at retirement*. That is, net borrowing is permitted prior to retirement but the liability must be extinguished to leave the household with exactly zero net worth at retirement.

In each case, introducing annuitization considerably increases wealth inequality. For example, table 3.5 shows that when all the factors are present, the introduction of social security increases the Gini coefficient from 0.57 to 0.71 (compare rows 10 in tables 3.3 and 3.5)—very close to the 0.73 value of the SCF wealth distribution. Wealth inequality is increased because a sizable fraction of low earning households now arrives at retirement with low or zero wealth. In contrast, richer households—for whom the annuity is very small relative to consumption per capita—accumulate roughly the same amount of wealth that they would have accumulated in the absence of social security.

The introduction of social security changes qualitatively the impact of inheritances on intragenerational wealth inequality: now, inheritances *increase* wealth inequality. For example, the Gini coefficients for the experiments of rows 9 and 10 become 0.65 and 0.71 respectively. The explanation here is that the availability of annuities makes the distribution of bequeathable wealth much less equal and perpetuates wealth inequality across extended families. High-earning parents who accumulate positive wealth through retirement will bequeath a substantial sum if they die early. The receipt of inheritances by their children causes them to arrive at retirement with substantial wealth. Hence, they may, in turn, bequeath substantial wealth to their children and so on.

This sequence of bequests and accumulation by rich households stands in sharp contrast to that of poor households. The latter do not bequeath much wealth to their children. Indeed, those who are borrowing constrained arrive at retirement with zero wealth, live entirely off of social security during retirement, and make no bequests when they die. As a result, their children arrive at retirement with less wealth than otherwise. The annuitization of lifetime resources makes the distribution of inheritances much more unequal and increases persistence in the incidence of bequests across bequeathing and nonbequeathing households. Consequently, the inheritance process reinforces rather than reduces wealth inequality at retirement. Social security's role in reducing bequests through its provision of annuities is also evident in its impact on the ratios of aggregate and cross-generational bequests to aggregate labor income: both ratios fall to about 30 percent of their values in table 3.3.

Turn next to table 3.6's wealth distributions. In the row 10 simulation, the top 1, 5, and 10 percent of 66-year-old households hold 22.7, 51.0, and 64.3 percent of aggregate wealth, respectively. These figures are much closer to the SCF wealth distribution than those in table 3.4. Almost all of the increase in the concentration of wealth arises from the introduction of social security. That said, this simulation is not particularly realistic given that it assumes perfect marital sorting and perfect inheritance of skills.

Sensitivity to the Assumed Degree of Actuarial Fairness of Social Security Benefits

The simulation findings turn out to be highly sensitive to the degree to which United States social security benefits are assumed to be fair. If we assume that social security (including medicare) pays benefits that equal, in present value, 35 percent of the present value of contributed taxes, the wealth Gini for the row 10 case of table 3.7 increases from 0.71 to 0.80. Moreover, the top 1, 5, and 10 percent of 66-year-old households now hold 27.5, 60.6, and 75.3 percent of aggregate wealth, making the upper tail of the wealth distribution noticeably more skewed than that found in the SCF data (see table 3.2).

Sensitivity to the Assumed Interest Rate

We also ran our table 3.5, row 10 simulation assuming a 6 percent real rate of interest (and a 6 percent time preference rate). In so doing, we left unchanged the level of social security benefits provided

Table 3.7
Inequality and bequest flows—adding partial marital sorting, partial skill inheritances, rate of return heterogeneity, consumption growth, and adjusting for the top tail in the lifetime earnings distribution

Row	Simulation	Gini W	Gini C	Total B/L (%)	X-Gen B/L (%)	C/L (%)
1	Inheritances, skill differences, perfect marital sorting, and perfect inheritance of skills (table 3.5, row 10)	0.711	0.527	2.5	0.8	54.2
2	Partial marital sorting	0.661	0.476	2.6	0.8	54.8
3	Partial inheritance of skills	0.712	0.530	2.4	0.8	54.0
4	Rate of return heterogeniety	0.717	0.525	2.6	0.8	52.9
5	Consumption growth	0.613	0.516	5.1	1.6	39.5
6	Top earnings tail adjustment	0.721	0.713	2.4	0.8	66.7
7	Partial marital sorting, partial inheritance of skills, rate of return heterogenity, and top earnings tail adjustment, and consumption growth	0.674	0.670	5.5	1.7	47.0

Note: All wealth and consumption distributions are across 66-year-old households in the simulation. W—wealth, C—consumption, B—aggregate bequest, L—aggregate labor earnings, X-Gen—cross generational, I—inherited wealth.

each worker. Interestingly, neither the Gini coefficient nor the upper tail of the wealth distribution is much affected by the choice of interest rate. The Gini coefficient for this run is 0.71, and the top 1, 5, and 10 percent of wealth holders account for 21.6, 50.5, 64.8 percent of total wealth. These values are almost identical to those reported in rows 10 of tables 3.5 and 3.6. The explanation for this is that a higher interest rate, by lowering the price of future consumption, permits households to consume more at every age. This is true notwithstanding the reduction in the present value of their human wealth and social security benefits due to the higher interest rate. Although planned pre- and postretirement consumption is higher, the assets at retirement needed to finance postretirement consumption are not necessarily larger—again because of the lower price of postretirement consumption. Hence, a higher interest rate materially alters neither household assets at retirement nor the distribution of those assets.

Toward a More Realistic Simulation

The previous simulations invoked extreme assumptions with respect to marital sorting, the inheritance of skills, and the uniformity across households of rates of return. These assumptions were made to clarify the nature of the effects of these and other factors on bequests and wealth inequality. In the remainder of the chapter, we show how more realistic assumptions alter our findings. In this regard, we also consider a lower rate of time preference and what appears to be a more realistic upper tail of the distribution of lifetime labor earnings.

Imperfect Marital Sorting and Imperfect Inheritablity of Skills

There is little solid evidence to use to calibrate the degree of marital sorting and inheritability of skills. But what evidence exists, together with our priors, leads us to consider 0.5 rank correlation coefficients between the lifetime earnings of husbands and wives. Solon (1992) and Solon and Zimmerman (1992) suggest a value of 0.5 for the inheritability coefficient (the correlation between parents' and childrens' earnings). But this value generates what appears to us to be a bit too much wealth mobility. Consequently, we choose a value of 0.7 for our final simulations.[12] This decision does not materially alter simulated wealth concentration at retirement.

Including Interest Rate Heterogeneity

Different individuals face different rates of return in capital markets. To incorporate rate-of-return heterogeneity, we use data on the portfolio holdings of households from the 1995 SCF. We classify household reported assets into several categories, assign a rate of return to each category, and compute each household's portfolio-weighted rate of return.[13] The weighted frequency of households for rates of return ranging from zero to 10+ percent in steps of 0.5 percent is used to randomly allocate the *average* rate of return within each step to households in the simulation. Households are assumed to earn their assigned rate of return in each year of their lives, and there is zero correlation between rates of return earned by parent and child households.

Calibrating the Rate of Time Preference

In addition to including unrealistic assumptions about assortative mating and inheritance of skills, the simulation in row 10 of table 3.5 produces two ratios that are unrealistic—one is a 1.9 ratio of aggregate wealth to aggregate labor income, the other is a .025 ratio of the flow of bequests to aggregate labor income. In the United States, these two ratios are roughly 6 and .06, respectively. To produce a more realistic set of results, we modified our assumption of zero life-cycle growth in consumption per adult, apart from that arising from liquidity constraints and the receipt of inheritances. Specifically, we assumed that consumption per equivalent adult rises at 1.5 percent per year through age 66. This produces a longitudinal age-consumption profile that accords much more closely with the actual U.S. profile. We refer below to this adjustment in terms of a reduction in the time preference rate through the age of retirement.

Adjusting for the Upper Tail of the Distribution of Lifetime Earnings

As mentioned, the econometric functions comprising CORSIM's earnings module were estimated from the PSID. Although the PSID has many advantages, sampling high income and high wealth households is not one of them. Consequently, CORSIM's earnings module appears to considerably understate the degree of skewness in the actual distribution of lifetime earnings. For example, the present value of earnings of the highest earning male in CORSIM is only 4.4 times as large as that of the male in the 95th percentile. For females the corresponding earnings multiple is 12.7. Across the 4,000 males and females, the present value of earnings has a Gini coefficient of 0.129. In the SCF however,the earnings multiple is 65.3 for the highest earning male and 44.7 for the highest earning female. To incorporate a more realistic earnings distribution in the simulation, we replace the top 5 percent of the CORSIM earnings distribution with that obtained from the 1995 SCF.[14] Despite the adjustment, the Gini for the present value of earnings across the 4,000 individuals increases only slightly to 0.133.

Results Based on More Realistic Assumptions

Tables 3.7 and 3.8 show how the more realistic assumptions just described alter the results. The first row of each table begins with the respective row 10 results of tables 3.5 and 3.6. Rows 2–6 in each table show the impact of deviating from the previous row 10 assumptions by respectively incorporating partial marital sorting, partial inheritance of skills, rate of return heterogeneity, a lower time preference rate through retirement, and the top earnings tail adjustment. The last row, row 7, in each table simultaneously invokes all five of the new assumptions.

Although we ran the simulations involving the top earnings tail adjustment out for over two hundred years, the distribution of wealth fluctuated from year to year to a much greater degree than was the case for all the other simulations. For example, in the last fifteen years, the Gini coefficient for the run with all five new assumptions fluctuated between .624 and .729 and the wealth share of the richest 1 percent fluctuated between 24.7 percent and 41.1 percent. To deal with this issue, we report in rows 6 and 7 the average values of variables over the last fifteen years of the simulations.

The major new messages of tables 3.7 and 3.8 are the importance of both the rate of time preference and the shape of the top tail of the lifetime earnings distribution to wealth inequality. As row 5 shows, a lower rate of time preference prior to retirement age reduces wealth concentration. The top 1 percent of wealth holders now hold only 16.3 percent of total wealth, compared to 22.6 percent when there is no desired growth in consumption per adult equivalent. This makes

Table 3.8
Inequality and bequest flows—adding partial marital sorting, partial skill inheritances, rate of return heterogeneity, and adjusting for the top tail in the lifetime earnings distribution

		Percent of wealth held by top								
Row	Simulation	99%	95%	90%	75%	50%	25%	10%	5%	1%
1	Inheritances, skill differences, perfect marital sorting, and perfect inheritance of skills	100.0	99.8	99.4	97.3	91.0	79.9	64.3	51.0	22.7
2	Partial marital sorting	100.0	99.7	99.1	96.5	89.4	76.8	57.1	41.6	16.4
3	Partial inheritance of skills	100.0	99.8	99.4	97.4	91.3	80.3	64.0	50.1	21.7
4	Rate of return heterogeniety	100.0	99.9	99.6	97.6	91.5	80.4	64.4	50.8	22.6
5	Consumption growth	100.0	99.7	99.1	96.1	87.1	71.2	52.2	39.1	16.3
6	Top earnings tail adjustment	100.0	99.8	99.5	97.8	91.7	78.9	63.6	54.7	39.7
7	Partial marital sorting, partial inheritance of skills, rate of return heterogenity, and top earnings tail adjustment and consumption growth	100.0	99.7	99.3	96.9	89.6	75.2	58.8	49.4	32.8

Note: All wealth distributions are across 66-year-old households in the simulation.

sense. The lower time preference rate produces relatively more wealth accumulation at the bottom end of the wealth distribution, which is otherwise almost exclusively dependent on social security benefits in retirement. Although it makes wealth concentration too low, this change in assumptions dramatically raises the economy's ratios of wealth to labor income and bequests to labor income. The two ratios are now 5.4 and .05.

Adding just the top-tail adjustment to the distribution of lifetime earnings considerably increases the degree of wealth inequality as measured by the share of wealth of the top 1 percent. Now the top 1 percent have 39.7 percent of total wealth. In considering this result, it's important to bear in mind that our top-tail earnings adjustment is crude for two reasons. First, the SCF doesn't provide information about lifetime earnings. Second, try as it may, the SCF is unlikely to be sampling the Bill Gateses of this world, whose annual labor earnings run into the hundreds of millions if not billions, thereby understating earnings as well as wealth inequality.

As the row 7 results show, including the top tail adjustment with all the modifications in the other assumptions generates wealth shares for the top 1, 5, and 10 percent of 32.8 percent, 49.4 percent, and 58.8 percent. These figures are very close to the corresponding SCF values of 30.4 percent, 51.0 percent, and 62.5 percent. Thus, based on the combined set of more realistic assumptions, our model appears capable of reproducing actual U.S. wealth inequality. Furthermore, under these assumptions, the model generates realistic ratios of wealth to labor income and bequests to labor income. The respective values of 6.0 and .055 are quite close to their empirical counterparts.

V. Intergenerational Wealth Mobility

This section considers the degree of intergenerational wealth mobility arising in our final simulation (the last row of table 3.7).[15] Table 3.9 presents a wealth mobility matrix in which the rows represent parent-household wealth positions and the columns indicate child-household wealth positions, both at age 66. The numbers in each row show the probability (in percentage terms) of the child being in the column wealth range given the parent wealth range represented by that row.[16] Consider a wealth value of 18 in the table. This is the cutoff value for the top 20 percent of wealth holders. According to

Table 3.9
Transition matrix: wealth at retirement for parent- and child-households (skill differences, marital sorting, and inherited skills; partial marital sorting and inheritance of skills; skewed earnings distribution at upper tail; and rate of return consumption growth = 1.5% through age 66; 0% thereafter.)

	j														
i	0–6	6–12	12–18	18–24	24–30	30–36	36–42	42–48	48–54	54–60	66–72	72–78	78–84	84–90	90+
0–6	47.4	41.0	7.1	2.2	0.9	0.4	0.3	0.1	0.1	0.1	0.0	0.0	0.0	0.0	0.3
6–12	23.3	45.9	15.5	6.6	3.0	1.6	1.0	0.6	0.4	0.3	0.2	0.2	0.1	0.1	1.2
12–18	9.8	41.7	22.3	10.4	5.3	2.9	1.9	1.1	0.7	0.5	0.3	0.3	0.2	0.2	2.3
18–24	5.7	35.0	25.1	13.2	6.9	3.7	2.6	1.5	1.1	0.6	0.5	0.4	0.3	0.2	3.1
24–30	3.9	28.1	27.1	15.1	8.0	4.9	2.9	2.0	1.2	0.8	0.5	0.5	0.4	0.6	3.7
30–36	3.3	23.5	25.1	16.9	10.0	5.5	4.2	2.7	1.9	1.2	0.5	0.7	0.3	0.2	4.0
36–42	2.3	21.8	25.6	18.4	10.1	6.3	4.5	2.2	1.7	1.4	0.4	0.8	0.5	0.3	3.6
42–48	2.3	18.0	24.7	20.8	11.5	6.3	4.5	3.2	1.4	1.0	0.6	0.8	0.4	0.3	4.2
48–54	2.5	14.2	22.5	18.9	11.5	7.8	5.4	3.5	2.2	1.7	1.0	1.0	0.5	0.4	6.7
54–60	2.1	14.0	22.3	20.7	12.6	7.9	5.6	2.1	2.8	1.5	0.8	1.1	0.2	1.3	4.9
66–72	1.1	14.8	21.3	15.6	14.3	9.2	5.9	2.2	3.2	2.4	0.8	1.3	1.1	0.3	6.5
72–78	3.2	13.6	21.2	19.2	10.6	8.8	6.2	4.7	2.1	0.9	1.5	1.2	1.2	0.6	5.0
78–84	3.0	13.2	18.4	14.3	15.8	12.0	7.5	3.0	3.0	2.3	1.1	0.4	0.8	0.8	4.5
84–90	2.5	15.2	17.3	20.3	9.1	10.2	6.6	5.1	2.5	2.0	1.0	1.5	0.0	0.5	6.1
90+	3.6	11.6	11.6	13.8	11.0	8.4	6.5	5.0	3.3	3.3	1.9	1.7	1.5	1.0	15.9

Source: Authors' calculations.
Note: Numbers indicate probability (%) that child-household will be in wealth range *j* given parent-household is in wealth range *i*.

the table, almost one half of children whose parents are in the top 20 percent of wealth holders at age 66 end up in the top 20 percent of wealth holders when they themselves reach age 66. This result is in rough agreement with the evidence in Wedgwood (1929), Harbury and Hitchens (1979), and Menchik (1979).[17]

Next, consider parents in the poorest group, whose wealth ranges from 0 to 6. The children of these parents have a 47.4 percent chance of finding themselves in the same wealth group when they reach age 66. And they have a similar likelihood of being in one of the next two higher wealth groups. So 95 percent of these children will end up poor as well. Indeed, the chance that these children will end up in one of the top 5 wealth ranges is only 0.5 percent.[18] For the children of the richest parents, this chance is 22 percent.[19] These results notwithstanding, table 3.9 shows that wealth mobility is fairly high from some perspectives. Take the richest parents. The probability that their children, at age 66, will be in one of the five lowest wealth ranges is 52 percent.

Wealth mobility is highly sensitive to our assumed degree of inheritability of skills. And for high degree of skill inheritance, wealth mobility is substantially reduced by assuming higher degrees of assortative mating. For example, the probability that the children of the super rich end up super-rich themselves rises from 15.9 percent to 49.3 percent if the correlation coefficient of inheritability is increased from 0.7 to 1.0. And holding this coefficient at 0.7, this probability rises from 15.9 percent to 20.9 percent if the correlation coefficient of assortative mating is raised from 0.5 to 1.0.

VI. Caveats and Conclusion

Many people intuitively believe that inheritances, because of their random nature and receipt by a lucky few, cause considerably greater wealth inequality among members of the same cohort than is actually the case, surprising as it may seem. Because the process underlying inheritances is largely unrelated to the earnings differences that are the key determinant of life cycle wealth accumulation, inheritances can be wealth-equalizing.

This chapter develops a large-scale, life-cycle simulation model to explore the role of inheritances and other factors in generating wealth inequality. The model includes uncertain longevity, fertility differences, skill differences, assortative mating, inherited skills, heterogeneous rates of return, annuitization via a social security system, and progressive income taxation. We find that skill differences, the annuitization of retirement savings, assortative mating, and the skewness of the upper tail of the earnings distribution, are the major factors underlying intragenerational wealth inequality. The inheritance of bequests is an important contributor to wealth inequality, but only in the presence of social security; that is, without social security, bequests actually reduce wealth inequality, albeit to a minor degree. Interestingly, the inheritance of skills from one's parents does not much affect wealth inequality. Most of wealth inequality stems from earnings inequality, and how members of a particular generation came to have their unequal earnings doesn't change the fact that their levels of accumulated wealth will differ. Another minor factor affecting wealth distribution is progressive income taxation.

All told, the factors examined in this chapter are capable of reproducing observed U.S. wealth inequality among married couples at retirement. What we believe to be our most realistic simulation produces a Gini coefficient of 0.65—not far from the .73 Gini coefficient found in the SCF. This same simulation leaves the top 1, 5, and 10 percent of wealth holders holding 31.6, 47.0, and 55.9 percent of aggregate wealth, respectively. These wealth shares are quite close to the corresponding 1995 SCF values of 30.4, 51.0 and 62.5 percent for married couples in their 60s.

We also learned that the inheritance of skills and its interaction with marital sorting, rather than inheritance of wealth, are the main factors in limiting intergenerational mobility across wealth levels. Under the most realistic calibration of the simulation, the probability is 15.9 percent that children of the super rich will themselves be super-rich.

We've taken our model through a number of paces, but left others for future research. These include adding heterogeneous saving preferences (i.e., differences in time preference rates), income- or wealth-correlated mortality probabilities, different ages of first marriage, changes in marital status, and a more detailed set of fiscal institutions, as in the impressive study by Hubbard, Skinner, and Zeldes (1994).[20]

Whatever the true merit in our preference and other assumptions, this chapter has, at a minimum, introduced some new technology for studying key factors underlying wealth inequality. Its rather surprising findings—that intentional bequests are not needed to generate either a very high degree of wealth concentration or a realistic stock of wealth relative to the size of the economy; that inheritances, absent social security, can equalize the wealth distribution; that social security is likely to make inheritances much more unequal; and that the skewness of the distribution plays a pivotal role in wealth inequality—may bring us somewhat closer to understanding the key factors underling the actual U.S. distribution of wealth.

Notes

The opinions expressed here are those of the authors and not necessarily those of Boston University, the Federal Reserve Bank of Cleveland, the National Bureau of Economic Research, or the National Institute for Economic and Social Research. We thank Steven Caldwell for providing fertility data from CORSIM, his detailed micro simulation model of the U.S. economy. We thank Pierre Pestieau and other participants of the ISPE conference "Bequests and Inequality Across Generations," participants at the Federal Reserve System's Committee on Money and Macroeconomics, James Poterba, and two referees for very valuable comments. Laurence J. Kotlikoff gratefully acknowledges research support from the National Institute of Aging.

1. Davies and Shurrocks (2001) provide an excellent review of the literature.

2. Optimal consumption over a fixed and certain lifespan is simulated for 500 couples. Each parent couple is identical in all but the following dimensions: parents' own inheritances, earnings, rate of return, rate of time preference, intensity of altruism toward children, and parents' age of first birth. Random draws of these variables from distributions calibrated to Canadian data are allocated to each couple before computing its optimal consumption path and desired bequest. Bequests occur when parents die, which, given there is no lifespan uncertainty, occurs at a common age. Bequests are distributed among children equally or, alternatively, in a compensatory manner based on children's earnings. Assuming constant rates of income and population growth over time, a single simulation over 500 couples suffices to generate a cross-sectional distribution of wealth, income, and lifetime resources.

3. Davies also attempts to explore the impact of the different sources of heterogeneity on inequality. Unfortunately, the multigeneration (dynamic) simulations required to explore the long-run level of bequests and inequality that results from removing, in turn, the heterogeneity in each of the variables was precluded by limits on computational capacity. Consequently, Davies was forced to consider these experiments assuming no bequests.

4. Menchik's findings are suggestive of wealth immobility, but are certainly not definitive evidence. First, the sample is quite small. Second, there are major issues of sample selection, foremost of which is that the 1,050 original decedents are hardly representative of the population as a whole. $40,000 was a considerable sum in the 1930s and 1940s, and the parent-child wealth correlation might be quite different in a complete and random sample. Third, the ages of death of both parents and children are highly varied, and there is no correction for life-cycle differences in wealth accumulation by age. Thus the high parent-child wealth correlation could simply reflect a

correlation in the ages of death of parents and children. Finally, most of the 199 children are married, but there is no analysis of the correlation of the household wealth of the child and that of the child's spouse's parents (the child's in-laws). If the children of the rich tend to marry children of the middle and poorer classes, their spouse's parents will likely have modest amounts of wealth. Were they included in the sample, the parental-child wealth correlation might be much lower than Menchik reports.

5. Sixty-six-year-olds have children aged between 23 and 44; 65-year-olds have children aged between 22 and 43; and so on through 45-year-olds who have children aged between 2 and 23.

6. The mortality probabilities are based on the latest U.S. mortality tables. Conditional mortality probabilities below age 67 are set to zero and the conditional mortality probability at age 88 is set to unity. The probability of dying at age $= a, d_a$, is calculated as

$$d_a = (1 - \sigma_a) \prod_{s=67}^{a-1} \sigma_s,$$

where σ_s is the conditional probability of surviving at age s.

7. Hall (1988) reports that there is "... no strong evidence that the elasticity of intertemporal substitution is positive. Earlier findings of substantial positive elasticities are reversed when appropriate estimation methods are used."

8. We say "up to" because during years in which the household is age 66 and over, it has neither living parents nor living grandparents, and during years in which the household is age 44 through 65, it has no living grandparents.

9. The fact that even supercomputers would have difficulty solving this problem in a reasonable amount of time raises the question of how mere mortals can actually deal with this complexity.

10. The net worth calculation is based on computer code provided in the SCF documentation. The net worth percentiles are calculated using the final nonresponse-adjusted sample weights provided in the SCF.

11. Introducing progressive income taxation by itself does not qualitatively change the results reported in table 3.3. As expected, wealth inequality at retirement is lower in all cases simply because households with higher income face higher average tax rates. In addition, consumption inequality is lower than wealth inequality at retirement because greater wealth cannot be converted into a proportionally greater consumption stream at retirement: the asset income generated along the way is taxed at higher average income tax rates. Table 3.3's result that inheritances reduce rather than increase wealth inequality at retirement is not overturned by the introduction of progressive income taxes alone. However, the impact of progressive income taxation in the presence of social security *is* qualitively different. Apparently, progressive income taxation in the presence of social security acts like higher levels of social security benefits in limiting the wealth accumulation of the poor and the middle class and disenfranchising their children with respect to inheritances. This causes a reduction in the flow of bequests as a share of labor income. On the other hand, the differentially higher burden that progressive income taxation imposes on high-income households limits their wealth accumulation as well. The net impact is this rather minor decline in wealth inequality.

12. Matching spouses by skill levels (or associating child-parent skill levels) to deliver a correlation coefficient close to the selected value in each year of the simulation is achieved by taking a linear combination of the two extreme cases of perfect matching and random matching of individuals by skill.

13. The asset categories are liquid assets, government bonds, private bonds and bond mutual fund shares, stocks and stock mutual funds, real estate, and other nonfinancial assets. Liability categories include mortgages and real estate debt and other debt. In forming a weighted average rate of return on each household's portfolio, we used the absolute value of liabilities. For liquid assets we assumed the geometric average annual real rate of return (0.68 percent) on U.S. Treasury bills during the period 1926–97. For government bonds we use the geometric average annual real rate of return on long and intermediate term government bonds between 1926 and 1997 (2.09 percent). For private bonds and bond mutual funds we use the geometric average rate of return on long-term corporate bonds between 1926 and 1997 (2.52 percent). For stocks and stock mutual funds, we use the weighted average of real rates of return on large and small company stocks (8.00 percent). The weights for the two stock market returns were obtained from analysts at the Wilshire 5000 company. The source for the aforementioned average rates of return is the *1998 Yearbook* published by Ibbotson Associates. The average rates of interest on mortgages and other real estate debt was constructed using data from Case and Shiller (1990) who report annualized excess returns (excess over the three-month T-bill return) on home purchases for each quarter between 1971 and 1986 in four large U.S. metropolitan areas. We computed the total returns by adding the annualized real T-bill return for each quarter, calculated the geometric mean over the period of the study, and averaged the rates of return over the four metropolitan areas. This procedure yields a real rate of return of 0.45 percent. Finally the rate of return for mortgage and real estate debt was calculated as the geometric average nominal mortgage rate between 1973 and 1997 divided by the geometric average rate of inflation over the same period. This yielded 3.91 percent. The average real rate on other debt was assumed to be 13.54 percent—the rate applicable for 1995—obtained from the *Statistical Abstract for the United States, 1998*, table 820.

14. This is accomplished by rescaling the CORSIM longitudinal profiles for the top 100 skill ranks for both males and females. The CORSIM skill ranks are based on present values of earnings of the longitudinal earnings profiles calculated using a 4 percent rate of discount. The 1995 SCF skill ranks are based on the wage and salary levels of randomly selected samples of 2,000 males and 2,000 females aged 35 to 45. We used this age range because we felt that the distribution of annual earnings would better approximate the distribution of lifetime earnings at these ages than at other ages. First, the skill levels for both the CORSIM and the SCF skill distributions are normalized to make the skill level at the 95th percentile equal to unity in each. Second, each CORSIM longitudinal skill profile corresponding to the 100 ranks higher than the 95th percentile are rescaled by the ratio of the SCF normalized skill level to the CORSIM normalized skill level for that skill rank. Finally, the entire set of 2,000 CORSIM longitudinal profiles are renormalized to deliver a total wage flow of $176,000 in each period of the simulation.

15. Transition matrices for other simulations are available from the authors upon request.

16. Each child household has two parent households. Hence, in forming the probabilities in the transition matrices of Table 3.9, we count each child household twice.

First we pair the child's household wealth at age 66 with the male spouse's parent household wealth at age 66 and enter this pairing in the appropriate cell of the transition matrix. Next, we pair the child's household wealth with the female spouse's parent household wealth at age 66 and enter this pairing again in the appropriate cell of the transition matrix. These entries are aggregated for all child households after the 132nd year of the simulation. Thus, the transition probabilities reflect both parent household wealth positions. The probabilities reported are those of the child household's wealth position (column) conditional of the parent household's wealth position (row).

17. Note, however, that these studies do not control for the age at which wealth of parents and children is observed, and it is unclear to which segments of the wealth distribution their samples correspond.

18. This number does not correspond to the sum of those reported in the table because of rounding.

19. The correlation coefficient of parental and child age-66 wealth in this final run is 10 percent. This is much smaller than the correlation reported by Menchik, but, as argued above, Menchik's is correlating wealth at different ages and doing so on a restricted subset of the population.

20. Including a distribution of time preference rates would generate even greater wealth inequality if the propensity to save were correlated with the level of lifetime earnings or inherited wealth. On the other hand, if saving behavior were uncorrelated with economic resources, the dispersion in time preference rates would produce a larger dispersion in wealth at retirement, but not necessarily larger measures of wealth concentration. One could also consider preferences espoused by Carroll (1998) and others in which people accumulate wealth for the sake of power and status, rather than to finance consumption. Incorporating earnings uncertainty (as in Hubbard, Skinner, and Zeldes 1994), health-care expenditure uncertainty, and rate of return uncertainty are additional key elements to consider in future work. Incorporating higher survival probabilities for those with greater economic resources (more money buys better health care) would reduce the model's wealth inequality and immobility. The reason is that the richest elderly would live the longest and would, as a group, spend down a larger fraction of their wealth before they died. This, of course, means reduced inheritances for the children of the rich, making the wealth holding of these children and their contemporaries less concentrated and less correlated with that of their parents. The forgoing argument postulates causality from resources to longevity. However, the opposite possibility cannot be ruled out. If longevity affects saving behavior, the wealth distribution across each *retiring* cohort may well exhibit greater inequality as longer-lived households saved more to finance a lengthier retirement.

References

Abel, A., Kotlikoff, L. J. 1994. "Intergenerational Altruism and the Effectiveness of Fiscal Policy: New Tests Based on Cohort Data." In *Savings and Bequests*. Ann Arbor, Michigan: University of Michigan Press.

Altonji, J. G., Hayashi, F., Kotlikoff, L. J. 1992. "Is the Extended Family Altruistically Linked? Direct Tests Using Micro Data." *The American Economic Review* 82 (December) 1177–98.

Altonji, J. G., Hayashi, F., Kotlikoff, L. J. 1997. "Parental Altruism and Inter Vivos Transfers: Theory and Evidence." *Journal of Political Economy* 105(6) 1121–66.

Atkinson, A. B. 1980. "Inheritance and the Redistribution of Wealth." In G. M. Heal and Hughes, eds., *Public Policy and the Tax System*. London: Allen and Urwin.

Atkinson, A. B. 1971. "The Distribution of Wealth and the Individual Life Cycle." *Oxford Economic Papers* 23:239–54.

Atkinson, A. B., Harrison, A. J. 1978. *Distribution of Personal Wealth in Britain*. Cambridge, England: Cambridge University Press.

Atkinson, A. B., Stiglitz, J. 1980. *"Lectures in Public Economics."* Singapore: McGraw-Hill.

Auerbach, A. J., Gokhale, J., Kotlikoff, L. J., Sabelhaus, J., and Weil, D. 1999. "The Annuitization of Americans' Resources—A Cohort Analysis." Mimeo, Boston University.

Becker, G. S., Tomes, N. 1986. "Human Capital and the Rise and Fall of Families." *Journal of Labor Economics* 4(3) Part II S1–39.

Becker, G. S. and Nigel, T. 1979. "An Equilibrium Theory of the Distribution of Income and Intergenerational Mobility." *Journal of Political Economy* 87(6) 1153–89.

Blinder, A. S. 1973. "A Model of Inherited Wealth." *Quarterly Journal of Economics*. 87(4) 608–26.

Blinder, A. S. 1974. *Toward An Economic Theory of Income Distribution*. Cambridge, MA: MIT Press.

Blinder, A. S. 1976. "Inequality and Mobility in the Distribution of Wealth." *Kyklos* 29:607–38.

Boskin, M. J., Kotlikoff, L. J. 1985. "Public Debt and U.S. Saving: A New Test of the Neutrality Hypothesis." *Carnegie-Rochester Conference Volume Series*.

Caldwell, S., Favreault, M., Gantman, A., Gokhale, J., Johnson, T., Kotlikoff, L. J. 1999. "Social Security's Treatment of Postwar Americans." In *Tax Policy and the Economy*, NBER vol. 13. Cambridge, MA: MIT Press.

Carroll, Christopher D. 2000. "Why Do the Rich Save So Much?" In Slemrod, Joel B., ed., *Does Atlas Shrug? The Economic Consequences of Taxing the Rich*. Cambridge: Harvard University Press.

Case, K., and Shiller, R. J. 1990. "Forecasting Prices and Excess Returns in the Housing Market." *AREUEA Journal*, 18(3) 253–73.

Davies, J. B. 1982. "The Relative Impact of Inheritance and Other Factors on Economic Inequality." *Quarterly Journal of Economics* 97(3) 471–98.

Davies, J. B. and Kuhn, P. J. 1991. "A Dynamic Model of Redistribution, Inheritance, and Inequality." *Canadian Journal of Economics* 24(2) 324–44.

Davies, J. B., and Shorrocks, A. 1971. "Assessing the Quantitative of Inheritance in the Distribution of Wealth." *Oxford Economic Papers* 30(1) 239–54.

Davies, J. B., and Shorrocks, A. F. 2001. "The Distribution of Wealth." In Atkinson, A. B., and Bourguignon, F., eds., The Handbook of Income Distribution. New York: North Holland.

Flemming, J. S. 1976. "On the Assessment of the Inequality of Wealth." In *Selected Evidence Submitted to the Royal Commission: Report No. 1, Initial Report of the Standing Reference (Royal Commission on the Distribution of Income and Wealth, HMSO, London)* 34–70.

Flemming, J. S. 1979. "The Effects of Earnings Inequality, Imperfect Capital Markets, and Dynastic Altruism on the Distribution of Wealth in Life Cycle Models." *Economica* 46:363–80.

Gokhale, J., Kotlikoff, L. J., and Sabelhaus, J. 1996. "Understanding the Postwar Decline in United States Saving: A Cohort Analysis." *The Brookings Papers on Economic Activity* Vol. 1.

Harbury, C. D. and Hitchens, D. M. W. N. 1979. *Inheritance and Wealth Inequality in Britain*. London: Allen and Unwin.

Hall, Robert E. 1988. "Intertemporal Substitution in Consumption." *Journal of Political Economy* 96(2):339–57.

Hubbard, R. G., Skinner, J. S., and Zeldes, S. P. 1994. "The Importance of Precautionary Motives for Explaining Individual and Aggregate Saving." In Meltzer, A. H. and Plosser, C. I., eds., *The Carnegie-Rochester Conference Series on Public Policy* 40:59–126.

Huggett, M. 1996. "Wealth Distribution in Life Cycle Economies." *The Journal of Monetary Economics* 38:469–94.

Hurd, M. D. 1990. "Research on the Elderly: Economic Status, Retirement and Consumption & Saving." *Journal of Economic Literature* 28:565–637.

Hurd, M. D. 1992. "Measuring the Bequest Motive: the Effect of Children on Saving by the Elderly in the United States." In Tachibanaki, T., ed., *Savings and Bequests*. Ann Arbor, Michigan: University of Michigan Press, 111–36.

Laitner, J. 1979a. "Household Bequests, Perfect Expectations, and the National Distribution of Wealth." *Econometrica* 47(5) 1175–93.

Laitner, J. 1979b. "Household Bequest Behaviour and the National Distribution of Wealth." *Review of Economic Studies* 46(3) 467–83.

Laitner, J., and Juster, F. T. 1996. "New Evidence on Altruism: A Study of TIAA-CREF Retirees." *American Economic Review* 86(4) 893–908.

Loury, G. 1981. "Intergenerational Transfers and the Distribution of Earnings." *Econometrica* 49(4) 843–67.

Meade, J. E. 1964. *Efficiency, Equality, and the Ownership of Property*. London: Allen and Unwin.

Meade, J. E. 1966. "Life-Cycle Savings, Inheritance and Economic Growth." *Review of Economic Studies*. 33:61–78.

Meade, J. E. 1976. *The Just Economy*. London: Allen and Unwin.

Menchik, P. 1979. "Intergeneration Transmission of Inequality: An Empirical Study of Wealth Mobility." *Economica* 46:349–62.

Miles, D. 1997. "Demographics and Saving: Can we Reconcile the Evidence." Paper presented to National Institute Conference on the macroeconomics of inequality. Churchill College, Cambridge.

Oulton, N. 1976. "Inheritance and the Distribution of Wealth." *Oxford Economic Papers* 28:86–101.

Pryor, F. 1973. "Simulation of the Impact of Social and Economic Institutions on the Size Distribution of Income and Wealth." *American Economic Review* 63:50–72.

Solon, G. 1992. "Intergenerational Income Mobility in the United States." *American Economic Review* 82(3) 393–408.

Solon, G. and Zimmerman, D. J. 1992. "Regression toward Mediocrity in Economic Stature." *American Economic Review* 82(3) 409–29.

Stiglitz, J. E. 1969. "Distribution of Income and Wealth among Individuals." *Econometrica* 37(3) 382–97.

Tomes, N. 1981. "The Family, Inheritance, and the Intergenerational Transmission of Inequality." *Journal of Political Economy* 89(5) 928–58.

Wedgwood, J. 1929. *The Economics of Inheritance*, London: Ecorge Routledge & Sons.

Wilhelm, M. O. 1996. "Bequest Behavior and the Effect of Heirs' Earnings: Testing the Altruistic Model of Bequests." *American Economic Review* 86(4) 874–92.

Wilhelm, M. O. 1997. "Inheritance, Steady-State Consumption Inequality, and the Lifetime Earnings Process." *Manchester School of Economic and Social Studies* 65(4) 466–76.

Wolfson, M. 1977. "The Causes of Inequality in the Distribution of Wealth: A Simulation Analysis." Ph.D. thesis, Cambridge University.

Wolfson, M. 1979. "The Bequest Process and Causes of Inequality in the Distribution of Wealth." In J. D. Smith, ed., *Modelling the Intergenerational Transmission of Wealth*. New York: NBER.

II Altruism

4 Intergenerational Altruism and the Effectiveness of Fiscal Policy—New Tests Based on Cohort Data

with Andrew B. Abel

In recent years Barro's (1974) ingenious model of intergenerational altruism has taken its place among the major theories of consumption and saving. The model, which starts with the simple assumption that parents care about the welfare of their children, yields the remarkably strong conclusion that, apart from distorting marginal incentives, deficits and all other government redistributions between generations have no effect on the economy. The possibility that deficits, unfunded social security, and similar policies do not matter has received considerable attention.

Despite its policy importance, there have been few direct tests of the intergenerational altruism model. The main difficulty in directly testing the model at the microlevel is the relative lack of data detailing both the consumption and resources of altruistically linked households. In addition, it is difficult to determine from the data which households are altruistically linked to each other. Direct tests of the model with macrodata are also problematic because they require the aggregation of different clans (sets of altruistically linked households) each of which may have a different utility function.

In this essay we present a new direct test of the altruism model. The test is based on a property of the model that, as of the first draft of this essay, had not previously been exploited. This property is that the Euler errors (i.e., disturbances in the Euler equations) of altruistically linked members of clans are identical. Assuming utility is homothetic and time separable, this equality of Euler errors means that, controlling for clan preferences about the age distribution of consumption, the percentage changes over time in consumption of all clan members are equal. Intuitively, since consumption of each clan member is based on overall clan resources, and not on the distribution of resources over clan members, any shocks to the resources of specific clan members will be spread across all clan members. Under the homotheticity and time separability assumptions, spreading shocks over all clan members means changing the consumption of all members by the same percentage.

Ideally, one would test this proposition by simply comparing changes in the consumption of different clan members. Unfortunately, the requisite clan-specific data is not generally available (see Altonji, Hayashi, and Kotlikoff 1992 for an exception); indeed, it may be very difficult to determine who is and who is not a member of a particular altruistically linked clan. As indicated by Kotlikoff (1989) and Bernheim and Bagwell (1988), clans may be quite large because of current as well as potential intermarriage.

How can we use our Consumer Expenditure Survey data on household consumption to test intergenerational altruism when we cannot identify which households should be grouped together in clans? Our test is based on the implication of the altruism model that, after controlling for demographics, all clan members should change their consumption by the same percentage in any given period. If clans are large, and all clans have the same age structure, then the average Euler error in each age group of households in our sample should be the same, under intergenerational altruism. However, the assumption of identical age structures within each clan seems too strong. A weaker assumption is that the age structure of clans is independent of their Euler errors; that is, the fact that a clan accounts for a larger than average fraction of households in an age group does not help predict how its Euler error will differ, on average, from the average Euler error across clans. Even with this weaker assumption we can test the intergenerational altruism hypothesis by comparing the average Euler errors of different age groups.

Testing the altruism model by comparing average cohort percentage changes in consumption is particularly advantageous because it is nonparametric; in determining whether the average consumption of different age cohorts moves together we place no restrictions on preferences beyond the assumptions of homotheticity and time separability. In particular, each clan can have quite different preferences.

The new quarterly Consumer Expenditure Survey (CEX), which, as of the time of this study, is available from the middle of 1980 through the middle of 1985, provides an excellent data set for determining whether the consumption of different age groups moves together. The CES records the consumption of each sample household for up to four quarters, and thus can be used to determine the average quarterly percentage change in consumption of households in a given age group.

The null hypothesis of our test is that, after controlling for demographics, cohort differences in the average percentage change in consumption (average Euler errors) are due simply to sampling and measurement error. Alternative hypotheses, suggested by the life-cycle model, are that, after controlling for demographics, (1) the percentage changes in the average consumption of any two cohorts are more highly correlated the closer in age are the two cohorts, (2) the variance in the percentage change in consumption is a monotone function of the age of the cohort, and (3) cohort differences in consumption changes depend on cohort differences in resource shocks, which may be proxied by cohort differences in income changes. While the data do not reject the altruism model against alternatives (1) and (2), they do reject the altruism model against alternative (3); that is, we find no age structure to the variance-covariance matrix of cohort Euler errors, but we do find that cohort differences in Euler errors are significantly correlated with cohort differences in income changes.

This chapter proceeds in the next section by reviewing briefly the empirical literature bearing on the intergenerational altruism hypothesis. The third section presents the model of altruistically linked households and develops the proposition that Euler errors are equal for all clan members. The fourth section derives a statistical model to test this proposition. The fifth section discusses the statistical implications of the selfish life-cycle model, which represents at least one important alternative to the altruism model. The sixth section describes the data. The seventh section contains the empirical results. The last section summarizes the findings and concludes with a discussion of the implications of the findings for the effectiveness of fiscal policy.

Empirical Research Bearing on the Altruism Hypothesis

The largest body of empirical literature bearing on the altruism hypothesis relates the time series of aggregate consumption to the time series of social security wealth. Chief among these studies are those of Feldstein (1974), Darby (1979), and Leimer and Lesnoy (1980). Studies relating the consumption time series to other aspects of fiscal policy include Kormendi (1983), and Aschauer (1985). The results of this body of research can be summarized with one word: ambiguous. Even were the results all in agreement, it would be difficult to know precisely what had been learned; as pointed out by Auerbach and Kotlikoff (1983) and Williamson and Jones (1983), if the life-cycle model is taken as the null hypothesis in these studies, the models are misspecified because of the inability to aggregate the behavior of different age groups. Auerbach and Kotlikoff (1983) show that the regression procedures would reject the life-cycle model even using data taken from a pure life-cycle economy. An alternative view of these regressions is that the Barro model is the null hypothesis. But in this case many of the regressions also seem to be misspecified both because of aggregation and because they ignore the government's intertemporal budget constraint.

Recent papers by Boskin and Kotlikoff (1986) and Boskin and Lau (1988) directly test the implication of the intergenerational altruism model that the age distribution of resources does not affect the age distribution of consumption. Both reject the proposition that aggregate consumption is invariant to the age distribution of resources. The findings of these two papers accord with the findings reported here that link cohort differences in Euler errors to cohort differences in income changes. Mace (1991) uses the same CES data that we use to test risk sharing. Her findings in support of risk sharing are strongly contradicted by the results reported here as well as by the findings in Altonji, Hayashi, and Kotlikoff 1989.

A different body of literature that is relevant to the altruism model as well as other neoclassical models is the Euler equation studies of Hall (1978), Flavin (1981), Hall and Mishkin (1982), Mankiw, Rothenberg, and Summers (1982), Lawrence (1983), Shapiro (1984), Altonji and Siow (1987), Zeldes (1989), and others. These studies test intertemporal expected utility maximization, specifically its implication that the Euler error is uncorrelated with previous information. A rejection of this null hypothesis would rule out the altruism model as well as other neoclassical consumption models. The time series tests of the Euler equation provide mixed results. In contrast, most microlevel studies appear to accept the Euler equation restriction for the majority of households. For example, both Zeldes (1989) and Lawrence (1983) use the limited consumption data in the Panel Study of Income Dynamics and reach the conclusion that the Euler equation holds for the great majority of households.

The microlevel studies that are closest to our own are Altonji, Hayashi, and Kotlikoff 1992, Townsend 1989, and Cochrane 1991. Altonji, Hayashi, and Kotlikoff use matched consumption and income data on the households of parents and their adult children; their findings strongly reject the altruism model's prediction that the distribution of consumption between parents and children is independent of the distribution of resources between the parent and children. In contrast, Townsend (1989) and Rosenzweig (1988) study the consumption and transfer behavior of households within Indian villages. Townsend reports that the consumption changes of households within each village are highly correlated and Rosenzweig reports substantial income-smoothing transfers; these findings are consistent either with altruism or risk sharing among villagers. Cochran tests for perfect insurance markets with microdata on consumption and certain types of income changes. Not surprisingly, he rejects the proposition that insurance markets are perfect, although he does report that certain income shocks are reasonably well insured.

Finally, there is a microliterature on transfers (see Cox 1987 and Kotlikoff 1988 for summaries) that appears, on balance, to reject the altruism model. Cox (1987), for example, finds that transfers rise with the level of recipients' incomes, and Menchik (1984) reports that, far from being equalizing, most bequests are divided perfectly evenly between children.

The Equal Euler Error Proposition

In this section we model the consumption decisions of households and show that all households within an altruistically linked clan will have the same Euler errors in every period. To model the consumption decisions we must introduce the utility function of the clan. The clan utility function depends on the consumption of present and future households within the clan. We begin by discussing the utility function of a household within a clan at a point in time. After discussing this intratemporal utility function, we combine the intratemporal utility functions of all households in the clan at all points of time.

The Intratemporal Household Utility Function

Let U_{ikt} denote the utility in period t of household k in clan i. The assumptions that the intertemporal utility function is homothetic and time-separable implies that the intratemporal household utility function is isoelastic; that is,

$$U_{i,k,t} = \sum_{a=0}^{D} P_{i,k,t,a}\theta_{i,k,t,a}\frac{c_{i,k,t,a}^{1-\gamma_i}}{(1-\gamma_i)}, \tag{1}$$

where $P_{i,k,t,a}$ is the number of members age a in household k, clan i at time t; D is the maximum age of life; $\theta_{i,k,t,a}$ is the weight household k in clan i places on the utility of members age a at time t; and $c_{i,k,t,a}$ is the consumption of the members of clan i who are in household k and are age a at time t. The utility function in equation 1 is written as a function of the consumption of each of the members of the household. For the isoelastic utility function we can express household utility simply as a function of total household consumption at time t. Let $C_{i,k,t}$ denote household k's total consumption at time t, then:

$$C_{i,k,t} = \sum_{a=0}^{D} P_{i,k,t,a}c_{i,k,t,a}. \tag{2}$$

The optimal allocation of consumption across the individual members of the household is determined by maximizing the intratemporal utility function in equation 1 subject to equation 2. Performing this optimization and substituting the optimal values of $c_{i,k,t,a}$ into equation 1 yields

$$U_{i,k,t} = \phi_{i,k,t_i}\frac{C_{i,k,t}^{1-\gamma_i}}{(1-\gamma_i)} \tag{3a}$$

where

$$\phi_{i,k,t} = \left(\sum_{a=0}^{D} P_{i,k,t,a}\theta_{i,k,t,a}^{1/\gamma_i}\right)^{\gamma_i}. \tag{3b}$$

Equation 3a expresses the utility of the household as a function of total household consumption.

The Clan's Intertemporal Utility Function

The intertemporal utility function of a clan of altruistically linked households is obtained by summing the intratemporal household utility functions across all households in the clan and across the present and all future periods of time, taking account of time preference. Let α_i denote the time preference discount factor for all households in clan i, and let N_{is} denote the number of households in clan i at time s. At time t, the objective function of the clan is

$$V_{i,t} = E_t \sum_{s=t}^{\infty} \alpha_i^{s-t} \sum_{h=1}^{N_{i,s}} \phi_{i,h,s} \frac{C_{i,h,s}^{1-\gamma_i}}{1-\gamma_i}. \tag{4}$$

The clan maximizes equation 4 subject to:

$$W_{i,t+1} = (W_{i,t} + e_{i,t} - C_{i,t} - G_t)(1 + r_{i,t}), \tag{5}$$

where,

$$C_{i,t} = \sum_{h=1}^{N_{i,t}} C_{i,h,t},$$

is total clan i consumption at time t. The term $e_{i,t}$ stands for the possibly uncertain labor earnings of the clan at time t; $r_{i,t}$ is the possibly uncertain rate of return earned by clan i at time t on its portfolio of nonhuman wealth, and $W_{i,t}$ is clan i's net nonhuman wealth at time t. In addition to $e_{i,t}$ and $r_{i,t}$, $\phi_{i,h,s}$ for $s > t$ in equation 4 may be uncertain at time t due to life span uncertainty and uncertainty about clan fertility.

The term G_t in equation 5 stands for government consumption at time t. This is the only way in which fiscal policy enters the clan's budget constraint. Government consumption spending produces an income effect on private consumption spending, because the clan must finance this spending out of its (the economy's) collective output. But regardless of the size of government spending, the budget constraint is invariant to the choice by the government of which clan members will "pay" (mail the government its tax payments) for its spending. The reason is that the clan does its own redistribution across its members, so any redistribution by the government is automatically offset by clan redistribution. The fact that equation 5 does not include any information about the identity of taxpayers automatically implies that government redistribution in this model is ineffective.

The First-Order Conditions

Maximization of equation 4 subject to equation 5 implies the static first-order conditions

$$\phi_{i,k,t}C_{i,k,t}^{-\gamma_i} = \phi_{i,h,,t}C_{i,h,t}^{-\gamma_i}, \tag{6}$$

and the intertemporal first-order conditions

$$E_t[\alpha_i\phi_{i,k,t+1}C_{i,k,t+1}^{-\gamma_i}(1 + r_{i,t+1})] = \phi_{i,k,t}C_{i,k,t}^{-\gamma_i}. \tag{7}$$

The static first-order conditions in equation 6 characterize the optimal allocation of consumption between households h and k within clan i. The intertemporal first-order condition in equation 7 holds for each household within clan i. Let $\varepsilon_{i,k,t+1}$ denote the Euler error at time $t + 1$ for household k in clan i. The Euler error is defined by

$$\alpha_i\phi_{i,k,t+1}C_{i,k,t+1}^{-\gamma_i}(1 + r_{i,t+1}) = E_t[\alpha_i\phi_{i,k,t+1}C_{i,k,t+1}^{-\gamma_i}(1 + r_{i,t+1})]\varepsilon_{i,k,t+1}, \tag{8}$$

where $E_t\varepsilon_{i,k,t+1} = 1$. Using the definition of the Euler error in equation 8 we can rewrite equation 7 as

$$\alpha_i\phi_{i,k,t+1}C_{i,k,t+1}^{-\gamma_i}(1 + r_{i,t+1}) = \phi_{i,k,t}C_{i,k,t}^{-\gamma_i}\varepsilon_{i,k,t+1}. \tag{7'}$$

Equations 6 and 7′ together imply that the Euler errors of all households in clan i are identical. That is,

$$\varepsilon_{i,k,t+1} = \varepsilon_{i,h,t+1} \equiv \varepsilon_{i,t+1}. \tag{9}$$

Note that in deriving this result we did not need to restrict different households in a given clan to have identical age compositions or to receive identical weights in the clan utility function.

Are Euler Errors Equalized under the Life-Cycle Model with Perfect Risk Sharing?

An alternative nonaltruistic model with the implication of equal Euler errors across households is the selfish life-cycle model under the assumption of perfect risk sharing and identical isoelastic preferences and identical time preference rates. To see this, note that the equilibrium of such a life-cycle economy with perfect risk sharing may be represented as the solution to a planning problem in which the planner maximizes a weighted sum of individual household expected intertemporal utilities subject to a collective budget constraint (see Townsend 1989). The division of total consumption at each point in time will depend on the household's weight; that is, equation 6 will hold. In addition, since there is a single budget constraint in this problem, the weighted marginal utility of each household's consumption will be equated to the shadow value of this budget constraint at each point in time. Hence, changes (over time) in the weighted value of each household marginal utility will equal the changes (over time) in these shadow prices; i.e., equation 7′ will hold. Since the shadow prices and their changes are not household specific, the weighted ratio of changes in marginal utilities of consumption will be the same for each household. Hence, equation 9, the equal Euler error proposition, will hold.

A Test of the Equal Euler Error Proposition Based on Cohort Data

In this section we develop a method of testing the equal Euler error proposition using cohort data. We start by taking logarithms of equation 7′, yielding

$$\log(C_{i,k,t+1}/C_{i,k,t}) = (1/\gamma_i)\log(\alpha_i\phi_{i,k,t+1}/\phi_{i,k,t}) - \log[\varepsilon_{i,t+1}/(1+r_{i,t+1})] \tag{10}$$

Consider all households in clan i whose heads are age a. Take the average of equation 10 over all such households. The resulting average of equation 10 is given by equation 11 where we define the averages of the left-hand side and the two terms on the right-hand side of equation 10 respectively by

$$Y^a_{i,t+1} = \psi^a_{i,t+1} + \mu_{i,t+1}. \tag{11}$$

Note that the term $\mu_{i,t+1}$ is not indexed by age since the Euler errors of each household in clan i are identical. Next average equation 11 over all clans. This produces equation 12 where $s^a_{i,t}$ is the fraction of age a households that belong to clan i at time t, and M is the total number of clans.

$$\sum_{i=1}^{M} s^a_{i,t}Y^a_{i,t} = \sum_{i=1}^{M} s^a_{i,t}\psi^a_{i,t} + \sum_{i=1}^{M}\mu_{i,t}/M + \sum_{i=1}^{M} s^a_{i,t}\left(\mu_{i,t} - \sum_{j=1}^{M}\mu_{j,t}/M\right) \tag{12}$$

In equation 12 the cohort average value of $\mu_{i,t}$ is written as the simple unweighted average of the Euler errors across all clans (the second term on the right-hand side of the equation) plus the cohort average value (weighted by each clan's fraction of all cohort households) of the deviation of the clan's Euler error from the unweighted average Euler error over all clans. We assume that this third term on the right-hand side, which is the population covariance between a clan's Euler error and its share of the population in the age group, is zero.

We can rewrite the remaining terms in equation 12 more compactly by letting $\bar{Y}_t^a$ denote the left-hand side of equation 12, $\bar{\psi}_t^a$ denote the first term on the right-hand side of equation 12, and $\bar{\mu}_t$ denote the second term on the right-hand side of equation 12.

$$\bar{Y}_t^a = \bar{\psi}_t^a + \bar{\mu}_t \qquad (12')$$

Equation 12′ states that the cohort average value of the percentage change in consumption (more precisely, the log of the ratio of consumption at $t+1$ to consumption at time t) equals a term, $\bar{\psi}_t^a$, which depends on age and time, plus a term $\bar{\mu}_t$, which is independent of age.

Because of sampling and measurement error, the true population mean, $\bar{Y}_t^a$, is not observable. Hence, in equation 13, we set the observed population-weighted sample mean of the logarithm of the ratio of consumption at time $t+1$ to consumption at time t, $\hat{\bar{Y}}_t^a$, equal to the true population mean, $\bar{Y}_t^a$, plus a term, η_t^a, that reflects sampling and measurement error. Our null hypothesis is that $\eta_t^a = \omega_t^a / h_t^a$, where ω_t^a is an independently and normally distributed random variable with mean zero and variance σ^2, and h_t^a adjusts for the sampling error in our weighted estimate of $\bar{Y}_t^a$. Specifically, h_t^a equals $\Sigma_k {w_{tk}^a}^2 / (\Sigma_k w_{tk}^a)^2$, where w_{tk}^a is the CEX population weight at time t for household k in cohort a. In equation 12′ the term $\bar{\psi}_t^a$ reflects the average growth in consumption due to demographic changes in household composition. Since we are dealing with data over only a five year interval, in equation 13 we drop the time subscript and treat $\bar{\psi}_t^a$ as a time-invariant, but age-specific constant.

$$\hat{\bar{Y}}_t^a = \bar{\psi}^a + \bar{\mu}_t + \eta_t^a \qquad (13)$$

Equation 13 forms the basis for our statistical test of the equality of average cohort percentage changes in consumption. Under the null hypothesis of equal Euler errors, ω_{at} is i.i.d. across ages a and time periods t with variance equal to σ^2.

If the null hypothesis fails to hold and the weighted average Euler errors differ across age cohorts, the error term η_t^a will capture not only measurement and sampling noise, but also each cohort's time t average Euler error after controlling for age and time effects. Our alternative hypothesis is, therefore, that the ω_{at}s are not simply i.i.d., but depend on age as specified below.

$$E(\omega_{it}\omega_{js}) = 0 \quad \text{if } s \neq t$$

$$E(\omega_{it}\omega_{jt}) = \rho^{|i-j|}\sigma^2 v^{i+j} \qquad (14)$$

According to equation 14 the variance of ω_{it} increases or decreases with age depending on whether v exceeds or falls short of unity, and the correlation of ω_{it} and ω_{jt} for $i \neq j$ depends on the size of the age gap, $|j - i|$. For example, if ρ exceeds zero, equation 14 says that the correlation of ω_{it} and ω_{jt} for age groups i and j is larger the closer in age are the age groups i and j. The case in which $\rho = 0$ and $v = 1$ corresponds to the null hypothesis. Values of ρ and v as well as the age and time effects in equation 13 are estimated by maximum likelihood. The Appendix presents the likelihood function and derives the estimators.

Another testable implication of equation 13 is that η_t^a is uncorrelated with changes in cohort a's resources, which may be proxied by changes in its income. To see this note that in equation 13 the term $\bar{\mu}_t$, which equals the common (across cohorts) average Euler error, fully controls for resource changes under the altruism model. Hence, if one adds cohort a's income change to the implicit regression model in equation 13, the coefficient on the cohort's income change should be zero. Another way of saying this is that differences across cohorts with respect to consumption changes should depend only on differences in their demographics (the $\bar{\psi}^a$ terms) and not on the distribution across cohorts of income changes. In addition to testing whether there is a significant age pattern to the variance-covariance matrix of the η_t^as, we add the cohort's income change to equation 13 and estimate the model by ordinary least squares. This procedure is, in differences, the fixed effects test of altruism developed in Altonji, Hayashi, and Kotlikoff 1989.

Consumption Behavior of Selfish Life-Cycle Households: An Alternative Hypothesis

This section motivates the assumption of an age-dependent variance-covariance matrix of the η_t^as under the alternative life-cycle model. The null hypothesis of operative altruistic linkages is that the Euler error is identical across households within a clan; hence, within a clan the Euler error is independent of the age of the household head. In contrast, under the life-cycle model Euler errors of different households within a clan bear no special relation to one another, but we would expect that the variance-covariance matrix of Euler errors across unrelated as well as related households would depend on the households' ages. This section illustrates, with two different preference structures and types of uncertainty, why ρ is likely to differ from zero and v is likely to differ from unity if the life-cycle model holds.

Example 1: Logarithmic Utility

The first example is based on Samuelson 1969 and assumes only uncertainty with respect to the rate of return. Let $c_{t,a}$ be the consumption at time t of a household whose head is age a; $w_{t,a}$ is the wealth at time t of a household whose head is age a. The decision problem at time t, when the household is age a, is to maximize

$$E_t\left[\sum_{j=0}^{D-a}\beta^j u(c_{t+j,a+j})\right], \tag{15}$$

and

$$w_{t+1,a+1} = (w_{t,a} - c_{a,t})R_{t+1,a+1}, \tag{16}$$

where D is the age at which the household head dies and $R_{t+1,a+1}$ is the gross rate of return on the portfolio from period t to period $t+1$. Now suppose that the utility function is logarithmic, $u(c) = \log c$. This optimization problem can be solved by stochastic dynamic programming (Samuelson 1969) to obtain

$$c_{t,D-j} = g_j w_{t,D-j}, \tag{17a}$$

where

$$g_j = \left(\sum_{k=0}^{j}\beta^k\right)^{-1}. \tag{17b}$$

This solution holds regardless of the temporal dependence of the process generating returns $R_{t+1,a+1}$.

Now consider the growth rate in consumption from period t to period $t+1$. It follows directly from equation 17a that

$$c_{t+1,a+1}/c_{t,a} = (g_{j-1}/g_j)(w_{t+1,a+1}/w_{t,a}). \tag{18}$$

The ratio of wealth in successive periods can be rewritten using equations 16 and 17a as

$$w_{t+1,a+1}/w_{t,a} = (1-g_j)R_{t+1,a+1}. \tag{19}$$

Substituting equation 19 into equation 18 yields

$$c_{t+1,a+1}/c_{t,a} = (g_{j-1}/g_j)(1 - g_j)R_{t+1,a+1}. \tag{20}$$

Finally, we can use the expression for g_j in equation 17b to simplify the expression for the growth rate of consumption in equation 20 to obtain

$$c_{t+1,a+1}/c_{t,a} = \beta R_{t+1,a+1}. \tag{21}$$

The growth rate of consumption is proportional to the realized gross rate of return from period t to period $t+1$. If the gross rate of return on a household's portfolio is independent of the age of the household head then $R_{t+1,a+1} = R_{t+1}$ for all a. In this case, all households will have the same Euler error regardless of the age of the household head.

Taken at face value, this example suggests that the Euler error is independent of the age of the household head. However, this conclusion depends on the assumption that $R_{t+1,a+1} = R_{t+1}$ for all a. This assumption would be warranted if all households held the same portfolios (up to a scale factor) regardless of age. However, as documented in King and Leape 1984 the composition of actual U.S. household portfolios is significantly different depending on the age of the household head. Young and middle-age households tend to hold a large portion of their wealth in the form of negative holdings of fixed income securities (mortgages), significant holdings of housing, and small holdings of stocks and bonds. Older households, in contrast, hold much more of their wealth in the form of home equity (i.e., their outstanding mortgages are much smaller) and in stocks and bonds.

Because the allocation of portfolios varies systematically with age, and because the rates of return on different assets reflect different stochastic processes, we might expect the conditional variances of the portfolio rates of return, $R_{t+1,a+1}$, to vary systematically with age. Furthermore, because the composition of portfolios is more similar for similar aged households than for households of very different ages, we might expect the Euler errors to be more highly correlated for households of similar age than for households of very different ages.

Example 2: Quadratic Utility

In order to focus on the role of human wealth, as distinct from nonhuman wealth, we change the framework slightly. Now we suppose that utility is quadratic and that the rate of return on nonhuman wealth is constant. In addition, assume that the gross rate of return on nonhuman wealth, R, is equal to β^{-1} (the reciprocal of the time preference discount factor). The only uncertainty that the household faces is in labor income $y_{t,a}$. In this case, it is straightforward to apply the certainty equivalence principle to obtain:

$$E_t(c_{t+j,a+j}) = c_{t,a} \quad \text{for } j = 0, 1, 2, \ldots, D-a. \tag{22}$$

The lifetime budget constraint of the household implies that the present value of revisions in future labor income, $E_{t+1}(y_{t+1+j,a+1+j}) - E_t(y_{t+1+j,a+1+j})$, is equal to the present value of revisions in future consumption, $E_{t+1}(c_{t+1+j,a+1+j}) - E_t(c_{t+1+j,a+1+j})$. Such that

$$\sum_{j=0}^{D-a-1} R^{-j}[E_{t+1}(y_{t+1+j,a+1+j}) - E_t(y_{t+1+j,a+1+j})]$$
$$= \sum_{j=0}^{D-a-1} R^{-j}[E_{t+1}(c_{t+1+j,a+1+j}) - E_t(c_{t+1+j,a+1+j})]. \tag{23}$$

Equation 22 implies that the revisions in expectations of future consumption are equal to the change in consumption between period t and period $t+1$, hence:

$$E_{t+1}(c_{t+1+j,a+1+j}) - E_t(c_{t+1+j,a+1+j}) = c_{t+1,a+1} - c_{t,a} \equiv \Delta c_{t+1,a+1}. \tag{24}$$

To calculate the revision in expectations of future labor income, we first specify the moving average representation of the process for labor income as

$$y_{t,a} = \sum_{k=0}^{a} \xi_k e_{t-k,a-k} + \bar{y}_{t,a}, \tag{25}$$

where $E_{t-1}\{e_{t,a}\} = 0$. With this time series process for labor income, the revisions in expected future (between time t and time $t+1$) labor income at time $t+1$ are

$$E_{t+1}(y_{t+1+j,a+1+j}) - E_t(y_{t+1+j,a+1+j}) = \xi_j e_{t+1,a+1}. \tag{26}$$

Substituting the revisions in future consumption equation 24 and the revisions in future labor income equation 26 into equation 23 we obtain

$$\Delta c_{t+1,a+1} = \Gamma_a e_{t+1,a+1}, \tag{27a}$$

where

$$\Gamma_a \equiv \left(\sum_{j=0}^{D-a-1} R^{-j} \xi_j \right) \Bigg/ \left(\sum_{j=0}^{D-a-1} R^{-j} \right). \tag{27b}$$

The variance of the unforecastable change in consumption, which in this example is equal to the variance of the actual change in consumption, is

$$\text{var}(\Delta c_{t+1,a+1}) = \Gamma_a^2 \text{ var}(e_{t+1,a+1}). \tag{28}$$

Note that even if the variance of the innovation to the labor income process, $\text{var}(e_{t+1,a+1})$, is independent of age, the variance of the unforecastable change in consumption is age-dependent because Γ_a is, in general, age-dependent. For instance, if the labor income process is i.i.d., then $\xi_0 = 1$ and $\xi_j = 0$ for all nonzero j. In this case,

$$\Gamma_a = \left(\sum_{j=0}^{D-a-1} R^{-j} \right)^{-1},$$

which is an increasing function of age. Alternatively, if the labor income process is a first-order auto-regressive progress with AR coefficient ρ, then $\xi_j = \rho^j$. In this case, $\Gamma_a = [(1 - R^{-1})/(1 - \rho/R)] \times [1 - (\rho/R)^{D-a})/(1 - (1/R)^{D-a})]$. If the process is stationary and ρ is nonnegative, then Γ_a is increasing with age. For a random walk, $\rho = 1$ and $\Gamma_a = 1$ independent of age. If ρ is greater than 1, then Γ_a is decreasing with age.

Equation 28 gives the variance of the Euler error expressed in terms of the change in the level of consumption rather than the change in the logarithm of consumption. In this model, the age-consumption profile will, on average, be flat. Hence, on average, the variance of the percentage change in consumption will vary with age if the variance of the absolute change in consumption varies by age.

The Data

The ongoing Consumer Expenditure Survey (CEX), which began in the first quarter of 1980, interviews approximately 4,500 households in each quarter. Most households are interviewed four times in the CES. The four interviews always ask a common set of questions about consumption, but some questions are asked only in the first and fourth interviews, and others are asked only in the fourth interview. Some households are interviewed fewer than four times because they drop out of the sample. Others are interviewed fewer than four times because of the sample design; in an effort to maintain in each quarter the same fraction of households responding to a first, second, third, and fourth interview, the CEX administers the second, third, or fourth interviews to some households as their initial interview. If the household's initial interview is a second interview, the household will be interviewed two more times. If a household's initial interview is a third interview, the household will be interviewed once more. And if the household's initial interview is a fourth interview, the household will not be reinterviewed.

The approximately 4,500 interviews in each quarter are spread over each month of the quarter. In the interviews households are asked about their consumption expenditures in the previous three months. Hence, a household interviewed in January 1981 reports consumption expenditures for October, November, and December 1980, while a household interviewed in March 1981 reports consumption expenditures for December 1980 and January and February 1981. Unfortunately, for most expenditure items, households only report total expenditures in the previous three full months and do not provide a month-to-month breakdown of those expenditures. As a consequence, the data for a household interviewed, say, in January cannot readily be combined with data from a household interviewed in February since the two quarterly observations cover overlapping, rather than identical quarters. In effect, each wave of the Consumer Expenditure Survey provides three overlapping sets of observations on quarterly consumption. In our analysis we treat each of the three quarterly data sets separately and refer to them as "quarterly sample" 1, 2, and 3.[1] For purposes of analyzing the quarterly data we considered fifty-eight age cohorts corresponding to ages 23 through 80.

Given the lumpiness of some nondurable consumption expenditures, such as vacation trips, it is useful to test the equal Euler error proposition with semiannual as well as quarterly data. For those households who were interviewed four times, the four quarterly observations can be combined to form observations on semiannual consumption. There are six possible semiannual data sets. For example, households interviewed in January, April, July, and October in year t provide an observation on the ratio of consumption over the period April–September in year t to consumption over the period October in year $t-1$–March in year t. Households interviewed in July and October of year t and January and April of year $t+1$ provide an observation on the ratio of consumption over the period October in year t–March in year $t+1$ to consumption over the period April–September in year t. These types of observations produce a single data set of semiannual changes in consumption. One can also form a data set using households interviewed for the first of four times in April and other households interviewed for the first of four times in October. Hence, the April-July-October-January sequence provides two semiannual data sets. The May-August-November-February sequence provides another two semiannual data sets; and the June-September-December-March sequence provides the final two semiannual data sets.

Because of the smaller number of households who completed all four surveys, we constructed three-year age cohorts; i.e., we combined ages 23, 24, and 25 into one age group, ages 26, 27, and 28 into another age group, etc., up to the age group covering ages 77, 78, and 79. This difference in the definition of an age cohort should be kept in mind when comparing the quarterly and semiannual results presented in the next section; because of the difference in definitions, one would expect the estimated values of ρ and ν based on the semiannual data to be roughly the cube of their respective values based on the quarterly data.

The definition of aggregate consumption used in this study is total consumption expenditures excluding expenditures on housing, insurance, and consumer durables. We exclude housing both because adjustments to housing consumption are infrequent and because it is very difficult to impute quarterly or semiannual rent accurately for homeowners. Insurance expenditures were excluded because such expenditures represent risk pooling as opposed to consumption per se. In addition, the data records both negative and positive amounts of insurance expenditures, where a negative amount corresponds to a claim payment. Expenditures on durables should clearly be excluded from the definition of consumption. In contrast, imputed rent should be included; unfortunately, data on the stocks of durables are not sufficient for that purpose.

The CEX provides population weights in each quarter for each household interviewed. These weights depend on the age of the household head as well as other economic and demographic characteristics. We use the time $t+1$ sample weights in determining the cohort-specific weighted average value of the logarithm of the ratio of consumption at time $t+1$ to consumption at time t; that is, we construct a weighted value of $\bar{Y}_{at}$.

Households that reported less than \$150 of quarterly expenditure on food were excluded from the sample. This is the only form of sample selection in our analysis. Some preliminary analysis indicated that including households with very small quarterly food expenditure would not materially alter the results.

Empirical Findings

Changes in the Age-Consumption Profile over the Sample Period

As a prelude to examining estimates of ρ and v, figure 4.1 illustrates how the age-consumption profile changed over the period 1980

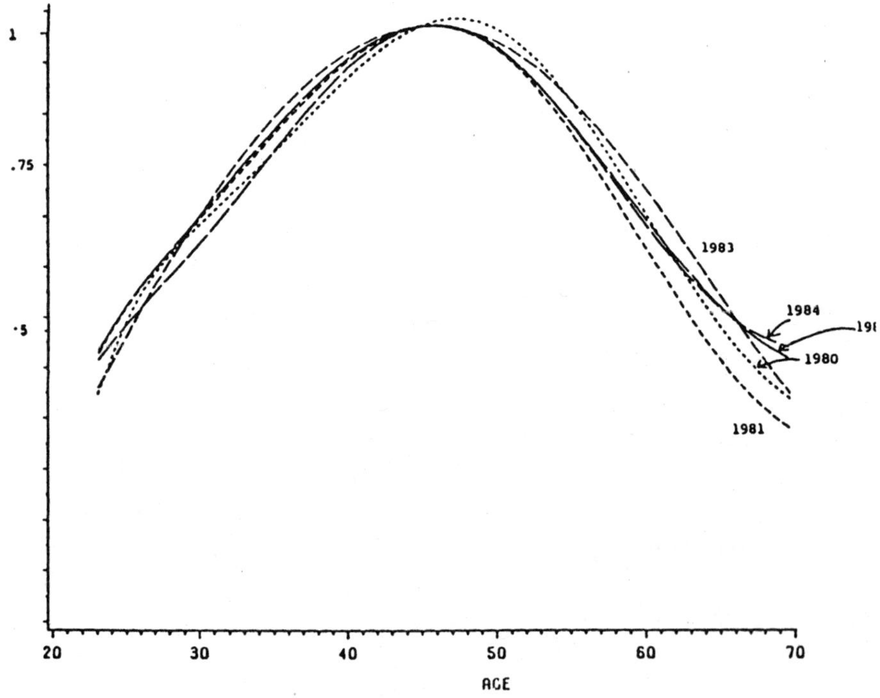

Figure 4.1
Age consumption profile, 1980–1985

through 1984. Ignoring demographic change, the proposition that each cohort's consumption should change, on average, by the same percentage, implies a time-invariant age-consumption profile. In forming figure 4.1 we calculated the annual weighted average of quarterly consumption (measured in 1985 dollars) at each individual age for households interviewed in April, August, and December of each of the five years. We combined these weighted averages within each calendar year to produce annual values of average consumption by age of the household. Next we divided annual consumption in year t at each age by the average consumption of 45-year-old households in year t. Finally, we smoothed these relative consumption values for each year by regressing them against an intercept and a fourth order polynomial in age. In these regressions the R^2 values each exceed 0.9. Figure 4.1 plots the resulting five smoothed polynomials of consumption at a particular age relative to consumption at age 45. ries: 23–29, 30–39, 40–49, 50–59, 60–69, and 70+. For each of these six age groups we report quarterly values of 100 times the deviation of the weighted average $\hat{\bar{Y}}_t^a$ from the mean value, $\Sigma_{t=1}^{19} \hat{\bar{Y}}_t^a$, taken over the nineteen quarters in our sample. According to equation 12′ and ignoring measurement and sampling error, these deviations, which we refer to as average adjusted Euler errors, should be identical for each of the six age groups. In addition to presenting these deviations, table 4.1 reports the standard deviations of these deviations. These standard deviations are based on information on the variation across households in the percentage change in consumption within age-time cells.

Table 4.1 indicates that these average adjusted Euler errors are typically different across the six age categories. However, these differences could well be due to within cell variation. The standard errors of the entries in table 4.1 are quite large.

Another informal way to assess the data is to regress $\hat{\bar{Y}}_t^a$ on a set of age group dummies and time dummies, either quarterly or semiannual.[2] The results from this regression can be compared with the results from regressing the same dependent variable on age dummies and the interaction of each of the time dummies with each of the age dummies.[3] According to equation 13, given a particular time period t, the age-time interactions should have identical coefficients. For purposes of this regression using quarterly data, we constructed six age dummies corresponding to the six age groups of table 4.1. The F values for quarterly samples 1, 2, and 3 are 1.470, 1.237, 0.746,

Table 4.1
Quarterly estimates of average adjusted Euler errors, quarterly sample I

Age group	1980.3	1980.4	1981.1	1981.2
23–29	−.033 (0.204)	.055 (.178)	.074 (.178)	−.105 (.181)
30–39	−.101 (0.210)	.057 (.181)	.052 (.178)	−.087 (.174)
40–49	−.084 (0.198)	.100 (.182)	−.004 (.175)	−.082 (.192)
50–59	−.154 (0.179)	.041 (.175)	−.002 (.181)	−.027 (.183)
60–69	−.130 (0.193)	.015 (.220)	.024 (.169)	.006 (.207)
70+	−.109 (0.185)	.010 (.202)	.099 (.170)	−.020 (.202)
	1981.3	1981.4	1982.1	1982.2
23–29	−.050 (.187)	−.007 (.183)	−.115 (.182)	.031 (.175)
30–39	.056 (.181)	.017 (.189)	−.061 (.185)	−.055 (.193)
40–49	−.060 (.199)	.031 (.199)	−.076 (.179)	−.024 (.201)
50–59	−.074 (.180)	.004 (.181)	−.020 (.180)	−.032 (.179)
60–69	−.038 (.204)	−.071 (.223)	−.023 (.173)	−.094 (.199)
70+	−.154 (.198)	.105 (.236)	−.123 (.174)	.140 (.196)
	1982.3	1982.4	1983.1	1983.2
23–29	−.006 (.182)	.020 (.184)	.029 (.179)	−.048 (.177)
30–39	−.014 (.201)	−.010 (.197)	.111 (.182)	−.052 (.178)
40–49	−.008 (.200)	.008 (.195)	.088 (.177)	−.038 (.181)
50–59	−.062 (.180)	−.016 (.188)	.052 (.174)	−.020 (.209)
60–69	−.035 (.193)	−.077 (.202)	.049 (.175)	−.101 (.200)
70+	−.108 (.209)	.009 (.219)	.112 (.179)	−.110 (.222)
	1983.3	1983.4	1984.1	1984.2
23–29	.032 (.184)	−.003 (.175)	.015 (.176)	−.076 (.205)
30–39	−.031 (.181)	.011 (.230)	.008 (.187)	−.061 (.183)
40–49	−.004 (.183)	.065 (.180)	−.011 (.176)	−.060 (.181)
50–59	.042 (.207)	.012 (.183)	.011 (.174)	−.027 (.186)
60–69	−.020 (.221)	.012 (.217)	−.064 (.173)	−.003 (.181)
70+	−.020 (.212)	.019 (.196)	−.012 (.178)	.009 (.190)
	1984.3	1984.4	1985.1	
23–29	−.021 (.213)	.046 (.207)	−.011 (.188)	
30–39	.020 (.185)	.027 (.185)	.034 (.185)	
40–49	.025 (.183)	.034 (.185)	.032 (.186)	
50–59	.007 (.191)	−.034 (.194)	−.065 (.181)	
60–69	−.011 (.178)	−.046 (.180)	.014 (.176)	
70+	−.015 (.186)	−.029 (.190)	.016 (.176)	

Note: Standard deviations are in parentheses.

Table 4.2
Maximum likelihood estimates and χ^2 values: quarterly samples

	Consumption measured per household						
	Unconstrained		$\rho = 0$		$v = 1$		$\rho = 0$ $v = 1$
Sample	ρ	v	v	χ^2	ρ	χ^2	χ^2
Sample 1	0.020	1.002	1.002	0.958	0.003	1.307	2.345
Sample 2	−0.024	1.000	1.000	0.611	−0.024	0.000	0.611
Sample 3	0.031	1.000	1.000	1.066	0.031	0.000	1.066

Note: Five percent critical values for χ^2 are 5.991 for two restrictions and 3.841 for one restriction.

respectively. Since the $F(90, 987)$, 5 percent critical value is 1.27, the age-time interactions are significantly different in only one of the three quarterly samples. The $F(25, 103)$ values in the corresponding regressions for the six semiannual samples are 0.912, 2.414, 2.538, 1.485, 1.768, and 0.612. The 5 percent critical value in this case is 1.61. Hence, age-time interactions are significantly different in three of the six semiannual samples.

Table 4.2 presents our maximum likelihood estimates for ρ and v for the three quarterly data sets based on individual age cohorts from age 23 through age 80. None of the reported estimates of these parameters is significantly different from the values predicted by the null hypothesis of intergenerational altruism. Indeed, in the case of v, two of the three estimates are equal to 1, to three decimal places, and the third value of 1.002 implies that the variance of ω_{it} for 70-year-olds is only about 15 percent larger than the corresponding variance for 20-year-olds. One of the three point estimates for ρ is negative; a negative value of ρ, even were it significant, seems highly unlikely from the perspective of the life-cycle model. The other two non-negative values of ρ suggest a very small correlation between the consumption of adjacent age groups. Even if these estimates were significant, their values seem quite small.

The likelihood functions associated with table 4.2 are rather sharply peaked; hence, one can reject values of ρ and v that are substantially different (in an economic sense) from the maximum likelihood estimates. Table 4.3 presents the range of values of ρ and v that fall within 95 percent chi-squared confidence intervals around the maximum likelihood estimates.[4] According to the table, even if one takes the largest values of ρ and v that cannot be rejected by the data,

Table 4.3
95 Percent confidence intervals for ρ and v: quarterly estimates

	Consumption measured per household					
	Maximum likelihood		v Range		ρ Range	
Sample	ρ	v	High	Low	High	Low
Sample 1	0.020	1.002	1.005	0.999	.095	−0.030
Sample 2	−0.024	1.000	1.003	0.997	.020	−0.099
Sample 3	0.031	1.000	1.003	0.997	.106	−0.044

the resulting estimates provide no strong evidence of substantial departure from the null hypothesis of intergenerational altruism.

Since many of the consumption expenditures included in our definition of nondurable expenditure may not be made each quarter, the results in table 4.2 may, in part, reflect the lumpiness of nondurable expenditures; that is, the variance in consumption changes due to the lumpiness of expenditures may dominate the results. Hence, it may be useful to repeat the analysis using simply food expenditure, which is much less lumpy than, for example, clothing expenditure or vacation trips. The results based on quarterly food expenditures are quite similar to the results based on total nondurable, non-housing consumption expenditure. The point estimates in the three samples of ρ are −0.059, −0.068, and 0.002. The point estimates of v in the three samples are 1.001, 0.998, and 1.003. The estimates of ρ and v are not jointly significantly different from 0 and 1, respectively; the respective x^2 values for the three samples for the joint test that $\rho = 0$ and $v = 1$ are 4.087, 4.991, and 4.757—all of which lie below the 5 percent critical value of 5.991.

Another way to consider the lumpiness of expenditures is to repeat the analysis with semiannual data. Table 4.4 presents the results based on the six semiannual consumption data sets, which, as mentioned, combine three ages into a single-age cohort. Once again, none of the estimates of ρ and v are separately or jointly significantly different from the null hypothesis values of $\rho = 0$ and $v = 1$. Three of the six point estimates of v lie above 1 and three lie below 1. Three of the six point estimates of ρ are positive and three are negative. Hence, like the quarterly estimates, there is no suggestion in the data that the null hypothesis is strongly disfavored. Unlike the quarterly results, however, several of the estimates of v are economically more

Table 4.4
Maximum likelihood estimates and χ^2 values: semiannual samples

	Consumption Measured per household						
	Unconstrained		$\rho = 0$		$v = 1$		$\rho = 0$ $v = 1$
Consumption category	ρ	v	v	χ^2	ρ	χ^2	χ^2
Sample 1	−0.133	1.007	1.009	2.531	−0.136	0.409	3.101
Sample 2	−0.142	1.008	1.009	2.945	−0.142	0.478	3.490
Sample 3	0.087	0.990	0.991	0.024	0.080	0.706	1.585
Sample 4	0.055	0.991	0.992	0.467	0.049	0.555	0.918
Sample 5	−0.072	0.984	0.984	0.719	−0.069	2.377	3.054
Sample 6	0.050	1.022	1.022	0.353	0.051	3.679	4.048

Note: Five percent critical values for χ^2 are 5.991 for two restrictions and 3.841 for one restriction.

important. For example, the estimate for v in the sixth sample of 1.022 implies that the variance of ω_{it} for very old households is over 1.7 times the variance for very young households. In addition, for each of the six samples the confidence intervals around v include economically significant as well as economically insignificant values. Thus the semiannual results do not provide as strong evidence against the life-cycle model as do the quarterly results. It may be that quarterly changes and even semiannual changes in consumption reflect quite lumpy expenditures and that testing the equal Euler error proposition on annual or even biannual would be more appropriate. Unfortunately, appropriate data for such an analysis do not currently exist.

One might question whether we have properly controlled for demographic change in treating $\bar{\psi}^a$ as an age-specific, time-invariant constant. One way to consider whether the results are sensitive to treatment of demographics is to reestimate the model defining household consumption as household consumption per household member or per adult equivalent in the household; in forming adult equivalents we treat each child under age 18 as equal to 0.5 adults. We tried each of these alternative definitions of household consumption. The quarterly results are essentially the same as those in table 4.2.[5] The semiannual results are only slightly different from those in table 4.4; when consumption is measured either as household consumption per member or per equivalent adult, the null hypothesis is rejected in only two of the six semiannual samples.[6]

Are Cohort Euler Errors Correlated with Cohort Changes in Income?

One question that may be raised with respect to the empirical findings in the above subsection is the power of the tests against the life-cycle alternative. While we have argued that the variance-covariance matrix of cohort Euler errors is likely to be age-dependent under the life-cycle model, there are some combinations of life-cycle preference structures and distributions of cohort-specific resource shocks that also satisfy the null hypothesis of $v = 1$ and $\rho = 0$. A potentially more powerful method for testing altruism against the life-cycle alternative is to ask whether, in addition to age dummies and time dummies (that control for common resource shocks), cohort-specific income changes enter significantly in a regression explaining cohort average percentage changes in consumption. Because the CEX asked about income only in its first and fourth interviews, we only have two observations on income. Hence, we considered only households with four complete surveys and formed, for each of the three-year age groups, the average percentage change in income and consumption between the first and fourth interviews. We did this for each of the three quarterly samples.

Table 4.5 reports the income change coefficients for two different sets of regressions. In the first set we control for common resource shocks by including time dummies. In the second set we exclude the time dummies. Table 4.5 contains the results from the regressions for each of the quarterly samples, plus the results from pooling the three quarterly samples. In the case of the pooled regression with time dummies, we include different time dummies for each quarterly sample since, as described above, the quarterly samples cover somewhat different time intervals.

Table 4.5
Cohort average income change coefficients

	Regressions with time dummies		Regressions without time dummies	
Sample	Coefficient	*t*-statistic	Coefficient	*t*-statistic
Quarterly sample 1	.035	1.52	.011	.38
Quarterly sample 2	.068	3.58	.027	.85
Quarterly sample 3	.066	2.70	.034	1.19
Pooled sample	.052	3.57	.026	1.53

Consider the regressions including the time dummies. In two of three quarterly samples and in the case of the pooled regression, the coefficients on cohort income changes are statistically significant. In addition, the point estimates are economically large in the sense that they are even larger than the point estimates one obtains if one does not control for common resource shocks through the time dummies. These results constitute evidence against the altruism model and evidence for the life-cycle model.[7]

The Implications of the Findings for the Effectiveness of Fiscal Policy

In this chapter we have used cohort data to test the standard model of operative altruistic linkages. The altruism model in contrast to the standard (no-risk-sharing) life-cycle model suggests that (1) after controlling for demographics, consumption changes for different cohorts should, on average, be identical and (2) that, after controlling for demographics, differences across cohorts in their changes in consumption should not be correlated with their income changes. The life-cycle model plus the assumption of perfect risk sharing also delivers these two testable propositions. We tested the first implication by asking whether, after controlling for demographics and common resource shocks, the variance-covariance matrix of consumption changes is age-dependent; we tested the second implication by determining whether differences across cohorts in consumption changes depend on differences across cohorts in their income changes.

We were not able to reject the first implication of the altruism model, but we were able to reject the second. Hence, on balance, our results reject the altruism model and, by extension, the life-cycle model with risk sharing in favor of the standard (no-risk-sharing) life-cycle alternative. An important attribute of these results is that they are nonparametric in nature; specifically, in comparing the average change in consumption across age groups, we place no restrictions on preferences beyond the assumptions of homotheticity and time separability. Our rejection of risk sharing based on cohort data accords with the findings on microdata of Altonji, Hayashi, and Kotlikoff (1992).

While our findings rule out the standard model of altruism in which information is symmetric, one can construct more elaborate models of altruism with information asymmetries in which clan member Euler errors do depend on the clan members' particular income realizations. For example, Kotlikoff and Razin (1988) present a model in which altruistic parents cannot observe their children's work efforts. To avoid being manipulated by children who take it easy and claim their earnings are low because they have low ability, parents will condition their transfers on the observable earnings of their children. In this model, government redistribution between parents and children, assuming it is observable, would not change the parents' information sets and would, therefore, be completely offset by the parents in their private transfer behavior.

However, for this asymmetric information model to be plausible one would expect to see annual or at least periodic inter vivos transfers to children, with these transfers depending on the donor's income. But all the cross-section studies of U.S. private transfers suggest that, apart from the very wealthy, the vast majority of U.S. citizens neither receive nor make transfers on a routine basis. In addition, the evidence on U.S. bequests indicates that they are almost always divided equally among children with no regard to their children's current, let alone past, earnings. These facts seem strong evidence against altruism models with asymmetric information.

If one rejects, as do we, the standard as well as more elaborate varieties of the altruism model, one is left with the following implication: government redistribution between cohorts will raise the consumption of cohorts receiving the transfers and lower the consumption of those making the transfers. But what is the implication of this for national consumption and national saving? In the case of policies that redistribute from future generations to current generations, the implication is clearly an increase in national consumption and a decline in national saving. Even policies that simply redistribute between currently living cohorts will lower national saving if the redistribution runs from younger to older cohorts. The reason is that older cohorts, at least in the United States, appear to have substantially higher propensities to consume than do younger cohorts out of their remaining lifetime resources.[8]

The deleterious impact of intergenerational redistribution on national saving is more than a theoretical possibility. In the past four decades the U.S. government has engineered a massive intergenerational redistribution toward older generations of the day and away from all generations coming behind them (see Kotlikoff 1992). Simulation studies of life-cycle models suggest that such redistribution would seriously lower U.S. savings and capital formation. This is indeed what has transpired. Since 1980 the United States has been saving at about two-fifths the rate observed in the prior three decades. This reduced saving cannot be attributed to increased government consumption since government spending on goods and services relative to NNP has remained roughly constant since the mid-1950s. Rather it reflects an increase in the rate of private sector consumption out of the annual output left over after government consumption is netted out. If this increase in private sector consumption is due to redistribution toward the elderly, one would expect to observe a shift since the 1950s in the shape of the cross-section, age-consumption profile, with the relative consumption of the elderly increasing over time. This is precisely what is emerging from preliminary analysis of the 1962–63, 1972–73, and the 1980s Consumer Expenditure Survey (see Gokhale, Kotlikoff, Sabelhaus 1996).

To conclude, this chapter contributes to a growing body of findings that document the effectiveness of intergenerational redistribution in raising the consumption of generations receiving income from the government and lowering the consumption of generations giving income to the government. While the precise effect of postwar U.S. intergenerational redistribution on U.S. saving may never be known, the available evidence from this and other studies suggest that past and present U.S. intergenerational redistribution may well be the main reason for the long term and continuing decline in U.S. saving.

Appendix: The Likelihood Function and The Derivation of The Estimators

Under our assumption that the η_t^as are normal and independent across time, the log of the likelihood function, L, is given by:

$$L = \log K - \frac{1}{2}\sum_{t=1}^{T} \log|V_t| - \frac{1}{2}\sum_{t=1}^{T} \eta_t' V_t^{-1} \eta_t \tag{A.1}$$

where $\eta_t = Y_t - \psi - \mu_t^i$. The term Y_t is a column vector whose elements are $\hat{Y}_t^a$. The vector ψ captures the time-invariant, age-specific constants arising in equation (4.13) when $\bar{\psi}_t^a$ is time invariant. The vector i is a column vector of 1s. The term T equals the number of time periods in our data set.

The matrix V_t equals $H_t'VH_t$, and V is defined by

$$V = \sigma^2 \begin{vmatrix} v^2 & \rho v^3 & & \cdot & \cdot \\ \rho v^3 & v^4 & \cdot & & \\ \cdot & \cdot & \cdot & \cdot & \cdot \\ \rho^{N-2} v^N & \rho^{N-3} v^{N+1} & \cdot & v^{2N-2} & \rho v^{2N-1} \\ \rho^{N-1} v^{N+1} & \rho^{N-2} v^{N+2} & & \rho v^{2N-1} & v^{2N} \end{vmatrix}$$

where N is the number of age cohorts (58 in the case of quarterly data and 19 in the case of semiannual data) in our data, and

$$H_t = \begin{vmatrix} h_{1t} & 0 & \cdot & \cdot & \cdot & 0 \\ 0 & & \cdot & \cdot & & \cdot \\ \cdot & & & & \cdot & 0 \\ 0 & & \cdot & \cdot & 0 & \cdot & h_{nt} \end{vmatrix} \quad \text{where}$$

h_{at} equals $\sum_k w_{atk}^2 \Big/ \left(\sum_k w_{atk}^2 \right)$ and

where w_{atk} is the CEX population weight of household k, which is age a at time t.

The first-order conditions resulting from maximizing equation A.1 with respect to ψ, μ_t, and σ^2 are given respectively in equations A.2, A.3, A.4:

$$\sum_{t=1}^{T} V_t^{-1} \eta_t = 0 \tag{A.2}$$

$$i V_t'^{-1} \eta_t = 0 \tag{A.3}$$

$$NT = \sum_{t=1}^{T} \eta'_t V_t^{-1} \eta_t \tag{A.4}$$

From equation A.3 we have

$$\mu_t = (i V_t^{-1} i)^{-1} (Y_t - \psi) \tag{A.5}$$

Equations A.5 and A.2 imply

$$\sum_{t=1}^{T} V_t^{-1}[I - (i'V_t^{-1}i)ii'](Y_t - \psi) = 0 \tag{A.6}$$

Normalizing the sum of the μ_ts to zero yields

$$s^2 \sum_{t=1}^{T} (iV_t'^{-1}i)^{-1} i'V_t^{-1}(Y_t - \psi) = 0 \tag{A.7}$$

Multiplying equation A.7 by i and adding the resulting expression to equation A.6 leads to

$$\hat{\psi} = \sum_{t=1}^{T} [V_t^{-1} - (iV_t'^{-1}i)^{-1}(V_t^{-1} - I)i'V_t^{-1}]^{-1}$$

$$\left\{ \sum_{t=1}^{T} [V_t^{-1} - (i'V_t^{-1}i)^{-1}(V_t^{-1} - I)ii'V_t^{-1}]Y_t \right\} \tag{A.8}$$

Given knowledge of the V_ts, we can use equation A.8 plus equation A.5 to determine estimates of the μ_ts and the elements of ψ. Rather than solve analytically for the estimates of ν and ρ, we searched over a grid of alternative pairs of these parameters. For each choice of these parameters we formed by V_t matrices and used equations A.8 and A.5 to calculate the corresponding values of ψ and the μ_ts.

Notes

The earlier version of this chapter (entitled "Does the Consumption of Different Age Groups Move Together? A New Nonparametric Test of Intergenerational Altruism," NBER Working Paper, no. 2490, 1988) appears to have been the first in a series of papers by economists, including Townsend (1989), Altonji, Hayashi, and Kotlikoff (1992), Cochran (1991), and Mace (1991) to test the equality in Euler errors implied by risk sharing, whether the risk sharing is altruistically motivated or not. We thank Joseph Altonji, Robert Barsky, Gary Becker, Jinyong Cai, Gary Chamberlain, Jagadeesh Gokhale, Fumio Hayashi, Robert Lucas, Kevin Murphy, Sherwin Rosen, Robert Townsend, Lawrence Weiss, and seminar participants at Brown University, the University of Chicago, and at the National Bureau of Economic Research's summer workshop on financial markets for very helpful comments. Jinyong Cai and Jagadeesh Gokhale provided outstanding research assistance. This research was funded by the National Science Foundation. Our data are from the 1980 through 1985 Consumer Expenditure Surveys, which are publicly available through the Bureau of Labor Statistics.

1. Quarterly sample 1 corresponds to households interviewed in April, July, October, and January. Quarterly sample 2 corresponds to households interviewed in May, August, November, and February. Quarterly sample 3 corresponds to households interviewed in June, September, December, and March. In constructing the data for

quarterly sample 1, as an example, we form ratios of (*a*) the July reported quarterly consumption to the April reported quarterly consumption, (*b*) the October reported quarterly consumption to the July reported quarterly consumption, (*c*) the January reported quarterly consumption to the October reported quarterly consumption, and (*d*) the April reported quarterly consumption to the January reported quarterly consumption. In forming the average logarithm of the ratio of consumption say in January 1983 to consumption in October 1982, all households who were surveyed in both October 1982 and January 1983 were included.

2. In this regression time dummies, age dummies, and the residuals account, respectively, for 81.3 percent, 4.2 percent, and 14.5 percent of the variance of the dependent variable.

3. To illustrate these two regressions, consider the case of two age groups, ages 1 and 2, and two time periods, time 1 and 2. Then the initial regression is: $\hat{Y}_t^a = \delta_1 A_1 + \delta_2 A_2 + \tau T_2$, where the δs and τs are coefficients, and A_1, A_2 and T_2 are dummies for age group 1, age group 2, and time period 2, respectively. The alternative model is: $\hat{Y}_t^a = \delta_1 A_1 + \delta_2 A_2 + \lambda A_1 T_2 + l A_2 T_2$, and the test is whether $\lambda = l = \tau$.

4. These bounds were constructed by holding one of these parameters fixed at its maximum likelihood value and varying the other parameter until the resulting likelihood was significantly (at the 5 percent level) different from the maximum likelihood.

5. With household consumption defined as consumption per person, the point estimates for ρ for samples 1, 2, and 3 are 0.034, –0.043, and 0.044, respectively. For ν the corresponding point estimates are 1.001, 1.000, and 1.000. With household consumption defined as consumption per equivalent adult, the three point estimates for ρ are 0.032, –0.035, and 0.039, while the three point estimates for ν are 1.001, 1.000, and 1.000. The χ^2 values for testing the null hypothesis that $\rho = 0$ and $\nu = 1$ are 2.094, 1.952, and 0.395 for the three quarterly samples when consumption is measured per person, and 2.240, 1.352, and 1.667 for the three quarterly samples when consumption is measured per equivalent adult.

6. With household consumption defined as consumption per person the point estimates for ρ for semiannual samples 1, 2, 3, 4, 5, and 6 are –0.1260, 0.0450, –0.0840, –0.1360, 0.0570, and –0.0060, respectively. For ν the corresponding point estimates are 1.0010, 0.9710, 0.9700, 1.0140, 0.9970, and 1.023. With household consumption defined as consumption per equivalent adult, the six point estimates for ρ are –0.1270, 0.0770, –0.0900, –0.1310, 0.0480, and .0100, while the six point estimates for ν are 1.0090, 0.9730, 0.9740, 1.015, 0.9940, and 1.0210. The six respective semiannual χ^2 values for testing the null hypothesis that $\rho = 0$ and $\nu = 1$ are 3.0763, 7.3924, 8.710, 3.807, 0.493, and 4.220 when consumption is measured per person, and 3.0441, 6.699, 7.284, 3.735, 0.533, and 3.581 when consumption is measured per equivalent adult.

7. The simple Keynesian model, in which consumption depends only on contemporaneous income, also is supported by these findings. But there appears to be more support in the results for the life-cycle model than the Keynesian model. The reason is that the time dummies in the first set of regressions in table 4.5 are highly significant. Ignoring measurement error, the Keynesian model (at least the simple version of it) predicts that only changes in current income explain changes in consumption. In the Keynesian model, therefore, the time dummies, which control for common resource shocks, should not enter the regression explaining changes in cohort consumption. In contrast, the life-cycle model would suggest that the time dummies as well as the income change variable would be significant. The reason is that the income change

variable does not, under the life-cycle hypothesis, control perfectly for the cohort's change in resources; if the life-cycle model holds and the Euler errors of different age groups are correlated, then the time dummies should pick up that component of the common shock to the different cohorts' Euler errors that are not captured by the change in income. This point was first made in Altonji, Hayashi, and Kotlikoff 1989.

8. This statement is based on research in progress by Jagadeesh Bokhala and Laurence J. Kotlikoff to measure how the propensity to consume varies with age.

References

Altonji, Joseph, Fumio Hayashi, and Laurence J. Kotlikoff. "Is the Extended Family Altruistically Linked? New Tests Based on Micro Data." *American Economic Review* (Dec. 1992): 1177–98.

Altonji, Joseph, and Aloysius Siow. "Testing the Response of Consumption to Income Changes with (Noisy) Panel Data." *Quarterly Journal of Economics* 102 (May 1987): 293–328.

Aschauer, David. "Fiscal Policy and Aggregate Demand." *American Economic Review* 75, no. 1 (March 1985): 117–27.

Auerbach, Alan J., and Laurence J. Kotlikoff. "An Examination of Empirical Tests of Social Security Savings." In *Social Policy Evaluation: An Economic Perspective*, ed. Elhanan Helpman et al. New York: Academic Press, 1983.

Barro, Robert J. "Are Government Bonds Net Wealth?" *Journal of Political Economy* 82, no. 6 (Nov./Dec. 1974): 1095–1117.

Bernheim, B. Douglas, and Kyle Bagwell. "Is Everything Neutral?" *Journal of Political Economy* 96 (1988): 308–38.

Boskin, Michael J., and Laurence J. Kotlikoff. "Public Debt and U.S. Saving: A New Test of the Neutrality Hypothesis." *Carnegie-Rochester Conference Volume Series*, Autumn, 1985.

Boskin, Michael J., and Lawrence Lau. "An Analysis of U.S. Post War Consumption and Saving." 2 parts. National Bureau of Economic Research Working Paper, no. 2605; no. 2606. National Bureau of Economic Research, 1988.

Cochrane, John. "A Simple Test of Consumption Insurance." *Journal of Political Economy* 99 (October 1991): 957–76.

Cox, Donald. "Motives for Private Income Transfers." *Journal of Political Economy*, 95 (June 1987): 508–46.

Darby, Michael R. *Effects of Social Security on Income and the Capital Stock*. Washington, DC: Amer. Ent. Inst., 1979.

Feldstein, Martin. "Social Security, Induced Retirement, and Aggregate Capital Accumulation." *Journal of Political Economy* 82, no. 5 (Sept./Oct. 1974): 905–26.

Flavin, Marjorie A. "The Adjustment of Consumption to Changing Expectations about Future Income." *Journal of Political Economy* 89, no. 5 (October 1981): 974–1009.

Hall, Robert E. "Stochastic Implications of the Life Cycle–Permanent Income Hypothesis: Theory and Evidence." *Journal of Political Economy* 86, no. 6 (December 1978): 971–87.

Hall, Robert E., and Frederic Mishkin. "The Sensitivity of Consumption to Transitory Income: Estimates from Panel Data on Households." *Econometrica* 50, no. 2, (March 1982): 461–81.

Hayashi, Fumio. "The Effects of Liquidity Constraints on Consumption: A Cross Sectional Analysis." *Quarterly Journal of Economics*, no. 1 (Feb. 1985): 183–206.

King, Mervyn A., and Jonathan I. Leape. "Wealth and Portfolio Composition: Theory and Evidence." National Bureau of Economic Research Working Paper, no. 1468, 1984.

Kormendi, Roger. "Government Debt, Government Spending, and Private Sector Behavior." *American Economic Review* 73, no. 4 (December 1983): 994–1010.

Kotlikoff, Laurence J. "Intergenerational Transfers and Savings." *Journal of Economic Perspectives* 2, no. 2 (Spring 1988): 41–58.

Kotlikoff, Laurence J. "Altruistic Extended Family Linkages, A Note." In *What Determines Savings?*, by Kotlikoff. Cambridge, MA: MIT Press, 1989.

Kotlikoff, Laurence J. *Generational Accounting*. New York, NY: Free Press, 1992.

Kotlikoff, Laurence J., and Assaf Razin. "Making Bequests without Spoiling Children." National Bureau of Economic Research Working Paper, no. 2735, 1988.

Kotlikoff, Laurence J., Jagadeesh Gokhale, and John Sabelhaus. "Understanding the Postwar Decline in U.S. Saving." *Brookings Papers on Economic Activity* 1 (1996): 315–90.

Lawrence, Emily. "Do Transfers to the Poor Reduce Savings?" Yale University, 1983. Mimeo.

Leimer, Dean R., and Selig D. Lesnoy. "Social Security and Private Saving: A Reexamination of the Time Series Evidence Using Alternative Social Security Wealth Variables." Working Paper, no. 19. Washington, DC: Social Security Administration, Office of Research and Statistics, 1980.

Mace, Barbara. "Full Insurance in the Presence of Aggregate Uncertainty." *Journal of Political Economy* 99 (October 1991): 928–56.

Mankiw, N. Gregory, Julio J. Rothenberg, and Lawrence H. Summers. "Intertemporal Substitution in Macroeconomics." *Quarterly Journal of Economics* 48: 1983.

Menchik, Paul L. "Unequal Estate Division: Is it Altruism, Reverse Bequests, or Simply Noise?" Paper presented to the 1984 Seminar on Modeling the Accumulation and Distribution of Wealth, Paris, France, 1984.

Rosenzweig, Mark R. "Risk, Implicit Contracts, and the Family in Rural Areas of Low Income Countries." *Economic Journal* 98 (December 1988): 1148–70.

Samuelson, Paul. "Lifetime Portfolio Selection by Dynamic Stochastic Programming." *Review of Economics and Statistics* 51, no. 3 (August 1969): 239–46.

Shapiro, Matthew. "The Permanent Income Hypothesis and the Real Interest Rate: Some Evidence from Panel Data." *Economics Letters* 14 (1984): 93–100.

Townsend, Robert M. "Risk and Insurance in Village India." University of Chicago, 1989. Mimeo.

Williamson, Samuel H., and Warren L. Jones. "Computing the Impact of Social Security Using the Life Cycle Consumption Function." *American Economic Review* 73, no. 5 (December 1983): 1036–52.

Zeldes, Stephen. "Consumption and Liquidity Constraints: An Empirical Investigation." *Journal of Political Economy* 97 (1989).

5 Is the Extended Family Altruistically Linked? Direct Tests Using Micro Data

with Joseph G. Altonji, and
Fumio Hayashi

What is the basic economic decision-making unit? Is it the household or the extended family? For questions of public policy, knowing the size and scope of economic decision-making units is of great importance. As Robert Barro (1974) and Gary Becker (1974, 1981) stressed, nondistortionary government redistribution among members of an altruistically linked economic unit will not alter the collective budget constraint and, therefore, will not alter any of the unit's economic choices. If large altruistically linked economic units exist, this line of argument implies that private behavior will neutralize most, if not all, of the government's intergenerational and intragenerational redistribution.

In this paper we use extended-family data from the Panel Study of Income Dynamics (PSID) to test directly the assumption of operative altruistic linkages between parents and children against the alternative of zero linkage.[1] On an ongoing basis, the PSID surveys child "split-offs." These are children of the original 1968 respondents who subsequently became heads or spouses in their own households. By combining data on food consumption, income, assets, transfers, and household characteristics for these split-off adult children with the same data for their parents (the original survey respondents who have also been continually reinterviewed), one can use the PSID to form a unique and rich data set covering at least a portion of the extended family.[2]

The intuition behind our tests is quite simple. If parents and children are altruistically linked, their consumption will be based on a collective budget constraint, and the distribution of consumption between parents and children will be independent of the distribution of their incomes. In contrast to the altruism model, the nonaltruistic pure life-cycle model predicts that the distribution of incomes is a critical determinant of the distribution of consumption between parent and children.

While this simple idea underlies our tests, the actual form of our tests involves specifications of food demand functions. Under both the altruism and life-cycle models, one can express the consumption and leisure choices of parents (children) as functions of the parents' (children's) marginal utility of income and of prices.[3] An implication of the altruism model's single-collective-budget constraint is that parents and children have the same marginal utility of income. In contrast, under the life-cycle model, parents and children maximize their own preferences subject to their own budget constraints and have different marginal utilities of income.

The marginal utility of income is captured by a fixed effect in our food demand regressions. Given that we control for this fixed effect, according to the altruism model, the exogenous incomes and asset positions of parents (children) should not enter into our estimated demand functions for the parents' (children's) food consumption. Under the life-cycle hypothesis, in contrast, knowing the parent's fixed effect will not control perfectly for the child's fixed effect, and vice versa; hence, the exogenous incomes and asset positions of parents and children should enter into our estimated demand functions.

After estimating demands at a point in time, we combine the data over time and estimate the first differences of the demand functions. We find strong evidence against the altruism model both in the levels and first-differenced estimates of the food demand functions.[4] At a point in time, the distribution of consumption between parents and children is highly dependent on the distribution of their incomes; and over time, the distribution of consumption changes between parents and children is highly dependent on the distribution of their income changes. As we discuss below, the first-difference results rule out the possibility that the correlation we find in the levels reflects a correlation between parental preferences for particular children and the permanent incomes of those children.

In addition to showing that the distribution of extended-family resources matters for extended-family consumption, we test the life-cycle model by asking whether only own resources matter (i.e., whether the resources of extended-family members have no effect on a household's consumption). Our results indicate that extended-family member resources have at most a modest effect on household consumption after one has controlled for the fact that extended-family resources help predict a household's own permanent income.

The chapter proceeds in Section I by developing our empirical tests of altruism. Section II describes the linked PSID data. Sections III and IV contain, respectively, our findings from static and dynamic tests of altruism. Section V presents results of tests that take the life-cycle model, rather than the altruism model, as the null hypothesis. Section VI summarizes and concludes the chapter.

I. Testable Implications of the Altruism Model

A Static Illustration

To see in the simplest possible terms the force of altruism, consider the case of a parent who is altruistic toward a child, but the child is not altruistic toward the parent. Suppose the parent's utility function is given by $U_p = \theta_p U(C_p) + \theta_k U(C_k)$, where C_p stands for the parent's consumption, C_k stands for the child's consumption, and θ_p and θ_k are the respective weights the parent attaches to his own utility from consumption, $U(C_p)$, and to the child's utility, $U(C_k)$. The child's consumption, C_k, will equal the child's resources, R_k, plus T, the transfer made to the child (i.e., $C_k = R_k + T$). The parent's consumption will equal the parent's resources less the transfers to the child (i.e., $C_p = R_p - T$). These two constraints imply the combined budget constraint: $C_k + C_p = R_k + R_p$.

Suppose that the child takes the parent's transfer as given. Then the parent's choice of his own consumption and transfer (assuming it is positive) leads the parent to set $\theta_p U'(C_p) = \theta_k U'(C_k) = \lambda$, where λ is the marginal utility of income. This first-order condition and the collective-budget constraint can be used to solve for C_p and C_k. Hence, as first shown by Becker (1974) and Barro (1974), the parent and child act as if they are maximizing the parent's utility function subject to the combined-budget constraint. This type of outcome is generic in one-sided, two-sided, or, indeed, many-sided altruistic models assuming that recipients of transfers take such transfers as given [i.e., the game between the donor and recipient is noncooperative Nash and there are positive (operative) transfers].[5]

Next assume that the utility function is of the isoelastic form, $U(C) = C^{1-\gamma}/(1-\gamma)$. From the first-order conditions, we have $\log C_p = -(1/\gamma)\log\lambda + (1/\gamma)\log\theta_p$ and $\log C_k = -(1/\gamma)\log\lambda + (1/\gamma)\log\theta_k$.

Obviously, C_p will exceed C_k if θ_p is greater than θ_k. If the true values of C_p and C_k differ from the measured values, C_p^m and C_k^m, by multiplicative errors, whose logarithms we denote u_p and u_k, respectively, we have the following statistical representation of the demand system:

$$\log(C_{ip}^m) = -\left(\frac{1}{\gamma_i}\right) \log \lambda_i + \left(\frac{1}{\gamma_i}\right) \log \theta_{ip} + u_{ip}, \tag{1}$$

$$\log(C_{ik}^m) = -\left(\frac{1}{\gamma_i}\right) \log \lambda_i + \left(\frac{1}{\gamma_i}\right) \log \theta_{ik} + u_{ik}. \tag{2}$$

In equations (1) and (2) the subscript i refers to parent-child pair i. With data on a sample of parent-child pairs one can estimate (1) and (2) jointly treating the terms $\log \lambda_i$ for each parent-child pair as a fixed effect.[6] Since controlling for the fixed effect fully controls for the combined resources of the parent and child, one can test the model by asking whether the parent's resources, R_{pi}, enter into the parent's consumption equation and whether the child's resources, R_{ki}, enter into the child's consumption equation.[7] The altruism model predicts zero coefficients on own resources, controlling for combined resources. In contrast, the life-cycle and Keynesian models predict that own resources are significant determinants of own consumption. As we show below, this basic test procedure carries over to more realistic dynamic models with multiple consumption goods, uncertainty, and endogeneous labor supply.

Two-Sided Altruism

Before turning to those issues we need to remark on how the results of the proposed test should be interpreted if altruism is two-sided. By two-sided altruism we mean that the child cares about the parent's utility and vice versa. It is easy to show that with two-sided altruism there will be different transfer regimes (three in the case of a single parent and a single child) determined by the division of resources between the parent and child. As the share of joint resources owned by the parent increases from zero to unity, the regime shifts from one in which the child transfers to the parent to one in which there are no transfers and then to one in which the parent transfers to the child. Changes in the resource distribution between the parent and child that are large enough to shift the transfer regime will be associated with changes in the ratio of the parent's consumption to the child's consumption.

Hence, one response to a finding of a significant own-resource coefficient in the fixed-effect test discussed above is that extended families are indeed altruistic but that the test is simply capturing the fact that transfer regimes change as the distribution of resources changes between parent and child. While this may be true, its implication with respect to Barro's neutrality proposition, at least for large government redistributions between parents and children, is the same as if there is no altruism, namely, that such government redistribution is not neutral. One way to test whether the Barro proposition holds for small government redistributions—those that are not likely to alter the transfer regime—is to focus on the subset of parent-child pairs in which the parent's resource share is much larger than that of the child. For this subset of observations one would expect no correlation between consumption and resource shares. While we do not know precisely the resource shares of our parent-child pairs, we can conduct this more refined test of altruism by running our fixed-effects test for parent-child pairs in which the parent has high income and the child has low income.

A Dynamic Formulation

Given that within a transfer regime the standard altruism model can be summarized by the maximization of a single objective function subject to a single collective budget constraint, we proceed by referring to the extended family as the dynasty and by expressing the general problem of the dynasty as

$$\max E_t \left\{ \sum_{s=t}^{\infty} b^s U(Z_s, \mathbf{p}_s; \mathbf{x}_s) \right\}, \tag{3}$$

subject to

$$A_{t+1} = (1 + r_t)A_t + Y_t - Z_t,$$

where

$$Y_t = \sum_{k=1}^{m_t} Y_{kt},$$

and where

E_t = expectation operator,

m_t = number of households in the dynasty at time t,

Y_{kt} = labor earnings of the kth household of the dynasty at time t,

Z_t = total nominal consumption expenditure by the dynasty at t,

A_t = the dynasty's wealth at time t,

r_t = nominal interest rate at time t,

$\mathbf{x}_{kt}$ = vector of demographics for the kth household at time t,

$\mathbf{x}_t$ = vector consisting of $\mathbf{x}_{kt}$ $(k = 1, \ldots, m_t)$,

$\mathbf{p}_t$ = vector of commodity prices, and

b = discount factor.

In (3) we assume that labor supply is exogenous. The dynasty's indirect intertemporal utility function $U(Z_t, \mathbf{p}_t; \mathbf{x}_t)$ is defined as the maximized value of the following static optimization problem:

$$\max_{\{\mathbf{C}_{kt}\}} \sum_{k=0}^{m_t} u(\mathbf{C}_{kt}; \mathbf{x}_{kt}), \tag{4}$$

subject to

$$\mathbf{p}_t' \sum_{k=0}^{m_t} \mathbf{C}_{kt} \leq Z_t,$$

where $u(\mathbf{C}_{kt}; \mathbf{x}_{kt})$ is the dynasty's time-t utility from the vector of consumption of household k, $\mathbf{C}_{kt}$, with demographic characteristics $\mathbf{x}_{kt}$. The term $\mathbf{p}_t$ stands for the time-t price vector.

The key prediction of this more general model—namely, that resources are shared by altruistically linked individuals within the dynasty and, therefore, by households within the dynasty—can be formalized as follows. Let λ_t be the scalar shadow price for the budget constraint in (3). Then the first-order conditions from the maximization in (4) imply the demand functions:

$$\mathbf{C}_{kt} = f(\lambda_t, \mathbf{p}_t; \mathbf{x}_{kt}) \quad k = 0, 1, \ldots, m_t. \tag{5}$$

As suggested above, the important point here is that the scalar shadow price λ_t, which is a "sufficient statistic" for dynasty resources at time t, is common across dynasty members, while in the life-cycle hypothesis it depends on the household identifier k. For a wide range of utility functions the shadow price λ_t can be treated as a component of a fixed effect. In the case of exogenous labor supply, since the price vector $\mathbf{p}_t$ is also common across dynasty members, the fixed effect can also depend on prices. Since the only consumption component available in our data is food consumption, we now focus on the food component of (5) and require that the demand function for food be of the form:

$$f_{kt} = h(\mathbf{x}_{kt}, \mathbf{p}_t) + \alpha(\mathbf{p}_t, \lambda_t) \tag{6}$$

where f_{kt} is either the level or the logarithm of food consumption. Since the $\alpha(\cdot, \cdot)$ function does not depend on k, we treat it as a fixed effect. As described in Altonji et al. (1989), a large class of utility functions satisfy the demand specification given in (6). The class includes the familiar constant-elasticity-of-substitution (CES) functions and constant-absolute-risk-aversion functions.[8]

Testing the Dynasty Model

With (6) as our starting point, our statistical representation is given by

$$f_{kt} = \boldsymbol{\beta}_t'\mathbf{x}_{kt} + \alpha_t + u_{kt} \quad k = 0, 1, \ldots, m_t, \tag{7}$$

where α_t is the fixed effect. The error term u_{kt} accommodates measurement error for food consumption and unobserved household characteristics that are unrelated to $\mathbf{x}_{kt}$ and α_t.

To implement tests of the dynasty model, we have to resolve a few problems. First, we do not observe all the dynasty member households. Let $\{0, 1, 2, \ldots, n\}$ stand for the set of dynasty members we can observe in the PSID, with $k = 0$ being the parent household and $k = 1, 2, \ldots, n$ representing split-offs. The second problem is that this n varies across dynasties and over time. Third, we do not have a specific model of how the marginal utility of dynasty income, λ_t, is related to observable variables.

To see how these problems can be resolved, we suppress the time subscript in (7), but add the dynasty index i to obtain

$$f_{ik} = \boldsymbol{\beta}'\mathbf{x}_{ik} + \alpha_i + u_{ik} \quad k = 0, 1, \ldots, n_i \quad i = 1, 2, \ldots, N, \tag{7'}$$

where N is the number of dynasties with at least one split-off in the sample and n_i is the number of split-offs of dynasty i. This is exactly the fixed-effect model for panel data. Because the fixed effect controls for household preferences/characteristics and measurement errors that are common across all members of the dynasty, the error term u_{ik} consists of household deviations in preferences and measurement error from the dynasty mean.

We can nest this model with the life-cycle alternative by augmenting (7′) to include an earnings term:

$$f_{ik} = \boldsymbol{\beta}'\mathbf{x}_{ik} + \psi Y_{ik} + \alpha_i + u_{ik} \quad k = 0, 1, \ldots, n_i \quad i = 1, 2, \ldots, N, \tag{8}$$

where Y_{ik} stands for earnings of member-household k of dynasty i. This additional variable Y need not be restricted to earnings. Under the life-cycle hypothesis, variables like nonlabor income, assets, and the history of earnings should matter even when the fixed effect is controlled for. As discussed below, if we allow for variable labor supply, then nonlabor income, assets, possibly current wage rates, and lagged wage rates can be used to test the altruism model.

We now make the basic identifying assumption that the error term u (which consists of consumption measurement error and unobservable household characteristics unrelated to the observable characteristics $\mathbf{x}$) is uncorrelated with earnings (or our other controls for household k's resources). According to the dynasty model the fixed effect α_i (which is time-specific) should be correlated with earnings Y_{ik} (or our other controls for household k's resources), but the earnings coefficient ψ is, nonetheless, identified to be zero under the null hypothesis of the dynasty model. This is because the fixed effect is removed in the estimation. Note that if some (or all) of the dynasties in the sample are linked, the fixed effect α_i will be numerically the same for each of these dynasties. Hence, our fixed-effect test is robust to altruistic linkages across dynasties.

In contrast to the dynasty model, which predicts a value of ψ equal to zero, under the life-cycle and Keynesian alternatives, ψ should be positive. The reason is that under these alternatives to the dynasty model consumption depends not on the collective resources of one's extended family, but rather simply on one's own resources. Hence, under the alternative models controlling for extended-family resources by controlling for the marginal utility of income of the extended family will not control for the resources used in making consumption decisions. Indeed, under the life-cycle or Keynesian alternatives the fixed effect α_i has the interpretation of common environmental and genetic components of the unobservable characteristics common to the family, rather than the interpretation of a transform of the extended family's marginal utility of income.

Does Variable Labor Supply Alter the Test Procedure?

If labor supply is variable, the price vector $\mathbf{p}_t$ in (6) includes the wage rates of different household members, which could differ across member households within the dynasty as well as across members within particular dynasty households. Thus, the $\alpha(\cdot,\cdot)$ function in (6) cannot, in general, be treated as a fixed effect, and we have to restrict preferences further to ensure that the $\alpha(\cdot,\cdot)$ function is independent of wage rates, which may differ across households. One can show (see Richard Blundell, 1986) that for the demands to take this form the utility function must be either homogeneous or additively separable as in (7′).

For the case in which f_{kt} stands for the level of food expenditure, Martin Browning et al. (1985) provide a complete characterization of preferences in which demand functions can be written as the sum of an $\alpha(\cdot,\cdot)$ function that does not depend on wage rates plus an $h(\cdot,\cdot)$ function that may include wage rates. Constant absolute risk aversion, expanded to include leisure, is one example of such a preference structure. For this particular preference structure cross-price effects do not arise in the demands; hence the demand function is of the form given by (6), but $h(\cdot,\cdot)$ depends only on demographics and the price of food (and not wage rates), and $\alpha(\cdot,\cdot)$ depends only on λ_t. For other preferences described by Browning et al. the $h(\cdot,\cdot)$ function, but not $\alpha(\cdot,\cdot)$, may depend on wage rates. For this latter set of preferences in which $h(\cdot,\cdot)$ may include wage rates, the significance of own wage rates in the food demand does not constitute evidence against altruism. However, for these preferences, one can test altruism by including own nonlabor income and own assets in addition to wage rates.

Since nonlabor income and assets may reflect idiosyncratic tastes that are not fully captured by our demographic controls and, therefore, enter the error term u_{ik} in (8), we also estimate specifications that include both current and lagged wage rates. If preferences are time-separable, past wage rates will not enter $h(\cdot,\cdot)$, and they will affect consumption only through the marginal utility of income. Consequently, we can test the altruism model by determining whether the lagged wage rate is significantly greater than zero.

Dynamic Tests

A dynamic version of the static fixed-effect equation is derived from the time-differencing of equation (8), which yields

$$\Delta f_{ikt} = \boldsymbol{\beta}'\Delta \mathbf{x}_{ikt} + \theta \Delta Y_{ikt} + \Delta\alpha_{it} + \Delta u_{ikt}, \tag{9}$$

where $\Delta f_{ikt} = f_{ikt} - f_{ikt-1}$ in the case of one-year differences and $\Delta f_{ikt} = f_{ikt} - f_{ikt-2}$ in the case of two-year differences. The term $\Delta\alpha_{it}$ equals the corresponding difference over time in dynasty i's logarithm of its marginal utility of income (i.e., it equals $\alpha_{it} - \alpha_{it-1}$ in the case of first differences and $\alpha_{it} - \alpha_{it-2}$ in the case of second differences).[9] Since $\Delta\alpha_{it}$ does not depend on the household identifier k, it is the same across all dynasty households (although its value differs in the case of one-year and two-year differences). Assuming exogenous labor supply, one can test the dynamic version of the altruism model by including the change in current earnings, ΔY_{ikt}, where $\Delta Y_{ikt} = Y_{ikt} - Y_{ik,t-1}$ in the case of one-year differences and $\Delta Y_{ikt} = Y_{ikt} - Y_{ik,t-2}$ in the case of two-year differences. If the altruism model holds, the coefficient on this variable will be zero. This is true despite the fact that the income-change term is correlated over time with changes in the marginal utility of income. The reason is that the fixed-effect technique fully controls for changes in the marginal utility of income. Thus, the proposed dynamic test of the dynasty model is simply the fixed-effect first-differenced version of the static fixed-effect test.[10]

The dynamic test, however, does have one advantage over the static test. It controls for the remote possibility that the dynasty's preferences toward its member households are correlated with their earnings capacity. Such a correlation could arise if parents invested more in the human-capital accumulation of favorite children. Such preferences could be represented by a household-specific constant in equation (8). However, these constants would drop out in the time-difference results; that is, favorite children may get to consume more and, as a result of past investments, earn more, but their change in consumption should depend on the dynasty's total change in income, not on the particular income change they experience.

The dynamic test also raises the issue of risk sharing. The dynamic test can distinguish the altruism model from the life-cycle model with no risk sharing, but it does not have power against the life-cycle model with selfish risk sharing among extended-family members.

To see why not, take the case of a selfish parent and selfish child who overlap for, in the simplest case, two periods, time t and $t+1$. Suppose the parent's and child's incomes at time s ($s = t, t+1$) are Y_{ps} and Y_{ks}, respectively. The parent and child must make consumption decisions at time t knowing Y_{pt} and Y_{kt}, but not knowing Y_{pt+1} and Y_{kt+1}. Let V_p and V_k stand, respectively, for the expected utilities of the parent and child, where

$$V_p = C_{pt}^{1-\gamma}/(1-\gamma) + bE_t C_{pt+1}^{1-\gamma}/(1-\gamma)$$

$$V_k = C_{kt}^{1-\gamma}/(1-\gamma) + bE_t C_{kt+1}^{1-\gamma}/(1-\gamma),$$

and where E_t is the expectation operator at time t conditional on information at time t and C_{ps} (C_{ks}) stands for the parent's (child's) consumption at time s. Suppose the selfish parent and child choose to pool their income risk and that they reach an efficient bargain. In this case their behavior can be described as a decision to maximize $\theta_p V_p + (1-\theta_p)V_k$, where the bargaining weight θ_p agreed to by the parent and child will depend on the known values of Y_{pt} and Y_{kt} and the distributions of Y_{pt+1} and Y_{kt+1}. At time s ($s = t, t+1$) this maximization will lead to

$$\log C_{ps} = \left(\frac{1}{\gamma}\right) \log \theta_p - \left(\frac{1}{\gamma}\right) \log \lambda_s,$$

and

$$\log C_{ks} = \left(\frac{1}{\gamma}\right) \log (1-\theta_p) - \left(\frac{1}{\gamma}\right) \log \lambda_s,$$

where λ_s is the Lagrangian multiplier for the time-t parent-child combined-budget constraint. From these relations we have

$$\log C_{pt+1} - \log C_{pt} = -\left(\frac{1}{\gamma}\right)(\log \lambda_{t+1} - \log \lambda_t),$$

and

$$\log C_{kt+1} - \log C_{kt} = -\left(\frac{1}{\gamma}\right)(\log \lambda_{t+1} - \log \lambda_t).$$

With the addition of measurement error and taste variations, this is the dynamic fixed-effect model specified in (11). Hence, selfish risk sharing, like altruism, can lead to identical changes in the logarithm of the marginal utility of income for extended-family members. The dynamic test must, therefore, be viewed as a test of the altruism/life-cycle models with risk sharing against the Keynesian/life-cycle models with no risk sharing.[11]

Using Extended-Family Data to Test the Life-Cycle Model

The discussion thus far has centered on tests that can lead to the rejection of the altruism model; but the altruism model is not the only interesting null hypothesis. For example, one would also like to test the pure life-cycle model against its alternatives. By pure life-cycle model we mean that households neither fully nor partially share resources with their extended-family members. This rules out selfish risk sharing as well as altruism. The new data on the extended family provide an opportunity for testing the pure life-cycle model's prediction that the household's resources and only the household's resources affect its consumption. The test is simply to determine whether extended-family resources affect a household's consumption after one has controlled for the fact that extended-family resources help predict the household's permanent income.

Consider again equation (7), but modified in accordance with the life-cycle model's prediction to permit the marginal utility of income to be household-specific:

$$f_{kt} = \boldsymbol{\beta}_t'\mathbf{x}_{kt} + \alpha_{kt} + u_{kt} \quad k = 0, 1, \ldots, m_t. \tag{10}$$

According to the life-cycle model α_{kt} in equation (10) will depend on household-specific resources, although in general this dependence will not be simple. We proxy this relationship by considering the projection of α_{kt} on the household's current wealth, A_{kt}, its current nonasset income, e_{kt}, and z lags of past nonasset income, $e_{kt-1}, \ldots, e_{kt-z}$. Hence, we can write $\alpha_{kt} = \alpha_{kt}(A_{kt}, e_{kt}, \ldots, e_{kt-z})$. Assuming that the elements of the α_{kt} projection fully capture the household's marginal utility of income and assuming that the life-cycle model is true, the corresponding dynasty-average values of wealth and current and past nonasset income should not enter significantly in the regression equation given in (11):

$$\begin{aligned} f_{kt} = {} & \boldsymbol{\beta}_t'\mathbf{x}_{kt} + \ell_1 A_{kt} + \ell_2 e_{kt-1} + \cdots + \ell_{z+1} e_{kt-z} \\ & + \bar{\ell}_1 \bar{A}_{kt} + \bar{\ell}_2 \bar{e}_{kt-1} + \cdots + \bar{\ell}_{z+1} \bar{e}_{kt-z} + \varepsilon_{kt}. \end{aligned} \tag{11}$$

In addition to incorporating the substitution of the α_{kt} projection into equation (10), equation (11) permits household food consumption to depend on the dynasty-average values of $A_{kt}, e_{kt}, \ldots, e_{kt-z}$, where the dynasty averages (denoted with overbars, "–") at time t are taken over all time-t members of the dynasty in the data including the own household. We test the life-cycle model by considering whether the $\bar{\ell}_i$s $(i = 1, \ldots, z+1)$ are zero.

With additional assumptions one can refine the testing strategy underlying equation (11). Assume that utility is quadratic and that households face only earnings uncertainty. Then α_{kt} can be written as the sum of the present expected value of human wealth plus nonhuman wealth, where f_{kt} now stands for the level of food consumption. Let us further assume that the household's labor earnings e_{kt} equal the sum of a permanent component, e^p_{kt}, which evolves as a random walk, and an independent and identically distributed transitory component, $\tilde{e}_{kt}$; that is,

$$e_{kt} = e^p_{kt} + \tilde{e}_{kt}. \tag{12}$$

Assume that the present expected value of human wealth may be approximated by e^p_{kt} divided by the interest rate plus $\tilde{e}_{kt}$. Together these assumptions imply the following specification of (10):

$$f_{kt} = \boldsymbol{\beta}_t' \mathbf{x}_{kt} + \delta_1 A_{kt} + \delta_2 e^p_{kt} + \delta_1 \tilde{e}_{kt} + \varepsilon_{kt}. \tag{13}$$

The econometric problem in estimating (13) is that we do not have independent measures of the permanent and transitory components of e_{kt}. Substituting into (13) for e^p_{kt} from (12) and allowing for the possibility that the dynasty-average values of A_{kt} and e_{kt}, $\bar{A}_{kt}$ and $\bar{e}_{kt}$, enter the equation yields

$$f_{kt} = \boldsymbol{\beta}_t' \mathbf{x}_{kt} + \delta_1 A_{kt} + \delta_2 e_{kt} + \bar{\delta}_1 \bar{A}_{kt} + \bar{\delta}_2 \bar{e}_{kt} + \varepsilon'_{kt}, \tag{13'}$$

where, under the life-cycle hypothesis, the error term $\varepsilon'_{kt} = \varepsilon_{kt} + (\delta_1 - \delta_2)\tilde{e}_{kt}$. Since e_{kt} is correlated with ε'_{kt}, we estimate (13′) using instrumental variables. Our test of the life-cycle model is that $\bar{\delta}_1$ and $\bar{\delta}_2$ equal zero.

Unfortunately, the PSID has data on assets and liabilities only for 1984. Hence, we conduct the test in equation (11) and the test in equation (13′) for 1984. In order to use data from the other years, we again estimate (11) but use, instead of the nonasset income and wealth variables, the following variables: current and lagged values of own and dynasty-average total income and current values of own and dynasty-average home equity. Equation (13′) can also be estimated in the absence of wealth data by using own and dynasty-average current total income in the place of current own and dynasty-average nonasset income and current wealth and by instrumenting own and dynasty-average current total income. This formulation is simply Friedman's permanent-income hypothesis augmented to allow the average permanent income of the dynasty to affect household consumption. In conducting our tests of (11) and (13′) we measure food consumption both in the levels and in the logs.

A final test that we conduct of the life-cycle model is to regress the change in the logarithm of food consumption against changes in the log of household's total income (head's wage rate) and changes in the average value of dynasty total income (heads' wage rates). Considering whether changes in relatives' resources affect a household's consumption may more sharply test the life-cycle model than tests based on the level of relatives' resources. The reason is that even if the life-cycle model is true, dynasty resource variables, which are correlated with household resource variables, will enter into equation (11) if we have not controlled properly for the household's marginal utility of income. In contrast, while dynasty resources may help predict the level of a household's resources, changes in dynasty resources are less likely to help predict changes in a household's resource position.

II. Data and Sample Selection

The PSID

The PSID began in 1968 with a sample of over 5,000 households. The PSID has reinterviewed the heads and spouses of the initial sample each year since 1968. In the case of divorce or separation, the PSID has followed both the head and spouse into their new households. Such new households that are added to the PSID are referred to as "split-offs." In addition to split-offs from divorce or separation, there are child split-offs that arise whenever one of the children of the 1968 respondents, who was not living independently of the respondents in 1968, leaves the respondents' household to form (or become a spouse in) his or her own household.[12] The same set of information that has been collected for the parent households has also been collected for all split-offs. Hence, the PSID provides a matched data set of parents together with at least a subset of their independent children.

Our data come from the 1985 PSID, specifically the families and individuals tape that does not include households who dropped out of the PSID prior to 1985. The 1985 tape contains data collected for 1984 as well as for all previous years. We first identify all individuals in the 1985 PSID who are listed, in 1968, as children. We then identify the 1968 parents of these children. These parents are referred to as the "earliest parents," since they may or may not be the natural parents. Our second step is to follow, starting in 1968, each identified child and determine whether and when he or she formed an independent household, by which we mean became a head or spouse in a household different from that of the child's earliest parents. The third step involves collecting data on consumption, labor supply, income, and so forth for such independent children in each year that they are independent together with contemporaneous data for the households that include their earliest parents. If there is only one earliest parent or if both earliest parents are still living together, we collect data on the single households containing such earliest parents. If there are two earliest parents but they are no longer living together, we collect contemporaneous data on the two households containing each of the two earliest parents, including data on possible step-parents. Hence, in a given year there will be data for one or two earliest-parent households for each independent child. We are able to link the data on each of the independent-children households to the data for their independent siblings as well as to the data for their earliest parents. In order to run the fixed-effect model, we need at least two observations on extended-family members in a given year. Hence, if data are available on an independent child who has no independent siblings and who has no parents (because of death, missing data, or attrition from the sample), we exclude the observation from the analysis. We also require that each dynasty in the regression samples contain at least one parent and one child.

Since there are new split-offs every year, the number of independent-child household observations in the data increases over time. The number of earliest-parent household observations also changes through time because of divorce, remarriage, death, and sample attrition. Table 5.1 reports for each year the number of earliest-parent households as well as the number of independent-child households used in our analysis after we have applied the

Table 5.1
Enumeration of independent-child and earliest-parent household observations

	Independent children				Earliest parents			
			Two parents					
Year	Total	1 Parent	Married	Divorced/separated	Total	One child	Two children	Three or more children
1976	713	314	386	13	544	396	121	27
1977	775	315	447	13	576	411	129	36
1978	971	387	563	21	692	462	173	57
1979	1,201	481	685	35	792	484	211	97
1980	1,384	524	816	44	883	508	258	117
1981	1,550	591	900	59	945	515	280	150
1982	1,731	635	1,017	79	1,019	522	307	190
1983	1,892	699	1,114	79	1,068	512	332	224
1984	2,043	725	1,219	99	1,129	530	341	258
1985	2,178	764	1,293	121	1,171	531	344	296
Total:	14,438	5,435	8,440	563	8,819	4,871	2,496	1,452

sample selection rules described below. The table also distinguishes the number of independent-children observations according to whether they are associated with one or two earliest-parent households. Finally, it distinguishes the number of earliest-parent households by the number of associated independent-child households. The table, as well as our empirical work, begins with the 1976 data; prior to 1976 there are relatively few observations on independent children, and information needed to construct our income measure is missing.

The number of independent children increases from 713 in 1976 to 2,178 in 1985. The corresponding figures for earliest parents are 544 in 1976 and 1,171 in 1985. To understand the table, take 1985 as an example. In that year 764 of the 2,178 independent children have only one earliest parent, while the rest (1,293 + 121) have two earliest parents. Of those children with two earliest parents in the 1985 PSID, 121 have two earliest parents who are living in separate households in 1985. Next consider the 1,171 earliest parents listed in the table for 1985. A total of 531 of these parents have only one independent child in the data set; 344 have two children in the data set, and the rest (296) have three or more children in the data set.

As mentioned, the PSID so far has included a complete list of assets and liabilities only for the 1984 wave. Our 1984 wealth measure uses the 1984 PSID data on holdings of stocks, bonds, real estate, vehicles, business and farm assets, checking and saving accounts, house value, and the value of outstanding mortgages. For years other than 1984, when relatively complete asset data are not available, we can use information on the house value less the remaining mortgage. We also use data on nonlabor income, which includes income from assets and income from exogenous sources (e.g., social security benefits).

Additional Sample Selection Criteria

The PSID's survey questions about income and consumption for a particular year refer to income earned in the previous year and consumption expenditures at the time of the survey (typically March or April). Since children who are first recorded as independent in year t are asked about income and consumption during year $t-1$, some or all of which time may have been spent with their earliest parent(s), we exclude from the analysis data from the year in which a child is

Table 5.2
A description of the data

	Child households		Parent households		Total	
Variable	Mean	SD	Mean	SD	Mean	SD
Household income	8,608	5,599	9,297	9,740	8,869	7,452
Dynasty income	7,871	3,965	9,103	7,752	8,336	4,227
Total food	1,234	691	1,326	751	1,269	716
Food away from home	259	279	214	307	242	291
Food at home	975	610	1,112	633	1,027	622
Black	0.310	0.463	0.315	0.464	0.312	0.463
Asian	0.002	0.049	0.002	0.042	0.002	0.047
American Indian	0.002	0.053	0.003	0.057	0.003	0.054
Other nonwhite	0.005	0.070	0.004	0.065	0.005	0.068
Married	0.699	0.458	0.683	0.465	0.693	0.461
Divorced	0.074	0.262	0.106	0.307	0.086	0.280
Female	0.503	0.500	0.362	0.480	0.449	0.497
Age of head	29.1	3.96	56.7	7.71	39.5	14.5

first reported as independent. For the same reason, data are excluded on parents who split off by divorcing or separating in the first year the parents are reported as split-offs. Parents and children must also be either a head or a spouse. In addition, we exclude household observations in which either reported annual income is less than \$500 or annual consumption is less than \$250, where both numbers refer to 1967 dollars. Finally, we require that the age of parent is greater than 38 and the age of each child is greater than 24. Table 5.2 reports, for both child and parent households, means and standard deviations of many of the variables used in this analysis.

III. Results of Static Tests of Altruism

Static Tests Based on Current Income

The first row of table 5.3 reports the income coefficients from the static fixed-effect test for both logarithm and level specifications. These are the results of fitting equation (8) to the data pooled across years. As described in Altonji et al. (1989), disaggregating by year has no material effect on the results. Income is defined here as total

Table 5.3
Regression estimates of the effect of income on food consumption

	Fixed effect		No fixed effect		Sample size	
Test	Log	Level	Log	Level	Log	Level
Static Tests of Altruism						
Food	0.240 (23.289)	0.021 (4.163)	0.286 (33.067)	0.028 (5.083)	23,257	23,257
Food at home	0.165 (14.940)	0.010 (3.732)	0.201 (22.868)	0.014 (4.573)	23,148	23,257
Food away from home	0.383 (17.545)	0.010 (4.085)	0.497 (24.156)	0.013 (5.268)	19,723	23,257
Food lagged one year	0.242 (22.802)	0.020 (4.016)	0.279 (31.231)	0.026 (4.954)	20,565	20,565
Rich parent, poor child	0.228 (12.567)	0.057 (10.888)	0.246 (17.457)	0.062 (14.885)	7,036	7,036
Nonlabor income	0.028 (5.144)	0.014 (1.944)	0.041 (7.865)	0.019 (2.068)	12,534	12,534
Instrumental variable for income with education/occupation	0.306 (9.510)	0.042 (7.972)	0.340 (13.500)	0.046 (10.016)	15,687	15,687
Dynamic Tests of Altruism						
One-year difference in food	0.063 (5.013)	0.002 (1.518)	0.074 (7.108)	0.002 (1.295)	18,189	18,189
Two-year difference in food	0.137 (10.425)	0.003 (1.005)	0.144 (13.352)	0.005 (1.191)	15,439	15,439

Note: Numbers in parentheses are *t* statistics testing the null hypothesis that the coefficient is zero.

family income less transfers received by the household head from family members living outside the household. Hence, the income variable consists of labor income plus nonlabor income, where the latter variable includes asset income plus government transfers but excludes private transfers. The demographic controls in these and subsequent static regressions are the number of males and females in the household in 11 age brackets,[13] dummies for the household's race, dummies for the household's marital status, a fourth-order polynomial in the age of the head, a dummy for the sex of the head, a dummy for whether the household is a child or parent household,[14] the square of the number of children, the number of adults squared, and the square of the household's size. The standard errors in this and subsequent regressions are White standard errors (see Halbert

White, 1984). Specifically, they allow for an arbitrary co-variance pattern of errors across years and households for each extended family.

In contrast to the altruism model's prediction of zero income coefficients when one controls for the fixed effects, both the log and level income coefficients are positive and highly significant. From the double logarithmic specification it is immediate that the income elasticities are economically large and reasonable. These income coefficients are also quite large when compared with the income coefficients that arise if one omits the fixed effects. In the case of the log specification the fixed-effect coefficient is 84 percent as large as the non-fixed-effect coefficient; in the level specification the fixed-effect coefficient is 75 percent as large.

While the income coefficients are larger when the fixed effects are omitted, one would expect such an outcome if the life-cycle model were true and current income were not a perfect measure of permanent income. To see this, suppose each dynasty member had an identical permanent income. In this case the fixed effects would control perfectly for the household's permanent income and, given that one has controlled for permanent income, the coefficient on current income should be zero. Now clearly, the permanent income of different dynasty members will differ; but if they are correlated, which is surely the case, the force of the argument should go through.[15]

The strong rejection of the altruism model found in the first row of table 5.3 is robust to the definition of food consumption. Rows 2 and 3 of the table report the income coefficients for food at home and food away from home. All four of these coefficients are statistically significant and economically significant when compared with the size of the coefficients when fixed effects are omitted.

The rejection of altruism is also robust to the temporal pairing of the consumption and income data. In the base case we pair year t's response to the consumption question with year t's response to the income question. However, the year-t income question refers to income in the previous year, while the year-t consumption question refers to the respondent's household's usual weekly consumption expenditure (although the data are reported on an annual basis). It may be that the response to the consumption question refers to consumption in the current year. In row 4 of table 5.3 we regress year $t-1$'s consumption against year t's income. The results are quite similar to those in the first row of table 5.3.

One response to these findings is that, while the altruism model may not hold for all parent and child pairs, it may hold for a subset of households such as those that engage in transfers with one another. Unfortunately, there are relatively few observations across all the years in which the household head reports receiving transfers from other family members. A larger sample that might be likely to satisfy the predictions of altruism and also avoid the problem discussed in Section II of switches in transfer regimes is the sample of parents with incomes above the median for parents together with that subset of their children whose incomes are below the median for children. Row 5 of table 5.3 reports the results for this sample of rich parents and poor children. The results also very strongly reject the altruism model.

Static Tests Based on Nonlabor Income, Wage Rates, and Assets

Row 6 of table 5.3 repeats the fixed-effect tests but uses nonlabor income rather than total income when estimating equation (8). We restrict the sample to households with \$50 or more of nonlabor income. The results again reject the altruism model. Table 5.4A reports a regression that replaces income with the wages of the head and spouse plus the household's nonlabor income. For the level regression, wage rates and nonlabor income are entered in their levels, while in the logarithmic regression these variables are entered in their logs. An additional sample selection rule imposed here is that wage rates exceed \$0.50 per hour in 1967 dollars. The regression sample in this case includes wives with reported wages less than \$0.50. To control for such wives, many of whom simply do not work, we included a dummy.

The findings in table 5.4A add to the case against the altruism model. In the fixed-effects regressions the coefficients on annual wage rate are significant statistically and economically, which, depending on the form of preferences, may itself constitute evidence against the altruism model. The nonlabor-income coefficient in the log regression is highly significant. In addition, the nonlabor-income coefficients are close in magnitude (the level coefficients are identical to three digits) for the fixed-effects and non-fixed-effects regressions. We also estimated the models of table 5.4A but excluded nonworking wives. The regression results are quite similar.

Table 5.4
Regression estimates including wage rates and dummy for nonworking wife

A. *Current Wage Rates and Nonlabor Income*

Regression	Fixed effect: Head's wage	Fixed effect: Spouse's wage	Fixed effect: Nonlabor income	No fixed effect: Head's wage	No fixed effect: Spouse's wage	No fixed effect: Nonlabor income	Sample size
Levels	0.379	0.180	0.012	0.549	0.339	0.012	8,237
	(5.540)	(1.871)	(1.683)	(7.491)	(3.669)	(1.419)	
Logs	0.136	0.071	0.030	0.178	0.107	0.047	8,237
	(10.255)	(3.838)	(5.252)	(14.183)	(6.867)	(8.967)	

B. *Current and Lagged Wage Rates*

Regression	Fixed effect: Head's wage	Fixed effect: Spouse's wage	Fixed effect: Lagged wage	No fixed effect: Head's wage	No fixed effect: Spouse's wage	No fixed effect: Lagged wage	Sample size
Levels	0.354	0.257	0.293	0.412	0.406	0.401	14,421
	(6.469)	(3.126)	(4.653)	(7.683)	(5.070)	(6.299)	
Logs	0.114	0.065	0.069	0.134	0.097	0.099	14,421
	(9.588)	(4.466)	(5.752)	(13.063)	(7.705)	(9.793)	

Note: Numbers in parentheses are t statistics testing the null hypothesis that the coefficient is zero.

Next we estimated pooled regressions for a sample defined like that of table 5.4A (including wives with wages less than \$0.50), except that home equity rather than nonlabor income was used to test the altruism model. In these regressions (not reported), we required that households have \$1,000 or more of home equity to be included in the sample. In the fixed-effects regressions (sample size = 6,257) the levels coefficient on home equity is 0.004 ($t = 1.97$), and the log coefficient is 0.042 ($t = 3.39$). The corresponding non-fixed-effects coefficients are 0.008 ($t = 5.15$) and 0.075 ($t = 7.43$). Again, contrary to the altruism model's prediction, the fixed-effects coefficients are nontrivial compared with the non-fixed-effects coefficients.

Finally, in table 5.4B we use the lagged wage of the household head to test the altruism model. The regressions also include current wages of the household head and spouse. Recall that if the dynasty's utility function is time-separable, current wages may enter the demand functions, but lagged wages will not. The advantage of testing altruism with lagged wages is that, compared with nonlabor income, they are less likely to be correlated with that component of the error term that reflects household preferences not captured by our demographic controls. The lagged wage coefficients are highly significant in both rows. While the lagged wage coefficients are larger if one excludes the fixed effects, the lagged wage coefficients in the fixed-effects regressions are, nevertheless, quite substantial.

Static Tests of Altruism Under Asymmetric Information

One response to these results is that they only reject the symmetric-information altruism model. If dynasty members are imperfectly informed about each other's income, then the component of dynasty members' income that is unobservable may affect the members' consumption. If parents are altruistic toward children and wealthier than them and if children are less altruistic toward parents, then the component of a child's household income that is unobservable to parents will affect the child's consumption relative to other members of the extended family. Income components that parents know about will not be related to the distribution of consumption in the dynasty. In this case, parents may act to neutralize intergenerational government transfers (which they can observe), even though our results show that they do not neutralize all within-dynasty differences in income.

We allow for this possibility in the seventh row of table 5.3 by instrumenting income with education and two-digit occupation dummies of the household head under the assumption that these are observable to all dynasty members. The sample consists of 15,687 household-year observations with valid data on the occupation and education variables and excludes persons who left the survey in 1986 or 1987, but the departure from our basic sample does not affect the results. The coefficient on the instrumented log of income is 0.306 with a t statistic of 9.51 when fixed effects are included, which compares to 0.340 ($t = 13.5$) when fixed effects are excluded. In the linear case, the instrumented regression coefficient is 0.042 with a t statistic of 7.92 when fixed effects are included and 0.046 when they are excluded. Evidently, the dynasty does not neutralize income differences that are easily observable.

IV. Dynamic Tests

The results from estimating the basic model in one-year and two-year differences are given in the last two rows of table 5.3. These are the results of fitting equation (9) to the pooled data. As the table indicates, the magnitudes of the income-change coefficients are very similar whether one includes or excludes the fixed effects. The effect of changes in own income on household consumption appears to be equally large whether or not one controls for changes in the resource positions of the household's relatives. For example, the coefficient on the second difference in the log of income is 0.137 ($t = 10.425$) in the fixed-effect regression and 0.144 ($t = 13.352$) in the non-fixed-effect regression. The low t statistics in the linear regressions may reflect the problem of greater noise relative to signal associated with first-differencing (see Zvi Griliches and Jerry Hausman, 1986).

These dynamic results reject the standard altruism model and a modified altruism model in which favorite children receive more human capital and, as a result, end up with higher earnings. The results also reject the hypothesis of selfish risk sharing among extended-family members.

V. Can One Reject the Life-Cycle Model?

Table 5.5 reports the ordinary least-squares (OLS) results of estimating equation (11). Recall that this equation relates food consumption to current and two lagged values of own and dynasty nonasset income and current own and dynasty values of wealth. The results in both the logs and the levels (columns 1 and 2) seem, on balance, to suggest a role for dynasty resources in influencing household consumption. In the case of the logs, the sum of the dynasty nonasset income coefficients is about two-fifths the corresponding sum for household nonasset income. The dynasty asset coefficient, although insignificant, is 38 percent of the household asset coefficient.

Table 5.5 also contains the results for 1984 from estimating equation (13′) by instrumental variables (IV). Recall that (13′) arises from assuming that utility is quadratic and that nonasset income consists of a random walk plus a transitory component. In this structural model, consumption is determined by current wealth and the instrumented value of current income. The instrumental variables we use for current (1984) nonasset incomes of the household and dynasty are the demographic controls, household and dynasty wealth, and the separate means (across years) of nonasset income for the household and for all dynasty households. In forming these means we exclude data for 1984.

Table 5.5
The effects of household and dynasty nonasset income and wealth on the log of food consumption, 1984

	OLS		IV on current nonasset income	
Variable	Logs	Levels	Logs	Levels
Household nonasset income in 1984	0.124	0.013	0.281	0.040
	(4.08)	(1.96)	(10.63)	(5.02)
Household nonasset income in 1983	0.049	0.007		
	(1.46)	(0.906)		
Household nonasset income in 1982	0.041	0.014		
	(1.35)	(2.23)		
Household wealth in 1984[a]	0.00142	2.27	0.0011	1.823
	(2.96)	(2.46)	(2.60)	(1.347)
Dynasty nonasset income in 1984	0.113	0.021	0.057	0.0069
	(2.44)	(2.31)	(1.71)	(2.15)
Dynasty nonasset income in 1983	−0.058	−0.020		
	(1.22)	(2.01)		
Dynasty nonasset income in 1982	0.035	0.013		
	(0.825)	(1.61)		
Dynasty wealth in 1984[a]	0.00054	1.397	0.0007	1.523
	(0.671)	(2.46)	(1.09)	(1.22)
Sum of household income coefficients	0.214	0.034		
	(9.43)	(7.66)		
Sum of dynasty income coefficients	0.090	0.015		
	(2.80)	(2.31)		
Number of households:	2,045	2,045	2,507	2,507
X^2 statistic[b] on dynasty income and wealth [P value]:	15.10 [0.005]	18.84 [0.001]	6.70 [0.035]	6.98 [0.030]

Notes: Numbers in parentheses are t statistics testing the null hypothesis that the coefficient is zero.

a. Wealth is measured in thousands of 1967 dollars.

b. The chi-square test statistics in columns 1 and 2 (3 and 4) have 4 (2) degrees of freedom.

The IV results suggest a smaller role of dynasty resources than the previous reduced-form results. In the log regression, the point estimate of the coefficient on dynasty current nonasset income is only one-fifth that of the household; in addition, the dynasty wealth coefficient, though numerically large, is insignificant. Even these results may overstate the true size of the dynasty coefficients since modeling income as a random walk plus a white-noise component may be inappropriate, and the dynasty variables may be correlated with the misspecification error.

The findings of table 5.5 are reinforced by those in table 5.6. Table 5.6 is another reduced-form version of (11), but one that uses data for all past years. Since data on wealth are not available, the regressions of table 5.6 include home equity as well as current and two lags of nonasset income. In the pooled log results the sum of the dynasty income coefficients are almost 30 percent of the corresponding sum of household income coefficients. The dynasty home-equity coefficient is three-quarters the size of the household's home-equity coefficient and is significant.

Table 5.7 returns to the structural permanent-income formulation [equation (13′)] but uses the data for all the years. Since wealth data is available only for 1984, we used total income and instrumented total income with the mean (over past and future years) of total income. The IV coefficients on dynasty income are much smaller than the IV coefficient on own income. In the case of the pooled log IV regression the coefficient on dynasty income is not statistically significant, and it is one-eighteenth of the coefficient on household total income.[16] Note that, as predicted, the difference between the own-income and dynasty coefficients is larger for the IV estimates than for the OLS estimates.

Table 5.8 considers how changes in household and dynasty total income and wage rates (of heads) influence changes in household consumption. The results here are slightly more supportive of the life-cycle model. Consider first one-year changes in consumption. Here, the change in dynasty income has an insignificant influence on the change in consumption, although the magnitude of the point estimate is not trivial. In the case of two-year changes, the two-year change in dynasty income has zero (to three decimal places) effect on the two-year change in household consumption. The wage-rate changes of the dynasty are uniformly insignificant, even after we

Table 5.6
The effects of current and lagged household and dynasty nonasset income and home equity on food consumption

Variable	Pooled regression: Logs	Pooled regression: Levels
Household income in year		
t	0.151	0.013
	(10.42)	(3.39)
$t-1$	0.030	0.006
	(2.27)	(2.07)
$t-2$	0.027	0.011
	(2.34)	(3.32)
Dynasty income in year		
t	0.061	0.016
	(3.20)	(2.14)
$t-1$	−0.0066	0.001
	(0.34)	(0.22)
$t-2$	0.008	−0.002
	(0.42)	(0.48)
Home equity		
Household	0.0027	4.59
	(3.69)	(3.06)
Dynasty	0.0020	2.40
	(1.44)	(1.02)
Sum of income coefficients		
Household	0.208	0.031
	(13.97)	(8.43)
Dynasty	0.062	0.015
	(3.04)	(3.68)
Number of households:	11,905	11,905
X^2 [P value]:	19.58	19.10
	[0.0006]	[0.0007]

Notes: Numbers in parentheses are t statistics testing the null hypothesis that the coefficient is zero. X^2 statistics and associated P values are for the joint test that dynasty income and wealth variables are all zero.

Table 5.7
Tests of the life-cycle model

		OLS estimates		IV estimates	
Pooled regression	Number of households	Household total income	Dynasty total income	Household total income	Dynasty total income
Logs	21,711	0.261 (25.3)	0.048 (3.29)	0.337 (21.4)	0.023 (1.12)
Levels	21,711	0.0219 (4.11)	0.0142 (5.52)	0.040 (7.01)	0.010 (3.02)

Note: Numbers in parentheses are t statistics testing the null hypothesis that the coefficient is zero.

instrument the wage measure with an alternative wage measure to reduce bias from measurement error.

VI. Summary and Conclusion

In recent years the infinite-horizon altruism model has played an important role in theoretical analysis and policy debate. This is surprising, given the lack of direct micro empirical support for the model. The long delay in testing the model with micro data reflects the paucity of data on the extended family. Fortunately, the ongoing PSID now provides sufficient extended-family data to test the operative altruism model. The key prediction of the altruism model is that altruistically linked family members fully share resources in the sense that the division of their total consumption should be independent of the division of their collective resources.

This chapter directly tests whether the distribution of resources affects the distribution of consumption among parents and children. We find overwhelming evidence that it does. Our test procedure is attractive because it does not require solving the extended family's dynamic programming problem or knowing either the precise level of extended-family resources or the boundaries of the altruistically linked extended family. According to the altruism model, all members of the extended family will have the same marginal utility of income, and their consumption demands can be written as functions of this variable and relative prices. Once one controls (through the fixed-effect technique) for the extended family's marginal utility of

Table 5.8
Dynamic tests of the life-cycle model: the Effects of household and dynasty income and wage-rate changes on changes in food consumption

Variable	One-year changes OLS	One-year changes OLS	One-year changes IV	Two-year changes OLS	Two-year changes OLS	Two-year changes IV
Household variables						
Change in log of household income	0.065 (5.39)			0.138 (13.2)		
Change in log of wage of household head		0.035 (2.67)	0.455 (2.86)		0.061 (5.05)	0.280 (3.77)
Dynasty variables						
Change in log of average dynasty income	0.022 (1.16)			0.000 (0.013)		
Change in log of wage of average dynasty head		−0.014 (0.728)	−0.228 (1.31)		−0.026 (1.37)	0.086 (0.80)
Number of observations:	18,200[a]	12,203	6,621	14,284	9,747	5,038

Notes: All equations include year dummies and controls for changes in demographics. The equations that include wage rates also include dummy variables for year t and $t-j\,(j=1,2)$ that equal 1 if a wife was present in the given year and worked a positive number of hours in the previous year at an hourly wage rate greater than \$0.50.

The wage rate in the consumption equation is annual labor earnings of the head divided by annual hours. It refers to the calendar year before the survey. The samples for columns 2 and 3 (columns 5 and 6) exclude households in which the household head did not work or had an average wage rate of less than \$0.50 in either year t or year $t-1$ (t and $t-2$). The principal instrument for the change in the average hourly wage in columns 3 and 6 is the change in a second wage measure that refers to the job held at the time of the survey. This second wage measure is based on a direct question about the hourly wage in the case of hourly workers and is imputed from a question about earnings per week, per month, and so forth in the case of salaried workers. The other instruments are the mean of this alternative wage-change measure taken across households in the dynasty and all the control variables that appear in the consumption-change equation. The sample in column 3 (6) is further restricted to households for which both wage measures are available in years t and $t-1$ (t and $t-2$). However, the difference in the samples has little to do with the increase in the absolute value of the coefficients that arises when instruments are used. Altonji (1986) discusses the properties of this instrumental-variables estimator. The large increase in the coefficient estimates when instruments are used is due to the correction for measurement error and the fact that the second wage measure and the consumption data both refer to the time of the survey.

a. Due to a minor discrepancy in the computation of lagged values, the sample for column 1 exceeds the sample for the dynamic fixed-effects test of the life-cycle model by 11 observations. This has no effect on the results.

income, the resource position of particular extended-family members should not influence the consumption of those members.

In our tests we use total income, nonlabor income, home equity, and wage rates as proxies for the resource position of particular extended-family members. We find that each of these proxies is a significant variable in explaining the consumption of extended-family members even after one has controlled for the extended family's marginal utility of income. The strong rejection of the altruism model holds up for the subset of the sample consisting of rich parents and poor children. It also holds up whether or not labor supply is viewed as endogenous and whether or not the tests are run in levels or first differences.

In addition to showing that own resources matter given extended-family resources, we test the life-cycle model by asking whether only own resources matter (i.e., whether the resources of extended-family members have no effect on a household's consumption). Our results suggest that extended-family member resources have at most a modest effect on marginal household consumption decisions after one has controlled for the fact that extended-family resources help predict a household's own permanent income.

Despite our findings, we do believe that significant altruistically motivated transfers occur in the United States, particularly among the wealthy, who are underrepresented in the PSID. Our findings suggest, however, that very few U.S. households are altruistically linked at the margin in the sense that redistribution between the donor and recipient will be neutralized. The altruistically motivated transfers that one observes in the United States may come in the form of less than fully efficient educational support to liquidity-constrained children (as described by Becker [1974] and Allan Drazen [1978]), in-kind transfers by paternalistic altruists (as described by Robert A. Pollak [1988]), incentive-oriented transfers by altruistic parents concerned about free-riding children (as described by Kotlikoff and Assaf Razin [1988]), and end-of-life transfers by parents concerned that children will squander what they receive at an early age and ask for more (as described by Kotlikoff [1987], Lindbeck and Weibull [1988], and Bruce and Waldman [1989, 1991]).

While liquidity-constrained, paternalistic, and strategically constrained altruism may abound, our findings nevertheless indicate that changing the distribution of resources within the extended family significantly changes its distribution of consumption. Given this finding, the notion that an extended family, let alone an entire country, can be modeled as a single representative consumer with an infinite horizon seems highly questionable.

Notes

We are very grateful to Paul Taubman for assisting our acquisition of data. We thank Robert Barro, Gary Becker, Fischer Black, Richard Blundell, Steve Davis, Gary Chamberlain, V. Chari, Bill English, Zvi Griliches, Dale Jorgenson, Kevin Lang, Bruce Lehrman, Robert Lucas, Greg Mankiw, Jeff Miron, Kevin Murphy, Michael Riordan, Sherwin Rosen, Mark Rosenzweig, Robert Townsend, Paul Taubman, Laurence Weiss, Stephen Zeldes, and seminar participants at a number of universities for very helpful comments. Patricio Arrau, Jinyong Cai, Jagadeesh Gokhale, and Christian Stadlinger provided outstanding research assistance. We are grateful to the National Institute of Aging (grant no. 1RO1AG8655-01) and to the Center for Urban Affairs and Policy Research, Northwestern University, for research support. The 1985 Panel Study of Income Dynamics used in this study is available through the University of Michigan Survey Research Center.

1. One might think that directly studying transfers (see Donald Cox [1987] for a survey of the literature) would be a more appropriate way to test altruism than studying consumption. However, in the absence of liquidity constraints (see Becker, 1974; Allan Drazen, 1978; David Altig and Steven Davis, 1989) or strategic considerations (see Assar Lindbeck and Jörgen Weibull, 1988; Neil Bruce and Michael Waldman, 1989, 1991), the timing of transfers is arbitrary in altruistic models. Secondly, transfers are difficult to measure since they may be in kind or in forms whose prices are not available (e.g., partnership shares). Third, transfers may arise for nonaltruistic reasons, and the mere occurrence of transfers is not, in itself, evidence of altruism.

2. Other studies that have used the PSID child split-offs include Altonji (1988), Jere Behrman et al. (1989), Gary Solon et al. (1987), and Solon (1992). While food expenditures comprise the only consumption data in the PSID (other than expenditures on utilities and information on housing and automobiles, for which rental services would need to be imputed), food is a nondurable and is a major component of nondurable consumption expenditure. Food expenditures should respond to altruistic transfers unless those transfers are in kind and the amount of such in-kind transfers exceeds what the household would voluntarily purchase if the transfer had instead been made in cash.

3. These are Frisch demand functions.

4. Our first-difference results accord with those in the revised version of Andrew Abel and Kotlikoff (1988) and John Cochrane (1991). Other studies in this literature are Mark R. Rosenzweig (1988), Robert M. Townsend (1989), and Barbara Mace (1991).

5. See Kotlikoff et al. (1990) for a model in which transfers are not taken as given.

6. See James Heckman and Thomas MaCurdy (1980) and MaCurdy (1981) for an early use of fixed-effects methods in estimating Frisch demand functions from panel data on individuals.

7. The fixed-effect estimation in this case of only one child and one parent is equivalent to taking the difference between the logarithm of C_{pi} and the logarithm of C_{ki} as

the dependent variable. Clearly, the fixed effect drops out of this regression, and the log difference of the parent's and child's consumption should depend only on the weights θ_p and θ_k and not on the difference between the parent's and child's incomes.

8. As described in note 8 of our working paper (Altonji et al., 1989) a CES function leading to (6) can be viewed as an indirect utility function that incorporates optimal within-household allocation of the total household consumption of each good.

9. If the dynasty is not liquidity-constrained, this difference plus a term involving the time-t interest rate equals the logarithm of the multiplicative Euler error. Note that our dynamic tests, as well as our static tests, are valid even if the dynasty is liquidity-constrained.

10. In contrast to the Euler-equation approach to testing intertemporal consumption choice (see Hayashi [1987] for a survey), our test of the altruism model against the life-cycle/Keynesian alternatives controls for the Euler error through the fixed-effect estimation and, as such, does not require any assumption about the correlation (or lack thereof) across households of the time-t Euler error with information available at time $t-1$.

11. Note that the static fixed-effects test of altruism verses the Keynesian/life-cycle models remains valid even if there is selfish life-cycle risk sharing. At a point in time s, life-cycle risk sharing leads to the fixed-effect model: $\log C_{ps} = (1/\gamma) \log \theta_p - (1/\gamma) \log \lambda_s$ and $\log C_{ks} = (1/\gamma) \log \theta_k - (1/\gamma) \log \lambda_s$. If one regresses the log of consumption against the fixed effect $-(1/\gamma) \log \lambda_s$, demographics, and household income, household income will enter significantly because the bargaining weights, θ_p and θ_k, will depend on the initial resource position of the parent and child. This is not the case in the altruism model, in which utility weights reflect preferences, not bargaining power.

12. We include divorced parents in the dynasty because their altruism for their children will lead to altruistic linkages between them (see Kotlikoff, 1983; B. Douglas Bernheim and Kyle Bagwell, 1988).

13. We constructed the age-sex variables by counting the number of persons who were in a particular household and in a particular age-sex category in a given year. See Altonji et al. (1989 note 16) for a description of the construction of these variables.

14. In terms of the simple model described in equations (1) and (2), the child dummy captures the terms involving θ_{ip} and θ_{ik}.

15. For evidence on this correlation found in the PSID data see Solon et al. (1987) and Solon (1992).

16. The R^2 values for the first stage of the pooled IV estimation underlying Table 5.7 are 0.714 for Y_{ikt} and 0.764 for Y_{it}. The R^2 of the pooled OLS consumption regression is 0.381.

References

Abel, Andrew and Kotlikoff, Laurence J., "Does the Consumption of Different Age Groups Move Together? A New Nonparametric Test of Intergenerational Altruism," National Bureau of Economic Research (Cambridge, MA) Working Paper No. 2490, 1988.

Altig, David and Davis, Steven J., "Altruism, Borrowing Constraints, and Social Security," mimeo, Hoover Institution, May 1989.

Altonji, Joseph G., "Intertemporal Substitution in Labor Supply: Evidence from Micro Data," *Journal of Political Economy*, June 1986, *94*, S176–S215.

Altonji, Joseph G., "The Effects of Family Background and School Characteristics on Education and Labor Market Outcomes," mimeo, Northwestern University, December 1988.

Altonji, Joseph G., Hayashi, Fumio and Kotlikoff, Laurence J., "Is the Extended Family Altruistically Linked? Direct Tests Using Micro Data," National Bureau of Economic Research (Cambridge, MA) Working Paper No. 3046, July 1989.

Barro, Robert, "Are Government Bonds Net Wealth?" *Journal of Political Economy*, November–December 1974, *82*, 1095–1117.

Becker, Gary, "A Theory of Social Interactions," *Journal of Political Economy*, November–December 1974, *82*, 1063–93.

Becker, Gary, *A Treatise on the Family*, Cambridge, MA: Harvard University Press, 1981.

Behrman, Jere, Pollak, Robert and Taubman, Paul, "The Wealth Model; Efficiency in Education and Equity in the Family," mimeo, Department of Economics, University of Pennsylvania, 1989.

Bernheim, B. Douglas and Bagwell, Kyle, "Is Everything Neutral?" *Journal of Political Economy*, April 1988, *96*, 308–38.

Blundell, Richard, "Econometric Approaches to the Specification of Life Cycle Labour Supply and Commodity Demand Behavior," *Econometric Reviews*, 1986, *5*(1), 89–146.

Browning, Martin, Deaton, Angus and Irish, Margaret, "A Profitable Approach to Labor Supply and Commodity Demand over the Life-Cycle," *Econometrica*, May 1985, *53*, 503–44.

Bruce, Neil and Waldman, Michael, "The Rotten-Kid Theorem Meets the Samaritan's Dilemma," *Quarterly Journal of Economics*, February 1989, *105*, 155–65.

Bruce, Neil and Waldman, Michael, "Transfers in Kind: Why They Can Be Efficient and Nonpaternalistic," *American Economic Review*, December 1991, *81*, 1345–51.

Cochrane, John, "A Simple Test of Consumption Insurance," *Journal of Political Economy*, October 1991, *99*, 957–76.

Cox, Donald, "Motives for Private Income Transfers," *Journal of Political Economy*, June 1987, *95*, 508–46.

Drazen, Allan, "Government Debt, Human Capital, and Bequests in a Life Cycle Model," *Journal of Political Economy*, June 1978, *86*, 505–16.

Griliches, Zvi and Hausman, Jerry, "Measurement Error in Panel Data," *Journal of Econometrics*, February 1986, *31*, 93–110.

Hayashi, Fumio, "Tests for Liquidity Constraints: A Survey and Some New Observations," in T. Bewley, ed., *Advances in Econometrics II, Fifth World Congress*, Cambridge: Cambridge University Press, 1987, pp. 91–120.

Heckman, James J. and MaCurdy, Thomas E., "A Life-Cycle Model of Female Labour Supply," *Review of Economic Studies*, January 1980, *47*, 47–74.

Kotlikoff, Laurence J., "Altruistic Linkages Within the Extended Family, A Note," Sloan Foundation Proposal, 1983; reprinted in Laurence J. Kotlikoff, *What Determines Savings?*, Cambridge, MA: MIT Press, 1989.

Kotlikoff, Laurence J., "Justifying Public Provision of Social Security," *Journal of Policy Analysis and Management*, Spring 1987, *6*, 674–89.

Kotlikoff, Laurence J. and Razin, Assaf, "Making Bequests without Spoiling Children," National Bureau of Economic Research (Cambridge, MA) Working Paper, October 1988.

Kotlikoff, Laurence J., Razin, Assaf and Rosenthal, Robert, "A Strategic Altruism Model in which Ricardian Equivalence Does Not Hold," *Economic Journal*, December 1990, *100*, 1261–8.

Lindbeck, Assar and Weibull, Jörgen W., "Altruism and Time Consistency: The Economics of Fait Accompli," *Journal of Political Economy*, December 1988, *96*, 1165–82.

Mace, Barbara, "Full Insurance in the Presence of Aggregate Uncertainty," *Journal of Political Economy*, October 1991, *99*, 928–56.

MaCurdy, Thomas E., "An Empirical Model of Labor Supply in a Life Cycle Setting, *Journal of Political Economy*, December 1981, *89*, 1059–85.

Pollak, Robert A., "Tied Transfers and Paternalistic Preferences," *American Economic Review*, May 1988 (*Papers and Proceedings*), *78*, 240–4.

Rosenzweig, Mark R., "Risk, Implicit Contracts, and the Family in Rural Areas of Low Income Countries," *Economic Journal*, December 1988, *98*, 1148–70.

Solon, Gary, "Intergenerational Income Mobility in the United States," *American Economic Review*, June 1992, *82*, 393–408.

Solon, Gary, Corcoran, May, Gordon, Roger and Laren, Debra, "The Effect of Family Background on Economic Status: A Longitudinal Analysis of Sibling Correlations," National Bureau of Economic Research (Cambridge, MA) Working Paper No. 2282, June 1987.

Townsend, Robert M., "Risk and Insurance in Village India," mimeo, University of Chicago, February 1989.

White, Halbert, *Asymptotic Theory for Econometricians*, Orlando, FL: Academic Press, 1984.

6

Parental Altruism and Inter Vivos Transfers: Theory and Evidence

with Joseph G. Altonji and Fumio Hayashi

I. Introduction

Family exchange is a fundamental economic issue. Families can redistribute income among their members, insure their members against economic risk, and extend their members credit.[1] Two motives compete to explain family exchange: altruism and self-interest. Distinguishing between the two matters. The effectiveness of government redistribution, the intergenerational transmission of inequality, and the degree of risk sharing all hinge on the nature and extent of family exchange.

This paper tests altruism. Specifically, it checks the following implication of altruism: reducing the income of donor parents by one dollar and increasing the income of a recipient child by one dollar reduces the amount transferred by one dollar. Ours is not the first test of transfer-income derivatives.[2] But it uses what we think are better data and a better econometric procedure. Our data set is the 1968–89 Panel Study of Income Dynamics (PSID), particularly the 1988 wave, which contains a supplemental survey on family transfers. The PSID collects separate panel data on parents and most of their adult children. Consequently, we can control for the principal theoretical determinants of money transfers: the current and permanent incomes of the parents, the child, and the child's siblings. We also control for unobserved heterogeneity by using Altonji and Ichimura's (1996) sample selection–corrected derivative estimator.

In Altonji, Hayashi, and Kotlikoff (1992), we used consumption data to test the joint hypotheses that (*a*) family economic links are motivated by altruism and (*b*) all families have operative altruistic linkages. Specifically, we examined the prediction that altruistically linked family members would share their incomes in deciding how much to consume. We found strong evidence that such income sharing, if it occurs, is not ubiquitous. The present study complements our previous work, as well as related consumption studies, by testing for altruism among just those parents who are actually transferring money to their children.[3]

Reliable estimation of transfer-income derivatives requires dealing with unobserved heterogeneity and sample selection bias and doing so without imposing strong functional form assumptions. As we illustrate, transfers are not likely to be an additively separable function of observed factors such as income and unobserved determinants. Consequently, standard estimation methods, such as the Tobit model or Heckman's two-step estimator, cannot be used. In contrast, our derivative estimator is robust to the functional form relating parental utility to consumption and to observed and unobserved preference characteristics. It is also robust to the distribution of unobserved heterogeneity and to certain types of measurement error in reported transfers.

One question about testing altruism with transfer data involves timing. Is the timing of parents' transfers determinant, or just their present value? The answer, in realistic settings, is that timing matters. Indeed, as we discuss in the text and prove in the appendix to this chapter, uncertainty about their child's future income leads parents to delay making transfers as long as possible. This preference for delay is balanced by other factors. Capital market imperfections, considered by Drazen (1978), Becker (1991), and Altig and Davis (1992), are one of them. In concert, these elements produce a time path of transfers that (*a*) balances the desire to delay transfers in order to resolve uncertainty against the desire to relieve recipients' liquidity constraints and (*b*) satisfies the transfer-income derivative restriction where current income is the relevant income measure.[4]

Our findings are striking. Our estimated transfer-income derivatives decisively fail to satisfy the restriction of altruism. In our data, a reduction in parents' income by one dollar reduces their transfer by less than five cents and a one-dollar increase in the child's income reduces the transfer she receives by less than eight cents. Consequently, shifting one dollar in current income from the parents to the child leads to less than a 13-cent reduction in the transfer. This, obviously, is a far cry from the one-dollar reduction predicted by the altruism model.

The chapter is organized in the following manner. Section II discusses the timing of transfers in the context of a two-period model in which altruistic parents are uncertain about their child's future income, but may nonetheless make first-period transfers to relieve their child's liquidity constraint. Section III describes our method of controlling for unobserved heterogeneity in measuring transfer-income derivatives. Sections IV, V, and VI describe the data, present findings, and draw conclusions.

II. A Two-Period Model of Altruistic Inter Vivos Transfers

Consider a model in which parents and a child overlap for two periods. Parents care about their own consumption. They also care about their child's utility and are prepared to make transfers to her.[5] Whether and when they do so depends on the child's second-period income (which is uncertain as of the first period) as well as on the degree to which the child is liquidity-constrained. For example, the child may end up with sufficiently high second-period income that the parents transfer nothing to her in that period. Given this possibility and if their child is not liquidity-constrained, the parents will refrain from making any transfers in the first period until they have had a chance to observe their child's second-period income. There are two reasons for this. First, there is the chance that the child will strike it rich in the second period, in which case the parents will wish to make a negative transfer. Since parents cannot compel the repayment of past gifts, their best option is to wait and see whether their child really needs their help. This is true regardless of the child's likelihood of striking it rich. Even the prospect that their children will win the lottery will lead parents who would otherwise be indifferent to delay making their transfers. True, parents care about their children's utility and therefore want them to intertemporally optimize with respect to current and future consumption. But the parents do not need to make transfers to the child to get this to happen. Instead, the child will do this on her own because doing so is in her self-interest.

The second reason parents will wait to make transfers is to keep their child from overconsuming in period 1 in order to appear relatively poor and elicit a larger transfer in period 2.[6] This motivation to delay transfers also hinges on uncertainty about the child's second-period income. In the absence of uncertainty and liquidity constraints, the parents cannot affect their child's free-riding by delaying their transfers. Giving their child a dollar less in period 1 will not lead her to reduce her consumption in period 1 because she will realize that maintaining her period 1 consumption level will have no effect on her period 2 consumption. True, her own period 2 assets will be lower, but total period 2 family assets will remain the same. This means that her consumption in period 2, which is based on total family resources, will remain the same. Uncertainty alters the story. With uncertainty, the child knows that maintaining her period 1 consumption level in response to a one-dollar reduction in period 1 transfers will come at the cost of lower period 2 consumption in those second-period states of nature in which she has relatively high income and receives no transfers. So, with uncertainty, the parents can, in part, keep their child from overconsuming by delaying their transfers.

Liquidity constraints temper the parents' preference for delay. Now the child cannot intertemporally optimize without first-period transfers from the parents. In this case the parents, in period 1, trade off the benefits to their child of immediate transfers, which translate into immediate consumption, against the cost of being more likely to end up in the second period wishing they could get a transfer from their child. Thus, in the presence of uncertainty, first-period transfers, whether they are zero or positive, represent precisely the amount the parents wish to give in that period rather than the first installment on a certain present value of lifetime transfers that could just as well be paid with interest in the second period. As we show, when the first-period transfer is positive, the difference in the partial derivatives of the transfer with respect to the parents' first-period income and the child's first-period income equals one.

The Model

The parents have a time-separable utility function defined over their own and their child's consumption in periods 1 and 2, that is,

$$V_{p1} = u(c_{p1}) + \eta u(c_{k1}) + E_1[u(c_{p2}) + \eta u(c_{k2})], \tag{1}$$

where $u(\cdot)$ is the concave, point-in-time utility of consumption function, E_1 is the period 1 expectation operator, η is the weight the parents place on the child's utility, c_{p1} stands for consumption of the parents at time 1, and c_{k1} and the other consumption variables are defined analogously.[7] For simplicity, assume that only the second-period income of the child is uncertain.

The dynamic programming needed to maximize the parents' utility starts in period 2. When the parents and child enter that period, the child receives her previously uncertain second-period income, Y_{k2}. Given this value, the parents decide how much (including zero) to transfer to the child. The parents' second-period transfers can, thus, be written as a function of the parents' and child's second-period resource positions. The child, in turn, takes as given this period 2 transfer function as well as any period 1 transfer she receives in choosing the level of period 1 consumption that maximizes her lifetime utility. The child's optimum period 1 consumption can, consequently, be written as a function of her period 1 resource position, including period 1 transfers, and her parents' period 2 resource position. The parents use this period 1 child consumption function in deciding how much to consume and transfer in period 1.

The Appendix lays out this dynamic program and proves that first-period transfers will be positive only if the child is liquidity-constrained, a condition in which the child faces a higher cost of funds than her parents. In this circumstance, it is easy to see that the transfer-income derivative restriction applies. In the objective function and constraints that determine the model's consumption levels, c_{k1}, c_{p1}, c_{k2}, c_{p2}, and first- and second-period transfers, R_1, and R_2, the parents' and child's first-period incomes Y_{p1}, Y_{k1}, and R_1 appear in the linear combination $Y_{p1} - R_1$ or $Y_{k1} + R_1$. Consequently, if we increase Y_{p1} by ε and decrease Y_{k1} by ε, then R_1 will increase by ε and all the other variables will be unchanged. Hence we have

$$\frac{\partial R_1}{\partial Y_{p1}} - \frac{\partial R_1}{\partial Y_{k1}} = 1, \tag{2}$$

which forms the basis of our test of altruism.[8]

III. Econometric Issues and Methods

Our method for estimating income-transfer derivatives is based on the following version of (6.2):

$$\frac{\partial R(\mathbf{Z}, \boldsymbol{\eta})}{\partial Y_{pt}} - \frac{\partial R(\mathbf{Z}, \boldsymbol{\eta})}{\partial Y_{kt}} = 1, \tag{3}$$

which holds provided that R is positive. The terms Y_{pt} and Y_{kt} are the current nonasset income of the parents and child, respectively. The variable $\mathbf{Z}$ denotes the vector $\{Y_{pt}, Y_{kt}, \mathbf{X}\}$, where the vector $\mathbf{X}$ contains current wealth, the determinants of expected future income, and observed preference shifters. The variable $\boldsymbol{\eta}$ is redefined to be a vector (as opposed to a scalar function) of unobservable preference variables.

There are two problems in implementing a test based on (3). First, $\boldsymbol{\eta}$ is unobserved, so (3) cannot be evaluated for any particular family. Second, one needs to estimate the transfer-income derivatives that enter (3) taking account of the fact that the restriction (3) holds only when $R > 0$. Standard approaches to sample selection such as the Tobit model or Heckman's (1979) two-step estimator cannot be used to form consistent estimates of the derivatives with respect to Y_{pt} and Y_{kt} of $R(\mathbf{Z}, \boldsymbol{\eta} \mid \mathbf{Z}, R > 0)$ because $R(\mathbf{Z}, \boldsymbol{\eta})$ cannot be written as the sum of functions of Y_{pt}, Y_{kt}, and $\mathbf{X}$ and a function of $\boldsymbol{\eta}$.[9] Generalizing the maximum likelihood Tobit procedure to models that are nonseparable in $\mathbf{Z}$ and $\boldsymbol{\eta}$ and have nonnormal errors requires a specific assumption about how the unobservables interact with the observables. Using the wrong form could lead to a mistaken rejection of the restriction.

We deal with the first problem by basing our test on the expectation over $\boldsymbol{\eta}$ of the $\boldsymbol{\eta}$-constant income derivatives. In so doing, we take advantage of the fact that under the null hypothesis the restriction (3) holds for all families with $R > 0$. We deal with the second problem by using Altonji and Ichimura's (1996) selection-corrected derivative estimator for nonseparable limited dependent variables models, which we now briefly describe as it applies to the transfer problem.

Let $\boldsymbol{\eta}^*(\mathbf{Z})$ be the set of values of $\boldsymbol{\eta}$ such that $R > 0$ and $g(\boldsymbol{\eta})$ the density of $\boldsymbol{\eta}$. We assume that the distribution of $\boldsymbol{\eta}$ is independent of $\mathbf{Z}$, although we note below that parental investments in human capital may invalidate this assumption. Let $P_R(\mathbf{Z})$ be the probability that R is greater than zero given $\mathbf{Z}$. For a given value of $\mathbf{Z}$, the expected value over observations with positive transfers of the difference in transfer-income derivatives is

$$E\left[\frac{\partial R(\mathbf{Z}, \boldsymbol{\eta})}{\partial Y_{pt}} - \frac{\partial R(\mathbf{Z}, \boldsymbol{\eta})}{\partial Y_{kt}} \middle| \mathbf{Z}, R > 0\right] = \int_{\boldsymbol{\eta}^*(\mathbf{Z})} \left[\frac{\partial R(\mathbf{Z}, \boldsymbol{\eta})}{\partial Y_{pt}} - \frac{\partial R(\mathbf{Z}, \boldsymbol{\eta})}{\partial Y_{kt}}\right] \cdot \frac{g(\boldsymbol{\eta})\, d\boldsymbol{\eta}}{P_R(\mathbf{Z})}$$

$$= \int_{\boldsymbol{\eta}^*(\mathbf{Z})} 1 \cdot \frac{g(\boldsymbol{\eta})\, d\boldsymbol{\eta}}{P_R(\mathbf{Z})} = 1, \qquad (4)$$

where the last equality reflects the application of (3). Thus our answer to the first problem is to exploit the fact that since the restriction (3) is true for all $\boldsymbol{\eta}$, it carries over to the expected value over $\boldsymbol{\eta}$ of (3).

To estimate the left-hand side of (4), we work with the conditional expectation function

$$\bar{R}(\mathbf{Z}) \equiv E[R(\mathbf{Z},\boldsymbol{\eta}) \mid \mathbf{Z}, R > 0] = \int_{\boldsymbol{\eta}^*(\mathbf{Z})} R(\mathbf{Z},\boldsymbol{\eta}) \frac{g(\boldsymbol{\eta})\, d\boldsymbol{\eta}}{P_R(\mathbf{Z})}, \tag{5}$$

which can be estimated given that R and $\mathbf{Z}$ are all observable. Specifically, we work with the derivatives of the conditional expectation function $\bar{R}(\mathbf{Z})$. Because selection into the sample with $R > 0$ is not random, we need to correct the income derivatives of $\bar{R}(\mathbf{Z})$ for sample selection. We begin by differentiating (5) with respect to Y_{jt} $(j = p, k)$, obtaining

$$\frac{\partial \bar{R}}{\partial Y_{jt}} = E\left[\frac{\partial R}{\partial Y_{jt}} \,\middle|\, \mathbf{Z}, R > 0\right] + A_j^2(\mathbf{Z}) + A_j^3(\mathbf{Z}), \tag{6}$$

where

$$A_j^2(\mathbf{Z}) = R(\mathbf{Z},\boldsymbol{\eta}^*(\mathbf{Z}))\frac{g(\boldsymbol{\eta}^*(\mathbf{Z}))}{P_R(\mathbf{Z})}\frac{\partial \boldsymbol{\eta}^*(\mathbf{Z})}{\partial Y_{jt}} = 0 \tag{7}$$

by virtue of the fact that on the boundary transfers are zero. The term A_j^3 is more problematic:

$$\begin{aligned} A_j^3(\mathbf{Z}) &= \int_{\boldsymbol{\eta}^*(\mathbf{Z})} R(\mathbf{Z},\boldsymbol{\eta}) \frac{g(\boldsymbol{\eta})}{P_R(\mathbf{Z})}\left[\frac{-\partial P_R(\mathbf{Z})/\partial Y_{jt}}{P_R(\mathbf{Z})}\right] d\boldsymbol{\eta} \\ &= \frac{-\partial P_R(\mathbf{Z})/\partial Y_{jt}}{P_R(\mathbf{Z})}\bar{R}(\mathbf{Z}). \end{aligned} \tag{8}$$

Since $\partial P_R/\partial Y_{kt} < 0$ and $\partial P_R/\partial Y_{pt} > 0$, A_k^3 is positive and A_p^3 is negative.[10] Fortunately, one can estimate $A_j^3(\mathbf{Z})$ by first estimating $P_R(\mathbf{Z})$ from data on an indicator variable for $R > 0$ and $\mathbf{Z}$ and then substituting the estimate of $P_R(\mathbf{Z})$, the estimate of $\bar{R}(\mathbf{Z})$, and the associated estimates of the derivatives $\partial P_R/\partial Y_{jt}$ into (8). Consequently, our estimator of the difference in the transfer-income derivatives is given by

$$\begin{aligned} &E\left[\frac{\partial R(\mathbf{Z},\boldsymbol{\eta})}{\partial Y_{pt}} \,\middle|\, \mathbf{Z}, R > 0\right] - E\left[\frac{\partial R(\mathbf{Z},\boldsymbol{\eta})}{\partial Y_{kt}} \,\middle|\, \mathbf{Z}, R > 0\right] \\ &\quad = \left[\frac{\partial \bar{R}(\mathbf{Z})}{\partial Y_{pt}} - A_p^3(\mathbf{Z})\right] - \left[\frac{\partial \bar{R}(\mathbf{Z})}{\partial Y_{kt}} - A_p^3(\mathbf{Z})\right], \end{aligned} \tag{9}$$

where we replace the terms on the right-hand side with sample estimates. Our test of the transfer-income derivative restriction compares our estimate of (9) to one for various values of $\mathbf{Z}$. The first and second terms in brackets are the estimators of $E[\partial R(\mathbf{Z}, \boldsymbol{\eta})/\partial Y_{pt} \,|\, \mathbf{Z}, R > 0]$ and $E[\partial R(\mathbf{Z}, \boldsymbol{\eta})/\partial Y_{kt} \,|\, \mathbf{Z}, R > 0]$.

An Empirical Formulation

Altonji and Ichimura (1996) discuss both parametric and nonparametric approaches to estimating $\bar{R}(\mathbf{Z})$ and $P_R(\mathbf{Z})$. Because of the large number of variables involved in our analysis and sample size considerations, we take a flexible parametric approach. Let θ_1 denote the parameters of the function $\bar{R}(\mathbf{Z}; \theta_1)$. We estimate these parameters by running the following least-squares regression on the sample for which $R > 0$:

$$R = \bar{R}(\mathbf{Z}; \theta_1) + u, \tag{10}$$

where u is uncorrelated with $\mathbf{Z}$ because $\bar{R}(\mathbf{Z}; \theta_1)$ is the conditional expectation of R. We specify $\bar{R}(\mathbf{Z}; \theta_1)$ to contain a third-order polynomial in the nonasset incomes of the parents and child with interactions among all first- and second-order terms, third-order polynomials in the assets of both parties and the product of the assets, and third-order polynomials in the permanent incomes Y_p and Y_k of the parents and child as well as the product of Y_p and Y_k. The function also includes a large number of demographic controls, which are listed in table 6.1 below and the notes to tables 6.5 and 6.6.

In choosing a flexible specification for $P_R(\mathbf{Z})$, we are guided by the fact that, as discussed by Amemiya (1981), a conditional probability function can always be approximated by the convolution of a particular conditional distribution function $\Phi(\cdot)$ and a function $h(\mathbf{Z}; \theta_2)$, provided that $h(\mathbf{Z}; \theta_2)$ is sufficiently flexible, with

$$P_R(\mathbf{Z}) = \Phi(h(\mathbf{Z}; \theta_2)). \tag{11}$$

We choose the standard normal conditional distribution function for $\Phi(\cdot)$ and a polynomial specification for $h(\mathbf{Z}; \theta_2)$ that is the same as the specification for $\bar{R}(\mathbf{Z}; \theta_1)$. In this case the elements of θ_2 are the coefficients of the probit index, and we can use standard probit estimation routines to estimate $P_R(\mathbf{Z})$. Given the flexibility in $h(\mathbf{Z}; \theta_2)$, we doubt whether allowing additional flexibility through either Φ or $h(\mathbf{Z}; \theta_2)$ would make much difference.

Table 6.1
Means by transfer category

Variable	Total sample ($N = 3{,}402$)	If no transfer ($N = 2{,}715$)	If transfer ($N = 687$)
Parent gave kid money 0/1 ($R > 0$)	.202	.000	1.000
Amount of money parent gave kid (R)	297.0	.000	1,507.8
	(2,064.5)	(.000)	(4,453.5)
Kid is unmarried female	.230	.228	.240
Kid is unmarried male	.167	.148	.245
Kid is married female	.304	.316	.256
Number of children in kid's household	1.237	1.318	.917
Number of children in single kid's household	.295	.307	.245
Parent is divorced, unmarried father	.023	.024	.019
Parent is divorced, remarried father	.043	.044	.038
Parent is widowed, unmarried father	.026	.028	.016
Parent is widowed, remarried father	.017	.019	.012
Parent is divorced, unmarried mother	.093	.094	.086
Parent is divorced, remarried mother	.05	.05	.049
Parent is widowed, unmarried mother	.184	.194	.144
Parent is widowed, remarried mother	.032	.035	.022
Parents married but live apart	.021	.023	.01
Kid reports race other than white	.357	.385	.246
Age of kid	30.527	30.891	29.087
	(5.802)	(5.786)	(5.642)
Age of parent	58.719	58.965	57.745
	(8.349)	(8.257)	(8.642)
Health of kid in 1988 (1 = excellent, 5 = poor)	2.096	2.117	2.016
	(.947)	(.956)	(.907)
Health of parent in 1988 (1 = excellent, 5 = poor)	3.115	3.171	2.894
	(1.173)	(1.176)	(1.135)
Distance to parent house (estimated)	141.454	139.432	149.447
	(210.737)	(209.739)	(214.604)
Parent resides with kid	.069	.063	.093
Parent lives with another relative	.018	.0200	.013
Inverse of number of kids	.273	.260	.321
	(.181)	(.173)	(.201)
Parent's permanent income: time-averaged method ($\bar{Y}_p$)	54.746	51.481	67.649
	(30.821)	(27.510)	(38.814)
Kid's permanent income: time-averaged method ($\bar{Y}_k$)	48.171	47.644	50.254
	(24.286)	(23.868)	(25.785)
Parent's permanent income: autoregressive method ($\hat{Y}_p$)	53.403	50.976	62.996
	(23.682)	(21.350)	(29.335)
Kid's permanent income: autoregressive method ($\hat{Y}_k$)	46.207	45.949	47.223
	(14.942)	(14.869)	(15.195)

Note: Standard deviations are in parentheses. The sample is unweighted.

Inference is complicated by the fact that the derivative estimators are a complicated nonlinear function of $\hat{\theta}_1$ and $\hat{\theta}_2$. Furthermore, one must account for the fact that the samples used to estimate $\hat{\theta}_1$ and $\hat{\theta}_2$ contain more than one observation from some families, and heteroscedasticity is likely to be present in (10). While one can use the "delta method" to derive asymptotic standard errors for $E[\partial R(\mathbf{Z}, \boldsymbol{\eta})/\partial Y_{pt} \mid \mathbf{Z}, R > 0; \hat{\theta}_1, \hat{\theta}_2]$, $E[\partial R(\mathbf{Z}, \boldsymbol{\eta})/\partial Y_{kt} \mid \mathbf{Z}, R > 0; \hat{\theta}_1, \hat{\theta}_2]$, and their difference from the asymptotic joint distribution of $\hat{\theta}_1$ and $\hat{\theta}_2$, the approximation may not be reliable. Consequently, we use a bootstrap procedure to estimate the standard errors of these derivatives for various values of **Z** and for the sample average of the derivatives over the distribution of **Z** for those who receive transfers.[11] To simplify the notation, we refer to these derivatives as $E\partial R/\partial Y_{pt}$, $E\partial R/\partial Y_{kt}$, and $\Delta E\partial R/\partial Y_{jt}$.

Controlling for Information about Future Income

The derivatives in (3) hold constant variables in the information set used to forecast future income. Our econometric analysis tries to control for these variables. To the extent that it fails, the predicted difference in transfer-income derivatives will likely exceed one. Why? Because unobservables that raise future income are also likely to raise current income. Consequently, $\partial R/\partial Y_{pt}$ will be larger than if the unobservables had not changed because higher values of the parents' future income will induce the parents to make larger transfers in the present as well as in the future. While we could not sign the effect of the child's future income on current transfers in the model because of the role of liquidity constraints in the timing of transfers, $\partial R_1/\partial Y_{k1}$ will be smaller in the likely event that higher values of the child's future income reduce present as well as future transfers. We address the issues of measurement error in current income, assets, and transfers in Section V.

Endogeneity of the Child's Income?

The estimator we use assumes that the unobserved components of the preference vector $\boldsymbol{\eta}$ are independent of Y_{kt}. Parental investments in their child's human capital will influence current and permanent income of the child and may depend on $\boldsymbol{\eta}$. The derivative restriction (6.3) will hold, but the endogeneity of Y_{kt} may lead to bias in the estimate of $E\partial R/\partial Y_{kt}$. The bias is likely to be positive, leading to an underestimate of $\Delta E\partial R/\partial Y_{jt}$.[12]

IV. Data

This section discusses the sample as well as the construction and quality of key variables.

The Sample

Our data are taken from the 1988 Panel Study of Income Dynamics (PSID), which includes a special supplement on transfers between relatives.[13] Using the PSID overcomes a key problem in the study of intergenerational transfers, namely obtaining reliable data on the economic resources of both parents and adult children. Our sample consists of parents and their children who were in 1968 PSID families and were heads or wives of 1988 PSID households. Only about 2 percent of the children were students in 1988. We have 1988 data on the income and family composition of the households in which these individuals reside as well as pre-1988 data on their assets, health status, income, and other variables. Those 1988 households containing heads or wives who were children in the 1968 study are matched to the 1988 households of their parents. An observation consists of one such matched pair. Given that a child's mother and father may be in separate households, each child may appear in one or two records. Parents with multiple children appear in as many records as they have respondent children. The effective sample for most of the multivariate analyses consists of 3,402 parent-child pairs, including 687 pairs with positive transfers.[14]

The Transfer Data

Information on R is based on the following two-part question: (1) During 1987, did you/your family living here receive any loans, gifts, or support worth \$100 or more from your parents? (2) About how much were those loans, gifts, or support worth altogether in 1987? Separate questions are asked about transfers from the father and transfers from the mother if the parents are divorced, and as noted above, we treat these transfers as separate observations. If the child is married at the time of the 1988 survey, the question is asked first about the husband's parents and then about the wife's parents. Persons who married into PSID households were not interviewed, so we use information on the transfers from either the wife's parents or the husband's parents depending on whether the wife or the husband was in the original 1968 PSID sample.[15]

Several points about this question deserve mention. First, the question specifically refers to loans. Nonetheless, we treat the responses as transfer measures since we have no evidence on the fraction of the transfers that are actually loans. In this regard, Altonji et al. (1996) find that transfers are no more likely to be reported among those children who became new homeowners between the 1986 and 1987 or the 1987 and 1988 surveys. Second, in the interest of simplicity we ignore the \$100 threshold in the question, although we doubt that this makes much difference.[16] Third, we have little direct information on the quality of the data. Presumably, the fact that the question directly asks about help from parents is an advantage over questions that do not specify the relationship.[17] Although the incidence of money transfers is higher than in most other studies,[18] we still think that there is substantial measurement error in the transfer reports. However, to repeat, our derivative estimator is robust to random failure to report transfers and to random variation in the fraction of transfers that households report.

Income and Wealth Measures

Nonasset net family income in 1987 is our measure of current income of the parents and the child (Y_{pt}, Y_{kt}). We exclude asset income because it may be affected by prior transfers but control for assets and permanent family income (including asset income) separately. We also use two alternative measures of permanent income: Y_p of the parents and Y_k of the kids. Both are based on the regression model

$$\log(Y_{it}) = \mathbf{X}_{yit}\beta + e_{it}, \tag{12}$$

where Y_{it} is the family income of person i in year t and the vector $\mathbf{X}_{yit}$ consists of a fourth-order polynomial in age, a set of marital status dummies, year dummies, and counts of number of children. The first measure assumes that $e_{it} = v_i + u_{it}$, where the serial correlation in u_{it} is assumed to be sufficiently weak to be ignored in computing permanent income. We first estimate the parameter β from gender-specific OLS regressions using all observations in which the person was a head or wife.[19] We estimate v_i as the mean of the residuals from the regression for each person. We obtain our first measure of permanent income for parents by adding the estimate of v_i to the prediction from the regression for a person who is aged 40, is married, and had no children in 1988 and taking the antilog.[20] We call these measures $\bar{Y}_p$ and $\bar{Y}_k$, where the overbar reflects the fact that they are basically time averages of current and past income adjusted for demographic variables and time.

For the second measure, we model e_{it} as a third-order autoregressive process with coefficients that depend on a third-order polynomial in age, Age_{it} of person i in year t:

$$e_{it} = (1, \text{Age}_{it}, \text{Age}_{it}^2, \text{Age}_{it}^3)\gamma_1 e_{it-1} + (1, \text{Age}_{it}, \text{Age}_{it}^2, \text{Age}_{it}^3)\gamma_2 e_{it-2}$$
$$+ (1, \text{Age}_{it}, \text{Age}_{it}^2, \text{Age}_{it}^3)\gamma_3 e_{it-3} + u_{it},$$

where γ_1, γ_2, and γ_3 are 4×1 vectors of parameters and u_{it} is serially uncorrelated. We estimate β from (12) using OLS and estimate γ_1, γ_2, and γ_3 using the OLS residuals from the sample estimate of (12).[21] We then use the chain rule of forecasting to forecast future values of e for the periods $t+1$ to $t+6$; combine the forecasts into an index with weights that decline geometrically at rate $1/1.07$ and sum to one; add the index to the prediction based on the estimate of (12) for a person who is aged 40, is married, and had no children in 1988; and take antilogs. We call these measures $\hat{Y}_p$ and $\hat{Y}_k$. They allow time dependence in the stochastic income component to depend on age and place more weight on the recent past than the time-averaged measures.

The quality of the permanent income measures deserves discussion. The minimum number and fifth percentile of the number of observations used to construct $\bar{Y}_p$ are 10 and 21, respectively. The fifth, fiftieth, and ninetieth percentiles for the number of observations used to construct $\bar{Y}_k$ are one, nine, and 18. The fact that these measures are averaged from several years of data suggests that transitory income and measurement error will have only a minor effect on them.[22]

Our measure of assets of the parents is based on the 1984 wealth supplement to the PSID, which is the most recent year prior to 1988 in which detailed information on assets was collected. Since this variable refers to the wealth of the head and wife (if present) of the individual's 1984 household, we interact this variable with a dummy equal to zero if the household head changed since 1984 and one otherwise and add the dummy variable to the list controls. We construct the asset measure and a change in household head dummy for the child household in the same way. We also explore the issue of measurement error by experimenting with data from the 1989 wealth supplement.

In some of our estimation we use the average of permanent incomes of siblings who are heads or wives in the PSID as a control for the resources of siblings.[23]

Table 6.1 presents the unweighted means and standard deviations of selected variables for our sample and for the subsets with and without positive transfers. The means of age are 30.5 for the children and 58.7 for the parents. One implication of our model of the timing of transfers is that the transfer probability should fall with the age of the child as earnings rise relative to permanent income. This is consistent with the table as well as with the multivariate probits (not shown). Only 2.9 percent of the children who were heads of household and reported a positive transfer in 1987 were students at the time of the 1988 survey. The comparable percentage for wives is 0.6 percent. The percentages who were students in 1987 are similar, so few of the transfers would appear to be related to recent schooling expenditures.

V. Results

This section is divided into five subsections. Subsection *A* describes the distribution of transfers. Subsection *B* presents a probit model of the probability of a transfer. Subsection *C* presents estimates of the transfer-income derivatives. Subsection *D* shows that these results are robust to a large number of changes in the specification, data, and estimation method. Subsection *E* discusses the source and interpretation of our findings.

A. The Distribution of Transfers

Table 6.2 reports the mean probability of a transfer and the mean, standard deviation, and fifth, twenty-fifth, median, seventy-fifth, and ninety-fifth percentiles of the distribution of positive transfers. It also reports corresponding statistics for the ratio of the transfer

Table 6.2
Distribution of positive transfers

	Fraction > 0	Mean	Mean > 0	Standard deviation > 0	5th Percentile	25th Percentile	Median	75th Percentile	95th Percentile	Maximum
Transfer amount	.233	421.20	1,810	26,833	100	200	500	1,000	5,000	50,000
Ratio to parent: time-averaged permanent income	.233	.0057	.0246	.3214	.0015	.0037	.0078	.0171	.0737	.6586
Ratio to kid: time-averaged permanent income	.233	.0091	.0390	.5163	.0017	.0046	.0102	.0236	.1341	.9567
Ratio to parent: autoregressive permanent income	.233	.0060	.0260	.3451	.0017	.0038	.0082	.0177	.0801	.7310
Ratio to kid: autoregressive permanent income	.233	.0088	.0377	.5063	.0020	.0047	.0094	.0224	.1228	.9921
Ratio to parent: current income	.231	.0122	.0527	.9605	.0022	.0061	.0141	.0374	.1687	3.084
Ratio to kid: current income	.233	.0200	.0859	1.147	.0027	.0089	.0216	.0579	.3724	2.314

Note: Sample sizes vary slightly because of missing values. Estimates are weighted. Transfers from parents living in separate households are combined.

Table 6.3
Probability of money transfer to child and mean transfer amount by permanent income of parent and permanent income of child

	Permanent income quintile of child					
Permanent income quintile of parent	Lowest (23,821) (1)	Second (39,059) (2)	Third (49,746) (3)	Fourth (62,119) (4)	Highest (89,904) (5)	Total (52,926) (6)
Lowest (28,030):						
Probability	.150	.093	.114	.104	.194	.126
Mean	491	279	1,035	548	780	567
Second (42,864):						
Probability	.266	.215	.125	.176	.175	.193
Mean	724	1,589	2,083	2,722	558	1,477
Third (55,040):						
Probability	.257	.260	.232	.235	.190	.234
Mean	677	1,248	2,233	1,098	1,796	1,408
Fourth (69,505):						
Probability	.473	.331	.277	.250	.269	.302
Mean	1,201	1,110	3,536	930	747	1,465
Highest (109,639):						
Probability	.489	.371	.330	.280	.342	.345
Mean	2,707	2,243	4,214	1,862	3,434	3,015
Total (62,584):						
Probability	.268	.241	.220	.224	.268	.244
Mean	1,173	1,412	3,066	1,476	2,222	1,851

Note: The permanent income measures are $\bar{Y}_p$ and $\bar{Y}_k$ and refer to family income. Transfers from parents living in separate households are combined. Estimates are weighted using the 1988 person weights of the children.

amount to the income of the parents and the income of the child. Tables 6.2, 6.3, and 6.4 aggregate transfers received from and given to parents living separately, so each person with living parents appears only once in the sample used to compute these tables.[24] For married couples the parents are either the parents of the husband or the parents of the wife, depending on whether the husband or the wife was a child in the original 1968 PSID sample.

The probability that R is positive is .23. The overall mean transfer is \$421 (in 1988 dollars), and the mean and median of the positive transfers are \$1,810 and \$500. When R is positive, the median and ninety-fifth percentile of the ratio of R to the child's 1988 income are .022 and .372 for the sample with positive transfers. The median and ninety-fifth percentile of the ratio of R to the parents' 1988 income are .014 and .169.

Table 6.4
Probability of money transfer to child and mean transfer amount by current income of parent and current income of child

	Current income quintile of child					
Current income quintile of parent	Lowest (23,821) (1)	Second (39,059) (2)	Third (49,746) (3)	Fourth (62,119) (4)	Highest (89,904) (5)	Total (52,926) (6)
Lowest (1,618):						
Probability	.156	.121	.172	.080	.156	.138
Mean	630	896	432	1,746	828	777
Second (19,176):						
Probability	.257	.176	.233	.100	.146	.182
Mean	403	4,681	3,320	636	1,911	2,337
Third (30,125):						
Probability	.336	.184	.252	.265	.174	.243
Mean	961	695	1,593	2,205	1,646	1,420
Fourth (46,019):						
Probability	.550	.330	.220	.291	.157	.299
Mean	1,111	2,224	753	674	1,212	1,217
Highest (100,371):						
Probability	.518	.393	.437	.299	.307	.377
Mean	2,420	2,689	1,822	2,779	4,865	2,885
Total (39,721):						
Probability	.321	.234	.261	.210	.192	.244
Mean	1,170	2,328	1,719	1,776	2,701	1,851

Note: See note to table 6.3. The current income measure is family income.

Table 6.3 presents weighted estimates for the matched sample of the probability of transfers and the mean amount given a positive transfer by permanent income quintile of the parents and child using $\bar{Y}_p$ and $\bar{Y}_k$ as the measures. Mean income for each quintile is also shown.

According to the table, the probability of a transfer is negatively related to the child's income when the parents' income quintile is held constant. The bottom row shows that there is no correlation if one does not hold the parents' quintile constant. The transfer amounts are essentially unrelated to the child's income when the parents' income is held constant. However, the bottom row shows that they increase substantially with Y_k when parents' income is not held constant. Evidently, the strength of the relationship between the child's income and the transfer amount is exaggerated by a failure to control for parental income.[25]

When the child's income is held constant, parents' income bears a positive relationship to the transfer probability and, in the case of a positive transfer, to the transfer amount. Column 6 shows that the probability of a transfer rises from .126 in the lowest quintile of Y_p, to .234 in the third quintile, and to .345 in the top quintile. The mean of the transfers also rises with parental income, from $567 in the lowest quintile to $3,015 in the highest. The relationship appears to be stronger than the relationship between transfers and the child's income. However, the increase in transfer amounts as the parents' income increases (with the child's income held constant) is only a small fraction of the increase in the parent's income, which has a mean of $28,030 in the first quintile and $109,639 in the fifth quintile.

Table 6.4 repeats table 6.3, but with permanent income replaced by current income. The results are qualitatively similar to those for permanent income. The main difference is a stronger negative relationship between the child's current income and the transfer probability. This partially reflects the fact that our permanent income measure adjusts for the age of the child, whereas our current income measure does not, and age has a negative effect on the transfer probability.

One way to summarize tables 6.3 and 6.4 is to regress the cell means for the transfer amounts against the cell means for the parents' income and the child's income. When the permanent income measures in table 6.3 are used, the coefficient (uncorrected OLS standard error) or parents' income is .025 (.006) and the coefficient on the child's income is .003 (.007). When table 6.4 is used, the coefficient on parents' current income is .017 (.007), whereas the coefficient on the child's income is .009 (.010). Thus inspection of tables 6.3 and 6.4 and the summary regressions suggest that $\Delta E\partial R/\partial Y_j$ is much closer to zero than the value of one implied by altruistic preferences. There are, of course, many problems with these simple cross tabulations. However, the basic results are qualitatively consistent with what we obtain below using the derivative estimator based on (9), although $E\partial R/\partial Y_{kt}$ is negative and statistically significant in the multivariate model.

B. *The Effects of Income and Wealth on the Probability of a Transfer*

Column 2 of table 6.5 reports probit estimates of the effects of the current and permanent income of the child and the parents on the probability that the child receives money from the parents and a detailed set of controls, with $\bar{Y}_p$ and $\bar{Y}_k$ used as the measures of Y_p and Y_k. In column 3 we use $\hat{Y}_p$ and $\hat{Y}_k$ as the measures with little effect on the results. Since the relationship between transfers and income is likely to be nonlinear, the model contains cubics in Y_{pt} and Y_{kt}, cubics in the measures of Y_p and Y_k, the product of Y_p and Y_k, cubics in the assets of both parties, and the product of the assets. The income and wealth variables are measured in \$1,000s.[26]

Column 2, row 2, of the table reports that, for this specification, the sample mean of the derivative of the transfer probability with respect to Y_{kt} is $-.0021$, which implies that a \$10,000 increase in the current family income of the child will lower the odds of a transfer by .021. Rows 3, 4, and 5 report the predicted transfer probability evaluated at the median, twentieth percentile, and eightieth percentile of Y_{kt}; the median of Y_p, Y_k, and Y_{pt}; and the mean of all other variables. The probability is .145 at the median of Y_{kt}, .176 at the twentieth percentile, and .116 at the eightieth percentile. Rows 8, 9, and 10 report a similar set of calculations on the effects of parental income Y_{pt}, showing that the transfer probability is .127 at the twentieth percentile of Y_{pt} and .183 at the eightieth percentile.

An increase in the permanent income of the child from the twentieth to the eightieth percentile has a small negative effect on the probability (rows 14 and 15). On the other hand, a comparable increase in the permanent income of the parents raises the transfer probability from .096 to .197 in rows 19 and 20, which is about double the effect of parents' current income. In column 1 we report estimates that exclude current income measures and wealth. They confirm a strong positive effect of the permanent income of the parents and a significant negative effect for the permanent income of the child on the odds of a transfer.[27]

C. *Estimates of the Effects of Income on Transfer Amounts*

Table 6.6 reports the derivatives of transfers with respect to current nonasset income Y_{pt} and Y_{kt} of the parents and kids based on the estimator in Section III. In panel A we use $\bar{Y}_p$ and $\bar{Y}_k$ as the measures of permanent income. In panel B we report results using $\hat{Y}_p$ and $\hat{Y}_k$.[28] Columns 1 and 3 of the table report the uncorrected derivatives $\partial\bar{R}(\mathbf{Z})/\partial Y_{pt}$ and $\partial\bar{R}(\mathbf{Z})/\partial Y_{kt}$. Columns 2 and 4 report the corrected derivatives $E\partial R/\partial Y_{pt}$ and $E\partial R/\partial Y_{kt}$ based on (9). The sample selection

Table 6.5
Effects of income and wealth on the probability of a transfer: Probit estimates

	Permanent income measure*				
	$\bar{Y}_k, \bar{Y}_p$		$\hat{Y}_k, \hat{Y}_p$	Earnings (time-averaged)	
	(1)	(2)	(3)	(4)	(5)
Current income	excluded	nonasset income	nonasset income	earnings	excluded
Assets	excluded	yes	yes	yes	yes
	Effects of kid's current income				
1. Probit coefficient, linear specification		−.0044 (.0021)	−.0039 (.0021)	−.0037 (.0022)	
2. Mean of derivatives		−.0021	−.0020	−.0020	
Probability of transfer:					
3. At median		.145	.145	.137	
4. At 20th percentile		.176	.176	.165	
5. At 80th percentile		.116	.117	.116	
	Effects of parents' current income				
6. Probit coefficient, linear specification		.0036 (.0011)	.0039 (.0011)	.0047 (.0013)	
7. Mean of derivatives		.0014	.0016	.0016	
Probability of transfer:					
8. At median		.145	.145	.137	
9. At 20th percentile		.127	.124	.120	
10. At 80th percentile		.183	.186	.172	
	Effects of kid's permanent income				
11. Probit coefficient, linear specification	−.0038 (.0012)	−.0021 (.0016)	−.0042 (.0028)	−.0106 (.0050)	−.0041 (.0013)
12. Mean of derivatives	−.0013	−.0003	−.0006	−.0027	−.0015
Probability of transfer:					
13. At median	.170	.145	.145	.137	.154
14. At 20th percentile	.198	.152	.149	.150	.181
15. At 80th percentile	.148	.139	.136	.120	.133
	Effects of parents' permanent income				
16. Probit coefficient, linear specification	.0105 (.0010)	.0075 (.0013)	.0092 (.0017)	.0088 (.0023)	.0061 (.0010)
17. Mean of derivatives	.0036	.0024	.0028	.0039	.0025
Probability of transfer:					
18. At median	.170	.145	.145	.137	.154
19. At 20th percentile	.095	.096	.100	.101	.100
20. At 80th percentile	.262	.197	.192	.203	.215

Table 6.5 (continued)

	Permanent income measure*				
	$\bar{Y}_k, \bar{Y}_p$		$\hat{Y}_k, \hat{Y}_p$	Earnings (time-averaged)	
	(1)	(2)	(3)	(4)	(5)
	Effects of kid's wealth				
21. Probit coefficient, linear specification		.00001 (.00069)	.00008 (.00069)	.00025 (.00066)	−.00028 (.00067)
22. Mean of derivatives		.00005	.00005	.00014	−.00016
Probability of transfer:					
23. At median		.145	.145	.137	.154
24. At 20th percentile		.145	.144	.136	.155
25. At 80th percentile		.146	.146	.140	.149
	Effects of parents' wealth				
26. Probit coefficient, linear specification		.00040 (.00020)	.00041 (.00020)	.00072 (.00021)	.00067 (.00020)
27. Mean of derivatives		.00054	.00056	.00080	.00076
Probability of transfer:					
28. At median		.145	.145	.137	.154
29. At 20th percentile		.120	.119	.104	.119
30. At 80th percentile		.190	.190	.201	.219

Note: Conventional asymptotic standard errors for the probit estimator are in parentheses. They do not correct for correlation across observations involving siblings or mothers and fathers who are in separate households. The models also control for the demographic variables listed in table 1 and cubic polynomials in the age of the child and in the age of the parent. Col. 1 contains 3,402 observations and 687 positive transfers, cols. 2 and 3 contain 3,062 observations and 618 positive transfers, and col. 4 contains 2,850 observations and 601 positive transfers. Probit coefficients and standard errors for the linear specification come from models that contain only linear income (and wealth and current income) terms (rows 1, 6, 11, 16, 21, and 26). All other results are based on models that include a cubic in the income (and wealth) measures and an interaction between the level income terms. Wealth is measured in thousands of dollars. Probabilities are evaluated at the mean of the included variables and the median of the income and wealth variables.

*The methods used to construct the "time-averaged" permanent income measures $\bar{Y}_k$ and $\bar{Y}_p$ and the "autoregressive" measures $\hat{Y}_k$ and $\hat{Y}_p$ are described in Sec. IV.C.

Table 6.6
Effects of the parents' and child's current income on transfers: Derivative estimator for nonlinear limited dependent variables models

Evaluation point	Parents' income (Y_{pt}) Uncorrected derivative* (1)	Parents' income (Y_{pt}) Corrected derivative† (2)	Child's income (Y_{kt}) Uncorrected derivative* (3)	Child's income (Y_{kt}) Corrected derivative† (4)	$\Delta E\partial R/\partial Y_{jt}$: Difference in Derivatives (Col. 2–Col. 4) (5)
	A. Time-averaged measure of permanent income: $\bar{Y}_k, \bar{Y}_p$‡				
1. Average of derivatives	.014	.023	−.052	−.066	.089
	(.014)	(.077)	(.047)	(.091)	(.141)
2. Sample means	.009	.035	−.048	−.088	.123
	(.011)	(.015)	(.026)	(.036)	(.037)
3. Sample means: $Y_{pt} = 80\%$, $Y_{kt} = 20\%$	.006	.038	−.055	−.126	.164
	(.016)	(.018)	(.060)	(.079)	(.096)
4. Sample means: $Y_{pt} = 20\%$, $Y_{kt} = 80\%$	.020	.035	−.057	−.090	.125
	(.019)	(.023)	(.028)	(.033)	(.040)
	B. Autoregressive measure of permanent income: $\hat{Y}_k, \hat{Y}_p$‡				
1. Average of derivatives	.016	.026	−.054	−.067	.093
	(.014)	(.070)	(.035)	(.120)	(.165)
2. Sample means	.010	.031	−.050	−.079	.110
	(.011)	(.014)	(.026)	(.034)	(.035)
3. Sample means: $Y_{pt} = 80\%$, $Y_{kt} = 20\%$	.007	.028	−.059	−.104	.132
	(.015)	(.018)	(.058)	(.077)	(.093)
4. Sample means: $Y_{pt} = 20\%$, $Y_{kt} = 80\%$	.021	.043	−.058	−.072	.115
	(.019)	(.022)	(.028)	(.031)	(.040)

Note: See Sec. III for a description of the estimation procedure and the bootstrap method used to compute the standard errors (in parentheses). The sample used to estimate eq. (10) contains 666 observations. The sample used to estimate (11) contains 3,402 observations. Equations also control for permanent income of the parent, permanent income of the child, assets of the parent in 1984, and assets of the child in 1984; separate dummy variables for whether assets of the parent in 1984 are missing, assets of the child in 1984 are missing, or assets of either the parent or the child are missing; the demographic variables listed in table 1; and cubics in the age of the parent and the age of the child.

* $\partial\bar{R}(\mathbf{Z})/\partial Y_{jt}$; $j = p$ in col. 1 and k in col. 3.

† $[\partial\bar{R}(\mathbf{Z})/\partial Y_{jt}] + \{[\bar{R}(\mathbf{Z})\partial P_R(\mathbf{Z})/\partial Y_{jt}]/P_R(\mathbf{Z})\}$; $j = p$ in col. 2 and k in col. 4.

‡ Permanent income is calculated using the time-averaged method in panel A and the autoregressive method in panel B (see Sec. IV.C).

correction factors are the terms defined in equation (8). The results indicate that the correction factors are often substantial relative to the uncorrected derivatives and almost always have the expected sign, with $A_p^3(\mathbf{Z}) < 0$ and $A_k^3(\mathbf{Z}) > 0$. Column 5 reports the estimates of the difference between $E\partial R/\partial Y_{pt}$ and $E\partial R/\partial Y_{kt}$ evaluated at various points.

In row 1 of panel A, we take the sample mean of all the terms evaluated at the values of $\mathbf{Z}$ for each observation in the sample with positive transfers. In row 2 of panel A, we evaluate the derivatives at the sample means of all variables. The corrected estimates of $E\partial R/\partial Y_{pt}$ and $E\partial R/\partial Y_{kt}$ evaluated at the sample means are .035 (.015) and $-.088$ (.036). The implied value for $\Delta E\partial R/\partial Y_{jt}$ is .123 (.037), which is far below one.[29] The corresponding estimate using the alternative measures of permanent income in panel B is .110. The sample average of $(E\partial R/\partial Y_{pt}) - (E\partial R/\partial Y_{kt})$ is .089 (row 1 of panel A), although the standard error is relatively large. The largest estimate of the difference in derivatives is .164, which we obtain when we use $\bar{Y}_p$ and $\bar{Y}_k$ as the controls for permanent income and evaluate the derivatives at the mean of $\mathbf{X}$ and the eightieth and twentieth percentile values of Y_{pt} and Y_{kt} (respectively).

In summary, the difference in the derivatives of transfers with respect to the current incomes of the parents and child is about 0.1 rather than the value of one implied by the altruism model. The result reflects two basic facts about the PSID data that are also consistent with evidence from other data sets, such as the National Longitudinal Survey (see Dunn's [1993] results and his survey of other studies). First, the derivative of transfer amounts with respect to parents' current income (and permanent income) is relatively small. A small value is perfectly consistent with the theory and depends on the form of preferences and the distribution of resources. However, altruism implies that in this case the derivative of the transfer amounts with respect to the child's income must be negative and large in absolute value. In fact, transfer amounts are not very responsive to the child's income. This basic fact does not appear to be the result of bias from selection into the sample with positive transfers, because our methodology corrects the effects of bias on the income derivatives.

In table 6.7 we drop the current income terms and report the derivatives with respect to Y_p and Y_k. Although the theory suggests that the current income of the child (with permanent income held

Table 6.7
Effects of the parents' and child's permanent income on transfers

Evaluation point	Parents' income (Y_p): Uncorrected derivative* (1)	Parents' income (Y_p): Corrected derivative† (2)	Child's income (Y_k): Uncorrected derivative* (3)	Child's income (Y_k): Corrected derivative† (4)	$\Delta E \partial R/\partial Y_j$: Difference in Derivatives (Col. 2–Col. 4) (5)
	A. Time-averaged measure of permanent income: $\bar{Y}_k, \bar{Y}_p$				
1. Average of derivatives	.026	.044	−.002	−.010	.054
	(.008)	(.009)	(.006)	(.006)	(.011)
2. Sample means	.013	.037	−.008	−.017	.053
	(.012)	(.014)	(.008)	(.009)	(.017)
3. Sample means: $Y_p = 80\%$, $Y_k = 20\%$	−.008	.006	.006	−.005	.011
	(.023)	(.025)	(.025)	(.027)	(.046)
4. Sample means: $Y_p = 20\%$, $Y_k = 80\%$	.049	.059	−.021	−.030	.089
	(.021)	(.022)	(.013)	(.013)	(.028)
	B. Autoregressive measure of permanent income: $\hat{Y}_k, \hat{Y}_p$				
1. Average of derivatives	.031	.054	−.001	−.012	.066
	(.010)	(.011)	(.008)	(.009)	(.013)
2. Sample means	.018	.050	.006	−.009	.059
	(.012)	(.017)	(.015)	(.017)	(.027)
3. Sample means: $Y_p = 80\%$, $Y_k = 20\%$	−.000	.018	.025	.013	.005
	(.026)	(.030)	(.034)	(.038)	(.063)
4. Sample means: $Y_p = 20\%$, $Y_k = 80\%$	.068	.105	−.010	−.024	.129
	(.029)	(.029)	(.021)	(.021)	(.042)

Note: See note to table 6.6. Current incomes of the parent and child are excluded.
* $\partial \bar{R}(\mathbf{Z})/\partial Y_j$; $j = p$ in col. 1 and k in col. 3.
† $[\partial \bar{R}(\mathbf{Z})/\partial Y_j] + \{[\bar{R}(\mathbf{Z}) \partial P_R(\mathbf{Z})/\partial Y_j]/P_R(\mathbf{Z})\}$; $j = p$ in col. 2 and k in col. 4.

constant) is the relevant variable, there are some pragmatic reasons having to do with measurement error to look at the derivatives with respect to permanent income. Also, the size of these derivatives provides information about the extent to which differences in permanent income are mitigated through transfers. In panel A, which is based on $\bar{Y}_k$ and $\bar{Y}_p$, $E\partial R/\partial Y_p$ is .037 at the sample mean with a standard error of .014, whereas $E\partial R/\partial Y_k$ is $-.017$ with a standard error of .009. It is also interesting to note that $E\partial R/\partial Y_{kt}$ ($-.088$ in row 2 of panel A of table 6) is substantially larger than $E\partial R/\partial Y_k$, whereas $E\partial R/\partial Y_p$ and $E\partial R/\partial Y_{pt}$ are very similar. This is consistent with the view that liquidity constraints are important for a substantial fraction of the younger households but not important for older households.

The estimate of $(E\partial R/\partial Y_p) - (E\partial R/\partial Y_k)$ is reported in column 5. At the sample mean this parameter is .053 with a standard error of .017, which is far below one. We obtain similar results using $\hat{Y}_k$ and $\hat{Y}_p$ in panel B, and the results are not very sensitive to where the derivatives are evaluated. We conclude that the flow of money transfers is only weakly related to the difference in the permanent incomes of parents and children.[30]

The estimates of the effects of assets on transfers should also satisfy the derivative restriction, although the results should be taken with a large grain of salt given measurement error and the fact that the model implies that assets are a choice variable and will be influenced by past transfer behavior and preferences. Furthermore, the fact that the wealth distribution is highly skewed may reduce the robustness of the estimates. At the sample means, an extra dollar of parental assets raises the transfer amount by 1.1 cents (not shown). An increase in the child's assets leads to a transfer increase of 3.7 (.024) cents, which has the wrong sign. The difference in the derivatives is $-.026$ (.023), which is not significantly different from zero and is a far cry from one.[31]

D. *Additional Experiments*

In this subsection we examine the sensitivity of the results to changes in the specification and estimation methods.

Controlling for the Incomes and Numbers of Siblings

One objection to these results is that we have not controlled for the income of other relatives to whom the parents may be altruistically linked. We added the average of $\bar{Y}_k$ for siblings of the child who are in the sample and found that this has almost no effect on the difference in the derivatives.[32] We also added interactions between the income variables and $1/(1 + \text{number of siblings})$ as well as the level and the square of the average income of siblings in this specification. In this analysis, we exclude people who have siblings but do not have siblings who were PSID split-offs. At the sample means for all variables except number of siblings, the difference in derivatives is .161 for only children and .113 for children with three siblings (table 6.8, panel A).

The decline in the difference in derivatives with the number of children has implications for some alternative theories of transfers. One possible explanation for the failure of the test of income derivatives is that it is costly for parents to differentiate among children. Although it seems ad hoc, one could simply add an "aversion to inequality in transfer amounts" argument to the parental utility function in our model. This would break the restriction that $\Delta E\partial R/\partial Y_{jt}$ must equal one. It would also lower $E\partial R/\partial Y_{pt}$ because part of the increase in transfers would be wasted on rich children. A modification to the basic altruism model that is perhaps more appealing on theoretical grounds and has similar implications involves the following assumptions. (1) Children care deeply about how much their parents love them.[33] (2) Children are hurt if they feel that the parents prefer a sibling. (3) Children have imperfect information about the actual needs of their siblings. (4) Children make inferences about their parents' feelings for them based on the amount of help that they and their siblings receive, and parental transfers cannot be fully hidden from other siblings. If these assumptions are correct, then altruistic parents whose utility functions do not depend directly on transfers may choose not to differentiate much among their children when giving gifts. They will be concerned about the utility losses associated with the inferences that children draw about parental preferences from the differentiated gifts. This type of signaling model is qualitatively consistent with a number of facts. First, it implies that bequests, which are public, will be less sensitive to the relative incomes of siblings than inter vivos transfers. The results of Menchik (1980) and Wilhelm (1996) show that bequests are evenly divided among children in most cases and insensitive to the relative incomes of the children. The results of Dunn (1993) and Altonji et al. (1996) show that transfers do depend on the relative incomes of siblings.

Table 6.8
Alternative estimates of the effect of parents' and child's current income on transfers

Evaluation point	$E\partial R/\partial Y_{pt}$	$E\partial R/\partial Y_{kt}$	$\Delta E\partial R/\partial Y_{jt}$
	A. Effects of the parents' and child's income on transfers by number of siblings*		
Sample mean	.028	−.087	.115
0 siblings	.017	−.144	.161
3 siblings	.031	−.082	.113
	B. Estimates using instruments for the parents' and child's current income†		
Sample mean	−.004	−.145	.141
	C. Estimates using net assets in 1989 as the wealth measure‡		
Sample mean	.033	−.100	.133
	D. Estimates using instruments for the parents' and child's current income and 1989 wealth#		
Sample mean	−.013	−.106	.119

Note: All the results in the table are based on models that control for the demographic variables listed in table 1 and cubics in the age of the child and the parent.

*We added interactions between 1/(number of siblings + 1) and the linear current income terms, the permanent income terms, and assets of the parent and child to the probit model (11) and the regression model (10). The number of siblings is the number of siblings the child reports, regardless of whether they have become split-offs by 1988. All other variables are evaluated at the sample mean. Sample sizes used to estimate probit model (11) and regression model (10) are 2,914 and 560, respectively. The permanent income measures are $\hat{Y}_p$ and $\hat{Y}_k$ throughout the table.

†We replaced the level, square, cube, and the interaction terms involving the parents' and kid's current nonasset income with predicted values from a regression against the income of the parent and kid in the previous year, the average of the siblings' reports of their parents' income in 1987, the square and cube for this average, and all other variables in the transfer equation (including all terms involving permanent income and asset terms).

‡We constructed the asset minus debt measure from the detailed information on assets and debts contained in the 1989 household information. We obtained similar results using the measure of net worth in 1989 provided on the public use tape. We set the measure of assets minus debt in 1989 to zero if data are missing or if the head of the household in 1989 is not the same as in 1988. We included three dummies for whether asset data are missing for the parent, the child, or either the parent or the child in the probit model (11) and the regression model (10). In 1989, 2.9 percent of the kids and 2.6 percent of the parents did not respond.

See n. † for the instruments used for current income. We used the same instruments for 1989 wealth. A dummy is assigned to parents and kids with missing data on 1989 wealth. The sample size for (11) is 3,402, and the sample size for (10) is 666. We evaluate the derivatives at the means of the predicted income and wealth measures among the sample of children receiving transfers. Restricting the sample to families with valid asset data in both 1984 and 1989 had little effect on the results.

Since there is no information extraction problem in the case of only children, our finding that the difference in transfer-income derivatives is larger for only children is qualitatively consistent with the theory. However, the fact that the difference is only .161 even for only children and that the coefficient on parents' income is actually smaller for only children (.017 vs. .031 for persons with three siblings) suggests that costs of unequal treatment of children are only a minor part of the story.

Interactions with Other Demographic Variables

We also investigated the possibility that the income derivatives depend on demographic variables that influence the probability of a transfer. The results, reported in Altonji et al. (1995), show that the transfer-income derivatives are not very sensitive to the value of the transfer probability.

Measurement Error in Income

We noted earlier that measurement error in the current income of the parents and child could bias the results below the theoretical value of one. We investigated this issue by forming instruments for the level, square, cube, and the interaction terms involving the parents' and child's nonasset income. The instrumental variables consist of powers of the income in 1986 (which the parents and child report in the 1987 survey), the average of the siblings' reports of their parents' 1987 income, the square and cube of this average, and all other variables in the transfer equation (including all terms involving permanent income and assets).[34] At the sample mean the estimate of $E\partial R/\partial Y_{pt}$ is $-.004$, and $E\partial R/\partial Y_{kt}$ is $-.145$ (table 6.8, panel B). Thus the difference in derivatives is .149. This is 35 percent higher than the estimate that ignores measurement error, suggesting that there is a substantial amount of measurement error in the current income measures. However, measurement error does not go very far in squaring the estimated values of the difference in derivatives with the value of 1.0 predicted by the altruism model.

The Measure of Income

Our results were not very sensitive to the use of alternative measures of current family income, including after-tax family income, family income minus help from relatives, family income net of both taxes and help from relatives, and total family income (including income from assets).[35]

Measurement Error in Assets

The 1989 wave of the PSID contains a wealth supplement that asks questions very similar to the questions asked in 1984. We have reestimated the model substituting the 1989 measures for the 1984 measures. The estimate of $(E\partial R/\partial Y_{pt}) - (E\partial R/\partial Y_{kt})$ evaluated at the sample mean rises from .110 to .133 (table 6.8, panel C). When we form instruments for the current income variables *and* the 1989 asset measures using the instruments mentioned above along with the 1984 asset measures, at the sample means $E\partial R/\partial Y_{pt}$ is $-.013$, which has the wrong sign but remains small; $E\partial R/\partial Y_{kt}$ is $-.106$, and the difference is .119 when evaluated at the sample means. In summary, there is little evidence that measurement error in wealth or income or both has a large effect on the income results.

Sensitivity to Outliers, Functional Form for Transfers and Income, and Estimation Method

We noted earlier that the distribution of transfers is skewed to the right. We have reestimated the model after excluding 35 cases of transfers in excess of \$5,000. The results in panel A of table 6.9 show that this has the effect of *lowering* the transfer-income derivatives by about 60 percent.

Since the heavy skewness in the transfer distribution may be affecting the robustness of our estimates, we have also estimated the conditional expectation function $\overline{R}(\mathbf{Z})$ by first estimating a regression model for the log of transfers and then using the parameter estimates and the estimated error variance of that model of compute $\overline{R}(\mathbf{Z})$.[36] The results are close to but somewhat smaller than those in table 6.6, columns 2, 4, and 5.

The level of income is approximately lognormal, so a few large values of income could have a large effect on our estimates, particularly since we use a polynomial form. We estimated $\overline{R}(\mathbf{Z})$ from a regression model for the log of transfers as the dependent variable after replacing the polynomials in the levels of the current income and permanent income with polynomials in the logs. Observations with nonasset income below \$1,000 are excluded. The average of the difference in derivatives declines from .093 (table 6.6, row 1) to .056 (not shown), and the difference in derivatives at the sample mean declines from .110 (table 6.6, row 2) to .041 (table 6.9, panel C).

As a final check, we used the least absolute deviation (LAD) regression to estimate the conditional mean function on the grounds

Table 6.9
Experiments with alternative functional forms and sample exclusions

Panel	Functional form and sample exclusions	Estimation method for transfer eq. (10)	$E\partial R/\partial Y_{pt}$	$E\partial R/\partial Y_{kt}$	$\Delta E\partial R/\partial Y_{jt}$
A	Exclude 35 cases of transfers >$5,000; transfers and income in levels*	OLS	.013	−.02	.033
B	Transfers in logs, income in levels†	OLS	.012	−.034	.046
C	Transfers and income in logs, income >$1,000‡	OLS	.006	−.035	.041
D	Transfers and income in levels#	LAD	.002	−.008	.01

*The sample sizes for the probit model (11) and the regression model (10) are 3,367 and 631. The permanent income measures are $\hat{Y}_p$ and $\hat{Y}_k$ throughout the table.
†We estimated the conditional expectation function $\bar{R}(\mathbf{Z})$ by first estimating a regression model for the log of transfers and then using the parameter estimates and estimated error variance of that model to compute $\bar{R}(\mathbf{Z})$ under the assumption that the error term in the *log* transfer equation is additive and has a lognormal distribution. The sample sizes underlying (11) and (10) are 3,335 and 647.
‡Observations with Y_{kt} and/or Y_{pt} below $1,000 were excluded. Polynomials in the logs of current income and permanent income were used in (10) and (11). See n. † for how the regression model for the log of transfers was used to estimate the conditional expectation function $\bar{R}(\mathbf{Z})$. The sample sizes underlying (11) and (10) are 3,309 and 636.
#Least absolute deviation (LAD) regression was used to estimate (10). The sample sizes underlying (11) and (10) are 3,402 and 666.

that the LAD regression may be more robust even though it is an inconsistent estimator of the conditional mean function when errors are skewed. The income derivatives decline in absolute value (panel D). In summary, our basic conclusion that the income derivatives are small appears to be quite robust.

E. Discussion of Findings

Are there additional problems with the data and methods or modifications to the model that can reconcile the empirical results with altruistic preferences? Measurement error in the transfer reports is one possibility. In Altonji et al. (1995) (see also Altonji and Ichimura 1996), we analyze a measurement error model in which some respondents randomly report their receipt of transfers and some who receive transfers report a random fraction ε of what they actually receive. We show that random reporting error of this type will bias the derivative estimator downward by the factor $1 - \bar{\varepsilon}$, where $\bar{\varepsilon}$ is the mean of ε, even if a fraction of transfer recipients fails to report transfers.[37] One can reconcile the estimates with the theory if respondents who report positive transfers on average report only 13 percent of the transfers they receive, that is, $\bar{\varepsilon} = .13$. However, if one were to multiply average transfers of $1,810 by 1/.13, one would conclude that average transfers are, on average, $13,923 per year. This seems far too high, particularly given that many parents have more than one child. Underreporting of transfer amounts may be able to explain a part of the gap between .13 and one, but it does not seem likely that it can explain all or even most of it.

A second issue is the consequences for our test of departures from optimality in the timing of transfers. We show in section II that the timing of transfers is determinant if future income (or needs) is uncertain and credit markets are imperfect. It may be, however, that the utility loss from minor variation in the timing is small for families with relatively stable income streams. Even for these families the model in section II describes how transfer flows are determined over a period of time, and actual transfers should match the flow implied by the model if both are aggregated over a few years. However, some families may not make a transfer in the year we examine, and some may receive a transfer that is larger than what they receive in an average year over a period of 2 or 3 years (say).

Would such indeterminacy invalidate the test? We have considered the case in which both the frequency of transfer flows and the size of each transfer are positively related to the average transfer flow. We have also considered the case in which the frequency of transfer flows is independent of the average transfer flow. In both cases the transfer-income derivative test statistic derived will be greater than or equal to one if the altruism hypothesis is correct.[38] Consequently, indeterminacy in the timing of transfers seems, if anything, to strengthen the rejection of altruism.

We also investigated whether random variation around the optimal division between transfers in period t and bequests would affect the results.[39] We investigated a model in which transfers $R(\mathbf{Z})$ in t are equal to a positive random variable q times the value implied by our model, and bequests equal the value implied by the model plus $(1 - q)\beta(t)R(\mathbf{Z})$, where q has mean $\bar{q}$ and $\beta(t)$ is a discount factor chosen so that the present discount value of transfers plus bequests is not affected by q. In this case, $\Delta E\partial R/\partial Y_{jt}$ will equal $\bar{q}$ under the null. Consequently, random variation around the optimal timing, with $\bar{q}$ equal to one, has no effect on our analysis. A very large departure from optimality would be required to rationalize an estimate of the difference in transfer-income derivatives of .13 with the altruism model.[40]

If one accepts the results, it is useful to ask what models are more consistent with them. One possibility is that preferences are altruistic, but parents know little about the incomes of their children. It is easy to show in a static model that this would reduce $E\partial R/\partial Y_{kt}$ in absolute value and reduce the difference in test statistics. However, given the estimates of $E\partial R/\partial Y_{pt}$, the parents would have to be almost completely ignorant of their child's current income for this explanation to work.[41]

A second possibility is that efforts by parents to "tax" Y_{kt} will distort the hours of work and effort decisions of children. This would appear to be an important issue if one takes our estimates of $E\partial R/\partial Y_{pt}$ of .03–.05 seriously. These estimates imply that parental preferences are such that they would prefer to reduce transfers by .95–.97 for each extra dollar of Y_{kt}. Thus the disincentive effects may be a major constraint on parental behavior, particularly if children are not very concerned about the utility of their parents. (If parents and children have the same objective function, there would be no disincentive effects.) In view of our findings, it would be interesting to draw on the optimal taxation literature to conduct an analysis of how large the child's labor supply response would have to be to square our low estimates of $E\partial R/\partial Y_{kt}$ and $E\partial R/\partial Y_{pt}$ with altruism. A third possibility is that the derivative restriction fails if parents and children can use bargaining strategies other than the reaction function that we assume.[42]

Given the large discrepancy between the results and the prediction of the basic altruism model, a satisfactory model of transfers is likely to involve factors in addition to altruism. First, suppose that parents get utility from R independently of the child's utility. This warm-glow motive tends to reduce the difference in derivatives. Second, Cox's (1987) theoretical analysis implies that, at least in a static context, the difference in derivatives is less than one if transfers are made in exchange for services from the child. Bernheim et al. (1985), Cox (1987), and Cox and Rank (1992) provide some direct evidence on child services (such as visits and phone calls) that supports a role for exchange. However, in Altonji et al. (1996), we analyze the 1988 PSID data on time help provided to parents and find that it has little relationship to the parents' income or wealth, in contrast to the predictions of simple exchange models. Also, we find that differences between siblings in the receipt of money transfers depend on the relative incomes of the siblings but have little to do with the relative amounts of time they spend helping their parents. Finally, we find that while sibling differences in distance from parents have a strong effect on flows of time help, they have little effect on flows of money help. In an exchange model, the reduction with distance in time flows should lead to a reduction in money flows.

VI. Conclusion

This chapter uses matched panel data on parents and their adult children and a new econometric methodology to produce consistent estimates of the derivatives of transfers with respect to the parents' income and the child's income. We then use our estimates to test a fundamental prediction of altruistic preferences: the difference in the derivatives should equal one. The chapter's econometric approach may be useful in analyzing other consumer choice problems that involve overlapping budget constraints and limited dependent variables, such as estimating the effects of public transfers on private transfers or charitable giving, testing whether public transfers crowd out private transfers, and analyzing the effects of the endowments of the wife and husband on resource allocation within the household.

We find that parents increase their transfers by a few cents for each extra dollar of current or permanent income they have, which in itself is consistent with altruism. The inconsistency arises because we also find that parents reduce transfers by only a few cents for each extra dollar of income their child has. As we show in section II, the difference in the transfer-income derivatives should be one, whereas our estimates are concentrated in the .04–.13 range depending on the choice of income measure and the point at which the derivatives are evaluated. Our results, which constitute a strong rejection of operative intergenerational altruism, are robust to changes in functional form, outliers, the number of siblings, the definition of current and permanent income, and measurement error in income and wealth.

Appendix

This appendix shows that uncertainty about a child's future income leads parents to delay making transfers unless their child is liquidity-constrained. It also derives the transfer-income derivative restriction. Our model's utility function is

$$V_{p1} = u(c_{p1}) + \eta u(c_{k1}) + E_1[u(c_{p2}) + \eta u(c_{k2})], \tag{A1}$$

where c indexes consumption, p indexes parents, k indexes the child, and 1 and 2 index periods 1 and 2. For future reference, Y is income, A is assets, and R is the transfer amount.

For simplicity, assume that parents have no second-period non-asset income, are not liquidity-constrained, and earn a zero rate of return on their savings. After learning the value of Y_{k2}, the parents choose the second-period transfer, R_2, to maximize their second-period utility; that is, they solve

$$\max_{R_2} u(A_{p2} - R_2) + \eta u(A_{k2} + Y_{k2} + R_2)$$
$$\text{subject to } R_2 \geq 0, A_{p2} - R_2 \geq 0, A_{k2} + Y_{k2} + R_2 \geq 0, \tag{A2}$$

where $u(\cdot)$ is strictly concave with $u'(0) = \infty$. In (A2), the child takes the transfer of the parents as given so that her second-period consumption is just $A_{k2} + Y_{k2} + R_2$.[43] The solution to (A2) satisfies

$$u'(c_{p2}) \geq \eta u'(c_{k2}), \tag{A3}$$

where $c_{p2} = A_{p2} - R_2$ and $c_{k2} = A_{k2} + Y_{k2} + R_2$. This equation holds as an equality and $R_2 > 0$ provided that Y_{k2} is less than or equal to a critical value, $\bar{Y}_{k2}$, that solves

$$u'(A_{p2}) = \eta u'(A_{k2} + \bar{Y}_{k2}). \tag{A4}$$

Equation (A4) implicitly defines $\bar{Y}_{k2}$ as a function of A_{p2} and A_{k2}. Denoting this function by $z(\cdot\,,\cdot)$, we get

$$\bar{Y}_{k2} = z(A_{p2}, A_{k2}). \tag{A5}$$

Parents' second-period utility can be expressed as one of two indirect utility functions:

$$\begin{aligned} &M(A_{p2} + A_{k2} + Y_{k2}) \quad \text{for } Y_{k2} \leq z(A_{p2}, A_{k2}),\\ &N(A_{p2}, A_{k2} + Y_{k2}) \quad \text{for } Y_{k2} > z(A_{p2}, A_{k2}). \end{aligned} \tag{A6}$$

Note that when $Y_{k2} = \bar{Y}_2$, the $M(\cdot)$ and $N(\cdot\,,\cdot)$ functions are equal.

Now consider the first period in which the child faces the intertemporal budget constraint:

$$A_{k2} = \rho(A_{k1} + Y_{k1} - c_{k1} + R_1), \tag{A7}$$

where the function $\rho(\cdot)$ determines the gross return on the child's saving. For levels of child saving above a critical value $x^*, \rho(x) = x$. That is, the child's gross return is simply the amount she saved, so her rate of return on additional saving is zero, the same value her parents are assumed to earn on their saving. For values of child saving below x^*, the child's rate of return on saving (as well as the interest rate she pays on borrowing) exceeds zero; that is, $\rho'(x) > 1$ when $x < x^*$. Finally, we assume that, for $x < x^*$, $\rho(\cdot)'' \leq 0$; that is, for $x < x^*$, $\rho(\cdot)$ is an increasing concave function with a marginal rate of return above one and an average rate of return below one. The value x^* could be negative but is probably positive. The properties of $\rho(\cdot)$ capture the idea of soft credit market constraints; borrowing rates are higher than lending rates and the cost of borrowing rises as one's net worth falls.

Parents' assets obey

$$A_{p2} = A_{p1} + Y_{p1} - c_{p1} - R_1. \tag{A8}$$

Parents choose their first-period transfer, R_1, and their first-period consumption, c_{p1}, to solve

$$\max_{c_{p1}, R_1} u(c_{p1}) + \eta u(c_{k1}(A_{k1} + Y_{k1} + R_1, A_{p2})) + V(A_{p2}, A_{k2}|I_1), \tag{A9}$$

where $R_1 \leq 0$,

$$V(A_{p2}, A_{k2}|I_1) = \int_0^{z(A_{p2}, A_{k2})} M(A_{p2} + A_{k2} + Y_{k2}) f(Y_{k2}|I_1)\, dY_{k2}$$
$$+ \int_{z(A_{p2}, A_{k2})}^{\infty} N(A_{p2}, A_{k2} + Y_{k2}) f(Y_{k2}|I_1)\, dY_{K2}, \tag{A10}$$

and

$$c_{k1}(A_{k1} + Y_{k1} + R_1, A_{p2}) \equiv \operatorname*{argmax}_{c_{k1}} u(c_{k1})$$
$$+ \int_0^{z(A_{p2}, A_{k2})} u(A_{k2} + Y_{k2} + R_2(A_{p2}, A_{k2} + Y_{k2})) f(Y_{k2}|I_1)\, dY_{K2}$$
$$+ \int_{z(A_{p2}, A_{k2})}^{\infty} u(A_{k2} + Y_{k2}) f(Y_{k2}|I_1)\, dY_{k2} \tag{A11}$$

subject to (A7) and (A8). In (A10) and (A11), $f(Y_{k2}|I_1)$ is the density function for Y_{k2} conditional on the information I_1 available in period 1, which includes Y_{k1}, Y_{p1}, and other relevant variables. The function $V(\cdot\,,\cdot)$, which depends on I_1, is the expected utility of the parents conditional on their entering the second period with A_{p2} in assets and their child's entering the second period with A_{k2} in assets. The function $R_2(A_{p2}, A_{k2} + Y_{k2})$ relates transfers in the second period to second-period resources of the parent and child.

The solution to problem (A9) satisfies

$$u'(c_{p1}) - \eta u'(c_{k1})\frac{\partial c_{k1}}{\partial A_{p2}} = \frac{\partial V}{\partial A_{p2}} \tag{A12}$$

and

$$\eta u'(c_{k1})\left(\frac{\partial c_{k1}}{\partial R_1} - \frac{\partial c_{k1}}{\partial A_{p2}}\right) \leq \frac{\partial V}{\partial A_{p2}} - \frac{\partial V}{\partial A_{k2}}\rho'(\cdot)\left(1 - \frac{\partial c_{k1}}{\partial R_1} + \frac{\partial c_{k1}}{\partial A_{p2}}\right), \tag{A13}$$

where $\partial c_{k1}(\cdot)/\partial R_1$ is determined by differentiating the first-order conditions defining the solution to (A11). If (A13) holds as a strict inequality, first-period transfers, R_1, will be zero.

We shall now show that (A13) is a strict inequality and R_1 must be zero if two conditions hold. Condition 1 is that the child is not liquidity-constrained, which means that the child has a marginal interest rate of $\rho'(A_{k1} + Y_{k1} + R_1 - c_{k1}(\cdot\,,\cdot)) = 1$ when $R_1 = 0$. Note that in this case A_{k2} must exceed x^* since the interest rate is zero when the child is not liquidity-constrained. Condition 2 is that $f(Y_{k2}|I_1)$ is positive for at least some values of $Y_{k2} > z(A_{p2}, A_{k2})$ for all values of (A_{p2}, A_{k2}) that are feasible given first-period assets and income and that satisfy the no liquidity constraint condition $A_{k2} > x^*$. Condition 2 says that there are some states of the world in period 2 in which the parent will not want to make a second-period transfer. It means that parents have an incentive to delay transfers.

To see why these two conditions imply that (A13) holds as an inequality, consider the following two equalities:

$$\frac{\partial V}{\partial A_{k2}} = \eta E_1 u'(c_{k2}) \tag{A14}$$

and

$$E_1\left[u'(c_{k2})\left(1 + \frac{\partial R_2}{\partial A_{k2}}\right)\right] = \frac{u'(c_{k1})}{\rho'(A_{k1} + Y_{k1} + R_1 - c_{k1})}. \tag{A15}$$

Equation (A14) follows from differentiating (A10) with respect to A_{k2}. Equation (A15) is the first-order condition arising in problem (A11), where we use the fact that $\partial R_2/\partial A_{k2} = 0$ when $Y_{k2} > \bar{Y}_{k2}$. Setting $\rho'(\cdot)$ to one because we are considering the case of no liquidity constraints (condition 1) and using (A14) and (A15) to rewrite (A13) yields

$$\eta E_1 \left[u'(c_{k2}) \left(\frac{\partial R_2}{\partial A_{k2}} \right) \right] \left(\frac{\partial c_{k1}}{\partial R_1} - \frac{\partial c_{k1}}{\partial A_{p2}} \right) \leq \frac{\partial V}{\partial A_{p2}} - \frac{\partial V}{\partial A_{k2}}. \tag{A16}$$

By differentiating (A10), one may easily show that the right-hand side of (A16) is positive.[44] Consequently, first-period transfers must by zero if the left-hand side of (A16) is negative, which one may establish by differentiating (A15). To see this, let $W_2 = A_{p2} + Y_{k2} + A_{k2}$ by the sum of the parents' and child's resources in the second period. When $\rho'(\cdot) = 1$, (A15) may be rewritten as

$$u'(c_1) - \int_0^{z(A_{p2}, A_{k2})} u'(c_{k2}(W_2)) \left[1 + \frac{\partial R_2(W_2)}{\partial A_{k2}} \right] f(Y_{k2}|I_1)\, dY_{k2}$$
$$- \int_{z(A_{p2}, A_{k2})}^{\infty} u'(A_{k2} + Y_{k2}) f(Y_{k2}|I_1)\, dY_{k2} = 0,$$

where we have used the fact that $R_2 = 0$ when $Y_{k2} < z(A_{p2}, A_{k2})$ and the fact that c_{k2} and R_2 depend on W_2 only when $Y_{k2} \geq z(A_{p2}, A_{k2})$. Differentiating with respect to R_1 and A_{p2} yields, respectively,

$$K_1 \frac{\partial c_{k1}}{\partial R_1} - K_2 \left(1 - \frac{\partial c_{k1}}{\partial R_1} \right) - K_3 \left(1 - \frac{\partial c_{k1}}{\partial R_1} \right) = 0 \tag{A17a}$$

and

$$K_1 \frac{\partial c_{k1}}{\partial A_{k2}} - K_2 \left(1 - \frac{\partial c_{k1}}{\partial A_{k2}} \right) - K_3 \left(\frac{\partial c_{k1}}{\partial A_{p2}} \right) = 0, \tag{A17b}$$

where $K_1 = u''(c_{k1})$, and

$$K_2 = \int_0^{z(A_{p2}, A_{k2})} \left\{ u''(c_{k2}(W_2)) \left[1 + \frac{\partial R_2(W_2)}{\partial A_{k2}} \right] + u'(c_{k_2}(W_2)) \left[\frac{\partial^2 R_2(W_2)}{\partial^2 A_{k2}} \right] \right\}$$
$$\times f(Y_{k2}|I_1)\, dY_{k2},$$

$$K_3 = \int_{z(A_{p2}, A_{k2})}^{\infty} u''(A_{k2} + Y_{k2}) f(Y_{k2}|I_1)\, dY_{k2}.$$

Using (A17a) and (A17b) to solve for $\partial c_{k1}/\partial R_1$ and $\partial c_{k1}/\partial A_{k2}$ and taking the difference establishes that

$$\frac{\partial c_{k1}}{\partial R_1} - \frac{\partial c_{k1}}{\partial A_{p2}} = \frac{K_3}{K_1 + K_2 + K_3} > 0. \tag{A18}$$

To establish the inequality in (A18), note first that the denominator $K_1 + K_2 + K_3$ is the second derivative of the child's first-period objective function (A11) with respect to c_{k1}, so $K_1 + K_2 + K_3 < 0$ at the value of c_{k1} chosen by the child. (The condition $u'(0) = \infty$ guarantees that the child's first-period problem has an interior solution.) The numerator $K_3 < 0$ because $u''(\cdot) < 0$ by concavity and because condition 2 says that $f(Y_{k1}|I_1)$ is positive for at least some values of $Y_{k2} > z(A_{p2}, A_{k2})$. The first-order condition (A3) for R_2 and concavity guarantee that $\partial R_2/\partial A_{k2} < 0$ when $Y_{k2} < z(A_{p2}, A_{k2})$, and $\partial R_2/\partial A_{k2} = 0$ if $Y_{k2} > z(A_{p2}, A_{k2})$. Consequently, the left-hand side of (A16) must be negative.

Note that the right-hand side of (A16) captures the option value to the parents of waiting to make a transfer; its positive sign means that the expected utility to parents of holding an extra dollar at the beginning of period 2 exceeds their expected utility from having their child hold an extra dollar. The negative sign of the left-hand side of (A16) reflects the parents' decision to hold back transfers to keep their child from overconsuming. The inclusion of the term $\partial R_2/\partial A_{k2}$ in (A15) and, as a consequence, (A16) captures the propensity of the child to free-ride on the parents' generosity by overconsuming when young.

Now take the case in which the child is liquidity-constrained; that is, $\rho'(A_{k1} + Y_{k1} + R_1 - c_{k1}(\cdot)) > 1$ when $R_1 = 0$. In this case, the left-hand side of (A16) and the last term on the right-hand side of (A16) are multiplied by $\rho'(\cdot)$. Although the negative sign of the left-hand side of (A16) remains, the right-hand side may now also be negative, leading the parents to make period 1 transfers. In this case, the marginal loss to the parents from reducing A_{p2} by a dollar and increasing A_{k2} by a dollar (i.e., from transferring a dollar), which is given by $(\partial V/\partial A_{k2}) - (\partial V/\partial A_{p2})$, is smaller than the marginal gain from being able to transfer to a child facing a value of ρ' in excess of one, which is given by $(\rho' - 1)(\partial V/\partial A_{k2})$.[45] The transfer income derivatives restriction $(\partial R_1/\partial Y_{p1}) - (\partial R_1/\partial Y_{k1}) = 1$ when $R_1 > 0$ follows immediately from the fact that Y_{p1}, Y_{k1}, and R_1 always enter the equations of the problem in the combinations $Y_{p1} - R_1$ and $Y_{k1} - R_1$. See (A7), (A8), and (A9).

Notes

This research was supported by the National Institute of Aging (grant 1RO1AG8655-01), the Japan Economic Foundation, and the Institute for Policy Research, Northwestern University Charles Pierret and Daniel Aaronson provided excellent research assistance. We are grateful to Agar Brugiavini, Bo Honore, Donald Cox, Anne Laferrere, Costas Meghir, Bruce Meyer, and Chistopher Udry; participants in the SPES conference on Dynamic Models of Household Behavior in Sardinia, Italy (June 1993); participants in seminars at the Institut National de la Statistique et des Etudes Economiques–Centre de Recherche en Economie et Statistique, Oxford University, Northwestern University, the University of Chicago, Vanderbilt, Johns Hopkins, Yale, Princeton, University of California at Los Angeles, and the National Bureau of Economic Research; and the referee for valuable comments on earlier drafts.

1. Barro (1974), Becker (1974, 1991), Ben-Porath (1980), Kotlikoff and Spivak (1981), Pollak (1985), and numerous other studies discuss the family's role in performing these functions.

2. Cox and Rank (1992) use the National Survey of Family and Households to study transfers. They strongly reject the restriction on transfer-income derivatives. Their estimation method differs from ours in that they use Heckman's (1979) two-step estimator to correct for sample selection. This estimator is inappropriate for transfer models, which involve nonseparable error terms. Their data set also lacks direct measures of parents' income. The measurement error in their proxy for parents' income may be biasing downward their estimate of the effect on parents' transfers of an increase in their income, and the failure to adequately control for parents' income may lead to a positive bias in their estimate of the effect of the child's income on transfers. However, these biases would have to be large to square their results with the altruism model. With the exception of the study by Cox and Rank, we know of no previous empirical studies that have directly tested the transfer-income derivative restriction. Several studies have examined the effects of either parental income or the child's income on transfers, and a few have simultaneously estimated the effects of both parental and child's income without assessing the transfer-income derivative restriction. Dunn (1993) reviews these studies. A few generalizations may be made. First, with the exception of studies by Dunn (1993), Rosenzweig and Wolpin (1993, 1994), and Altonji, Hayashi, and Kotlikoff (1996), which use matched intergenerational panel data from the National Longitudinal Surveys of Labor Market Experience, most studies are based on a single cross-section survey that reports only the income of the donor. Second, few studies distinguish among the effects of permanent income and current income of both the parent and the child or control for the incomes of siblings. Third, most of the studies that examine transfer amounts use ordinary least squares (OLS), Tobit, or generalized Tobit as the estimation procedure. Cox (1987) estimates the response of parental transfers to the child's income but does not test the income-transfer derivative restriction. Gale and Scholz (1994) provide a useful descriptive analysis of transfer patterns using the Survey of Consumer Finances and other sources.

3. See, e.g., Thomas (1990) and Browning (1992) on intrahousehold resource allocation and Abel and Kotlikoff (1994), Hayashi (1995), and Hayashi, Altonji, and Koltikoff (1996) on intergenerational resource allocation and risk sharing.

4. In their conclusion (p. 1219), Altig and Davis speculate that uncertainty about incomes and longevity will give parents an incentive to delay transfers. They also call for research on a model with both capital market imperfections and uncertainty. Although tax considerations can also pin down the timing of transfers, we leave them out of our analysis. Gift and estate taxes are a minor issue for most families since parents can shelter from taxes up to $1.2 million in bequests and up to $20,000 per child per year in gifts. Differences in parents' and children's marginal capital income tax rates are also likely to be small given the tax schedule of the late 1980s.

5. They care neither about the amount per se transferred to the child (as in Blinder [1976] and Andreoni [1989]) nor about services provided them by their child (as in Bernheim, Shleifer, and Summers [1985] and Cox [1987]). For a recent survey of these and other theories of the family, see Bergstrom (1993).

6. This is the Samaritan's dilemma analyzed by Buchanan (1975), Kotlikoff (1987), Laitner (1988), Lindbeck and Weibull (1988), Bruce and Waldman (1990), and others.

7. We also assume that $u'(0) = \infty$ to guarantee interior solutions to the parents' and child's consumption choice problem in periods 1 and 2. The point-in-time utility functions of the parents and child may differ. They may also depend on additional person- and time-specific preference shifters. But we ignore these possibilities, as well as the time preference factor, to simplify the notation. The analysis in the Appendix also goes through if the child cares about the parents. In this case, there are regimes in the first period and in the second period in which the child would make a transfer to the parent. The possibility that the child will return money in the second period if she turns out to be less needy than the parents reduces the parents' incentive to delay transfers to the second period.

8. As we discuss below, the derivative restriction holds in an extended model in which parents may choose to invest in their child's human capital in period 0. At the other end of the life cycle, adding a period 3 to the model with uncertainty about whether the parents will survive does not change the result. Parents will make transfers in period 2 or period 1 or both if the children are liquidity-constrained and the restriction (2) will hold. The child will receive a bequest at the end of period 2 if the parent dies.

9. A simple static model illustrates this point. Assume that the parents' utility, V^p, is logarithmic in their own consumption, c_p, and the consumption of their child, c_k, i.e., $V^p = \log c_p + \eta \log C_k$, where η is the unobserved relative weight the parents place on the child's log consumption and is distributed across parents according to the density $g(\eta)$. The condition for positive transfers from the parents to the child is $\eta > Y_k/Y_p$. The amount that is transferred, if transfers are positive, is $R = (-Y_k + \eta Y_p)/(1+\eta)$. Note that the unobservable η enters the formula for R in a nonseparable way. This non-separability between preferences and incomes is generic to the transfer models based on altruism.

10. Intuitively, higher (lower) values of the child's (parents') income shift the distribution of η over which transfers occur to include values that are associated with larger transfers for any given value of the child's and parents' income. The effects of selection are transparent in the example in n. 9, where η is a scalar. Transfers rise with η given Y_k and Y_p, and η must exceed Y_k/Y_p for a transfer to occur.

11. We partition the sample by the number of observations from each extended family, lumping together the handful of observations from families with eight, nine, or ten observations. Let N_j be the number of families with j observations in our actual sample. For each bootstrap replication m and each j, we draw with replacement from

the sample until we obtain a new sample of N_j families. The mth bootstrap replication sample is the combination of the samples drawn for each j. By drawing the bootstrap samples so that N_j families come from each group j, we preserve the correlation structure that arises because the observations are clustered by families. We then implement the derivative estimator and compute estimates $E[\partial R(\mathbf{Z}, \boldsymbol{\eta})/\partial Y_{pt}|\mathbf{Z}, R > 0; \hat{\theta}_1^m, \hat{\theta}_2^m]$, $E[\partial R(\mathbf{Z}, \boldsymbol{\eta})/\partial Y_{kt}|\mathbf{Z}, R > 0; \hat{\theta}_1^m, \hat{\theta}_2^m]$, and the difference between them, where m denotes the particular bootstrap replication. We performed 125 bootstrap replications. We computed standard errors from the tenth and ninetieth percentile values of 125 derivative estimates. The standard errors are based on the assumption that the derivative estimator has a normal distribution and make use of the relationship between the variance of a normal and the distance between the tenth and ninetieth percentile values. Note that in tables 6.6 and 6.7 we evaluate the derivatives at various values of $\mathbf{Z}$. In the bootstrap replications we always use the distribution of the original sample to determine the points (such as the mean) at which to evaluate the derivatives.

12. Drazen (1978), Becker (1991), and others have investigated models in which altruistic parents choose between investing in a child's human capital and making monetary transfers when the child has left school. We have analyzed a three-period version of our model in which in period 0 parents may choose to make transfers to adolescent children to overcome liquidity constraints that would limit schooling investments or to induce children who are misinformed about the value of school to stay in school longer. Parents do not make all transfers in period 0 for the same reason that they wish to delay transfers in our two-period model. The restriction (2) holds for period 1 transfers even though the child's income and the parents' wealth will be affected by earlier investments, but the model implies that the child's income and the parents' wealth will depend on preferences $\boldsymbol{\eta}$. Altonji and Ichimura (1996) provide a related estimator for the case of endogenous regressors when instruments are available. Their estimator is not practical in the current case given our relatively small sample size and the limited explanatory power of the instruments available to us, such as income innovations.

13. Other recent papers using the PSID transfer data include Hill and Soldo (1993), Ioannides and Kan (1993), Schoeni (1993), Pollak (1994), and Altonji et al. (1996). We also make limited use of the wealth data from the 1989 wave of the PSID.

14. The distribution of parent household records by number of children is as follows: 644 parent households have been matched to only one child, 454 to two children, 235 to three children, 135 to four children, 60 to five children, 27 to six children, 11 to seven children, 7 to eight children, 0 to nine children, and 1 to ten children. The sample contains 3,018 children who are matched to one parent household and 192 children who are matched to two parent households.

15. The respondent for a PSID household is usually either the head of the household or the spouse, so in some cases the husband provides information about transfers from the wife's parents, and vice versa.

16. The derivative estimator may easily be modified to take this threshold into account by subtracting \$100 from the reported transfers prior to estimation (see Altonji and Ichimura 1996). This would have no effect on the uncorrected derivative estimates in cols. 1 and 3 of tables 6.6 and 6.7 and lead to only a small change in the corrected derivative estimates.

17. In Altonji et al. (1996), we use the fact that the parents provide information on transfers given to others to check on the information provided by the children. The

parental responses suggest a lower incidence of transfers. We argue that the fact that the question about money help provided to others does not identify the specific relationship to the recipient leads to underreporting.

18. See Dunn (1993) for a recent survey.

19. We use all those heads of household and wives in the PSID who have valid data in a given year rather than only those individuals in our matched intergenerational sample.

20. We included all years of data in which respondents were either a head of household or the wife of the head. Consequently, if a divorce occurs, the data for women include observations from the years in which she was married as well as the later years. Note, however, that the regressions control for marital status. An alternative would be to use family income in the years since the most recent change in marital status. The measures $\hat{Y}_p$ and $\hat{Y}_k$ based on the autoregressive model discussed below do not place any weight on values of e_{it} that are more than three years in the past and, consequently, are less sensitive to this issue.

21. The samples used to estimate the autoregression for e_{it} are restricted to observations for which three lags of income are available. Lagged family income residuals cannot be constructed for children who became heads or wives for the first time in 1986 or 1987 or for whom family income is missing for other reasons. To avoid dropping these observations, we set the 1985 value of e_{it} to the 1986 value (if available) or 1987 if not. We set missing data for 1986 equal to the 1987 value.

22. Note that the income from assets, annuities, and pensions is reflected in our permanent income measures. The annuity value of assets that do not generate an income stream, such as a home, will not be reflected in the permanent income measures but will be reflected in controls for wealth. Since asset income may be affected by past transfers, we also experiment with measures of permanent labor earnings of the husband and wife.

23. When no independent siblings are present in the sample, we set the measure of sibling income to zero. We control for whether or not independent siblings are present with a dummy variable. All specifications include a control for the inverse of the number of siblings, whether or not they are in independent PSID households. Not surprisingly, transfers to a given child are negatively related to the number of siblings (see Altonji et al. 1996).

24. In practice, this makes little difference. We attempt to approximate a representative sample of independent children with one or more living parents by using the 1988 person weights in tables 6.2, 6.3, and 6.4. In tables 6.3 and 6.4 the incomes of parents living in separate households are the average of the two households. Statistics reported in the paper are based on unweighted samples unless otherwise indicated. The multivariate analyses are unweighted. The sample for tables 6.2, 6.3, and 6.4 is slightly larger than the samples for the other tables because it includes observations that are missing data on one or more variables needed for the multivariate analyses. The discrepancy between table 6.1 and table 6.2 in the probability of a transfer (.202 vs. .233) reflects aggregation across parents and weighting in table 6.2.

25. We noted earlier that most previous studies use proxies for parental income that may not provide an adequate control.

26. Rows 1, 6, 11, and 16 report the probit coefficient (standard error) on Y_{kt}, Y_{pt}, Y_k, and Y_p, respectively, for a model including only the linear terms in these variables. In

col. 2 the coefficient (standard error) on Y_{kt} is $-.0044$ (.0021), the coefficient on Y_{pt} is .0036 (.0011), the coefficient on Y_k is $-.0021$ (.0016), and the coefficient on Y_p is .0075 (.0013).

27. Columns 2 and 3, rows 23–25, report that the partial effect of the child's wealth is essentially zero, whereas an increase in parental wealth from the twentieth to the eightieth percentile raises the transfer probability from .120 to .190 (col. 2, rows 29–30). Since the assets of the kid, particularly early in the life cycle, may be heavily influenced by previous transfers, the coefficient on the child's assets in probably biased upward (toward a positive value) in the likely event that there are unobserved, serially correlated factors influencing monetary transfers. Parental assets will also be influenced by past monetary transfers and investments in human capital. As a result, serial correlation in the factors influencing transfers will lead to a downward bias in the coefficient on parental assets. On the other hand, if parents accumulate assets in anticipation of providing transfers to children, then the coefficient on parents' assets may be overstated in absolute terms. Also keep in mind that our measures of permanent income include income from assets, which makes it a bit difficult to interpret the asset variable separately. In col. 4 we report estimates after substituting current earnings and permanent earnings of the head and wife (based on the fixed-effect specification) for family income and adding cubic specifications for net assets of the parents and the kids (measured in 1984). For the parents the effects of assets are larger when earnings are used, with a twentieth to eightieth percentile shift in wealth associated with a .097 increase in the transfer probability. The effect of the child's assets remains very small but becomes positive. In col. 5 we drop the current earnings measures and obtain results for permanent earnings analogous to those in col. 1 for permanent income. The effect of the child's assets becomes negative. The coefficient on the child's assets in col. 5, row 11, is based on a linear specification and is not statistically significant. However, the coefficients of the cubic specification in the child's assets are jointly significant, and the probability of a transfer falls from .155 for a child in the twentieth percentile of the wealth distribution to .149 for a child in the eightieth percentile.

28. The specification of the nonasset income and asset terms in (10) and (11) appears following eq. (10). We include dummies for missing asset data for parents, the child, and either the parents or the child. We include the same demographic controls used in the probit models in table 6.5. The detailed regression estimates and probit estimates underlying the results in tables 6.6 and 6.7 are available on request.

29. As described in Altonji et al. (1996), the Tobit estimate of the difference in derivatives is only .096.

30. When we control for current income, the derivative of transfers is positive for our measures of Y_p and negative but very small for Y_k. The positive transfer response to Y_p is predicted by the theoretical model. We are unable to sign the effect of an increase in Y_k when Y_{kt} is held fixed. On one hand, higher future income exacerbates liquidity constraints and reduces the need for future transfers, leading the parent to increase the first-period transfer. On the other hand, higher future income means that the child has more resources to shift into the first period, lessening the marginal utility of first-period transfers. Cox (1990) presents a somewhat different model in which the child's future income has a positive effect on the transfer amount today.

31. The derivatives evaluated at the eightieth percentile value for parental assets and the twentieth percentile value for the child's assets are similar. The estimates are not sensitive to replacing assets in 1984 with assets measured in 1989 or to the use of the 1984 asset measures to form instruments for the 1989 measures.

32. Sibling income has a positive effect on transfers. In Altonji et al. (1996), we control for family fixed effects and find that richer siblings are less likely to receive money transfers from parents and more likely to give money transfers to parents.

33. In the model in sec. II, $u(c_k)$ would depend on the child's belief about η, which is based on parental behavior, including transfers given.

34. The 1988 supplement on transfers asked about the income of parents. We set the average of the sibling report of parents to zero and include a missing data dummy when the kid's reports of parental income are missing for all the siblings from a given family who are in the matched sample. We estimated prediction equations using the full sample used to estimate the probit model for the probability of a transfer and inserted the predicted values of the income terms into the probit model (11) and the regression model (10) for positive transfer amounts. Such two-stage approaches are usually inconsistent in nonlinear models, but we do not have an alternative to it.

35. As noted above, the question about help from relatives is separate from questions about transfers in the 1988 transfer supplement.

36. See panel B of table 6.9. In going from the log regression model to the conditional expectation function (10) for the level of R, we assume that the error term in the *log* transfer equation is additive and has a lognormal distribution. We then use the formula for the expectation of a lognormal random variable.

37. Let R^* be the observed transfer amount. Altonji et al. (1995) consider the measurement error model $R^* = I \varepsilon R$, where I is a Bernoulli random variable equal to one with fixed probability p_I and zero with probability $1 - p_I$, and ε is a positive random variable that is independent of R with a mean of $\bar{\varepsilon}$ if $R > 0$. The estimator is consistent if $\bar{\varepsilon} = 1$ even if a fraction of transfer recipients fail to report transfers. One may easily extend the analysis in Altonji et al. (1995) to show that if the probability of reporting a transfer is a positive function of the transfer amount and $\bar{\varepsilon} = 1$, then the difference in derivatives will be positively biased.

38. Notes describing this analysis are available from the authors.

39. We point out in n. 8 that adding a period 3 with uncertainty about whether the parents will survive to the model in sec. II does not change the derivative restriction.

40. The 1984 wave of the PSID has some limited information on expected inheritances that could be used to estimate the derivatives of bequests with respect to Y_{pt} and Y_{kt}, with the other variables held constant. Unfortunately, there are no comparable transfer data in that year.

41. In Altonji et al. (1992), we studied the link between the distributions of income and consumption in the extended family and we found that replacing family income with the component of income that is predictable on the basis of schooling and the two-digit occupation actually strengthened the evidence against the joint hypothesis of altruistic preferences and operative altruistic links. This finding suggests that parents know quite a bit about the permanent incomes of their children, although it leaves open the possibility that they do not know much about current income conditional on permanent income.

42. Bergstrom, Blume, and Varian (1986) (theorem 7 and p. 47, par. 2) consider a model that may be interpreted as a static model in which parents care about their own consumption and the consumption of each of their children, and the children care only about their own consumption. The model seems to imply that if there is a Nash equi-

librium in the transfer amounts that involves a positive transfer R to a particular child j and perhaps other children, then following an exogenous increase in the parents' income of one dollar and a reduction of j's income by one dollar, transfers of $R+1$ to child j and the original amounts to the other children are a Nash equilibrium. This suggests that the derivative restriction may carry over to some other bargaining models.

43. Kotlikoff and Rosenthal (1993) make the alternative assumption that the child can refuse the receipt of a transfer as part of a strategy to induce the parents to increase their transfer.

44. In differentiating (A10) with respect to A_{p2} and A_{k2} to sign the right-hand side of (A16), recall that $M(A_{p2}+A_{k2}+\bar{Y}_{k2}) = N(A_{p2}, A_{k2}+\bar{Y}_{k2})$. Also recall that in those states in which $Y_{k2} \leq \bar{Y}_{k2}$, $\partial M(A_{p2}+A_{k2}+\bar{Y}_{k2})/\partial A_{p2} = \partial M(A_{p2}+A_{k2}+\bar{Y}_{k2})/\partial A_{k2}$, whereas in those states in which $Y_{k2} > \bar{Y}_{k2}$, $\partial N(\cdot,\cdot)/\partial A_{p2} = u'(c_{p2}) > u'(c_{k2}) = \partial N(\cdot,\cdot)/\partial A_{k2}$.

45. In the case in which the parents are also subject to liquidity constraints, one may show that transfers will be zero if, when $R_1 = 0$, the marginal interest rate faced by the parents is greater than or equal to the marginal interest rate faced by the child. Transfers may be positive if the child faces an interest rate that is sufficiently higher than that facing the parents when $R_1 = 0$.

References

Abel, Andrew, and Kotlikoff, Laurence J. "Intergenerational Altruism and the Effectiveness of Fiscal Policy: New Tests Based on Cohort Data." In *Savings and Bequests*, edited by Toshiaki Tachibanaki. Ann Arbor: Univ. Michigan Press, 1994.

Altig, David, and Davis, Steven J. "The Timing of Intergenerational Transfers, Tax Policy, and Aggregate Savings." *A.E.R.* 82 (December 1992): 1199–1220.

Altonji, Joseph G.; Hayashi, Fumio; and Kotlikoff, Laurence J. "Is the Extended Family Altruistically Linked? Direct Tests Using Micro Data." *A.E.R.* 82 (December 1992): 1177–98.

Altonji, Joseph G.; Hayashi, Fumio; and Kotlikoff, Laurence J. "Parental Altruism and Inter Vivos Transfers: Theory and Evidence." Working Paper no. 5378. Cambridge, Mass.: NBER, December 1995.

Altonji, Joseph G.; Hayashi, Fumio; and Kotlikoff, Laurence J. "The Effects of Income and Wealth on Time and Money Transfers between Parents and Children." Working Paper no. 5522. Cambridge, Mass.: NBER, April 1996.

Altonji, Joseph G., and Ichimura, Hidehiko. "Estimating Derivatives in Nonseparable Models with Limited Dependent Variables." Manuscript. Evanston, Ill.: Northwestern Univ., 1996.

Amemiya, Takeshi. "Qualitative Response Models: A Survey." *J. Econ. Literature* 19 (December 1981): 1483–1536.

Andreoni, James. "Giving with Impure Altruism: Applications to Charity and Ricardian Equivalence." *J.P.E.* 97 (December 1989): 1447–58.

Barro, Robert J. "Are Government Bonds Net Wealth?" *J.P.E.* 82 (November/December 1974): 1095–1117.

Becker, Gary S. "A Theory of Social Interactions." *J.P.E.* 82 (November/December 1974): 1063–93.

Becker, Gary S. "*A Treatise on the Family*. 2d ed. Cambridge," Mass.: Harvard Univ. Press, 1991.

Ben-Porath, Yoram, "The F-Connection: Families, Friends, and Firms and the Organization of Exchange." *Population Development Rev.* 6 (March 1980): 1–30.

Bergstrom, Theodore C. "A Survey of Theories of the Family." Manuscript. Ann Arbor: Univ. Michigan, May 1993.

Bergstrom, Theodore C.; Blume, Lawrence; and Varian, Hal. "On the Provision of Public Goods." *J. Public Econ.* 29 (February 1986): 25–49.

Bernheim, B. Douglas; Shleifer, Andrei; and Summers, Lawrence H. "The Strategic Bequest Motive." *J.P.E.* 93 (December 1985): 1045–76.

Blinder, Alan S. "Intergenerational Transfers and Life Cycle Consumption." *A.E.R. Papers and Proc.* 66 (May 1976): 87–93.

Browning, Martin. "Children and Household Economic Behavior." *J. Econ. Literature* 30 (September 1992): 1434–75.

Bruce, Neil, and Waldman, Michael. "The Rotten-Kid Theorem Meets the Samaritan's Dilemma." *Q.J.E.* 105 (February 1990): 155–65.

Buchanan, James M. "The Samaritan's Dilemma." In *Altruism, Morality, and Economic Theory*, edited by Edmund S. Phelps. New York: Sage Found., 1975.

Cox, Donald. "Motives for Private Income Transfers." *J.P.E.* 95 (June 1987): 508–46.

Cox, Donald. "Intergenerational Transfers and Liquidity Constraints." *Q.J.E.* 105 (February 1990): 187–217.

Cox, Donald, and Rank, Mark R. "Inter-Vivos Transfers and Intergenerational Exchange." *Rev. Econ. and Statis.* 74 (May 1992): 305–14.

Drazen, Allan. "Government Debt, Human Capital, and Bequests in a Life-Cycle Model." *J.P.E.* 86 (June 1978): 505–16.

Dunn, Thomas A. "The Distribution of Intergenerational Income Transfers between and within Families." Manuscript. Syracuse, N.Y.: Syracuse Univ., May 1993.

Gale, William G., and Scholz, John Karl. "Intergenerational Transfers and the Accumulation of Wealth." *J. Econ. Perspectives* 8 (Fall 1994): 145–60.

Hayashi, Fumio. "Is the Japanese Extended Family Altruistically Linked? A Test Based on Engel Curves." *J.P.E.* 103 (June 1995): 661–74.

Hayashi, Fumio; Altonji, Joseph G.; and Kotlikoff, Laurence J. "Risk-Sharing between and within Families." *Econometrica* 64 (March 1996): 261–94.

Heckman, James J. "Sample Selection Bias as a Specification Error." *Econometrica* 47 (January 1979): 153–61.

Hill, Martha, and Soldo, Beth. "Intergenerational Transfers: Economic, Demographic and Social Perspectives." Manuscript. Ann Arbor: Univ. Michigan, 1993.

Ioannides, Yannis M., and Kan, Kamhon. "The Nature of Two-Directional Intergenerational Transfers of Money and Time: An Empirical Analysis." Manuscript. Blacksburg: Virginia Polytechnic Inst. and State Univ., Dept. Econ., March 1993.

Kotlikoff, Laurence J. "Justifying Public Provision of Social Security." *J. Policy Analysis and Management* 6 (Summer 1987): 674–89.

Kotlikoff, Laurence J., and Rosenthal, Robert W. "Some Inefficiency Implications of Generational Politics and Exchange." *Econ. and Politics* 5 (March 1993): 27–42.

Kotlikoff, Laurence J., and Spivak, Avia. "The Family as an Incomplete Annuities Market." *J.P.E.* 89 (April 1981): 372–91.

Laitner, John. "Bequests, Gifts, and Social Security." *Rev. Econ. Studies* 55 (April 1988): 275–99.

Lindbeck, Assar, and Weibull, Jörgen W. "Altruism and Time Consistency: The Economics of Fait Accompli." *J.P.E.* 96 (December 1988): 1165–82.

Menchik, Paul L. "Primogeniture, Equal Sharing, and the U.S. Distribution of Wealth." *Q.J.E.* 94 (March 1980): 299–316.

Pollak, Harold, "Informal Transfers within Families." Ph.D. dissertation, Harvard Univ., September 1994.

Pollak, Robert A. "A Transaction Cost Approach to Families and Households." *J. Econ. Literature* 23 (June 1985): 581–608.

Rosenzweig, Mark R., and Wolpin, Kenneth I. "Intergenerational Support and the Life-Cycle Incomes of Young Men and Their Parents: Human Capital Investments, Coresidence and Intergenerational Financial Transfers." *J. Labor Econ.* 11, no. 1, pt. 1 (January 1993): 84–112.

Rosenzweig, Mark R., and Wolpin, Kenneth I. "Parental and Public Transfers to Young Women and Their Children." *A.E.R.* 84 (December 1994): 1195–1212.

Schoeni, Robert F. "Private Interhousehold Transfers of Money and Time: New Empirical Evidence." Working Paper no. 93-26. Santa Monica, Calif.: Rand Corp., Labor and Population Program, July 1993.

Thomas, Duncan. "Intra-household Resource Allocation: An Inferential Approach." *J. Human Resources* 25 (Fall 1990): 635–64.

Wilhelm, Mark O. "Bequest Behavior and the Effect of Heirs' Earnings: Testing the Altruistic Model of Bequests." *A.E.R.* 86 (September 1996): 874–92.

7 A Strategic Altruism Model in Which Ricardian Equivalence Does Not Hold

with Assaf Razin and
Robert W. Rosenthal

It is now many years since Robert Barro (1974) wrote his ingenious article showing how love of children (intergenerational altruism) can economically link current and future generations and thereby neutralize intergenerational redistribution by the government (Ricardian Equivalence). Several critics have pointed out reasons why the requirement for Ricardian Equivalence of interior transfers may not be satisfied (e.g., Barro, 1974; Drazen, 1978; Laitner, 1979 and 1988, and Feldstein, 1988). Others (Kotlikoff, 1983 and Bernheim and Bagwell, 1988) have cast doubt on the model by showing how intermarriage across Barro dynasties can lead to incredibly large groups of intragenerationally linked individuals, redistribution among whom will also be neutralized.

None of the critics has, however, questioned whether Ricardian Equivalence necessarily follows from the basic elements in Barro's study. This article does just that. It examines the strategic game between an altruistic parent and a possibly altruistic child[1] and shows, under the Extended Nash Bargaining Solution,[2] that Ricardian Equivalence will almost never hold.

Barro does not make explicit the game he models between an altruistic parent and child, but in his formulation the child appears to be quite passive and simply takes whatever transfer is given. There is no scope for the child to manipulate the parent by threatening to refuse transfers that are below a specified level and/or by threatening to transfer funds to the parent if the parent is not sufficiently generous. Stated differently, there is no scope for strategies associated with statements such as "If that's the best you can do, forget it." The apparent restrictions on the actions of children in the Barro model become more apparent if parents not only are altruistic with respect to their children but children are also altruistic with respect to their parents. While parents and children may care for each other, they are unlikely to agree on the exact net amount to be transferred between them. For families with reciprocal altruism (presumably most families) the problem then is one of competing altruism in which parents may be trying to transfer to their children at the same time that the children are trying to transfer to their parents. In such a setting the assumption that each player simply accepts whatever is offered seems unrealistic. Individuals seem equally empowered both to make and to refuse gifts.[3]

The next section computes both the ordinary and extended Nash Bargaining Solutions (which turn out to be the same) to a game involving a parent and child, at least one of whom is altruistic towards the other. Section II shows why the solution will almost never be neutral with respect to government redistribution between the two players. Section III discusses the differences between cooperative and noncooperative solutions to this game and suggests a way of distinguishing empirically between the two. Section IV concludes and presents ideas for future research that would expand on the framework presented here.

I. The Extended Nash Bargaining Solution in a Two-person Altruism Game

There are two stages in this altruism game. In the second stage the players agree to maximize the product of their utility gains relative to the respective values of utility at the threat point that results from the first stage.[4] From this maximization one can compute the indirect utility of each player as a function of the threat point. In the first stage the players choose threat strategies noncooperatively. The payoffs in the resulting two-stage game are the indirect utilities for the point resulting from any pair of threat strategies.

The Second Stage

Equation (1) expresses the Nash product N for the second stage. The terms $V_p(C_p, C_k)$ and $V_k(C_p, C_k)$ stand for the utility functions of the parent and child, respectively. Their arguments, C_p and C_k, are the respective consumptions of the parent and child. The terms $\overline{V}_p$ and $\overline{V}_k$ stand for the respective threat-point utilities of the parent and child, which are constants in this stage.

$$N(C_p, C_k) = [V_p(C_p, C_k) - \bar{V}_p][V_k(C_k, C_p) - \bar{V}_k]. \tag{1}$$

To keep matters simple we assume that $V_p(\,,\,)$ and $V_k(\,,\,)$ are of the forms:

$$V_p(C_p, C_k) = u(C_p) + w(C_k) \tag{2}$$

$$V_k(C_k, C_p) = m(C_k) + n(C_p), \tag{3}$$

where the functions $u(\,), w(\,), m(\,)$; and $n(\,)$ are continuously differentiable, increasing, and concave.[5]

The expression for N is maximised subject to the collective parent-and-child budget constraint:

$$C_p + C_k = E_p + E_k = E, \tag{4}$$

where E_p and E_k are the endowments of the parent and child, respectively, and subject to the constraint that both factors in brackets on the right-hand side of (1) be non-negative. Any solution to this maximization problem satisfies:

$$[u'(C_p) - w'(C_k)][m(C_k) + n(C_p) - \bar{V}_k]$$
$$+[m'(C_k) - n'(C_p)][u(C_p) + w(C_k) - \bar{V}_p] = o. \tag{5}$$

There are two different ways equation (5) could be satisfied. One way is for both terms in (5) to be zero (i.e., at least one of the factors of each term to be zero). This can occur, for instance, if both parent and child remain at the threat point or if the factors involving derivatives are both zero. The second way is for the ratio of $\partial V_p(C_p, E - C_p)/\partial C_p$ (the first factor in square brackets in (5)) to $\partial V_k(E - C_p, C_p)/\partial C_p$ to equal minus the ratio of the parent's utility gain to the child's utility gain.

Figure 7.1 depicts $V_p(C_p, E - C_p)$ and $V_k(C_k, E - C_k)$ under the assumptions that: (i) $u'(o) = w'(o) = m'(o) = n'(o) = \infty$ and (ii) $x > y$ where x and y are defined by $u'(x) = w'(E - x)$ and $n'(y) = m'(E - y)$. In the figure, C_k is measured from left to right on the horizontal axis and C_p from right to left, their sum being fixed at E. The first assumption ensures that the parent's and child's most preferred allocations (their respective bliss points) lie between o and E on the horizontal axis. The second assumption ensures that the parent's (child's) bliss point involves more consumption by the parent (child) than does the child's (parent's) bliss point. Points A and B indicate allocations corresponding to the bliss points of the parent and child,

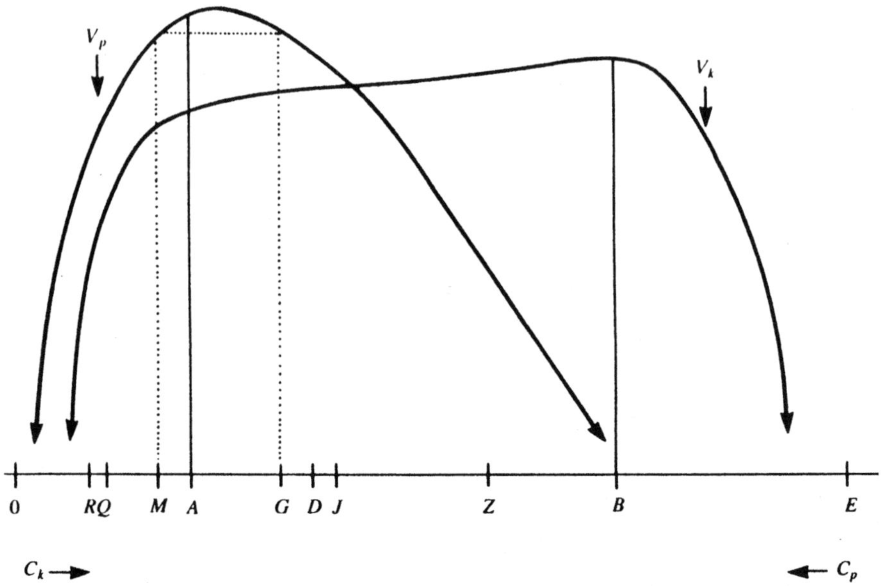

Figure 7.1
A strategic altruism model

respectively. Any allocation lying between points A and B, such as Z, is a Pareto-optimal allocation.

As described below, the first-stage game leads to the determination of a threat-point allocation on the horizontal axis. The threat values of the parent's and child's utility, $\overline{V}_p$ and $\overline{V}_k$, correspond to the values of $V_p(\ ,\ )$ and $V_k(\ ,\ )$ evaluated at this threat-point allocation. If the result of the first-stage game is a threat allocation such as Z that lies between A and B, the solution to the second stage is for the players to consume the allocation Z. This is a simple consequence of Pareto optimality and corresponds to the first instance of the first type of solution to equation (5). In contrast, if the first-stage game leads to a threat allocation to the right of B or to the left of A, such as R, N can be increased beyond the value obtained by consuming the allocation R. The solution in this case occurs at a point like D, where the ratio of the slope of V_p to that of V_k equals minus the ratio of the parent's utility gain to the child's utility gain. (The point D necessarily lies between points A and B because to the left of A and to the right of B the slopes of V_p and V_k have the same sign, making their ratio nonnegative.) Note that the point D resulting from R is uniquely determined: between A and B the absolute value of the ratio of the slopes increases in C_k, while the ratio of the utility gains falls.

In the case that the parent's bliss point lies to the right of the child's bliss point, threat-point allocations lying between the two bliss points will again be decisive in that each player will consume at the threat-point allocation. For points to the left of the child's bliss point and to the right of the parent's bliss point the bargaining solution will again map to a point between the two bliss points. In the case that the child does not care about the parent ($n(C_p) = o$, violating assumption (i)), the graph corresponding to figure 7.1 is similar except that V_k rises monotonically between $C_k = o$ and $C_k = E$.

In the case that the two bliss points coincide there is only one Pareto optimum (at the coincident bliss points), and the solution to (5) involves both derivative factors being zero.

The First Stage

We model the first-stage game strategies for the parent and child as choices of how much to offer each other and how much to accept from each other. These should be thought of as maxima in all cases; for instance, if the parent offers α and accepts β, while the child offers γ and accepts δ, then $\min(\alpha, \delta) - \min(\beta, \gamma)$ is the net transfer from parent to child. Since the two players start out with the total endowment and nothing is wasted, the result of the first-stage game is simply a reallocation (here representable as a point on the horizontal axis in figure 7.1).

The solution to the first stage game is quite simple. The equilibrium threat-point allocation always turns out to be just the point of initial endowments of the players. This is an immediate consequence of the fact that each player can enforce the initial endowment point as the outcome of the first stage. Since for each solution to the first stage game, the second stage results in a Pareto optimum, any move from the endowment point in the first stage must be worse overall for one of the players who will, therefore, veto it.

II. The Failure of Ricardian Equivalence

Ricardian Equivalence means that any government transfer is subsequently undone by the private actions of parent and child, so that the government's redistribution has no real consequences. This property almost never holds for the model considered above. To see this examine again figure 7.1. Any government redistribution that results in an endowment between A and B is not altered. A government redistribution that leaves the endowment to the left of point A or leaves the endowment to the right of point B, while it leaves unchanged the direction of the bargained net transfer, will, nonetheless, change the threat point in stage 1 and, therefore, the solution.

In the figure, government redistribution from the parent to the child that moves the endowment point, and therefore the threat point, from point R to point Q moves the solution from point D to point J. In the figure, point J lies to the right of D (though it need not in general). Hence, the government policy is successful in increasing both the consumption and welfare of the child; that is, in this example, private transfers do not fully offset the government's transfers.

Private transfers may, however, more than fully offset government redistribution. As an example, if the government redistributes from the parent to the child by moving the endowment from point R to point M, the solution will move from point D to a point between A and G. The solution must lie to the left of G because to the right of G the parent is made worse off than remaining at the threat point M. Compared with point D, a solution to the left of point G involves smaller net transfers to the child: that is, private transfers more than offset the government's transfers. From the figure it is clear that, in general, if the government redistributes enough to the net recipient of private transfers, but not so much as to move the endowment point into the region between A and B, the private response will more than offset the government policy. Thus, if the government takes away too much of the net transferee's bargaining leverage, the net transferee will end up worse off.

There can be isolated instances where the government's transfer is exactly offset; here Ricardian Equivalence holds. Also in the case $A = B$ the unique Pareto-optimal allocation is the solution in the second stage no matter what transfers occur; hence, for this case Ricardian Equivalence holds.

III. Comparing the Extended Nash Bargaining Solution to the Noncooperative Equilibrium

The noncooperative equilibrium in this same static framework exhibits Ricardian Equivalence in more cases than the isolated ones above.[6] In the one-stage noncooperative equilibrium each player takes the other player's maximum offer and acceptance as given and chooses his best response. In terms of figure 7.1 if the endowment point lies between points *A* and *B*, the only noncooperative equilibrium is the same as the cooperative solution, resulting in each player consuming his endowment. If the endowment lies to the left of point *A* the following describes all the equilibria: the parent offers to transfer just enough funds to the child to move the allocation to the parent's bliss point *A* and the parent accepts nothing. The child offers nothing and accepts the amount of the parent's offer (or more). The obvious analogy holds to the right of *B*. Starting from endowments to the left of *A* (or to the right of *B*), government redistributions that keep the endowment to the left of *A* (or to the right of *B*) leave unchanged the equilibrium outcome. The players still move to the same bliss point with the same utility payoffs. For these cases Ricardian Equivalence holds.

One might argue that the noncooperative solution is more plausible than the cooperative solution. Rather than agree to play the cooperative game, why does the potential net transferor not simply call the other player's bluff. For example, if the endowment lies to the left of point *A*, why does the parent not simply tell the child "take it or leave it," and why does the child not simply take it. One answer is that since the child knows the parent's altruistic utility, the child calls the parent's bluff. This assumes the parent has no last-mover advantage.

Another answer may be that the child cares about the bargaining process as well as the outcome. If the child feels he is being told "take it or leave it," he may leave it because he resents being treated in that manner. The child may also feel a loss of pride in accepting a transfer, so that transfer may need to be conveyed to the child in a manner that preserves the child's pride.

In the model presented here the noncooperative equilibria happen to be Pareto optimal, so Pareto improvements do not justify the cooperative solution. However, extensions of the model lead to cases in which the noncooperative equilibrium is not Pareto optimal. As an example, take the case in which the parent has two children each of whom cares about the parent, but who are not altruistic toward each other. Also suppose that the parent is not altruistic toward the children. In this case the noncooperative equilibrium, if it involves both children transferring to the parent, will not be Pareto optimal (see

Nerlove et al., 1984). In making their transfers to the parent, each child ignores the external benefit to the other. As a consequence, the noncooperative equilibrium involves too little being transferred to the parent.

One way to test empirically the cooperative model against the noncooperative model is to determine whether the distribution of consumption among family members who are parties to net transfers depends on the distribution of initial resources among these members. For example, suppose one had a sample of parents each transferring to his child. According to the cooperative model presented here, the distribution of endowments between the parent and child will affect the distribution of consumption between the parent and child. Such is not the case in the noncooperative model.

IV. Ideas for Future Research and Conclusion

This article demonstrates that Ricardian Equivalence does not necessarily hold in models with altruistic transfers once one takes into account the strategic behavior of recipients as well as donors. The model we have used to make this point is, however, static and highly stylised. It does not take into account that parents and children can bargain over many periods and that their bargaining positions may depend on their life expectancies. It also takes a particular view of both the bargaining process and the strategies available to the players (although more realistic alternatives are not obvious). Finally, it does not consider how the bargaining outcome is affected by the presence of more than one child and/or more than one parent.

Specifying alternative noncooperative and cooperative strategic-altruism models in finer detail may represent a fruitful line of research. We suspect that for the most part such models will not, however, satisfy Ricardian Equivalence because, as in the cooperative model of this paper, interior transfers can result from non-interior strategic postures and because noninterior strategies (e.g., accepting nothing) are likely to be aspects of equilibria.

Notes

We are grateful to the National Science Foundation (grant no. SES8808362) and to the National Institute of Aging (grant no. 1P01AG05842-01) for research support. We thank Andy Weiss and a referee for helpful comments.

1. Bernheim et al. (1985) also consider strategic interplay between parents and children but in a model in which altruistic parents wish to procure services from their children.

2. Nash (1953). See also Luce and Raiffa (1957) chapter 6 for a summary with critical comments.

3. Abel (1987) and Kimball (1986) rule out the refusal of gifts a priori. In their analyses of "two way" altruism they develop conditions on preferences that will, in part, ensure that transfers are never refused in a noncooperative game in which each player chooses transfers taking the transfers of others as given.

4. There is an extensive literature beginning with Nash (1950) justifying the product-of-the-utility gains solution. See Roth (1979) for a recent survey.

5. These forms for the utility functions $V_p(\,,)$ and $V_k(\,,)$ are consistent with the parent (the child) caring about his own consumption and the utility of the child (the parent). For example, use (3) to write the following expression: $C_k = m^{-1}[V_k - n(C_p)]$. The insertion of this expression into (2) yields $V_p(C_p, C_k) = H_p(C_p, V_k) = u(C_p) + w(m^{-1}[V_k - n(C_p)])$.

6. Noncooperative models are examined by Carmichael (1982), Burbridge (1983), Weil (1987), Abel (1987), and Kimball (1986).

References

Abel, Andrew B. (1987). "Operative gift and bequest motives." *American Economic Review*, vol. 77, no. 5, (December), pp. 1037–47.

Barro, Robert J. (1974). "Are government bonds net wealth?." *Journal of Political Economy*, vol. 82, (November/December), pp. 1095–117.

Bernheim, Douglas B., Scheifer, Andrei and Summers, Lawrence H. (1985). "The strategic bequest motive." *Journal of Political Economy*, vol. 93, no. 6, (December), pp. 1045–77.

Bernheim, Douglas B., Scheifer, Andrei and Bagwell, Kyle (1988). "Is everything neutral? The implications of intergenerational altruism in an overlapping generations model with marriage." *Journal of Political Economy*, vol. 96, no. 2, (April), pp. 308–38.

Burbridge, John B. (1983). "Government finance in an overlapping generations model with gifts and bequests." *American Economic Review*, (March), pp. 222–7.

Carmichael, Jeffrey. (1982). "On Barrow's theorem of debt neutrality: the irrelevance of net wealth." *American Economic Review*, (March), pp. 202–13.

Drazen, Alan. (1978). "Government debt, human capital, and bequests in a life cycle." *Journal of Political Economy*, vol. 86, (March), pp. 505–16.

Feldstein, Martin. (1988). "The effects of fiscal policies when incomes are uncertain: a contradiction to Ricardian Equivalence." *American Economic Review*, (March), pp. 14–23.

Kimball, Miles. (1986). "Making sense of two-sided altruism." mimeo, Harvard University, (December).

Kotlikoff, Laurence J. (1983). "Altruistic extended family linkages, a note." mimeo, National Bureau of Economic Research, also published in Laurence J. Kotlikoff, *What Determines Savings?* Cambridge, Mass: MIT Press, 1989, p. 86.

Laitner, John. (1979). "Household bequest behavior, perfect expectations, and the national distribution of wealth." *Econometrica*, vol. 47, no. 5, (September), pp. 1175–94.

Laitner, John. (1988). "Bequests, gifts, and social security." *Review of Economic Studies*, no. 55 (2), no. 182, (April), pp. 275–300.

Luce, R. Duncan and Raiffa, Howard. (1957). *Games and Decisions: Introduction and Critical Survey*, New York: John Wiley and Sons.

Nash, John F. (1950). "The bargaining problem." *Econometrica*, vol. 18, (April), pp. 155–62.

Nash, John F. (1953). "Two-person cooperative games." *Econometrica*, vol. 21, (January), pp. 128–40.

Nerlove, Marc, Razin, Assaf and Sadka, Efraim (1984). "Bequests and the size of population when population is endogenous." *Journal of Political Economy*, (June), pp. 527–31.

Roth, Alvin E. (1979). *Axiomatic Models of Bargaining*, Berlin, W. Germany: Springer-Verlag.

Weil, Philippe. (1987). "Love thy children": reflections on the Barro debt neutrality theorem, *Journal of Monetary Economics*, vol. 19, (May), pp. 377–91.

8

Making Bequests without Spoiling Children: Bequests as an Implicit Optimal Tax Structure and the Possibility that Altruistic Bequests Are Not Equalizing

with Assaf Razin

I. Introduction

The assumption that parents know perfectly the abilities of their children underlies most, if not all, of the theoretical research on intergenerational transfers. This assumption has a strong implication, namely that altruistic parents will make transfers to their children that are independent of their children's work efforts. As this paper demonstrates, if altruistic parents do not know their children's abilities and cannot observe their work effort, they will condition their transfers on the level of their children's labor earnings. To keep their children from pretending (by working and earning less) to be of low ability in order to garner a larger transfer, parents are likely to make larger transfers to high-earning children and smaller transfers to low-earning children. Indeed, in addressing their information problem, altruistic parents may produce more inequality in the final consumption of children than would arise if parents were not altruistic. To help keep their children from freeloading, parents may also make their transfers, at the margin, a function of their children's labor earnings. As a consequence children's marginal returns to labor supply can differ, and potentially greatly, from their observed after-tax wages.

Those familiar with the optimal income tax literature (Mirrlees 1971; Sadka 1976; Stiglitz 1987) may sense a parallel between a parent who redistributes among children of unobserved abilities and a government that redistributes among citizen of unobserved abilities. Indeed, the two problems are essentially isomorphic. An immediate implication of this proposition is that if government and parental preferences about the distribution of welfare coincide there may be no optimal income tax role for the government; that is, parental choice of average and marginal transfers may substitute perfectly for the government's optimal tax structure.

The next section, section II, contains a simple model that illustrates the nature of the parent's information problem. The model is used to show how the parent's total and marginal transfers depend on the child's observed earnings. Section III calculates for a specific utility function and a specified list of parameters the values of transfers, the implicit marginal tax associated with transfers, and other endogenous variables. Section IV discusses the model's implications concerning debt neutrality pointing out that, as in Feldstein (1988), Ricardian Equivalence will not hold in states of nature in which transfers are operative, provided that in other states of nature transfers are inoperative. States of nature refer here to the realized abilities of children. Section IV also concludes the chapter with suggestions for additional research.

II. The Choice of Transfers under Asymmetric Information

A static model suffices to clarify the problem of an altruistic parent who wishes to transfer to a child, but does not know the child's ability and cannot observe the child's effort. The parent must infer from his (her) observation of the child's earnings the ability and effort of the child. The parent's utility depends on the parent's own consumption and the utility of the child. The utility of the child, in turn, is a concave function of the child's own consumption and the child's effort. Prior to observing the child's labor earnings, the parent announces a set of transfers to the child conditional on the child's labor earnings. Hence, the parent maximizes his (her) expected utility over the different possible states corresponding to different levels of the child's ability. The constraints in this maximization problem include the parent and child's combined budget constraint, self-selection constraints, and nonnegativity constraints on transfers from parents to children. The self-selection constraints ensure that the child will truthfully reveal his (her) ability.

With the exception of the nonnegativity constraints on transfers, the problem is isomorphic to that of a government maximizing a weighted average of its own utility from consumption and the utility of low- and high-ability workers in the case that ability is unobservable. In place of an optimal income tax, the parent uses his (her) transfer to the child both to redistribute and to provide the proper marginal incentives necessary for truthful revelation.

To illustrate the problem in the simplest manner, let the child have two possible ability levels, A_l and A_h, where $A_l < A_h$. Earnings of the low- and high-ability children are denoted by E_l and E_h, respectively. The relationships between earnings, ability, and effort of the low- and high-ability children, L_l and L_h, are given by

$$\begin{aligned} E_l &= A_l L_l \\ E_h &= A_h L_h \end{aligned} \tag{1}$$

In equation (1) the wage per unit of effective labor supply is normalized to 1.

The expected utility function of the parent is given by

$$W_p = q[U(C_{pl}) + \beta V(C_{kl}, E_l/A_l)] + (1-q)[U(C_{ph}) + \beta V(C_{kh}, E_h/A_h)], \tag{2}$$

where q is the probability the child is of low ability, C_{pl} and C_{ph} are the consumption values of the parent if the child turns out to have low or high ability respectively, and $V(,)$ is the utility function of the child which depends on his (her) consumption (C_{kl} for the low-ability child and C_{kh} for the high-ability child) and his or her effort L_l or L_h. In (2) these effort levels are replaced (using (1)) by earnings divided by ability.

The parent's problem is to maximize (2) with respect to C_{pl}, C_{kl}, C_{ph}, C_{kh}, E_l, and E_h subject to the budget constraints given in (3) and (4), the self selection constraints given in (5) and (6), and the non-negativity constraints on transfers given in (7) and (8). In the budget constraints, Y stands for the parent's income. Note that $Y - C_{pl}$ is the parent's transfer to the low-ability child, and $Y - C_{ph}$ is the parent's transfer to the high-ability child.

$$Y + E_l \geq C_{pl} + C_{kl} \tag{3}$$

$$Y + E_h \geq C_{ph} + C_{kh} \tag{4}$$

$$V(C_{kh}, E_h/A_h) \geq V(C_{kl}, E_l/A_h) \tag{5}$$

$$V(C_{kl}, E_l/A_l) \geq V(C_{kh}, E_h/A_l) \tag{6}$$

$$Y \geq C_{pl} \tag{7}$$

$$Y \geq C_{ph} \tag{8}$$

Let us associate the Lagrangian multipliers θ_l and θ_h with the constraints (3) and (4), respectively; the multipliers λ_l and λ_h with the constraints (5) and (6), respectively; and the multipliers μ_l and μ_h with the constraints (7) and (8), respectively. Equations (9)–(14) present the first order conditions for the choices of C_{pl}, C_{ph}, C_{kl}, C_{kh}, E_l, and E_h under the assumptions that (5) is binding, that (6) is not binding, and that transfers are nonnegative, that is, that μ_l and μ_h are 0.

$$qU'(C_{pl}) - \theta_l = 0 \tag{9}$$

$$(1-q)U'(C_{ph}) - \theta_h = 0 \tag{10}$$

$$q\beta V_1(C_{kl}, E_l/A_l) - \theta_l - \lambda_h V_1(C_{kl}, E_l/A_h) = 0 \tag{11}$$

$$(1-q)\beta V_1(C_{kh}, E_h/A_h) - \theta_h + \lambda_h V_1(C_{kh}, E_h/A_h) = 0 \tag{12}$$

$$q\beta V_2(C_{kl}, E_l/A_l)\frac{1}{A_l} + \theta_l - \lambda_h V_2(C_{kl}, E_l/A_h)\frac{1}{A_h} = 0 \tag{13}$$

$$(1-q)\beta V_2(C_{kh}, E_h/A_h)\frac{1}{A_h} + \theta_h + \lambda_h V_2(C_{kh}, E_h/A_h)\frac{1}{A_h} = 0 \tag{14}$$

The combinations of (9) and (11) and (10) and (12) indicate that the parent equates his (her) marginal utility of consumption to β times the child's marginal utility of consumption plus a term that indicates how increasing the child's consumption through an increase in transfers (since transfers equal Y minus parent's consumption) affects the self-selection constraint (5). In the case of equation (11) transferring another dollar to the child (increasing the child's consumption by a dollar) raises the high-ability child's utility when he pretends to be of low ability; this makes the self-selection more difficult to satisfy and therefore raises, at the margin, the cost of transferring to the child. The opposite occurs with respect to equation (12).

The addition of equations (12) and (14) indicate that the high-ability child's marginal rate of substitution $-(V_2/V_1)$ between consumption and effort is equated to his (her) marginal productivity (A_h). This is not the case for the low-ability child. The addition of (11) and (13) indicates that the low-ability child faces an implicit marginal tax at rate τ, where τ is given by

$$\tau = \frac{\lambda_h}{(q\beta - \lambda_h)V_1(C_{kl}, E_l/A_l)}H, \tag{15}$$

and

$$H = V_1(C_l, E_{kl}/A_h) - V_1(C_l, E_{kl}/A_l)$$
$$+ V_2(C_{kl}, E_l/A_h)\frac{1}{A_h} - V_2(C_{kl}, E_l/A_l)\frac{1}{A_l} \qquad (16)$$

If $V_{12} \leq 0$, that is, the marginal utility of consumption decreases with the amount of effort (increases with the amount of leisure), $q\beta - \lambda_h$ (from equation (11)) and H (from equation (16)) are positive. Hence, the tax rate on the low-ability child is positive since λ_h is positive.

If the self-selection constraint on the low-ability child's utility (equation (6)) is binding, a similar argument indicates that the low-ability child will face a zero implicit marginal tax, while the high-ability child will face an implicit marginal subsidy.

In the case of full information, there are no self-selection constraints, so the solution can be found by simply setting λ_h or λ_l equal to zero in the first-order conditions for the choice of C_{pl}, C_{ph}, C_{kl}, C_{kh}, E_l, and E_h. In this case there is, of course, no distortion of the child's work effort, and the parent equates his (her) marginal utility of consumption to β times the child's marginal utility of consumption.

Figure 8.1 depicts the case in which the self-selection constraint on the high-ability child is binding. The diagram, which is, except for symbols, identical to that in Sadka (1976), plots the utility of the child in consumption and earnings space assuming $V_{12} \leq 0$. At any point in this space the slope of the high-ability child's indifference curve is smaller than that of the low-ability child. At the optimum the high-ability child is at point A and faces no implicit marginal tax (i.e., the slope of his [her] indifference curve is 1). At point A the high-ability child is indifferent between truthfully revealing his (her) ability and pretending to be of low ability by earning E_l and consuming C_{kl} at point B. The low-ability child ends up at point B with the slope of his (her) indifference curve less than 1, indicating a positive implicit tax.[1]

III. Comparisons of the Asymmetric and Perfect Information Solutions

The log-linear utility function given in equation (17) is useful for illustrating differences between the full information and asymmetric information problems.

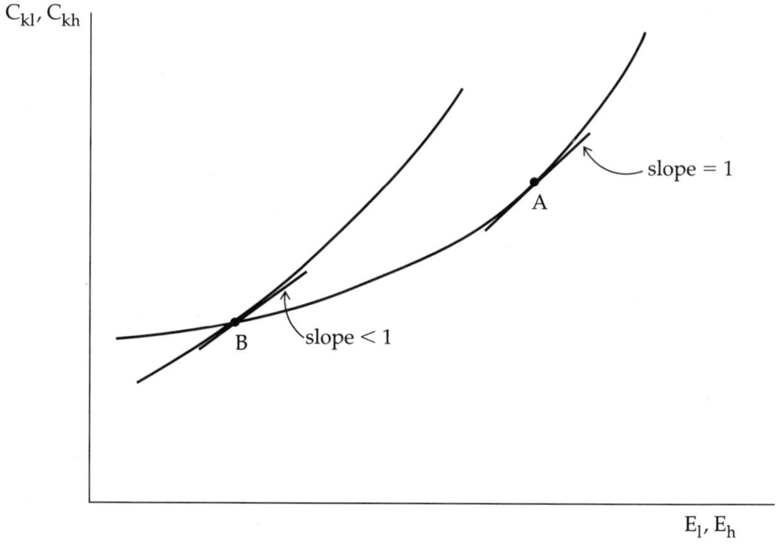

Figure 8.1
Using bequests as an implicit tax to sort children

$$W_p = q[\log C_{pl} + \beta(\log C_{kl} - \alpha(E_l/A_l))] + (1-q)[\log C_{ph} + \beta(\log C_{kh} - \alpha E_h/A_h))] \quad (17)$$

It is easy to show for this function that the two self-selection constraints cannot simultaneously be binding. From the first-order conditions it is easy to confirm the following relationships, where the superscript f stands for the case of full information and the superscript a stands for the case of asymmetric information.

$$C_{pl}^a > C_{pl}^f$$
$$C_{kl}^a < C_{kl}^f$$
$$C_{ph}^a < C_{ph}^f$$
$$C_{kh}^a = C_{kh}^f$$
$$E_h^a < E_h^f$$
$$E_l^a \; ? \; E_l^f \quad (18)$$

In words, in the asymmetric information case the parent of the high-ability child consumes less and makes a larger transfer (since

Table 8.1
Calculations based on the log-linear utility function

	Benchmark		$\beta = .75$		$q = .25$		$\alpha = .40$		$A_h = 1.25$	
	AI	FI	AI	FI	AI	FI	AI	FI	AI	FI
C_{pl}	1.96	1.58	2.43	2.00	2.20	1.58	2.46	1.97	2.26	1.58
C_{ph}	1.66	2.10	2.15	2.67	1.87	2.10	2.09	2.63	1.75	2.63
C_{kl}	1.36	1.50	1.39	1.50	1.30	1.50	1.72	2.24	1.07	1.50
C_{kh}	2.00	2.00	2.00	2.00	2.00	2.00	2.50	2.50	2.50	2.50
E_l	.34	.08	.83	.50	.50	.08	1.18	.85	.33	.08
E_h	.67	1.11	1.15	1.67	.87	1.11	1.58	2.13	1.25	2.13
T_l	1.04	1.42	.57	1.00	.80	1.42	.54	1.03	.74	1.42
T_h	1.34	.09	.85	.33	1.13	.90	.91	.37	1.25	.37
τ*	.09	.00	.07	.00	.13	.00	.08	.00	.28	.00

Note: Except where indicated, all parameters are the benchmark parameters. The benchmark parameters are $Y = 3$, $A_l = .75$, $A_h = 1$, $q = .5$, $\beta = .95$, $\alpha = .50$.
*τ stands for the implicit marginal tax on the low ability child. It is defined by $\text{MRS}_i = A_i(1 - \tau_i)$ for $i = l, h$, where MRS is the marginal rate of substitution between consumption and effort.

transfers equal $Y - C_{ph}$), while the parent of the low-ability child consumes more and makes a smaller transfer. Hence, transfers are less equalizing for this utility function when information is asymmetric, and as presently described, under asymmetric information, the transfer to the high-ability child can exceed that to the low-ability child, while the reverse holds under full information. The equations in (18) also indicate that the high-ability child consumes the same, but earns less, in the asymmetric information case with increased transfers making up for the lower earnings. The low-ability child consumes less in the asymmetric case, but his (her) earnings may be larger or smaller.

Table 8.1 compares the asymmetric and full information solutions for this utility function for a range of parameter values. The results are quite striking. For each of the sets of parameters, asymmetric information leads parents to transfer more to the high-ability child than to the low-ability child, that is, transfers are not equalizing. For example, for the benchmark parameters, the transfers, under full information, are 1.42 to the low-ability child and .9 to the high-ability child. With incomplete information, however, the transfers are almost the reverse, with only 1.04 going to the low-ability child and 1.34 going to the high-ability child. The counterpart of these differences in transfers is that the consumption of parents will be quite different when information is asymmetric than when it is not. For the benchmark parameters, parents of high-ability children consume 2.10 under full information, but only 1.66 under asymmetric information; while parents of low ability children consume 1.58 under full information but 1.96 under asymmetric information.

The consumption of low-ability children in the benchmark case is 1.50 with full information, but only 1.36 with asymmetric information; for high-ability children, earnings adjust to maintain the same consumption level under full and asymmetric information. Hence, compared with the case of full information, the consumption of high- and low-ability children is less equal when information is asymmetric. Indeed, when information is asymmetric the process of parents transferring to their children can lead to more inequality in their children's consumption than would occur if parents were not altruistic and made no transfers to their children. For the benchmark parameters, but with $\beta = 0$, the high-ability child's consumption is 2.00, while the low-ability child's consumption is 1.50 (as in the full information case with $\beta = .95$).

The implicit marginal tax rates on the low-ability child listed in table 8.1 range from 7 percent to 28 percent. The 28 percent figure is particularly interesting. This implicit tax rate arises when A_h equals 1.25 while A_l remains at .75. Compared with the benchmark case, the implicit marginal tax rate is over three times larger, although the total transfer to the low-ability child is almost 25 percent smaller. This comparison indicates that implicit marginal taxation through parental bequests and intervivos transfers can be quite large despite the fact that total transfers are small.

The different parameter combinations considered in the second two columns of table 8.1 suggest that children's labor earnings can be quite sensitive to the extent of altruism (the level of β). Columns 5 and 6 of this table consider a lower value of the probability q of having a low-ability child. In the case of asymmetric information, the smaller value of q leads to smaller transfers to both the high- and low-ability children, but to a higher implicit tax on the low-ability child.

IV. Implications for Debt Neutrality and Conclusions

Any new model of intergenerational transfers should be immediately examined with respect to Robert Barro's (1974) debt neutrality proposition (Ricardian Equivalence). As in Feldstein (1988), the model presented here will not exhibit Ricardian Equivalence in states of nature when altruistic transfers are operative unless transfers are operative in all states of nature. To see this, suppose that the solution to the parent's problem involves zero transfers to the high-ability child, but positive transfers to the low-ability child. The self-selection constraint, (5) in this case, may still be binding because the high-ability child may try to disguise himself (herself) as a low-ability child to receive a transfer. If the government redistributes from the parent to the child, independent of the child's earnings (in a lump sum fashion), the utility of the high-ability child will increase. But this will alter the self-selection constraint (5) and, thereby, alter the outcome when the child is of low ability. In particular, by increasing the left-hand side of (5) the government policy relaxes this self-selection constraint evaluated at the pregovernment transfer optimum. As a consequence, the total (government plus parent) transfers to the low-ability child will likely be greater as a result of the government's policy. Hence, the policy will likely be effective in redistributing to the child regardless of whether the child turns out to be of high or low ability.

To summarize this chapter's findings, the inability of parents to know or to monitor perfectly their children's work efforts can significantly alter parental transfers to children. Parents are likely to respond to their information problem by making larger bequests to higher-earning children and by using their transfers implicitly either to tax at the margin low-earning children or to subsidize at the margin high-earning children. These implicit tax rates may be quite large, despite the fact that total transfers are small. Hence, labor supply studies should take into account potential implicit family taxation as well as official government taxation. In addition, the fact that the family may play an implicit role in taxation means that there may be less need for the government to play such a role.

Note

1. To be more precise, the slope (the right derivative) of the budget constraint relating the child's preparent transfer earnings to his (her) postparent transfer consumption at point B must be less than unity. Indeed, this slope must be less than or equal to the slope of the high-ability child's indifference curve at point B; that is, the "marginal tax schedule" must have a kink at point B.

References

Barro, Robert J. "Are Government Bonds Net Wealth?" *Journal of Political Economy*, 48(6): 1095–118.

Feldstein, Martin, "The Effects of Fiscal Policies when Incomes are Uncertain: A Contradiction to Ricardian Equivalence," *American Economic Review*, March 1988.

Mirrlees, James, "An Exploration in the Theory of Optimum Income Taxation," *Review of Economic Studies*, 1971, vol. 38, 175–208.

Sadka, Efraim, "On Income Distribution, Incentive Effects and Optimal Income Taxation," *Review of Economic Studies*, 1976, vol. 43, 261–68.

Stiglitz, Joseph, "Pareto Efficient and Optimal Taxation and the New New Welfare Economics," in *The Handbook of Public Economics*. Amsterdam, Holland: North Holland, 1987.

III Life-Cycle Planning

9

Looking for the News in the Noise: Additional Stochastic Implications of Optimal Consumption Choice

with Ariél Pakes

1. Introduction

In neoclassical models of consumption under uncertainty, optimizing agents utilize only current information about present and future prices and endowments in making current consumption decisions. This proposition has two implications. First, what was learned in the past is relevant to current behavior only in so far as past experience is incorporated in current knowledge of distributions of present and future prices and endowments. Second, given current information, new information about distributions of prices and endowments completely govern changes in the consumption program over time.

This chapter, unlike much of the related literature,[1] focuses on the second implication of the life-cycle theory. Limiting ourselves to the special case of earnings uncertainty, we provide conditions under which the revision in the expected discounted value of lifetime earnings (the news) equals the revision in the expected discounted value of consumption (the noise). There are two implications of this result. First, since new information represents the resolution of past subjective uncertainty, the result can be used to measure the extent and the time resolution of earnings uncertainty. Second, since the revision in the expected discounted value of consumption need not equal the revision in the expected discounted value of lifetime earnings, one can measure the extent to which the revisions in consumption programs are, indeed, determined by revisions in earnings expectations; that is, one can test the news equals noise proposition. We present one such test, using time series data, which unambiguously rejects the news equals noise proposition.

In the course of deriving the noise equals news results we clarify the functional relationship between the disturbance in the Euler equation governing the evolution of the marginal utility of consumption and the underlying innovation in earnings. We also indicate conditions under which the expectation of future consumption, conditional on current information, depends only on current consumption, and the additional restrictions needed for this conditional expectation to be linear in current consumption.

The next section derives our main theoretical proposition. Section 3 discusses the implications of the proposition for measuring earnings uncertainty and testing the life-cycle model. We then illustrate the test of the noise equals news proposition by applying it to aggregate time series data (section 4). The results indicate that, at least at the level of aggregate data, the assumptions underlying a linear relationship between expected future consumption and current consumption are false, and that unexpected changes in aggregate labor earnings explain only a small portion of the variance in aggregate consumption innovations. Apparently, in aggregate consumption data, the noise greatly exceeds the news.

2. Relating Consumption Innovations to New Information on Life-time Earnings

In the life-cycle model with earnings uncertainty considered here current consumption and plans about future consumption depend on preferences, the level of current assets, and probability distributions governing the stream of lifetime labor earnings. Revisions in consumption plans between two different periods are determined by revisions in the probability distribution of lifetime earnings associated with new information gathered between the periods. Using this fact, and assuming that distributions of revisions in the expected present value of lifetime earnings do not depend on past information, the life-cycle model implies the existence of two functions, one depending only on c_{t+1}, and the other only on c_t, where c_t denotes period t consumption. The difference between these two functions is exactly equal to the revision in the expected discounted value of lifetime earnings between periods t and $t+1$.

This proposition and some of its corollaries are presented in this section. The first two corollaries consider implications of the proposition for the stochastic process generating consumption. In contrast to other results in the literature, these corollaries deal with consumption per se, which is observable, rather than the marginal utility of consumption, which is not. The third corollary concerns the relationship between the stochastic process generating consumption and that generating earnings. This corollary states that the covariance of realized lifetime earnings and the revision in the present expected value of consumption (defined in the proposition) equals the variance of the revision in consumption, which in turn, equals the variance in the unobservable revision in the expected discounted value of lifetime earnings. It is this corollary which provides a basis for both an empirical analysis of the extent of household uncertainty about earnings, and for testing the extent to which revisions in consumption programmes are indeed determined by revisions in expected earnings.

Assumption 1 (A1) provides the model of consumption behavior that underlies our results.

ASSUMPTION 1 (A1): The consumer chooses a consumption program to $\max E_t\left\{\sum_{\tau=0}^{T-t} \beta^\tau U(c_{t+\tau})\right\}$ subject either to $A_t = \sum_{\tau=0}^{T-t} R^{\tau+1}(c_{t+\tau} - w_{t+\tau})$, with probability one, or

$$A_t = E_t \sum_{\tau=0}^{T-t} R^{\tau+1}(c_{t+\tau} - w_{t+\tau}),$$

where U(.) is a monotonically increasing strictly concave utility function possessing a continuous second derivative, β is a subjective discount factor, T is the known length of economic life, t is the age of the agent, c_t is consumption in period t, $w_{t+\tau}$ is earnings in period $t+\tau$, A_t is nonhuman wealth at age t, $R = \dfrac{1}{1+r}$, where r is the known real interest rate, and E_t denotes the expectation operator conditional on the information set at time t (where required we explicitly denote this information set by I_t). Moreover, the consumption programme is assumed to be bounded away from zero with probability one.[2]

Proposition 1 (P1) underlies the results presented in Hall (1978).

PROPOSITION 1 (P1): (See Hall [1978]). Given A1,

$$U'(c_{t+1}) = \lambda U'(c_t) + \xi_{t+1}$$

where $E_t \xi_{t+1} = 0$ and $\lambda = \beta/R$.

Proposition 1 is the first-order condition arising from expected utility maximization. It states that the expected marginal utility of consumption in period $t+1$ conditional on the information set in period t is a function of only consumption in period t; that is, it does not depend on any other variable in I_t. Note, however, that P1 has implications only for the stochastic process generating the marginal utility of consumption. In particular, the expectation of future consumption could depend on any or all variables in the current information set without violating P1. Each of the following two assumptions is sufficient to restrict the elements of the current information set which determine the expectation of future consumption. A1 is an assumption about preferences, while A2 is an assumption about the stochastic earnings process. As indicated in corollary 2, under either assumption expected future consumption depends only on current consumption.

ASSUMPTION 2 (A2): The utility function is quadratic, that is, $U(c_t) = a_0 + a_1 c_t + a_2 c_t^2$.

ASSUMPTION 3 (A3): Let $\eta_{t+\tau} = (E_{t+\tau} - E_{t+\tau-1}) \sum_{j=\tau}^{T-t} R^{j-\tau} w_{t+j}$, and $F_{t+\tau}(\eta_{t+\tau}|I_{t+\tau-1})$ be the distribution of $\eta_{t+\tau}$ conditional on the information set in period $t+\tau-1$. Then

$$\{dF_{t+\tau}(\eta_{t+\tau}|I_{t+\tau-1}) = dF_{t+\tau}(\eta_{t+\tau})\}_{\tau=0}^{T-t}.$$

In A3 $\eta_{t+\tau}$ is the revision in the expected discounted value of lifetime earnings arising from information that accumulates between $t+\tau-1$ and $t+\tau$. Clearly, since revisions in expectations cannot be predicted, $E[\eta_{t+\tau}|I_{t+\tau-1}] = 0$. A3 states that not only the expectation, but also the entire distribution of $\eta_{t+\tau}$ is independent of $I_{t+\tau-1}$.

Proposition 2 is central to the remainder of this paper.

PROPOSITION 2 (P2): If A1 and either A2 or A3 are satisfied, then there exist monotonically increasing continuously differentiable functions,

$$\delta^{(t+1)}(c_{t+1}) \quad \text{and} \quad \boldsymbol{\delta}^{(t)}(c_t),$$

such that

$$\delta^{(t+1)}(c_{t+1}) = \mathbf{R}^{-1}\boldsymbol{\delta}^{(t)}(c_t) + \eta_{t+1},$$

where η_{t+1} is defined in A3 and, hence, $E_t\eta_{t+1} = 0$.

The proof of P2, presented in the appendix, shows that $\delta^{(t+1)}(c_{t+1})$ is equal to the expected discounted sum of consumption expenditures between $t+1$ and the end of the planning horizon condition on the information set in period $t+1$; $\boldsymbol{\delta}^{(t)}(c_t)/\mathbf{R}$ is the expectation of this same variable conditional on the information set in period t.[3] The proposition states that these expectations can be written as functions of only c_{t+1} and c_t, respectively. It follows from the budget constraint that the revision in the expectation of the discounted value of consumption expenditures must be equal to the revision in the expectation of the discounted value of lifetime earnings (η_{t+1}).

It is worth comparing P1 and P2. Both propositions establish the existence of two functions, one dependent only on c_{t+1} and one only on c_t, such that the difference between them is "unexpected"; that is, both differences have an expectation, conditional on the information set in period t, of zero. In P2, however, this difference is precisely the revision in the expected discounted value of lifetime earnings. P1, in itself, does not provide information on the source of $\xi_{t+1} = \mathrm{U}'(c_{t+1}) - \lambda \mathrm{U}'(c_t)$, nor does it indicate anything about the properties of ξ_{t+1} except that $\mathrm{E}_t\xi_{t+1} = 0$. It should be clear, however, that ξ_{t+1} is determined by η_{t+1}. In fact, given A3, there is a one to one relationship between the realizations of the two random variables (see the appendix).

We first use proposition 2 to clarify two properties of the stochastic process generating consumption, and then discuss how it can be used to investigate the stochastic relationship between consumption and earnings. Corollary 3 is an immediate consequence of P2 and provides sufficient conditions for Hall's (1978) statement that "no variable apart from current consumption should be of any value in predicting future consumption."

COROLLARY 3: If A1, and either A2 or A3 are satisfied, then there exists a (monotonically increasing and continuously differentiable) function, $g_t(c_t)$, such that[4]

$$c_{t+1} = g_t(c_t) + u_{t+1}$$

where

$$\mathrm{E}_t u_{t+1} = 0.$$

The assumptions underlying P2 and Corollary 3 are quite general, requiring no explicit specification of the utility function or stochastic process generating earnings. As a consequence, the function $g_t(.)$

could be quite complicated. Corollary 4 notes, however, that if the utility function either displays constant absolute risk aversion, as specified in A4, or is quadratic, then $g_t(.)$ is linear.

ASSUMPTION 4 (A4): The utility function exhibits constant absolute risk aversion, that is, $U'(c_t) = Be^{-\gamma c t}$ $(B, \gamma > 0)$.

COROLLARY 4 (proved in the appendix): Provided A1 and either A2, or A3 and A4, are satisfied, then $c_{t+1} = \alpha_{0t} + \alpha_1 c_t + \alpha_{2t}\eta_{t+1}$.

Many of the tests of proposition 1 presented in the literature assume $g_t(c_t)$ is linear in c_t (e.g., Hall [1978], Hall and Mishkin [1982], and Flavin [1981]). Corollary 4 indicates that those results are somewhat more general than noted by Hall (1978), who justified linearity by quadratic utility, since $g_t(c_t)$ will also be linear if A3 and A4 are satisfied. Note that in the case of constant absolute risk aversion, $\alpha_1 = 1$. Note also that if the assumptions underlying this corollary are valid, the revision in the expected discounted value of lifetime earnings is simply proportional to the difference between c_{t+1} and a linear function of c_t. Hence, under the assumptions of the corollary, the η_{t+1} revisions defined in P2, can be identified in a straightforward manner, and this identification does not require any additional information on the sequence of distribution functions $\{F_{t+1}(\eta_{t+1})\}$. Our final corollary concerns the relationship between η_{t+1} and the revisions in the expected discounted value of the consumption program in a more general setting. This corollary requires only the assumptions underlying proposition 2.

COROLLARY 5: Let $L_t = \sum_{\tau=0}^{T-t} R^{\tau} w_{t+\tau}$ and $r_{t+1} = \delta^{(t+1)}(c_{t+1}) - R^{-1}\boldsymbol{\delta}^{(t)}(c_t)$; and assume A1 and either A2 or A3. Then

$$E_{(j)}[r_{t+1}L_{t+1}] = E_{(j)}[r_{t+1}^2] = E_{(j)}[\eta_{t+1}^2]$$

for $j \leq t$.

L_{t+1} is the realized discounted value of labor earnings between t and the end of the planning horizon. It can be partitioned into the revision, between $t+1$ and the end of the planning horizon, in the expected discounted value of lifetime earnings, $(L_{t+1}E_{t+1}L_{t+1})$, the period $t+1$ revision in that expectation that occurred because of information accumulated between t and $t+1$, η_{t+1} (recall that $E_{t+1}L_{t+1} - E_tL_{t+1} = \eta_{t+1}$, and the period t expected discounted value of lifetime earnings (E_tL_{t+1}); that is

$$L_{t+1} = (L_{t+1} - E_{t+1}L_{t+1}) + \eta_{t+1} + E_tL_{t+1}.$$

Provided the assumptions underlying proposition 2 are correct, the revision in the expected discounted value of the consumption program, that is, $r_{t+1} = \delta^{t+1}(c_{t+1}) - R^{-1}\boldsymbol{\delta}^t(c_t)$, just equals η_{t+1}. Corollary 5 follows from noting that $L_{t+1} - E_{t+1}L_{t+1}$ cannot be correlated with any variable in I_{t+1} including η_{t+1}, while η_{t+1} cannot be correlated with any variable in I_t including E_tL_{t+1}.

Eden and Pakes (1981) appear to be the first to utilize the fact that the revision in consumption expenditures should contain information on changes through time in the expected discounted value of lifetime earnings. They note that the total variance in the individual's expected discounted value of lifetime earnings at time t is just

$$\sum_{j=1}^{T-t} R^{2(j-1)} E\eta_{t+j}^2,$$

and that the sequence $\{E\eta_{t+j}^2\}$ provides a measure of the age profile of the realizations of the variance in lifetime earnings. The article by Eden and Pakes (1981) assumes a quadratic utility function, and uses only information on consumption expenditures to estimate $E\eta_t^2$. Corollary 5 provides the analogue of the Eden and Pakes result for an arbitrary concave utility function, and indicates that there are, in principal, two unbiased estimates of $E\eta_{t+1}^2$. This latter fact has two implications, First it provides a basis for testing the model, since, in principal, we can compare the variance in the consumption innovation to the covariance between it and lifetime earnings. Section 3.2 illustrates this point. Second, but perhaps more important, the fact that there are two unbiased $E\Sigma\eta_{t+1}^2$ allows us to relax different assumptions and still extract information on the parameters of interest. In particular it permits us to allow for heterogeneity and errors in measurement when using micro panel data to analyze the uncertainty in earnings streams. Section 3.1 elaborates this point.

3. Some Implications

3.1. Panel Data

In this section we consider in more detail the special case of assumptions A1 and A2 (quadratic utility) or A3 plus A4 (the case where the one-period utility function exhibits constant absolute risk aversion, and the distributions of the revisions in expected lifetime earnings are independent of past information). Our purpose is to illustrate how the results of the last section enable us to account for heterogeneity and errors in measurement when constructing measures of earnings uncertainty from micro panel data sets. Partly for notational convenience we begin by explicitly incorporating (quite arbitrary) heterogeneity in the preference parameters, β and γ, and in the distributions of the revisions in expected lifetime earnings, $dF_{t+\tau}(\eta_{t+\tau})$; we assume, initially, correctly measured data. Under these assumptions, the results in the last section and those in the appendix imply that the change in consumption and the lifetime earnings of consumer i at age t can be written, respectively, as

$$\Delta C_{t+1,i} = C_{t+1,i} - C_{t,i} = \alpha_{0,i,t} + \alpha_{2,t+1}\eta_{t+1,i} \tag{1}$$

and

$$L_{t+1,i} = (L_{t+1,i} - E[L_{t+1,i}|I_{t+1,i}]) + \eta_{t+1,i} + E[L_{t+1,i}|I_{t,i}],$$

where

$$\alpha_{0,i,t} = \gamma_i^{-1} \ln\left\{\int \exp(-\gamma_i\eta_{t+1,i}/\alpha_{2,t+1})\, dF_{t+1,i}(\eta_{t+1,i}) - \ln(\beta_i/R)\right\},$$

and $\alpha_{2,t+1}^{-1} = \sum_{\tau=0}^{T-(tm+1)} R^{\tau}$.

Suppose that we have N observations on the couple $(\Delta C_{t+1,i}, L_{t+1,i})$ in each of J different population groups, and that we were interested in estimating and comparing the means of

$$E[\eta_{t+1,i}^2|I_{i,t}] \equiv \int \eta_{t+1,i}^2\, dF_{t+1,i}(\eta_{t+1,i}),$$

say comparing the means of $E_{(i)}E[\eta_{t+1,i}^2|I_{i,t}] = \sigma_{t+1}^2$ in the different groups. (The first expectation is understood to be taken with respect to the measure of consumers in the group of interest; when we wish to distinguish more explicitly between groups, we will use a superscript j.) We consider using the group sample covariance of $\Delta C_{t+1,i}$ and $L_{t+1,i}$, say $S_{t+1}^{2(j)}$, as an estimate of $\sigma_{t+1}^{2(j)}$, and we seek conditions under which

$$S_{t+1}^{2(j)} = 1/N \sum_{i\in j}(\Delta C_{t+1,i} - \Delta\bar{C}_{t+1}^{(j)})(L_{t+1,i} - \bar{L}_{t+1}^{(j)}) \xrightarrow{P} \sigma_{t+1}^{2(j)}\alpha_{2,t+1} \tag{2}$$

where $\Delta\bar{C}^{(j)}_{t+1} = N^{-1}\sum_{i\in j}\Delta C_{t+1,i}$, $\bar{L}^{(j)}_{t+1} = N^{-1}\sum_{i\in j} L_{t+1,i}$, and $\xrightarrow{P}$ reads converges in probability to. Clearly, provided the sample realizations of $(\Delta C_{t+1,i}, L_{t+1,i})$ are mutually independent, and

$$E\Delta C_{t+1,i}(L_{t+1,i} - \bar{L}^{(j)}_{t+1}) = \sigma^{2(j)}_{t+1}\alpha_{t+1}$$

for all $i \in j$ (and some finite $\sigma^{2(j)}_{t+1}$), the strong law of large numbers will insure that property (2) is indeed satisfied for every j (see, for example, Rao [1973] chapter 2).

It is worth considering situations in which the first two conditions may be questionable. The independence assumption is likely to be problematic if all observations are drawn in the same year, since then there may be market factors whose realizations affect all the $\eta_{t+1,i}$ in a given group. In this case, what we can (and cannot) learn from the data depends upon the structure of the dependence induced by the market factors. In the case where $\eta_{t+1,i} = \zeta_{t+1,i} + \theta_{t+1}$ for all i, and the $\{\zeta_{t+1,i}\}$ are mutually independent, we could still obtain consistent estimates of the difference between the $\sigma^{2(j)}_{t+1}$ among different groups, though not of the level of any of them. In considering the second condition, recall that the model implies that

$$\alpha_{2,t+1}E[\eta_{t+1,i}L_{t+1,i}|I_{i,t}] = \alpha_{2,t+1}E[\eta^2_{t+1,i}|I_{i,t}],$$

and this insures that

$$\alpha_{2,t+1}E[\eta_{t+1,i}E[\eta_{t+1,i}L_{t+1,i}] = \alpha_{2,t+1}E_{(i)}E[\eta_{t+1,i}L_{t+1,i}|I_{i,t}] = \alpha_{2,t+1}\sigma^2_{t+1}.$$

It follows that

$$E\Delta C_{t+1,i}(L_{t+1,i} - \bar{L}^{(j)}_{t+1}) = \alpha_{2,t+1}\sigma^{2(j)}_{t+1} \quad (\text{for } i \in j),$$

provided $E\alpha(L_{t+1,i} - \bar{L}^{(j)}_{t+1}) = 0$, that is, provided the covariance between $\alpha_{0,i,t}$ and lifetime earnings vanishes. Since the model assumes that the individual knows his preference parameters and the distributions of the revisions in lifetime earnings, and since these determine $\alpha_{0,i,t}$, there should be no correlation between $\alpha_{0,i,t}$ and the revisions in the expectation of lifetime income. However, there may be a cross-sectional correlation between $\alpha_{0,i,t}$ and the initial (period zero) expected discounted value of lifetime earnings, and this could cause some inconsistency.

In order to determine the effect of errors in measurement on our results, we must specify how these errors are generated. Under the classical assumption of additive measurement errors which are uncorrelated with the true deviates and with each other—that is, under the assumption that we observe couples $(\Delta C_{it}^m, L_{it}^m)$ governed by

$$\begin{cases} \Delta C_{i,t}^m = \Delta C_{i,t} + V_{i,t}^C \\ L_{i,t}^m = L_{i,t} + v_{i,t}^L \end{cases} \tag{3}$$

where $E[v_{i,t}^q L_{i,t}] = E[v_{i,t}^q C_{i,t}] = E[v_{i,t}^L v_{i,t}^C] = 0$ (for $q = L, C$), and $(\Delta C_{i,t} L_{i,t})$ abide by the model in equation (1)—it is clear that the presence of measurement error does not affect the consistency property described in equation (2). In this case, then, both $S_{L,\Delta C}^{(j)}$ and $S_{L^m,\Delta C^m}^{(j)}$ (within group covariance of the observed deviates) are consistent estimators for $\alpha_{t+1}\sigma_{L,\Delta C}^{2(j)}$. On the other hand, $S_{L^m \Delta C^m}$ will be a less precise estimator for $\alpha_{t+1}\sigma_{L,\Delta C}$, and presumably one could derive more precise estimates for $\alpha_{t+1}\sigma_{L,\Delta C}^2$ than $S_{L^m \Delta C^m}^{(j)}$.[5]

3.2. *A Time Series Example*

Having considered applying corollary 5 to measuring earnings uncertainty, we now turn to an aggregate time series example that uses corollary 5 to test the new equals noise proposition. Here we ignore issues of aggregation over individuals, let T (the planning horizon) approach infinity, and assume the stochastic process generating earnings is (strictly) stationary and normal.[6] These assumptions simplify the testing procedure considerably.

The assumption of stationarity allows us to write the earnings process as an infinite autoregression with an independent and identically distributed disturbance. This disturbance is proportional to η_{t+1}, the revision in expected lifetime earnings between t and $t+1$ (see Anderson [1971] and the definition of η_{t+1} in A3). That is

$$w_{t+1} = \sum_{\tau=0}^{\infty} \gamma_\tau w_{t-\tau} + \varepsilon_{t+1}, \tag{4}$$

and

$$\eta_{t+1} = \theta\varepsilon_{t+1},$$

where $\{\varepsilon_{\tau+1}\}$ is a sequence of independently and identically distributed random variables.[7]

Given stationarity of the earnings process, it is assumed that $\delta^{t+1}(.) \to \delta^*(.)$ as $T \to \infty$, where the function $\delta^*(.)$ can be expressed as the nth-order polynomial

$$\delta^*(c_t) = \sum_{i=0}^{n} m_i c_t^i. \tag{5}$$

Note that if $m_i = 0$, for $i \geq 2$, the assumption of a quadratic or constant absolute risk aversion utility function (corollary 4), and the corresponding linear predictor function for c_{t+1} used in previous analyses (e.g., Flavin [1981], Hall and Mishkin [1982]), is valid.

To provide a more informative summary of the data than can be obtained from the value of a test statistic, we allow a disturbance term, say v_{t+1}, to affect the revision in the consumption programme [i.e., $r_{t+1} = \delta^{t+1}(c_{t+1}) - \mathbf{R}^{-1}\boldsymbol{\delta}^t(c_t)$]. We then ask what percentage of the variance in r_{t+1} (the noise) is accounted for by the disturbance, and what percentage is accounted for by the revision in the expected discounted value of lifetime earnings, i.e., by the news, η_{t+1}.

Letting $\{v_t\}$ be a sequence of independent random variables whose joint distribution is assumed to be independent of the joint distribution of earnings (and whose realizations cannot, therefore, be accounted for by the life-cycle model with earnings uncertainty), we write

$$r_{t+1} = \eta_{t+1} + v_{t+1} \tag{6a}$$

and consider estimates of ρ^2, where

$$\rho^2 = \frac{E\eta_{t+1}^2}{E\eta_{t+1}^2 + Ev_{t+1}^2} \tag{6b}$$

To obtain the system of equations to be estimated, we use the relation $\boldsymbol{\delta}^t(c_t) = \delta^t(c_t) - c_t$ (see the appendix). Equation (7*a*) is derived from this fact, (4), (5), (6) and the definition of r_{t+1} presented in corollary 5, while equation (7*b*) comes directly from (4). This produces the system

$$c_{t+1} = k_0 + R^{-1} \sum_{i=1}^{n} k_i c_t^i - \sum_{i=2}^{n} k_i c_{t+1}^i + \theta m_1^{-1} \varepsilon_{t+1} + m_1^{-1} v_{t+1} \tag{7a}$$

$$w_{t+1} = \sum_{\tau=0}^{\infty} \gamma_\tau w_{t-\tau} + \varepsilon_{t+1}, \tag{7b}$$

where $k_0 = m_0(\mathrm{R}^{-1} - 1)/m_1$, $k_1 = (m_1 - 1)/m_1$, and $k_i = m_i/m_1$ $(i = 2, \ldots, n)$. Note that, if the model is correct, the coefficient of c_t^i in equation (7*a*) should be opposite in sign, and a bit larger (in absolute value) than the coefficient of c_{t+1}^i $(i = 2, \ldots, n)$ with the difference determined by R. Thus, for $i \geq 2$ we can obtain an estimate of R, and for $i > 2$ we can test the model's implications by testing if the coefficient of c_t^i equals R^{-1} times the coefficient of c_{t+1}^i.

Since both ε_{t+1} and v_{t+1} are determinants of c_{t+1} they will, in general, be correlated with powers of that variable. Therefore, consistent estimates of the coefficients in equation (7*a*) require the use of instruments for c_{t+1}^i $(i = 2, \ldots, n)$. Clearly, the assumptions of the model imply that

$$\mathrm{E}(c_t^i v_{t+1}) = \mathrm{E}(c_t^i \varepsilon_{t+1}) = \mathrm{E}(w_{t-\tau} v_{t+1}) = \mathrm{E}(w_{t-\tau}\varepsilon_{t+1}) = 0 \quad \text{for } i, \tau \geq 0.$$

In the example in section 3 equation (7*a*) is estimated by two-stage least squares using current and lagged earnings and powers of current consumption as instruments. Equation (7*b*) is estimated by ordinary least squares. Let e_{t+1}^c and e_{t+1}^w be the estimated residuals from the consumption and earnings equations, respectively, that is

$$e_{t+1}^c = c_{t+1} - \hat{k}_0 - \mathrm{R}^{-1} \sum_{i=1}^{n} \hat{k}_i c_t^i - \sum_{i=2}^{n} \mathrm{R}^{-1} \hat{k}_i c_{t+1}^i, \tag{8}$$

and

$$e_{t+1}^w = w_{t+1} - \sum_{\tau=0}^{\infty} w_{t-\tau} \hat{\gamma}_\tau,$$

where a circumflex over a variable indicates its estimated value. Then, letting $\mathrm{S}(x, y)$ represent the sample covariance of x and y,

$$r_{e^c e^w}^2 = \frac{\mathrm{S}(e^w, e^c)^2}{\mathrm{S}(e^w, e^w)^2 \mathrm{S}(e^c, e^c)^2} \xrightarrow{\mathrm{P}} \frac{\theta^2 \mathrm{E}\varepsilon^2}{\theta^2 \mathrm{E}\varepsilon^2 + \mathrm{E}v^2} = \rho^2, \tag{9}$$

where $\xrightarrow{\mathrm{P}}$ reads converges in probability, and the last equality follows from the fact that $\eta = \theta\varepsilon$ (equation (4)) and the definition of ρ^2 (equation (6*b*)). That is, the r^2 from the residuals of the two equation system in (7) provides us with a consistent estimate of ρ^2, the fraction of the variance in the revision in the expected discounted value of consumption expenditures that is accounted for by the life-cycle model with earnings uncertainty.

4. Results from an Illustrative Test of the Noise Equals News Proposition

The data used to carry out the illustrative time series test described above are National Income Accounts (NIA) quarterly observations of consumption of nondurables and services and quarterly NIA observations of wages and salaries.[8] There are 147 observations corresponding to the first quarter of 1947 through the third quarter of 1983. All observations were expressed in percapita terms and converted to 1972 dollars using a weighted average of the NIA nondurables deflator and the NIA services deflator, with the fixed weight determined by the average share of nondurables consumption in total consumption of nondurables plus services. Since our empirical approach assumes stationarity in earnings, we detrended wages and salaries with the trend path estimated by regressing the logarithm of wages and salaries against a constant and time.

Empirical Results

Table 9.1 presents the coefficients from estimating equation (7*a*) assuming first through fourth order polynomial functions for $\delta^*(.)$ (equation (5)). Estimation of the linear model is by OLS, while the second-, third-, and fourth-order models are estimated by two stage least squares.[9]

The higher order terms in each of the regressions are highly significant suggesting that the linear model posited by Flavin (1981) and Hall and Mishkin (1982) is inappropriate. The appropriateness of a higher-order model is also suggested by a test of the linearity of the function $g_t(.)$ of corollary 3. Specifically, we regressed c_{t+1} on successive higher order polynomials of c_t. In the regression of c_{t+1} on c_t and c_t^2 the coefficient of c_t^2 has a t ratio of -2.30 which is significant at the 5 percent level. The F statistic for the inclusion of third order terms in the approximation for $g_t(.)$ was (marginally) insignificant.

Recall that if the model is appropriate the coefficient of c_t^i equals minus R^{-1} times the coefficient of c_{t+1}^i for $i \geq 2$ (see equation (7*a*)). Looking at the unconstrained parameters estimates in Table 9.1 it is clear that they are close to satisfying these constraints. However, a formal test of these constraints clearly rejects them; the observed value of the F(2, 131) test statistic is 21.36. This occurs because the fourth order model has a near perfect fit, making even those alter-

Table 9.1
Regression results: First-order through fourth-order consumption models*

Variable	First-order model	Second-order model	Third-order model	Fourth-order model
Constant	−3.417	−2.914	14.986	−22.224
	(5.973)	(8.818)	(12.825)	(10.845)
C_t	1.006	1.006	.988	1.040
	(.002)	(.007)	(.014)	(.017)
C_t^2		−.184E-3	−.405E-3	−.583E-3
		(.805E-5)	(−.158E-4)	(.115E-4)
C_{t+1}^2		.183E-3	.407E-3	.557E-3
		(.843E-5)	(.180E-4)	(.908E-5)
C_t^3			−.521E-9	.140E-8
			(.380E-10)	(.459E-10)
C_{t+1}^3			.521E-9	−.133E-12
			(.406E-10)	(.475E-10)
C_t^4				−.123E-12
				(.631E-14)
C_{t+1}^4				.116E-12
				(.677E-14)
Ratio of standard error of regression to mean value of consumption	.00542	.00116	.00024	.00003

*Two stage least squares estimates of equation (5*a*). $w_{t-\tau}$ and c_t^i ($\tau = 0, 1, \ldots, 7$ and $i = 1, \ldots, N$) are used as instruments. There are 129 observations. Numbers in parentheses below coefficient estimates are estimated assymptotic standard errors. E1 is 10.

natives that are close to the null hypothesis very powerful. The estimate of R^{-1}, that is of one plus the annual real interest rate, obtained from the constrained 4th order model has the reasonable value of 1.032 with a standard error of .018.

Table 9.2 provides the estimated fractions of the variance in consumption innovations (noise) explained by earnings information (news) (see equation (6*b*)). As indicated by equation (9), this ratio is equal to the squared correlation coefficient between the residuals in the consumption and the earnings equations (7*a*) and (7*b*). The earnings equation was estimated using eight lagged values of quarterly earnings. We also conducted the analysis using four rather than eight lags of earnings and obtained results essentially identical to those reported in Table 9.2.

All of the ratios reported in Table 9.2 are quite small. In the first-order, linear model the innovation in earnings explains less than a

Table 9.2
Estimated ratios of news to noise and estimated asymptotic standard errors

Model	Ratio of news to noise	Standard error of ratio
First Order	.181	0.77
Second Order	.511E-3	.084
Third Order	.743E-2	.84
Fourth Order	.020	.050

fifth of the innovation in consumption. For the higher order models "news" is 2 percent or less of "noise." Only in the first-order model is the estimated ratio of news to noise statistically significantly different from zero.

5. Summary and Conclusion

This chapter provides conditions under which the life-cycle model with earnings uncertainty implies a simple functional relationship between revisions in the expected discounted value of consumption programmes and revisions in the expected discounted value of lifetime earnings. This relationship can be used to infer the extent and time resolution of uncertainty from panel data on consumption choices. The chapter also indicates conditions under which the expected discounted value of future consumption depends only on current consumption. Finally, the paper presents a new test of optimal consumption choice under earnings uncertainty.

Applying the results of this chapter to micro panel data should be particularly fruitful since they permit comparisons across demographic and occupational groups of the magnitude and time resolution of earnings uncertainty. Much of the uncertainty in earnings in the cross section is, of course, averaged out in macro data. Indeed, in illustrating our theoretical results on aggregate time series data, we find that new information about earnings has little bearing on aggregate consumption innovations.

Appendix

Proof of P2: Let $\{c_{j+\tau}^{(j)}\}_{\tau=0}^{T-j}$ be the optimal consumption program for period j. Since this program must satisfy the budget constraint in year j,

$$E_j \sum_{\tau=0}^{T-j} R^{\tau} c_{j+\tau}^{(j)} = A_j R^{-1} + E_j \sum_{\tau=0}^{T-j} R^{\tau} w_{j+\tau}.$$

Using this condition for period t and $t+1$, and the fact that

$$A_{t+1} = A_t R^{-1} + w_t - c_t,$$

one can show that

$$\delta_{t+1} = R^{-1} \boldsymbol{\delta}_t + \eta_{t+1}, \tag{10}$$

where

$$\delta_{t+1} = E_{t+1} \sum_{\tau=0}^{T-(t+1)} R^{\tau} c_{t+1+\tau}^{(t+1)}, \quad \text{and} \quad \boldsymbol{\delta}_t = \delta_t - c_t.$$

The term δ_{t+1} equals the expected discounted value of current and future consumption conditional on the information set in period $t+1$ and is, therefore, a function of I_{t+1}; that is, $\delta_{t+1} = \delta_*^{(t+1)}(I_{t+1})$; and $\boldsymbol{\delta}_t = \boldsymbol{\delta}_{*t}^{(t)(I)}$. To prove the proposition, it suffices to prove the following lemma.

LEMMA: If A1 and either A2 or A3 is satisfied then for $t = 1, \ldots, T-1$, $\delta^{(t)}(I) = \boldsymbol{\delta}^{(t)}(c_t)$; with $\boldsymbol{\delta}^{(t)}(c_t)$ monotonically increasing and continuously differentiable in c_t.

Proof: If the utility function is quadratic (A2), then the lemma follows directly from proposition 1 and the definition of $\boldsymbol{\delta}_t$, for quadratic utility implies that $E_t[c_{t+\tau}^{(t)}] = (\lambda^{\tau} - 1)\alpha_0 + \lambda^{\tau} c_t$ for $\tau \geq 0$; where $\lambda = \beta/R$, and α_0 is determined by the parameters of the utility function. If A2 is not satisfied but A3 is, the lemma is proved by induction. Thus assume $\delta_*^{(j+1)}(I_{j+1}) = \delta^{(j+1)}(c_{j+1})$, the latter function being monotonically increasing and continuously differentiable in c_{j+1}. Then equation (10) and the implicit function theorem imply the existence of a continuously differentiable monotonically increasing function $Q^{j+1}(.)$ such that

$$c_{j+1} = Q^{(j+1)}(\boldsymbol{\delta}_j R^{-1} + \eta_{j+1}). \tag{11}$$

Also from proposition 1,

$$U'(c_{j+1}) = \lambda U'(c_j) + \xi_{j+1} \quad \text{with} \quad E_j \xi_{j+1} = 0. \tag{12}$$

Substituting (11) into (12) and taking expectations we have

$$\mathrm{H}^{(j+1)}(\boldsymbol{\delta}_j, c_j) = \int [\mathrm{U}'\{\mathrm{Q}^{(j+1)}(\boldsymbol{\delta}_j\mathrm{R}^{-1} + \eta_{j+1})\}]\, d\mathrm{F}_{j+1}(\eta_{j+1}) - \lambda \mathrm{U}'(c_j) = 0, \tag{13}$$

with $\mathrm{H}^{(j+1)}_{\boldsymbol{\delta}_j} = \mathrm{R}^{-1}\int \mathrm{U}''\{\mathrm{Q}^{(j+1)'}(\mathrm{R}^{-1}\boldsymbol{\delta}_j + \eta_{j+1})\}\, d\mathrm{F}_{j+1}(\eta_{j+1})$, which is negative and continuous in $\boldsymbol{\delta}_j$ by virtue of the continuity of $\mathrm{U}''(.)$ and $\mathrm{Q}^{j+1'}(.)$; and $\mathrm{H}'_{cj} = -\lambda \mathrm{U}''(c_j)$, which is positive and continuous in c_j. The implicit function theorem therefore implies the existence of a monotonically increasing continuously differentiable function $\boldsymbol{\delta}^{(j)}(c_j)$ such that $\boldsymbol{\delta}_j = \boldsymbol{\delta}^{(j)}(c_j)$. Since $\delta_j = \boldsymbol{\delta}_j + c_j$, it follows that $\delta^{(j)}_*(\mathrm{I}_j) = \mathrm{R}[\boldsymbol{\delta}^j(c_j) + c_j] = \delta^{(j)}(c_j)$, is also monotonically increasing and continuously differentiable in c_j. To complete the inductive argument one need only observe that $\delta^{(\mathrm{T})}_*(\mathrm{I}_\mathrm{T}) = c_{\mathrm{T}'}$ and construct $\boldsymbol{\delta}^{\mathrm{T}-1}(c_{\mathrm{T}-1})$ from equations (11), (12), and (13) substituting $\mathrm{T}-1$ for j. □

Two points are worthy of note here. First the proof clarifies the roles of assumptions 2 and 3 in the text in deriving proposition 2. If the utility function is quadratic (assumption 2) the both $\mathrm{Q}^{j+1}(.)$ and $\mathrm{U}'(.)$ are linear. In that case equation (13) involves integrating over a linear function of η_{j+1}, so that $\mathrm{H}^{j+1}(.)$ depends on the distribution of η_{j+1}, only through $\mathrm{E}_j\eta_{j+1}$, which is zero by construction. For quadratic utility then the proposition is true regardless of whether the conditional distribution of η_{j+1} depends on any variables in I_j. If the utility function is not quadratic, then equation (13) involves integrating over a convex function of η_{j+1}. The integral will then depend on higher order moments of η_{j+1}, and though $\mathrm{E}_j\eta_{j+1} = 0$, the conditional variance, say, of η_{j+1} may depend on variables in I_j. Thus, without either quadratic utility or assumption 3, $\mathrm{H}^{j+1}(.)$ will be a function of more variables in I_j than c_j, and neither proposition 2 nor the statement that E_jc_{j+1} is only a function of c_j are true. The second point is that the proof is constructive in the sense that given any $\mathrm{U}(.)$, and any sequence $\{d\mathrm{F}_{j+1}(\eta_{j+1})\}$, the proof explains exactly how to construct $\{\delta^{j+1}(c_{j+1})\}$ and $\{\boldsymbol{\delta}^j(c_j)\}$.

Proof of Corollary 4: If A2 is satisfied then corollary 4 follows directly from the proof of proposition 2. To prove the corollary when A3 and A4 are satisfied we first use an inductive argument to show that $\{\delta^{(t+1)}(c_{t+1}) = \psi_{0,t+1} + \psi_{1,t+1}c_{t+1}\}_{t=1}^{\mathrm{T}-t}$ and then derive the implied relationship between c_{t+1} and c_t. Assuming $\delta^{(t+1)}(c_{t+1}) = \psi_{0,t+1} + \psi_{1,t+1}c_{t+1}$, equation (A2) in the proof of proposition 2 becomes,

$$c_{t+1} = \frac{1}{\psi_{1,t+1}}(\boldsymbol{\delta}_t \mathrm{R}^{-1} + \eta_{t+1} - \psi_{0,t+1}).$$

Substituting this equation into (12) and solving (13) for $\boldsymbol{\delta}_t$ yields:

$$\boldsymbol{\delta}_t = \mathrm{R}\boldsymbol{\psi}_{1,t+1} c_t + \frac{\mathrm{R}\psi_{1,t+1}}{\gamma} \log\left(\frac{k_{t+1}}{\lambda}\right) + \psi_{0,t+1}\mathrm{R},$$

where

$$k_{t+1} = \int e^{-(\gamma/\psi_{1,t+1}\mathrm{R})\eta_{t+1}}\, d\mathrm{F}_{t+1}(\eta_{t+1}).$$

Noting that $\delta_t = (\boldsymbol{\delta}_t + c_t) = \delta^{(t)}(c_t)$, and that $\delta^{\mathrm{T}}(c_{\mathrm{T}}) = c_{\mathrm{T}}$, completes the inductive argument. Clearly this argument implies that the sequences $\{\psi_{0,t}\}$ and $\{\psi_{1,t}\}$ are determined by the recursions

$$\psi_{1,t} = \psi_{1,t+1}\mathrm{R} + 1, \quad \psi_{0,t} = \frac{\mathrm{R}\psi_{1,t+1}}{\gamma} \log \frac{k_{t+1}}{\lambda} + \psi_{0,t+1}\mathrm{R},$$

with initial conditions $\psi_{1,\mathrm{T}} = 1$; and $\psi_{0,\mathrm{T}} = 0$. This solution and equation (10) in the proof of proposition 2, imply the corollary. Assuming that the limit of the solution to the finite horizon problem converges to the solution of the infinite problem and assuming a stationary distribution of η_t, then as $\mathrm{T} \to \infty$, $\psi_{1,t} \to \frac{1}{1-\mathrm{R}}$, and

$$\psi_{0,t} \to \frac{1}{\gamma}\frac{\mathrm{R}}{(1-\mathrm{R})^2} \log \frac{k^*}{\lambda}, \quad \text{where } h^* = \int e^{-\gamma((1-\mathrm{R})/\mathrm{R})\eta}\, df(\eta). \quad \square$$

Notes

The authors thank Chris Sims, Fumio Hayashi, Greg Mankiw, and an anonymous referee for helpful comments and John Bound, Linus Yamane, and Tom Abbott for excellent research assistance.

1. Recently, considerable attention has been given to testing for optimal intertemporal consumption choice in stochastic environments. In principle both implications noted above provide a basis for testing the theory. A test of the first implication is that theoretically irrelevant information is in fact irrelevant to current consumption choices. A test of the second implication is that, given current information, new information about prices and endowments fully determines the precise time path of consumption. While the two implications are closely related, one can easily construct examples of non optimizing consumption choice that satisfy tests of one implication but not of the other. Nevertheless, most past tests have focused on the first implication, defined a revision in the consumption programme (more precisely in the programme for the marginal utility of consumption), and then tested whether this revision is correlated

with information available before it was made (see Hall [1978], Hansen and Singleton [1983], Mankiw, Rotenberg and Summers [1982]). One difficulty in evaluating these studies as a group is that they involve repeated use of much the same data for consumption and leisure choices while using a variety of different time series that incorporate past information. In a finite sample revisions in marginal utility will be significantly correlated with a multitude of variables in the "past" information set, and one will surely find many such variables in repeated searches.

2. More precisely we require that there exists an $\varepsilon > 0$, such that $\mathbf{C}^t \geq \varepsilon$ with probability one, where $\mathbf{C}^t$ denotes the consumption programme formulated in period t. This assumption underlies the proof of the result in Hellwig [1978] (recorded here as proposition 1). It can be insured by appropriately restricting the utility function and the statistic process generating earnings (i.e., the primitives of the model; see for example, Hellwig [1977]). Finally, note that the propositions and corollaries presented here will be true under either the "probability" or the "expectational" specification of the budget constraint (it is possible for a property of the consumption programme to be true for one specification, but not the other).

3. It should be noted that the proof is constructive in that it provides a method of calculating these functions from the utility function and probability distributions of revisions in the expected discounted values of lifetime earnings.

4. P2 and the implicit function theorem imply the existence of a monotonically increasing continuously differentiable function $\mathrm{Q}^{(t+1)}(.)$ such that $c_{t+1} = \mathrm{Q}^{(t+1)}\{\mathrm{R}^{-1}\boldsymbol{\delta}^{(t)}(c_t) + \eta_{t+1}\}$. The function $g_t(c_t)$ is constructed by integrating $\mathrm{Q}^{t+1}(.)$ over the probability measure, $d\mathrm{F}_{t+1}(\eta_{t+1})$.

5. This is because earnings and consumption levels, as well as other household characteristics, are likely to contain extractable information on the extent of measurement error.

6. Strictly speaking, the assumption of stationarity is not necessary in our framework. Under mild regularity conditions on the boundedness of the variance of the earnings process, the fact that $\mathrm{R} < 1$, implies that, as T grows, the difference,

$$\sum_{\tau=0}^{\mathrm{T}} \mathrm{T}^{\tau} w_{j+\tau} - \sum_{\tau=0}^{\infty} \mathrm{R}^{\tau} w_{j+\tau},$$

converges, in mean square, to zero. That is, if we formed

$$\mathrm{L}_j^{(\mathrm{T})} = \sum_{\tau=0}^{\mathrm{T}} \mathrm{R}^{\tau} w_{j+\tau},$$

then, by choosing T large enough, we can insure that the difference $r_j\mathrm{L}_j^{(\mathrm{T})} - r_j\mathrm{L}_j^{(\infty)}$ is smaller than any positive ε with probability very close to one. On the other hand the larger is T, the less data is available to form sample averages

$$\left(\mathrm{J}^{-1} \sum_{j=0}^{\mathrm{J}} r_j \mathrm{L}_j^{(\mathrm{T})} \quad \text{and} \quad \mathrm{J}^{-1} \sum_{j=0}^{\mathrm{J}} r_j \mathrm{L}_j^{(\infty)} \right)$$

and the larger will be the standard error of these estimates of $\mathrm{EJ}^{-1} \sum r_j \mathrm{L}_j^{\tau}$ and $\mathrm{EJ}^{-1} \sum r_j^2$.

We actually tried to form these means sample averages empirically for the special case of quadratic utility functions (see corollary 4), but it became clear that sufficiently large T resulted in the loss of too many degrees of freedom.

7. If the process generating earnings has a convergent autoregressive representation, then θ can be expressed as a function of the autoregressive coefficients (the γ_τ), and one could impose, or test, this constraint. In the empirical work the value of θ varied with the order of the autoregression we assumed, though the estimated variance of the disturbance from the wage equation, and its covariance with the residual in the consumption equation did not vary significantly. This is another example of the familiar observation that the residuals formed after estimating a stationary process do not vary much with the precise form of the process estimated, though other properties of the estimated process may vary substantially. Since our theoretical results are independent of the precise form of the earnings process, we thought it best to leave θ unconstrained. We also used NIA observations on compensation of employees as the earnings variable. None of the empirical results were materially affected by using employee compensation rather than wages and salaries.

8. We also used NIA observations on compensation of employees as the earnings variable. None of the empirical results were materially affected by using employee compensation rather than wages and salaries.

9. At this stage the analysis is indistinguishable from estimating the first-order condition (M) with a polynomial approximation of the utility function.

References

Anderson, T. W. (1971). *The Statistical Analysis of Time Series*, John Wiley and Sons Inc.

Eden, B. and Pakes, A. (1981). "On Measuring the Variance-Age Profile of Lifetime Earnings", *Review of Economic Studies*, 48, pp. 385–94.

Flavin, M. A. (1981). "The Adjustment of Consumption to Changing Expectations about Future Income", *Journal of Political Economy*, 89, 5, pp. 974–1009.

Hall, R. E. (1978). "Stochastic Implications of the Life Cycle-Permanent Income Hypothesis: Theory and Evidence", *Journal of Political Economy*, 86, 6, December, pp. 971–87.

Hansen, L. P. and Kenneth, J. S. (1983). "Stochastic Consumption, Risk Aversion, and the Temporal Behavior of Asset Returns", *Journal of Political Economy*, 91, 2, April, pp. 249–65.

Hellwig, F. (1977). "A Model of Borrowing and Lending with Bankruptcy", *Econometrica*, 45, 8, November, pp. 1879–1907.

King, M. (1982). "The Economics of Saving", *National Bureau of Economic Research Working Paper*, 1247, October.

Mankiw, G., Rotenberg, J. J. and Summers, L. H. (1982). "International Substitution in Macroeconomics", *National Bureau of Economic Research Working Paper*, 898, June.

Rao, C. R. (1973). *Linear Statistical Inference and Applications*, John Wiley and Sons, New York.

Sargent, T. J. (1978). "Rational Expectations, Econometric Exogeneity, and Consumption", *Journal of Political Economy*, 86, 4, August, pp. 673–700.

10

Can People Compute? An Experimental Test of the Life-Cycle Consumption Model

with Stephen Johnson and William Samuelson

I. Introduction

The assumption of rational choice is a cornerstone of modern economic theory. Rational choice requires that individuals correctly value their present and future resources, that they make consistent decisions, and that they obey the axiom of revealed preference. This chapter presents the results of an experimental study of consumption in which subjects were asked to make consumption decisions under hypothetical economic conditions. The questions in the experiment are designed to test the assumption of rational choice and to elicit information about preferences. The subjects' responses suggest a widespread inability to make coherent and consistent consumption decisions. Errors in consumption decision-making appear to be substantial and, in many cases, systematic. In addition, the experiment's data strongly reject the standard life-cycle model of consumption choice.

The principal specific findings of the laboratory experiment are as follows: (a) Subjects displayed significant inconsistencies in their consumption decisions; each of the subjects, in at least two pairs of economically identical situations, chose consumption values that differed by 20 percent or more. From the perspective of the standard life-cycle model, error in decision-making accounts, on average, for roughly half of the variation in individual consumption choices. (b) A sizeable fraction of subjects valued discounted future earnings less than present assets. (c) Almost all subjects exhibited oversaving behavior, apparently because they underestimated the power of compound interest. (d) The hypotheses that intertemporal consumption preferences are either homothetic or uniform across individuals are strongly rejected. (e) Consumption choice is only weakly correlated with subjects' stated intertemporal preferences.

In recent years an increasing body of research in experimental economics has sought to test many of the basic axioms of economic theory. Important experimental studies of rational decision-making include those of Allais and Hagen (1979), Grether and Plott (1979), Kahneman and Tversky (1979), and Tversky and Kahneman (1974). Laboratory exeriments have been used to study market and non-market institutions including competitive markets (Smith 1967), oligopolistic price setting (Plott 1982), public goods mechanisms (Smith 1982), auctions (Cox, Smith, and Walker 1985), and bargaining and negotiation procedures (Samuelson and Bazerman 1985). To our knowledge, however, this is the first experiment of consumption behavior.

Our laboratory experiment tests directly the life-cycle model of saving (Modigliani and Brumberg 1954; Ando and Modigliani 1963). A large body of theoretical and empirical research is based on the life-cycle model. Its influence on research and macroeconomic policy notwithstanding, tests of the life-cycle model with field data have proven inconclusive for reasons of data quality, inability to identify the consumer unit, incomplete knowledge of the consumer unit's information set, and lack of information about financial and other constraints confronting the consumer. It has proved particularly difficult to test directly the model's most basic assumption of intertemporal optimization by consumers. Recourse to experimental testing is, therefore, attractive because it alleviates a host of data and information problems.

The experiment was implemented by an interactive computer program in which subjects key in consumption choices in response to a series of questions. Forty-nine subjects (MBA students and undergraduates at Boston University) were paid to participate in the life-cycle simulation. Subjects were asked what consumption choices they would make if they were single, faced no uncertainty, had specified levels of future earnings and current assets, knew their ages of retirement and death, and could borrow and save at a specified interest rate.

The experiment presents subjects with two kinds of decision tasks. In parts I, II, and VI of the experiment, subjects are asked to make consumption and savings decisions year by year over their life cycle (from age 35 until death at age 75). In the other parts of the experiment, subjects made single year consumption choices under varying economic conditions (asset levels, earnings, interest rates). With the experiment's data one can examine whether subjects tend to over- or undersave, whether subjects make identical consumption choices in economically equivalent (but different) situations, whether preferences are homothetic, and whether the present value of labor earnings and current assets, which together constitute the present value of resources, have an equal impact on consumption spending.

As experimental economists (see Vernon Smith, 1982) have forcefully argued, in certain respects experimental data permit more effective tests of theoretical models than does field data. The advantages of experimental analysis are those of control and measurement: the experimenter can control perfectly the exogenous economic environment and can measure all relevant economic variables without error. Since field data is subject to measurement errors and lack of controls, it may be difficult or impossible to determine from nonexperimental data whether changes in behavior are due to differences in preferences or economic circumstances as opposed to nonoptimizing behavior.

The countervailing criticism of the experimental approach, of course, is that individual behavior in laboratory experiments may differ from real world decision-making. Vernon Smith (1982) uses the term "parallelism" to denote the extent to which the laboratory setting mimics the real world. In our view, the parallelism issue in our experimental setting is a matter of degree. Certainly our experimental setting is far simpler than the real world setting. However, parallelism need not be diminished (indeed, it may be enhanced) by simplification as long as the main factors affecting behavior in actual practice are captured in the design of the experiment. Though simplified, the description of the life-cycle setting contained in the experiment certainly resembles the kind of consumption and saving choices faced by individuals in their own lives.

Granted that the settings are parallel, it is obvious that both the analytical resources available to the individual and his decision-making incentives may differ between the experiment and the real world. In making real-world consumption and saving choices, individuals have more time and incentive to consider their decisions and to revise them. They also have the option to avail themselves of expert advice and observe the behavior of their friends and relatives. On the other hand, real world intertemporal optimization problems are far more complex than those presented in our experiment. They involve a variety of uncertainties and financial constraints, problems of joint utility maximization in the case of families, and significant problems of information updating. Furthermore, our own casual empiricism suggests that individuals do not freely discuss their saving decisions, that the number who consult accountants and other professionals on these matters is relatively small, and that many individuals make their decisions without significant analysis. Thus, in providing responses to the experiment's questions, subjects may be acting quite similarly to the way they would act if actually faced with the comparable situation in the real world. Hence, experimental analysis may shed considerable light on actual consumption and saving decisions.

Section II provides a summary and review of the testable implications of the life-cycle model of consumption under certainty. Section III describes the design of the experiment and the subject population, and section IV presents the main results. Section V presents consumption choices and demographic characteristics. Section VI summarizes the findings and indicates our plans for additional experimental research on consumption.

II. Testable Implications of the Life Cycle Model Under Certainty

The life-cycle model under certainty posits that an individual chooses his consumption spending over his lifetime to maximize a concave utility function:

$$U = U(C_1, \ldots, C_d) \quad \text{subject to} \tag{1}$$

$$\sum_{j=1}^{d} C_j \underset{s=2}{\overset{j}{\pi}} R_s = A_1/R_1 + H_1, \tag{2}$$

where C_j is consumption at age j; d is the age of death; $R_s = 1/(1 + r_s)$, where r_s is the interest rate at time s; A_1 is initial assets; and H_1 is the present value of labor earnings (human wealth) as of age 1.

The fundamental presumption of this intertemporal optimization problem is that the individual's lifetime consumption and savings decisions are made without error. Thus, in an experimental setting that imposes constraint (2), a subject should make consumption decisions in precise accordance with life-cycle predictions. Two implications, stated as hypotheses, follow immediately from the general model.

HYPOTHESIS I: The individual should exhaust his resources at the time of his death (there are no leftover assets).

HYPOTHESIS II: An individual's consumption choice in a given year depends directly on the present value of resources and is independent of the mix of assets and the present value of lifetime labor earnings.

In addition, if consumption at each age is a normal good, we have

HYPOTHESIS III: An increase in the present value of resources leads to increases in consumption at each age.

If the utility function is homothetic and time separable, utility can be written as

$$U = v(C_1) + \beta v(C_2) + \cdots + \beta^{d-1} v(C_d), \tag{3}$$

where $\beta = 1/(1+\delta)$, and δ is the individual's time preference rate. In this case, the individual's optimal consumption expenditure at age j can be expressed as:

$$C_j = PVR_j / \left[\sum_{s=j}^{d} \underset{i=j+1}{\overset{s}{\pi}} R_i h(R_i/\beta) \right], \tag{4}$$

where PVR_j is the present value of resources at age j, and where the function $h^{-1}(\ )$ is the marginal rate of substitution between consumption at different dates, that is,

$$C_{s+1}/C_s = h(R_{s+1}/\beta) \tag{5}$$

From (4) and (5) one sees that the assumption of separable utility implies the following strengthening of hypothesis III:

HYPOTHESIS IIIB: With the time path of the interest rate held constant, consumption in a given year is proportional to the present value of resources as of that date. Equivalently, the average and marginal propensities to consume are equal and independent of the level of PVR_j.

HYPOTHESIS IIIC: If the interest rate is constant, an individual's average and marginal propensities to consume are increasing functions of age.

Hypothesis IIIC holds because the right-hand-side divisor in (4) is smaller the larger is the initial age j at which the summation begins.

Finally, in the case that the utility function is of the isoelastic form

$$v(C_s) = C_s^{1-\lambda}/(1-\lambda), \tag{6}$$

expression (5) can be rewritten in logs as

$$\log(C_{s+1}/C_s) = -1/\lambda \log \beta + 1/\lambda \log R_{s+1}. \tag{5$'$}$$

In this instance, one can regress the log of the ratio of consumption in adjacent periods on a constant plus the log of R_{s+1} and thereby estimate β and λ.

III. Description of the Experiment

The life-cycle experiments were conducted at Boston University in three sessions using paid student volunteers as subjects. The majority of subjects were MBA students; the others were undergraduate business majors and graduate economic students. There was no time limit for completing the computerized questionnaire. Most subjects took about an hour and a half to finish; some finished within an hour, and some took as long as two hours. Collaboration of any kind and the use of calculators were prohibited. Sixty students completed the questionnaire. However, eleven questionnaires were excluded from the analysis either because they contained key punch errors or because the subject failed to complete one or more sections. Therefore, the results to be discussed are based, in most cases, upon 49 sets of responses.

It was strongly and repeatedly emphasized at the beginning of the experiment that subjects do their best to respond to all questions on the basis of what would make them most happy given the situation described. Furthermore, subjects were told that if they were conscientious in expressing their true preferences, they would receive a bonus at the end of the experiment. In parts I and II of the questionnaire, subjects were reminded that they should attempt to spend all of their earnings over their lifetimes. The appendix reproduces the experimental questionnaire and its instructions.

The questionnaire's basic economic setting can be summarized as follows. The individual in the experiment has just turned 35 and will live to his 75th birthday on which day he dies (with certainty). In his job he earns an annual salary of $25,000 until he retires on his 65th birthday—that is, he works for thirty years and is retired for ten. The individual can save or borrow as much money as he wishes at 4 percent interest. Subjects were instructed that in the questionnaire setting there is no inflation, deflation, or taxes, no dependents to support, no current or potential health problems, and no uncertainty about the future. All durable goods are rented by the year. Finally, it was assumed that annual consumption expenditures occur, and the labor earnings are received on January 1st of each year and that the individual's birthday is also January 1st.

The computer questionnaire consists of eight parts soliciting annual consumption spending choices for various combinations of age, assets, interest rates, future earnings, and retirement ages. In total, each subject makes 145 such choices. Part I asks the subject to specify his desired level of consumption spending for each year from age 35 to 75. In this section, the subject receives no feedback concerning the level of assets accumulating (at 4 percent interest) in his savings account. Part II solicits the same information, but updates the subject's asset position before each annual consumption decision is made.

In parts III through V, subjects are asked to make consumption choices for four ages—35, 46, 55, and 69—under varying economic conditions. In part III subjects report consumption choices at these ages at different levels of assets (with future earnings unchanged). Part IV varies the individual's retirement age (with the level of assets and annual earnings fixed). Part V varies the stream of earnings (with assets and the age of retirement fixed). In parts VI and VII subjects report consumption decisions under varying interest rates. Finally, part VIII asks subjects to rank in order of preference five lifetime consumption profiles.

In all parts, except part I, subjects were prompted to make their consumption decisions sequentially, that is, although they were allowed to modify a current response, they were not allowed to return to modify previously given answers. In addition, subjects were prohibited (and prevented by the computer program) from returning and changing any previously completed part of the experiment.

Several economic situations were repeated more than once to permit tests of consistency in the subjects' choices. For example, in part III subjects were asked to choose consumption spending at ages 35, 46, 55, and 69 given the same amount of assets and the same lifetime earnings they had at those ages in part II. In this, as in other cases of exactly identical circumstances, subjects were not alerted to the fact that the circumstances were identical. Other pairs of situations, while not precisely the same, presented the subjects with the same present value of resources (assets plus the present value of future earnings) at the same age, but differed in the relative contribution of assets and earnings to total resources. In addition, several pairs had the same level of assets and present value of labor earnings, but differed with respect to the lifetime profile of earnings.

Subjects were asked to make nine consumption decisions at age 35, three pairs of which had the same present value of resources. For age 46, there were thirteen decisions, including four pairs with the same present value of resources. For age 55, there were nine decisions, including four pairs with the same resources; and for age 69, there were seven decisions, including one pair with the same resources.

Listed below is a brief summary of the eight parts of the consumption experiment.

Part I—Annual Consumption Choices without Feedback

In this section the subject is asked to choose the level of annual consumption spending for each year from age 35 to age 74, inclusive (40 choices in all). The subject is allowed to modify his consumption choices until he is satisfied with them, but throughout, he receives no information about his accumulated balance in his savings account.

Part II—Annual Consumption Choices with Savings Feedback

Again, the subject reports his annual consumption expenditure for each year from age 35 to age 74, inclusive. In contrast to part I, however, the subject is informed of the accumulated balance in his savings account at the time he must make his next year's consumption choice. Consumption choices are made in chronological order—that is, the subject is not permitted to change an earlier consumption choice.

Part III—Consumption with Specified Assets at Selected Ages

Here the subject is presented with sixteen age/asset pairs and is asked to choose the level of consumption spending at that age given the specified balance in his savings account. The following are the age/asset pairs.

	Age			
	35	46	55	69
	Assets			
A.	43500	43500	43500	43500
B.	214000	214000	214000	214000
C.	130000	130000	130000	130000
D.	*	*	*	*

*Assets in D were set equal to accumulated assets at the same age in part II.

Part IV—Consumption with Different Retirement Ages

This section varies the retirement age and assets. The subject is asked to choose his consumption spending at age 46 assuming the following retirement ages and asset levels.

	Assets	Retirement Age
A.	500000	72
B.	100000	56
C.	100000	61
D.	100000	68

Part V—Consumption with Different Lifetime Earnings

In this part subjects are presented with ten different earnings profile/asset/age combinations and asked to choose consumption expenditure in each case.

		Age			
		35	46	55	69
	Earnings Profile*	Assets			
A.	23200/47800/32500	65000	65000	65000	
B.	33000/33000/33000	65000	465000	65000	
C.	20700/31000/42500	65000	65000	65000	65000

*The three numbers are the annual earnings in the three decades of work: ages 35–44, 45–54, and 55–64, respectively.

Part VI—Consumption at Different Interest Rates

Here the subject chooses consumption at age 46 given assets of $90,000 at each of five interest rates (0 percent, 2 percent, 4 percent, 6 percent, and 8 percent).

Part VII—Consumption with Changing Interest Rate

The subject is asked to choose his consumption spending in each year between age 45 and age 75, with the annual interest rate varying according to the chart below. The subject initially has $50,000 in his savings account at age 45, and his asset balance is updated each year.

Age	Interest Rate	Age	Interest Rate
45–52	2%	61–67	6%
53–60	4%	68–74	3%

Part VIII—Ranking Different Lifetime Consumption Profiles

The participant is asked to rank, in order of preference, five different lifetime consumption profiles each of which is financially feasible, that is, exactly exhausts his resources at age 75. The profiles assume that the individual begins his working life at age 35 with no initial assets and earns $25,000 of labor income each year until retirement at age 65.

1. $21,841 per year, every year.
2. $16,008 at age 35, growing by 2 percent per year thereafter.
3. $11,240 at age 35, growing by 4 percent per year thereafter.
4. $28,592 at age 35, falling by 2 percent per year thereafter.
5. $23,420 from age 35 until age 65, then $10,921 from 65 to 75.

IV. Experimental Results

This section presents first some general features of the data, many of which accord with predictions of the life-cycle model. One central feature of the data is the extent of heterogeneity in consumption choices. Next we discuss the extent of inconsistent choice and explore

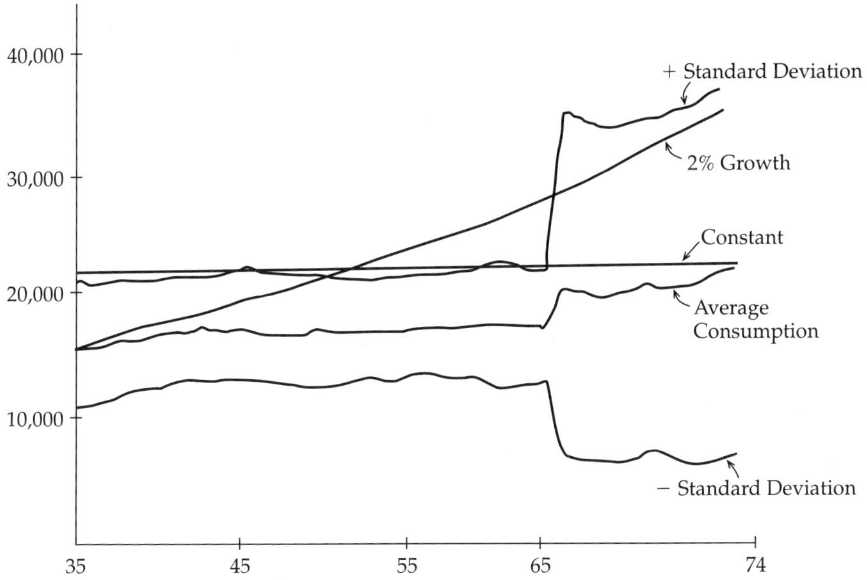

Figure 10.1
The average age—consumption profile (part II)

the degree to which consumption errors are systematic. Subsection *c* considers the evidence on normality and homotheticity and presents more formal tests of the standard life-cycle model. Subsection *d* considers the extent of oversaving. Subsection *e* examines the correlation between actual consumption choices in part II and part Viii's preferred options among a group of alternative feasible consumption paths. The final subsection indicates what rates of time preference and intertemporal elasticities of substitution might be inferred from these data.

Summary of Consumption Behavior

Figure 10.1 displays the average level of consumption chosen by the 49 subjects at each age in part II (with savings feedback). The dotted lines represent a band of one standard deviation in consumption responses at each age. The large size of these standard deviations indicates considerable diversity of consumption choices. Table 10.1 reports the data depicted in figure 10.1. Listed is the average consumption profile as well as the coefficient of variation, the minimum

Table 10.1
Summary of lifetime consumption behavior

Age	Average	Coefficient of variation	25th percentile	75th percentile	Minimum	Maximum
35	17663	.248	15000	20000	9600	25000
36	17891	.223	15000	20000	10000	24000
37	18258	.198	15000	20000	10000	23000
38	18705	.187	16000	21000	10000	24500
39	18568	.192	15000	20000	10000	25000
40	19523	.214	17000	21000	10000	35600
41	19747	.155	18000	21000	14000	30000
42	19522	.171	18000	21000	12000	30000
43	19577	.196	17500	21963	8000	30000
44	19605	.169	18000	21963	10000	29000
45	19965	.141	19000	22000	15000	25000
46	20514	.233	18000	22000	15000	45000
47	19701	.160	18000	22000	10000	25000
48	20107	.171	18000	22000	10000	30000
49	20352	.238	18000	22000	15000	40000
50	21393	.217	18800	23000	15000	40000
51	21069	.265	18000	22000	11000	45000
52	20754	.217	19000	22000	15000	40000
53	20522	.186	19000	22000	14000	30000
54	20595	.188	19000	22000	15000	33000
55	20638	.172	19000	22000	15000	30000
56	21456	.163	19000	24000	15000	30000
57	21438	.193	19000	24000	12000	34000
58	21687	.261	19000	24000	13500	50000
59	21732	.260	20000	23000	13000	50000
60	22213	.287	19000	24000	14500	50000
61	22114	.267	20000	24000	15000	50000
62	22438	.299	19000	25000	10000	50000
63	22669	.350	19000	25000	10000	60000
64	24004	.491	19000	25000	10000	90000
65	27679	.343	20000	35000	9000	50000
66	27852	.295	22000	33000	10000	50000
67	30335	.366	22000	35000	17495	80000
68	31203	.341	23000	40000	8500	58000
69	34471	.461	24000	40000	10000	100000
70	36742	.419	25000	45000	8000	70000
71	37276	.477	25000	45000	8000	100000
72	37605	.503	25000	42000	4000	100000
73	35666	.449	23000	45000	4000	75000
74	55556	1.063	25631	64100	3000	311991

and maximum responses, and the levels of consumption at the 25th and 75th percentiles of the consumption distribution.

The average consumption expenditure rises throughout the course of the life cycle. Average consumption spending first exceeds $25,000, the amount of annual earnings, in the first year of retirement. The growth of average consumption is slow prior to retirement and very substantial after retirement; the ratio of average consumption at age 44 to that at age 35 is 1.11. In contrast, the age 74 to age 65 ratio is 2.01. This end-of-life rapid growth of consumption appears to be the result of oversaving. Although their asset balance is updated year by year, subjects do not appear to appreciate fully the amount of assets they are accumulating. Thus, in the last years of their life, they play "catch up."

There are sizable differences in saving behavior across subjects. The coefficient of variation averages nearly 20 percent from age 35 to 57 and increases steadily and substantially thereafter. Another measure of dispersion is the ratio of the 75th percentile consumption choice to the 25th percentile consumption choice. This ratio is 1.33 at age 35, 1.16 at age 45, 1.16 at age 55, 1.75 at age 65, and 2.50 at age 74. A third measure is the ratio of the maximum to the minimum consumption choice. This ration is 2.60 at age 35, 1.67 at age 45, 2.00 at age 55, 5.56 at age 65, and 104.00 at age 74. This increase with age in the dispersion of the consumption distribution suggests that not all subjects oversaved; some may have undersaved and those that oversaved may have oversaved in different degrees.

Table 10.2 presents summary data on subject consumption choices for the representative ages 35, 46, 55, and 69 as reported in parts III–V of the experiment. Recall that in these parts of the experiment each subject is asked for consumption choices at particular ages given an exogenously specified level of assets, a time path of future earnings, and a retirement age. The interest rate is 4 percent throughout these parts of the experiment. The table lists average average propensity to consume (APCs) and (MPCs) as well as key percentiles of the APC and MPC distributions at the four ages. Table 10.2 also indicates APCs for benchmark cases corresponding to lifetime consumption paths with −2 percent, 0 percent, 2 percent, and 4 percent constant yearly growth.

As predicted by the life-cycle model, the average APCs increase with age (hypothesis iiic). The dispersion of APCs, measured by the ratio of the 75th to the 25th percentile, is largest at age 69, where it is

Table 10.2
APCs and MPCs by age

	Age							
	35		46		55		69	
	APC	MPC	APC	MPC	APC	MPC	APC	MPC
Mean	.042	.049	.052	.048	.069	.072	.202	.187
Median	.041	.038	.049	.044	.064	.052	.185	.155
25th percentile	.036	.025	.045	.021	.058	.019	.166	.108
75th percentile	.045	.060	.054	.064	.071	.115	.227	.209
Benchmark profiles								
2% decline	.064	.064	.070	.070	.083	.083	.192	.192
Constant	.049	.049	.057	.057	.071	.071	.183	.183
2% increase	.036	.036	.045	.045	.060	.060	.175	.175
4% increase	.025	.025	.034	.034	.050	.050	.167	.167

1.37. This is somewhat surprising; one might expect less difficulty and more similarity in consumption choice after retirement because the present value of future labor earnings need not be computed.

The average MPCs are similar in magnitude to the average APCs, however, the dispersion of MPCs is much greater. The median MPCs are smaller than the median APCs at each age; at ages 55 and 69 the differences are sizeable.

Prior to age 69 the median APC falls between the constant and 2 percent increase benchmark APCs. At age 69, however, the median APC is slightly larger than that of the constant growth rate path.

The variation across subjects in APCs appears to be systematic. A total of 17 of the 49 subjects recorded APCs above the table 10.2 averages for all four ages; 14 other subjects exceeded the average in three of four cases. At the other extreme, 15 subjects recorded consumption below the average in three or more cases. In short, the population of subjects appears to be divided into two distinct groups of "big" and "small" savers.

Inconsistencies and Errors in Consumption Choice

Hypothesis II states that individuals should make the same consumption choice when facing the same present value of resources and the same interest rate. We tested this hypothesis by constructing in parts II–V 17 pairs of situations in which subjects faced identical economic resources (at a 4 percent interest rate). Table 10.3 lists the percentage difference between each subject's chosen consumption expenditure for each economically equivalent (EE) situation. Percentage differences are computed in this table with the second minus the first case in the numerator and the first case in the denominator. To illustrate, the first column compares the subject's consumption choice in part II at age 35 to his later choice made at the same age and given the same economic circumstances in part III question *d*. The percentage errors of all subjects are listed in ascending order for each EE pair.

For all but three of the 17 EE cases in table 10.3, the average absolute error exceeds 20 percent. Clearly, this constitutes strong evidence of widespread consumption inconsistency and strongly contradicts hypothesis ii. Moreover, consumption errors are widespread across the subjects. As documented in table 10.4, each of the 49 subjects made at least two large consumption mistakes—an error in excess of 20 percent in absolute value. Thirty-seven of the 49 subjects made five or more large consumption errors in the 17 cases. Thirty-nine subjects made 1 or more very large errors—errors in excess of 40 percent in absolute value and, of these subjects, 11 made five or more very large errors.

A closer examination of table 10.3 and the summary information in table 10.3a indicates that many of the consumption errors are systematic. Consider, for example, the age 35 comparison of part III.C with part V.C. In III.C the asset level is $130,000, while it is $65,000 in V.C. Since total resources are equal in the two cases, the ratio of the present value of earnings to total resources is greater in V.C. In addition, the timing of labor earnings differs. In III.C the earnings path is a constant $25,000 until retirement. In V.C it is $20,700 from age 35 to age 44, $31,000 from age 45 to age 54, and $42,500 from age 55 to age 64. Taking III.C as the base, the median percentage change in consumption between III.C and V.C is negative 25 percent. Of the 30 subjects who answered these two questions (V.C was added after some initial experiments were conducted), only 3 had nonnegative errors (i.e., they increased their consumption from III.C to V.C). Some of the errors are quite sizable: 3 subjects reduced their consumption choice by more than 50 percent although they were in exactly the same economic choice situation.

The age-35 comparison of III.B with V.A also involves an increase in the earnings-resource ratio. Again, the median percentage error is

Table 10.3
Consumption errors

		Age 35		
II–IIId	IIIc–Vc	Va–Vb	Vb–IIIb	IIIb–Va
–.500	–.625	–.250	–.250	–.800
–.500	–.622	–.250	–.242	–.770
–.200	–.513	–.250	–.219	–.763
–.150	–.400	–.250	–.219	–.714
–.080	–.400	–.077	–.207	–.700
–.042	–.375	–.000	–.200	–.667
–.006	–.370	.000	–.200	–.600
.000	–.333	.000	–.179	–.600
.000	–.320	.000	–.175	–.514
.000	–.280	.000	–.120	–.500
.000	–.250	.000	–.120	–.460
.000	–.240	.018	–.107	–.438
.000	–.240	.100	–.107	–.389
.000	–.227	.111	–.107	–.370
.000	–.217	.136	–.100	–.333
.000	–.214	.136	–.083	–.304
.000	–.200	.143	–.074	–.300
.000	–.200	.154	–.074	–.280
.000	–.200	.167	–.074	–.250
.000	–.189	.183	–.069	–.249
.000	–.167	.190	–.048	–.242
.000	–.150	.207	–.028	–.229
.000	–.138	.227	–.011	–.212
.000	–.133	.250	.000	–.200
.000	–.119	.250	.000	–.200
.000	–.100	.250	.000	–.200
.000	–.074	.259	.000	–.170
.000	.000	.273	.000	–.167
.000	.167	.280	.042	–.130
.000	.200	.316	.056	–.120
.000		.333	.100	–.120
.000		.333	.125	–.098
.000		.350	.167	–.080
.000		.350	.320	–.072
.000		.353	.333	–.072
.020		.391	.333	–.053
.029		.400	.471	–.050
.050		.422	.500	–.045

Table 10.3 (continued)

Age 35				
II–IIId	IIIc–Vc	Va–Vb	Vb–IIIb	IIIb–Va
.059		.462	.522	–.040
.067		.500	.600	–.007
.067		.500	.630	.000
.091		.500	.818	.000
.091		.579	.852	.000
.095		.600	1.000	.000
.105		.667	1.000	.040
.111		.739	1.500	.136
.133		.765	1.667	.143
.143		.813	2.333	.160
.200		.840	3.667	.667

Age 46					
II–IIId	IIIa–IVc	IIIc–IVd	IVa–Vb	IVa–IVb	IIIb–Vc
–.532	–.700	–.756	–.600	–.547	–.793
–.489	–.567	–.655	–.600	–.450	–.600
–.310	–.250	–.653	–.400	–.333	–.556
–.250	–.205	–.520	–.333	–.156	–.535
–.250	–.183	–.425	–.300	–.130	–.500
–.217	–.167	–.423	–.178	–.105	–.500
–.079	–.167	–.400	–.175	–.083	–.458
–.067	–.150	–.348	–.057	–.071	–.442
–.045	–.150	–.333	.000	.000	–.440
–.043	–.143	–.250	.000	.000	–.355
–.006	–.130	–.250	.000	.037	–.343
.000	–.100	–.222	.000	.080	–.333
.000	–.100	–.200	.000	.120	–.300
.000	–.091	–.200	.000	.143	–.243
.000	–.087	–.200	.000	.200	–.200
.000	–.053	–.191	.000	.250	–.200
.000	–.050	–.182	.086	.273	–.148
.000	–.050	–.167	.100	.450	–.133
.000	–.043	–.167	.111	.599	–.130
.000	–.024	–.143	.136		–.120
.000	.000	–.130	.167		–.120
.000	.000	–.100	.250		–.100
.000	.000	–.100	.277		–.100
.000	.000	–.091	.333		–.091
.000	.000	–.087	.500		–.065

Table 10.3 (continued)

Age 46					
II–IIId	IIIa–IVc	IIIc–IVd	IVa–Vb	IVa–IVb	IIIb–Vc
.022	.000	–.087	.500		–.033
.050	.000	–.083	.600		.000
.050	.000	–.080	.600		.000
.050	.000	–.056	.714		.000
.056	.016	–.042	.750		.000
.071	.029	–.021			.000
.100	.059	.000			.000
.100	.087	.000			.000
.111	.097	.000			.039
.125	.100	.000			.040
.130	.111	.006			.043
.150	.132	.042			.064
.156	.133	.043			.080
.167	.136	.050			.081
.176	.143	.053			.120
.211	.211	.057			.130
.222	.286	.058			.150
.222	.294	.095			.160
.250	.333	.100			.200
.353	.389	.200			.250
.375	.400	.200			.250
1.500	.469	.333			.350
1.900	.933	.333			.364
2.636	1.000	.750			.417

Age 55					Age 69
II–IIId	Va–IIIc	IIIc–Vb	Vb–Va	Vc–IIIb	I–IIId
–.480	–.400	–.750	–.375	–.612	–.450
–.130	–.385	–.583	–.333	–.423	–.350
–.120	–.354	–.483	–.231	–.400	–.333
–.120	–.321	–.333	–.200	–.383	–.193
–.111	–.320	–.267	–.200	–.375	–.167
–.091	–.308	–.222	–.200	–.375	–.143
–.091	–.280	–.200	–.185	–.371	–.143
–.087	–.276	–.167	–.167	–.353	–.126
–.041	–.259	–.167	–.130	–.333	–.113
–.019	–.250	–.167	–.120	–.286	–.100
–.006	–.250	–.167	–.107	–.286	–.091
.000	–.240	–.163	–.100	–.267	–.059

Table 10.3 (continued)

Age 55					Age 69
II–IIId	Va–IIIc	IIIc–Vb	Vb–Va	Vc–IIIb	I–IIId
.000	−.233	−.150	−.091	−.265	−.050
.000	−.200	−.128	−.091	−.263	−.050
.000	−.200	−.107	−.071	−.233	−.040
.000	−.200	−.091	−.063	−.233	−.008
.000	−.167	.000	−.050	−.233	.000
.000	−.158	.000	−.012	−.200	.000
.000	−.143	.000	.000	−.194	.000
.000	−.063	.000	.000	−.167	.000
.000	−.045	.000	.000	−.148	.000
.024	−.040	.000	.000	−.132	.000
.042	−.022	.042	.000	−.118	.029
.043	.000	.043	.000	−.100	.040
.045	.000	.050	.000	−.042	.042
.045	.000	.050	.000	−.040	.080
.050	.000	.059	.000	.000	.117
.053	.000	.105	.000	.000	.167
.068	.000	.111	.000	.000	.178
.105	.000	.136	.024	.000	.200
.136	.013	.136	.071	.000	.200
.167	.022	.150	.075	.000	.220
.179	.034	.167	.080	.029	.250
.222	.037	.167	.080	.030	.250
.263	.100	.182	.100	.087	.300
.316	.100	.190	.121	.103	.308
.333	.100	.211	.130	.143	.333
.364	.111	.227	.143	.231	.364
.364	.119	.250	.176	.250	.366
.412	.200	.250	.190	.278	.389
.438	.200	.278	.190	.280	.500
.500	.200	.333	.217	.346	.500
.667	.200	.375	.250	.361	.550
.733	.433	.381	.286	.372	.786
.750	.500	.381	.318	.724	.818
.818	.600	.400	.333	.875	1.000
1.857	.933	.667	.389	1.000	1.074
2.161	1.233	.750	.500	1.581	1.083
3.091	1.667	.957	.500	4.435	1.955

Table 10.3a
Summary information for table 10.3

	Average	Median	Absolute average	Type	d(Erns / Res)
Age 35					
II–IIId	−.004	.000	.056	1	.000
IIIc–Vc	−.231	−.250	.255	2	.112
Va–Vb	.255	.250	.298	3	.000
Vb–IIIb	.286	.000	.409	2	−.223
IIIb–Va	−.232	−.200	.279	2	.223
Age 46					
II–IIId	.141	.000	.234	1	.000
IIIa–IVc	.040	.000	.179	2	−.144
IIIc–IVd	−.107	−.087	.202	2	.066
IVa–Vb	.083	.080	.259	3	.038
IVa–IVb	.015	.037	.212	2	.068
IIIb–Vc	−.104	−.065	.216	2	.268
Age 55					
II–IIId	.264	.045	.317	1	.185
Va–IIIc	.034	.000	.243	2	−.009
IIIc–Vb	.059	.050	.228	2	.056
Vb–Va	.030	.000	.141	3	.026
Vc–IIIb	.088	−.042	.366	2	−.015
Age 69					
II–IIId	.198	.042	.296	1	.165

Type 1 = Identical circumstances.
Type 2 = Same resources, different earns / res.
Type 3 = Same resources, same earns / res, different earns pattern.

Table 10.4
The distribution of subjects by number of consistency mistakes and size of mistake

Percentage mistake	Number of subjects with specified number of mistakes										
	0	1	2	3	4	5	6	7	8	9	10+
20%+	0	0	3	3	6	6	11	5	6	3	6
40%+	10	13	5	5	5	3	2	3	0	1	2

negative; it is negative 20 percent. In this case, 10 of the 49 subjects reduced their consumption by 50 percent or more in switching from the III.B circumstances to the V.A circumstances. The age-35 V.B and III.B comparison is quite similar; here the earnings-to-resource ratio falls, and while the median error is zero, the mean is .29, with 12 of 49 errors in excess of positive 50 percent. Overall, in 8 of 10 type-two cases in which the earnings-to-resource ratio changes, the average error has the opposite sign of the change in the earnings-to-resource ratio.

In the age-35 comparison of V.A and V.B the earnings-to-resources ratio is unchanged. Compared with V.B, earnings in V.A occur earlier in the life cycle. Again, there seems to be an undervaluation of future earnings. In this case the median consumption error in switching to V.B is positive 25 percent, and 20 of 49 subjects increase their consumption by 30 percent or more.

Normality, Homotheticity, and Regression Tests of the Standard Life-Cycle Model

The standard life-cycle model assumes that preferences are homothetic and time separable, implying that consumption at a given age is proportional to the present value of resources (hypothesis iiib). Thus, the elasticity of consumption at each age, with respect to the present value of resources, should equal unity. To test the standard model we calculated income elasticities for each subject between each pair of consumption observations at specific ages. In this analysis we treated pairs of observations with identical resources as a single observation with the level of consumption equal to the average of the two choices.

For each subject there are ten income elasticities at age 35, 28 at age 46, 10 at age 55, and 15 at age 69. Table 10.5 indicates the distribution of elasticities for each age across all subjects, organized by the size of the elasticities. The fraction of elasticities that are negative are .30 at age 35, .25 at age 46, .43 at age 55, and .25 at age 69. These fractions are sizeable and raise serious doubt about the validity of the normality assumption. It is particularly surprising that normality is violated so frequently at age 69; at this age the subjects are retired and need consider only their assets. A number of subjects repeatedly violated normality. For example in their age-55 responses, 17 of the 49 subjects have negative income elasticities in a quarter or more of

Table 10.5
The distribution of income elasticities of the entire sample by the size of income elasticity

	Fraction of elasticities of size							
Age	<−1	−1 to −.5	−.5 to −0	0 to .5	.5 to .75	.75 to 1.25	1.25 to 1.5	1.5+
35	.13	.05	.12	.15	.04	.13	.04	.33
46	.11	.05	.09	.11	.08	.13	.06	.36
55	.22	.07	.14	.13	.06	.09	.04	.27
69	.10	.05	.10	.19	.12	.19	.05	.20

the possible cases; 7 of these 17 have negative income elasticities in half or more of the possible cases.

The negative income elasticities obviously contradict the homotheticity assumption. Moreover, the positive elasticities are also often far from unity. Indeed, at age 35 only 13 percent of the calculated elasticities fall between .75 and 1.25, and at age 46 it is also only 13 percent; it is only 9 percent at age 55; and it is only 19 percent at age 69.

Another test of the standard life-cycle model is provided by estimating a regression equation at each age of the form:

$$C = \alpha + \gamma R + u, \tag{7}$$

where R denotes the present value of lifetime resources, and u is an error term. Finding a significant regression intercept leads to a rejection of the homotheticity assumption. Separate regressions were estimated for each subject at each of the ages 35, 46, 55, and 69. The number of observations (i.e., resource and consumption pairs) for the regressions at these ages are 9, 13, 9, and 6, respectively.

The results of these regressions show that a significant minority of subjects displayed nonhomothetic consumption behavior. At age 35, the hypothesis of a zero intercept was rejected at the 5 percent significance level in 10 cases (of 49), at age 46 in 24 cases, at 55 in 4 cases, and at age 69 in 8 cases. The age-46 regressions contained the largest number of observations (16 compared to the next largest number 10). Of the 196 estimated constants (49×4), 36 intercepts were significantly positive while only 10 were significantly negative. Thus, for the bulk of nonproportional subjects, the predicted APC falls with income.

Table 10.6
Tests of the importance of the resource mix to consumption

	Number of regressions (fraction of regressions)				
Age	Total	$\sigma 1$, $\sigma 2$ Pos	$\sigma 1 > \sigma 2$	$\sigma 1$, $\sigma 2$ Signif Diff	$\sigma 1$ Signif $> \sigma 2$
35	49	35	36	14	14
46	49	44	24	11	6
55	49	45	17	16	5
Total	147	124	77	41	25

An additional test of homotheticity was conducted by including a quadratic term in the value of resources as an independent variable in the regressions. Of a total of 196 regressions, the coefficient on squared resources was significant (at the 5 percent level) in 24 cases. Thus, there appears to be evidence of some nonlinear consumption behavior.

Retaining the linear specification, a test that consumption is independent of the mix of resources (hypothesis ii) can be conducted by estimating regressions of the form

$$C = \alpha + \sigma_1 A + \sigma_2 E + u, \quad (8)$$

where A denotes the subject's accumulated savings to date, and E denotes the present value of his future earnings. Of course, the irrelevance of the mix of resources implies that σ_1 should equal σ_2. We estimated (8) separately for ages 35, 46, and 55 (at age 69 future earnings were zero). Table 10.6 presents a summary of the distribution of assets and earnings coefficients.

In 85 percent of the cases (124 of 147 regressions), the earnings and assets coefficients are both positive as predicted by the life-cycle model. The coefficient on assets exceeded that on earnings in slightly more than half of the 147 regressions. In total, 41 of 147 (or 28 percent) of the regressions displayed coefficients that are statistically different from one another at the 5 percent level. In these 41 cases, the coefficient on assets exceed that on earnings by 25 times. Finally, there is only a single, insignificant asset coefficient (which is negative), but 16 negative earnings coefficients, 8 of which are significant. From these results it appears that a significant minority of subjects undervalue earnings relative to assets, while a somewhat smaller minority overvalue earnings. Table 10.6 summarizes these findings and presents the age-specific results.

Tables 10.7a–10.7d consider whether nonhomotheticity and the resource mix are significant in pooled regression analysis. The table displays the coefficients of four regression models estimated for the four key ages with the data pooled across all subjects. Model A explains consumption only in terms of total resources. Model B differs from A by the addition of an intercept. Model C modifies B by entering assets and earnings separately. Model D adds the squares of assets and earnings and the product of assets and earnings.

The model B intercepts in each of the four tables, 10.7a through 10.7d, are highly significant. Thus, these pooled regressions reject the homotheticity hypothesis. The model B coefficients on resources also contradict the life-cycle model's prediction that the marginal propensity to consume increases with age. Although all are insignificant, the coefficients at ages 35, 46, 55, and 69 display no strong positive correlation with age.

Given that an intercept belongs in the relation between consumption and resources, is it also the case that earnings and assets enter with the same coefficient? That is, do subjects value equally a dollar in assets and a dollar in human wealth? According to F-tests of model B vs. C, reported in table 10.8, the assumption of equal valuation of assets and earnings is strongly rejected for the pooled age-35 data, but accepted for the pooled age-46 and pooled age-55 data. In the age-35 model C regression, the assets coefficient is over seven times greater than the earnings coefficient. These results may reflect an inability of subjects to discount properly far distant earnings streams; that is, at ages 46 and 55 the future earnings streams extend for a shorter interval than at age 35.

The results on model G reinforce a view of undervaluation of future earnings. The APC is negatively related to the earnings-to-resources ratio at each of the three ages 35, 46, and 55. The earnings-to-resources coefficient is highly significant at ages 35 and 46. Hence, the larger the share of the present value of earnings in total resources, the smaller the average propensity to consume.

One may also question whether higher-order powers of assets and earnings help explain consumption. As indicated in table 10.8 (in the C vs. D F-test) these additional variables are jointly significant for the age-35 and the age-46 regressions. Table 10.8 also reports the results of a Chow test, assuming model B, indicating whether it is appro-

Table 10.7a
Age 35 pooled regression coefficients (standard errors)

Model	Res	Const	Earn	Assets	Earn*Assets	Squared		Earn/Res	$\bar{R}^2$
						Earn	Assets		
A	.042								.151
	(.001)								
B	.051	−4989							.156
	(.006)	(3461)							
C		11791	.012	.085					.249
		(4061)	(.008)	(.007)					
D		234167	−.851	−.431	.547	.821E−6	.683E−6		.263
		(88865)	(.340)	(1.101)	(1.173)	(.318E−6)	(.145E−5)		
(Dep Var is APC)									
G	.085							−.049	.088
	(.007)								(.008)

Table 10.7b
Age 46 pooled regression coefficients (standard errors)

						Squared			
Model	Res	Const	Earn	Assets	Earn*Assets	Earn	Assets	Earn/Res	$\bar{R}^2$
A	.049								.185
	(.001)								
B	.038	6625							.207
	(.004)	(2033)							
C		7234	.036	.039					.207
		(2681)	(.007)	(.005)					
D		2075	.026	.128	−.024	.242E−7	−.146E−7		.224
		(10363)	(.058)	(.175)	(.252)	(.677E−7)	(.136E−6)		
(Dep Var is APC)									
G	.052							−.100	.000
	(.006)							(.008)	

Table 10.7c
Age 55 pooled regression coefficients (standard errors)

						Squared			
Model	Res	Const	Earn	Assets	Earn*Assets	Earn	Assets	Earn/Res	$\bar{R}^2$
A	.007								.066
	(.002)								
B	.056	−4367							.069
	(.010)	(3833)							
C		1961	.068	.053					.072
		(4362)	(.014)	(.011)					
D		−15173	−.165	−.440	.398	−.136E−6	−.828E−6		.085
		(29221)	(.233)	(.646)	(.923)	(.366E−6)	(.103E−5)		
(Dep Var is APC)									
G	.061							−.012	.003
	(.008)							(.011)	

Table 10.7d
Age 69 pooled regression coefficients (standard errors)

Model	Res	Const	$\bar{R}^2$
A	.176		.40
	(.005)		
B	.034	8404	.15
	(.005)	(2575)	

Table 10.8
Significance values of F tests for pooled regressions

	Age			
Test	35	46	55	
B vs. C	.404E−7	.728	.249	
C vs. D	.024	.014	.075	
B Pooled vs. Unpooled	.955E−7	.111E−15	.001E−18	.115E−15

priate to pool the data. Pooling the data is very strongly rejected for each of the four ages; that is, there is very significant heterogeneity in individual model B regression coefficients.

A final way to evaluate the performance of the standard life-cycle model is in terms of *R*-bar square. If the model is correct, the *R*-bar squares in the regressions of consumption against resources (model A) should be unity. This is far from the case. Table 10.9 reports the distribution of *R*-bar squares from subject-specific regressions for several of the models of tables 10.7a–10.7d for each of the four reference ages. For a large percentage of subjects the standard time-separable homothetic model, model A, explains only a modest fraction of the total variance in consumption choice. For example, at age 46 one half of the *R*-bar squares are below .5; 30 percent fall below .25. The *R*-bar squares for models C and D are somewhat higher, but even for model D at least a third of the *R*-bar squares at each age are less than .75.

Evidence of Oversaving

Perhaps the most severe challenge to accurate choice is posed in the year-by-year consumption decisions of parts I and II. Recall that in part I, subjects make their year-by-year decisions without feedback

Table 10.9
Distribution of $\bar{R}^2$s from alternative regression models

		Fraction of $\bar{R}^2$s of size					
Model	Age	<0	0–.25	.25–.5	.5–.75	.75–.85	.90–1
A	35	.22	.18	.29	.20	.08	.02
	46	.20	.12	.18	.31	.14	.04
	55	.27	.16	.24	.24	.06	.02
	69	.14	.02	.06	.22	.10	.45
C	35	.20	.06	.22	.27	.14	.10
	46	.12	.08	.14	.37	.14	.14
	55	.12	.10	.12	.39	.10	.16
D	35	.22	.08	.08	.24	.04	.33
	46	.04	.06	.06	.33	.12	.39
	55	.10	.06	.14	.10	.16	.43

(i.e., without any information concerning the accumulated balance in their savings account). In part II, subjects received this feedback year-by-year. Clearly, the information provided in part II better conforms to the information available in "real world" consumption and saving decisions. Our objective in studying the nonfeedback settings was to gain insight into subjects' abilities to discount and also to compare consumption choices with and without asset feedback.

In part I the overwhelming majority of subjects left significant positive asset balances at the conclusion of their lives. While the average value of age-74 consumption chosen is $25,709, the average value of assets unspent at age 75 is an astounding $250,000. Overall, 36 of 46 subjects (three subjects' responses to part I were invalidated by key punch errors) left balances at age 75 in excess of $50,000; nearly two-thirds of the subjects left assets in excess of $200,000, and over one-third left assets in excess of $300,000.

Table 10.10 lists the amount of assets not spent by the end of life in part I in ascending order in the first column. The second column considers the subjects in the same order as the first column and indicates the level of consumption at age 74 chosen by the subjects in part I. The third column gives the ratio of the first to the second column. The fourth column expresses the present value of the amount of end-of-life unspent resources as a percent of the initial age-35 present value of resources. The average ratio of unspent end-of-life assets to age-74 consumption is 13.97, and the median ratio is 13.26.

Table 10.10
Part I Oversaving behavior

End-of-life assets	Age 74 consumption	Ratio of column 1 to column 2	Ratio of the present value of end-of-life assets to the present value of resources
−385233	100000	−3.85	−.178
−93992	50000	−1.88	−.044
−58329	24000	−2.43	−.027
−25614	40000	−.64	−.012
1	21000	.00	.000
6064	25000	.24	.003
9294	20000	.46	.004
17526	25000	.70	.008
35865	20000	1.79	.017
41740	100000	.42	.019
71726	15000	4.78	.033
98152	40000	2.45	.045
114038	15000	7.60	.053
126193	12000	10.52	.058
133541	16000	8.35	.062
181975	20000	9.10	.084
201976	15000	13.47	.094
209846	25000	8.39	.097
217359	20000	10.87	.101
243476	16000	15.22	.113
254577	15000	16.97	.118
257139	18000	14.29	.119
265955	22100	12.03	.123
280801	19000	14.78	.130
280844	25000	11.23	.130
293823	30000	9.79	.136
307669	18500	16.63	.143
308462	25000	12.34	.143
319849	22000	14.54	.148
333265	20000	16.66	.154
352145	26550	13.26	.163
354585	25000	14.18	.164
368681	25000	14.75	.171
378563	25000	15.14	.175
394742	17000	23.22	.183
401699	20000	20.08	.186
419154	18000	23.29	.194
439242	25000	17.57	.203

Table 10.10 (continued)

End-of-life assets	Age 74 consumption	Ratio of column 1 to column 2	Ratio of the present value of end-of-life assets to the present value of resources
443701	25000	17.75	.206
482401	24000	20.10	.223
527973	35000	15.08	.245
529761	30000	17.66	.245
566066	18000	31.45	.262
605157	10000	60.52	.280
676817	16000	42.30	.314
765124	10000	76.51	.354

In total, 28 of the 46 subjects who answered part I failed to spend 10 percent or more of their lifetime resources; 9 of the 46 failed to spend 20 percent or more of their lifetime resources; and 2 of the 46 failed to spend 30 percent or more.

Further suggestion of oversaving comes from comparing the age-consumption profiles of part I with those of part II. Figure 10.2 displays the two profiles of one of the subjects. Note that the part I profile is generally below the part II profile. In the initial working years the two profiles closely track one another. In later years, after observing a significant amount of accumulated assets in part II, the subject rapidly readjusts his consumption spending upward.

Though consumption behavior varies markedly across subjects, the general characteristics of figure 10.2 are quite similar for many subjects. For 36 of 48 subjects, part II consumption profiles exceed part I profiles for all but a small number of years. A quantitative measure of the relative consumption behavior with and without feedback is provided by comparing accumulated savings at a given age. At age 69, 44 of 48 subjects had significantly smaller asset balances in part II than in part I. In part II, the average level of age-69 assets was $250,000; in part I it was $350,000.

With the benefit of asset feedback in part II, subjects exhibited what might be termed "adaptive" consumption behavior. However, even in part II it is clear that subjects did not succeed in choosing optimal consumption profiles. Rather they appear to oversave in the early stages of their working lives and then to engage in rapid spending, especially during their last ten to fifteen years. To illustrate this point, we calculated for part II the number of years of age-64

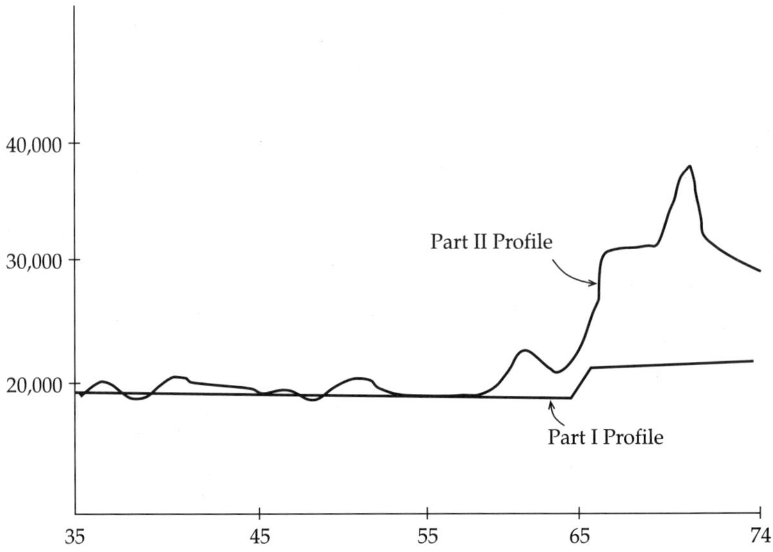

Figure 10.2
Comparison of part I and part II profiles

consumption that could be financed by the subject's age-65 assets. If the individual's aim was to have constant consumption over the last decade of life, then his age-65 assets would be sufficient only to finance ten years of the age-64 consumption level. In fact, for a significant minority of the subjects, age-65 assets are sufficient to finance their age-64 level of consumption for many more than ten years.

Table 10.11 presents the part II consumption choices of subjects in the last ten years of life. The table's first column lists in ascending order the level of assets at age 65; the second column presents the corresponding age-64 level of consumption; the third column presents the largest level of consumption over the remaining ten years, age 65 through 74. The forth column gives the number of years of consumption at the age-64 level that could be financed with age-65 assets.

A total of 29 of the 49 subjects had assets at age 65 that could finance ten or more years of their age-64 level of consumption; 9 had sufficient resources to finance twenty or more years of age-64 consumption; and 5 had enough assets at age 65 to finance thirty or more years of age-64 consumption. Those subjects who could finance twenty or more years of age-64 consumption realized at some point in their remaining ten years of part II that they had sizeable amounts of assets, at which point they dramatically adjusted upward their consumption. A comparison of columns two and three of the table indicates that the high-savers (those for whom column five exceeds 20), for at least one of their remaining ten years, chose a consumption level that, on average, equaled 6.5 times their age-64 consumption.

Comparisons of Actual Consumption Choices with Expressed Preferences

Recall that in part VIII subjects were asked to rank in order of preference five feasible consumption profiles: a constant profile, profiles with 2 percent, 4 percent, and −2 percent annual growth, and a step function with $23,000 in annual consumption prior to retirement and $10,000 thereafter. A natural question is whether the life-cycle consumption paths chosen by subjects in part II are consistent with their preference rankings reported in part VIII. In principal, one would like to have precise information about each subject's utility function. But the difficulty in eliciting such information makes that approach impractical. Instead, we compare a given subject's actual consumption choice with his preference ranking of the part VIII alternatives.

Table 10.12 indicates the fraction of subjects listing each profile as their first or second ranked alternative. Three-quarters of all subjects listed the 2 percent growth path as their first or second choice. The constant path is next in popularity, followed by the 4 percent growth path. The great majority of subjects also displayed "single peaked" preferences, choosing as their second profile choice a profile close to their first choice.

It is interesting to compare the part II profiles chosen by subjects with their consumption profile rankings. A useful measure of the closeness of these choices is the average annual absolute percentage difference between the part II profile and the most preferred part VIII. For those whose first choice in VIII is a constant profile the mean percentage deviation is 15 percent; for those with first choice profiles of 2 percent, 4 percent, −2 percent, and the step function mean deviations are 21 percent, 25 percent, 37 percent, and 46 percent. These mean percentage differences are quite large.

A second comparison of consumption choice with part VIII expressed preferences is summarized in table 10.13. The second row of this table lists the number of subjects whose actual part II choices

Table 10.11
Part II Oversaving behavior

Age 65 assets	Age 64 cons.	Largest post-64 cons.	Years of age 64 consumption affordable from age 65 assets
35885	30000	20000	1
108895	90000	25000	1
109107	18000	32526	6
113478	20000	40000	6
114490	21963	21002	5
123102	22000	39546	6
126668	27500	39157	4
127440	22000	31199	6
140088	22000	30000	7
142006	40000	50000	3
145527	20000	31000	8
161457	28000	35000	6
171288	24000	40000	8
172429	30000	38000	6
173850	19000	70954	11
176054	25000	50000	8
176701	30000	45000	6
183500	18000	66199	12
192288	22000	60000	10
193384	15000	39529	17
194727	25000	50000	9
195945	18000	40000	13
197989	25000	50000	9
198271	20000	55830	12
203607	28000	45000	8
204173	24000	52615	10
205148	15900	56000	17
212663	20000	47000	13
213833	19000	127000	14
224233	41129	41130	6
233823	19000	55000	16
244782	25000	70000	12
256051	24000	70000	13
256887	30000	66925	10
260740	20000	51598	17
261302	28000	65754	11
267808	25000	90715	13
294322	20000	140000	21
296081	23000	60000	17

Table 10.11 (continued)

Age 65 assets	Age 64 cons.	Largest post-64 cons.	Years of age 64 consumption affordable from age 65 assets
300673	10000	70000	∞
307186	10000	91936	∞
319143	19700	143000	24
321064	28000	100000	14
328270	19000	80000	27
335706	15000	100000	50
337159	20000	100000	26
343607	25000	70000	19
395443	15000	255789	∞
406827	20000	50000	38

∞ Resources can finance a perpetuity.

Table 10.12
Ranking of alternative consumption profiles

	Fraction of subjects choosing alternative profiles				
	0%	2%	4%	−2%	Step
First choice	.23	.31	.25	.13	.08
Second choice	.23	.44	.15	.11	.17

Table 10.13
Correlation of part II choices with part VIII ranking

	Profiles				
	0%	2%	4%	−2%	Step
# of subjects	11	15	12	6	4
Closest	5	10	4	0	0
2nd Closest	4	5	3	0	0
3rd Closest	0	0	0	4	3
4th Closest	0	0	0	0	1
5th Closest	2	0	5	2	0

came closest in terms of mean percentage error to their top ranked choice in VIII. The third row lists the number of subjects whose consumption choice more closely resembles their second ranked profile in VIII, and so on. It is clear that many subjects failed to choose profiles that came closest to their ranking in VIII; only 19 of 48 subjects chose in II a profile that came closest to their most preferred in VIII.

Estimates of Time Preference Rates and Intertemporal Elasticities of Substitution

The time preference rate and the intertemporal elasticity of substitution are key parameters in standard analyses of the supply of savings and the efficiency gains from tax reform (see, for example, Summers, 1981 and Auerbach and Kotlikoff, 1987). Estimates as large as 18 percent for the rate of time preference have been reported by Hausman (1979), but most estimates appear to center around 1.5 percent (Lawrence 1985). In the case of the intertemporal elasticity of substitution, the majority of estimates range from 0.2 to 0.5 (Auerbach, Kotlikoff, and Skinner 1983). These parameters have often been estimated assuming homothetic, time-separable preferences. While our data reject such preferences, it is still useful to determine whether estimates of these parameters based on experimental data are in accord with those based on actual data. If they were substantially different one would presumably be more skeptical of the quality of these experimental data.

We can calculate these preference parameters using the data from part VII which asked subjects to choose a time path of consumption in the presence of time-varying interest rates. Estimation of (5′) based on the pooled data yields an estimate of .376 for the intertemporal elasticity of substitution and .018 for the time preference rate. The standard error of the elasticity of substitution is .578; given the estimate of the elasticity of substitution, a standard error in the intercept of (5′) implies values of the time preference rate ranging from −.042 to .081.

The individual estimates of (5′) are, however, significantly different from the pooled estimates. The *F*-test, determining whether individual coefficients in the regression of equation (5′) equal the pooled coefficients, is significant at the .003 percent level.

Estimating (5′) separately for each subject yields only three significant estimates of the intertemporal substitution elasticity. A total of

Table 10.14
Regressions of APCs on demographic characteristics

	Coefficients (standard errors)			
	Age 35	Age 46	Age 55	Age 69
Constant	.324E−1 (.632E−2)	.735E−1 (.828E−2)	.843E−1 (.113E−1)	.308 (.447E−1)
Male	.448E−2 (.215E−2)	.304E−2 (.275E−2)	.152E−1 (.383E−2)	.182E−1 (.152E−1)
Age	.913E−3 (.294E−3)	−.210E−3 (.424E−3)	.241E−3 (.524E−3)	−.266E−2 (.298E−2)
Yrs Col	−.358E−2 (.800E−3)	−.372E−2 (.144E−2)	−.743E−2 (.143E−2)	−.123E−1 (.566E−2)
Italian	−.109E−1 (.433E−2)	−.148E−1 (.655E−2)	−.181E−2 (.772E−2)	−.346E−1 (.306E−1)
Jewish	.746E−2 (.337E−2)	.541E−2 (.440E−2)	.251E−1 (.602E−2)	.466E−2 (.239E−1)
Catholic	−.438E−3 (.268E−2)	−.753E−2 (.379E−2)	.504E−2 (.478E−2)	−.282E−1 (.189E−1)
Asian	−.908E−3 (.281E−2)	−.142E−1 (.355E−2)	−.118E−3 (.502E−2)	−.663E−1 (.199E−1)
Hispanic	.380E−2 (.312E−2)	−.424E−2 (.366E−2)	−.438E−3 (.556E−2)	.620E−2 (.220E−1)
Black, Ot.	−.613E−2 (.322E−2)	−.104E−1 (.524E−2)	−.569E−2 (.574E−2)	−.487E−1 (.227E−1)
Poor parents	.941E−2 (.424E−2)	.159E−1 (.617E−2)	.138E−1 (.756E−2)	.762E−1 (.300E−1)
Rich parents	−.982E−2 (.201E−2)	−.119E−1 (.271E−2)	−.238E−1 (.358E−2)	−.536E−1 (.142E−1)
Exp to be Rich	−.635E−3 (.202E−2)	.486E−2 (.304E−2)	−.556E−2 (.360E−2)	.210E−1 (.143E−1)

24 of 49 substitution elasticities are negative; of the remaining 25 elasticities only 3 are less than 0.5; 15 exceed 1. Of the 49 estimates of the rate of time preference, 4 are negative; 18 are between zero and .03; and 5 exceed .10.

V. Consumption Choices and Demographic Characteristics

One way to exhibit consumption choice differences by demographic groups is to regress APCs against characteristics. Table 10.14 reports the coefficients from such regressions for ages 35, 46, 55, and 69, where all the data in parts II through V which assume a 4 percent interest rate are pooled. The demographic variables include dummy variables for males, Italian, Jewish, Catholic, Asian, Hispanic, Black and others. There are also dummies for the income position of the subject's parents. "poor parents" and "rich parents" are dummies for subjects with parents who they consider to be in lower income and upper income groups, respectively. "Exp to be Rich" is a dummy for subjects who expect to be in high-income groups later in life. The excluded group is female, white Protestants, with middle-income parents, who do not expect to be in the high-income group. In addition to these dummy variables, "Age" is the subject's age and "Yrs Col" is the subject's number of years of college.

The combined set of demographic variables are highly significant in all four regressions, thus adding further evidence about consumption heterogeneity. The specific results suggest that males consume significantly more than females, that Asians, Italians, and Blacks consume less than White Protestants, that Jews consume more than white Protestants, and that those with more years of college consume less than those with fewer years of college. The significant Asian dummies are not surprising, but the coefficients on the dummies for Italians, Blacks, and Jews are rather surprising.

The last three dummy variables in the regressions are also quite interesting. Subjects with poor parents consumed significantly more and those with rich parents significantly less than those with middle-income parents. One may speculate that rich parents have imbued their children with stronger saving ethics than poor parents. The insignificance of the "Exp to be Rich" dummy suggests that subjects were able to abstract from their own personal circumstances in responding to the experiment. If such abstraction were quite difficult, one would expect this coefficient to be significantly positive.

A second interesting question is which subjects are more likely to make consumption mistakes. A pooled regression of the absolute percentage errors from table 10.3 (but redefined with the smaller consumption value in the denominator) on the explanatory variables of table 10.14 produced significant positive male and Jewish coefficients, and a significantly positive coefficient on "Poor parents." In addition, the coefficient on "Yrs Col" was significantly negative.

VI. Summary and Conclusion

A variety of findings in our life-cycle consumption experiment raise serious questions about the life-cycle model's ability to describe consumption choice. In their life-cycle consumption choices, many subjects repeatedly made substantial errors; they chose quite different levels of consumption in identical economic situations, and they oversaved, typically by very sizeable amounts. These errors are often systematic and appear to reflect a widespread inability to discount properly future earnings streams. Many subjects clearly undervalue future earnings streams, while a smaller number overvalue future earnings. Given these errors, it is not surprising that the standard life-cycle model typically explains less than half the variance in consumption. In addition, the experiment's data significantly reject the hypotheses that intertemporal consumption preferences are either homothetic or uniform across individuals. Indeed, differences in preferences appear to be substantial and are correlated, in part, with demographic characteristics.

These findings have important policy implications. If large segments of the population undervalue future income streams, then policies, such as social security and tax cuts, will alter saving because they change the timing of income. Thus a fully funded, actuarially fair social security system that provides future benefits in exchange for current payroll taxes will depress consumption and increase saving if future benefits are undervalued. Alternatively, a cut in current income tax receipts coupled with an equal present value increase in future income tax receipts will stimulate consumption and lower saving.

The findings also suggest that Keynesian models, which place greater emphasis on current relative to future income streams, may better describe actual consumption choice. But the Keynesian model, while perhaps a better descriptive tool, is probably too naive, just as the life-cycle model appears to be too sophisticated. What is needed is a better model of choice in the context of bounded rationality.

We believe that experimental research on consumption choice can provide a set of empirical regularities that will instruct the development of models of bounded rationality. In addition, experiments incorporating policy variables may prove a useful tool in policy formulation and analysis. In our future experimental research we intend to explore the responses to policy variables. In addition, we hope to gain more insight into the nature of consumption mistakes by examining directly whether subjects can discount and by correlating mistakes in discounting with mistakes in consumption choices. A third area of future experimental research is consumption choice under uncertainty.

Appendix: Consumption, Study Instrument

Introduction

We are interested in learning how people make saving decisions. We are going to ask you how much you would choose to consume in the following hypothethical circumstances.

General Circumstances

You are age 35, unmarried, and about to start your first job. You will work on this job until you retire at age 65. Each year you must decide how much money to spend on consumption and how much money to save. When you retire, your salary will cease. After you retire you will live for ten more years and die at age 75.

Your Specific Circumstances

1. You are single and will never get married. You have no children, parents, or other relatives to care for. You are going to spend all of your money over your lifetime on your own consumption.

2. You face no uncertainty whatsoever about the future. You will live for certain until age 75. You will be in excellent health and never have to pay a cent for medical or dental care. You will work full-time until age 65 when you retire.

3. Any money you save is deposited in your savings account and earns 4 percent interest per year. You may borrow money at any time in which case you must pay 4 percent interest on your borrowings.

4. There is never any inflation or deflation in your economy; that is, prices never change.

5. There are no taxes in your economy.

6. All events in your life occur on January 1. You were born on January 1. You get paid—in advance—for the coming year's work on January 1. You will retire on January 1. You receive interest on savings or pay interest on borrowing on Jan. 1. In addition, you make all your consumption expenditures for the year on January 1. You will die on December 31st, 2026, the day before you turn 75.

7. Consumption expenditures include purchases of food and clothing, payment for vacations during the year, payment for utilities for the year, and rental of housing and durable goods.

8. You always rent housing by the year as well as all durable goods like cars, refrigerators, furniture, stoves, televisions, air conditioners, etc. On January 1 of each year you pay all of the rent for the coming year. There are no moving costs, hassle costs, or any other costs of your renting a bigger house or apartment or, for example, of renting a smaller car or bigger dishwasher.

Basic Fact Sheet

General

This questionnaire has eight parts and should take from one to one-and-a-half hours to complete. We recognize the experiment is somewhat lengthy but ask that you try to be as conscientious as possible throughout. Please take your time and try to answer every question thoughtfully, on the basis of what would make you most happy given the situation described to you. We suggest that after you complete part IV you take a five-minute break. At that time, please help yourself to the refreshments we have provided.

If you have any questions *whatsoever* during the experiment, please stop and speak to one of the proctors. We strongly discourage guessing when at all in doubt.

Summary of Your Facts of Life

1. You begin working at age 35 with no savings.

2. You retire at the end of your 64th year, so 64 is the last year you work and earn a salary. (The only exception to this is part IV, which varies the retirement age.)

3. You die, *with certainty*, at the end of your 74th year, so 74 is the last year in which you can consume.

4. With the exception of part V, you always earn a $25,000 salary each year until you retire.

5. The interest rate is always 4 percent (except in Parts VI and VII). Your savings account will earn interest at that rate; you may always borrow as much as you wish at that interest rate.

6. Interest Computation: Your assets on January 1 of any year are equal to 1.04 times the sum of your assets on January 1 of the previous year plus your earnings on January 1 of the previous year less your consumption on January 1 of the previous year. Thus, if assets

last January 1 were \$10,000, earnings were \$25,000, and consumption was \$23,000, then assets this January 1 would equal 1.04 times (\$10,000 + \$25,000 − \$23,000) = 1.04 × \$12,000 = 12,480.

Operating the Computer

• In responding to any question, type *only* numerals, no commas, dollar signs, decimals, etc.

• With the exception of part I, part VII, and part VIII, entry of an answer requires two steps. First, you key the number you wish to enter and press the return key. Second, once you have looked at the number you have typed on the screen to make sure you've typed it correctly, type the ampersand (&—shift 7) to confirm the entry. The computer will then accept the answer and move on to the next question.

• If you wish to correct an entry *after* you have hit return, but before you have confirmed it with an ampersand, simply retype the number and hit return again.

• If you wish to correct an entry *before* you have hit return, use the backspace key (←, upper right on the keyboard) to begin the number again or to rekey part of the number.

• After you have typed the ampersand to confirm an entry, there is no way to correct it—so CHECK EACH ENTRY CAREFULLY BEFORE YOU CONFIRM IT.

• If the word "TEXT" lights up after you have hit the return key, but *before* you have confirmed with an ampersand, retype your entry.

• At the end of the Background and Introduction screens, and at the end of parts I, VII, and VIII, you must type the ampersand to advance to the next screen. IMPORTANT: Sometimes it will be necessary to type the ampersand several times, so if you've typed it and, within a second or two, have not advanced to the next screen, type it again.

• IMPORTANT: *On part II*, if you accidentally confirm a number that was typed incorrectly, stop immediately and tell a proctor.

• On parts I and VII, you may change any entry you wish by moving to the entry with the up or down arrows (to the far right of the keyboard). To move all the way to the beginning of these screens to review all of your entries, press the HOME key (next to the up arrow). DO NOT PRESS THE HOME KEY ON ANY OTHER PART OF THE EXPERIMENT.

Part I—Annual Consumption (Press down arrow to page down.)

Today is January 1, 1987 and you have just turned 35. This is your first day of work. You receive $25,000 today, payment in advance for working over the year. You will continue to work for the next 30 years earning $25,000 each year. On Jan. 1, 2016 you will be 64 and will start your last year of work and receive your last paycheck. Your last day of work is December 31, 2016. After retiring you will live for ten more years and die on December 31, 2026.

You have no initial savings. Below is a list of earnings you receive at each age over your lifetime. At each age please fill in the total amount of money you would choose to spend on consumption during that year.

Before you fill in your consumption choices, we want to make sure you understand how interest on your savings or borrowings is compounded. Since the interest rate is 4 percent, your assets on January 1 of each year are equal to 1.04 times the sum of your assets on January 1 of the previous year plus your earnings on January 1 of the previous year less your consumption on January 1 of the previous year. Thus, if assets last January 1 were $10,000, earnings were $25,000 and consumption was $23,000, then assets this January 1 would equal 1.04 times ($10,000 + $25,000 − $23,000) = 1.04 × $12,000 = $12,480.

Remember, at the end of your life YOU SHOULD NOT END UP IN DEBT. On the other hand, you do not want to leave behind any unspent money. In deciding your consumption at each age, choose, on the basis of what would make you most happy, given what you can afford.

(Type "&" to begin part I.)

Part I—Annual Consumption

Please enter your desired consumption for each year. Enter only numerals, no commas or other punctuation.

Age	Date	Earnings	Consumption
35	Jan. 1, 1987	25000	0
36	Jan. 1, 1988	25000	0
37	Jan. 1, 1989	25000	0
38	Jan. 1, 1990	25000	0

Age	Date	Earnings	Consumption
39	Jan. 1, 1991	25000	0
40	Jan. 1, 1992	25000	0
41	Jan. 1, 1993	25000	0
42	Jan. 1, 1994	25000	0
43	Jan. 1, 1995	25000	0
44	Jan. 1, 1996	25000	0
45	Jan. 1, 1997	25000	0
46	Jan. 1, 1998	25000	0
47	Jan. 1, 1999	25000	0
48	Jan. 1, 2000	25000	0
49	Jan. 1, 2001	25000	0
50	Jan. 1, 2002	25000	0
51	Jan. 1, 2003	25000	0
52	Jan. 1, 2004	25000	0
53	Jan. 1, 2005	25000	0
54	Jan. 1, 2006	25000	0
55	Jan. 1, 2007	25000	0
56	Jan. 1, 2008	25000	0
57	Jan. 1, 2009	25000	0
58	Jan. 1, 2010	25000	0
59	Jan. 1, 2011	25000	0
60	Jan. 1, 2012	25000	0
61	Jan. 1, 2013	25000	0
62	Jan. 1, 2014	25000	0
63	Jan. 1, 2015	25000	0
64	Jan. 1, 2016	25000	0
65	Jan. 1, 2017	0	0
66	Jan. 1, 2018	0	0
67	Jan. 1, 2019	0	0
68	Jan. 1, 2020	0	0
69	Jan. 1, 2021	0	0
70	Jan. 1, 2022	0	0

Age	Date	Earnings	Consumption
71	Jan. 1, 2023	0	0
72	Jan. 1, 2024	0	0
73	Jan. 1, 2025	0	0
74	Jan. 1, 2026	0	0
75	Jan. 1, 2027	YOU ARE NOW DEAD	

Part II—Consumption With Knowledge of Money in Savings Account

We are now going to repeat the previous question, but this time before you tell us how much you wish to consume in a given year we will tell you the amount of savings you have at the beginning of that year. If you are in debt at the beginning of a particular year your savings will be negative. Keep in mind that while you are free to borrow money from the bank, you cannot end up in debt at the end of your life. Also recall that your yearly earnings are $25,000 per year until you retire at the beginning of your 65th year and that you will die when you reach age 75.

(After reading, type "&" to begin part II.)

You are 35 years old. You will earn $25,000 per year until age 65. Your savings in your bank account is $0.00.

How much do you wish to spend to consumption this year?

Age	Money in Savings Account	Consumption	Interest Income	Labor Earnings
35	0		0	25000
		(Enter number. Then type "&" to confirm.)		

Part III—Consumption With Specified Savings at Selected Ages

We are now going to ask you to imagine you are a particular age and have a certain amount of money in your savings account. Please tell us how much you would spend on consumption at that age, given the savings indicated. The questionnaire will ask you to respond to 16 different age/savings combinations. Be sure to read BOTH age and savings before responding. Remember, you will continue to work until age 65 earning $25,000 per year.

(After reading, type "&" to begin Part III.)

You are 35 years old. You will earn $25,000 per year until age 65. Your savings in your bank account is $43,500.

How much would you consume at this age?

Age	Money in Savings Account	Consumption	Earnings
35←	43500←		25000
		(Enter number. Then type "&" to confirm.)	

Part IV—Consumption With Different Retirement Ages

Next we want to find out how much you'd spend on consumption if your retirement age were different from 65. We will ask you what you would consume at age 46, with $100,000 in your savings account, if you are to retire at some specified retirement age. We will ask you at 4 different retirement ages.

As usual, your earnings will be 25,000 per year until you reach the given retirement age.

(After reading, type "&" to begin Part IV.)

You are 46 years old. You earn $25,000 per year until retirement. Your savings account balance is $500,000.

How much would you consume at this age if you retire at age 72?

Age	Money in Savings Account	Consumption	Retirement Age
46	500000		72←
		(Enter number. Then type "&" to confirm.)	

Part V—Consumption with Different Lifetime Earnings

Now assume again that you will retire at 65 but that your earnings vary throughout your working life. We will hold your initial savings fixed at $65,000. Then we will show you an earnings profile and ask how much you would consume at 3 different ages, given those earnings. We will repeat this 3 times, showing you a different earnings profile each time. You will be asked for a total of 9 responses.

(After reading, type "&" to begin part V.)

You are 35 years old, and your savings account balance is $65,000. Your annual earnings are listed below—notice you retire at age 65.

How much would you consume at this age, given these earnings?

Age	Money in Savings Account	Earnings
35←	65000	23200 from age 35 through age 44
	Consumption	47800 from age 45 through age 54
	(Enter number. Then type "&" to confirm.)	32500 from age 55 through age 64

Part VI—Consumption with Different Interest Rates

Next we want to find out how much you'd spend on consumption if the interest rate were different from 4%. We will ask you what you would consume at age 46, with $90,000 in your savings account given the interest rate indicated. We will repeat this 5 times, changing the interest rate each time. Your earnings will be $25,000 per year until age 65.

(After reading, type "&" to being part VI.)

You are 46 years old. You earn $25,000 per year until age 65. Your savings in your bank account is $90,000.

How much would you consume at this age if the interest rate were 0%?

Age	Money in Savings Account	Consumption	Interest Rate
46	90000		0%←
		(Enter number. Then type "&" to confirm.)	

Part VII—Consumption With Changing Interest Rate

Next we want to see how your consumption and saving decisions are influenced by changes in interest rates over the course of your lifetime. Imagine that you are age 45, that you work until 65, earning $25,000 per year, and that you die at age 75. The interest rate you receive on your savings is not, however, fixed. The following table summarizes the interest rate you will face at each age. (They will be repeated on the next screen.)

(After reading, type "&" to begin part VII.)

Part VII—Consumption with Changing Interest Rate

Now assume you are age 45 and will earn $25000 per year, you retire at age 65, and that you will die at age 75.

Please enter your desired consumption for each year, and the interest rate in each case. Type "&" after completing the entire column.

Age	**Date**	**Earnings**	**Consumption**	**Interest Rate**
45	Jan. 1, 1997	25000	0	2%
46	Jan. 1, 1998	25000	0	2%
47	Jan. 1, 1999	25000	0	2%
48	Jan. 1, 2000	25000	0	2%
49	Jan. 1, 2001	25000	0	2%
50	Jan. 1, 2002	25000	0	2%
51	Jan. 1, 2003	25000	0	2%
52	Jan. 1, 2004	25000	0	2%
53	Jan. 1, 2005	25000	0	4%
54	Jan. 1, 2006	25000	0	4%
55	Jan. 1, 2007	25000	0	4%
56	Jan. 1, 2008	25000	0	4%
57	Jan. 1, 2009	25000	0	4%
58	Jan. 1, 2010	25000	0	4%
59	Jan. 1, 2011	25000	0	4%
60	Jan. 1, 2012	25000	0	4%
61	Jan. 1, 2013	25000	0	6%
62	Jan. 1, 2014	25000	0	6%
63	Jan. 1, 2015	25000	0	6%
64	Jan. 1, 2016	25000	0	6%

Age	Date	Earnings	Consumption	Interest Rate
65	Jan. 1, 2017	0	0	6%
66	Jan. 1, 2018	0	0	6%
67	Jan. 1, 2019	0	0	6%
68	Jan. 1, 2020	0	0	3%
69	Jan. 1, 2021	0	0	3%
70	Jan. 1, 2022	0	0	3%
71	Jan. 1, 2023	0	0	3%
72	Jan. 1, 2024	0	0	3%
73	Jan. 1, 2025	0	0	3%
74	Jan. 1, 2026	0	0	
75	Jan. 1, 2027		YOU ARE NOW DEAD	

Part VIII—Ranking Different Lifetime Consumption Profiles

Again assume you are age 35 and will earn $25,000 per year until you retire at age 65, and that you will die at age 75.

Each of the following consumption plans will leave you with exactly zero dollars on the day you die. Rank them from 1 to 5, giving 1 to your most preferred and 5 to your least preferred. (When finished, type "&" to exit.)

Rank

A. $21841 per year, every year

B. $16008 at age 35, growing 2% per year thereafter

C. $11240 at age 35, growing 4% per year thereafter

D. $28592 at age 35, falling by 2% per year thereafter

E. $23420 from age 35 until age 65, then $10921 from 65 to 75.

Consumption in Selected Years

Age	A	B	C	D	E
35	21841	16008	11240	28592	23420
46	21841	19905	17303	22895	23420
65	21841	28997	36455	15597	10921
74	21841	34654	51887	13004	10921

Part IX—Build Your Own Consumption Path

You have 20 points to distribute among the age ranges to show the relative amounts you'd like to consume at various times in your life. For example, if you wish to consume the same amount in every year, put "5" in each column. If you'd rather consume more while you're young, and less while you're old, enter larger numbers first, then smaller numbers. The program will translate the numbers you type into consumption in each age range. You can modify your numbers until you're satisfied with your lifetime consumption path. Remember, you can type any numbers you like provided they add up to twenty. (NOTE: You still earn $25,000 per year until retiring at age 65.)

(Type "&" to begin Part IX.)

Allot your twenty points to the four decades of your life. You still earn $25,000 per year until retirement at age 65. Below the numbers you type will appear a translation of your points into consumption for the decade. ONCE YOU'VE ENTERED YOUR POINTS, TYPE "!" FOR TRANSLATION. YOU MAY DO THIS AS MANY TIMES AS YOU WISH. WHEN YOU ARE FINALLY SATISFIED WITH THE CONSUMPTION PATHS YOU HAVE CONSTRUCTED, TYPE "&" TO FINISH THE EXPERIMENT.

Interest/AGE	35–44	45–54	55–64	65–74
.04	20	0	0	0
	53299	0	0	0
.08	20	0	0	0
	41944	0	0	0

Note

We thank Richard Zeckhauser for helpful comments. The data used in this study are available from the authors. We gratefully acknowledge research support provided by National Science Foundation grants #SES=8511221 and #SES-8520757 and a National Institute of Aging grant #P01-AG05842-01. The research reported here is part of the NBER's research program in taxation and project in aging. Any opinions expressed are those of the authors and not those of the National Bureau of Economic Research.

References

Allais, M. and O. Hagen, eds., *Expected Utility Hypotheses and the Allais Paradox*, D. Reidel Publishing Co.: Dordrecht, Holland, 1979.

Ando, Albert, and Franco Modigliani, "The Life Cycle Model: Aggregate Implications and Tests," *American Economic Review*, 53(1): 55–84, 1963.

Auerbach, Alan J., and Laurence J. Kotlikoff, *Dynamic Fiscal Policy*, Cambridge, England: Cambridge University Press, 1987.

Auerbach, Alan J., Laurence J. Kotlikoff, and Jonathan Skinner, "The Efficiency Gains from Dynamic Tax Reform," *International Economic Review*, vol. 24(2) 1983.

Cox, J. C., V. L. Smith, and J. M. Walker, "Expected Revenue in Discriminative and Uniform Price Sealed Bid Auctions," in V. L. Smith, ed., *Research in Experimental Economics*, vol. 3, 1985.

Grether, D. M. and C. R. Plott, "Economic Theory of Choice and the Preference Reversal Phenomenon," *American Economic Review*, vol. 69, 1979.

Hausman, Jerry, "Individual Discount Rates and the Utilization of Energy-Using Durables," *Bell Journal of Economics*, Spring 1979.

Kahneman, D. and A. Tversky, "Prospect Theory: An Analysis of Decision under Risk," *Econometrica*, vol. 47, 1979.

Lawrence, Emily, "Do the Poor Save More," mimeo, Yale University, 1985.

Modigliani, Franco and Richard Brumberg, "Utility Analysis and the Consumption Function: An Interpretation of Cross-section Data," in *Post-Keynesian Economics*, Kenneth K. Kurihara, ed., New Brunswick, N.J.: Rutgers University, 1954.

Plott, C. R., "Industrial Organization and Experimental Economics," *Journal of Economic Literature*, vol. 20, 1982.

Samuelson, W. and M. Bazerman, "The Winner's Curse in Bilateral Negotiations," in V. L. Smith, ed., *Research in Experimental Economics*, vol. 3, 1985.

Smith, V. L., "Experimental Economics: Induced Value Theory," *American Economic Review*, vol. 66, 1976.

Smith, V. L., "Experiments with a Decentralized Mechanism for Public Goods Decisions," *American Economic Review*, vol. 70, 1980.

Smith, V. L., "Microeconomic Systems as an Experimental Science," *American Economic Review*, vol. 72, 1982.

Summers, Lawrence H., "Capital Taxation and Capital Accumulation in a Life Cycle Model," *American Economic Review*, vol. 71: 533–544, 1981.

Tversky, A. and D. Kahnman, "Judgements under Uncertainty: Heuristics and Biases," *Science*, vol. 185, 1974.

11 Life Insurance of the Elderly: Adequacy and Determinants

with Alan J. Auerbach

The general economic status of the elderly has improved significantly in the past several decades. In contrast to 1960, when over a third of elderly households had incomes below the official poverty level, the current figure is below 15 percent. Despite the general reduction in poverty among the aged, the poverty rate among elderly nonmarried women, including widows, remains high. Today roughly one-third (31 percent) of elderly nonmarried women, compared with only 8 percent of elderly married women, are poor.[1]

That fact suggests a significant economic risk to women from the dissolution of marriage through divorce or a husband's death. Divorce insurance may not exist, but life insurance is readily available. Many households, however, may fail to buy enough life insurance. Concern about insufficient life insurance presumably underlies the provision of survivor and death benefits by the social security system. This chapter examines the adequacy of the life insurance protection conferred by the combination of private and public insurance. It also investigates the determinants of private life insurance purchases.

Three central questions are addressed in this chapter:

- How large are private life insurance holdings relative to the amounts needed to maintain the previous standard of living of surviving spouses?
- Do social security survivor benefits significantly increase the amount of life insurance protection?
- Is the pattern of private insurance purchases in general accord with the predictions of economic theory, particularly the proposition that social security survivor insurance should substitute (under assumptions specified below) dollar for dollar for private life insurance?

The answers to these questions clearly are important for understanding the cause of poverty among widows, the extent of government intervention in the life insurance market, and the effectiveness of that intervention in increasing the sum of private and public life insurance. Despite the importance of these issues, there has been relatively little research to date on the adequacy of insurance. Two articles by Holden, Burkhauser, and Myers appear to be the only other analyses related to the problem of inadequate life insurance purchase.[2] These articles suggest that the probability for women of being below the poverty level is increased significantly by the death of their husbands.

The data set chosen for this study, the Retirement History Survey (RHS), is attractive because it focuses on the elderly and because it permits the observation of household economic status before and after the death of a spouse.[3] These data, however, are deficient in several respects for the study of life insurance. First, they include the face value, but not the cash value, of life insurance policies. Second, although various questions about retirement plans and expected future income were posed to RHS participants, a considerable number for respondents did not answer many of these questions. Understanding the magnitude of expected future income, particularly labor earnings, is obviously important in assessing the adequacy of life insurance holdings. Given these data problems, our results should be viewed cautiously. In some important respects, however, correcting biases that arise from missing data would likely strengthen our conclusions.

The principal inferences we draw from this study are the following:

• Combined private and public life insurance is inadequate for a significant minority of elderly households.

• Almost one-half of households at risk (those for whom a significant portion of household resources take the form of earnings and benefits that cease with the death of the husband or wife) are inadequately insured.

• Empirical estimation of the demand for life insurance produces many results that are greatly at odds with theoretical predictions.

• Households do not appear to offset significantly the provision of social security survivor insurance by reducing their private purchase of life insurance.

There are five remaining sections in the chapter. The first presents general descriptive information about the extent and adequacy of life insurance. Adequacy of life insurance is assessed in terms of the ability of surviving spouses to maintain their previous standard of living. Comparisons of previous and current standards of living are made for households in which a spouse died between 1969 and 1971. In addition, similar comparisons for hypothetical surviving spouses are made for all married households in 1969. After presenting these comparisons of standards of living before and after the death of a spouse, we discuss six potential biases in the comparisons. These six sources of bias taken together lead us to believe that our calculations have understated the inadequacy of life insurance holdings.

The second section examines the optimal choice of life insurance holdings within a simple two-period model. The substitutability of private and public insurance is considered, as well as the proper valuation of future income streams under the assumption of an incomplete (or imperfect) market in life insurance and annuities.

The two-period model illustrates the interdependence of choices of life insurance made by husbands and wives. As stressed in the section, the insurance demand of one spouse depends on whether the other spouse has positive or no life insurance. The model assumes that private annuities are unavailable. As Yaari has pointed out, purchasing private annuities is in effect equivalent to having negative holdings of life insurance.[4] Negative holdings of life insurance are ruled out because annuities appear on the private market only at actuarially unfair rates.[5] None of the households in the RHS sample used here reported holding private annuities.

The theoretical model of the second section motivates the econometric specification of a two-indicator, switching-regressions model in the third section. The fourth section discusses the empirical findings and uses the results to evaluate the effect of social security on the purchase of private insurance. The last section summarizes the paper's findings and suggests directions for further research.

The Adequacy of Life Insurance: A Conceptual Framework

This section considers the adequacy of life insurance by comparing standards of living before and after either the actual or hypothetical death of a spouse. The definition of standard of living is obviously arbitrary; by the term we mean the sustained level of consumption of goods and services that can be afforded on the basis of a household's current assets and current and future income. Calculating affordable consumption annuities both before and after the death of a spouse requires information on the net worth, future labor earnings, private pensions, and social security benefits available to the couple when both spouses are alive as well as those resources available to the actual or hypothetical surviving spouse. Life insurance obviously increases the resources available to surviving spouses and its purchase can protect surviving spouses from a reduction in their affordable standards of living.

The size of consumption streams that can be financed from a given amount of resources depends on actuarial factors such as the interest rate, the extent to which annuities are implicitly if not explicitly available, and household economies of scale in joint consumption. Economies of scale refers here to the proposition that "two can live cheaper than one." Many goods—such as heating, lighting, and other housing services—are jointly consumed by married couples. Other goods, such as food and clothing, not have this feature of being public goods.

To see the importance of economies of scale, consider at one extreme that all goods consumed by couples are local public goods such as heating. For surviving spouses to maintain a previously affordable standard of living, they need to be able to purchase the same commodities when single that they and their spouses would have purchased when married. To do so obviously requires the same economic resources. With full insurance of the survival-contingent income stream of each spouse, the standard of living of the surviving spouse will be fully insured.

Fully insuring the survival-contingent income stream maintains the standard of living of survivors when all household consumption is joint, but this relationship fails in the absence of significant economies of scale. Consider the case of no joint consumption by married couples. The surviving spouse will then suffer a drop in the affordable standard of living only if the uninsured decedent's survival-contingent income stream would have financed more than the decedent's own stream of consumption. In other words, fully insuring the surviving spouse requires buying insurance equal to the difference between the value of the decedent's future income stream and the value of the decedent's future consumption. If this difference is negative—that is, if the value of the future income stream the decedent would have earned is less than the potential future value of the decedent's consumption—the surviving spouse's standard of living will be higher than it would have been had the decedent lived.

Because we do not know the precise extent of the economies of scale, we present calculations of the adequacy of life insurance under the assumption that economies of scale do not exist. We then discuss the likely bias arising from that assumption. Standard of living is measured in the calculations as the level annuity that could be financed with available resources. We calculate the combined resources of the couple before the actual or hypothetical death of a spouse and compute the level annuity, A_m, that could be purchased for each spouse under the assumption that each spouse receives an equal annuity. Next we determine the annuity that could be afforded by the surviving spouse, A_s. The ratio of the second annuity to the first annuity (A_s/A_m) is the measure used for the adequacy of insurance. Ratios below 0.75 are described as inadequate.

In more formal terms, let PVR_m be the present value of resources of the couple when they are both alive and let PVR_s be the present value of resources of the surviving spouse. We calculate A_s/A_m, where A_m (the annuity of the surviving spouse when married) and A_s (the annuity of the surviving spouse after the partner's death) are determined by

$$PVR_m = (D_h + D_w)A_m \tag{1m}$$

$$PVR_s = D_sA_s, \quad s = h, w. \tag{1s}$$

In equations (1), D_h and D_w are discount factors for the husband and wife; D_h equals the present value of a dollar received annually by the husband until his death, and D_w is correspondingly defined for the wife; D_s represents the discount factor for the surviving spouse, where s equals h or w. (Throughout the equations, the subscripts m, s, d, h, and w denote respectively "married," "surviving spouse," "deceased spouse," "husband." and "wife." For clarity, these same symbols have been suffixed to equation numbers—where they appear in roman type—to differentiate among the equations.)

As discussed in the literature and as indicated in the examination of potential biases later in this section, the proper valuation of future income streams in the presence of life-span uncertainty depends critically on the nature of explicit and implicit insurance arrangements.[6] At one extreme one could assume perfect markets in annuities and life insurance in which insurance premiums are actuarially fair. PVR_m and PVR_s would then correspond to the present expected values of the resources of married couples and surviving spouses, where the expectation is taken over survival probabilities. Similarly, D_h, D_w, and D_s would be the discount factors of those expected values.

Even if there were no public market in annuities, Kotlikoff and Spivak have indicated that risk sharing among family members (that is, parents and children) can closely approximate perfect annuity insurance even when the number of family members is as small as four.[7] Although families are not as effective in hedging the loss of future income streams (that is, in providing life insurance) as they are in hedging the duration of future consumption streams (that is, in providing annuity insurance), life insurance that is close to actuarially fair combined with family annuity insurance arrangements may approximate the situation of perfect life and annuity insurance. In this case, using actuarially fair discounting in forming PVR_m, PVR_s, D_h, and D_w would be roughly appropriate.

If public insurance markets are far from perfect, so that market insurance is in effect unavailable, and if family insurance arrangements do not arise, then simple discounting by only the interest rate is appropriate if it is assumed that borrowing and lending are unconstrained. Between the case of perfect insurance and no insurance is a range of partial insurance environments in which future income streams are priced (discounted) by using survival probabilities that depend to some extent on the availability and pricing of particular insurance policies. The next subsection examines such cases.

Because assessing the precise degree to which the insurance market is complete is difficult if not impossible, we examine the A_s/A_m ratios under alternative assumptions—at one extreme, perfect insurance and, at the other, no insurance. In our view the assumption of perfect insurance is an approximation closer to the experience of the RHS sample than is the assumption of no insurance; 65 percent of the 1969 RHS sample of elderly couples reported positive life insurance for both spouses, and another 22 percent of couples had positive life insurance for at least one spouse. At least some of this life insurance surely was in the form of term insurance; as Yaari has demonstrated, buying additional life insurance is equivalent to selling an annuity.[8] For at least those couples in which both spouses have term life insurance, one can therefore argue that annuities were available at the margin: had these couples purchased less in term insurance, they would have had more in annuities. In addition, the ability of parents to insure implicitly longevity risk for their children leads us to view the benchmark of perfect insurance as more appropriate than the benchmark of no insurance.

In the following subsection we describe the detailed data definitions that permit us to measure the adequacy of insurance for respondents in the RHS.

Description of Variables, Data, and Sample Selection

The terms for family resources, PVR_m and PVR_s, are defined as

$$PVR_m = NW_m + PVE_h + PVE_w + PVP_h + PVP_w + PVB_h + PVB_w + PVS_h + PVS_w \tag{2m}$$

$$PVR_s = NW_s + PVE_s + PVP_s + PVB_s + PVS_s + F_d, \tag{2s}$$

where NW stands for net worth, PVE is the present expected value of labor earnings, PVP denotes the present expected value of non-social-security pension benefits, PVB is the present expected value of social security retirement benefits, PVS stands for the present expected value of social security survivor benefits, and F represents the insurance on the decedent's life. The subscripts m, h, w, s, and d are as defined earlier. When s equals h, d equals w; when s equals w, d equals h.

As indicated in equation (2s), in calculations of hypothetical annuities for surviving spouses in 1969, PVR_s includes the insurance on the life of the hypothetical deceased spouse, F_d. In comparisons of the 1971 value of A_s with the 1969 value of A_m, reported values of NW_s presumably include unspent proceeds from the deceased spouses' life insurance; hence F_d is not included in forming PVR_s. This formulation of equations (2) treats reported life insurance as if it were only term insurance. We indicate below how the distribution of the A_s/A_m ratios would be affected by making the opposite assumption—that is, that the unreported cash value of life insurance equals the reported face value.

Net worth equals the sum of the reported values of assets less the reported values of liabilities. Observations were deleted if the market value of real estate was not reported, if the value of mortgages was not reported, or if more than two kinds of financial assets has missing values.

Present Values of Earnings and Private Pensions

The present value of earnings was calculated by assuming that current real earnings continue to the reported expected age of retirement. Respondents who indicated that they would never retire were assigned an expected retirement age, calculated in the following manner. Using the RHS records of social security earnings and other RHS data, we determined the actual retirement ages for those nongovernmental workers who stated in 1969 that they would never retire but did stop working before 1975. With these data we were able to calculate age-specific probabilities of retiring at each age between ages 58 and 67. We assumed that those who did not retire by age 67 retired, on average, at age 70. From this information we calculated the expected age of retirement for respondents who stated in 1969 that they never intended to retire because of age.

Similar calculations were made for respondents with positive 1969 labor earnings who indicated that they were partially retired but did not give an expected age of full retirement. Also included in this group were 1969 respondents who reported positive labor earnings but stated that they were fully retired. Because spouses of respondents were not asked in 1969 when they expected to retire, the same technique was used to estimate the expected retirement ages for those spouses with positive labor earnings in 1969. In this case we calculated age-specific probabilities of retiring between ages 51 and 67 and again assumed an average retirement age of 70 for spouses not retiring before age 67.

For employed respondents and spouses, current earnings equal 1968 social security reported earnings (obtained from the RHS records of social security earnings) valued in 1969 dollars, if these earnings were below the 1968 ceiling for such earnings, but above the 1968 earnings reported by the respondent and spouse. If 1968 social security reported earnings were above the ceiling or below 1968 self-reported earnings, 1968 self-reported earnings valued in 1969 dollars were used.

The stream of non-social-security pension benefits equals currently reported pension benefits before the expected retirement age and current pension benefits or reported expected retirement benefits, whichever is larger, after the expected retirement age. Because there is no information on whether these pensions provide joint survivor benefits, we have assumed that such benefits accrue solely to the husbands. It is our under-standing that before the passage of the Employee Retirement Income Security Act (ERISA) in 1974, joint survivor annuities were relatively rare. Because pension benefits of the wife were not reported in the 1969 survey, we have included only those of the husband in the analysis. This omission biases our calculation of A_w/A_m downward and biases our calculation of A_h/A_m upward.

Present Value of Social Security Benefits

The stream of future social security benefits was calculated by first determining the primary insurance amount (PIA) at age 62 for each respondent and spouse. Earnings before 1969 that were used in calculating the PIA were obtained from the RHS social security earnings records. Earnings between 1969 and the year in which the respondent or spouse would reach age 62 are projected as just described. The wife's social security benefit is her own benefit or the dependent's benefit once the wife is eligible for that benefit (that is, she has exceeded age 62, and her husband is receiving benefits or is dead), whichever is larger. Before eligibility for the dependent's benefit, the wife may be eligible to collect her own benefit. For respondents and spouses who indicated they were already retired, expected to retire before age 62, or were earning less than $1,680 (the social security exempt amount), the actuarially reduced stream of benefits commences at age 62. For respondents and spouses who expected to retire after age 62 or were earning more than $1,680, actuarially reduced benefits commence at the indicated expected retirement age if that age is less than or equal to 65. Between ages 65 and 72, respondents and spouses who had not yet retired (according to stated or imputed expectations) were assigned benefits according to an earnings test. Past age 72 non-earnings-tested benefits were available for all respondents and spouses.

If the husband was the decedent, survivor benefits were available. As described above, these benefits are provided on an actuarially reduced basis and are earnings-tested where appropriate. Although our calculations of total benefits have followed the social security law, we define the stream of social security survivor benefits to be the excess of the surviving wife's benefit over what she would have received had her husband lived.

In the projections of future real social security benefits, households are assumed to expect that current social security law will continue unchanged except for increased future benefits to adjust for inflation.

Data Characteristics

After deletion of observations with missing data, the 1969 RHS sample of married households numbered 5,131. A total of 4,295 husbands and 3,389 wives reported positive life insurance. Table 11.1 presents mean values of life insurance holdings as well as components of *PVR* cross-classified by the level of *PVR*, which is the present value of family resources. In forming present values, all future earnings, social security, and pension streams were actuarially discounted by using probabilities of mortality and assuming a 4 percent real interest rate. The overall average holdings of life insurance on the husband's life is $9,360, which may be compared with the mean value of family resources, *PVR*, which is $108,886. Life insurance is small relative to family resources, but is it small relative to the amount of the husband's future earnings and social security and other pension benefit streams that could be insured?

The answer is that the mean value of insurance on the husband's life is less than one-fifth the sum of the mean values of his insurable future income streams. Insurance holdings on wives are even smaller relative to their insurable streams; the ratio of these means is less than 6 percent. These figures would be inconsequential were future income streams only a trivial fraction of current family resources, *PVR*. This is not the case. The future income streams of husbands make up 44 percent of the total *PVR* of households in the sample; those of wives are 19 percent. The table also indicates that social security survivor benefits represent almost the fourth of the combined private and public insurance on the husband's life. Even if any offsetting from private insurance is ignored, social security survivor benefits make only a very small contribution to reducing the gap between husband's insurable income streams and private insurance on their lives.

Table 11.1 suggests that insurance is much more adequate for those with a *PVR* less than $25,000. For couples with a *PVR* above $250,000, insurance on the husband's life is also larger relative to *PVR*; for this group the husband's future income streams are less than one-fifth of *PVR*. The concern about inadequate insurance is therefore much more of an issue for middle-class households with a *PVR* between $25,000 and $250,000.

Table 11.1
Components of family wealth, 1969 (mean values; 1969 dollars)

	Present value of resources (PVR)[a]						
	<10,000	10–25,000	25–50,000	50–100,000	100–250,000	250,000+	Total
Item	(55)	(179)	(714)	(2,040)	(1,922)	(221)	(5,131)
Husband							
Earnings	307	1,099	5,316	16,822	33,312	42,431	21,772
Percent of *PVR*	5	6	13	22	24	9	20
Benefits	2,059	6,959	13,138	17,304	20,025	18,971	17,269
Percent of *PVR*	36	38	32	23	14	4	16
Pension	0	759	2,561	5,670	13,663	29,357	9,020
Percent of *PVR*	0	4	6	8	10	6	8
Insurance	1,247	2,057	2,582	5,042	12,057	55,914	9,360
Percent of *PVR*	22	11	6	7	9	12	9
Wife							
Earnings	67	973	2,044	5,981	12,271	11,864	7,804
Percent of *PVR*	1	5	5	8	9	3	7
Benefits	922	3,348	6,354	9,506	12,154	11,389	9,824
Percent of *PVR*	16	18	16	13	9	2	9
Survivor benefits	571	1,531	2,818	3,551	3,505	4,133	3,348
Percent of *PVR*	10	8	7	5	3	1	3
Insurance	251	487	687	1,018	1,419	1,260	1,103
Percent of *PVR*	4	3	2	1	1	0	1
Couple							
Net worth	1,825	3,803	8,484	16,329	44,975	352,834	39,849
Percent of *PVR*	32	21	21	22	32	75	37
PVR	5,751	18,472	40,715	75,163	139,905	470,978	108,886

Source: Authors' calculations from 1969 Retirement History Survey (RHS) data. Data were aggregated by *PVR* class.
a. The numbers of observations are in parentheses.

Annuity Ratios

Table 11.2 compares the annuity that actual surviving wives could purchase in 1971 with the corresponding annuity they could have purchased in 1969 when their husbands were alive (with it assumed, as stated earlier, that an annuity of equal amount was purchased for their husbands). In tables 11.2–11.7 the assumption of perfect insurance is maintained; hence the annuity ratios are based on discounting by both mortality and interest rates. Over one-third of surviving spouses are unable to afford an annuity as large as 75 percent of the annuity that was affordable while the deceased spouse was alive. For 15 percent of the sample, the affordable annuity is less than half of what could have been purchased (under the assumption of perfect insurance) before the death of a spouse. At the other extreme, a sizable fraction of widows appear economically better off after the death of their husbands. For over a quarter of the sample of surviving widows, the annuity affordable in 1971 is over 25 percent larger than the annuity affordable in 1969.

Table 11.3 presents similar calculations for men who were actually widowed between 1969 and 1971. Although the sample of such men is small, it appears that the percentage of widowers who experienced a large drop in consumable resources after the death of their wives is smaller than the corresponding figure for widows. Only 13 percent of the widowers have annuity ratios less than 0.75, and 30 percent have ratios greater than 1.25.

Table 11.4 considers the entire 1969 sample of households and compares the annuity that a wife could have purchased at the time of the RHS interview with the annuity that she could have puchased had her husband died immediately after the interview. This distribution of hypothetical widows by their annuity ratios is quite similar to that in table 11.2. About 25 percent of the sample have an annuity ratio below 0.75; almost 50 percent have a ratio less than 1.00. A sizable fraction, 33 percent, have an annuity ratio above 1.25.

A dramatically different situation obtains for hypothetical widowers (table 11.5). Only 2 percent have annuity ratios below 0.75; 95 percent of these men have ratios above 1.00, and 73 percent have ratios above 1.50. Clearly there is little reason for concern about inadequate life insurance for wives in this sample.

Another way of examining the adequacy of insurance coverage is to limit the investigation to those couples for whom substantial

Table 11.2
Widows' annuity ratios, 1971

Fraction of potential 1969 annuity	PVR class (1969 dollars)[a]						
	<10,000	10,000–25,000	25,000–50,000	50,000–100,000	100,000–250,000	250,000+	Total
	(5)	(5)	(19)	(42)	(16)	(2)	(89)
<0.10							
Number	0	0	0	0	1	0	1
Percent	0	0	0	0	6	0	1
0.10–0.25							
Number	0	0	0	1	0	1	2
Percent	0	0	0	2	0	50	2
0.25–0.50							
Number	1	0	1	4	5	0	11
Percent	20	0	5	10	31	0	12
0.50–0.75							
Number	0	1	5	10	2	1	19
Percent	0	20	26	24	13	50	21
0.75–1.00							
Number	1	1	5	12	3	0	22
Percent	20	20	26	29	19	0	25
1.00–1.25							
Number	0	1	2	7	1	0	11
Percent	0	20	11	17	6	0	12
1.25–1.50							
Number	0	0	3	3	3	0	9
Percent	0	0	16	7	19	0	10
1.50–1.75							
Number	0	0	0	3	0	0	3
Percent	0	0	0	7	0	0	3
1.75–2.00							
Number	1	0	0	2	1	0	4
Percent	20	0	0	5	6	0	4
>2.00							
Number	2	2	3	0	0	0	7
Percent	40	40	16	0	0	0	8

Source: Authors' calculations from 1969 and 1971 RHS data.
a. The numbers of observations are in parentheses.

Table 11.3
Widowers' annuity ratios, 1971

Fraction of potential 1969 annuity	PVR class (1969 dollars)[a]						
	<10,000	10,000–25,000	25,000–50,000	50,000–100,000	100,000–250,000	250,000+	Total
	(0)	(6)	(7)	(21)	(13)	(0)	(47)
<0.10							
Number	0	0	0	0	0	0	0
Percent	0	0	0	0	0	0	0
0.10–0.25							
Number	0	0	0	0	1	0	1
Percent	0	0	0	0	8	0	2
0.25–0.50							
Number	0	0	0	0	1	0	1
Percent	0	0	0	0	8	0	2
0.50–0.75							
Number	0	0	0	3	1	0	4
Percent	0	0	0	14	8	0	9
0.75–1.00							
Number	0	1	2	8	2	0	13
Percent	0	17	29	38	15	0	28
1.00–1.25							
Number	0	2	2	6	4	0	14
Percent	0	33	29	29	31	0	30
1.25–1.50							
Number	0	1	0	3	4	0	8
Percent	0	17	0	14	31	0	17
1.50–1.75							
Number	0	1	1	0	0	0	2
Percent	0	17	14	0	0	0	4
1.75–2.00							
Number	0	0	0	0	0	0	0
Percent	0	0	0	0	0	0	0
>2.00							
Number	0	1	2	1	0	0	4
Percent	0	17	29	5	0	0	9

Source: Authors' calculations from 1969 and 1971 RHS data.
a. The numbers of observations are in parentheses.

Table 11.4
Wives' annuity ratios if husbands die, 1969

Fraction of potential 1969 annuity	PVR class (1969 dollars)[a] <10,000 (55)	10,000–25,000 (179)	25,000–50,000 (714)	50,000–100,000 (2,040)	100,000–250,000 (1,922)	250,000+ (221)	Total (5,131)
<0.10							
Number	1	0	5	1	0	0	7
Percent	2	0	1	0	0	0	0
0.10–0.25							
Number	0	4	9	10	3	1	27
Percent	0	2	1	0	0	0	1
0.25–0.50							
Number	3	19	75	155	83	1	336
Percent	5	11	11	8	4	0	7
0.50–0.75							
Number	13	42	156	391	280	4	886
Percent	24	23	22	19	15	2	17
0.75–1.00							
Number	7	35	183	514	418	9	1,166
Percent	13	20	26	25	22	4	23
1.00–1.25							
Number	3	8	131	458	478	16	1,094
Percent	5	4	18	22	25	7	21
1.25–1.50							
Number	6	18	56	306	329	29	744
Percent	11	10	8	15	17	13	15
1.50–1.75							
Number	4	15	37	114	213	56	439
Percent	7	8	5	6	11	25	9
1.75–2.00							
Number	8	11	23	57	83	70	252
Percent	15	6	3	3	4	32	5
>2.00							
Number	10	27	39	34	35	35	180
Percent	18	15	5	2	2	16	4

Source: Authors' calculations from 1969 RHS data.
a. The numbers of observations are in parentheses.

Table 11.5
Husbands' annuity ratios if wives die, 1969

Fraction of potential 1969 annuity	PVR class (1969 dollars)[a]						
	<10,000	10,000–25,000	25,000–50,000	50,000–100,000	100,000–250,000	250,000+	Total
	(0)	(6)	(7)	(21)	(13)	(0)	(47)
annuity	(55)	(179)	(714)	(2,040)	(1,922)	(221)	(5,131)
<0.10							
Number	1	2	3	0	0	0	6
Percent	2	1	0	0	0	0	0
0.10–0.25							
Number	1	2	0	3	0	0	6
Percent	2	1	0	0	0	0	0
0.25–0.50							
Number	2	3	12	8	2	1	28
Percent	4	2	2	0	0	0	1
0.50–0.75							
Number	0	6	9	39	8	1	63
Percent	0	3	1	2	0	0	1
0.75–1.00							
Number	0	7	29	76	30	0	142
Percent	0	4	4	4	2	0	3
1.00–1.25							
Number	4	22	58	133	116	1	334
Percent	7	12	8	7	6	0	7
1.25–1.50							
Number	11	37	151	313	256	3	771
Percent	20	21	21	15	13	1	15
1.50–1.75							
Number	16	46	217	596	457	23	1,355
Percent	29	26	30	29	24	10	26
1.75–2.00							
Number	5	30	158	634	621	63	1,511
Percent	9	17	22	31	32	29	29
>2.00							
Number	15	24	77	238	432	129	915
Percent	27	13	11	12	22	58	18

Source: Authors' calculations from 1969 RHS data.
a. The numbers of observations are in parentheses.

insurance would be needed to keep a surviving spouse from suffering a large drop in consumable resources. This approach would exclude couples with most of their wealth held in current net worth, since the death of a spouse in such cases would have little effect on the total family resources (excluding insurance) available to the survivor. We therefore repeat in tables 11.6 and 11.7 the calculations done for tables 11.4 and 11.5, this time for the subsamples of husbands and wives who are "at risk," which we define as those for whom the other spouse's survival-contingent resources (labor earnings, pension benefits, and social security benefits) constitute over half of the couple's total resources.

By this measure, over half of the wives in the full sample are at risk. Of this group, over 45 percent have an annuity ratio of less than 0.75 (table 11.6). For wives and husbands at risk who are in poorer households, the extent of underinsurance is more significant. Consider, for example, wives at risk in households with a *PVR* of \$25,000–\$50,000 (table 11.6). Fifty-five percent of this group have an annuity ratio below 0.75, and 20 percent have a ratio below 0.50. Table 11.7 indicates that 28 percent of husbands at risk have hypothetical annuity ratios below 0.75. The number of husbands at risk, however, is small. These results reinforce the finding that underinsurance, particularly of husbands, is potentially a quite serious problem.

Potential Biases in Calculation of Annuity Ratios

Six sources of potential bias can affect the calculation of the annuity ratios. Each of these sources is examined below in turn.

Ignoring Cash Value of Life Insurance

To see how excluding the unobserved cash value of life insurance affects the results in tables 11.4 and 11.5, consider again equations (1) and (2). For hypothetical surviving wives, PVR_m is too small by an amount equal to the cash value of the husband's and wife's insurance, whereas PVR_s, which includes the face value and thus the cash value of the insurance on the deceased spouse's life (F_d), is too small by an amount equal to only the cash value of the surviving spouse's insurance. Because the average value of insurance on the husband's life is over eight times larger than that on his wife's, one would expect the cash value of the husband's insurance to exceed greatly that of the wife's. As a consequence, the omission of cash value implies

Table 11.6
Wives' annuity ratios if husbands die, wives at risk, 1969

Fraction of potential 1969 annuity	PVR class (1969 dollars)[a]						
	<10,000	10,000–25,000	25,000–50,000	50,000–100,000	100,000–250,000	250,000+	Total
	(28)	(99)	(446)	(1,201)	(972)	(30)	(2,776)
<0.10							
Number	1	0	5	1	0	0	7
Percent	4	0	1	0	0	0	0
0.10–0.25							
Number	0	4	9	10	3	1	27
Percent	0	4	2	1	0	3	1
0.25–0.50							
Number	3	19	75	155	83	1	336
Percent	11	19	17	13	9	3	12
0.50–0.75							
Number	13	42	156	391	280	4	886
Percent	46	42	35	33	29	13	32
0.75–1.00							
Number	7	25	152	454	376	7	1,021
Percent	25	25	34	38	39	23	37
1.00–1.25							
Number	2	3	35	146	171	8	365
Percent	7	3	8	12	18	27	13
1.25–1.50							
Number	0	4	7	36	41	5	93
Percent	0	4	2	3	4	17	3
1.50–1.75							
Number	1	2	5	3	9	1	21
Percent	4	2	1	0	1	3	1
1.75–2.00							
Number	0	0	0	2	6	2	10
Percent	0	0	0	0	1	7	0
>2.00							
Number	1	0	2	3	3	1	10
Percent	4	0	0	0	0	3	0

Source: Authors' calculations from 1969 RHS data. "At risk" refers to wives for whom the husband's survival-contingent resources constitute over half of the couple's total resources.

a. The numbers of observations are in parentheses.

Table 11.7
Husbands' annuity ratios if wives die, husbands at risk, 1969

Fraction of potential 1969 annuity	PVR class (1969 dollars)[a]						
	<10,000	10,000–25,000	25,000–50,000	50,000–100,000	100,000–250,000	250,000+	Total
	(5)	(24)	(62)	(180)	(101)	(2)	(374)
<0.10							
Number	1	2	3	0	0	0	6
Percent	20	8	5	0	0	0	2
0.10–0.25							
Number	1	2	0	3	0	0	6
Percent	20	8	0	2	0	0	2
0.25–0.50							
Number	2	3	12	8	2	1	28
Percent	40	13	19	4	2	50	7
0.50–0.75							
Number	0	6	9	39	8	1	63
Percent	0	25	15	22	4	50	17
0.75–1.00							
Number	0	7	27	74	29	0	137
Percent	0	29	44	41	29	0	37
1.00–1.25							
Number	0	4	10	52	54	0	120
Percent	0	17	16	29	53	0	32
1.25–1.50							
Number	0	0	1	3	8	0	12
Percent	0	0	2	2	8	0	3
1.50–1.75							
Number	1	0	0	1	0	0	2
Percent	20	0	0	1	0	0	1
1.75–2.00							
Number	0	0	0	0	0	0	0
Percent	0	0	0	0	0	0	0
>2.00							
Number	0	0	0	0	0	0	0
Percent	0	0	0	0	0	0	0

Source: Authors' calculations from 1969 RHS data. "At risk" refers to husbands for whom the wife's survival-contingent benefits constitute over half of the couple's total resources.

a. The numbers of observations are in parentheses.

that the ratio PVR_w/PVR_m is biased upward and that the ratio PVR_h/PVR_m is biased downward. This relation in turn implies an upward bias in the calculation of the hypothetical widows' annuity ratios (A_w/A_m) and a downward bias in the calculated annuity ratios of hypothetical widowers (A_h/A_m).

To consider the possible extent of this bias, we recalculated table 11.4 under the assumption that the cash value of husbands' and wives' insurance equals the face value; that is, that there is no term insurance. This assumption increases the fraction of hypothetical widows with annuity ratios below 0.75 from 25 percent to 27 percent. The bias with respect to the values of A_h/A_m in table 11.5 moves in the opposite direction; making the extreme assumption of no term insurance increases the annuity ratio for hypothetical widowers. Again the potential bias is small; the fraction of hypothetical widowers with annuity ratios above 1.50 rises from 73 percent to 74 percent.

Economies of Scale

Ignoring economies of scale in household consumption biases upward both widows' and widowers' annuity ratios, if the annuity is viewed as the level stream of consumption that can be financed. Suppose, for example, that household consumption were a pure public good. In this case the consumption stream that could be financed with A_m would equal twice the value of A_m if both spouses remain alive. For a widow with an annuity ratio of 0.75, according to this reasoning, the death of her spouse has meant a 62.5 percent [(2.0 − 0.75)/2] decline in consumption and an adjusted annuity ratio of 0.375 (0.75/2). Tables 11.2–11.7 may therefore significantly understate the potential welfare decline experienced by surviving spouses.

Bequests to Children and End-of-Life Expenses

The hypothetical annuity ratios also ignore possible bequests to children, end-of-life uninsured medical and funeral expenses, and, for those few observed households with considerable wealth, estate taxes. Inclusion of these factors would reduce the hypothetical annuity ratios below the reported values. This point is supported by the finding that the actual annuity ratios of surviving spouses (tables 11.2 and 11.3) are smaller than those of hypothetical surviving spouses (tables 11.4 and 11.5): 36 percent of actual widows, but only

25 percent of hypothetical widows, have ratios below 0.75; 13 percent of actual widowers, but only 2 percent of hypothetical widowers, have ratios below 0.75.

Valuing Future Streams if Insurance is Imperfect

The annuity distributions in tables 11.2–11.7 are quite sensitive to the assumption of perfect insurance. For example, if one discounts future streams only by the interest rate, which would be appropriate in the absence of any explicit or implicit insurance arrangement, the fraction of those hypothetical widows at risk and with inadequate insurance protection drops from over 45 percent to only 20 percent. For hypothetical widowers at risk, in contrast, the fraction with inadequate insurance protection rises from 28 percent to 40 percent. The direction of these changes reflects the fact that the discount factor for husbands relative to wives rises when discounting by only the interest rate rather than by both interest and mortality rates. Husbands in the sample are older and have higher age-specific death rates than their wives. Although we mention this alternative assumption to permit the reader to draw his or her own conclusion, in our view the calculations based on the assumption of close-to-perfect insurance arrangements better approximate the insurance environment of the RHS sample.

Income Taxes and Choice of Real Interest Rate

In calculating the annuity ratios we did not attempt to estimate taxes that would be paid on earning and pension streams. Nor did we estimate the marginal effective income tax rate to form an after-tax rate of return for discounting future income streams. We believe that these adjustments taken together would lower the annuity ratios. Present-value calculations of this kind are highly sensitive to the choice of discount rate. Realistic inclusion of tax factors would lead to discounting by an after-tax real rate of return substantially below 4 percent, which would raise considerably the present values of those income streams that would be lost in the event of a spouse's death. Because the ratio of discount factors for husbands and wives, D_h/D_w, is a decreasing function of the discount rate, and if the husband is older than the wife, adjusting for taxes would lower the annuity ratios of widows by more than it would for surviving husbands.

Uncertainty of Earnings

The calculations of annuity ratios assume that future real earnings are certain. The exception is the uncertainty that death poses for earnings. Although we have not closely examined the bias from ignoring other kinds of uncertainty in earnings, we believe that, roughly speaking, uncertain future earnings should be discounted by a risk-adjusted discount rate—a rate that could well be higher than the 4 percent real rate used here. Hence, by ignoring earnings uncertainty, we are probably biasing downward the calculated annuity ratios and, on this score, exaggerating somewhat the need for additional life insurance.

A Model of Life Insurance Demand

This section develops an estimable model of the demand for life insurance by married couples under the assumption of expected utility maximization. The model focuses on the life-cycle consumption of husbands and wives and ignores possible parental bequest motives and longevity risk sharing between parents and children. It also ignores uncertainty in earnings. The purposes of estimating a model of life insurance demand are twofold: first, to determine whether the actual purchase of life insurance is in general accord with the predictions of economic theory; second, to determine the extent to which households reduce their purchase of private life insurance in response to provision of social security survivor insurance. If insurance on the husband's life is assumed to be positive, theory predicts that properly valued income streams of the wife—including her labor earnings, public and private pension benefits, and survivor benefits—should substitute at the margin, dollar for dollar, for the insurance on her husband's life. Similar arbitrage relationships should hold at the margin between the wife's insurance and the properly valued income streams of the husband.

Life insurance transfers income across states of nature and thereby alters the amounts that can be consumed in those different states. The optimal choice of life insurance is thus determined simultaneously with the optimal choice of desired consumption in those states. If insurance markets are complete and actuarially fair, life insurance will be purchased (or sold) up to the point at which the marginal utility of consumption is equalized across each state of nature. Deviation of insurance pricing from actuarially fair values changes the effective prices of consuming in different states of nature and implies differences in the marginal utility of consumption across those different states. These points are illustrated in the equations below.

Our model has two periods. During the first, both the husband and wife are alive. During the second period there are four states of nature, corresponding to only the husband surviving, only the wife surviving, both surviving, and neither surviving. We denote consumption in the first period as C; consumption in the three states in which at least one member of the couple survives is denoted as C_h, C_w, and C_{hw}, respectively. In the first period and in state hw, in which both spouses are alive, *each* spouse separately consumes the amount C and C_{hw}, respectively. If there are no economies of scale, the couple spends $2C$ and $2C_{hw}$ in the first period and in the hw state, respectively. If consumption by a married couple is a pure public good, the couple spends only C and C_{hw} in the two states, although each spouse still consumes C and, if they both survive, C_{hw}. The couple's expected utility maximization problem is therefore

$$\max[p_h(1-p_w)U(C,C_h) + (1-p_h)p_wU(C,C_w) + p_hp_wU(C,C_{hw}) + (1-p_h)(1-p_w)U(C,0)], \tag{3}$$

where p_s is the probability that spouse s survives, and s equals h or w.

If both the husband and wife purchase positive amounts of life insurance, then the following equations constrain the choice of consumption in the three states of nature in which at least one member of the couple survives:

$$C_h = E_h + B_h + F_w + (A - \lambda C - \pi_h F_h - \pi_w F_w)(1+r) \tag{4h}$$

$$C_w = E_w + B_w + B_w^* + F_h + (A - \lambda C - \pi_h F_h - \pi_w F_w)(1+r) \tag{4w}$$

$$\lambda C_{hw} = E_w + B_w + E_h + B_h + (A - \lambda C - \pi_h F_h - \pi_w F_w)(1+r), \tag{4hw}$$

where A is the couple's tangible wealth in the first period, F_s is the face value of insurance purchased for spouse s, π_s is the corresponding premium paid per dollar for face value in the first period, E_s is wages of spouse s in the second period, B_s is the spouse's social security and pension benefits, and B_w^* is the survivor benefits to which the wife is entitled in the event of the husband's death. The terms r and λ are prices: r is the first-period interest rate, and λ is the price of second-period joint consumption. If λ equals 2, there are no economies of scale in consumption; if λ equals 1, household consumption is a pure public good.

These budget constraints are written under the assumptions that husbands will not be entitled to survivor benefits and that all private insurance is term insurance. The former assumption is consistent with observations in the sample. The second is more problematic. To the extent that policies are "whole-life" and not term policies, they will have a cash or asset value corresponding to the insurance policy's previous savings component, or "inside build-up." A whole-life policy may be viewed as a combination of a savings account with liquid assets equal to the policy's cash value and a term insurance policy with a death benefit equal to the difference between the policy's face value and cash value. If we knew how much cash value each policy had, we would subtract this amount from the face value F in equations (4) and add it to A. Unfortunately, no such information is available. We defer further discussion of this data problem until the empirical implementation of the model is considered.

In the case of positive insurance purchases for both spouses, we may use expressions (4h), (4w) and (4hw) to eliminate F_h and F_w, thus obtaining a single expression in consumption levels that may be interpreted as the household budget constraint:

$$\begin{aligned}\lambda C + \pi_h C_h + \pi_w C_w + \lambda[1/(1+r) - \pi_h - \pi_w]C_{hw} \\ = A + (E_h + B_h)[1/(1+r) - \pi_h] + (E_w + B_w)[1/(1+r) - \pi_w] + \pi_h B_w^*,\end{aligned} \tag{5}$$

where λ, π_h, π_w and $\lambda[1/(1+r) - \pi_h - \pi_w]$ are the "prices" of the four consumption levels, and the right-hand side is a weighted sum of the different resource components. We assume that insurance is actuarially fair:

$$\pi_h = (1 - p_w)/(1+r); \quad \pi_w = (1 - p_h)/(1+r). \tag{6}$$

Combination of expressions (5) and (6) yields a simpler and more intuitive version of the budget constraint:

$$\begin{aligned}\lambda C + [(1 - p_w)/(1+r)]C_h + [(1 - p_h)/(1+r)]C_w \\ + \lambda[p_h p_w - (1 - p_h)(1 - p_w)]/(1+r)]C_{hw} \\ = A + [p_h/(1+r)](E_h + B_h) + [p_w/(1+r)](E_w + B_w) \\ + [(1 - p_h)/(1+r)]B_w^*.\end{aligned} \tag{7}$$

Note how this result differs from what would obtain in the presence of complete and actuarially fair markets for annuities and life insurance, which would permit state-contingent purchases of consumption. In that case, the present value of resources would equal the sum of the expected values, based on the associated survival probabilities, of each of the components of wealth. The right-hand side of equation (7) differs from the present expected value of resources in that the survivor benefit B_w^* is multiplied only by the husband's death probability rather than by the product of his death probability and the wife's survival probability. This difference is because, without the availability of private annuities, resources that are available when the husband and wife both die are of no value. Put another way, the survivor benefit has the value it would have if it also paid off when both the husband and the wife die.

The implicit prices for second-period, state-contingent consumption also differ from those in the case of complete, actuarially fair insurance markets. The prices for C_h and C_w are higher, representing the fact that, in states in which one spouse dies, the household must commit resources regardless of whether the remaining spouse actually lives. This fact also makes the price of consumption lower in the state in which both spouses survive. The intuition is that, by providing resources for the state in which both live, the household reduces the amount it must waste in the state when both die; that is, increased expenditures for C_{hw} also increase consumption in the states in which one member of the couple survives, so that fewer direct expenditures are necessary.

Expected utility maximization by the household of equation (3) subject to budget constraint (7) leads to an optimal consumption vector that is a function of the implicit prices and the present value of resources given by the right-hand side of budget constraint (7). We label these prices q and the present value of resources PVR. Next, we derive expressions for the demands for life insurance. Subtracting expression (4hw) from (4w) yields

$$F_h = (C_w - \lambda C_{hw}) + (E_h + B_h - B_w^*). \tag{8h}$$

From expressions (4h) and (4hw) we obtain

$$F_w = (C_h - \lambda C_{hw}) + (E_w + B_w). \tag{8w}$$

Each expression has a clear interpretation, calling for the purchase of insurance for the husband or wife equal to the net loss in resources if that spouse dies plus the additional consumption that must be financed. The latter term may well be negative, depending on the value of λ and the tastes of the household.

Substituting the optimal consumption demands in expressions (8h) and (8w) yields demand functions for insurance:

$$F_h = H(q, PVR) + (E_h + B_h - B_w^*) \tag{9h}$$

$$F_w = W(q, PVR) + (E_w + B_w), \tag{9w}$$

where $H(\ )$ and $W(\ )$ are the consumption demands for C_h and C_w in excess of joint consumption expenditures when both spouses survive (that is, $C_w - \lambda C_{hw}$ and $C_h - \lambda C_{hw}$, respectively).

Equations (9h) and (9w) are appropriate only when both F_h and F_w are positive, since by assumption neither F_h nor F_w can be negative. We next consider situations in which one or both spouses are constrained at zero in the purchase of life insurance. In such situations the couple faces an optimization problem of reduced dimension, with different implicit prices for consumption and different weights used to calculate *PVR*. For example, suppose that the value of F_w satisfying equation (9w) is negative, requiring that it be constrained to zero. Then, in place of expression (8w) we have

$$0 = (C_h - \lambda C_{hw}) + (E_w + B_w), \tag{8w$'$}$$

which implies that the family can no longer independently determine C_h and C_{hw}. Substituting this restriction into expression (7) obtains a new budget constraint that omits C_{hw}:

$$\begin{aligned}\lambda C &+ [p_h/(1+r)]C_h + [(1-p_h)/(1+r)]C_w \\ &= A + [p_h/(1+r)](E_h + B_h) + [(1-p_h)/(1+r)](E_w + B_w + B_w^*).\end{aligned} \tag{7w$'$}$$

Note that the implicit price of the husband's consumption is now the probability of his own survival, rather than the probability of his wife's death. Similarly, the wife's wages and benefits are no longer weighted by her survival probability, but by her husband's death probability. Because only the husband may buy insurance, his insurance decision determines the allocation of resources between C_h and C_w, and the cost of this insurance determines the relative prices of these states of consumption. Because the wife cannot transfer resources to her husband through insurance, her survival probability does not enter into the budget constraint.

Letting q_h and PVR_h be the implicit price vector and present value of resources given by the right-hand side of equation (7w′), we obtain from equation (8h) the husband's demand for life insurance when his wife is constrained at zero life insurance:

$$F_h = H(q_h, PVR_h) + (E_h + B_h - B_w^*). \tag{9h′}$$

In an analogous fashion, we may derive prices q_w and the present value of resources PVR_w for the case in which the husband's insurance is constrained to equal zero and obtain the wife's insurance demand function:

$$F_w = W(q_w, PVR_w) + (E_w + B_w). \tag{9w′}$$

Four possible demand regimes therefore exist:

- husband and wife unconstrained,

$$F_h = H(q, PVR) + (E_h + B_h - B_w^*)$$

$$F_w = W(q, PVR) + (E_w + B_w);$$

- husband unconstrained but wife constrained,

$$F_h = H(q_h, PVR_h) + (E_h + B_h - B_w^*)$$

$$F_w = 0;$$

- wife unconstrained but husband constrained,

$$F_h = 0$$

$$F_w = W(q_w, PVR_w) + (E_w + B_w);$$

- both spouses constrained,

$$F_h = 0$$

$$F_w = 0.$$

Estimation of the demand for insurance across these regimes involves a switching-regressions model with censored dependent variables. We discuss different estimation strategies in the next section.

A problem involved in estimating the insurance demand functions (9h), (9h′), (9w), and (9w′) is that the RHS data do not report term insurance, which corresponds to F_h and F_w in the equations, but only the face value of insurance. An alternative approach that is robust for this particular problem is to estimate expressions (4h) and (4w) directly. Rearranging terms in equation (4w) and substituting in the demands for consumption, we obtain

$$F_h + (A - \pi_h F_h - \pi_w F_w)(1 + r) = \hat{H}(q, PVR) - (E_w + B_w + B^*_w), \qquad (10h)$$

where $\hat{H}(\,)$ is the expenditure on first-period consumption times $1 + r$ plus the wife's second-period consumption when widowed; that is, $\lambda C(1 + r) + C_w$. If we ignore the insurance premiums or assume that assets are measured net of insurance premiums, and assume that interest rates are small, then we have in equation (10h) an expression for the sum of insurance on the husband's life plus family assets, which does not require separation of the cash value from the term value of insurance. Equation (4h) provides a corresponding expression (10w) for F_w:

$$F_w + (A - \pi_h F_h - \pi_w F_w)(1 + r) = \hat{W}(q, PVR) - (E_h + B_h). \qquad (10w)$$

As with the previous insurance demand equations, to estimate this model consistently one must allow for different regimes in which the husband's or wife's insurance demand may be constrained to zero. When the wife's insurance is zero but the husband's is positive, $\hat{H}(q, PVR)$ is replaced by $\hat{H}(q_h, PVR_h)$; when the husband's insurance is zero but the wife's is positive, the function $\hat{W}(q, PVR)$ is replaced by $\hat{W}(q_w, PVR_w)$.

Econometric Specification

The model presented in the previous section can be specified as set forth below.

A Two-Indicator, Switching-Regression Model

Let I_h and I_w be zero-one indicators for zero versus positive values of the husband's and wife's insurance, respectively, and expressed as

$$\begin{aligned} I_h &= -c_h + \mu_h \\ I_w &= -c_w + \mu_w \end{aligned} \qquad (11)$$

where μ_h and μ_w are errors with zero means, and the critical values c_h and c_w and linear combinations of vectors of observable economic and demographic characteristics X_h and X_w:

$$c_h = -B_h X_h$$
$$c_w = -B_w X_w. \tag{12}$$

In equations (12), B_h and B_w are coefficient vectors. Referring to discussion of equations (9) and (10), we express the choices of F_h and F_w in the four possible regimes as follows:

- if $I_h > 0$ and $I_w > 0$,

$$F_h = \gamma_h Z_h + \varepsilon_h$$
$$F_w = \gamma_w Z_w + \varepsilon_w; \tag{13}$$

- if $I_h > 0$ and $I_w \leq 0$,

$$F_h = \theta_h Z_h' + \psi_h$$
$$F_w = 0; \tag{14}$$

- if $I_h \leq 0$ and $I_w > 0$,

$$F_h = 0$$
$$F_w = \theta_w Z_w' + \psi_w; \tag{15}$$

- if $I_h \leq 0$ and $I_w \leq 0$,

$$F_h = 0$$
$$F_w = 0. \tag{16}$$

In equations (13)–(15), Z_h, Z_w, Z_h', and Z_w' are vectors of explanatory variables, and γ_h, γ_w, θ_h, and θ_w are coefficient vectors. We assume that the six error terms—μ_h, μ_w, ε_h, ε_w, ψ_h, and ψ_w—have zero means and are distributed joint-normally. The elements of the covariance matrix of this distribution are denoted by σ_{ij}, where i, j references μ_h, μ_w, ε_h, ε_w, ψ_h, ψ_w.

Estimation Strategy

We can consistently estimate the econometric model represented by equations (11)–(16) by first estimating the choice of regimes (equations (11) and (12)) with a bivariate probit and then using the results of this probit to correct for sample selection in the regressions for the levels of F_h and F_w in equations (13)–(15). The appropriate Mills-ratio factors to correct selection bias differ in this case from those suggested by Heckman because the ones used here are based on a bivariate error process.[9] To illustrate the appropriate Mills-ratio formula, consider estimating the regression for F_h in equation (13). As derived in the appendix to this paper, the expected value of ε_h—given that $I_h > 0$ and $I_w > 0$—is

$$E(\varepsilon/I_h > 0, I_w > 0) = E(\varepsilon_h/\mu_h > c_h, \mu_w > c_w)$$
$$= \frac{[1 - F(c_h)][1 - F(c_w)]}{1 - \phi(c_h, c_w)}$$
$$\cdot [E(\varepsilon_h/\mu_h > c_h) + E(\varepsilon_h/\mu_w > c_w)]. \quad (17)$$

In equation (17), $F(\ )$ is the cumulative normal function, and $\phi(\ )$ is the bivariate cumulative normal function. The last bracketed term on the right-hand side of equation (17) contains the two univariate Mills ratios. If μ_h and μ_w were independent, the term $1 - \phi(c_h, c_w)$ would equal $[1 - F(c_h)][1 - F(c_w)]$, and equation (17) would reduce to the sum of two separate Mills ratios. In this case one could run two separate probits for $I_h > 0$ and $I_w > 0$ to form $E(\varepsilon_h/\mu_h > c_h)$ and $E(\varepsilon_h/\mu_w > c_w)$. When μ_h and μ_w are not independent, however, the term $\phi(c_h, c_w)$ must be estimated from a bivariate probit.

Empirical Results

In this section we report estimates for husbands' and wives' life insurance demands for the two models described in the previous section. We used Green's LEMDEP routine to estimate the model.[10] LEMDEP correctly calculates standard errors in the selection equations. The results are given in table 11.8 for husbands and in table 11.9 for wives.

Of the 5,110 total observations in the sample, there were 3,251 households in which both spouses had insurance, 1,024 households in which only the husband had insurance, 128 households in which only the wife had insurance, and 707 households in which neither family member had positive insurance.

We examined first the results for husbands' life insurance demands. We looked at two samples of households in which the husband's insurance was positive: those in which wives also purchased positive amounts of insurance, and those in which wives

Table 11.8
Husband's insurance demand, positive levels only

	Model 1[b]		Model 2[c]	
Variable[a]	Wife's insurance > 0 (3,251)	Wife's insurance = 0 (1,024)	Wife's insurance > 0 (3,251)	Wife's insurance = 0 (1,024)
Constant	−16,425 (−10,130)	−53,467 (−32,660)	−16,030 (−13,360)	−427,320 (−163,300)
Husband earnings	−0.0232 (−0.0428)	0.656 (0.1231)	. . .	. . .
Social security benefits	−0.0254 (−0.05018)	0.327 (0.157)	. . .	. . .
Pension	−0.02363 (−0.02266)	0.288 (0.075)	. . .	. . .
$PVR(h)^2$	−0.00387 (−0.00073)	0.0043 (0.0015)	−0.0039 (−0.00073)	0.0063 (0.0015)
$PVR(h)^3$	0.0000288 (0.0000062)	−0.00005 (−0.00001)	0.000028 (0.0000062)	−0.000065 (−0.000011)
Age	−725.16 (−194.7)	−99.69 (−557.3)	−608.54 (−321.7)	3,352.3 (1,614)
Age × $PVR(w)$	0.66259 (0.1040)	−0.70 (−0.209)	0.692 (0.93)	0.299 (0.179)
Mills ratio	6.2033 (0.65)	4.07 (0.86)	5.647 (0.97)	−8.477 (−3.8)
Wife earnings	. . .	. . .	−0.05 (−0.038)	−0.35 (−0.1611)
Social security benefits	. . .	. . .	−0.0405 (−0.3329)	−4.39 (−1.624)
Survivor benefits	−0.04199 (−0.07210)	−0.349 (−0.205)	0.0697 (0.0661)	−0.434 (−0.196)
$PVR(w)$	−0.18159 (−0.04930)	0.299 (0.1214)	−0.1901 (−0.0339)	−0.212 (−0.97)
Age	397.97 (103.50)	627.7 (231.3)	395.28 (156.3)	1,738.7 (538.3)
Age × $PVR(h)$	0.4926 (0.7846)	−0.26 (−0.153)	−0.014 (−0.0815)	0.022 (0.1513)
Mills ratio	2.9189 (0.36)	2.05 (0.68)	1.9127 (1.97)	−15.206 (−5.8)
Net worth	. . .	. . .	0.0356 (0.207)	0.029 (0.065)
$\bar{R}^2$	0.28	0.32	0.29	0.31

Source: Authors' calculations. The numbers in parentheses in the body of the table are standard errors.
a. Symbols h and w denote husband and wife.
b. Model 1 is based on equation 9h. The numbers of observations are in parentheses.
c. Model 2 is based on equation 10h. The numbers of observations are in parentheses.

Table 11.9
Wife's insurance demand, positive levels only

	Model 1[b]		Model 2[c]	
Variable[a]	Husband's insurance > 0 (3,251)	Husband's insurance = 0 (128)	Husband's insurance > 0 (3,251)	Husband's insurance = 0 (128)
Constant	871.9 (3,557)	−30,244 (−25,900)	8,140 (2,420)	12,266 (10,810)
Husband earnings	. . .	. . .	−0.47 (−0.019)	−0.41 (−0.17)
Social security benefits	. . .	. . .	−0.0079 (−0.025)	−0.44 (−0.19)
Pension	. . .	. . .	−0.0062 (−0.1777)	−0.32 (−0.107)
$PVR(h)$	0.081 (0.021)	0.43 (0.1)	−0.038 (−0.018)	−0.125 (−0.070)
Age	−87.3 (−81.9)	430 (447)	−77.802 (−48.0)	−277 (−194)
Age × $PVR(w)$	−0.116 (−0.04)	−0.6 (−0.18)	0.093 (0.020)	0.166 (0.082)
Mills ratio	0.901 (0.228)	−0.19 (−1.04)	−0.065 (−0.159)	−0.127 (−1.168)
Wife earnings	0.122 (0.019)	0.41 (0.093)	. . .	. . .
Social security benefits	0.207 (0.077)	−0.27 (−0.45)	. . .	. . .
Survivor benefits	. . .	. . .	. . .	. . .
$PVR(w)^2$	−0.0002 (−0.00017)	−0.00058 (−0.0012)	−0.2E-03 (−0.17E-03)	−0.0026 (−0.0028)
$PVR(w)^3$	0.24E-05 (0.15E-05)	−0.22E-05 (−0.2E-05)	−0.22E-05 (−0.15E-05)	0.71E-04 (0.62E-04)
Age	−93.7 (−34.7)	13.9 (147)	−15.8 (−24.5)	−176 (−199)
Age × $PVR(h)$	0.012 (0.018)	−0.07 (−0.08)	−0.010 (−0.019)	−0.12 (−0.086)
Mills ratio	1.3 (0.46)	−0.38 (−1.56)	0.333 (0.120)	−0.581 (−0.812)
Net worth	. . .	. . .	0.0075 (0.0179)	−0.179 (−0.061)
$\bar{R}^2$	0.16	0.58	0.15	0.54

Source: Authors' calculations. The numbers in parentheses in the body of the table are standard errors.

a. Symbols *h* and *w* denote husband and wife.

b. Model 1 is based on equation 9w. The numbers of observations are in parentheses.

c. Model 2 is based on equation 10w. The numbers of observations are in parentheses.

purchased no insurance. The first two columns is table 11.8 present estimates for model 1, based on equation (9h), for the two samples. The last two columns present estimates for model 2, based on equation (10h). Recall that the second model may be preferred because it does not require distinguishing between the cash and face value of insurance. In all cases, we included *PVR*, the present value of family resources, PVR^2, PVR^3, the husband's and wife's age, and interaction terms between these ages and *PVR* to account for the consumption demand functions $H(\ )$ and $\hat{H}(\ )$. The ages are meant to proxy for the survival probabilities that determine the state-contingent prices of consumption. The terms q_w defined by the right-hand side of equation (9h), and q_h, defined by the right-hand side of equation (9h′), were used for the regime under which the husband's demand is unconstrained but the wife's demand is constrained.[11]

Consider first the results for model 1 in table 11.8. To evaluate the performance of the model, note that the components of husbands' receipts should each have a coefficient of 1, the survivor benefits a coefficient of −1. Each of these independent variables is calculated as the present expected value of the relevant income stream. For the sample in which the wife's insurance is positive, the coefficients of the husband's earnings, social security, and pension benefits have the wrong sign, whereas survivor benefits have the right sign but are over seven standard deviations from −1. The results are somewhat better in the sample in which the wife's insurance is zero; these coefficients, albeit positive and significant, are nevertheless significantly below 1. For this sample the wife's survivor benefits have the wrong sign. The two bivariate Mills ratios are highly significant for both samples. Note that the standard errors of the coefficients tend, in general, to be quite small, thus implying a fairly precise rejection of the theoretical model.

The estimates for model 2 in table 11.8 are not much closer to those predicted by the theoretical model. The model predicts that the wife's social security benefits, survivor benefits, and earnings should all enter with a coefficient of −1; in the two subsamples only four of the eight coefficients have the correct negative sign, and only two are significant. The large −4.39 coefficient in the $F_w = 0$ regression in model 2 for the wife's social security benefits is hard to take seriously in light of the other results. The net worth variable (A) is positive in both samples, although quite small in absolute value; recall that its predicted value is −1. The overall goodness of fit for model 2 is quite similar to that for model 1.

Table 11.9 presents estimates for the analogous two models of wives' life insurance demands. (Models 1 and 2 in table are based on equations (9w) and (10w), respectively.) The two samples considered (all for wives who had positive life insurance) were for husbands who had insurance and husbands who had no insurance. The second sample was quite small, as one would expect—only 128 households.

In the two models in table 11.9 the components of husbands' and wives' earnings and benefits enter with the correct signs in eight of ten cases, and seven of these eight coefficients are significant. None of these coefficients, however, is close to 1 in absolute value. As in table 11.8, standard errors are typically quite small. The results for model 2 in which the husbands have zero insurance come closest to the theoretical prediction. For this sample each of the husband's streams, as well as net worth, has a negative coefficient as predicted, and each of these coefficients is significant.

Conclusions

A significant minority of elderly households appears to have inadequate life insurance. In addition, estimates of life insurance demand functions are to a great extent at odds with theoretical predictions. There appears to be little systematic response of private life insurance holdings to social security's provision of survivor benefits; hence social security is apparently effective in raising the welfare of widows and widowers through its provision of survivor insurance.

The poor econometric results make us skeptical about the usefulness of the RHS data for estimating sophisticated econometric models that describe the patterns of asset accumulation in households.

Given the significant poverty rates among elderly widows, this paper suggests the need for a reevaluation of the appropriate size of survivor benefits relative to retirement benefits under the social security system. It also suggests that poverty among elderly widows could be reduced by government programs to increase the public's purchase of private life insurance.

Appendix: Derivation of the Bivariate Mills Ratio Sample Selection Correction

Let $x = (\mu_1, \mu_2, \varepsilon) \sim \nu(0, \Sigma)$, where the elements of Σ are σ_{ij}. The correction for sample selection is

$$E(\varepsilon/\mu_1 > c_1 \text{ and } \mu_2 > c_2)$$

$$= \frac{\int_{c_1}^{\infty}\int_{c_2}^{\infty}\int_{-\infty}^{\infty} \varepsilon f(\mu_1, \mu_2, \varepsilon)\, d\varepsilon\, d\mu_1\, d\mu_2}{\int_{c_1}^{\infty}\int_{c_2}^{\infty}\int_{-\infty}^{\infty} f(\mu_1, \mu_2, \varepsilon)\, d\varepsilon\, d\mu_1\, d\mu_2}$$

$$= \frac{\int_{c_1}^{\infty}\int_{c_2}^{\infty}\int_{-\infty}^{\infty} \varepsilon \exp\left(-\frac{1}{2}x'\Sigma^{-1}x\right) d\varepsilon\, d\mu_1\, d\mu_2}{1-\phi(c_1, c_2)}, \tag{A1}$$

where $\theta(c_1, c_2)$ is the bivariate cumulative density function for (μ_1, μ_2).

Consider the numerator of equation (A1). Call it Q and write:

$$Q = \int_{c_1}^{\infty}\int_{c_2}^{\infty}\int_{-\infty}^{\infty} \varepsilon \exp -\frac{1}{2}(\mu_1^2\sigma^{11} + 2\mu_1\mu_2\sigma^{12} + \mu_2^2\sigma^{22}$$

$$+ \varepsilon^2\sigma^{33} + 2\varepsilon\mu_1\sigma^{13} + 2\varepsilon\mu_2\sigma^{23})\, d\varepsilon\, d\mu_2\, d\mu_1$$

$$= \int_{c_1}^{\infty}\int_{c_2}^{\infty} \exp -\frac{1}{2}\left[\mu_1^2\sigma_z^{11} + 2\mu_1\mu_2\sigma^{12} + \mu_2^2\sigma^{22} - \frac{(\mu_1\sigma^{13} + \mu_2\sigma^{23})^2}{\sigma^{33}}\right]$$

$$\times \int_{-\infty}^{\infty} \varepsilon \exp -\frac{1}{2}\sigma^{33}\left(\varepsilon + \frac{\mu_1\sigma^{13} + \mu_2\sigma^{23}}{\sigma^{33}}\right)^2 d\varepsilon\, d\mu_2\, d\mu_1, \tag{A2}$$

where σ^{ij} is the ijth element of Σ^{-1}.

Let $Z = \varepsilon + (\mu_1\sigma^{13} + \mu_2\sigma^{23})/\sigma^{33})$, and let N be the last integral on the right-hand side of equation (A2). Then

$$N = \int_{-\infty}^{\infty} Z \exp\left(-\frac{1}{2}\sigma^{33}Z^2\right) dZ - \frac{\mu_1\sigma^{13} + \mu_2\sigma^{23}}{\sigma^{33}}\int_{-\infty}^{\infty} \exp\left(-\frac{1}{2}\sigma^{33}Z^2\right) dZ$$

$$= 0 - \frac{\mu_1\sigma^{13} + \mu_2\sigma^{23}}{\sigma^{33}},$$

and

$$Q = -\int_{c_1}^{\infty}\int_{c_2}^{\infty} \left(\frac{\mu_1\sigma^{13} + \mu_2\sigma^{23}}{\sigma^{33}}\right) \exp -\frac{1}{2}\left[\mu_1^2\left(\sigma^{11} - \frac{\sigma^{13^2}}{\sigma^{33}}\right)\right.$$

$$\left. + \mu_2^2\left(\sigma^{22} - \frac{\sigma^{23^2}}{\sigma^{33}}\right) + 2\mu_1\mu_2\left(\sigma^{12} - \frac{\sigma^{13}\sigma^{23}}{\sigma^{33}}\right)\right] d\mu_1\, d\mu_2. \tag{A3}$$

Let $\Delta = |\Sigma^{-1}|$. Then

$$\frac{\sigma^{13}}{\sigma^{33}} = \frac{-1/\Delta(\sigma_{13}\sigma_{11} - \sigma_{23}\sigma_{12})}{1/\Delta(\sigma_{11}\sigma_{22} - \sigma_{12}^2)} = -\frac{\sigma_{13} - \sigma_{23}(\sigma_{12}/\sigma_{22})}{\sigma_{11} - \sigma_{12}(\sigma_{12}/\sigma_{22})} = -\frac{\sigma_{31\cdot2}}{\sigma_{11\cdot2}}.$$

Likewise, $\sigma^{23}/\sigma^{33} = -\sigma_{32\cdot1}/\sigma_{22\cdot1}$, and

$$Q = \int_{c_1}^{\infty}\int_{c_2}^{\infty}\left(\frac{\sigma_{31\cdot2}}{\sigma_{11\cdot2}}\mu_1 + \frac{\sigma_{32\cdot1}}{\sigma_{22\cdot1}}\mu_2\right)\exp -\frac{1}{2}\left[\mu_1^2\left(\sigma^{11} - \frac{\sigma^{13^2}}{\sigma^{33}}\right)\right.$$
$$\left. + \mu_2^2\left(\sigma^{22} - \frac{\sigma^{23^2}}{\sigma^{33}}\right) + 2\mu_1\mu_2\left(\sigma^{12} - \frac{\sigma^{13}\sigma^{23}}{\sigma^{33}}\right)\right] d\mu_2\, d\mu_1. \tag{A4}$$

Note that

$$\sigma^{11} - \frac{\sigma^{13^2}}{\sigma^{33}} = \frac{1 + \sigma_{12}^2/(\sigma_{11}\sigma_{22} - \sigma_{12}^2)}{\sigma_{11}} = \frac{1}{\sigma_{11} - \sigma_{12}^2/\sigma_{22}} = \frac{1}{\sigma_{11\cdot2}},$$

$$\sigma^{22} - \frac{\sigma^{23^2}}{\sigma^{33}} = \frac{1}{\sigma_{22\cdot1}},$$

$$\sigma^{12} - \frac{\sigma^{13}\sigma^{23}}{\sigma^{33}} = \frac{1}{\sigma_{12} - (\sigma_{11}\sigma_{22}/\sigma_{12})}.$$

These expressions and the last formula for Q imply:

$$Q = \int_{c_1}^{\infty}\int_{c_2}^{\infty}\left(\frac{\sigma_{31\cdot2}}{\sigma_{11\cdot2}}\mu_1 + \frac{\sigma_{32\cdot1}}{\sigma_{22\cdot1}}\mu_2\right)\exp$$
$$-\frac{1}{2}\left(\frac{\mu_1^2}{\sigma_{11\cdot2}} + \frac{\mu_2^2}{\sigma_{22\cdot1}} + \frac{2\mu_1\mu_2}{\sigma_{12} - [\sigma_{11}\sigma_{22}/\sigma_{12}]}\right) d\mu_2\, d\mu_1$$
$$= \frac{\sigma_{31\cdot2}}{\sigma_{11\cdot2}}\int_{c_2}^{\infty}\int_{c_1}^{\infty}\mu_1 b(\mu_1,\mu_2)\, d\mu_1\, d\mu_2 + \frac{\sigma_{32\cdot1}}{\sigma_{22\cdot1}}\int_{c_1}^{\infty}\int_{c_2}^{\infty}\mu_2 b(\mu_1,\mu_2)\, d\mu_2\, d\mu_1, \tag{A5}$$

where $b(\ )$ is the bivariate density function. Denote by A the first term on the righthand side of (A5):

$$A = \frac{\sigma_{31\cdot2}}{\sigma_{11\cdot2}}\int_{c_2}^{\infty}\exp\left(-\frac{1}{2}\frac{\mu_2^2}{\sigma_{22\cdot1}}\right)\int_{c_1}^{\infty}\mu_1 \exp$$
$$-\frac{1}{2}\left(\frac{\mu_1^2}{\sigma_{11\cdot2}} + \frac{2\mu_1\mu_2}{\sigma_{12} - (\sigma_{11}\sigma_{22}/\sigma_{12})}\right) d\mu_1\, d\mu_2;$$

and define:

$$B = \int_{c_1}^{\infty} \mu_1 \exp -\frac{1}{2}\left(\frac{1}{\sigma_{11\cdot 2}}(\mu_1^2 + \frac{2\mu_1\mu_2\sigma_{11\cdot 2}}{\sigma_{12} - (\sigma_{11}\sigma_{22}/\sigma_{12})}\right) d\mu_1.$$

It can be shown that

$$\frac{\sigma_{11\cdot 2}}{\sigma_{12} - \sigma_{11}\sigma_{22}/\sigma_{12}} = \frac{-\sigma_{12}}{\sigma_{22}}$$

and

$$B = \int_{c_1}^{\infty} \mu_1 \exp -\frac{1}{2}\left[\frac{1}{\sigma_{11\cdot 2}}\left(\mu_1^2 - 2\mu_1\mu_2\frac{\sigma_{12}}{\sigma_{22}}\right)\right] d\mu_1$$

$$= \exp -\frac{1}{2}\left(-\frac{\sigma_{12}^2\mu_2^2}{\sigma_{22}^2\sigma_{11\cdot 2}}\right)\int_{c_1}^{\infty} \mu_1 \exp -\frac{1}{2}\left[\frac{1}{\sigma_{11\cdot 2}}\left(\mu_1 - \frac{\sigma_{12}}{\sigma_{22}}\mu_2\right)^2\right] d\mu_1.$$

Thus

$$A = \frac{\sigma_{31\cdot 2}}{\sigma_{11\cdot 2}}\int_{c_2}^{\infty} \exp -\frac{1}{2}\left[\mu_2^2\left(\frac{1}{\sigma_{22\cdot 1}} - \frac{\sigma_{12}^2}{\sigma_{22}^2\sigma_{11\cdot 2}}\right)\right]\int_{c_1}^{\infty} \mu_1 \exp$$

$$-\frac{1}{2}\left[\frac{1}{\sigma_{11\cdot 2}}\left(\mu_1 - \frac{\sigma_{12}}{\sigma_{22}}\mu_2\right)^2\right] d\mu_1\, d\mu_2.$$

But

$$\frac{1}{\sigma_{22\cdot 1}} - \frac{\sigma_{12}^2}{\sigma_2^2\sigma_{11\cdot 2}} = \frac{1}{\sigma_{22}};$$

hence

$$A = \frac{\sigma_{31\cdot 2}}{\sigma_{11\cdot 2}}\int_{c_2}^{\infty} \exp -\frac{1}{2}\frac{\mu_2}{\sigma_{22}}\left[\int_{c_1}^{\infty} \mu_1 \exp\left(-\frac{1}{2}\frac{\mu_1 - (\sigma_{12}/\sigma_{22})\mu_2}{\sigma_{11\cdot 2}}\right) d\mu_1\right] d\mu_2.$$

Let $Z = \mu_1 - (\sigma_{12}/\sigma_{22})\mu_2$, and P be the last integral on the right-hand side of the above equation. Then

$$V(Z) = \sigma_{11} - 2\frac{\sigma_{12}^2}{\sigma_{22}} + \frac{\sigma_{12}^2}{\sigma_{22}} = \sigma_{11} - \frac{\sigma_{12}^2}{\sigma_{22}} = \sigma_{11\cdot 2}.$$

Thus

$$P = \int_{c_1}^{\infty}\left(Z + \frac{\sigma_{12}}{\sigma_{22}}\mu_2\right) \exp\left(-\frac{1}{2}\frac{Z^2}{V(Z)}\right) dZ$$

$$= \int_{c_1}^{\infty} Zf(Z)\, dZ + \frac{\sigma_{12}}{\sigma_{22}}\mu_2 \int_{c_1}^{\infty} f(Z)\, dZ$$

$$= E(Z/Z > c_1)[1 - F(c_1)] + \frac{\sigma_{12}}{\sigma_{22}}\mu_2[1 - F(c_1)]$$

$$= [1 - F(c_1)]\left(E(Z/Z > c_1) + \frac{\sigma_{12}}{\sigma_{22}}\mu_2\right).$$

Thus

$$A = \frac{\sigma_{31\cdot 2}}{\sigma_{11\cdot 2}}\int_{c_2}^{\infty}\left(\exp -\frac{1}{2}\frac{\mu_2^2}{\sigma_{22}}\right)\left[[1 - F(c_1)]\left(E(Z/Z_1 > c_1) + \frac{\sigma_{12}}{\sigma_{22}}\mu_2\right)\right] d\mu_2$$

$$= \frac{\sigma_{31\cdot 2}}{\sigma_{11\cdot 2}}[1 - F(c_1)]\left(E(Z/Z > c_1)[1 - F(c_2)] + \frac{\sigma_{12}}{\sigma_{22}}E(Z/Z > c_2)[1 - F(c_2)]\right)$$

$$= \frac{\sigma_{31\cdot 2}}{\sigma_{11\cdot 2}}[1 - F(c_1)][1 - F(c_2)]\left(E(Z/Z > c_1) + \frac{\sigma_{12}}{\sigma_{22}}E(Z/Z > c_2)\right).$$

By symmetry, the second piece of Q is

$$\frac{\sigma_{32\cdot 1}}{\sigma_{22\cdot 1}}[1 - F(c_1)][1 - F(c_2)]\left(E(Z/Z > c_2) + \frac{\sigma_{12}}{\sigma_{11}}E(Z/Z > c_1)\right).$$

Thus

$$Q = [1 - F(c_1)][1 - F(c_2)]\left[E(Z/Z > c_1)\left(\frac{\sigma_{31\cdot 2}}{\sigma_{11\cdot 2}} + \frac{\sigma_{32\cdot 1}}{\sigma_{22\cdot 1}} \times \frac{\sigma_{21}}{\sigma_{11}}\right)\right.$$

$$\left. + E(Z/Z > c_2)\left(\frac{\sigma_{32\cdot 1}}{\sigma_{22\cdot 1}} + \frac{\sigma_{31\cdot 2}}{\sigma_{11\cdot 2}} \times \frac{\sigma_{12}}{\sigma_{22}}\right)\right].$$

But

$$\frac{\sigma_{31\cdot 2}}{\sigma_{11\cdot 2}} + \frac{\sigma_{32\cdot 1}}{\sigma_{22\cdot 1}} \times \frac{\sigma_{21}}{\sigma_{11}} = \sigma_{22} \times \frac{\sigma_{31} \quad \sigma_{32}(\sigma_{12}/\sigma_{22})}{\sigma_{22}\sigma_{11} - \sigma_{12}^2} + \frac{\sigma_{32} - \sigma_{31}(\sigma_{12}/\sigma_{11})}{\sigma_{11}\sigma_{22} - \sigma_{12}^2} \times \sigma_{21}$$

$$= \frac{\sigma_{31}}{\sigma_{11}},$$

and by symmetry,

$$\frac{\sigma_{32\cdot 1}}{\sigma_{22\cdot 1}} + \frac{\sigma_{31\cdot 2}}{\sigma_{11\cdot 2}} \times \frac{\sigma_{12}}{\sigma_{22}} = \frac{\sigma_{32}}{\sigma_{22}}.$$

Hence

$$E(\varepsilon/\mu_1 > c_1 \text{ and } \mu_2 > c_2)$$
$$= \frac{[1 - F(c_1)][1 - F(c_2)]}{1 - \phi(c_1, c_2)} \left(\frac{\sigma_{31}}{\sigma_{11}} E(Z/Z > c_1) + \frac{\sigma_{32}}{\sigma_{22}} E(Z/Z > c_2) \right).$$

Note that the terms in brackets are the two univariate Mills' ratios.

Notes

We thank Peter A. Diamond, Jagadeesh Gokhale, and Jerry A. Hausman for many useful comments and suggestions. Jagadeesh Gokhale provided excellent research assistance.

1. U.S. Department of Health and Human Services, Federal Council on the Aging, *The Need for Long-Term Care* (Government Printing Office, 1981).

2. Karen C. Holden, Richard V. Burkhauser, and Daniel A. Myers, "Pensioners' Annuity Choice: Is the Well-Being of Widows Considered?" Discussion Paper 802-86 (University of Wisconsin-Madison, Institute for Research on Poverty, 1986); and Daniel A. Myers, Richard V. Burkhauser, and Karen C. Holden, "The Transition from Wife to Widow: The Importance of Survivor Benefits to the Well-Being of Widows," Discussion Paper 806-86 (University of Wisconsin-Madison, Institute for Research on Poverty, 1986).

3. The RHS data are available on tapes. The data are described in Lola M. Irelan and others, *Almost 65: Baseline Data for the Retirement History Study*, U.S. Department of Health, Education, and Welfare, Social Security Administration, Office of Research and Statistics, Research Report 49 (GPO, 1976).

4. Menahem E. Yaari, "Uncertain Lifetime, Life Insurance, and the Theory of the Consumer," *Review of Economic Studies*, vol. 32 (April 1965), pp. 137–50.

5. Benjamin M. Friedman and Mark Warshawsky, "Annuity Prices and Saving Behavior in the United States," National Bureau of Economic Research Working Paper 1683 (Cambridge, Mass.: NBER, 1985).

6. See Yaari, "Uncertain Lifetime"; Laurence J. Kotlikoff and Avia Spivak: "The Family as an Incomplete Annuities Market," *Journal of Political Economy*, vol. 89 (April 1981), pp. 372–91; and Douglas Bernheim, "Social Security and Private Insurance Arrangements" (Stanford University, Department of Economics, 1985).

7. "Family as Incomplete Annuities Market."

8. "Uncertain Lifetime," p. 140.

9. James J. Heckman, "The Common Structure of Statistical Models of Truncation, Sample Selection, and Limited Dependent Variables and a Simple Estimator for such Models," *Annals of Economic and Social Measurement*, vol. 5 (Fall 1976), pp. 475–92.

10. William Green, *LEMDEP* Computer Program, rev. version (New York University, School of Business, 1985).

11. See above, the section entitled "A Model of Life Insurance Demand," the discussion below equation 9w′. See also equation 14.

12 Household Financial Planning and Financial Literacy: The Need for New Tools

with B. Douglas Bernheim

I. Introduction

Americans, old, middle-aged, and young, have a pressing need for sound financial planning. Indeed, low rates of personal saving, anemic real wage growth, ever longer lengths of retirement, and the government's likely future fiscal retrenchment make financial planning more important than ever.

Unfortunately, Americans, as a group, appear ill-equipped to formulate their own financial plans. Many Americans have little facility with financial matters. Even those with considerable financial acumen are unable to preform the complex calculations required for constructing sensible financial plans. These considerations would be of little concern if Americans could simply rely on traditional financial planning tools to formulate appropriate financial plans. Unfortunately, these tools fall far short of those needed to properly guide household financial decisions.

This chapter examines the state of Americans' financial planning and financial literacy. It also critically evaluates traditional financial planning that involves targeting financial liabilities and recommends its replacement with an alternative method of financial planning that involves consumption smoothing. In contrast to the targeted liability approach, the consumption-smoothing approach to financial planning is closely aligned to the economic theory of consumption, saving, and insurance.

The chapter continues in section II by examining the adequacy of Americans' saving and life insurance holdings. Section III considers the evidence on financial literacy, asking whether Americans appreciate and can be induced to reduce their financial vulnerabilities. Based on this evidence, section IV offers a new set of criteria for evaluating financial planning and uses it to evaluate the most common financial planning methodology. It proposes an alternative and more appropriate method of formulating saving and insurance plans based on the principal of consumption-smoothing (rather than income replacement). Finally, it presents three examples that illustrate the significant differences between these two approaches to financial planning.

II. The Adequacy of Personal Saving and Life Insurance

Recent research suggests that most Americans are not taking sufficient steps to assure their financial security. As a result, severe financial vulnerabilities, resulting from both meager saving and insufficient life insurance are widespread.

A. The Adequacy of Personal Saving

To evaluate the adequacy of retirement preparation by any individual or group of individuals, one must first establish a quantitative standard of adequacy. There is no "right" or "wrong" standard of adequacy; rather, the use of different standards corresponds to different questions about retirement prospects. The appropriateness of a given standard must be judged within the context of a particular issue. A standard that is appropriate in one context may be inappropriate in another.

In this chapter, we emphasize a measure of adequacy that evaluates a retiree's living standard relative to his or her own preretirement living standard. With this measure, inadequate saving implies that a household will be forced to accept a lower standard of living during retirement. This measure is particularly appropriate when the object is to provide households with financial guidance. Since most households wish to avoid sharp declines in living standard, financial prescriptions should balance preretirement and postretirement living standards. In contrast, it would be entirely inappropriate to base financial recommendations on an absolute measure of adequacy, such as avoiding poverty. The majority of households would, upon finding themselves living just above the poverty level after retirement, conclude that they had saved inadequately. Similarly, those who had achieved lifetime earnings substantially in excess of their parents' might be severely disappointed if their standard of living in retirement did not also exceed that of their parents.

Unfortunately, most Americans save far too little to maintain their own standards of living after retirement. Diamond (1977) and Hamermesh (1984) have found that the typical worker has, in the past, reached retirement with total savings that are insufficient to sustain their preretirement standards of living. Although Kotlikoff, Spivak, and Summers (1982) dispute this finding, they attribute the adequacy of retirement preparation to an enormous unanticipated increase in social security benefits, rather than to adequate saving.

Recent research on the adequacy of saving has focused primarily on the baby boom generation. According to Bernheim (1993, 1994a), the typical baby boom household is saving at one-third the rate required to finance a standard of living during retirement comparable to the standard of living that it enjoys before retirement. Although the saving shortfall is pervasive, affecting individuals with all levels of earnings and educational attainment, it is particularly acute for single individuals, for households with total earnings between $60,000 and $100,000, and for workers who are not covered by pensions, or who are only covered by voluntary salary reduction plans. Married individuals fare somewhat better than single individuals due to the existence of the social security spousal benefit, which generally provides them with higher earnings replacement. The progressivity of the social security benefit formulas also provides lower income individuals with higher earnings replacement, and the highest income groups (those with total household earnings over $100,000) save significantly larger fractions of their incomes. This leaves middle and upper-middle income groups the least well prepared.

It is important to emphasize that these calculations probably describe a "best-case" scenario. If anything, they overstate the adequacy of retirement preparation. In the worst-case scenarios (which assume deep cuts in social security), baby boomers are saving less than one-tenth of what is required to avoid a potentially precipitous decline in standard of living after retirement.[1] Even a relatively moderate increase in future taxes would reduce the index below 30 percent, and a relatively modest reduction in social security benefits would depress it even further, to less than 20 percent. Of course, the distributional effects of these alternative scenarios differ dramatically. Reductions in social security benefits result in much larger saving shortfalls for lower income individuals, whereas tax increases would fall more heavily on higher income groups.

A separate study conducted by Arthur D. Little, Inc. (1993) corroborates the central findings of Bernheim (1993). It concludes that households without pension plans typically will have 20–30 percent of what they need to retire, and that those with pension plans typically will have 50–60 percent of what they need to retire comfortably.

Even if baby boomers are unable to maintain their preretirement standards of living after retirement, they may still fare well in comparison to retirees of previous generations. According to a study conducted by the Congressional Budget Office (CBO) (1993), baby boomers have significantly higher real incomes and greater accumulated wealth than their parents did at comparable ages.[2] Kingson (1992), and others have reached similar conclusions. While these findings appear to suggest that baby boomers are on track to match or exceed their parents' standard of living during retirement, caution is warranted for several reasons.

- Discussions of wealth accumulation in these studies focus on the level of saving (the accumulated value of past saving), rather than on the rate of saving. Rates of saving among young workers may have been higher during the late 1950s and early 1960s than in the late 1980s and early 1990s.
- Baby boomers' parents earned significantly more during their 50s and early 60s than during their 30s and 40s (in large part because real wages grew rapidly during the 1960s, and in the first half of the 1970s).
- Baby boomers may receive less generous pension benefits than their parents (due to possible changes in social security and to lower private accumulation resulting from the switch to 401K plans).
- Baby boomers' parents benefitted from an enormous, unexpected increase in housing equity that is not likely to be repeated.
- Baby boomers are having their children later than their parents did, and therefore will have fewer post–child rearing years to accumulate resources for retirement at an accelerated rate.
- Baby boomers will live significantly longer than their parents, so their savings need to go further.

- Baby boomers will exhaust a larger fraction of their wealth sending their children to college. (This consideration may be offset, to some extent, by the fact that the baby boomers are having fewer children than their parents did.)

Certainly, there are some factors that tend to favor the baby boomers, relative to their parents, not the least of which are their larger real incomes at comparable ages. A minority of baby boomers may also receive significant inheritances.[3] However, given the range and quantitative importance of the factors discussed above, it is not evident that baby boomers are, on average, saving enough to achieve even their parents' standard of living during retirement, let alone the standard that they themselves are enjoying, and will continue to enjoy, prior to retirement.

B. The Adequacy of Life Insurance

So far, we have focused attention on the adequacy of saving. Similar issues arise in the context of life insurance. These issues have been taken up in a series of studies by Auerbach and Kotlikoff (chap. 11, this volume; 1991a, 1991b). The first and second of these studies demonstrate that a significant minority of retirement-age households have inadequate life insurance. Moreover, almost one-half of households at risk (those for whom a significant portion of household resources take the form of earnings and benefits that cases with the death of the husband or wife) are inadequately insured. As a result of this insurance shortfall, roughly one-third of new widows experience a substantial (25 percent or greater) reduction in their living standards when their husbands die. The reduction in living standard associated with the husband's death is more severe for younger widows and widows with greater income prewidowhood, indicating a greater insurance shortfall for these groups.

The third study (Auerbach and Kotlikoff 1991b) examines the adequacy of life insurance for middle-age households. It too finds that a significant minority of wives are highly underinsured with respect to the possible deaths of their husbands. Roughly 25 to 30 percent of wives would suffer a reduction in standard of living in excess of 30 percent in the event of being widowed. These findings are even more striking when one focuses on households in which over half of the couple's present expected value of resources is dependent on the husband's survival. Somewhere between 30 and 40 percent of middle-age American wives in need of life insurance protection are poorly insured.

Other studies have reached similar findings. Hurd and Wise (1989) considers the high incidence of poverty among widows and asks whether a widow's poverty status arises as the direct result of the death of her husband. The authors show that this is definitely the case; they point out that whereas only 9 percent of their sample of couples (in which the husband subsequently dies) are poor, approximately 35 percent of subsequent widows in this sample are poor. The decline in living standard for surviving widows is also documented by Holden, Burkhauser, and Myers (1986). One notable deficiency in this literature is the absence of specific evidence on the adequacy of life insurance among younger households. These are the households at greatest risk, since human capital accounts for the bulk of their resources, and since they are more likely to have young children.

C. *The Need for Further Research*

Although the studies cited in this section have shed considerable light on the adequacy of saving and insurance among the American population, there is still much to be learned. To date, research has been impeded by the limitations of available survey data. No survey contains comprehensive data on any individual. One cannot, for example, make any adjustments for a particular household's expectations about future income and possible inheritances, for plans concerning special expenditures (such as college education or bequests), for preferences about relative pre- and postretirement living standards, for plans concerning the purchase or sale of homes, or for contingent plans regarding employment subsequent to the death of a spouse. In addition, financial data on individual households is usually "noisy." Thus, although existing surveys can be used to obtain a reasonably good sense for the financial status and vulnerabilities of "typical" households, they do not permit us to draw reliable inferences about individual households. For this reason, relatively little is currently known about the distribution of financial vulnerabilities within the population. Further progress in this direction would require data drawn from a fairly large number of detailed case studies.

III. Financial Literacy

Why do most Americans make such poor financial decisions? One possibility is that they lack the training, skill, and knowledge to recognize financial vulnerabilities, and to formulate prudent plans. The existing literature contains a fair number of studies that shed considerable light on the general public's level of financial sophistication. Sophistication, or the lack thereof, is reflected in both knowledge and choices.

One common measure of economic knowledge is performance on the Test of Economic Literacy (TEL), which was developed under the sponsorship of the National Council on Economic Education (NCEE). The TEL has been used to evaluate economic literacy among high school students (see Walstad and Soper, 1988). The NCEE has also developed a Survey of American Economic Literacy (SAEL), which covered the general public, as well as student populations (see Walstad and Larsen 1992). It should be noted that the TEL and the SAEL focus to a great extent on knowledge that is relevant for the assessment of public policy issues and that may not be relevant for personal financial management. Other sources of information on economic literacy include the Survey of Adult Literacy in America, sponsored by the National Center for Education Statistics, U.S. Department of Education (see Jordan 1993), a study of high school competency tests sponsored by the Consumer Federation of America and the American Express Company (1991), and results from national high school equivalency tests (Crenshaw 1993). Collectively, these studies paint a rather bleak picture of economic literacy. For example, only 20 percent of adults can determine correct change using prices from a menu (Jordan 1993), and many have trouble determining whether a mortgage at 8.6 percent is better than a mortgage at 8 3/4 percent (Crenshaw 1993). The level of economic literacy has been found to differ between males and females (Jackstadt and Grootaert 1980; Ferber, Birnbaum, and Green 1983; Buckles and Freeman 1983; and Watts 1987), as well as across countries (Whitehead and Halil 1991).

The sophistication of choices has also been the subject of extensive study. Numerous authors have observed that decision-making under uncertainty gives rise to a variety of behavioral anomalies (see, e.g., Kahneman, Slovic, and Tversky 1982). A large number of papers provide formal tests of rational intertemporal choice, with many authors concluding that the life-cycle model does not accurately describe behavior (see, e.g., Shefrin and Thaler 1983, 1988; Levin 1992; or Kotlikoff, Johnson, and Samuelson 1987). Numerous authors have also identified particularly naive or unsophisticated patterns of financial behavior. Examples include: a widespread failure to take advantage of clear arbitrage opportunities (Warshawsky 1987), the common practice of waiting until the end of a tax year to contribute to an IRA (Feenberg and Skinner 1989), the use of rough rule-of-thumb saving targets (Bernheim 1994c), the frequency of identifiable errors in personal financial management, including insufficient diversification and excessive conservatism in selecting investments (O'Neill 1990, 1993), limited familiarity with all but the simplest investment instruments (O'Neill 1993), the use of costly methods of borrowing (Hira 1993), the frequency with which personal bankruptcy results from poor credit management (Hira 1993), the prevalence of "compulsive spending addictions" (Faber and O'Guinn 1989), and the high frequency with which individuals fall prey to financial scams (Alliance Against Fraud in Telemarketing 1992).

In summary, the existing literature demonstrates that most individuals know little about managing personal finances, and that their choices reflect this ignorance. While these findings are useful and important, they leave many central questions unanswered. Only limited information is available on the determinants of economic literacy. More importantly, the existing studies do not allow us to draw any inferences about the impact of financial knowledge on decision-making, or to opine on the subject of whether individuals can be taught to save adequately or invest wisely.

To shed new light on these important questions, we report on recent research findings, based on a novel source of household data. Many of these findings result from research in progress, and must therefore be regarded as somewhat preliminary.

A. *The Data*

In the fall of 1993, Luntz Webber Research and Strategic Services, in cooperation with Merrill Lynch, administered an unprecedented survey of economic literacy and financial choices to a nationally representative, random sample of individuals between the ages of 29 and 47 (the baby boom cohort). It consists of two separate "waves."

Both waves contain a detailed battery of questions concerning household assets, earnings, income, pension coverage, employment status, and demographic information. The first wave, which surveyed 1,209 households, also contains various self-assessments of current financial status, future financial needs, intended saving, and actual saving. It also measures beliefs and expectations concerning social security, including current and future benefit levels, and other information on attitudes and expectations concerning unfunded government obligations. The second wave, which surveyed 806 households, assesses economic literacy, financial knowledge, developmental experiences that may be relevant to financial behavior, and sources of financial information and advice.

Response rates on financial questions were extremely high. Since the survey was administered only to members of the baby boom cohort, it is impossible to verify the accuracy of information on earnings or net worth by comparing sample statistics to national aggregates. However, comparisons between these data and an appropriate subsample drawn from the 1989 Survey of Consumer Finances (SCF) provide little reason to suspect that earnings, assets, or liabilities are systematically under- or overreported.

B. An Assessment of Financial Literacy

The Luntz-Webber / Merrill Lynch survey contained eleven questions designed to assess the respondent's knowledge of economic matters. These questions are reproduced in table 12.1. We have divided the questions into two subcategories: those that concern financial issues, and those that concern macroeconomic issues.

1. An Analysis of Absolute Performance

Performance on these questions was generally poor. This is consistent with the evidence reviewed at the outset of this section. Even allowing for an appropriate margin of error on certain questions (such as the Dow Jones average), more than 80 percent of the sample answered at least five of the eleven questions incorrectly.

It is possible to characterize the nature of financial illiteracy more precisely. Nearly two-thirds of the sample would not hazard a guess as to the level of the Dow Jones average, despite the fact that this number is reported on the front page of virtually every business section in every daily newspaper, as well as on virtually every

Table 12.1
Literacy questions

Financial knowledge
What is the current Dow Jones Industrials average?
For people who pay federal income taxes, what is the lowest income tax bracket?
What is the 30-year conventional mortgage rate right now?
If you deposited $1,000 and earned 8%, compounded annually, over thirty years, at the end of this period would you have earned more or less than $5,000?
Why do mutual funds typically have higher rates of return than federally insured bank CDs? (Options: (1) It's the law; (2) Mutual funds are bigger; (3) Mutual funds are riskier; (4) Inflation)
Which investment situation would you prefer: a chance to earn 8% when inflation is at 6%, or a chance to earn 5% when inflation is at 1%?
Macroeconomic knowledge
What is the current national unemployment rate?
What is the national minimum wage?
What is the annual rate of inflation?
What is the size of the total federal debt?
What is the size of the total federal debt per household?

national television and radio news program. The median answer for those professing knowledge was 3400—more than 300 points below the true range of the average during the week of the survey.

More than 90 percent of the sample answered the questions concerning unemployment and inflation, but they thought that both unemployment and inflation are higher than they are. The median response concerning unemployment was 8 percent, compared to 6.7 percent nationally at the time of the survey, and roughly one-third named a figure of 10 percent or higher. Similarly, the median response concerning inflation was 4 percent, compared to a rate of 2.8 percent at the time of the survey.

Respondents severely underestimated the size of the federal debt, with one-third of the sample reporting a number below $1 trillion. Among those answering this question, the median response was $3 trillion, whereas the correct answer was nearly $4.4 trillion. This discrepancy may be partially attributable to confusion about the differences between the debt and the deficit, as well as to inadvertent errors in orders of magnitude (i.e., saying "billions" rather than "trillions"). The survey separately asked for the federal debt per household. In theory, this number is far more relevant to the typical taxpayer than the total federal debt, since it measures the amount of liabilities that the government has incurred on his or her behalf. It is therefore striking—but perhaps not too surprising—that respondents were far more ignorant of the federal debt per houehold. Whereas 17 percent professed ignorance of the federal debt, more than one-third, or nearly twice as many, would not hazard a guess as to the federal debt per household. Those answering the question on debt per household severely underestimated this liability. The median answer was $18,000, compared with an actual liability of $45,700.

As noted in chapter 10, this volume, and in other studies, individuals tend to underestimate the power of compound interest. Nearly one-third of the sample indicated that $1,000, left in the bank for 30 years at 8 percent interest, would earn less than $5,000, whereas the correct answer is more than $10,000. Many respondents also poorly understand common financial instruments. Roughly 42 percent could not identify the proper explanation for the difference in average returns between mutual funds and federally insured CDs.

Respondents did perform relatively well on a small number of questions. The median response concerning the national minimum wage was $4.35—only $0.10 high—and 34 percent of the sample said $4.25. Most respondents also provided reasonably accurate answers to the question about conventional mortgage rates, with homeowners performing noticeably better than renters.

2. *An Analysis of Relative Performance*

Despite the rather shocking nature of many of these findings, it is difficult to obtain a meaningful absolute measure of financial literacy, since any such measure is necessarily predicated on subjective judgements concerning the set of things that a well-informed household ought to know. Test questions, such as those contained in the Luntz-Webber/Merrill Lynch survey, are best suited for evaluating the relative sophistication of different population subgroups. For this purpose, we depart from the existing literature, which uses simple binary measures of knowledge (i.e., "right" and "wrong"). These binary measures are problematic (e.g., how close to the actual Dow Jones average would an answer need to be, to be scored as correct?).

To remedy this problem, we assign a "relative knowledge score" to each question. This score is defined as the fraction of the population who gave answers that were further in absolute value than the respondent's answer from the true answer.[4] This procedure has the

Table 12.2
Average test scores

Population subgroup	Overall score	Financial score	Macroeconomic score
Age			
29–34	63.5	70.1	55.7
35–40	63.1	69.8	55.0
41–47	64.2	70.6	56.6
Gender			
Male	68.5	74.0	62.0
Female	58.9	66.5	49.8
Race			
White	64.3	71.0	56.3
Black	55.9	62.0	48.6
Education			
College degree	68.3	74.8	60.4
No college degree	60.6	67.2	52.8
Earnings			
First quartile	59.4	65.8	51.8
Second quartile	64.1	69.9	57.2
Third quartile	65.5	72.4	57.1
Fourth quartile	67.3	74.2	59.0

additional benefit of normalizing the score on each question to reflect difficulty, so that no question (or group of questions) dominates the variation in total scores.

Average scores for different population subgroups are contained in table 12.2. To interpret differences in test scores between subgroups, it is helpful to keep in mind the following information. Scores range between 25.8 and 96.5, with 25 percent of the population scoring between 25.8 and 54.2, 25 percent between 54.2 and 64.2, 25 percent between 64.2 and 73.5, and 25 percent above 73.5. Thus, towards the central portion of the population distribution, a 10-point increase in an individual's score would move him or her past roughly one-quarter of the population.

Surprisingly, test scores do not rise or fall systematically with age. This may reflect the effects of various offsetting factors. For example, individuals both acquire new knowledge and forget old knowledge as they age. It is also important to keep in mind that all respondents were surveyed at roughly the same point in time. As a result, we cannot separately identify the effects of age and birth year. Younger cohorts may have received more—or less—financial training than older cohorts.

Several other clear patterns emerge from an examination of table 12.2. Males score higher than females, and whites score higher than blacks. Due to the size of the sample, it was impossible to draw reliable inferences for any other ethnic subgroup; indeed, even the sample of black respondents is relatively small, and a corresponding measure of caution is therefore warranted when evaluating differences between blacks and whites. Average scores rise with both education and income, although perhaps not by as much as one might have expected.

Similar patterns are observed for overall scores, financial scores, and macroeconomic scores. This reflects the fact that financial and macroeconomic scores are very highly correlated (the correlation coefficient is quite large—0.51—and highly statistically significant). This is reassuring, since it suggests that the questions are consistently measuring underlying characteristics.

One must exercise considerable caution when interpreting any of the patterns described above. Simple correlations, such as those depicted in table 12.2, are often misleading. For example, the positive correlation between earnings and test scores, noted above, is certainly consistent with the hypothesis that individuals with higher earnings have greater incentives to acquire financial knowledge, so that they can better manage their money. However, earnings are also highly correlated with education. Are the correlations between test scores and education, and between test scores and earnings, just measuring the same thing? Similarly, earnings and education are correlated with gender and race, thereby further confounding interpretations based on table 12.2.

We overcome these interpretive difficulties by conducting a multivariate analysis of the data. Results are presented in table 12.3. With respect to overall test scores, virtually all of the patterns noted in table 12.2 hold up. There is no systematic relation between test performance and age. Differences based on gender and race are statistically significant, even holding other variables (such as education and earnings) constant. More educated individuals generally obtain higher scores, and these differences are also statistically significant. Higher earnings are also associated with higher test scores, even controlling for education (as well as the other explanatory variables),

Table 12.3
Multivariate analysis of average test scores

Variable	Overall score	Financial score	Macroeconomic score
Age/10^4	0.464	−2.27	3.74
	(8.44)	(8.90)	(11.4)
Gender	0.0800	0.0580	0.106
	(0.0094)**	(0.0099)**	(0.013)**
Black	−0.0561	−0.0576	−0.0544
	(0.0232)*	(0.0245)*	(0.0315)
Earnings/10^7	1.39	3.19	−0.775
	(0.89)	(0.91)**	(1.17)
Employment status	0.0278	0.0261	0.0298
	(0.0139)*	(0.0147)	(0.0188)
High school only	0.0290	0.0409	0.0146
	(0.0289)	(0.0302)	(0.0388)
High school plus	0.0746	0.0848	0.0624
(no college degree)	(0.0283)**	(0.0299)**	(0.0383)
College degree	0.111	0.122	0.0977
	(0.028)**	(0.030)**	(0.0384)**
Constant	0.494	0.562	0.414
	(0.043)**	(0.046)**	(0.059)**

Notes: For the purpose of this table, the dependent variables (test scores) are normalized to a scale of 0 to 1, rather than 0 to 100. Estimates are based on ordinary-least-squares regression. Standard errors are in parentheses.
* Denotes statistical significance at 5% level.
** Denotes statistical significance at 1% level.

but this effect is not statistically significant at conventional levels. In table 12.3, we have also controlled for employment status, on the theory that gainfully employed individuals may be more knowledgeable about economic matters. Indeed, the estimates bear this out.

Further insight is obtained by examining results for financial knowledge and macroeconomic knowledge separately. These results are nearly identical, with one important exception: financial scores rise with earnings, and this increase is statistically significant, whereas earnings have essentially no effect on macroeconomic scores. Although macroeconomic scores are correlated with earnings (see table 12.2), this correlation disappears once one controls for education, gender, race, and employment status. This finding is intuitive. As noted earlier, individuals with higher earnings almost certainly have greater incentives to acquire *financial* knowledge. For example, those who are able to purchase homes are more likely to

Table 12.4
Mean test scores vs. self-assessed financial knowledge

Self-assessed knowledge	Overall score	Financial score	Macroeconomic score
Very financially knowledgeable	67.1	73.5	59.4
Somewhat financially knowledgeable	64.2	70.8	56.3
Only a little financially knowledgeable	59.7	65.9	52.3
Not at all financially knowledgeable	58.9	68.2	47.7

follow movements in mortgage rates, and those who own stock are certainly more likely to follow the Dow Jones average. Thus, it is not surprising that we find a very strong positive relation between earnings and financial test scores, even when we control for education and other factors. However, those with greater resources do not necessarily have greater incentives to acquire macroeconomic information. Indeed, those with fewer resources are more vulnerable to unemployment, and may therefore may pay more attention to employment statistics. Likewise, they may be more concerned about the minimum wage, and at least as worried about inflation. Thus, it is not surprising that, once one controls for education and other factors, there is essentially no relation between earnings and macroeconomic test scores. This finding has important implications for the analysis contained in subsection D.

3. *An Analysis of Self-assessed Financial Knowledge*

The Luntz-Webber/Merrill Lynch survey also contained an additional question designed to elicit a self-assessment of financial literacy. Specifically, respondents were asked:

- Do you consider yourself very financially knowledgeable, somewhat financially knowledgeable, only a little financially knowledgeable, or not at all financially knowledgeable?

Answers to this question reflect a blend of actual knowledge and self-confidence. It is therefore of interest to evaluate the accuracy of self-assessments by comparing them with test scores, and to examine systematic differences in self-assessments across population subgroups.

Table 12.4 provides average test scores (overall, financial, and macroeconomic) broken down by self-assessments of financial knowledge. This table reveals a strong correlation between self-assessments and test scores. Nevertheless, this correlation is, perhaps, less pronounced than one might imagine. The average overall score among those pronouncing themselves "very financially knowledgeable" was 67.1, corresponding to the 57th percentile, whereas the average overall score among those describing themselves as "not at all financially knowledgeable" was 58.9, corresponding to the 38th percentile. It is noteworthy that those who are, by their own account, "not at all financially knowledgeable" actually obtained a higher average financial score than those who called themselves "only a little financially knowledgeable." In contrast, the average macroeconomic score rises monotonically with self-assessed knowledge. This observation raises the possibility that self-assessments of *financial* knowledge might actually reflect *macroeconomic* knowledge more closely than financial knowledge. We return to this issue later in the chapter.

Table 12.5 provides summary statistics for self-assessed knowledge for various population subgroups. For each subgroup, we report the fraction of respondents describing themselves as either "very financially knowledgeable" or "somewhat financially knowledgeable." Most of the patterns here are similar to those noted for test scores (table 12.2). There is no apparent relation between age and self-assessed financial knowledge; the youngest and oldest baby boomers consider themselves equally well-informed on financial matters. Males generally believe themselves to be more financially knowledgeable than females, and self-assessed financial knowledge rises with education and earnings. There are, however, some notable differences between the patterns exhibited in tables 12.2 and 12.5. The quantitative impact of gender, education, and earnings are very similar in table 12.2 (test scores). For example, average overall scores for males and females differ by 9.6 points; scores for those with and without college degrees differ by 7.7 points; and scores for those in the top and bottom earnings quartiles differ by 7.9 points. In contrast, the relation between self-assessed knowledge and earnings is much more pronounced than the relation between self-assessed knowledge and education, which is in turn more pronounced than the relation between self-assessed knowledge and gender. Specifically, the difference between the summary statistics reported for those in the top and bottom earnings quartiles in table 12.4 is 0.201, compared to a difference of only 0.109 for those with and without college degrees, and a difference of 0.078 between men and women.

Table 12.5
Self-assessed financial knowledge

Population subgroup	Fraction considering themselves either somewhat or very financially knowledgeable
Age	
29–34	0.802
35–40	0.786
41–47	0.801
Gender	
Male	0.836
Female	0.758
Race	
White	0.802
Black	0.788
Education	
College degree	0.863
No college degree	0.754
Earnings	
First quartile	0.701
Second quartile	0.757
Third quartile	0.798
Fourth quartile	0.902

In addition, there is practically no difference in self-assessed financial knowledge between whites and blacks, despite the differences in test scores noted in table 12.2.

Of course, these preliminary observations are based on simple correlations. Results from a multivariate analysis are presented in table 12.6. The central patterns observed in table 12.5 are unchanged: men have higher self-assessed knowledge than women; self-assessed knowledge is essentially unrelated to race, but rises with education. Notably, self-assessed knowledge is strongly related to earnings. Recall that, once other variables were controlled for, financial test scores were strongly related to earnings, while macroeconomic test scores were not. In this important respect, self-assessed financial knowledge behaves more like financial test scores than like macroeconomic test scores.

A comparison of the results in tables 12.3 and 12.6 reveals that our explanatory variables affect test scores differently than they affect

Table 12.6
Multivariate analysis of self-assessed knowledge

Variable	Coefficient
Age/10^4	0.482 (1.04)
Gender	0.293 (0.116)*
Black	0.0913 (0.280)
Earnings/10^7	66.6 (21.0)**
Employment status	0.0968 (0.160)
High school only	1.06 (0.309)**
High school plus (no college degree)	1.16 (0.305)**
College degree	1.34 (0.309)
Constant	−1.07 (0.505)*

Notes: Estimates are based on probit regression. Standard errors are in parentheses.
*Denotes statistical significance at 5% level.
**Denotes statistical significance at 1% level.

self-assessed knowledge. Under the obviously debatable assumption that test scores accurately measure economic and financial knowledge,[5] this suggests that certain population subgroups may systematically overestimate or underestimate their financial sophistication. Young baby boomers are no more likely to be excessively or insufficiently confident than older baby boomers. The most obvious candidates for overconfidence include those with high earnings, those with high school diplomas, the nonworking, and blacks (alternatively, low-earners, those not finishing high school, workers, and whites may be underconfident). College-educated individuals and women may also, on average, be overconfident in their financial sophistication.

C. *Are Americans Aware of Their Financial Vulnerabilities?*

Low levels of financial literacy suggest that inadequate financial preparation may be attributable to poor appreciation of financial vulnerabilities. The purpose of this section is to examine awareness of financial vulnerabilities directly.

The Luntz-Webber / Merrill Lynch survey instrument contains several questions designed to elicit self-evaluations of financial status. These questions include the following:

• Would you describe the state of your own personal finances these days as very shaky, fairly shaky, fairly secure, or very secure?
• Overall, how well prepared do you think you are financially for your eventual retirement? (Very well prepared, somewhat prepared, somewhat unprepared, very unprepared, or not prepared at all.)
• Do you expect to have a standard of living that is much worse, somewhat worse, somewhat better, much better, or have the same standard of living after you retire as you do today?

Overall, the answers to these questions indicate a fairly high degree of optimism about personal finances: 67.6 percent respondents described their personal finances as fairly secure or very secure; 57.7 percent believed that they are very well prepared, or somewhat prepared for retirement; while only 19.0 percent described themselves as very unprepared or not at all prepared. Virtually identical fractions of the population expected better (31.2 percent) and worse (31.1 percent) standards of living in retirement.

Provided that we have some objective measure of financial vulnerabilities, the answers to questions about personal financial status can be sued to evaluate the extent to which individuals recognize their vulnerabilities. One possible measure of financial vulnerabilities is the ratio of wealth to earnings. A lower value of the wealth-to-earnings ratio does not, however, necessary indicate greater vulnerability. A particular value of this ratio may indicate vulnerability for households with certain characteristics, while indicating relative security for households with other characteristics.

We therefore separate the population into four "adjusted-wealth" quartiles. Intuitively, the approach taken here amounts to dividing the population into numerous subgroups based on age, earnings, gender, marital status, education, pension coverage, and number of children, and then further subdividing each of the groups into quartiles based on wealth-to-earnings ratios. The first, or lowest, adjusted-wealth quartile corresponds to those individuals in the lowest wealth-to-earnings quartile within each population subgroup. Thus, those individuals in the lowest adjusted-wealth quartile have very low levels of wealth compared to other individuals with identical

Table 12.7
Wealth and perceptions

	Adjusted wealth quartile			
	1	2	3	4
State of personal finances				
Secure / fairly secure	53.9%	71.0%	66.4%	78.3%
Shaky / very shaky	46.1%	28.6%	33.7%	21.7%
State of preparation for retirement				
Very well / somewhat	44.6%	55.2%	62.0%	68.2%
Very unprepared / not at all	29.9%	19.5%	13.0%	14.3%
Standard of living during retirement				
Better / much better	29.9%	28.6%	29.8%	36.4%
Worse / much worse	37.3%	32.9%	31.7%	23.0%

Source: Bernheim (1994b).

characteristics. The other three adjusted-wealth quartiles are defined similarly.[6]

A household's adjusted-wealth quartile is a good measure of its financial vulnerability, relative to that of similar households. If individuals understand their financial vulnerabilities, then those in higher adjusted-wealth quartiles should regard themselves as more secure than those in lower adjusted-wealth quartiles.

Table 12.7 examines this possibility. In this table, we report summary statistics for the answers to survey questions concerning household financial status, separately for each adjusted-wealth quartile. This table exhibits a moderately strong relation between actual and perceived financial vulnerability. The fraction of the population that regards its personal finances as secure or fairly secure rises significantly between the first and second adjusted-wealth quartiles, as well as between the third and fourth quartiles. Oddly, this fraction declines slightly between the second and third quartiles. The fraction of the population describing itself as very well or somewhat prepared for retirement rises monotonically with household's adjusted-wealth quartile. The respondent's expected relative standard of living in retirement shows the weakest relationship to adjusted wealth. The fraction of the population expecting a better standard of living in retirement is highest in the top adjusted-wealth quartile, but varies little across the first three quartiles. On the other hand, the fraction of the population expecting a worse standard of living in retirement falls significantly between the first and second quartiles, and again between the third and fourth quartiles (there is also a slight decline between the second and third quartiles).

Although these results indicate some awareness of relative financial vulnerabilities, they also exhibit an unrealistic degree of optimism. Within the lowest adjusted-wealth quartile—a group that is poorly prepared by any objective measure of adequacy—more than half (53.9 percent) regard their personal finances as secure or fairly secure, 44.6 percent believe that they are very well or somewhat prepared for retirement, and only 37.3 percent expect to achieve a lower standard of living during retirement. Thus, although many poorly prepared members of the population acknowledge that they save significantly less than they should (Bernheim 1994b), they simultaneously maintain an unrealistic level of optimism concerning personal finances and retirement prospects. For at least this fraction of the population, and possibly for others as well, the failure to save adequately may result both from limited financial knowledge and from self-deception.

D. Does Financial Literacy Affect Savings Behavior?

At this point, it is useful to summarize a number of key findings. A significant majority of Americans are not making adequate financial preparations for their futures. As a result, financial vulnerabilities are widespread. In addition, most Americans are financially illiterate. Although those with high earnings and college degrees tend to obtain higher scores for economic literacy, these scores still indicate substantial deficiencies. One manifestation of financial illiteracy is a failure to appreciate financial vulnerabilities. Americans generally exhibit an excessive degree of optimism concerning their financial status. Consequently, financial illiteracy may be at the root of the documented shortfall of saving and insurance.

The preceding observations raise the possibility that the most financially literate individuals may recognize potential financial vulnerabilities, and make more adequate financial preparations than those who are less financially literate. If so, efforts to promote financial education, training, and knowledge may have a profound effect on personal saving. The purpose of this section is to analyze the impact of financial training and literacy on behavior.

1. Do Those with Financial Training Save More?

One approach to measuring the impact of financial training on behavior is to ask whether those who have received training save more than those who have not. Although this agenda sounds simple, it is fraught with difficulties. For example, relatively few adults receive anything resembling formal financial training, and participation in such training is self-selected. Thus, a significant correlation between adult financial training and saving would not, by itself, establish that training alters behavior.

One solution to both of these problems is to examine the impact of developmental experiences (prior to adulthood) on adult decisions. Formal and informal modes of financial training prior to adulthood are both common and identifiable. In addition, individuals often have little control over their own early developmental experiences.

The Luntz-Webber/Merrill Lynch survey contains a battery of questions designed to assess early developmental experiences related to financial training. These questions include the following:

- When you were growing up, did your parents talk to you always, often, sometimes, rarely, or never about their personal financial decisions?
- When you were a child, did you receive a specific allowance from your parents?
- Prior to age 16, did you have any bank accounts, perhaps held jointly with a parent, to which you deposited your own money?
- Prior to age 16, did you own any securities, such as stocks or bonds (perhaps held jointly with a parent)?

Table 12.8 provides a quantitative interpretations of the data. Those who spoke with their parents always or often accumulated 43 percent more for retirement, expressed as a fraction of earnings, than those who spoke with their parents rarely or never. Those who had allowances, bank accounts, and securities saved 36 percent more, 108 percent more, and 40 percent more for retirement (again, expressed as a fraction of earnings) as adults, respectively. These differences are consistent with the hypothesis that financial training prior to adulthood has a profound effect on financial choices during adulthood.

Even the statistics on early experiences contained in table 12.8 do not establish a causal relation. These statistics summarize simple correlations. Once again, we caution the reader that simple correlations may be misleading. For example, children may simply inherit the attitudes of their parents. Then the children of frugal parents will also be frugal. Frugal parents may also be more inclined to give

Table 12.8
Developmental experiences and retirement saving[a]

Developmental experience	Difference in median retirement savings between those with and without the experience[b]
Talked with parents about financial decisions	43%
Received specific allowance	36%
Held bank account	108%
Held securities	40%

Note: To clarify the meaning of these figures, take the 36% in the second line. This means that, relative to their earnings, those who received allowances as children put away 36% more for retirement as adults than those who did not receive allowances as children.
a. Median savings are measured as a multiple of annual earnings. Therefore, differences between those with and without the developmental experiences listed below are not attributable to differences between the adult earnings of these groups.
b. For "Talked with parents about financial decisions," the difference is between those who talked with their parents "always" or "often," and those who talked with their parents "rarely" or "never."

their children allowances, bank accounts, securities, and so forth. Consequently, a correlation may exist even if developmental experiences have no direct impact on behavior. Multivariate analysis, with appropriate control variables, is therefore required. We will come to this analysis shortly.

2. Do Those with Greater Economic Knowledge Save More?
Even if one can establish the efficacy of financial training during childhood, this does not imply that training of adults or young adults will also be effective. In particular, certain developmental experiences (such as making regular deposits to a bank account) may affect adult behavior through habituation, rather than by promoting adult financial literacy. Indeed, our analysis of the Luntz-Webber/Merrill Lynch survey data reveals that there is practically no relation between these experiences and adult test scores. Once individuals reach adulthood, it may be impossible to affect behavior through habituation. Consequently, it is important to determine whether the promotion of adulthood financial literacy can affect behavior, independent of habituation.

There is, without any question, a powerful quantitative relation between economic knowledge and personal saving. As shown in table 12.9, the median ratio of retirement savings to earnings for

Table 12.9
Knowledge and retirement savings

Ratio of retirement savings to earnings	Median	Mean
Test score quartile		
1	0.149	0.421
2	0.222	0.528
3	0.283	0.697
4	0.376	0.873
Self-assess financial knowledge		
Very	0.413	1.26
Somewhat	0.264	0.624
Only a little bit	0.135	0.332
Not at all	0.0	0.316

those receiving the highest test scores (those in the fourth quartile) was roughly two-and-a-half times as large as the median ratio of retirement savings to earnings for those receiving the lowest test scores (those in the first quartile). Similarly, the typical individual who describes him/herself as "very financially knowledgeable" has accumulated more than three times as much as the typical individual who describes him/herself as "only a little financially knowledgeable." Moreover, among those who consider themselves "not at all financially knowledgeable," the median individual has accumulated nothing for retirement. Similar patterns are observed for sample means.

These results do not, however, establish that individuals save more in response to the acquisition of economic knowledge. They are equally consistent with the possibility that individuals acquire economic knowledge after accumulating significant wealth, in order to manage their resources with greater competence. As we observed in subsection B, individuals may pay little attention to mortgage rates until they have accumulated sufficient resources to purchase a house, and they may begin to follow the Dow Jones average only after making significant investments in the stock market. Consequently, the direction of causality in table 12.9 is far from clear and requires further analysis.

3. An Analysis of Causal Relations

The technical term for the problem described in the preceding paragraph is "endogeneity." One can overcome this problem by identifying an appropriate "instrumental variable." Intuitively, our statistical "cure" works as follows. Financial literacy varies in the population for a large number of reasons. One reason is that wealthier individuals have an incentive to gather more financial knowledge, in order to manage their finances more effectively. This is the source of the endogeneity problem. But fortunately, financial literacy also varies for other reasons. If we can identify a portion of the variation in financial literacy that does not result from differences in wealth, then we should be able to determine the effect of a change in financial literacy on the decision to accumulate wealth. This is done through the use of an instrumental variable. In this context, an instrumental variable must be correlated with financial literacy, but must not itself be affected by wealth.

Referring back to subsection B, it is evident that we already have an excellent candidate for an instrumental variable. In particular, although we found that financial test scores were strongly related to resources, macroeconomic test scores were not. We noted in section B that this result was intuitive, since those with greater resources do not necessarily have a greater incentive to acquire macroeconomic knowledge. At the same time, the correlation between financial knowledge and macroeconomic knowledge is extremely high. Thus, the macroeconomic test score is an ideal instrument.

Using this technique, table 12.10 shows that a positive change in financial literacy significantly increases retirement savings. The first relation (equation 1) explains the ratio of retirement savings to earnings as a function of financial test scores and a variety of other variables, including age, earnings, marital status, gender, education, number of children, and race.[7] The coefficient of the respondent's financial test score is quite large, and highly statistically significant. This implies that a change in financial literacy that does not result from the accumulation of wealth (i.e., that is "exogenous") leads to significantly higher saving for retirement.

Equation (2) shows that the "quantity" of developmental experiences strongly influences adulthood behavior, independently of any effect on financial literacy (most likely through habituation). Equation (2) is identical to equation (1), except that we have added a variable measuring the "quantity" of positive developmental experiences.[8] The addition of this variable does not significantly alter the effect of financial literacy, but the effect of developmental experiences on saving in adulthood is large and highly statistically significant.

Table 12.10
Multivariate analysis of retirement savings

Equation number	1	2	3	4
Estimated coefficient for				
Financial test score	7.26 (2.94)*	6.90 (2.89)*	6.78 (2.92)*	6.47 (2.96)*
Developmental experiences	—	0.572 (0.142)**	0.593 (0.143)**	0.571 (0.143)**
Other control variables	Age Earnings Marital status Gender Education Children Race	Age Earnings Marital status Gender Education Children Race	Age Earnings Marital status Gender Education Children Race Parental thrift Parental income High school quality	Age Earnings Marital status Gender Education Children Race Parental thrift Parental income High school quality Studied economics

Notes: For the purposes of this table, test scores are normalized to a scale of 0 to 1, rather than 0 to 100. Estimates are based on two-stage-least-squares regression, treating financial test score as endogenous, and using macroeconomic test score as an instrument. Standard errors are in parentheses.
*Denotes statistical significance at the 3% level.
**Denotes statistical significance at the 1% level.

As noted above, the estimated impact of developmental experiences on retirement saving could be spurious if children simply inherit the financial attitudes of their parents. We test this hypothesis by adding another set of control variables. Two of these measure parental attitudes towards thrift. These variables are constructed from the following survey question:

- Thinking back to your childhood, were your parents more thrifty than average, somewhat more thrifty than average, average, somewhat less thrifty than average, or much less thrifty than average?

A third variable measures parental income. This is constructed from the following survey question: *What occupation did your father spend most of his career in?* This information is used to impute household income using sample medians from the 1968 Current Population Survey. A final variable is intended to control for high school quality. It represents the fraction of the respondent's high school class that attended college.

Equation (3) in table 12.9 shows that the addition of these control variables does not appreciably affect the size or statistical significance of the coefficients of interest. Although the controls are obviously imperfect, there is no evidence that children inevitably inherit life-long attitudes towards saving directly from their parents. Rather, the evidence supports the view that frugal parents train their children to be frugal by providing experiences and activities that habituate saving.

Equation (4) adds a final control variable, which indicates whether the respondent took a course in economics, business/management, or accounting during college or junior college. We add this variable to control for the individual's innate interest in economic issues (which might be correlated both with knowledge and with behavior). The key results are essentially unaffected.

The analysis contained in this section therefore provides cogent evidence in favor of two central propositions: first, that improvements in financial literacy significantly enhance saving for retirement, and second, that early developmental experiences have a substantial effect on adulthood financial choices, most probably through habituation.

E. Do Individuals Process Financial Information Appropriately?

In this section, we examine evidence that sheds light on the manner in which individuals process certain forms of financial information. We find that, in addition to being financially illiterate, most individuals lack an authoritative and reliable source of financial advice and guidance. It is therefore highly doubtful that they adjust their behavior appropriately in response to new information. Indirect evidence confirms this suspicion.

1. Leading Sources of Financial Information and Advice

Table 12.11 summarizes survey responses concerning the relative importance of the five most common sources of financial information and advice (parents and other relatives, friends, personal judgement,

Table 12.11
Primary sources of financial information and advice

Population subgroup	Parents/ relatives (%)	Friends (%)	Personal judgment (%)	Financial professional (%)	Print media (%)
Age					
29–34	34.9	7.8	22.6	9.1	17.7
35–40	27.1	6.3	25.6	16.5	17.3
41–47	23.0	8.0	29.3	11.1	20.2
Gender					
Male	21.5	7.2	29.9	11.5	23.8
Female	34.6	7.7	22.2	13.1	13.3
Race					
White	28.0	7.6	24.9	13.3	20.0
Black	36.4	0.0	36.4	3.0	15.2
Education					
College degree	23.6	9.3	24.0	15.3	23.3
No college degree	31.1	6.2	27.3	10.4	15.3
Earnings					
First quartile	24.7	10.9	32.2	9.2	10.3
Second quartile	29.5	11.0	18.5	12.1	19.1
Third quartile	27.2	5.8	26.6	11.6	21.4
Fourth quartile	29.5	4.6	23.1	15.6	24.3

financial professionals, and print media). As in previous sections, the data are broken down by age, gender, race, education, and earnings. A number of interesting patterns are readily apparent. Younger baby boomers tend to rely more on parents and relatives, and less on their personal judgement. The use of financial professionals appears to peak between ages 35 and 40. For women, parents and relatives are, by far, the dominant source of financial information and advice. In contrast, for men, parents and relatives rank third behind personal judgement and print media. Blacks are much more likely to rely on parents and personal judgement, but these differences may not be representative given the small size of the black subsample. Surprisingly, college-educated individuals are, if anything, slightly less likely to rely on their own personal judgement. Parents and relatives are also less important as sources of financial information and advice for those with college degrees. College education and earnings are both correlated with greater reliance on financial professionals and print media. Those with higher earnings also tend to seek less information and advice from friends. Although those in the lowest earnings quartile rely to a much greater extent on personal judgement, and to a lesser extent on parents and relatives, earnings bear little systematic relation to the use of these sources beyond the lowest quartile.

Given the general state of financial literacy, it is worrisome that so many individuals rely primarily on their own judgement. In the majority of cases, reliance on parents, relatives, and friends amounts to the blind leading the blind. It is therefore noteworthy that somewhere in the neighborhood of 60 percent of virtually every population subgroup relies primarily on parents, relatives, friends, and personal judgement. The fraction relying on financial professionals and print media does not exceed 40 percent for any population subgroup. Thus, it seems likely that most individuals lack an authoritative, reliable source of information and advice. It is particularly noteworthy that negligible fractions of the population rely primarily on potentially objective authoritative sources, such as employers or government publications. Indeed, the fraction of the population using these two possible sources, combined, is less than the fraction that relies on "prayer" or the functional equivalent thereof.

2. *Is Behavior Appropriate, Given Beliefs?*

In light of our findings, it is doubtful that individuals adjust their behavior appropriately in response to new information, such as pension plan data. This is important, since individuals currently receive a great deal of raw pension information, and very little interpretative advice and guidance, from sources such as their employers and the government. For example, any worker can request the Social Security Administration to prepare a "Personal Earnings and Benefit Estimate Statement," much like the statements that many employees receive from their private pension plan sponsors, containing estimates of retirement benefits, based on actual earnings and current law.[9] As of 1995, older workers began to receive these statements automatically, regardless of whether or not they request them. In subsequent years, the Administration has begun to send these statements automatically to younger workers as well. The supposition is, presumably, that better information will help workers to make better decisions. But our analysis suggests that better raw, uninterpreted information may induce workers to make worse decisions.

Unfortunately, it is very difficult to observe the information that different individuals receive concerning their benefits. However, our survey does contain questions concerning beliefs about social security benefits. Information affects behavior by changing beliefs. If behavior responds inappropriately to beliefs, then it probably also responds inappropriately to information. We find that behavioral responses to differences in beliefs are not reasonable. In particular, those with confidence in social security save essentially nothing.

To analyze this issue, we make use of the following survey question:

- Thinking about your future social security benefits, when you retire do you expect to receive no social security benefits, or do you expect to receive more, less, or the same amount of social security benefits as current retirees receive?

Survey responses indicate that 56.6 percent of baby boomers expect to receive either less than current retirees, or nothing at all. Roughly one-quarter of baby boomers expect to receive the same benefits as current retirees, and 18.2 percent anticipate higher benefits.

How do individuals respond to different beliefs about the future of social security? To answer this question, we examined the relation between accumulated wealth and the respondent's degree of confidence in the social security system. Table 12.12 shows, strikingly, that confidence regarding social security benefits is inversely related to savings behavior. To provide a better sense for the relation between wealth accumulation and confidence in social security, table 12.13 shows the results of estimating wealth trajectories for households with different levels of confidence in social security, but otherwise identical characteristics. As of age 30, there are only minor differences between the wealth-to-earnings ratios for those who expect no social security benefits, those who expect lower benefits than current retirees, and those who expect the same benefits. However, by age 47 (the maximum age of respondents in the data sample), the differences are enormous. Between ages 30 and 47, we estimate that those with the least confidence in social security (i.e., those who say they expect to receive no benefits) accumulate incremental wealth equal to slightly more than one (1.045) year's worth of earnings. Likewise, those with the next lowest degree of confidence in social security (i.e., those who say they expect to receive lower benefits than current retirees) accumulate incremental wealth equal to slightly more than

Table 12.12
Multivariate analysis of net worth (excluding housing)

Estimated coefficient for:	
No benefits expected	−1.74 (0.662)*
Lower benefits expected	0.973 (0.545)
(No benefits)* age	0.0563 (0.0173)**
(Lower benefits)* age	0.0280 (0.0140)*
Other control variables	Earnings Marital status Gender Age Education Children Pension status Spouse's pension status Higher benefits expected Various interactions with age

Source: Bernheim (1994b).
Note: Estimates based on ordinary-least-squares regression. Standard errors are in parentheses.
* Indicates statistical significance at the 5% level.
** Indicates statistical significance at the 1% level.

Table 12.13
Asset accumulation and confidence in social security

Individual's expectation about future social security benefits (compared to current levels)	Wealth/earnings ratio		
	Age 30	Age 47	Change
No future benefits	0.320	1.365	1.045
Lower future benefits	0.283	0.846	0.563
Same future benefits	0.367	0.455	0.088

Source: Bernheim (1994b).

one-half (0.563) of one year's worth of earnings. In contrast, those who are confident in social security (i.e., those who reported that they expect to receive the same benefits as current retirees) accumulate very little incremental wealth—less than one-tenth (0.088) of one year's worth of earnings.

Two central points emerge from this analysis of this section. First, survey respondents are plainly misprocessing the raw information that they receive and behaving inappropriately given their beliefs. Second, these findings do not bode well for the impact of the Social Security Administration's new benefit statement policy or any other public or private policy to inform individuals about retirement income that does not also provide some kind of guidance. The widespread misprocessing of the raw information contained in the social security benefit statements and/or private pension accumulation statements could significantly exacerbate recipients' existing savings shortfall.

3. Implications for the Design of Financial Decision-making Tools

If individuals are inclined to misprocess raw information such as forecasts of pension benefits, how can they be induced to use information more appropriately? One alternative is to provide them with better tools for financial decision-making. The design of such tools should be guided by an understanding and appreciation of financial illiteracy.

It has, for example, been suggested that the materials accompanying social security benefit statements should include simple computational aids, such as tables that convert retirement income replacement rates into required rates of preretirement saving. There is, however, a serious problem with this approach. Simple computational tools place much greater responsibility on the user. For example, to use properly the kind of tables described above, an individual must take the initiative to account for all relevant factors, and must integrate retirement saving with other saving objectives. When more is left to the individual, there is a greater chance that the tool will be misused, or not used at all. Ironically, the proper use of less sophisticated financial decision-making tools requires greater sophistication on the part of the user, while the proper use of more sophisticated tools can—at least in principle—be far less demanding of the user. Sophisticated tools can and should be designed to require little or no *conceptual* initiative on the part of the user.

The proper design of financial decision-making tools must also recognize the fact that quantitative targets do not *by themselves* motivate changes in behavior. Evidence on this point is obtained by exploring the relation between survey answers to the following two questions:

- What percentage of your annual household income are you now saving for retirement?
- What percentage of your annual household income do you think you should save for retirement?

We will use the term "actual rates of saving" to denote answers to the first of these questions, and "target rates of saving" to denote answers to the second.

One striking characteristic of this data is that there is typically a large gap between target rates of saving and actual rates of saving. The typical individual reports that he or she should increase his or her rate of saving by roughly 10 percent of annual income. The fact that this large gap (e.g., $5,000 on a $50,000 income) exists suggests that individuals do not regard the saving targets as cogent. Further analysis of the data reveals that every six percentage-point increase in the target rate of saving is associated with roughly a one percentage-point increase in the actual rate of saving. This result suggests that changes in quantitative target rates of saving have very little impact on behavior. Indeed, the estimated relation may overstate the significance of this relation.[10] This confirms the suggestion that quantitative target rates of saving currently lack cogency.

The absence of cogency is not surprising. Recall the evidence presented in section III.C: despite the fact that they save significantly less than they think they should, most households nevertheless believe—contrary to good sense—that they will be all right. In other words, the target rate of saving is a quantitative abstraction. There is little if any connection between this abstraction and concrete, qualitative considerations that motivate changes in behavior. This observation poses a difficult challenge for designing appropriate financial planning tools. To be effective, a tool must not only require little in the way of economic sophistication and conceptual initiative; it must also help users to interpret quantitative targets in terms of concrete consequences, so that prescriptions are psychologically cogent.

A natural concern is whether, given the excessive optimism documented in section III.C, individuals will be receptive to the use of any financial planning tools. Our findings suggest that this concern is probably not well-founded. Relatively few individuals rate themselves as *very* (as opposed to *somewhat*) financially knowledgeable. Similarly, the vast majority of respondents did not express the highest degree of confidence in their finances (e.g., that they were *very well* prepared for retirement). Finally, roughly three-quarters of respondents already rely on external sources of financial information and advice (other than personal judgement). Since the youngest workers (ages 29–34) are least likely to rely on their own judgement (table 12.11), and since they are the most computer literate, they may well be the most receptive to new tools.

IV. The Need for Improved Financial Planning

Appropriate financial planning should assist households in achieving and preserving the highest stable living standard that is also affordable, given their current and projected economic resources. To be realistic, and to provide appropriate recommendations, financial planning should account for a variety of complex factors, including: (a) households' demographic circumstances, such as the numbers and ages of children, (b) economies to scale in shared living, (c) the need to make special expenditures, such as paying for children's college educations or leaving a bequest, (d) the consumption of housing services which are not easily adjusted, and (e) the fact that economic resources and special expenditure needs may be contingent on circumstances. For example, the labor earnings as well as day-care expenses of surviving spouses may differ from those of married spouses.

Financial planning must also remain, from the household's perspective, extremely simple, even though the underlying calculations may be highly complex. This requires soliciting from households no more information than is used under the traditional method of financial planning, and providing recommendations that are easy to understand. It also implies that households should not be required to take conceptual initiative, and make ad hoc adjustments before obtaining reasonable recommendations. The output of financial planning tools should be transparent; it must explain in an understandable fashion, even to those with relatively little financial sophistication, why the recommended saving and insurance amounts are precisely those needed to permit the household to maintain its living standard over time and through various contingencies, while still covering its special expenditures and housing plans.

Finally, financial planning tools should show households the consequences of failing to adhere to the prescribed plan. For example, households should be shown the potential decline in their future living standard if they fail to raise their saving to the level being recommended. They should also be shown the decline in living standards that survivors will suffer if recommended amounts of life insurance are not purchased.

A. The Targeted Liability Approach

We refer to the traditional approach to financial planning as the *targeted liability approach*. Under this approach, households are asked to specify their particular needs, called liabilities. Next, saving and insurance amounts are calculated to meet these liabilities. In the case of saving, liabilities refer to the receipt of a targeted level of post-retirement income, the future payment of college tuition, the accumulation of a downpayment for a house, etc. The targeted level of postretirement income is typically set through the choice of a ratio of post- to preretirement income—the income-replacement rate. Once a client's saving liabilities are determined, the planner calculates the constant (in real terms) amounts the client needs to save each year to meet (fund) these liabilities.

In the case of life insurance, an estate liability, measured as a present value, is established based on the amount of income the potential decedent wishes to provide to his or her survivors. The targeted level of survivors' income is chosen based on another income-replacement rate—the desired ratio of survivors' income to current household income. The recommended amount of life insurance is then calculated as the difference between the household's current assets and the estate liability.

There are several critical problems with the targeted liability approach.

1. *The absence of clear criteria* The traditional method provides no clear criteria for setting its most important target, namely the income-replacement target or ratio that determines retirement income. Absent such criteria, households (or their financial planners) typically fall back on conventional rules of thumb, such as "target to replace in retirement 70 percent of preretirement labor earnings."

But such targets can lead to highly inappropriate prescriptions. For households with high assets relative to labor earnings, a 70 percent replacement rate is likely to be much too low. Such households are induced to save relatively little (consume relatively a lot) prior to retirement. Consequently, they will experience a significant decline in their living standard in retirement. For households with low net wealth relative to labor earnings, a 70 percent replacement rate is likely to be much too high. Such households will be led to save relatively large amounts (consume relatively little) prior to retirement in order to finance a much higher living standard in retirement.

2. *Individual needs* The traditional approach fails to adjust properly for household characteristics. For example, the traditional approach recommends the same amount of current saving to meet future savings targets regardless of whether the household composition is expected to change through time (due to the anticipated arrival of new children, or to the departure of grown children), and irrespective of whether the household has temporarily high or low income or expenses. But it is perfectly appropriate for households to save less when dependent children are present. Similarly, households with temporarily high income (temporarily low expenses) will want to save more in the present and less in the future. The reverse is true for households with temporarily low incomes (temporarily high expenses).

3. *Natural communications* The traditional approach is not well-suited for describing concrete consequences, rather than quantitative abstractions. This approach generates recommended levels of saving and insurance, but it does not provide a natural framework for communicating the cogency of these recommendations. This problem is inherent, since the foundation for this approach is an arbitrary notion of income replacement, and since, as noted above, many relevant household characteristics are not formally considered. By ignoring systematic and predictable changes in a household's ability to save, the traditional method often produces highly unrealistic recommendations (see the examples in subsection C that follow). The planning process loses credibility when it asks a household to follow a prescription without regard to its current circumstances. In practical terms, this reduces the likelihood that the household will actually follow the financial plan.

4. *Saving vs. insurance* Traditional financial planning fails to integrate choices that concern saving and insurance.[11] Saving and insurance decisions are highly interdependent. Households that save more don't need to purchase as much insurance through time. Similarly, households that plan to purchase more life insurance through time need to do less precautionary saving to protect against the death of the head or spouse. Thus, saving and insurance choices need to be determined simultaneously and with reference to a consistent set of criteria.

5. *Multiple savings goals* The traditional approach fails to integrate multiple saving objectives, such as retirement income and college tuition. Instead, each objective is translated into an immediate, fixed saving requirement, and these saving requirements are simply added together. But most households do not, and should not, behave this way. For example, they save first primarily for their children's college and, once they have paid for college, start saving in earnest for their retirement. In so doing, they are expressing a preference for stable or *smooth* consumption (living standard) over time.

In practice, experienced financial planners adjust their recommendations to try to compensate for the shortcomings of the traditional financial planning methodology. But even the most experienced financial planners can't be assured that they are making the most appropriate adjustments, many of which involve complex calculations that can only be performed by computer. Moreover, households increasingly are using traditional financial planning methodology, embodied in software or worksheets, to formulate financial plans on their own. Given the low levels of financial literacy of American households, it's likely that most of these households do not know how to begin to adjust, even crudely, for the shortcomings of traditional financial planning. In the context of *personal* financial planning tools (as opposed to *professional* tools for experienced and sophisticated planners), the traditional methodology violates the premise that one should not demand *conceptual* initiative on the part of the user.

B. The Consumption-Smoothing Approach

As described in section II, economic theory provides a framework for evaluating the adequacy of saving and insurance. This same framework can also be used to guide households with respect to their financial decisions. The framework is based on the premise that households wish to smooth their consumption over different stages of their life cycles and also over different possible contingencies. For example, they would like to avoid the need to slash expenditures during periods when their incomes are temporarily low. Nor will they wish to suffer a severe decline in their living standard in the event of the untimely death of the principal earner. Saving and the purchase of insurance are the means by which households can achieve this life-cycle consumption smoothing.

In the simplest version of this life-cycle model, households wish to consume exactly the same amount in each period of life and under each potential contingency. More realistic versions of this model recognize that households have preferences about their life-cycle *pattern* of consumption; e.g., they may prefer to consume relatively more in retirement, or less in the event of the death of a spouse.

We have developed a financial planning software package, entitled Economic Security Planner (see www.ESPlanner.com), that embodies this modern approach to life-cycle decision-making, and that meets the criteria for improved financial planning expressed at the outset of this section.[12] It jointly calculates the amounts of saving households need to do, and the amounts of life insurance they need to purchase to maintain their living standard over time and in the eventuality that one or both spouses passes away. Although it performs calculations that are far more sophisticated than those used in traditional financial planning, it employs a simple, user-friendly interface, and requires no more information from households than the traditional methodology. Unlike traditional tools, the use of this software does not require conceptual initiative, and appropriate prescriptions are obtained without the need for ad hoc adjustments. Since the underlying methodology evaluates financial decisions with reference to standards of living, it also provides natural language for communicating the cogency of recommendations in concrete terms.

Due to its rapid execution time, the program can be designed to assist users in performing sensitivity analyses to alternative assumptions about future economic and demographic events, e.g., by modifying assumptions about future labor earnings. Moreover, the software's ease of use invites continual updating of household information and the recomputation of financial plans, so that financial planning becomes an ongoing, "state-contingent" exercise. Like other financial planning software, *Economic Security Planner* does not provide advice. Rather it represents a tool for households or financial planners serving households to formulate meaningful plans for determining how they should save and insure for the future.

C. A Comparison of the Targeted-Liability Approach and the Consumption-Smoothing Approach

To make our concerns about traditional financial planning more concrete, we present three examples that compare the traditional targeted-liability approach to financial planning to the consumption-smoothing approach, as embodied in Economic Security Planner (ESPlanner, for short). The first two examples demonstrate the importance of basing targets on clear criteria, rather than arbitrary replacement rates, as well as the importance of integrating saving and life insurance decisions. The third example shows why the consumption-smoothing approach produces more practical and affordable strategies for achieving financial targets. It also shows the critical importance of treating multiple saving objectives in an integrated fashion.

Case 1

The first example is the case of Mr. and Mrs. Doe. The Does' vital statistics appear in table 12.14. Table 12.15 shows the results of

Table 12.14
Case 1: Mr. and Mrs. Doe, personal data

Vital statistics	
Age	55
Total net worth	$725,000
Mr. Doe's annual after-tax earnings	$100,000
Projected future earnings growth	None
Mrs. Doe's annual after-tax earnings	None
Projected annual retirement income from pensions and social security, after-tax	$15,000
Dependent children	None
Special needs	None
Economic assumptions	
Real after-tax rate of return	3%
Rate of inflation	0%

Table 12.15
Case 1: Financial planning for Mr. and Mrs. Doe, traditional method

Financial prescriptions	
Target income replacement rate	70%
Required retirement saving out of labor income (assuming reinvestment of all capital income from retirement assets)	$775 per year
Implications	
Annual preretirement spending	$99,225
Annual postretirement spending	$70,000
Percentage change	−29.5%

applying the traditional approach based on a 70 percent income-replacement. With this replacement rate, the traditional methodology would prescribe saving out of labor income at the rate of $775 per year (over and above reinvestment of capital income). What are the implications of this prescription? In effect, the Does are being advised to spend up to $99,225 per year between now and retirement. Subsequent to retirement, however, they will be forced to reduce their expenditures by nearly 30 percent. If the Does do not anticipate a major decline in their needs immediately following retirement, their standard of living will fall precipitously. Why does the traditional methodology produce such imprudent advice? The answer is that its focus is on income, not living standards. Once one considers maintenance of the Does' living standard, it becomes clear that a 70 percent income-replacement target is too low.

Now consider ESPlanner's recommendations for the Does based on the assumption that the Does choose to maintain the same standard of living both before and after retirement and in the event of the death of the head or spouse. As table 12.16 reports, ESPlanner prescribes saving, over and above reinvestment of capital income, of more than $17,000 per year, as well as roughly $273,000 worth of life insurance on Mr. Doe.[13] The prescription allows the Does to spend just over $81,000 per year, and to maintain this level of spending through retirement. Thus, rather than advising the Does to save very little prior to retirement and finance this consumption spree through a 30 percent decline in their living standard after retirement, ESPlanner tells the Does the highest amount they can afford to spend now without suffering an undesired drop in their living standard through time.

Table 12.16
Case 1: Financial planning for Mr. and Mrs. Doe, consumption replacement method

Financial prescriptions (for first year, 1994)	
Retirement saving out of labor income (assuming reinvestment of all capital income from retirement assets)	$17,389
Life insurance, Mr. Doe	$272,904
Life insurance, Mrs. Doe	$0
Total life insurance premiums	$1,354
Implications	
Annual consumption, two survivors	$81,258
Annual consumption, surviving wife	$57,458
Percentage change in consumption after retirement	0%

ESPlanner's calculations also ensure that, if Mr. Doe dies, Mrs. Doe's living standard will stay the same. As table 12.16 indicates, this entails her spending just over $57,000 per year. This is more than one-half of the Does' expenditures when both spouses are alive, reflecting household economies of scale (two can live more cheaply than one).

Case 2

Our second example is the case of Mr. and Mrs. Nodoe. The Nodoes' vital statistics are presented in table 12.17. They are the same as the Does' in all respects, except that they have accumulated only $100,000 in assets. Table 12.18 depicts the results of applying the traditional approach to the Nodoes. An income-replacement rate of 70 percent is used. With this replacement rate, the traditional methodology recommends saving out of labor income at the rate of $74,044 per year (over and above reinvestment of capital income). What are the implications of this prescription? In effect, the Nodoes are being advised to spend only $25,956 per year between now and retirement, so that they can spend $70,000 after retirement! This prescription is clearly untenable, and it is highly unlikely that the Nodoes would take it seriously.

Now compare this with the prescription generated by ESPlanner (table 12.19), which prescribes saving, over and above reinvestment of capital income, of roughly $45,000 per year, as well as roughly $455,000 worth of life insurance on Mr. Nodoe. The prescription allows the Nodoes to spend just over $52,000 per year and to main-

Table 12.17
Case 2: Mr. and Mrs. Nodoe, personal data

Vital statistics	
Age	55
Total net worth	$100,000
Mr. Nodoe's annual after-tax earnings	$100,000
Projected future earnings growth	None
Mrs. Nodoe's annual after-tax earnings	None
Projected annual retirement income from pensions and social security, after-tax	$15,000
Dependent children	None
Special needs	None
Economic assumptions	
Real after-tax rate of return	3%
Rate of inflation	0%

Table 12.18
Case 2: Financial planning for Mr. and Mrs. Nodoe, traditional method

Financial prescriptions	
Target income replacement rate	70%
Required retirement saving out of labor income (assuming reinvestment of all capital income from retirement assets)	$74,044 per year
Implications	
Annual preretirement spending	$25,956
Annual postretirement spending	$70,000
Percentage change	+170%

tain this level of spending through retirement. If Mr. Nodoe dies, Mrs. Nodoe will spend $37,000 per year, providing her with an equivalent standard of living. Again, ESPlanner's prescription offers Mr. and Mrs. Nodoe a plan that provides them with the highest stable standard of living that they can sustain.[14]

A comparison of our first two examples also illustrates the importance of integrating savings and life insurance decisions. We have not calculated life insurance prescriptions under the traditional methodology. However, it is easy to see that, given the same income replacement target, the traditional methodology would prescribe $625,000 more life insurance on Mr. Nodoe, than on Mr. Doe (the reason being that the Doe's assets are $625,000 higher). Notice that

Table 12.19
Case 2: Financial planning for Mr. and Mrs. Nodoe, consumption replacement method

Financial prescriptions (for first year, 1994)	
Retirement saving out of labor income (assuming reinvestment of all capital income from retirement assets)	$45,366
Life insurance, Mr. Nodoe	$455,175
Life insurance, Mrs. Nodoe	$0
Total life insurance premiums	$2,258
Implications	
Annual consumption, two survivors	$52,377
Annual consumption, surviving wife	$37,036
Percentage change in consumption after retirement	0%

ESPlanner prescribes only $182,000 more in life insurance for Mr. Nodoe ($455,000 vs. $273,000). Obviously, the Nodoes require more insurance because they have fewer assets. But the difference in insurance requirements is not equal to the difference in net worth (as assumed in the traditional approach), because the Nodoes' affordable standard of living, which the insurance is meant to protect, is lower than that of the Does' (reflecting the fact that the Nodoes are poorer than the Does). Note that if the Does and Nodoes follow the traditional prescription, widow Nodoe and widow Doe will have the same standard of living, even through, when they are both alive, Mr. and Mrs. Doe would have a much higher standard of living (roughly four times as much spending) as Mr. and Mrs. Nodoe, when they are both alive.

In some instances, financial planners base life insurance prescriptions on simple rules of thumb, rather than on an income replacement calculation. For example, households are advised that they should purchase life insurance equal to six to ten times annual earnings. For both the Does and the Nodoes, this prescription is excessive. By age 55, most couples simply do not have as much future survival-contingent income to protect, and proper financial planning should reflect this.

Case 3

Our third example is the case of Mr. and Mrs. Young. The Youngs' vital statistics appear in table 12.20. Table 12.21 depicts the results of applying the traditional approach. Here, an income replacement rate

Table 12.20
Case 3: Mr. and Mrs. Young, personal data

Vital statistics	
Age	35
Total net worth	\$100,000
Mr. Young's annual after-tax earnings	\$100,000
Projected future earnings growth	1% annual
Mrs. Young's annual after-tax earnings	None
Mrs. Young's annual after-tax earnings and survivor benefits conditional on Mr. Young's death	\$30,000
Projected annual retirement income from pensions and social security, after-tax	\$15,000
Dependent children	Triplets, age 5
Special needs	College expenses (\$250,000 in 2006)
Economic assumptions	
Real after-tax rate of return	3%
Rate of inflation	0%

Table 12.21
Case 3: Financial planning for Mr. and Mrs. Young, traditional method

Financial prescriptions	
Target income replacement rate	80%
Required retirement saving out of labor income (assuming reinvestment of all capital income from retirement assets)	\$29,378 per year
Required supplemental saving for college expenses (through 2005)	\$15,541 per year

Implications

Annual household spending	Amount	Standard of Living (SOL) Index
Age 35	\$55,081	1.00
Age 45	\$65,543	1.19
Age 55	\$92,641	2.13
Age 65 (and after)	\$106,760	2.45

of 80 percent is used. The traditional methodology prescribes saving at the rate of $29,378 per year through retirement, and supplemental saving of $15,541 per year, through 2005, for college tuition. What are the implications of this prescription? In effect, the Youngs are being advised to spend only $55,081 currently. This amount will grow with earnings to $65,543 at age 45. Then, once the children have left the household and college expenses have been paid, their spending will jump to $92,641 at age 55. It will then continue to grow with earnings, to $106,760 at age 65.

This recommendation is unrealistic for the Youngs because it is insensitive to their circumstances. First, the traditional planning ignores changing needs related to changing household composition. Second, it ignores anticipated growth of income, and third, it fails to integrate the Youngs' two saving objectives (college and retirement). The Youngs are told to save the most when their needs are highest and their income is the lowest. They are told to increase their spending dramatically after their children leave the household, precisely when their needs decline. As a result, their standard of living (as measured by the "SOL index") more than doubles between ages 35 and 55. The Youngs would most likely discard this prescription, since it requires them to sacrifice too much when their needs are greatest.

Now compare this with the prescription generated by ESPlanner (table 12.22), which prescribes saving, over and above reinvestment

Table 12.22
Case 3: Financial planning for Mr. and Mrs. Young, consumption replacement method

Financial prescriptions (for first year, 1994)		
Retirement saving out of labor income (assuming reinvestment of all capital income from retirement assets)		$3,447
Life insurance, Mr. Young		$1,088,168
Life insurance, Mrs. Young		$0
Total life insurance premiums		$1,284
Implications		
Annual household spending		
	Amount	Standard of Living (SOL) Index
Age 35	$95,270	1.00
Age 45	$95,270	1.00
Age 55	$75,318	1.00
Age 65 (and after)	$75,318	1.00

of capital income, of just under $3,500 in 1994, or roughly 3.5 percent of after-tax earnings, as well as roughly $1.1 million worth of life insurance on Mr. Young. Note that our insurance prescription represents nearly eleven times earnings, and therefore exceeds the top end of the usual rule-of-thumb range (six to ten times earnings) used by financial planners. This is because the Youngs are especially vulnerable to the loss of Mr. Young's future earnings. Our saving target rises through time with earnings, and increases significantly once the Young's children have left their household. This prescription allows the Youngs to spend roughly $95,000 per year while their children are at home, and roughly $75,000 per year after their children leave home (which provides them with roughly the same standard of living).

V. Conclusions

In this chapter, we have reviewed existing evidence, and have presented new evidence, concerning the financial status of American workers. This evidence depicts a crisis in financial planning. Most Americans are not making prudent financial decisions. To a large extent, they are unaware of their financial vulnerabilities, and they lack the knowledge, sophistication, and/or authoritative guidance required to set them on the right track.

A rapidly increasing number of Americans are seeking tools for personal financial planning. Unfortunately, the mechanical application of tools based on the prevailing approach to financial planning often produces prescriptions that are inappropriate and unreasonable. The proper use of these tools requires considerable judgement, sophistication, and conceptual initiative. A new financial planning tool, based on an alternative methodology, provides more sensible and cogent prescriptions without demanding cleverness or sophistication on the part of the user.

Notes

1. A recent study by Auerbach and Kotlikoff demonstrates that deep cuts in social security, or steep increases in taxes, will be required to achieve long-run fiscal balance. Bernheim (1994a) analyzes the importance of these policy scenarios for the adequacy of saving by baby boomers.

2. More specifically, the comparison is between 25 to 44-year-olds in 1962 and 1989.

3. Calculations based on evidence presented in Avery and Rendall (1994) suggest, however, that the typical baby boomer will inherit no more than $20,000, and probably much less. It is also noteworthy that the ratio of national wealth to national income has declined significantly over the last few decades. This suggests that, relative to income, baby boomers will receive smaller bequests than previous generations. The baby boomers' parents are likely to bequeath smaller fractions of their lifetime resources because of increasing annuitization and decreasing life insurance (see Auerbach, Kotlikoff, and Weil, 1992).

4. Suppose, for example, that we ask three individuals, A, B, and C, the same question. Suppose that the true answer is "5," that A answers "6," B answers "8," and C answers "0." Then A would receive a score of 100, B would receive a score of 67, and C would receive a score of 33.

5. The test of economic knowledge contained in the Luntz-Webber/Merrill Lynch survey is obviously imperfect. Some discrepancies between self-assessed knowledge and test scores may be attributable to subtle biases. In particular, cultural bias may account for the disparate effects of race in tables 12.3 and 12.6. Consider, for example, the question on the national unemployment rate. It is well known that survey respondents often reinterpret questions, providing answers that are more relevant to their own circumstances. Blacks might well report an unemployment figure that is accurate for blacks, but not for the general population. A closer inspection of answers to this particular question reveals that, although the median rate of unemployment reported by blacks and whites is identical (8 percent), a far larger fraction of blacks report rates in excess of 15 percent. Thus, it appears that a sizable minority of black respondents may be interpreting the question differently than intended, and providing an answer that is both more relevant, and more accurate, for their circumstances.

6. Formally, this is accomplished by estimating three quartile regressions (median, first quartile, and third quartile), explaining the wealth-to-earnings ratio as a function of household characteristics. Households are then placed into adjusted-wealth quartiles based on the relation between their actual wealth-to-earnings ratios and the fitted ratios from the quantile regressions.

7. The dependent variable is actually $ln[(RS + 1)/(EARN + 1)]$, where ln is the natural log, RS is retirement savings, and $EARN$ is total household earnings. We take logs in recognition of the fact that the distribution of wealth is extremely skewed and to reduce the influence of outliers. We add 1 to the numerator and denominator to assure that the argument is strictly positive.

8. Each respondent is given one point for receiving an allowance, one point for holding a bank account, one point for owning securities, one point for "sometimes" talking with his/her parents about finances, and two points for "always" or "often" talking with his/her parents about finances. We use an aggregate measure of developmental experiences to conserve space and degrees of freedom. We have also estimated specifications that allow each experience to have a different quantitative effect. Each experience affects saving in the predicted direction, but the level of statistical significance varies. As in table 12.8, the most powerful effect appears to flow from holding a bank account.

9. Three estimates are provided, corresponding to retirement at age 65, retirement at the earliest age at which full benefits are available, and retirement at age 70. All estimates are in today's dollars.

10. Different individuals may implicitly measure saving in different ways, and this automatically creates a spurious correlation between actual rates of saving and target rates of saving in cross-sections. In addition, for some individuals, target rates of saving may reflect ex post rationalizations of behavior.

11. Insurance is not considered when setting saving objectives. Wealth is considered when setting insurance levels, but in an ad hoc and inappropriate way (see the examples in subsection IV.C).

12. This software is the property of our company, Economic Security Planning, Inc.

13. Incidentally, the life insurance premia used by ESPlanner in these examples are those of TIAA-CREF.

14. It is, of course, possible that the Nodoes would be unwilling to reduce their spending immediately to $52,000 per year. If so, ESPlanner would help guide them in revising their plan. In particular, it would suggest that they might want to consider accepting a 10 percent reduction (or more) in their standard of living after retirement, or after Mr. Nodoe's death. A new plan could then be calculated, based on these new parameters. In this way, ESPlanner would help the Nodoes to understand the tradeoffs between their standard of living today, and their standard of living either after retirement or after the death of Mr. Nodoe. ESPlanner would also suggest other ways to modify the financial plan, including postponing retirement and downsizing housing.

References

Alliance Against Fraud in Telemarketing, *Top Emerging Scams of 1992*, Washington D.C., Winter 1992.

Arthur D. Little, Inc., *America's Retirement Crisis: The Search for Solutions*, Final Report to Oppenheimer Management Corporation, June 1993.

Attanasio, Orazio P., "A Cohort Analysis of Saving Behavior by U.S. Households," CEPR Publication No. 256, June 1991.

Auerbach, Alan J. and Laurence J. Kotlikoff, "Life Insurance of the Elderly: Adequacy and Determinants," in G. Burtless, ed., *Work, Health, and Income Among the Elderly*, The Brookings Institution, Washington D.C., 1987, 229–68.

Auerbach, Alan J. and Laurence J. Kotlikoff, "Life Insurance Inadequacy—Evidence from a Sample of Older Widows," National Bureau of Economic Research working paper No. 3765, 1991a.

Auerbach, Alan J. and Laurence J. Kotlikoff, "The Adequacy of Life Insurance Purchases," *Journal of Financial Intermediation* 1(3), June 1991b, 215–41.

Auerbach, Alan J. and Laurence J. Kotlikoff, *The United States' Fiscal and Saving Crises and their Implications for the Baby Boom Generation*, Merrill Lynch, Pierce, Fenner and Smith, Inc., February, 1994.

Auerbach, Alan J., Laurence J. Kotlikoff, and David N. Weil, "The Increasing Annuitization of the Elderly—Estimates and Implications for Intergenerational Transfers, Inequality, and National Saving," mimeo, University of Pennsylvania, 1992.

Avery, Robert B. and Michael S. Rendall, "Estimating the Size and Distribution of Baby Boomers' Prospective Inheritances," in the *Proceedings of the 1993 Annual Meeting of the American Statistical Association*, 1994.

Bernheim, B. Douglas, "Social Security Benefits: An Empirical Study of Expectations and Realizations," in Rita Ricardo-Campbell and Edward P. Lazear, eds., *Issues in Contemporary Retirement*, Stanford: Hoover Institution Press, 1988, 312–45.

Bernheim, B. Douglas, *Is the Baby Boom Generation Preparing Adequately for Retirement? Summary Report*, Merrill Lynch, Pierce, Fenner and Smith, Inc., January, 1993.

Bernheim, B. Douglas, *The Merrill Lynch Baby Boom Retirement Index*, Merrill Lynch, Pierce, Fenner and Smith, Inc., July 1994a.

Bernheim, B. Douglas, "Do Households Appreciate Their Financial Vulnerabilities? An Analysis of Actions, Perceptions, and Public Policy," *Tax Policy and Economic Growth*, Washington, D.C.: American Council for Capital Formation, forthcoming, 1994b.

Bernheim, B. Douglas, "Personal Saving, Information, and Economic Literacy: New Directions for Public Policy," in *Tax Policy for Economic Growth in the 1990s*, Washington D.C.: American Council for Capital Formation, 1994c, 53–78.

Bernheim, B. Douglas and John Karl Scholz, "Private Saving and Public Policy," *Tax Policy and the Economy* 7, 1993, 73–110.

Bosworth, Barry, Gary Burtless, and John Sabelhaus, "The Decline in Saving: Some Microeconomic Evidence," *Brookings Paper on Economic Activity* 1, 1991, 183–241.

Buckles, Stephen, and Vera Freeman, "Male-Female Differences in the Stock and Flow of Economic Knowledge," *Review of Economics and Statistics* 65(2), May 1983, 355–58.

Cantor, Richard and Andrew Yuengert, "The Baby Boom Generation and Aggregate Savings," mimeo, Federal Reserve Bank of New York, 1994.

Congressional Budget Office, *Baby Boomers in Retirement: An Early Perspective*, September 1993.

Consumer Federation of America and the American Express Company, *High School Competency Test Report of Findings*, Washington D.C., 1991.

Crenshaw, Albert B., "For Too Many, Managing Money Isn't Child's Play," *The Washington Post*, October 3, 1993.

Diamond, Peter A., "A Framework for Social Security Analysis," *Journal of Public Economics* 8(3), December 1977, 275–98.

Easterlin, Richard A., Christine M. Schaeffer, and Diane J. Macunovich, "Will the Baby Boomers be Less Well Off Than Their Parents? Income, Wealth, and Family Circumstances Over the Life Cycle," mimeo, University of Southern California, 1993.

Faber, R. and T. O'Guinn, "Compulsive Consumption and Credit Abuse," *Journal of Consumer Policy* 11, 97–109.

Ferber, Marianne A., Bonnie G. Birnbaum, and Carole A. Green, "Gender Differences in Economic Knowledge: A Reevaluation of the Evidence," *Journal of Economic Education* 14(2), Spring 1983, 24–37.

Feenberg, Daniel and Jonathan Skinner, "Sources of IRA Saving," *Tax Policy and the Economy* 3, 1989, 25–46.

Hamermesh, Daniel S., "Consumption During Retirement: The Missing Link in the Life Cycle," *Review of Economics and Statistics* 66(1), February 1984, 1–7.

Hira, Tahira K., "Financial Management Knowledge and Practices: Implications for Financial Health," mimeo, Iowa State University, 1993.

Holden, K. C., R. V. Burkhauser, and D. A. Myers, "Pensioners' Annuity Choice: Is the Well-Being of Their Widows Considered?" University of Wisconsin, Institute for Research on Poverty discussion paper 802–86, 1986.

Hurd, Michael D., and David A. Wise, "The Wealth and Poverty of Widows: Assets Before and After the Husband's Death," in D. Wise, ed., *The Economics of Aging*, Chicago and London: University of Chicago Press, 1989, 177–99.

Jackstadt, Stephen L., and Christiaan Grootaert, "Gender, Gender Stereotyping, and Socioeconomic Background as Determinants of Economic Knowledge," *Journal of Economic Education* 12(1), Winter 1980, 34–40.

Jordan, Mary, "90 Million Lack Simple Literacy," *The Washington Post*, September 9, 1993.

Kahneman, D., P. Slovic, and A. Tversky, *Judgement Under Uncertainty: Heuristics and Biases*, Cambridge: Cambridge University Press, 1982.

Kingson, Eric, *The Diversity of the Baby Boom Generation: Implications for Their Retirement Years*, American Association of Retired Persons, April 1992.

Kotlikoff, Laurence, Steven Johnson, and William Samuelson, "Can People Compute? An Experimental Test of the Life-Cycle Consumption Model," NBER working paper # 2183, 1987.

Kotlikoff, Laurence, Avia Spivak, and Laurence Summers, "The Adequacy of Savings," *American Economic Review* 72(5), December 1982, 1056–69.

KPMG Peat Marwick, *Retirement Benefits in the 1990s*, September 1993.

Levin, Laurence, "Are Assets Fungible? Testing Alternative Theories of Life-Cycle Savings," mimeo, Santa Clara University, 1992.

Mankiw, N. Gregory and David N. Weil, "The Baby Boom, the Baby Bust, and the Housing Market," *Regional Science and Urban Economics* 19, May 1989, 235–58.

Ng, Yew Swang, "Do Individuals Optimize in Intertemporal Consumption/Savings Decisions? A Liberal Method to Encourage Savings," *Journal of Economic Behavior and Organization* 17(1), January 1992, 101–14.

O'Neill, Barbara, *How Real People Handle Their Money: 35 Financial Planning Case Studies*, New Brunswick, N.J.: Rutgers Cooperative Extension Publications, 1990.

O'Neill, Barbara, "Assessing America's Financial IQ: Realities, Consequences, and Potential For Change," mimeo, Rutgers Cooperative Extension, 1993.

Schieber, Sylvester J. and John Shoven, "The Consequences of Population Aging on Private Pension Fund Saving and Asset Markets," CEPR Publication No. 363, September 1993.

Shefrin, Hersh and Richard Thaler, "Life-Cycle vs. Self-Control Theories of Saving: A Look at the Evidence," mimeo, 1983.

Shefrin, Hersh, and Richard Thaler, "The Behavioral Life-Cycle Hypothesis," *Economic Inquiry* 26, 1988, 609–43.

Vaupel, James W., "Uncertainties and New Evidence about the Prospects for Longer Life Expectancy," mimeo, Odense University, Denmark, 1992.

Walstad, William B., and Max Larsen, "A National Survey of American Economic Literacy," National Council on Economics Education, July 1992.

Walstad, William B., and John C. Soper, "A Report Card on the Economic Literacy of U.S. High School Students," *American Economic Review* 78(2), May 1988, 251–56.

Warshawsky, Mark, "Sensitivity to Market Incentives: The Case of Policy Loans," *The Review of Economics and Statistics* 69(2), May 1987, 286–95.

Watts, Michael, "Student Gender and School District Differences Affecting the Stock and Flow of Economic Knowledge," *Review of Economics and Statistics* 69(3), August 1987, 561–66.

Whitehead, David J., and Tony Halil, "Economic Literacy in the United Kingdom and the United States: A Comparative Study," *Journal of Economic Education* 22(2), Spring 1991, 101–10.

Yakoboski, Paul and Celia Silverman, "Baby Boomers in Retirement: What Are Their Prospects?" *EBRI Special Report and Issue Brief* No. 151, July 1994.

13 How Much Should Americans Be Saving for Retirement?

with B. Douglas Bernheim, Lorenzo Forni, and Jagadeesh Gokhale

How much should Americans save as they approach retirement? This is a critical question for any generation in its 40s and 50s. But it's particularly apt for baby boomers given that their future social security income is so uncertain. This uncertainty reflects the perilous condition of the system's finances. According to social security's actuaries, paying the full amount of promised benefits over time necessitates an immediate and permanent 4.7 percentage point hike in the program's 12.4 percent payroll tax rate.[1] The prospect that Congress and the Administration will raise social security taxes by almost two-fifths seems remote. And the smaller the chances of a major tax hike, the larger the chances of a major benefit cut.

This study applies a new financial planning software program, Economic Security Planner or ESPlanner, to consider how much households close to retirement should save. ESPlanner was developed by Economic Security Planning, Inc. The program maximizes households' sustainable living standards subject to borrowing constraints. It simultaneously determines the amounts of saving and life insurance households need to preserve their living standards through time,[2] We perform our analysis under two assumptions—that social security pays its promised benefits in full and that the Social Security Administration permanently cuts benefits by 30 percent starting in fifteen years. Our data set is the Health and Retirement Survey (HRS), specifically households with heads aged 50 through 61.

To preview our conclusions, ESPlanner's recommended saving rates are fairly high for all but the poorest HRS households. In addition, if HRS households are saving under the assumption that social security benefits will be paid in full, they are saving far too little given the potential for major cuts in those benefits when the baby boomers retire.

The chapter proceeds with brief descriptions of ESPlanner, our HRS data set, social security's long-term finances, and our findings.

I. ESPlanner

Consider maximizing an intertemporally separable, isoelastic utility function, which is defined over survival-state-specific levels of consumption that are adjusted for household composition and economies in shared living. Let this maximization be subject to resource constraints, liquidity constraints, and nonnegativity constraints on life insurance purchases. ESPlanner finds the limit of the solutions to this problem as the intertemporal elasticity of substitution approaches zero.[3] In so doing, it smooths the living standards of household members to the extent permitted by the household's borrowing constraints.

In forming its calculations, ESPlanner treats special expenditures and housing expenses as "off-the-top" expenses that are not subject to consumption smoothing. Contributions to and withdrawals from tax-favored retirement accounts are also treated as exogenous. In addition to requiring these inputs, ESPlanner needs projections of future earnings, assessments of the size of current nontax-favored as well as tax-favored assets, information on defined benefit pensions, social security benefits for those currently collecting, and past and projected covered earnings for those not yet collecting.

ESPlanner uses covered earnings to estimate the size of social security benefits for those not yet collecting benefits. Its benefit calculator considers eligibility rules, early retirement reductions, delayed retirement credits, benefit recomputations, the phased increase in the normal retirement age, the earnings test, family benefit maximums, the wage indexation of average indexed monthly earnings, and the price indexation of benefits once they are received. All these elements feed into the determination of retirement, spousal, mother, father, children, and widow(er) benefits.

ESPlanner also calculates federal and state income and payroll taxes in the process of deciding how much a household can spend without outliving its resources. In the case of the federal income tax, for each year and survival state, the software computes itemizable deductions, and then determines whether the household should itemize or take the federal standard deduction. The software also incorporates federal deductions and exemptions, the partial taxation of social security benefits, the earned income tax credit, the child tax credit, the phase-out at higher income levels of itemized deductions, and the indexation of tax brackets to the consumer price index. In forming federal and state taxable income, ESPlanner deducts, as appropriate, contributions to tax-favored accounts and includes, as appropriate, withdrawals from these accounts. The program considers most, but not all, factors entering into saving and insurance decisions. Its biggest omission is the riskiness of future income and expenditures on health care and other necessities. One can partly compensate for this shortcoming by entertaining worst-case scenarios. Since we do not consider such scenarios in this study, our reported recommended saving rates are likely to understate the rates at which households near retirement should save.

II. The HRS

Our data are drawn from the 1992 wave of the HRS, which covers 12,652 respondents aged 51 to 61 and their families. In drawing its sample, the HRS interviewed 5,000 married couples in which both spouses responded, 200 married couples in which one of the two respondents refused to answer, and 2,452 single individuals. Our analysis considers only households whose heads are ages 50 through 61 and for whom covered social security earnings are available for the head, and, if married, his or her spouse.

The survey collects information on health, income, wealth, pensions, social security benefits, demographics, education, housing, food consumption, family structure and transfers, current and past employment, retirement plans, cognition, health and life insurance, inter vivos gifts, inheritances, and bequests.[4] Unfortunately, the HRS data fields do not match up perfectly with the inputs required by ESPlanner. Bernheim, Forni, Gokhale, and Kotlikoff (1999) detail our procedures for imputing missing data.

III. Social Security's Long-Term Funding Crisis

The 38 percent tax hike needed to shore up social security's long-term finances is more than twice the size of the requisite tax rise acknowledged in the Social Security Administration's Trustees'

Report (1999). The discrepancy between the two figures reflects the Trustees' Report's truncation of its projection horizon. The Trustees' Report looks out only 75 years, whereas the 38 percent figure is a truly long-term calculation. While 75 years may seem like a long-enough horizon, projected social security deficits in 76 years and beyond are extremely large. In this regard, it's important to note that a significant component of social security's current long-term financial problem is the result of the 1983 Greenspan Commission's not looking far enough into the future. Indeed, the Commission could have forecast back in 1983 that social security would face a massive 75-year financing shortfall in 1999 simply because of the addition of 16 years of large annual deficits into the 1999 75-year projection window.

Unfortunately, there is good reason to believe that even a 38 percent payroll tax hike would not suffice to address social security's problems. The 38 percent figure is calculated based on intermediate economic and demographic assumptions. But the "intermediate" nature of these assumptions has been called into question by top economists and demographers. Indeed, the Social Security Advisory Board's 1999 technical panel recommended changes in the assumed intermediate rates of longevity improvement, real wage growth, and interest on government securities. In combination, the modified assumptions appear to raise the Old Age Survivors and Disability Insurance (OASDI) tax hike needed for true long-run solvency to almost 6 percentage points, which translates into a nearly 50 percent tax rise!

IV. Recommended Saving Rates

Table 13.1 presents median recommended saving rates for HRS households whose heads are sorted into two age groups—50 to 55 and 56 to 61. The table also decomposes its results by household income, marital status, race, and education. Saving rates are presented assuming that social security benefits will be (a) paid in full or (b) cut permanently by 30 percent starting in 15 years. A cut of this magnitude in the not-too-distant future appears to us to be roughly what lies ahead for the system. The table's results are based on an assumed 6 percent nominal interest rate and a 3 percent inflation rate. The numerator of the saving rate is defined as nontax-favored

Table 13.1
ESPlanner's median recommended nontax-favored saving rates (ratio of nontax-favored saving to income by income and demographic group)

	$0–$15,000			$15,000–$45,000			$45,000–$100,000			$100,000+		
50–55	Full benefits	Benefit cut	Obs	Full benefits	Benefit cut	Obs	Full benefits	Benefit cut	Obs	Full benefits	Benefit cut	Obs
Total sample	.01	.06	243	.13	.20	533	.14	.19	502	.17	.20	116
Married	.00	.10	37	.09	.17	272	.14	.19	429	.17	.20	111
Single	.01	.05	206	.17	.24	261	.20	.24	73	.28	.29	5
Non White	.02	.06	126	.19	.25	169	.18	.22	61	.21	.23	17
Non College	.01	.05	226	.13	.20	445	.16	.21	317	.18	.21	52
56–61												
Total sample	.00	.03	320	.17	.23	582	.20	.25	454	.23	.25	109
Married	–.11	.01	48	.14	.21	310	.20	.25	408	.23	.25	99
Single	.02	.03	272	.23	.28	272	.23	.26	46	.19	.20	10
Non White	.01	.02	153	.23	.29	153	.24	.30	56	.06	.08	8
Non College	.00	.03	303	.18	.24	474	.22	.27	290	.23	.26	50

saving; that is, saving apart from contributions to or withdrawals from retirement accounts. The income measure used in the denominator also excludes net contributions to these accounts.

Consider first the results for the 50- to 55-year-old households, assuming benefits are paid in full. The median recommended saving rate for households with incomes of $0 to $15,000 is quite small, only 1 percent. On the other hand, for those with $100,000 or more in income, it is fairly high, 17 percent. For low-income households with incomes of $15,000 to $45,000 and moderate income households with incomes of $45,000 to $100,000, the recommended saving rates are 13 percent and 14 percent, respectively. The fact that the median recommended saving rate is close to zero for the low income group and that the rate rises with income is not surprising. Most low-income households will receive the majority of their postretirement incomes from social security. And the higher the level of income, the smaller is the fraction of preretirement income being replaced by social security. The older sample, aged 56 to 61, generates the same pattern of saving rates by income. But with the exception of those with very low income, the median recommended saving rates are significantly higher, ranging from 17 percent for households with $15,000 to $45,000 in income to 23 percent for households with $100,000 or more in income.

Can households achieve these high saving rates by simply saving/reinvesting the capital income they earn on the nontax-favored assets they've accumulated to date? To examine this question, we calculated recommended saving rates out of nonasset income. Specifically, we subtracted nontax-favored capital income from recommended saving to form the numerator of this revised saving rate. To form the denominator, we subtracted the same quantity from income. Hence, the denominator is income exclusive of nontax-favored asset income.

For the lowest and second-lowest income groups, median recommended saving rates are essentially unchanged for both age groups. For households with $45,000 to $100,000 in income, the new medians are 12 percent for younger households and 17 percent for older ones. The corresponding nonasset income medians for the highest income households are 13 percent for younger households and 17 percent for older ones. Hence, the answer to our question is no; while most households don't need to save as large a share of their nonasset income, they still need to save a nontrivial fraction of that income.

ESPlanner generally recommends higher saving rates for single households, nonwhite households, and noncollege-educated households. In some cases, the differences are substantial. Take nonwhite households aged 56 to 61 with $15,000 to $45,000 in income. Their median saving rate is 29 percent, which is 6 percentage points higher than the median for whites and nonwhites combined. Or compare the 28 percent median rate for single households with the 21 percent median for married households in the same income and age range. While there seem to be systematic differences here that merit future research, one should not exaggerate these differences. Within each cell there is a very considerable variation in recommended saving rates. So knowing the particular circumstances of a household is much more important than knowing its general demographic characteristics in formulating a useful saving rate recommendation.

V. The Impact of Potential Social Security Benefit Cuts

Table 13.1 also shows the impact of our hypothetical benefit cut. The results are, in many cases, dramatic. Take married households with very low incomes. Their median saving rate rises by 10 percentage points in the younger group and 12 percentage points in the older group. In the second-lowest income group, the recommended rates for the younger and older age groups increase by 8 and 7 percentage points, respectively. Among high-income households, the recommended saving rate increases are smaller, but nontrivial. Increases in the recommended rates of saving out of nonasset income are equally large. For the middle-income groups, the nonasset income saving rates now range from 16 to 22 percent.

To check the sensitivity of our results to the assumed real rate of return, we redid the analysis using a 8 percent nominal rate of return, which implies a 5 percent real return. For the 50 to 55-year-olds sample, recommended saving rates are 1, 11, 11, and 10 percent for the lowest through highest income classes. The corresponding table 13.1 values are 1, 13, 14, and 17 percent. In the case of the 56 to 61-year-olds sample, the new medians are 1, 16, 17, and 20 percent, compared with the 0, 17, 20, and 23 percent values reported in table 13.1. Thus, recommended saving rates are lower with the higher interest rate. However, earning a higher real interest rate does not mean the HRS households can ignore the possibility of a major social security benefit cut. With our assumed cut, the four saving rate medians are 4, 17, 16, and 12 percent for the younger income groups and 3, 21, 21, and 22 percent for the older ones. These rates are substantially higher than those that assume benefits will be paid in full.

VI. Conclusion

Because of date limitations, knowing precisely the rate at which HRS households save is not easy. Hence, we can't say for sure if HRS households are saving too little or too much. On the other hand, we can apply ESPlanner to the HRS to consider the rate at which Americans approaching retirement should be saving, assuming they wish to smooth their current and future living standards. ESPlanner's recommended saving rates center around zero for very low-income households. But for low, middle, and upper income households, median recommended saving rates are fairly high. For these households, meeting ESPlanner's recommendations requires much more than simply reinvesting asset income or counting on high real rates of return. This is doubly true when one takes into account the very real prospect of major cuts in social security benefits in the not-too-distant future. According to our findings, American households close to retirement, be their incomes high or low, need to save at much higher rates than would otherwise be the case because of the risk of major cuts in social security benefits.

Notes

We are very grateful to the National Institute of Aging for research support and to Economic Security Planning, Inc. for permitting the use of Economic Security Planner (ESPlanner) in this study. The opinions expressed in this chapter are those of the authors and not necessarily those of Stanford University, The National Bureau of Economic Research, The Federal Reserve Bank of Cleveland, The Bank of Italy, or Boston University.

1. This is an unpublished estimate provided by Stephen Goss, Deputy Chief Actuary of the Social Security Administration.

2. Gokhale, Kotlikoff, and Warshawsky (1999) provide numerous examples of ESPlanner's calculations.

3. Auerbach and Kotlikoff (1987) take a similar approach to modeling consumption-smoothing. But unlike their model, ESPlanner accounts for liquidity constraints, adjusts consumption for changes in household composition, and treats state and federal taxes and social security benefits in far greater detail.

4. Mitchell and Moore (1997a and 1997b) provide excellent descriptions of the HRS, in general, and the wealth accumulation of the HRS sample in particular.

References

Auerbach, Alan J. and Laurence J. Kotlikoff, "Life Insurance of the Elderly: Its Adequacy and Determinants," in G. Burtless, ed., *Work, Health, and Income Among the Elderly*, The Brookings Institution, Washington D.C., 1987, 229–68.

Bernheim B. Douglas, Lorenzo Forni, Jagadeesh Gokhale, and Laurence J. Kotlikoff, "The Adequacy of Life Insurance: Evidence from the Retirement History Survey," NBER working paper, no. 7372, 1999.

Gokhale, Jagadeesh, Laurence J. Kotlikoff, and Mark Warshawsky, "Financial Planning—The Economic vs. the Conventional Approach," mimeo, NBER working paper, no. 7321, 1999.

Kingson, Eric. *The Diversity of the Baby Boom Generation: Implications for Their Retirement Years*. Washington, D.C.: American Association of Retired Persons, 1992.

Mitchell, Olivia S. and James F., Moore, "Retirement Wealth Accumulation and Decumulation: New Developments and Outstanding Opportunities," NBER working paper, no. 6178, 1997a.

Mitchell, Olivia S. and James F., Moore, "Projected Retirement Wealth and Savings Adequacy in the Health and Retirement Study," NBER working paper, no. 6240, 1997b.

The 1999 Technical Panel on Assumptions and Methods: Report to the Social Security Advisory Board, Washington, D.C.: Social Security Advisory Board, November 1999.

The 1999 Annual Report of the Board of Trustees of the Federal Old-Age and Survivors Insurance and Disability Insurance Trust Funds, Washington, D.C.: Government Printing Office, March 30, 1999.

14 Comparing the Economic and Conventional Approaches to Financial Planning

with Jagadeesh Gokhale and Mark J. Warshawsky

I. Introduction

The conventional approach to retirement and life insurance planning asks households how much they want to spend after retirement and in the event of the untimely death of the head of household or spouse. It then determines the amounts of saving and life insurance needed to achieve these targets. This approach, which is used throughout the financial planning industry, has received remarkably little attention from economists. This is surprising not only because of the importance of understanding how people formulate their financial plans, but also because traditional financial planning may generate recommendations that are at odds with the economic approach.

The economic approach is based on the life-cycle model of saving developed by Ando and Modigliani (1963) and the canonical model of life insurance developed by Yaari (1965). The goal of the economic approach is to smooth households' living standards over their life cycles and to ensure comparable living standards for potential survivors. In the economic approach, spending targets are endogenous. The targets are derived by calculating the most that each household can afford to consume in the present given that it wants to preserve that living standard into the future. And as stressed by Hubbard and Judd (1987) among others, a household's ability to consume may in the short term also be circumscribed by its ability to borrow.

Although spending targets under the conventional approach can be adjusted to approximate those derived under the economic approach, there are practical limits to such "trial and error" retargeting. Because of the complexity of the relevant factors, these limits especially exist for households experiencing changing demographics, enjoying economies to shared living, or facing borrowing constraints. This chapter illustrates the different saving and insurance recommendations provided by economic financial planning software and conventional financial planning software. The economic financial planning software, Economic Security Planner (ESPlanner), is developed by Economic Security Planning, Inc., and the conventional financial planning software, Quicken Financial Planner (QFP), is developed by Intuit, Inc. Each program is run on twenty-four cases, twenty of which are stylized and four of which are actual households.

We used both programs in a manner that did not require data or information external to the program beyond that provided in direct interrogatives from the programs. In particular, for QFP, we tried to emulate how a somewhat sophisticated household might use the program. QFP begins by asking a household what it is currently spending and whether it wants to continue spending that amount in the future. We expect that most households would answer the latter question in the affirmative. Next, QFP asks the household to enter earnings, net worth, and a variety of other data. Finally, QFP determines if the household's specified time-path of expenditure is feasible. If its plan puts the household into debt (or further into debt if the household started in debt) at any point in the future, QFP tells the household that its plan has failed. A plan can also fail if there are insufficient resources to finance consumption in retirement.[1] By contrast, if a household saves lots of money, it will almost certainly get a passing grade. We then expect that the household would adjust its initial consumption spending to, as closely as possible, "die broke," that is, to end up with zero financial net worth at the end of its planning horizon. Thus, in running QFP on the twenty-four cases, we choose the level of consumption expenditure by iterating until the household's terminal net worth is close to zero. This "trial and error" iteration process is time-consuming, which reinforces our view that even sophisticated households are unlikely to further fine-tune their expenditure plans to deal with demographic change, particularly the arrival and departure of children from the household, or with borrowing constraints.

The two software programs recommend dramatically different levels of saving and life insurance in each of the twenty-four cases with the discrepancies between the two sets of recommendations generally increasing with the complexity of the case. In some cases ESPlanner recommends substantially more saving in early years and substantially less saving in later years than does QFP. In other cases, the opposite is true. The differences in life insurance recommendations are more systematic, with ESPlanner generally recommending significantly less life insurance than QFP.

The different saving recommendations primarily reflect ESPlanner's adjustments for household demographics, economies in shared living, and borrowing constraints, as well as its different, and more detailed, approach to the calculation of federal and state income taxes and social security retirement benefits. The two programs' different life insurance recommendations reflect these factors, ESPlanner's contingent planning, and ESPlanner's integration in its life insurance calculations of social security survivor benefits.

Our comparison of ESPlanner and QFP illustrates some, but certainly not all, of the differences in the conventional and economic approaches. There is a plethora of financial planning software programs adopting the conventional approach. Many of these programs have specific features that differ from those of QFP. Hence in comparing ESPlanner with just QFP, we may be over- or understating typical differences between the two approaches. In addition, although ESPlanner captures the essential items that economists would stress in financial planning, it does not incorporate labor earnings uncertainty, rate of return uncertainty, and other nonlife contingencies that can influence life-cycle consumption choice.[2] ESPlanner does not explicitly consider the premiums, paid whether by the employer or by the household, for health and long-term care insurance, nor the expenditures arising from uninsured health and long-term care contingencies. Nor does ESPlanner optimize, subject to legal constraints, contributions to tax-deferred retirement accounts. Furthermore, although ESPlanner considers life contingencies for the purpose of determining the optimal amount of life insurance, it does not evaluate the optimal amount of life annuities to hold in the retirement period of the life cycle. Hence in comparing ESPlanner only with QFP, which also does not consider these uncertainties and factors, we may be understating the differences between the two approaches.

The chapter proceeds as follows. Sections II and III describe ESPlanner and QFP, respectively. Section IV summarizes the main conceptual and technical differences between the two programs. Sections V and VI compare ESPlanner's and QFP's recommendations for the twenty stylized and four actual cases, respectively. Section VII summarizes the paper and draws conclusions.

II. Economic Security Planner

Economists Douglas Bernheim, Jagadeesh Gokhale, and Laurence Kotlikoff and software engineer Lowell Williams established Economic Security Planning, Inc. to develop ESPlanner, a software package whose primary goal is to foster appropriate saving and insurance decisions.[3] Their stimulus was the findings, in Kotlikoff, Spivak, and Summers (1982), Auerbach and Kotlikoff (1987, 1991), Bernheim (1991, 1995), and other studies, that a significant fraction of households undersaves and underinsures. Undersaving in these studies means that a household can't sustain its current living standard in the future, and underinsuring means it can't sustain its current living standard if the household head or spouse were to die. ESPlanner's objective is to permit households to achieve the highest living standard that they can afford to sustain both through time and in the event of the early death of the household head or spouse.

Unlike many other financial planning programs, ESPlanner's life insurance, consumption, and saving recommendations are fully integrated. The program's consumption and saving recommendations take into account the need to pay life insurance premiums, and its life insurance recommendations are set to ensure the same living standard through time for survivors as that afforded by the otherwise intact household.

What Factors Does ESPlanner Consider?

In determining the extent to which a household can smooth its living standard, ESPlanner takes into account the maximum amount of money the household says it can borrow apart from housing-related debt. It also considers the current and future labor, pension, social security, inheritance, and other income the household will receive and the federal and state income taxes and federal payroll taxes that it will pay. The appendix describes ESPlanner's tax and social security benefit calculations in detail. ESPlanner also takes account of 401(k), 403(b), and other tax-favored saving vehicles, housing plans, special expenditures, estate plans, and preferences about how the household would, if not borrowing constrained, like its living standard to change through time.[4] Finally, ESPlanner recognizes that a household's expenditures do not directly translate into its standard of living. Adjustments are made for household composition and household "economies of scale"—the fact that people can live more cheaply together than apart.[5] To be precise, ESPlanner provides for children until they reach age 19, and takes into account that children may cost more or less than adults and that the relative costs of children can vary by age. It also adjusts for the number of adult equivalents based on a user-specified degree of economies to scale in shared living.

ESPlanner's Recommendations

ESPlanner's principal outputs are recommended time-paths of consumption expenditure, taxable saving, and term-life insurance holdings (for each spouse in the case of married couples). All outputs are displayed in current-year (that is, real) dollars. Consumption in this context is everything the household gets to spend after paying for its "off-the-top" expenditures, that is, its housing expenses, special expenditures, life insurance premiums, taxes, and net contributions to tax-favored accounts. As mentioned, the amount of recommended consumption expenditures varies from year to year in response to changes in the household's composition. It also rises when the household moves from a situation of being liquidity constrained to one of being unconstrained. Finally, recommended household consumption will change over time if users intentionally specify that they want their living standard to change. For example, if users specify that they desire a 10 percent higher living standard after a certain year in the future, the software will incorporate that preference in making its recommendations, provided that it does not violate a borrowing constraint.

ESPlanner's recommended taxable saving in a particular year equals the household's total income (nonasset plus asset income) in that year minus that year's sum of (a) recommended spending on consumption and insurance premiums, (b) specified spending on housing and special expenditures, (c) taxes, and (d) net contributions to tax-favored accounts (contributions less withdrawals).

ESPlanner's recommendations for annual term insurance are either positive or zero.[6] If recommended term insurance is positive for a particular potential decedent (the household head or, if married, spouse) in a particular year and if the decedent dies at the end of that year, the surviving household will have precisely the same living standard as the household would have had absent the decedent's premature death. If the potential decedent's recommended insurance in a particular year is zero, the surviving household will have the same or higher living standard if the decedent dies in that year. These statements are, of course, conditional on the household actually buying the amounts of life insurance being recommended and on the correctness of its assumptions and information concerning future income, current asset holdings, rates of return, special expenditures, and so forth.

Checking ESPlanner's Recommendations

ESPlanner's algorithm is very complicated. But users of the software can check ESPlanner's reports to see that, given their data inputs, preferences, and borrowing constraints, the program recommends the highest and smoothest possible living standard over time. Take, as an example, case 1, the first and simplest of our twenty stylized cases. It involves a Massachusetts couple in which the husband, George, is initially age 29 and the wife, Jane, is initially age 27. (Cases appear at the end of the chapter, pp. 524–547.) George works through age 65 earning $50,000 each year in 1999 dollars. Jane doesn't work. They have no children, no special expenses, no housing expenses, no estate plans, no private defined benefit pension income, no self-employment income, no special receipts, no tax-favored saving accounts, no employer-funded defined contribution accounts, and no coverage under social security.

Turn, now, to table 14.1, which presents the nontax-favored balance sheet for case 1. All values reported in the table and all other ESPlanner reports are in 1999 dollars.[7] Because table 14.1 is a balance sheet, the changes from one year to the next in nontax-favored net worth equal the latter year's nontax-favored saving. Apart from this adding-up property, note that terminal nontax-favored net worth is zero, that is, the household's recommended time-path of spending precisely exhausts the household's economic resources assuming each spouse lives as long as possible. In this particular case, household spending simply includes consumption, life insurance premiums, and funeral expenses of $5,000 for each spouse. In general, spending also includes special expenditures and housing expenses.

This balance sheet tracks the evolution of the household's nontax-favored net worth assuming the household head and spouse both live to their maximum ages of life—assumed to be age 95. As just

Table 14.1
George's and Jane's nontax-favored balance sheet in case 1

Year	George's age	Jane's age	Income	Spending	Taxes	Nontax-favored saving	Nontax-favored net worth
1999	29	27	50,000	26,588	8,640	14,772	14,772
2000	30	28	50,430	26,562	8,872	14,996	29,769
2001	31	29	50,867	26,535	9,108	15,224	44,992
2002	32	30	51,310	26,509	9,347	15,454	60,446
2003	33	31	51,761	26,488	9,590	15,683	76,129
2004	34	32	52,217	26,460	9,837	15,920	92,049
2005	35	33	52,681	26,432	10,088	16,161	108,211
2006	36	34	53,152	26,435	10,342	16,375	124,586
2007	37	35	53,629	26,420	10,698	16,511	141,097
2008	38	36	54,110	26,422	11,083	16,605	157,702
2009	39	37	54,593	26,430	11,470	16,693	174,395
2010	40	38	55,079	26,421	11,859	16,799	191,195
2011	41	39	55,569	26,424	12,250	16,895	208,089
2012	42	40	56,061	26,437	12,644	16,980	225,069
2013	43	41	56,555	26,443	13,040	17,072	242,142
2014	44	42	57,053	26,445	13,437	17,171	259,312
2015	45	43	57,553	26,442	13,837	17,274	276,585
2016	46	44	58,056	26,425	14,240	17,391	293,976
2017	47	45	58,562	26,418	14,645	17,499	311,475
2018	48	46	59,072	26,388	15,053	17,631	329,106
2019	49	47	59,586	26,357	15,464	17,765	346,871
2020	50	48	60,103	26,320	15,878	17,905	364,777
2021	51	49	60,625	26,274	16,295	18,056	382,833
2022	52	50	61,150	26,218	16,716	18,216	401,050
2023	53	51	61,681	26,151	17,140	18,390	419,440
2024	54	52	62,217	26,063	17,569	18,585	438,025
2025	55	53	62,758	25,956	18,002	18,800	456,825
2026	56	54	63,306	25,820	18,440	19,046	475,871
2027	57	55	63,860	25,784	18,883	19,193	495,063
2028	58	56	64,419	25,784	19,331	19,304	514,368
2029	59	57	64,982	25,784	19,781	19,417	533,785
2030	60	58	65,547	25,784	20,233	19,530	553,316
2031	61	59	66,116	25,784	20,688	19,644	572,960
2032	62	60	66,688	25,784	21,146	19,758	592,719
2033	63	61	67,264	25,784	21,606	19,874	612,592
2034	64	62	67,842	25,784	22,069	19,989	632,582

Table 14.1 (continued)

Year	George's age	Jane's age	Income	Spending	Taxes	Nontax-favored saving	Nontax-favored net worth
2035	65	63	18,425	25,784	8,018	−15,377	617,205
2036	66	64	17,977	25,784	7,776	−15,583	601,622
2037	67	65	17,523	25,784	7,531	−15,792	585,830
2038	68	66	17,063	25,784	7,283	−16,004	569,826
2039	69	67	16,597	25,784	7,031	−16,218	553,608
2040	70	68	16,125	25,784	6,776	−16,435	537,173
2041	71	69	15,646	25,784	6,517	−16,655	520,518
2042	72	70	15,161	25,784	6,256	−16,879	503,639
2043	73	71	14,669	25,784	5,990	−17,105	486,534
2044	74	72	14,171	25,784	5,721	−17,334	469,201
2045	75	73	13,666	25,784	5,448	−17,566	451,635
2046	76	74	13,154	25,784	5,172	−17,802	433,833
2047	77	75	12,636	25,784	4,892	−18,040	415,793
2048	78	76	12,110	25,784	4,608	−18,282	397,512
2049	79	77	11,578	25,784	4,321	−18,527	378,985
2050	80	78	11,038	25,784	4,029	−18,775	360,210
2051	81	79	10,492	25,784	3,734	−19,026	341,184
2052	82	80	9,937	25,784	3,435	−19,282	321,903
2053	83	81	9,376	25,784	3,132	−19,540	302,363
2054	84	82	8,807	25,784	2,824	−19,801	282,562
2055	85	83	8,230	25,784	2,513	−20,067	262,495
2056	86	84	7,645	25,784	2,197	−20,336	242,159
2057	87	85	7,053	25,784	1,877	−20,608	221,551
2058	88	86	6,453	25,784	1,553	−20,884	200,667
2059	89	87	5,845	25,784	1,403	−21,342	179,326
2060	90	88	5,223	25,784	1,254	−21,815	157,511
2061	91	89	4,588	25,784	1,101	−22,297	135,214
2062	92	90	3,938	25,784	945	−22,791	112,424
2063	93	91	3,274	25,784	786	−23,296	89,129
2064	94	92	2,596	25,784	623	−23,811	65,318
2065	95	93	1,902	30,784	457	−29,339	35,980
2066		94	1,048	16,115	286	−15,353	20,627
2067		95	601	21,115	113	−20,627	0

suggested, ESPlanner's planning horizon extends through the maximum ages of life of the household head and, if married, his or her spouse. The emphasis here on the maximum, rather than the expected, length of life is a part of ESPlanner's general philosophy, namely to plan conservatively.

Consumption spending in this case is constant at $25,784 until George reaches age 95. It then declines to $16,115, the amount Jane gets to spend on herself after George has passed away. The former value is 1.6 times the latter value, reflecting the assumed degree of economies in shared living, namely that two can live as cheaply as 1.6. Hence, the household's living standard remains the same until its last possible year, when Jane reaches age 95. Table 14.1's total spending amounts differ from $25,784 when both George and Jane are alive by annual amounts equal to the life insurance premiums on George's recommended holdings of life insurance and their funeral expenses, $5,000 per person.

The fact that (a) the household just exhausts its resources when Jane dies at age 95 (i.e., does not die in debt) and that (b) the recommended consumption expenditure path entails a uniform living standard for all household members in each year the household exists means that ESPlanner has maximized the household's sustainable living standard given the household's economic resources. That is, raising consumption spending in each year to produce a slightly higher uniform living standard would lower saving in each year and leave the household in debt in its last period of existence. Married users can also check ESPlanner's survivor reports to verify that surviving spouses who follow ESPlanner's life insurance recommendations will, if the household's inputs assumptions prove correct, be able to maintain as high a living standard as the household would have had if the spouse had not died early.

The survivor reports for Jane (George) can be produced for any hypothetical ages at which George (Jane) might die. As an example, table 14.2 shows Jane's survivor nontax-favored balance sheet if George dies at age 51. Note that Jane's spending as a survivor, which, in this case, consists only of consumption, equals $16,115, precisely 62.5 (1 divided by 1.6) percent of the amount Jane and George would jointly spend on consumption were George not to die. Hence, Jane's recommended consumption as a widow entails the same living standard as she would have had when married. Table 14.2 also shows that Jane can, as a survivor, afford to spend this

Table 14.2
Jane's Survivor nontax-favored balance sheet in case 1

Year	Jane's age	Income	Spending	Taxes	Nontax-favored saving	Nontax-favored net worth
2021	49	518,691	0	0	518,691	518,691
2022	50	15,108	16,115	7,084	−8,091	510,599
2023	51	14,872	16,115	6,957	−8,200	502,399
2024	52	14,633	16,115	6,828	−8,310	494,090
2025	53	14,391	16,115	6,697	−8,421	485,668
2026	54	14,146	16,115	6,565	−8,534	477,134
2027	55	13,897	16,115	6,431	−8,649	468,486
2028	56	13,645	16,115	6,295	−8,765	459,722
2029	57	13,390	16,115	6,157	−8,882	450,840
2030	58	13,131	16,115	6,017	−9,001	441,839
2031	59	12,869	16,115	5,876	−9,122	432,718
2032	60	12,603	16,115	5,732	−9,244	423,475
2033	61	12,334	16,115	5,587	−9,368	414,107
2034	62	12,061	16,115	5,439	−9,493	404,615
2035	63	11,785	16,115	5,290	−9,620	394,995
2036	64	11,505	16,115	5,139	−9,749	385,246
2037	65	11,221	16,115	4,985	−9,879	375,366
2038	66	10,933	16,115	4,830	−10,012	365,354
2039	67	10,641	16,115	4,673	−10,147	355,208
2040	68	10,346	16,115	4,513	−10,282	344,926
2041	69	10,046	16,115	4,351	−10,420	334,507
2042	70	9,743	16,115	4,187	−10,559	323,947
2043	71	9,435	16,115	4,021	−10,701	313,247
2044	72	9,124	16,115	3,853	−10,844	302,402
2045	73	8,808	16,115	3,682	−10,989	291,413
2046	74	8,488	16,115	3,510	−11,137	280,276
2047	75	8,163	16,115	3,334	−11,286	268,990
2048	76	7,835	16,115	3,157	−11,437	257,553
2049	77	7,502	16,115	2,977	−11,590	245,963
2050	78	7,164	16,115	2,795	−11,746	234,217
2051	79	6,822	16,115	2,610	−11,903	222,314
2052	80	6,475	16,115	2,423	−12,063	210,252
2053	81	6,124	16,115	2,233	−12,224	198,028
2054	82	5,768	16,115	2,041	−12,388	185,640
2055	83	5,407	16,115	1,846	−12,554	173,086
2056	84	5,041	16,115	1,649	−12,723	160,364
2057	85	4,671	16,115	1,448	−12,892	147,472

Table 14.2 (continued)

Year	Jane's age	Income	Spending	Taxes	Nontax-favored saving	Nontax-favored net worth
2058	86	4,295	16,115	1,246	−13,066	134,406
2059	87	3,915	16,115	1,040	−13,240	121,166
2060	88	3,529	16,115	847	−13,433	107,733
2061	89	3,138	16,115	753	−13,730	94,003
2062	90	2,738	16,115	657	−14,034	79,969
2063	91	2,329	16,115	559	−14,345	65,625
2064	92	1,911	16,115	459	−14,663	50,963
2065	93	1,484	16,115	356	−14,987	35,976
2066	94	1,048	16,115	251	−15,318	20,658
2067	95	602	21,115	144	−20,657	0

amount each year on consumption and not end up in debt even if she lives to her maximum ago of life, 95. Also note that the initial amount of nontax-favored wealth with which Jane begins widowhood is $518,691. This amount equals (up to rounding error) the sum of George's and Jane's $382,833 in nontax-favored assets at age 50, plus the $140,858 amount of term insurance recommended for George at age 50, less $5,000 for George's funeral. Were ESPlanner to recommend even a dollar less in life insurance for George at age 50, Jane would not be able to finance the same living standard as a survivor without ending up in debt at age 95 if she were to live that long.

III. Quicken Financial Planner

There is an expanding universe of financial planning software programs and Internet sites available to the general public that offer advice on saving for retirement and other goals, as well as on asset allocation. These programs include proprietary packages offered by mutual-fund and insurance companies with investment and insurance products to sell, as well as independent packages marketed by financial experts and consumer software companies. In addition, there are packages sold to professional financial advisors who use these programs in the course of financial planning sessions given to clients.

The packages on the market differ in focus, sophistication, and level of detail. As mentioned above, however, they all share certain conceptual features. A goal is set by the household for the desired income or expenditure flow in retirement (usually a set percentage of earned income expected to be received just prior to retirement). Then the appropriate saving rate (usually assumed to be level over the work life) and optimal asset allocation are calculated by the program, given certain assumptions, preferences, and information provided by the household, to enable the household to reach its goal. This conventional approach is consistent with the way actuaries traditionally have designed pension plans, that is, a retirement income goal (a replacement rate) is set and the contribution rate (usually level) necessary to achieve that goal is calculated.

We employ the Quicken Financial Planner (QFP), which is representative of the conventional approach. QFP is manufactured by Intuit, Inc., makers of Quicken and Turbo Tax software. To our knowledge, QFP is the most sophisticated and comprehensive planning package available to the general public; it rivals professional software in its detail and use of advanced techniques. QFP seems appropriate for households at most income and wealth levels, perhaps with the exclusion of those households with unusual financial circumstances and those at the bottom and the very top of the income and wealth distributions. (QFP, and ESPlanner for that matter, provide little detail on government assistance programs and estate taxes.)

Inputs and Outputs of QFP

A detailed description of QFP is provided in the appendix of Warshawsky and Ameriks (2001, forthcoming). Here we summarize that discussion and highlight certain features of QFP that we employ in our analysis.

QFP is designed to aid in financial planning for retirement, children's college education, and life insurance needs; we ignore here its advice on asset allocation. Basic demographic and economic (both current and expected future) information is collected about the household. In the "income taxes" section, the respondent household inputs combined federal and state average income tax rates expected in the periods before and after retirement. The respondent is given a choice of two methods to do this estimation: (1) the "demographic average," that is, the average tax rate paid by the average person in the respondent's state of residence within the same range of household income and demographic situation, or (2) the "tax return" approach, that is, the average tax rate calculated based on the household's adjusted gross income and the actual taxes paid in the prior year. Because we do not know actual taxes paid in the prior year, we employ QFP's demographic average method in our analysis; an actual user might input his or her own tax information using the tax return approach.

QFP asks for a myriad of details concerning the household's current and expected future pension coverage, current investment, real estate holdings, loans, and mortgages outstanding. In the "living expenses" section, the respondent household is given a choice of two estimation methods, "rough estimate" and "itemized list." In the first method, QFP simply asks for the household's estimated living expenses before and after retirement, and offers as guidance an abbreviated statement for the current year of cash flow less "off-the-top" expenditures like taxes, loan payments, housing expenses, and planned contributions to pension and savings plans. In the second approach, the household fills out a detailed budget for the current and future years, and QFP sums up pre- and postretirement living expenses from this list. We employ the first method.

In the "social security estimated benefits" section, QFP again gives the user two choices in estimation methods, "rough estimate" and "Social Security Administration estimate." In the first method, the respondent household is asked to sort itself into one of four earnings bands; an estimate of social security benefits is then generated based on planned age at retirement. In the second method, the respondent is simply invited to input the number from the official response to the Request for Personal Earnings and Benefits Estimate Statement form mailed to the Social Security Administration. We employ the first method in our analysis.

QFP has certain advanced planning options allowing for more sophisticated modeling. In particular, in "cash shortfalls," the respondent household is asked whether it plans to sell investments to cover preretirement shortages; although the default answer, which is conservative, is no, in our analysis, we respond yes.[8] In "realized gains," the respondent is asked to estimate the percentage of the gains in the taxable investment portfolio subject to taxes every year; we employ the default answer of 100 percent. In "sweep," the respondent is asked what percent of surplus cash flow is swept into taxable savings; we answer 100 percent, although QFP suggests a more conservative answer of 0 percent. QFP defines surplus cash flow as the excess of planned sources over planned uses of annual money flows. With the cash shortfalls and sweep options employed, the QFP is able to produce nonconstant savings recommendations; these options are unusual in the conventional approach and narrow the contrast somewhat with the economic approach.

Another helpful feature of QFP is its comprehensive information about the current cost of college. Using data from the College Board, QFP reports, by state, for public and private colleges and universities and community colleges, the cost of (in-state and out-of-state) tuition, room and board, books, fees, and other expenses. A worksheet is also available to input expected financial aid, the student's own income, and gifts from relatives. This feature would seem to be especially valuable to households with children approaching the age of entry into college with knowledge about the type, or the specific identity, of the college their children will attend. Because all of the cases we examine involve young families we did not employ this feature of QFP, which is not available in ESPlanner.

QFP processes all this information in an easy-to-see fashion. It initially gives one result: whether or not the household can anticipate having the money needed to retire. If the news is bad, a brief statement regarding the nature of the problem is given, including the year when net worth becomes negative or assets are depleted. This is the manner in which QFP alerts users to infeasible plans as well as to violations of borrowing constraints. If the household provides QFP with an initial level of expenditure and tells it to maintain that expenditure level through time and if that expenditure level leads the household in any future year into debt or into more debt than the household initially had or into insufficient assets to finance retirement, QFP will announce that the household's plan has failed.

Once users have generated a plan that hasn't failed, they can perform the "what if" analysis. Specifically, users can change, one at a time, key assumptions and items of information, such as retirement age or pension contribution rate, and see whether their original consumption expenditure plan is still feasible with the new inputs.

QFP's Insurance Planner uses data already inputted on the household's demographic and economic makeup, and asks the respondent household for its preferences on the size of a desired estate and other postmortem expenses, such as children's college tuition and the spouse's living expenses, to be covered. The Insurance Planner then advises on the optimal amount of term insurance to hold in the first year of the financial plan. The Insurance Planner is semi-autonomous; none of its outputs, including the premiums on its recommended insurance coverage, is used in the main corpus of QFP.

IV. Conceptual and Technical Differences in ESPlanner and QFP

There are three main conceptual differences between the conventional approach to financial planning represented by QFP and the economic approach represented by ESPlanner: the determination of expenditure targets, the treatment of demographics and economies of scale, and the handling of borrowing constraints.

Smoothing a household's standard of living refers to maintaining the same living standard for each person in the household at each point in time. As mentioned above, ESPlanner does this for the household, subject to the household's resources (including social security), its exogenous housing expenses, its exogenous special expenses, its endogenous tax liabilities, and its exogenously specified nonmortgage debt limit. In solving for the time-path of consumption that smooths, to the maximum feasible and desired degree, the household's living standard, ESPlanner is endogenously determining the household's expenditure targets as well as the amounts the household must save, in nontax-favored form, and insure to achieve these targets.

By contrast, QFP asks households to set their own expenditure targets. It then accumulates the household's excess cash flow (income less expenses less all planned saving) and sees whether the accumulated sum ever becomes negative given its financial plans (or, if the household was initially in debt, whether its debt becomes more negative than the initial level of debt). If the household's accumulated cash flow never goes into the red (or too far into the red) and if enough assets are available to finance consumption in retirement and to meet other user-determined goals, the household's expenditure plan is scored a success. Indeed, QFP effectively scores such a plan a complete success in that it doesn't encourage users to adjust their expenditure target to keep them from, in effect, leaving money on the table. This practice is justifiable because households face lots of future risks, planning to leave money on the table which can be used on future rainy days is not such a bad thing. The counterargument is that the amount of money being left on the table may be far smaller or far greater than the household feels it needs to protect itself against future risks. Because, QFP, like ESPlanner, permits users to treat the accumulation of an emergency fund and bequests as special expenditures, the inclusion of these items would seemingly obviate the need to plan for unspent funds.

As mentioned in the introduction, for this research we ran QFP in a manner that avoids leaving money on the table and involves (a) setting an initial level of consumption expenditures, (b) telling QFP that we want to maintain the same level of expenditure through time, and (c) iterating on this initial level of consumption expenditure until the household has very few assets remaining at the end of life.

The second conceptual difference involves the goal of smoothing through time household members' living standards. ESPlanner does this by determining, at each point in time, the number of adult equivalents and adjusting for economies in shared living. QFP, in contrast, invites users to make these adjustments for themselves in setting their consumption expenditure targets.

The third conceptual difference is the treatment of borrowing constraints. ESPlanner builds borrowing constraints directly into its consumption expenditure recommendations. QFP, on the other hand, tells users whether their exogenously specified consumption trajectory will, at some point, violate the program's implicit zero constraint on future borrowing. QFP users whose plans are failed by the software because they run into borrowing constraints are free to rerun the program by lowering their current consumption and raising their future consumption. But users might also respond by lowering their initial consumption and continuing to tell QFP that they want to spend the same amount in the future as in the present. In so doing, they will arrive at an expenditure plan that passes QFP's feasibility criterion, but leaves money on the table.

Interestingly, in the twenty-four cases examined below, we never encountered negative net worth in our use of QFP. However, we quite often encountered borrowing constraints in our use of ESPlanner, which is due to the interaction of demographics with borrowing constraints. In those cases in which ESPlanner generates borrowing constraints, the household has young children and, therefore, higher consumption expenditure needs when young than when old. Our application of QFP ignores these demographic conditions. Consequently, compared to economic theory, our practical application of QFP set consumption expenditure too low when the household is young and too high when the household is old. Because the households we examine have relatively high housing and special expenditures when young, the inappropriately low short-run QFP consumption expenditures are needed to avoid short-run borrowing constraints. Also, in order to make the results of ESPlanner and QFP as comparable as possible, we set the maximum amount a household is able to borrow in ESPlanner to zero.

In addition to these conceptual differences, there are several technical differences between the two programs. First, ESPlanner formulates more precise estimates of federal and state income taxes as well as social security benefits compared to QFP's average approach. Second, QFP apparently does not adjust for inflation in the first year of planning, whereas ESPlanner does. This may, however, simply reflect a difference in the timing conventions of the two programs. Third, ESPlanner integrates life insurance with the financial plan; premiums need not be entered as an itemized expense. Fourth, ESPlanner assists users in comparing their actual current saving with the amount being recommended, whereas QFP encourages users to compare their actual current expenditures with the amount they ultimately end up targeting.

V. Comparing Economic Security Planner and Quicken Financial Planner

The main table of this publication, table 14.3 (p. 524), provides a detailed comparison of the output of the two software programs. The first twenty situations, labeled case 1 through case 20, are based on the same stylized household considered above, in which the husband, George, is aged 29 and the wife, Jane, is aged 27. George earns $50,000 per year in 1999 dollars and expects to retire at age 65. Each case adds some demographic or economic complexity to their initial situation. Cases 21 through 24 consider four actual households with quite different economic and demographic circumstances. To save space, we present results only for selected years of life, and only for key variables (stated in inflation-adjusted terms), namely, consumption, taxable savings, taxes, tax-deferred and taxable assets, and life insurance. We use ESPlanner's definitions of these variables and combine several items from QFP's output tables to make the numbers comparable.

For all cases and for both Planners, we make the following economic assumptions, unless otherwise stated. The expected nominal rate of return on investments (whether taxable or tax-favored) is 6 percent, and the expected general inflation rate is 3 percent. When relevant, the expected rate of inflation for college tuition is assumed to be 5 percent. Federal and state tax rates and rules, as well as government benefit programs (mainly social security), are expected to remain unchanged in the future. All households spend their entire lives in Massachusetts. Version 3.3 (r4) of QFP and version 1.10.37 of ESPlanner were used. Both programs were run with the computer's date set to January 1, 1999.

Case 1—Husband Works

ESPlanner's output for case 1 was discussed above. Recall that the household's living standard is perfectly smoothed with the couple spending $25,784 on consumption until the husband reaches age 95 and passes away. Thereafter, the surviving spouse, Jane, spends $16,115 on consumption, which suffices to maintain the same living standard she enjoyed when married. These and all other dollar figures discussed below are quoted in 1999 dollars.

QFP recommends a somewhat higher level of consumption expenditure in case 1: $27,810 when both George and Jane are alive and $16,686, when Jane is surviving by herself. It should be recalled, however, that premiums for life insurance are an "off-the-top" expenditure in ESPlanner, whereas they are (implicitly) included in living expenses in QFP. Although their 1999 income levels are identical, the two programs recommend quite different amounts of nontax-favored saving for 1999. ESPlanner recommends about $1,400 more nontax-favored saving in 1999 than QFP! The reason is that QFP calculates higher levels of taxes for 1999 than does ESPlanner. Although QFP generates higher taxes than ESPlanner when the couple is young, it generates lower taxes than ESPlanner when the couple is middle-aged and older.

In considering these differences, it is important to bear in mind that QFP is making approximations in calculating taxes. Specifically, QFP is applying a single average tax rate over time, independent of the household's expected schedule of taxable income over time. In contrast, as described in the appendix, ESPlanner makes very precise federal and state tax calculations that include determining whether or not the household should itemize its deductions, computing the household's taxable income, and using exact federal and state tax rate schedules to determine the household's tax liabilities. Correct calculation of state taxes is particularly important as households age and accumulate taxable capital income. The fact that ESPlanner produces much higher taxes when the couple has significant nontax-favored asset income reflects its incorporation of the very high rate of capital income taxation by the State of Massachusetts. This rate is roughly two times higher than the rate levied on labor income.[9]

Although the two programs recommend significantly different 1999 levels of nontax-favored saving, their 1999 life insurance recommendations are nearly identical. Neither program recommends life insurance for the nonworking wife. QFP's recommended life insurance for the husband is $680,000. ESPlanner's is $667,948. ESPlanner, but not QFP, provides life insurance recommendations for all future years as well: The husband's recommended level of life insurance declines over time, and is zero after he reaches age 57. At age 45, the recommended amount is $293,459.

Case 2—Wife Works

Case 2 assumes that Jane works through her sixty-fourth year of life and earns $25,000 per year in 1999 dollars. Because the couple has greater economic resources, it can sustain a higher living standard, which is what each program recommends. However, the two programs now differ by almost $6,000 annually with respect to the level of the couple's sustainable living standard. ESPlanner has George and Jane consuming $35,883 when both are alive, compared with QFP's $41,720, a 16 percent difference. Again, tax calculations and, to a lesser extent, life insurance premiums appear to explain this difference. ESPlanner's 1999 taxes are almost $3,000 higher than QFP's, and ESPlanner's taxes are significantly higher when the couple is middle-aged and approaching retirement. For example, when George is 45, ESPlanner's taxes are almost $8,000 higher. These differences appear to reflect ESPlanner's inclusion of Massachusetts's 12 percent tax on nontax-sheltered capital income as well as our use in QFP of the "demographic average" method.

Associated with these differences in recommended consumption are differences in recommended nontax-favored saving. ESPlanner recommends 1999 nontax-favored saving be set at $21,937, whereas QFP recommends it be set at $20,069. When George is age 45, ESPlanner's recommended nontax-favored saving is much less than QFP's—$24,352 versus $32,354. At George's age 65, ESPlanner's recommends much more dissaving than does QFP—$21,975 versus $13,491. Thus, compared with QFP, ESPlanner recommends slightly more saving when George and Jane are young, and less saving in middle age and the start of old age, when George and Jane face higher taxes than QFP says they will face.

The nontrivial differences between the two programs in saving recommendations and tax estimates eventuates in nontrivial differences in accumulated assets when the couple reaches retirement age. According to ESPlanner's plan, the couple has $871,921 in taxable assets when George reaches 65. According to QFP's plan, the couple taxable assets in George's sixty-fifth year are almost 15 percent larger—$996,629.

Turning to the life insurance recommendations, both programs tell George he needs less life insurance because Jane now has earnings that can help sustain her if George dies prematurely. ESPlanner is now recommending slightly more insurance than QFP, but the difference is quite small.

Case 3—Adding Social Security Benefits

Case 3 adds the assumption that both George and Jane are in social security–covered employment, and are, therefore, paying payroll taxes and can expect benefits at levels currently legislated. According to ESPlanner, George and Jane receive $18,843 and $10,515, respectively, in social security retirement benefits when each reaches age 65. These benefit levels are substantially higher than the corresponding $10,049 and $5,266 figures calculated by QFP. The differences here apparently reflect the wage indexation of social security earnings histories by ESPlanner. (ESPlanner follows very precisely the rules for determining social security benefits as detailed in the Social Security Handbook.[10])

Because ESPlanner expects the couple to receive significantly more in future social security benefits than does QFP, it recommends less saving prior to retirement. Indeed, ESPlanner's 1999 recommended level of nontax-favored saving of $9,629 is one-third lower than QFP's recommendation of $14,257. The couple's sustainable living standard is higher in case 3 than case 2 in both programs. For example, with social security, ESPlanner recommends that the couple consume $43,737 each year that both George and Jane are alive. Without social security it recommends they consume $35,883.[11]

Case 3's life insurance recommendations are not much different from those of case 2, which is not surprising. On the one hand, the availability of social security survivor benefits reduces the need for life insurance for George. On the other hand, the couple's higher living standard when both spouses are alive means that Jane's needs as a survivor are greater.

Case 4—Adding Housing

This case builds on case 3 by adding housing. Specifically, we assume that George and Jane own a home with a market value of $200,000, annual property taxes of $2,500, annual maintenance of $1,500, annual homeowners' insurance of $400, and a thirty-year mortgage with remaining balance of $170,000 and annual principal and interest mortgage payments of $1,124 (the mortgage interest rate is 8 percent). The couple is assumed to remain in their house until the end of their lives.

The need to pay housing expenses reduces the amount of resources that can be devoted to consumption. The consumption decline is over $10,000 in QFP and over $8,000 in ESPlanner. The difference between the two programs is again due to taxes. Because ESPlanner takes into account the deductibility of mortgage interest payments, ESPlanner's taxes decline by almost $3,000 annually in moving from case 3 to case 4. In contrast, QFP's taxes using the demographic average rates are essentially unchanged.

The need to pay off the household's mortgage and other housing expenditures raises recommended life insurance for George under both programs. And both programs, in an intuitive practice, now recommend roughly $60,000 in life insurance for Jane. Indeed, unlike Jane's consumption, which disappears if she dies, the household's housing expenditures are no different when Jane passes away. Because Jane's income contributes to meeting these expenditures when Jane is alive, insuring that income is important.

Case 5—Adding Children

In case 5 we add two children, one born in 1997 and the other born in 2001. Because QFP doesn't adjust for household demographics, its recommended annual levels of consumption and taxable saving are unchanged by the presence of children. Stated differently, our application of QFP involves smoothing consumption expenditures over the household's life cycle, rather than smoothing its living standard. Smoothing a household's living standard requires spending more (although not proportionately more) on consumption in those years when the household has more members.

Unlike QFP, ESPlanner aims at smoothing households' living standards to the extent the household desires a smooth living standard and to the extent such smoothing doesn't violate the household's borrowing constraint. Hence ESPlanner's consumption recommendations take into account the assumed changes over time in household composition. In particular, ESPlanner assumes that children remain in their parents' household through age 18. In determining how much additional consumption is needed to equalize the living standards of children with those of their parents, ESPlanner permits users to input child-adult consumption equivalency factors that are child-age specific. These factors together with the program's specification of economies to scale in shared living are used to determine how much household consumption rises or falls when children enter or leave the household. The household's recommended consumption expenditure will vary with changes in its demographic composition even during intervals of time when the household is liquidity or borrowing constrained.

For example, consider a household that desires a perfectly smooth living standard through time, that lives for sixty years (the household head or spouse specifies a maximum remaining lifespan of sixty years), and that is borrowing constrained over its first twenty years. ESPlanner will (a) smooth the household's living standard over the first twenty years, (b) smooth the household's living standard over the last forty years, and (c) make the discrepancy in living standards between the first twenty years and the last forty years as small as possible.

Case 5 illustrates these features of ESPlanner because the additional expenditures on consumption arising from the presence of the children pushes the household into a liquidity-constrained position. (We assume in all cases that no borrowing is possible.) Indeed, the household is liquidity constrained over its first thirteen years, by which we mean that its living standard in the first thirteen years is lower than in subsequent years. As the case 5 ESPlanner results show, initial (1999) consumption is $37,105 and initial taxable saving is $2,981. The corresponding QFP recommendations are $32,600 and $7,299.

Why is the household saving in 1999 in the ESPlanner results if it is liquidity constrained? The answer is that the household still attempts to smooth its living standard over the first thirteen years even if it can't perfectly smooth its living standard over its entire lifetime. To do so, it needs to save at the beginning of the thirteen-year interval in anticipation of the arrival of the second child. Once the second child is born, ESPlanner's recommended consumption expenditure (*but not the living standard per person*) rises to $43,383 and ESPlanner's recommended taxable saving becomes negative. The household slowly spends down its small stock of net worth, so that by 2008 its net worth is zero. Between 2009 and 2012 the household's consumption rises in step with increases in its disposable income—the income it has after paying for taxes and housing expenditures. After 2012 the household again saves positive amounts. In that year, its consumption equals $43,705. This level is lowered to $40,366 in 2016 when the first child leaves the household and reduced again to $32,933 when the second child leaves the household.

In addition to recommending markedly different levels of initial consumption and taxable saving, QFP and ESPlanner recommend quite different levels of life insurance for case 5. QFP's 1999 recommendations are $520,000 for George and $60,000 for the wife. The corresponding ESPlanner recommendations are $362,076 and zero. Although ESPlanner recommends no initial life insurance holdings for Jane, it does recommend she start buying life insurance in 2003.

What explains these differences? The answer is social security survivor benefits. The availability of these benefits reduces the need for life insurance on both the husband and the wife, and the timing of their potential receipt disproportionately reduces the need for life insurance during years when the children are young. ESPlanner includes these benefits in forming its life insurance recommendations. QFP, we suspect, does not.[12] The survivor benefits to which we refer here are not simply widow and widower benefits that are available to surviving spouses starting at age 60, but also child, and mother/father benefits that are available to survivor households with children. Because child benefits are paid in the form of annual income streams until the children reach age 19 and mother/father benefits are paid in the form of annual income streams until the children reach age 16, their remaining present values are smaller the older the children are when the household first begins receiving these benefits.

Case 6—Financing College Tuition for Children

Case 6 augments the previous case by incorporating special expenditures in the form of college tuition payments of $30,000 per year for each child between age 19 and 22. The need to save for these expenditures raises recommended 1999 taxable saving in both programs, but the recommended increase (relative to case 5) is almost 30 percent greater in ESPlanner than in QFP. And the need to guarantee payment of tuition regardless of who survives also alters life insurance recommendations. In this case the increases (relative to case 5) are roughly the same across the two programs.

The need to pay for future college expenses changes the timing of the household's liquidity constraints in ESPlanner's calculations. Now the household experiences one long period of liquidity-constrained consumption—between 1999 and 2023. The year 2023 (when George is 53 and Jane is 51) is the year their youngest child finishes college; that is, once George and Jane are free from paying college tuition they experience a discrete increase in their living standard.

Case 7—Establishing an Emergency Fund

Case 7 adds a need for a $50,000 (in 1999 dollars) emergency fund to be accumulated by 2035. Both software packages have the household put aside the $50,000 accumulated for an emergency fund in 2035, when George is age 65. This course of action is reflected in large negative savings at that age in both sets of results. However, QFP recommends that an additional $671 be saved in 1999, whereas ESPlanner recommends only $26 more be saved initially, but an additional $1,118 in 2024—the first year after the household has finished paying college tuition and is no longer liquidity constrained and is enjoying a higher living standard. Thus ESPlanner pays for the emergency fund when the couple can afford to, that is, when it doesn't have such pressing needs for other expenditures. In contrast, QFP pays for the emergency fund by reducing consumption in each year of the household's life, which is a measure consistent with the conventional approach's target-savings methodology.

Case 8—Adding Taxable Assets

Case 8 gives $50,000 in taxable assets to the household. ESPlanner uses these additional resources to finance additional consumption during the period 1999–2023 when the household is liquidity constrained. Hence, its recommended 1999 level of taxable saving decreases (compared with case 7) by $1,701, whereas QFP's recommended 1999 taxable saving rises by $1,679. ESPlanner has the household increase consumption by more than $2,000 in the liquidity-constrained years, whereas QFP recommends an annual increase of slightly more than $1,000 over the household's lifetime. Taxes are higher in QFP owing to the larger accumulation of taxable assets and the resulting investment income.

In contrast to this difference in taxable saving recommendations, there is little difference between the two programs in the response of their life insurance recommendations to the presence of the initial taxable net worth. Both programs recommend minor reductions in the life insurance holdings of both George and Jane.

Case 9—Adding Tax-Deferred Assets

Case 9 gives George $50,000 in nontaxable assets which he holds in a defined contribution plan. Because the household is liquidity constrained through 2023 and because the income from these assets is not accessible to the household until late in life, ESPlanner recommends essentially no changes (compared to case 8) in taxable saving for 1999. QFP, on the other hand, recommends that the household reduce its 1999 taxable saving by $1,858. Regarding consumption, QFP suggests a $1,800 increase over the household's lifetime, while ESPlanner increases consumption only slightly initially, but then bumps it up by about $3,000 for the remainder of life.[13]

Both programs recommend roughly similar reductions in life insurance holdings. This point notwithstanding, the recommended 1999 levels of life insurance for George and Jane remain quite different across the two programs. For example, QFP recommends Jane have $80,000 of life insurance, whereas ESPlanner recommends she have only $8,525.

Case 10—Adding Tax-Deferred Saving

In this case we assume that both George and his employer each contribute $2,500 to a defined contribution plan on behalf of George. Once again we find large differences in recommended taxable saving responses. QFP tells George and Jane to save almost $5,000 less in taxable form in 1999. ESPlanner tells them to save just $61 less. Because George has more future income (his employer's contributions) to protect, both programs recommend that George have more life insurance in 1999. But ESPlanner now recommends that Jane have no insurance whereas QFP still recommends she purchase $80,000 of coverage.

Case 11—Adding Bequests

This case adds a $50,000 special bequest by both George and Jane. QFP responds by raising recommended life insurance for each spouse. ESPlanner raises recommended life insurance just for George; that is, it continues to recommend no life insurance for Jane. The reason is that, were Jane to die, George would have enough resources from his own labor earnings, the couple's taxable net worth, and his taxable net worth to sustain a higher living standard on his own than if Jane were alive.

Case 12—Adding a Defined Benefit Pension

This case gives Jane a $10,000 (in 1999 dollars) defined benefit pension annuity beginning at age 63. The pension income is not indexed for inflation nor are there survivor benefits. Here again we have income coming to the household in the postliquidity-constrained period. Hence, ESPlanner recommends essentially no change in 1999 taxable saving or consumption. QFP, on the other hand, treats the household as effectively being able to spend this future income in the present. So it recommends a $1,600 higher level of 1999 consumption and a commensurate reduction in 1999 saving. Indeed, QFP's recommended saving for 1999 is now 13 percent less than ESPlanner's.

Both programs now recommend less life insurance for George. But QFP recommends $20,000 less in life insurance for Jane, while ESPlanner recommends $33,212 more. QFP's recommended reduction in life insurance for Jane is curious given that Jane now has more future income that she needs to protect for George against the possibility of her early death.

Case 13—Adding an Inheritance

Case 13 adds a $400,000 (in 1999 dollars) inheritance that Jane will receive in 2027 from her father, but only in the case that Jane is alive. Because this inheritance arrives too late to relieve the household's liquidity constraint, there is again very little change compared to case 12 in ESPlanner's 1999 saving recommendations. However, there is a very large increase in ESPlanner's recommended life insurance for Jane. This increase makes sense; Jane's inheritance is only available if she's alive, so she must take out additional insurance to make sure that George and her children will enjoy this inheritance. Quicken also recommends more initial life insurance for Jane, but the percentage increase (relative to case 12) is substantially smaller than for ESPlanner. This difference appears to reflect our specification in ESPlanner that Jane's inheritance is contingent on her being alive. Quicken, in contrast, does not differentiate between noncontingent and contingent receipts or, for that matter, special expenditures.

The initial amount of insurance recommended by ESPlanner for George declines (compared with case 12) because the inheritance (which is insured through Jane's life insurance) represents another asset George can use as a survivor to maintain his and the children's living standard.

QFP, because it ignores liquidity constraints, begins spending Jane's inheritance right away, raising consumption in 1999 by over $4,500 and reducing 1999 recommended saving to just $754. This $754 recommended level of saving stands in stark contrast to ESPlanner's $6,793 saving recommendation for 1999.

Both programs now recommend fairly similar initial levels of life insurance for Jane. But George's initial life insurance should, according to ESPlanner, be only about three-fifths of the level recommended by QFP. Interestingly, when Jane is 43, ESPlanner recommends more life insurance for Jane than for George. Why? Again, because Jane needs to guarantee that her inheritance will effectively be available to George and the children if she dies prior to receiving it.

Case 14—Adding Real Wage Growth

This case leaves out the inheritance of case 13 and instead assumes that George and Jane each experience 2 percent growth each year in their real labor earnings. Because the couple has a lot more income in the future than the present, each program advocates dissaving in the short run in order to permit a higher level of current consumption. But ESPlanner recommends almost $8,000 more in saving (actually, more than $800 less in dissaving) than does QFP. Again, liquidity constraints explain this difference. Once ESPlanner realizes that the couple can't perfectly smooth its living standard over its entire life, it focuses on smoothing the couple's living standard during the liquidity-constrained interval and the nonliquidity-constrained interval. This means consuming less than QFP recommends in the former interval and consuming more than QFP recommends in the later interval. QFP also suggests a withdrawal (with tax penalties) from the defined contribution plan in midlife, which ESPlanner will never recommend before age 59.

Case 15—Age 62 Retirement of Husband

This case is identical to case 12 (that is, no inheritance or real wage growth) except the husband retires at age 62. Earlier retirement increases QFP's recommended 1999 taxable saving by almost 30 percent, but leaves ESPlanner 1999 saving recommendation essentially unchanged. QFP reacts to the reduced lifetime earnings by lowering current as well as future recommended consumption and thus raising saving. ESPlanner, in contrast, reacts by cutting consumption in the period after George and Jane are no longer liquidity constrained—the period when they are otherwise enjoying a higher living standard.

Because George has less future labor income to protect, both programs advise George to purchase less life insurance. QFP's recommended reduction in insurance for George is, however, 40 percent greater than ESPlanner's recommended reduction. Both programs also advise Jane to buy less life insurance. Indeed, ESPlanner recommends zero life insurance for Jane, whereas QFP recommends a $100,000 policy.

Case 16—Five Percent Real Rates of Return

This case is identical to case 12 except it assumes 8 percent rather than 6 percent nominal rates of return on taxable and nontaxable assets. Because the inflation rate is still set at 3 percent, this implies real interest rates of 5 percent rather than 3 percent on these assets. Ignoring liquidity constraints, higher real interest rates permit higher levels of lifetime consumption. But the household is liquidity constrained. Indeed, the higher real interest rate generates so much accumulation in their nontaxable accounts that George and Jane now experience two intervals of liquidity constraints, one prior to their children completing college and the other between the time their children complete college and the time (when George is age 65) when they pay off their emergency fund, start withdrawing their nontaxable assets, and start collecting their social security benefits. Consequently, ESPlanner recommends very little change (compared with case 12) in initial consumption and, therefore, in initial taxable saving. At George's age 65, when the household is in the last year of its second constrained interval, consumption is $43,489; that is, $2,078 more than in case 12. At George's age 66, consumption rises to $61,057, which is $16,273 (36 percent) more than in case 12! In contrast to ESPlanner, QFP cuts initial saving by more than one half. Hence, ESPlanner's recommended 1999 level of saving is more than twice that of QFP. Again QFP recommends large midlife withdrawals from the household's defined contribution plan.

Case 17—Five Percent Inflation
This case differs from case 12 in assuming a 5 percent inflation rate. The higher inflation rate lowers real returns on taxable and nontaxable assets to 1 percent. It also reduces the real values of the couple's mortgage payments and Jane's pension benefits. QFP reacts to these offsetting factors by reducing (relative to case 12) household saving in 1999 by about one quarter. ESPlanner leaves 1999 saving roughly as is.

Case 18—Ages of Death Are 85
Lowering the latest ages at which George and Jane could die from 95 to 85 would, absent liquidity constraints, permit George and Jane to consume more each year. Thus, QFP's initial consumption rises (relative to case 12) from $31,270 to $35,570, lowering initial taxable saving from $5,994 to $4,653. ESPlanner's initial consumption is changed only slightly in reflection of a small change in recommended life insurance holdings and, thus, life insurance premium payments. Hence, initial ESPlanner taxable saving in case 18 is 46 percent higher than the amount recommended by QFP. QFP's recommended life insurance holdings are unaffected by the change in the maximum age of life, whereas ESPlanner's recommended holdings decline because the household does not need to insure its living standard for as long a period of time.

Case 19—Ten Percent Higher Postretirement Living Standard
In this exercise, we tell both programs that the household wishes to have a 10 percent higher living standard after George is age 65. Because the couple is liquidity constrained when young and would

otherwise experience more than a 10 percent rise in its living standard after retirement compared to their youth, this change in assumptions leads to essentially no change in ESPlanner's initial consumption and taxable saving recommendations. But QFP now recommends less initial consumption and more initial taxable saving. Consequently, the two programs recommend almost the same initial levels of taxable saving.

Case 20—Downsizing of Home at Retirement

In this scenario, the couple sells its home when George retires and moves into a rental property that charges $1,500 per month in rent. This decision frees up the couple's home equity for use in financing its consumption in retirement. On the other hand, it raises considerably the couple's postretirement housing expenses. On balance, the decision reduces the couple's ability to finance consumption.

QFP encourages the couple to immediately cut its consumption and raise its taxable saving in anticipation of the higher postretirement housing expenses. ESPlanner, in contrast, cuts future rather than immediate consumption and, thus, recommends roughly the same initial taxable saving. Both programs recommend that both spouses purchase more life insurance. However, as has been the case with the other scenarios, QFP's insurance recommendations are considerably higher than those of ESPlanner. Here, QFP's 1999 recommended insurance holdings, for George and Jane combined, total $800,000. The comparable ESPlanner figure is $561,041—a 30 percent smaller amount.

Summary of Findings For First Twenty Cases

In looking back at the twenty cases we've now considered, several things become clear. First, the two programs provide remarkably different recommendations even in simple settings despite the fact that each is designed to help households maintain their living standards or at least their consumption levels through time. Second, the two programs are calculating significantly different levels of taxes and social security benefits and these differences materially alter their saving and insurance recommendations. Because we have been able to check the accuracy of ESPlanner's tax and social security benefit calculations, it appears that QFP's calculation of these variables may be "soft." (Of course, there is a broader question, applicable to all software packages and planning exercises, about the accuracy of any projection of taxes and social security, decades into the future, although QFP does allow the user to lower the estimate of social security benefits to be paid in the future.) Third, the fact that QFP does not automatically adjust for household composition and liquidity constraints leads it in many cases to recommend either much less or more taxable saving compared to ESPlanner. Finally, QFP generally recommends more life insurance than what ESPlanner has determined households actually need in order to insure their current living standards for potential survivors; this tendency may reflect an incomplete estimation of social security survivor benefits.

VI. Comparing QFP and ESPlanner for Four Actual Households

This section examines the recommendations of the two software programs when applied to four actual households.

Case 21—A Young, Low-Income Couple

This case involves a couple in which each spouse is age 35 and each retires at age 65. They plan to have two children, one in 2001 and one in 2003. The husband earns $43,000 initially, declining by 2001 to $35,000 and staying constant thereafter. The wife earns $37,000 in 1999, zero in 2000, $35,000 in 2001, $36,000 in 2002, $37,000 in 2003, and $38,000 thereafter. The husband receives a gift of $10,000 from his father in 1999 and 2000. As for special expenditures, the couple makes a $15,000 down payment in 1999 to purchase a house and makes nominal truck loan payments of $4,500 in 1999 and 2000. The couple also plans to spend $20,000 on college tuition for each of the children between their ages of 19 and 22. The couple plans for funerals of $5,000 each, but doesn't wish to leave a bequest. The couple currently has $14,000 in taxable net worth, and the wife has $3,000 in an IRA. Otherwise the couple has no assets.

The wife intends to contribute $1,200 to her IRA annually until she retires. Her withdrawals from her IRA will begin at age 65 and will be taken out in equal annual payments. The couple is buying a house in 1999 for $150,000. Purchase of the house causes $2,500 in annual property taxes, $400 in annual homeowner's insurance payments, and $2,000 in annual maintenance. The couple intends in 1999 to take out a $135,000, thirty-year mortgage with monthly principal and interest payments of $990. Both spouses will begin collecting social security retirement benefits at age 65. They both entered past labor income, which is needed to compute their social security benefits in ESPlanner. The economic assumptions the couple chooses are ESPlanner's default values, including 6 percent nominal interest rates on taxable and nontaxable assets, a 3 percent inflation rate, and a zero nonmortgage borrowing constraint.

In running the couple's data through ESPlanner, we also solicited their current saving and insurance holdings. Prior to running the software the couple planned to save $19,620 in 1999. The wife has no life insurance, while the husband has $30,000.

In ESPlanner we find that the couple is never liquidity constrained. On the other hand, the couple never accumulates a significant stock of taxable assets. As the table for case 21 makes clear, the couple is advised to consume $26,866 initially and $38,500 when both children are at home. Our application of QFP, on the other hand, recommends constant consumption of $26,920 when both spouses are alive, regardless of the presence of children. Here, ESPlanner gives a more intuitive recommendation; children cost a lot of money and this must be reflected in household savings decisions.

QFP and ESPlanner agree that husband and wife should have equivalent life insurance holdings, reflecting their equivalent economic contribution to the household. Again, however, ESPlanner suggests lower life insurance than QFP.

Case 22—A Middle-Aged, Upper-Income Couple

This case involves a couple with a forty-year-old wife and a thirty-nine-year-old husband. They have two children, one born in 1991, the other born in 1993. The wife doesn't work. The husband works, earning $200,000 in 1999 and 2000. Starting in 2001 and continuing until his retirement at age 55, the husband expects to earn $100,000. They plan to send each of their children to college for four years at a cost of $30,000 per child per year. They have no special bequests and plan for funerals of $5,000 each. The husband currently has $800,000 in life insurance; the wife has none. The couple's taxable assets are $225,500. The wife has an IRA with a 1999 balance of $84,700, and the husband has a 401(k) with a 1999 balance of $148,000. Both plan to withdraw their nontaxable assets (and make them taxable) at age 59. The couple is currently saving $11,765 in taxable form. The husband plans to contribute $9,500 into his 401(k) plan each year and expects his employer to contribute $6,000. The wife does not intend to make additional IRA contributions. The couple owns a $475,000 house with annual property taxes of $5,200, annual maintenance of $1,500, annual homeowners' insurance of $500, and a twenty-nine-year-old $170,000 mortgage with monthly payments of $1,131. Each spouse intends to take his or her social security retirement benefits starting at age 62.

QFP and ESPlanner recommend vastly different amounts of consumption, taxable saving, and life insurance for this household. QFP recommends more than twice the life insurance for the husband than is recommended by ESPlanner. Differences in tax calculations, in the treatment of household composition, and in the treatment of liquidity constraints appear to explain the different consumption and saving recommendations. To begin, ESPlanner sets consumption much higher in earlier than in later years because it realizes that the couple needs to spend more when it has children. Second, ESPlanner calculates the couple's short-run taxes to be much higher than those generated by QFP, reflecting higher Massachusetts's income taxes on capital income. Note that QFP does not allow for the employer's matching contribution to the 401(k) plan to reflect inflation-induced increases in pay. Also QFP's social security benefits are lower than ESPlanner's.

Case 23—An Older, Very High Income Couple

This case involves a couple in which the husband is age 64 and the wife is age 57. The husband intends to work for two more years, earning close to $400,000 over the two years. The couple has a variety of large special expenses in the short run, including an expensive home renovation. The husband has two nominal pensions providing close to $200,000 annually that he expects to collect starting after retirement. Each spouse is planning for a $5,000 funeral. The couple also wants to give its children a $2 million gift in 2025. The couple's taxable net worth is close to $3 million. The wife has a very small IRA account, and the husband has a 401(k) account with balances that are close to three-quarters of a million dollars. Each spouse elects to withdraw the smallest amount of funds from these tax-favored accounts permitted by law. The couple owns a house with a market value of $1,200,000. The annual property taxes, maintenance, and homeowners' insurance total $6,000, $13,000, and $1,000, respectively. There is a twenty-five-year $525,000 mortgage on the property with a monthly payment of $3,318. The couple plans to sell its home in 2025 and use the proceeds as well as other funds to make the

$2 million gift. After selling its home, the couple plans to rent a home for $4,000 per month. The couple uses the default economic assumptions.

QFP and ESPlanner agree in this case that neither spouse needs life insurance, but they disagree very strongly about the amount of taxes the couple will pay initially and over time and the rate at which the couple should dissave (spend down) its taxable assets. ESPlanner calculates the couple's 1999 taxes at $182,449, whereas QFP calculates them at $237,681, which represents a 30 percent difference. ESPlanner takes into account the tax deductibility of special expenditures, and ESPlanner's much lower 1999 taxes may reflect the fact that some of the couple's very large 1999 special expenditures are tax deductible. Interestingly, ESPlanner's calculated taxes are higher than are QFP's when the husband is age 75, but then fall below QFP's.

Because ESPlanner calculates that the couple will generally pay less in taxes initially and over time, it recommends considerably higher consumption expenditures. In 1999, ESPlanner says the household can consume $204,510, whereas QFP tells the household not to consume more than $186,880. ESPlanner recommends the couple dissave $317,615 in 1999—a very large sum, which reflects, in large part, the couple's very substantial special expenditures in 1999. QFP, in contrast, recommends the couple dissave $138,380.

Case 24—A Middle-Aged Low-Income Divorcee

This case describes a fifty-nine-year-old divorcee who plans to work until age 70 and whose life expectancy is age 85. She earns $35,000 a year, has $32,000 in assets (evenly divided between taxable and tax-deferred accounts), is making a nominal loan repayment of $4,500 for the next three years, and pays $10,200 a year for rent. Her current employer contributes 20 percent of pay to a defined contribution plan, and she will receive $4,000 a year in nominal benefits from a prior employer's defined benefit pension plan.

ESPlanner gives a higher standard of living than QFP and allows greater savings withdrawals for this woman. These recommendations are almost entirely due to ESPlanner's higher estimate of social security benefits—$21,430 compared to $9,232 in QFP.[14] In fact, ESPlanner's higher estimate for social security benefits produces a liquidity constraint in the first decade of planning, because the replacement of income in retirement for this woman is so high.

VI. Summary and Conclusions

This chapter used Economic Security Planner and Quicken Financial Planner to illustrate and contrast the economic and conventional approaches to financial planning. After clarifying the main conceptual and technical differences between the two programs, the paper compared their consumption, saving, and insurance recommendations for twenty stylized and four actual households. These recommendations are remarkably different even for very simple cases. The differences are, however, readily explained. They are due to very different tax and social security benefits calculations and to very different treatments of demographics and borrowing constraints.

Table 14.3 Cases 1–24

Case 1

Husband works, wife doesn't work, no social security benefits, no housing, no children, no college, no emergency fund, no taxable assets, no tax-deferred assets, no tax-deferred saving, no bequests, no pensions, no inheritance, no real wage growth, age 65 retirement for husband, 3 percent real returns, 3 percent inflation, max. death ages are 95, desired stable standard of living, no downsizing of home at retirement

Age of husband	Age of wife	Consumption (living expenses)		Taxable saving		Taxes		Taxable assets		Husband's tax-deferred assets		Husband's life insurance		Wife's life insurance	
		Quicken	Esp	Quicken	Esp	Quicken	Esp	Quicken	Esp	Quicken	Esp	Quicken	Esp	Quicken	Esp
29	27	27,810	25,784	13,383	14,772	9,296	8,640	13,312	14,772	0	0	680,000	667,948	0	0
45	43	27,810	25,784	20,526	17,274	11,729	13,837	264,240	276,585	0	0	N.C.	293,458	N.C.	0
65	63	27,810	25,784	(9,653)	(15,377)	6,457	8,018	664,601	617,205	0	0	N.C.	0	N.C.	0
85	83	27,810	25,784	(20,963)	(20,067)	2,378	2,513	268,731	262,495	0	0	N.C.	0	N.C.	0
Deceased	95	16,686	16,115	(17,156)	(20,627)	10	113	1,064	0	0	0	N.C.	0	N.C.	0

Note: N.C. = not computed

Case 2

Husband works, *wife works*, no social security benefits, no housing, no children, no college, no emergency fund, no taxable assets, no tax-deferred assets, no tax-deferred saving, no bequests, no pensions, no inheritance, no real wage growth, age 65 retirement for husband, 3 percent real returns, 3 percent inflation, max. death ages are 95, desired stable standard of living, no downsizing of home at retirement

		Consumption (living expenses)		Taxable saving		Taxes		Taxable assets		Husband's tax-deferred assets		Husband's life insurance		Wife's life insurance	
Age of husband	Age of wife	Quicken	Esp	Quicken	Esp	Quicken	Esp	Quicken	Esp	Quicken	Esp	Quicken	Esp	Quicken	Esp
29	27	41,720	35,883	20,069	21.937	13,944	16,624	19,962	21,937	0	0	460,000	461,763	0	0
45	43	41,720	35,883	32,354	24,352	17,594	25,223	396,258	393,396	0	0	N.C.	129,531	N.C.	0
65	63	41,720	35,883	(13,491)	(21,975)	9,683	12,128	996,629	871,921	0	0	N.C.	0	N.C.	0
85	83	41,720	35,883	(30,437)	(28,678)	3,561	4,261	402,571	365,003	0	0	N.C.	0	N.C.	0
Deceased	95	25,032	22,427	(25,757)	(26,776)	9	129	888	0	0	0	N.C.	0	N.C.	0

Note: N.C. = not computed

Case 3
Husband works, wife works, *social security benefits*, no housing, no children, no college, no emergency fund, no taxable assets, no tax-deferred assets, no tax-deferred saving, no bequests, no pensions, no inheritance, no real wage growth, age 65 retirement for husband, 3 percent real returns, 3 percent inflation, max. death ages are 95, desired stable standard of living, no downsizing of home at retirement

		Consumption (living expenses)		Taxable saving		Taxes		Taxable assets		Husband's tax-deferred assets		Husband's life insurance		Wife's life insurance	
Age of husband	Age of wife	Quicken	Esp	Quicken	Esp	Quicken	Esp	Quicken	Esp	Quicken	Esp	Quicken	Esp	Quicken	Esp
29	27	42,700	43,737	14,257	9,629	18,564	21,093	14,182	9,628	0	0	420,000	449,205	0	0
45	43	42,700	43,737	21,867	10,724	21,156	24,882	281,513	173,344	0	0	N.C.	175,054	N.C.	0
65	63	42,700	43,737	(11,410)	(10,336)	8,897	7,464	706,929	384,790	0	0	N.C.	0	N.C.	0
85	83	42,700	43,737	(22,331)	(12,414)	4,986	2,939	285,399	155,930	0	0	N.C.	0	N.C.	0
Deceased	95	25,620	27,336	(17,480)	(13,124)	1,471	13	1,929	0	0	0	N.C.	0	N.C.	0

Note: N.C. = not computed

Case 4

Husband works, wife works, social security benefits, *housing*, no children, no college, no emergency fund, no taxable assets, no tax-deferred assets, no tax-deferred saving, no bequests, no pensions, no inheritance, no real wage growth, age 65 retirement for husband, 3 percent real returns, 3 percent inflation, max. death ages are 95, desired stable standard of living, no downsizing of home at retirement

		Consumption (living expenses)		Taxable saving		Taxes		Taxable assets		Husband's tax-deferred assets		Husband's life insurance		Wife's life insurance	
Age of husband	Age of wife	Quicken	Esp	Quicken	Esp	Quicken	Esp	Quicken	Esp	Quicken	Esp	Quicken	Esp	Quicken	Esp
29	27	32,600	35,586	7,299	2,967	18,527	18,166	7,260	2,968	0	0	580,000	588,754	60,000	63,873
45	43	32,600	35,586	16,082	6,796	20,141	21,688	175,623	85,798	0	0	N.C.	299,112	N.C.	0
65	63	32,600	35,586	(9,363)	(7,246)	7,596	4,900	573,110	277,120	0	0	N.C.	0	N.C.	0
85	83	32,600	35,586	(17,934)	(8,935)	4,485	1,890	233,830	114,104	0	0	N.C.	0	N.C.	0
Deceased	95	19,560	22,241	(15,759)	(7,577)	1,477	0	2,309	0	0	0	N.C.	0	N.C.	0

Note: N.C. = not computed

Case 5

Husband works, wife works, social security benefits, housing, *children*, no college, no emergency fund, no taxable assets, no tax-deferred assets, no tax-deferred saving, no bequests, no pensions, no inheritance, no real wage growth, age 65 retirement for husband, 3 percent real returns, 3 percent inflation, max. death ages are 95, desired stable standard of living, no downsizing of home at retirement

		Consumption (living expenses)		Taxable saving		Taxes		Taxable assets		Husband's tax-deferred assets		Husband's life insurance		Wife's life insurance	
Age of husband	Age of wife	Quicken	Esp	Quicken	Esp	Quicken	Esp	Quicken	Esp	Quicken	Esp	Quicken	Esp	Quicken	Esp
29	27	32,600	37,105	7,299	2,981	18,527	16,982	7,260	2,981	0	0	520,000	362,076	60,000	0
45	43	32,600	43,705	16,082	(66)	20,141	17,997	175,623	0	0	0	N.C.	325,241	N.C.	39,248
65	63	32,600	32,933	(9,363)	(5,054)	7,596	3,113	573,110	202,142	0	0	N.C.	0	N.C.	0
85	83	32,600	32,933	(17,934)	(6,465)	4,485	1,177	233,830	85,817	0	0	N.C.	0	N.C.	0
Deceased	95	25,620	20,583	(15,759)	(5,966)	1,477	0	2,309	0	0	0	N.C.	0	N.C.	0

Notes: Assume for QFP a $5,000 annual allowance per child in the life insurance calculator. N.C. = not computed

Case 6

Husband works, wife works, social security benefits, housing, children, *college,* no emergency fund, no taxable assets, no tax-deferred assets, no tax-deferred saving, no bequests, no pensions, no inheritance, no real wage growth, age 65 retirement for husband, 3 percent real returns, 3 percent inflation, max. death ages are 95, desired stable standard of living, no downsizing of home at retirement

		Consumption (living expenses)		Taxable saving		Taxes		Taxable assets		Husband's tax-deferred assets		Husband's life insurance		Wife's life insurance	
Age of husband	Age of wife	Quicken	Esp	Quicken	Esp	Quicken	Esp	Quicken	Esp	Quicken	Esp	Quicken	Esp	Quicken	Esp
29	27	28,270	31,189	11,768	8,773	18,550	16,982	11,706	8,773	0	0	580,000	414,718	120,000	50,578
45	43	28,270	36,466	(8,241)	7,904	20,751	20,440	232,922	122,396	0	0	N.C.	362,119	N.C.	78,886
65	63	28,270	31,592	(7,842)	(3,944)	6,597	2,213	470,249	164,404	0	0	N.C.	0	N.C.	0
85	83	28,270	31,592	(14,643)	(5,216)	4,087	822	192,892	71,712	0	0	N.C.	0	N.C.	0
Deceased	95	16,962	19,745	(13,056)	(5,152)	1,484	0	3,257	0	0	0	N.C.	0	N.C.	0

Note: N.C. = not computed

Case 7

Husband works, wife works, social security benefits, housing, children, college, *emergency fund*, no taxable assets, no tax-deferred assets, no tax-deferred saving, no bequests, no pensions, no inheritance, no real wage growth, age 65 retirement for husband, 3 percent real returns, 3 percent inflation, max. death ages are 95, desired stable standard of living, no downsizing of home at retirement

Age of husband	Age of wife	Consumption (living expenses)		Taxable saving		Taxes		Taxable assets		Husband's tax-deferred assets		Husband's life insurance		Wife's life insurance	
		Quicken	Esp	Quicken	Esp	Quicken	Esp	Quicken	Esp	Quicken	Esp	Quicken	Esp	Quicken	Esp
29	27	27,620	31,130	12,439	8,799	18,554	16,982	12,374	8,798	0	0	600,000	427,175	140,000	66,224
45	43	27,620	36,397	(7,193)	7,905	20,880	20,449	246,186	122,829	0	0	N.C.	378,165	N.C.	97,426
65	63	27,620	30,312	(59,154)	(52,587)	6,433	2,513	453,403	128,708	0	0	N.C.	0	N.C.	0
85	83	27,620	30,312	(14,208)	(4,021)	4,007	491	184,689	58,602	0	0	N.C.	0	N.C.	0
Deceased	95	16,572	18,945	(12,723)	(4,375)	1,460	0	863	0	0	0	N.C.	0	N.C.	0

Note: N.C. = not computed

Case 8

Husband works, wife works, social security benefits, housing, children, college, emergency fund, *taxable assets*, no tax-deferred assets, no tax-deferred saving, no bequests, no pensions, no inheritance, no real wage growth, age 65 retirement for husband, 3 percent real returns, 3 percent inflation, max. death ages are 95, desired stable standard of living, no downsizing of home at retirement

		Consumption (living expenses)		Taxable saving		Taxes		Taxable assets		Husband's tax-deferred assets		Husband's life insurance		Wife's life insurance	
Age of husband	Age of wife	Quicken	Esp	Quicken	Esp	Quicken	Esp	Quicken	Esp	Quicken	Esp	Quicken	Esp	Quicken	Esp
29	27	28,900	33,261	14,118	7,098	19,057	18,081	63,549	58,597	0	0	580,000	415,500	120,000	54,244
45	43	28,900	38,888	(7,518)	5,568	21,593	20,816	290,959	137,713	0	0	N.C.	373,522	N.C.	92,783
65	63	28,900	30,312	(59,838)	(52,587)	6,983	2,513	484,537	128,708	0	0	N.C.	0	N.C.	0
85	83	28,900	30,312	(15,211)	(4,021)	4,317	491	196,718	58,602	0	0	N.C.	0	N.C.	0
Deceased	95	17,340	18,945	(13,542)	(4,375)	1,464	0	247	0	0	0	N.C.	0	N.C.	0

Note: N.C. = not computed

Case 9

Husband works, wife works, social security benefits, housing, children, college, emergency fund, taxable assets, *tax-deferred assets*, no tax-deferred saving, no bequests, no pensions, no inheritance, no real wage growth, age 65 retirement for husband, 3 percent real returns, 3 percent inflation, max. death ages are 95, desired stable standard of living, no downsizing of home at retirement

Age of husband	Age of wife	Consumption (living expenses)		Taxable saving		Taxes		Taxable assets		Husband's tax-deferred assets		Husband's life insurance		Wife's life insurance	
		Quicken	Esp	Quicken	Esp	Quicken	Esp	Quicken	Esp	Quicken	Esp	Quicken	Esp	Quicken	Esp
29	27	30,700	33,437	12,260	7,030	19,047	18,081	61,701	58,530	53,000	53,000	540,000	370,828	80,000	8,525
45	43	30,700	39,094	(10,500)	5,567	21,309	20,791	254,150	137,527	83,902	83,902	N.C.	323,502	N.C.	39,567
65	63	30,700	34,034	(64,543)	(51,371)	6,027	3,601	385,117	91,156	148,987	141,832	N.C.	0	N.C.	0
85	83	30,700	34,034	(11,078)	(2,652)	5,113	2,175	141,897	46,955	86,088	61,304	N.C.	0	N.C.	0
Deceased	95	18,420	21,271	0	(6,635)	4,365	0	0	0	4,921	0	N.C.	0	N.C.	0

Note: N.C. = not computed

Case 10

Husband works, wife works, social security benefits, housing, children, college, emergency fund, taxable assets, tax-deferred assets, *tax-deferred saving*, no bequests, no pensions, no inheritance, no real wage growth, age 65 retirement for husband, 3 percent real returns, 3 percent inflation, max. death ages are 95, desired stable standard of living, no downsizing of home at retirement

Age of	Age of	Consumption (living expenses)		Taxable saving		Taxes		Taxable assets		Husband's tax-deferred assets		Husband's life insurance		Wife's life insurance	
husband	wife	Quicken	Esp	Quicken	Esp	Quicken	Esp	Quicken	Esp	Quicken	Esp	Quicken	Esp	Quicken	Esp
29	27	33,020	31,910	7,285	6,769	19,021	17,274	56,752	58,268	58,161	58,000	600,000	458,962	80,000	0
45	43	33,020	37,308	(18,640)	5,787	20,694	20,002	155,433	137,586	195,168	191,910	N.C.	303,522	N.C.	0
65	63	33,020	40,821	(74,300)	(48,332)	3,262	6,395	120,357	0	478,571	446,422	N.C.	0	N.C.	0
85	83	33,020	41,031	0	817	7,194	6,126	0	17,857	273,608	192,956	N.C.	0	N.C.	0
Deceased	95	19,812	25,645	0	(10,890)	4,650	5	0	0	1,770	0	N.C.	0	N.C.	0

Note: N.C. = not computed

Case 11
Husband works, wife works, social security benefits, housing, children, college, emergency fund, taxable assets, tax-deferred assets, tax-deferred saving, *bequests*, no pensions, no inheritance, no real wage growth, age 65 retirement for husband, 3 percent real returns, 3 percent inflation, max. death ages are 95, desired stable standard of living, no downsizing of home at retirement

		Consumption (living expenses)		Taxable saving		Taxes		Taxable assets		Husband's tax-deferred assets		Husband's life insurance		Wife's life insurance	
Age of husband	Age of wife	Quicken	Esp	Quicken	Esp	Quicken	Esp	Quicken	Esp	Quicken	Esp	Quicken	Esp	Quicken	Esp
29	27	32,670	31,851	7,646	6789	19,023	17,274	57,112	58,289	58,161	58,000	660,000	490,331	140,000	0
45	43	32,670	37,240	(18,036)	5,786	20,627	20,010	162,613	137,964	195,168	191,910	N.C.	335,521	N.C.	0
65	63	32,670	39,996	(73,432)	(47,454)	3,499	6,596	139,852	9,582	478,571	446,422	N.C.	0	N.C.	0
85	83	32,670	39,996	552	2,295	7,373	6,646	34,923	52,418	276,528	192,956	N.C.	0	N.C.	0
Deceased	95	19,602	24,998	(33)	(10,949)	14,842	713	0	0	1,943	0	N.C.	0	N.C.	0

Notes: In QFP, a bequest is entered separately in two locations: as a special expense at the end of the year of the wife's death and as a "specific bequest" in the life insurance calculator. N.C. = not computed

Case 12

Husband works, wife works, social security benefits, housing, children, college, emergency fund, taxable assets, tax-deferred assets, tax-deferred saving, bequests, *pensions*, no inheritance, no real wage growth, age 65 retirement for husband, 3 percent real returns, 3 percent inflation, max. death ages are 95, desired stable standard of living, no downsizing of home at retirement

Age of husband	Age of wife	Consumption (living expenses)		Taxable saving		Taxes		Taxable assets		Husband's tax-deferred assets		Husband's life insurance		Wife's life insurance	
		Quicken	Esp	Quicken	Esp	Quicken	Esp	Quicken	Esp	Quicken	Esp	Quicken	Esp	Quicken	Esp
29	27	34,270	31,870	5,994	6780	19,014	17,274	55,469	58,280	58,161	58,000	620,000	449,309	120,000	33,212
45	43	34,270	37,262	(20,826)	5,747	20,605	20,002	129,758	137,562	195,168	191,910	N.C.	293,091	N.C.	54,671
65	63	34,270	41,411	(67,672)	(41,814)	4,659	9,097	95,865	0	422,254	446,422	N.C.	0	N.C.	0
85	83	34,270	44,784	870	2,017	7,775	7,970	37,896	62,323	243,987	192,956	N.C.	0	N.C.	0
Deceased	95	20,562	27,990	(4,816)	(11,094)	14,087	1,753	0	0	835	0	N.C.	0	N.C.	0

Note: N.C. = not computed

Case 13

Husband works, wife works, social security benefits, housing, children, college, emergency fund, taxable assets, tax-deferred assets, tax-deferred saving, bequests, pensions, *inheritance*, no real wage growth, age 65 retirement for husband, 3 percent real returns, 3 percent inflation, max. death ages are 95, desired stable standard of living, no downsizing of home at retirement

Age of husband	Age of wife	Consumption (living expenses)		Taxable saving		Taxes		Taxable assets		Husband's tax-deferred assets		Husband's life insurance		Wife's life insurance	
		Quicken	Esp	Quicken	Esp	Quicken	Esp	Quicken	Esp	Quicken	Esp	Quicken	Esp	Quicken	Esp
29	27	38,930	31,813	754	6,793	19,336	17,274	50,266	58,293	58,161	58,000	520,000	315,383	220,000	202,813
45	43	38,930	37,196	(29,630)	5,785	20,766	20,011	30,305	138,000	195,168	191,910	N.C.	143,101	N.C.	248,239
65	63	38,930	55,126	(60,827)	(53,745)	8,619	16,234	503,385	294,359	116,943	446,422	N.C.	0	N.C.	0
85	83	38,930	55,126	(13,690)	(7,617)	6,640	10,802	237,575	174,230	67,572	192,956	N.C.	0	N.C.	0
Deceased	95	23,358	34,454	(52,462)	(17,431)	5,185	1,810	0	0	1,838	0	N.C.	0	N.C.	0

Note: N.C. = not computed

Case 14
Husband works, wife works, social security benefits, housing, children, college, emergency fund, taxable assets, tax-deferred assets, tax-deferred saving, bequests, pensions, No inheritance, *real wage growth*, age 65 retirement for husband, 3 percent real returns, 3 percent inflation, max. death ages are 95, desired stable standard of living, no downsizing of home at retirement

		Consumption (living expenses)		Taxable saving		Taxes		Taxable assets		Husband's tax-deferred assets		Husband's life insurance		Wife's life insurance	
Age of husband	Age of wife	Quicken	Esp	Quicken	Esp	Quicken	Esp	Quicken	Esp	Quicken	Esp	Quicken	Esp	Quicken	Esp
29	27	49,950	43,664	(13,320)	(5,292)	21,458	17,274	36,327	46,208	58,161	58,000	700,00	639,279	40,000	19,965
45	43	49,950	51,051	(18,332)	9,332	25,319	27,316	17,470	41,951	142,660	191,910	N.C.	477,309	N.C.	40,363
65	63	49,950	54,816	(66,546)	(53,488)	9,431	16,022	481,141	285,514	247,912	446,422	N.C.	0	N.C.	0
85	83	49,950	54,816	(12,251)	(7,328)	8,848	10,717	213,715	170,862	143,248	192,956	N.C.	0	N.C.	0
Deceased	95	29,970	34,260	(36,065)	(17,240)	9,667	1,808	0	0	1,172	0	N.C.	0	N.C.	0

Notes: In QFP, the social security benefits are increased compared to earlier cases because final salary, in real terms, is higher than current salary. N.C. = not computed

Case 15

Husband works, wife works, social security benefits, housing, children, college, emergency fund, taxable assets, tax-deferred assets, tax-deferred saving, bequests, pensions, no inheritance, no real wage growth, *age 62 retirement for husband,* 3 percent real returns, 3 percent inflation, max. death ages are 95, desired stable standard of living, no downsizing of home at retirement

Age of husband	Age of wife	Consumption (living expenses)		Taxable saving		Taxes		Taxable assets		Husband's tax-deferred assets		Husband's life insurance		Wife's life insurance	
		Quicken	Esp	Quicken	Esp	Quicken	Esp	Quicken	Esp	Quicken	Esp	Quicken	Esp	Quicken	Esp
29	27	32,580	31,921	7,739	6,767	18,043	17,274	57,204	58,266	58,161	58,000	580,000	373,288	140,000	77,831
45	43	32,580	37,322	(17,881)	5,744	20,736	19,995	164,459	137,232	195,168	191,910	N.C.	225,327	N.C.	105,337
65	63	32,580	39,337	(16,527)	(45,168)	4,168	7,619	57,671	8,216	462,204	374,185	N.C.	0	N.C.	4,578
85	83	32,580	39,337	1,694	1,489	7,599	6,754	24,230	62,050	257,751	161,733	N.C.	0	N.C.	0
Deceased	95	19,548	24,586	(765)	(8,116)	14,700	1,706	0	0	356	0	N.C.	0	N.C.	0

Note: N.C. = not computed

Case 16

Husband works, wife works, social security benefits, housing, children, college, emergency fund, taxable assets, tax-deferred assets, tax-deferred saving, bequests, pensions, no inheritance, no real wage growth, age 65 retirement for husband, *5 percent real returns*, 3 percent inflation, max. death ages are 95, desired stable standard of living, no downsizing of home at retirement

Age of husband	Age of wife	Consumption (living expenses)		Taxable saving		Taxes		Taxable assets		Husband's tax-deferred assets		Husband's life insurance		Wife's life insurance	
		Quicken	Esp	Quicken	Esp	Quicken	Esp	Quicken	Esp	Quicken	Esp	Quicken	Esp	Quicken	Esp
29	27	38,280	33,019	2,557	6,423	19,377	17,641	51,896	57,924	59,214	59,000	480,000	343,402	100,000	0
45	43	38,280	38,606	(26,219)	6,258	20,754	20,899	64,950	136,646	247,992	242,859	N.C.	221,604	N.C.	0
65	63	38,280	43,489	(72,394)	(27,374)	4,312	17,344	45,798	0	442,045	737,371	N.C.	0	N.C.	0
85	83	38,280	61,057	274	2,873	8,327	17,064	272	71,394	302,224	366,853	N.C.	0	N.C.	0
Deceased	95	22,968	38,161	0	(21,109)	15,538	2,299	0	0	2,616	0	N.C.	0	N.C.	0

Note: N.C. = not computed

Case 17
Husband works, wife works, social security benefits, housing, children, college, emergency fund, taxable assets, tax-deferred assets, tax-deferred saving, bequests, pensions, no inheritance, no real wage growth, age 65 retirement for husband, 3 percent real returns, *5 percent inflation*, max. death ages are 95, desired stable standard of living, no downsizing of home at retirement

Age of husband	Age of wife	Consumption (living expenses)		Taxable saving		Taxes		Taxable assets		Husband's tax-deferred assets		Husband's life insurance		Wife's life insurance	
		Quicken	Esp	Quicken	Esp	Quicken	Esp	Quicken	Esp	Quicken	Esp	Quicken	Esp	Quicken	Esp
29	27	36,200	32,944	5,013	5,714	19,175	17,466	54,326	58,214	59,214	59,000	640,000	523,737	80,000	0
45	43	36,200	38,518	(12,539)	5,705	20,499	20,867	121,785	130,820	196,577	192,255	N.C.	297,628	N.C.	17,509
65	63	36,200	42,473	(70,059)	(43,539)	5,555	9,048	129,525	0	477,833	442,959	N.C.	0	N.C.	0
85	83	36,200	42,854	117	1,715	8,243	7,855	52,689	68,786	273,140	190,622	N.C.	0	N.C.	0
Deceased	95	21,720	26,784	(3,510)	(12,185)	14,593	2,102	0	0	2,970	0	N.C.	0	N.C.	0

Note: N.C. = not computed

Case 18

Husband works, wife works, social security benefits, housing, children, college, emergency fund, taxable assets, tax-deferred assets, tax-deferred saving, bequests, pensions, no inheritance, no real wage growth, age 65 retirement for husband, 3 percent real returns, 3 percent inflation, *death at age 85*, desired stable standard of living, no downsizing of home at retirement

Age of husband	Age of wife	Consumption (living expenses)		Taxable saving		Taxes		Taxable assets		Husband's tax-deferred assets		Husband's life insurance		Wife's life insurance	
		Quicken	Esp	Quicken	Esp	Quicken	Esp	Quicken	Esp	Quicken	Esp	Quicken	Esp	Quicken	Esp
29	27	35,570	31,912	4,653	6,785	19,007	17,274	54,134	58,284	58,161	58,000	620,000	428,054	120,000	15,433
45	43	35,570	37,312	(23,169)	5,753	20,577	20,001	102,987	137,504	195,168	191,910	N.C.	288,392	N.C.	33,455
65	63	35,570	41,811	(69,568)	(37,751)	4,470	11,309	76,366	0	339,476	439,630	N.C.	0	N.C.	0
85	83	35,570	48,457	0	(52,075)	4,964	10,655	0	24,509	78,292	0	N.C.	0	N.C.	0
Deceased	85	21,342	30,286	0	(12,169)	15,205	1,899	0	0	518	0	N.C.	0	N.C.	0

Note: N.C. = not computed

Case 19

Husband works, wife works, social security benefits, housing, children, college, emergency fund, taxable assets, tax-deferred assets, tax-deferred saving, bequests, pensions, no inheritance, real wage growth, age 65 retirement for husband, 3 percent real returns, 3 percent inflation, max. death ages are 95, *10 percent higher post-retirement living standard*, no downsizing of home at retirement

Age of husband	Age of wife	Consumption (living expenses)		Taxable saving		Taxes		Taxable assets		Husband's tax-deferred assets		Husband's life insurance		Wife's life insurance	
		Quicken	Esp	Quicken	Esp	Quicken	Esp	Quicken	Esp	Quicken	Esp	Quicken	Esp	Quicken	Esp
29	27	33,550	31,871	6,738	6,779	19,018	17,274	56,208	58,279	58,161	58,000	640,000	449,185	120,000	32,823
45	43	33,550	37,264	(19,561)	5,748	20,650	20,002	144,552	137,550	195,168	191,910	N.C.	294,626	N.C.	54,213
65	63	36,355	44,900	(69,595)	(45,263)	4,736	9,254	103,720	3,282	467,578	446,422	N.C.	0	N.C.	0
85	83	36,355	44,900	1,021	1,909	8,233	8,001	37,987	63,541	249,381	192,956	N.C.	0	N.C.	0
Deceased	95	21,813	28,063	(3,074)	(11,165)	14,690	1,753	0	0	5,167	0	N.C.	0	N.C.	0

Note: N.C. = not computed

Case 20

Husband works, wife works, social security benefits, housing, children, college, emergency fund, taxable assets, tax-deferred assets, tax-deferred saving, bequests, pensions, no inheritance, no real wage growth, age 65 retirement for husband, 3 percent real returns, 5 percent inflation, max. death ages are 95, desired stable standard of living, *downsizing of home at retirement*

Age of husband	Age of wife	Consumption (living expenses)		Taxable saving		Taxes		Taxable assets		Husband's tax-deferred assets		Husband's life insurance		Wife's life insurance	
		Quicken	Esp	Quicken	Esp	Quicken	Esp	Quicken	Esp	Quicken	Esp	Quicken	Esp	Quicken	Esp
29	27	32,430	31,728	7,894	6,827	19,024	17,274	57,358	58,327	58,161	58,000	660,000	497,077	140,000	63,964
45	43	32,430	37,096	(17,624)	5,746	21,752	20,020	167,536	138,403	195,168	191,910	N.C.	341,353	N.C.	91,374
65	63	32,430	37,311	(73,194)	(49,802)	7,012	14,379	329,501	225,243	478,571	446,422	N.C.	0	N.C.	0
85	83	32,430	37,311	(5,664)	(3,241)	9,276	10,932	133,455	188,583	276,528	192,956	N.C.	0	N.C.	0
Deceased	95	19,458	23,319	(11,183)	(74,708)	15,383	3,291	0	0	2,820	0	N.C.	0	N.C.	0

Note: N.C. = not computed

Case 21
A young, low-income couple

Age of husband	Age of wife	Consumption (living expenses)		Taxable saving		Taxes		Taxable assets		Wife's tax-deferred assets		Husband's life insurance		Wife's life insurance	
		Quicken	Esp	Quicken	Esp	Quicken	Esp	Quicken	Esp	Quicken	Esp	Quicken	Esp	Quicken	Esp
35	35	26,920	26,866	7,863	5,424	19,901	20,355	21,683	19,845	4,419	4,380	340,000	242,122	340,000	236,396
45	45	26,920	38,500	16,947	3,447	19,222	16,812	132,998	46,839	18,400	17,984	N.C.	169,566	N.C.	197,139
65	65	26,920	26,866	21,667	(797)	16,439	312	374,766	43,794	64,356	59,321	N.C.	25,735	N.C.	31,197
85	85	26,920	26,866	(16,730)	(2,414)	3,083	96	266,097	11,375	36,592	15,489	N.C.	9,477	N.C.	10,813
90	90	13,460	26,866	0	(1,030)	3,316	7	0	0	3,013	0	N.C.	0	N.C.	0

Note: N.C. = not computed

Case 22
A middle-aged, upper-income couple

Age of husband	Age of wife	Consumption (living expenses)		Taxable saving		Taxes		Taxable assets		Couple's tax-deferred assets		Husband's life insurance		Wife's life insurance	
		Quicken	Esp	Quicken	Esp	Quicken	Esp	Quicken	Esp	Quicken	Esp	Quicken	Esp	Quicken	Esp
39	40	39,390	48,909	102,508	57,063	48,366	70,217	324,909	289,328	262,661	262,162	960,000	474,795	0	0
45	46	39,390	48,909	21,883	4,526	30,154	28,969	494,700	366,871	411,295	411,486	N.C.	184,907	N.C.	0
65	66	39,390	35,925	0	0	11,804	7,364	0	0	843,756	675,978	N.C.	0	N.C.	0
85	86	39,390	41,823	(632)	194	10,191	7,468	1489	3,130	343,461	288,373	N.C.	0	N.C.	0
95	Deceased	21,008	28,683	0	0	5,781	6,710	0	0	1,325	0	N.C.	0	N.C.	0

Notes: N.C. = not computed. QFP does not allow the employer's matching contribution to a tax-deferred account to reflect inflation-induced increases in pay.

Case 23
An older, very high income couple

Age of husband	Age of wife	Consumption (living expenses)		Taxable saving		Taxes		Taxable assets		Couple tax-deferred assets		Husband's life insurance		Wife's life insurance	
		Quicken	Esp	Quicken	Esp	Quicken	Esp	Quicken	Esp	Quicken	Esp	Quicken	Esp	Quicken	Esp
64	57	186,880	204,510	(138,380)	(317,615)	237,681	182,449	2,608,876	2,566,384	835,135	835,135	0	0	0	0
75	68	186,880	204,510	64,289	(64,357)	110,389	131,659	2,474,844	1,815,234	1,005,179	1,086,296	N.C.	0	N.C.	0
85	78	186,880	204,510	(37,627)	(133,145)	74,006	55,720	1,958,129	799,840	748,607	980,869	N.C.	0	N.C.	0
Deceased	90	24,917	127,819	0	(118,883)	8,961	46	0	0	7,131	0	N.C.	0	N.C.	0

Note: N.C. = not computed

Case 24
A middle-aged, low-income divorcee

	Consumption (living expenses)		Taxable saving		Taxes		Taxable assets		Tax-deferred assets		Life insurance	
Age	Quicken	Esp	Quicken	Esp	Quicken	Esp	Quicken	Esp	Quicken	Esp	Quicken	Esp
59	13,390	17,320	(119)	(5,517)	8,139	8,977	15,747	10,063	24,185	23,960	0	0
65	13,390	17,508	6,146	0	8,691	9,446	36,579	0	76,835	73,644	N.C.	0
70	13,390	21,654	(3,543)	987	3,865	1,550	60,103	987	114,696	106,266	N.C.	0
75	13,390	21,654	(5,592)	328	3,098	1,763	32,923	3,992	90,964	75,790	N.C.	0
85	1,116	21,654	0	(1,370)	326	2,007	0	0	2,053	0	N.C.	0

Note: N.C. = not computed

Appendix: ESPlanner's Tax and Social Security Benefit Calculations

This appendix describes ESPlanner's tax and social security benefit calculations.

Federal Income Tax Calculations

ESPlanner's calculations of federal income taxes in each future year take into account the household's year-specific marital status. Thus, in the case of married households, the marital status is married when both spouses are alive and single when one is deceased. Households that are married are assumed to file jointly. The tax schedules for each filing status are taken from the federal income tax booklet for the latest available tax year—usually the year prior to the "current" year entered by the user. The tax schedule is applied to the program's calculation of federal taxable income. Federal taxable income equals federal Adjusted Gross Income (AGI) less personal exemptions and less the standard or itemized deduction, whichever is larger.

AGI for each year includes projected incomes in current dollars from the following sources: labor income (wages and salaries), self-employment income, asset income projected by the program based on user inputs of initial nontax-favored net worth and rates of return, and on the optimal spending plan computed by the program. AGI also includes taxable asset income, taxable social security benefits, taxable special receipts, taxable distributions from defined benefit pension plans and taxable withdrawals from tax-favored saving plans. Each of these items is based upon the user's inputs and preferences. Nontaxable special receipts and withdrawals from nondeductible tax-favored accounts are not included in AGI. Deductible contributions to tax-favored retirement accounts are subtracted from income in calculating each year's AGI. Employer contributions to tax-favored retirement accounts are not included in AGI. However, withdrawals from these accounts are included.

The Tax Schedule

The tax schedules for the two types of filing statuses implemented in ESPlanner are taken from the federal income tax booklet for the 1998 tax year—the latest year for which the federal schedules are available. These schedules are as follows:

(1) If taxable income is over:	(2) but not over:	(3) the tax is:		(4) of the amount over:
Married filing jointly:				
$0	$42,350	———	15.0%	$0
42,350	102,300	$6,352.50 +	28.0%	42,350
102,300	155,950	23,138.50 +	31.0%	102,300
155,950	278,450	39,770.00 +	36.0%	155,950
278,450	———	83,870.00 +	39.6%	278,450
Single:				
$0	$25,350	———	15.0%	$0
25,350	61,400	$3,802.50 +	28.0%	25,350
61,400	128,100	13,896.50 +	31.0%	61,400
128,100	278,450	34,573.50 +	36.0%	128,100
278,450	———	88,699.50 +	39.6%	278,450

The Indexation of the Tax Schedule

Tax-rate brackets and inframarginal tax amounts (all of the dollar amounts listed in the tax schedules) are adjusted for inflation in each year over the household's lifetime. This is done to ensure that the schedule keeps pace with the growth of income in current dollars. The indexation is done using the user-specified rate of inflation.

Adjustment for the Current Year

Because the tax schedules listed above are applicable for the 1998 tax year whereas the user will enter 1999 as the current year, all tax brackets and inframarginal tax amounts [the dollar amounts shown in column (3) in the schedules listed above] are indexed for inflation at the user-specified annual rate. This is done to avoid subjecting 1999 taxable income to tax schedules appropriate for 1998, that is, based on the wage and price levels prevailing in 1998.

Standard Deductions and Exemptions

The standard deduction and personal exemption amounts are also taken from the tax year prior to the "current" year (tax year 1998 in the current version). The amount subtracted from AGI for each personal exemption was $2,700. The standard deductions were $7,100 for the "married filing jointly" filing status and $4,250 for the "single" filing status. These amounts are also indexed for inflation for each future year based on the user-specified future rate of inflation. The number of personal exemptions allowed equals two plus the number of children for "married and filing jointly" and one plus the number of children for the "single" filing statuses. The personal exemption amount that can be deducted from AGI in calculating taxable income is phased out if AGI is above certain dollar limits depending upon the filing status. ESPlanner takes account of the phase-out of personal exemptions based on these dollar limits indexed for inflation.

The Decision to Itemize

ESPlanner takes the maximum of the standard deduction or itemized deduction where the latter includes mortgage interest payments, property taxes, state and local income tax payments, and tax-deductible special expenditures that the user specifies—such as alimony payments, charitable contributions, and deductible medical expenses. Note that state and local income tax payments are deductible only if they are being withheld from pay or the user makes estimated tax payments during the tax year. ESPlanner assumes withholding or pre-payment in every case.

The Phase-Out of Itemized Deductions

Federal income tax rules phase out itemized deductions for high income taxpayers (both married filing jointly and single payers). For the 1998 tax year, the amount of the deduction is reduced by 3¢ for every dollar of AGI in excess of $124,500 with the total reduction limited to 80 percent of the original amount. The reduction does not apply to certain components of the itemized deductions claimed, such as medical care expenses, investment interest, and casualty and theft losses. Because ESPlanner does not distinguish between these and other sources of itemized deductions, the phase-out rules are applied to the entire itemized deduction.

The Child Tax Credit

The child tax credit equals $400 times the number of qualifying children in the household. The tax credit is phased out if AGI is over the threshold of $110,000 for the "married and filing jointly" status and of $75,000 for the "single" filing status. The phase-out rate is $50 for each $1,000 of income in excess of the applicable threshold. The amount of the child tax credit equals the computed amount or the federal income tax liability net of the earned income tax credit, whichever is less. If the earned income tax credit exceeds the federal income tax liability, the child tax credit is applied against the payroll tax liability.

The Earned Income Credit

The program's calculation of the earned income credit adheres to the EIC worksheet in federal Form 1040. ESPlanner first checks for eligibility to take EIC based on investment income and on taxable and nontaxable (employer contributions to 401(k) plans, for example) earned income thresholds for households with no qualifying child and those with at least one qualifying child (adopted, foster, step- and grand-children are excluded in ESPlanner's calculations). Next, EIC is computed based on the EIC schedule for taxable and nontaxable income. If the EIC is nonzero, it applies if AGI is less than certain dollar thresholds ($5,600 for households without a qualifying child and $12,300 for households with at least one qualifying child). If AGI is greater than these dollar amounts, EIC is based on the AGI.

Payroll Taxes

In each year, the payroll tax for a married household is the sum of the two spouses' payroll taxes. Each spouse's tax equals the employee share of the OASDI tax rate (6.2 percent) applied to labor earnings up to the taxable maximum level plus the employee share of the HI tax rate (1.45 percent) applied to total labor earnings. If earnings from self-employment are present, these are included in the calculation only to the extent that labor earnings fall short of the taxable maximum limit for the OASDI tax. The entire labor income from self-employment in taxed on account of the HI tax. In the case of self-employment income, the employer plus employee tax rates for OASDI and HI are applied.

The Taxation of Social Security Benefits

Social security benefits are taxed by including these benefits in the federal income tax base in the following manner. If the sum of AGI and 50 percent of social security benefits falls short of $25,000 (adjusted for inflation for future years) if single and $32,000 (same qualifier) if married, then none of the benefits are taxable. If the sum exceeds the applicable dollar threshold, but the excess is less than $9,000 if single ($12,000 if married), then the smaller of one-half of the excess or 50 percent of the benefit is taxable and is included in the federal income tax base. In addition, if the aforementioned excess is greater than the dollar thresholds, 85 percent of this excess or 85 percent of the benefit, whichever is smaller, is also added to the federal income tax base.

State Income Tax Calculations

State income taxes are calculated for each state that imposes an income tax according to the specific tax rules applicable in the user's state of residence. In most cases, the state income tax base equals the federal AGI readjusted for taxable social security benefits. State income tax calculations incorporate special features peculiar to each state: for example, some states (such as Massachusetts) impose special taxes on asset incomes. State-specific personal, spousal, and dependent exemptions (including additional exemptions for the elderly) and the applicable standard deductions are used to calculate the state taxable income. State taxes are calculated by applying the state's tax rate schedule to the taxable income.

Social Security Benefit Calculations

Retirement Benefits

Eligibility. Before ESPlanner provides you (and your spouse if married) social security retirement benefits, it checks that you are *fully insured*. Individuals must be *fully insured* to receive retirement benefits based on their earnings records. Becoming fully insured requires sufficient contributions at a job (including self-employment) covered by social security. For those born after 1929, acquiring forty *credits* prior to retirement suffices for fully insured status. Earnings between 1937 and 1951 are aggregated and divided by $400, and the result (rounded down to an integer number) are the pre-1952 credits which are added to the credits earned after 1950 in determining insured status. After 1951, workers earn one credit for each quarter of the year they work in social security–covered employment and earn above a specified minimum amount. The year of *first eligibility* for retirement benefits is the year in which the individual reaches age 62. The individual is *entitled* to retirement benefits after an application for benefits is submitted, but never before age 62.

Determination of Primary Insurance Amount (PIA). The PIA is the basis for all benefit payments made on a worker's earnings record. There are several steps in computing the PIA.

Base years are computed as the years after 1950 up to the first month of entitlement for retirement benefits begins. For survivor benefits, base years include the year of the worker's death.

Elapsed years are computed as those years after 1950 (or after attainment of age 21, whichever occurs later) up to (but not including) the year of first eligibility. The maximum number of elapsed years for an earnings record is forty (it could be shorter, for purposes of calculating survivor benefits if the person dies prior to age 62).

Computation years are calculated as the number of elapsed years less 5, or 2, whichever is greater. Earnings in base years (up to the maximum taxable limit in each year, and through age 60 or two years prior to death, whichever occurs earlier) are wage-indexed according to economy-wide average wages. Of these, the highest earnings in years equaling the number of computation years are added together and the sum is divided by the number of months in computation years to yield *Average Indexed Monthly Earnings* (AIME).

Bend Points. The AIME is converted into a PIA using a formula with *bend points*. The bend-point formula is specified as 90 percent of the first X dollars of AIME plus 32 percent of the next Y dollars of AIME plus 15 percent of the AIME in excess of Y dollars. The dollar amounts X and Y are also wage-indexed and are different for different eligibility years. The dollar amounts pertaining to the year of attaining age 60 (or, for survivor benefits, the second year before death, whichever is earlier) are applied in computing the PIA.

Benefits. A person who begins to collect benefits at his or her "normal retirement age" (currently age 65) receives the PIA as the monthly retirement benefit. In subsequent years, the monthly benefit is adjusted according to the Consumer Price Index (CPI) to maintain its purchasing power.

Increases in Normal Retirement Ages. After 2003, normal retirement ages are scheduled to increase by two months for every year that a person's sixty-fifth birthday occurs later than the year 2003. This progressive increase in the normal retirement age for those born later ceases between the years 2008 through 2020; those attaining age 65 in these years have a normal retirement age of 66. The postponement in retirement ages resumes after 2020 such that those born after 2025 have a normal retirement age of 67. All cohorts attaining age 65 after that year have a normal retirement age of 67.

Reductions for Age. A person who begins to collect retirement benefits earlier than the normal retirement age receives a *reduction for age.* The reduction factor is $\frac{5}{9}$ of 1 percent for each month of entitlement prior to the normal retirement age. The reduced benefit payment (except for the inflation adjustment) continues even after the person reaches or surpasses the normal retirement age. If the number of months of reduction exceeds thirty-six months (for example, in case of entitlement at age 62 when the normal retirement age is 67), then the reduction factor is $\frac{5}{12}$ of 1 percent for every additional month of early entitlement.

Delayed Retirement Credits. Those who begin to collect benefits after their normal retirement age (up to age 70) receive *delayed retirement credits.* The amount of the delayed retirement credit for each month of delayed entitlement depends on the year in which a person attains normal retirement age. For example, those attaining age 65 in 1997 receive an additional 5 percent in monthly benefits for each year of delay in entitlement. However, those attaining age 65 in the year 2008 will receive an additional 8 percent in benefits for each year of delayed entitlement.

Earnings Test. If a person continues to work and earn after the month of entitlement, benefits are reduced because of an *earnings test.* Beneficiaries under the normal retirement age lose $1 for each $2 earned above an earnings limit. Those older than the normal retirement age lose $1 for each $3 earned above a higher earnings limit. The earnings limits have already been specified through the year 2000 and are scheduled to grow with average wages in subsequent years. All benefits payable on a worker's earnings record, including the worker's own retirement benefits and spousal and child dependent benefits, are proportionally reduced by the testing of the worker's earnings.

Recomputation of Benefits. Earnings in any year after entitlement to benefits are automatically taken into account in a recomputation of the PIA for determining the subsequent year's benefit amount. However, these earnings are not indexed before they are included in the AIME calculation. If such earnings are higher than some prior year's earnings (indexed earnings through age 60 or unindexed earnings after age 60), they result in an increase in the PIA and benefit payable. If they are lower than all previous year's earnings, they will not lower the PIA or benefits since only the highest earnings in base years are included in the calculations.

Spousal and Child Dependent Benefits

Eligibility. Wives and husbands of insured workers (including divorced spouses) are entitled to *spousal benefits* if the couple was married for at least ten years at the time of application for spousal benefits, the spouse is over age 62 or has in care a child under age 16 entitled to benefits under the insured worker's record, and the insured worker is collecting retirement benefits. Children of insured workers under age 16 are entitled to *child dependent benefits* if the child is unmarried and the worker is collecting retirement benefits.

Benefits. Spousal and child benefits equal 50 percent of the insured worker's PIA (each). Child dependent benefits may be lower only if the *family maximum* applies. Spousal benefits may be lower due to the family maximum, a reduction for age, the application of the earnings test, or the spouse's receipt of retirement benefits based or her or his own earnings record.

Family Maximum. All benefits paid under a worker's record (except retirement benefits or divorced spousal benefits) are reduced proportionately to bring them within the family maximum benefit level. The maximum benefits payable on a worker's earnings record is determined by applying a bend-point formula to the PIA similar to that applied to the AIME in calculating the PIA. For example, the family maximum equals 150 percent of the first $\$X$ of PIA plus 272 percent of the next $\$Y$ of the PIA plus 134 percent of the next $\$Z$ of the PIA plus 175 percent of the PIA greater than $\$X + \$Y + \$Z$. The values X, Y, and Z are adjusted for each year of the calculation according to the growth in economy-wide average wages. In case the spousal benefit is eliminated for any reason, the benefits payable on the insured worker's record are subjected to the family maximum test again, treating the spouse as though he or she were not eligible for spousal benefits. This may result in higher benefits for children who may be eligible for dependent benefits under the worker's record.

Reduction of Spousal Benefits for Age. Spouses eligible for the spousal benefit may elect to receive (may become entitled to) their benefits before normal retirement age. In this case the spousal benefit is reduced by $\frac{25}{36}$ of 1 percent for each month of entitlement prior to normal retirement age. If the number of months of reduction exceeds thirty-six months (for example, in case of entitlement at age 62 when the normal retirement age is 67), then the reduction factor is $\frac{5}{12}$ of 1 percent for every additional month of early entitlement.

Earnings Testing and Redefinition of Spousal Benefits. If a spouse is earning above the amount allowed by the earnings test, the spousal benefits he or she is eligible to receive will be earnings tested according to the pre- and postnormal retirement schedule described above. If a spouse is already collecting retirement benefits, the spousal benefit is redefined as the greater of the excess of the spousal benefit over the spouse's own retirement benefit or zero.

Survivor Benefits (Widow(er), Father/Mother, and Children)

Eligibility. The surviving spouse of a deceased worker is eligible for *widow(er) benefits* if the widow(er) is at least age 60, is entitled to (has applied for) widow[er] benefits, the worker died fully insured, and the widow(er) was married to the deceased worker for at least nine months. The widow(er) of a deceased worker is eligible for *father/mother benefits* if the widow(er) is entitled to (has applied for) benefits, the worker died fully insured, and the widow(er) has in care a child of the worker. A surviving child is eligible for *child survivor benefits* on the deceased worker's record if the child is under age 18 and is entitled (an application has been filed) and the worker was fully insured.

Survivor Benefits. Monthly benefits equal 100 percent of the worker's PIA for a widow(er); they equal 75 percent of the PIA for father/mother and child survivor benefits. Widow(er) and child survivor benefits may be lower only if the family maximum applies.

Widow(er)s may become entitled to (elect to receive) survivor benefits earlier than normal retirement age, but not earlier than age 60. In this case the reduction is $\frac{19}{40}$ of 1 percent for each month of entitlement prior to normal retirement age. After the widow(er) is 62, he or she may become entitled to (elect to receive) retirement benefits based on her or his own past covered earnings record. In this case the widow(er) benefits are redefined as the excess over own retirement benefit or zero, whichever is greater. Finally, widow(er) survivor and own retirement benefits are also subject to the earnings test. If the deceased worker was already collecting a reduced retirement insurance benefit, the widow(er)'s benefit cannot be greater than the reduced widow(er) benefit or the greater of 82.5 percent of the worker's PIA or the worker's own retirement benefit. If the deceased worker was already collecting a retirement insurance benefit greater than the PIA because of delayed retirement, the widow(er) is granted the full dollar amount of the delayed retirement credit over and above the (reduced) widow(er) benefit. Father/mother benefits are not similarly augmented by delayed retirement credits that the deceased worker may have been receiving.

Father/Mother Benefits. These benefits may be reduced if the family maximum applies or if the father or mother is entitled to his or her own retirement benefit. In this case the father/mother benefit is redefined as the excess over the father or mother's own retirement benefit or zero, whichever is greater. Father/mother benefits are also subject to the earnings test. On the other hand, they are not reduced for age. For those eligible to receive both widow(er) and father/mother benefits, the program calculates both and takes the larger benefit.

Calculation of a Deceased Worker's PIA. The calculation of survivor benefits in the case of widow(er) uses the larger of two alternative calculations of the deceased worker's PIA. These are the "wage indexing" method and the "reindexing" method. Moreover, the year up to which the worker's wages are indexed may be different depending upon whether the deceased worker would have become age 62 before or after the widow(er) attains age 60.

The Wage-Indexing Method. The last year for indexing earnings is the earlier of (a) the year the worker dies minus two years or (b) the year worker would have attained age 60. Bend-point formula dollar amounts are taken from the earlier of the year the worker dies or the year the worker would have attained age 62. The PIA thus calculated is inflated by the CPI up to the year the widow(er) turns age 60 (if later) to obtain the PIA value on which widow(er) benefits would be based. Where applicable, these benefits are then adjusted for the family maximum, reduction for age, delayed retirement credits, and the earnings test.

The Reindexing Method. The worker's original earnings are indexed up to the earlier of (a) the year the widow(er) attains age 58 or (b) the year the worker attains age 60. The elapsed years are computed as the number of years from 1951 (or the worker's age 22 if later) through the year the widow(er) attains age 60. The computation years equal elapsed years minus five years (computation years cannot be less than two). Bend-point formula dollar values are applied from the year the widow(er) attains age 60. There is no subsequent indexing of the PIA for inflation.

The Sequencing of Widow(er) Benefit Calculations. Widow(er) benefit reductions follow the following steps. First the widow(er) plus children's benefits are subjected to the family maximum. Second, the widow(er) benefit is reduced for early entitlement (of the widow(er) prior to normal retirement age). Third, the widow(er) benefit is compared to the widow(er) own retirement benefit if entitled to the latter. Fourth, the widow(er) benefit is redefined as the excess over own benefit if own benefit is positive. Finally the earnings test is applied, first to the widow(er)'s own benefit and then to the widow(er) benefit that is in excess of own benefit. If the widow(er) benefit is eliminated as a result of these tests, the benefits payable on the insured worker's record are subjected to the family maximum test again, treating the widow(er) as though he or she were not eligible for the widow(er) benefit. This procedure can potentially increase children's benefits if the family maximum limit was binding the first time through.

Notes

Laurence Kotlikoff is grateful to the TIAA-CREF Institute and the National Institute of Aging for research support. Economic Security Planning, Inc. is grateful to the National Institute of Aging for research support through a STTR grant. John Ameriks and Stuart Gillan provided helpful comments. The opinions expressed here are those of the authors and do not necessarily reflect those of TIAA-CREF.

1. By this, we mean that the household's present value of resources doesn't suffice to pay for the present value of its targeted consumption expenditure, including its post-retirement consumption expenditure. As mentioned, the program will "fail" even if this restriction is satisfied, if the targeted trajectory of expenditure puts the household into debt or further into debt prior to reaching retirement.

2. See Hubbard, Skinner, and Zeldes (1995) for a treatment of consumption choice in the presence of lifespan and earnings uncertainty and Campbell et al. (1999) for a treatment of consumption choice in the presence of rate-of-return uncertainty.

3. The three economists are also using ESPlanner under two National Institute of Aging grants to study the adequacy of saving and insurance. The National Institute of Aging also supported research on ESPlanner through an STTR grant. Economic Security Planning, Inc., is willing to provide academic researchers with copies of the program for free. To contact the company, go to *www.ESPlanner.com.*

4. "Borrowing constrained" refers to a household's inability to get credit on the security of its future anticipated earnings, for example, through a credit card or an unsecured line of credit. "Liquidity constrained" often refers to that as well as to the inability to sell assets (whether financial or real) to finance consumption.

5. From the perspective of economic theory, the household is viewed as maximizing a Leontief intertemporal utility function with year-specific time preference and demographic weights subject to borrowing constraints and nonnegativity constraints on life insurance.

6. Negative life insurance is formally identical to the purchase of an inverted life annuity, that is, the receipt of annual payments for life purchased by, in a predetermined lump sum amount, the estate of the deceased.

7. ESPlanner produces the following main reports: current recommendations, annual recommendations, nontax-favored balance sheet, income, spending, nonasset income (for each spouse), housing, taxes, tax-favored balance sheets (for each spouse), estate reports (for each spouse and for couples if both spouses die in the same year), social security benefit reports (for the household and for each spouse). ESPlanner's survivor reports are essentially the same as its main reports.

8. Regardless of the answer to the cash shortfall question, QFP uses the following rules regarding sales of investments. After retirement, the mandatory minimum distributions from tax-deferred retirement accounts are made first. Then taxable investments are sold. Finally, if more resources are still needed, tax-deferred accounts are again drawn upon. Before retirement, shortfalls due to special expenses or home down payments are funded, first by the sale of taxable investments and then by withdrawals from tax-deferred accounts (along with the payment of tax penalties, if applicable). If the answer to the cash shortfall question is yes, then shortfalls due to taxes, living expenses, loan payments, and planned saving are covered by the sequential sale of taxable and tax-deferred investments.

9. The Massachusetts legislature is currently considering lowering the tax on personal capital income to the same rate as is levied on labor income.

10. ESPlanners's calculation of the "primary insurance amounts" for the earning members of the household, on which all benefits are based, is identical to that produced by social security's own ANYPIA program.

11. This difference may suggest that social security is, on balance, a plus for George and Jane in terms of their sustainable living standards. But this is not necessarily so

because in case 2 we did not ascribe to George and Jane the contributions their employers would otherwise be making on their behalf to social security. Those contributions represent a form of compensation to George and Jane that would, in the absence of social security, presumably be paid directly to them.

12. In moving from case 4 to case 5, QFP's recommended life insurance for the husband drops by $60,000, but we don't believe this is due to the presence of social security survivor benefits.

13. Taxes are higher in the last years of life in QFP compared to ESPlanner because taxable as well as tax-deferred assets are consistently higher in QFP. Also, QFP, as we utilize it, does not seem to recognize the special tax credits, deductions, and exemptions available to the elderly.

14. In part, the benefit is high because (a) our middle-aged divorcee doesn't plan to start collecting benefits until she is age 70, and (b) ESPlanner incorporates delayed retirement credits and benefit recomputations in its calculation of retirement benefits.

References

Ando, Albert, and Franco Modigliani. 1963. "The 'Life Cycle Hypothesis' of Saving: Aggregate Implications and Tests." *American Economic Review* 53.

Auerbach, Alan J., and Laurence J. Kotlikoff. 1987. "Life Insurance of the Elderly: Its Adequacy and Determinants." In Gary Burtless, ed., *Work, Health, and Income Among the Elderly*. Washington, D.C.: The Brookings Institution.

Auerbach, Alan J., and Laurence J. Kotlikoff. 1991. "The Adequacy of Life Insurance Purchases." *Journal of Financial Intermediation*, 1(3): 215–241.

Bernheim, B. Douglas. 1991. *The Vanishing Nest Egg: Reflections on Saving in America*. New York: Priority Press.

Bernheim, B. Douglas. 1995. "The Merrill Lynch Baby Boom Retirement Index: Update '95." Stanford University, mimeo.

Campbell, John Y., Joao F. Cocco, Francisco J. Gomes, and Pascal J. Maenhout. 1999. "Investing Retirement Wealth: A Life-Cycle Model." NBER Working Paper No. W7029.

Hubbard, R. Glenn, and Kenneth L. Judd. 1987. "Social Security and Individual Welfare: Precautionary Saving, Borrowing Constraints, and the Payroll Tax." *American Economic Review* 77:91–112.

Hubbard, R. Glenn, Jonathan Skinner, and Stephen P. Zeldes. 1995. "Precautionary Saving and Social Insurance." *Journal of Political Economy* 103(2): 360–399.

Kotlikoff, Laurence J., Avia Spivak, and Lawrence H. Summers. 1982. "The Adequacy of Saving." *American Economic Review* 72(5): 1056–69.

Warshawsky, Mark, and John Ameriks. 2001. "What Does Financial Planning Software Say About Americans' Preparedness for Retirement?" In Olivia S. Mitchell, P. Brett Hammond, and Anna Rappaport, eds., *Forecasting Retirement Needs and Retirement Wealth*. Pension Research Council.

Yaari, Menahem E. 1965. "Uncertain Lifetime, Life Insurance, and the Theory of the Consumer." *Review of Economic Studies* 32:137–50.

Index